Mastering Database Technologies

Mastering Database Technologies

By
Ivan Bayross

BPB PUBLICATIONS
B-14, CONNAUGHT PLACE, NEW DELHI-110001

FIRST INDIAN EDITION 2006

Distributors:

MICRO BOOK CENTRE
2, City Centre, CG Road,
Near Swastic Char Rasta,
AHMEDABAD-380009 Phone: 26421611

COMPUTER BOOK CENTRE
12, Shrungar Shopping Centre, M.G. Road,
BANGALORE-560001 Phone: 5587923, 5584641

MICRO BOOKS
Shanti Niketan Building, 8, Camac Street,
KOLKATTA-700017 Phone: 22826518, 22826519

BUSINESS PROMOTION BUREAU
8/1, Ritchie Street, Mount Road,
CHENNAI-600002 Phone: 28410796, 28550491

DECCAN AGENCIES
4-3-329, Bank Street,
HYDERABAD-500195 Phone: 24756400, 24756967

MICRO MEDIA
Shop No. 5, Mahendra Chambers, 150 D.N. Road,
Next to Capital Cinema V.T. (C.S.T.) Station,
MUMBAI-400001 Ph.: 22078296, 22078297

BPB PUBLICATIONS
B-14, Connaught Place, **NEW DELHI-110001**
Phone: 23325760, 23723393, 23737742

INFO TECH
G-2, Sidhartha Building, 96 Nehru Place,
NEW DELHI-110019
Phone: 26438245, 26415092, 26234208

INFO TECH
Shop No. 2, F-38, South Extension Part-1
NEW DELHI-110049
Phone: 24691288, 24641941

BPB BOOK CENTRE
376, Old Lajpat Rai Market,
DELHI-110006 PHONE: 23861747

Price : Rs. 450/-

ISBN 81-8333-130-0

Published by Manish Jain for BPB Publications, B-14, Connaught Place, New Delhi-110 001 and Printed by him at Akash Press, New Delhi.

Foreword

The Oracle Database Server is the world's largest selling RDBMS product. It is estimated that the combined sales of both these Oracle database products account for around 80% of the RDBMSystems sold worldwide. These products are constantly undergoing change and evolving. Their cost of ownership is being brought down and their functionality ever expands. A popular version, of this product is Oracle9i.

The natural language of this RDBMS product is ANSI SQL and PL/SQL. PL/SQL is a superset of ANSI SQL.

This book has been written to address the needs of students who wish to have a ready reference book, with real life examples, which covers SQL and PL/SQL the core languages of Oracle9i.

Exception handling has been covered in some depth. This is the area of interest to students wishing to grow commercial application development skills and then working on large, enterprise wide, multi-user commercial applications.

I've tried to use my extensive application development experience in Oracle to produce this book that should cover most of the areas that seem to puzzle students when learning database technologies.

This foreword will not be complete without my thanking the many people who encouraged me and put up with the many revisions of the manuscript with patience and tolerance.

My sincere **THANKS** go to:

- ❑ My publisher Mr. Manish Jain. He has brought enormous changes in my life. This is a debt of gratitude I will never be able to pay in full.
- ❑ Mrs. Vaishali Shah who personally, laid out the manuscripts logic flow, tested the logic flow, grabbed the screens and structured much of the material. Vaishali without your tender, loving, care this manuscript would never have come together as it did. Your attention to detail was superb, you've done a really terrific job.
- ❑ Mr. Sharanam Shah the Tech lead on this project, your attention to detail in ANSI SQL syntax and its binding to commercial applications was excellent, you've done a really splendid job.
- ❑ Ms. Viraj Joshi who checked and double-checked all the hands on exercises code spec and the solutions that accompanied the exercises. Thanks for being meticulous in your checking.
- ❑ The many SQL programmers who read this material, without you all I would not be an author. I welcome both your brickbats and bouquets. You can contact me via BpB, New Delhi else you could check out my web site appropriately named ivanbayross.com. Regretfully it's forever in a development stage.
- ❑ Finally, my wife Cynthia who has always encouraged me whenever I thought that I'd never get a manuscript ready for publishing. You have always helped to keep my feet firmly on the ground, with you I am truly blessed.

Ivan N. Bayross

Table of Contents

Section-I: Database Concepts

1. *Introduction to Database* 1

Introduction to DBMA 1
What is Database Management Systems (DBMS) 2
Benefits of DBMS 3
Areas Where DBMS is Used 3
Types of Database Systems 3
What is a Relational Database Management System (RDBMS) 4
Object Oriented Database 4
Traditional Applications 4
New Applications 4
Excepted DB Features for New Applications 5
The Object-Oriented Data Model 5
Dr. E.F. Codd's Rules for RDBMS 6
DBMS V/S RDBMS 7

2. *Data Models and Data Integrity* 8

Data Models 8
Data Models Classification 8
File-Based Systems or Primitive Models 8
Traditional Data Models 8
Semantic Data Models 8
Entity Relationship Model 8
Relational Data Model 9
Network Data Model 9
Hierarchical Model 10
Data Integrity 10
DBA's Role in Managing Data Integrity 11

3. *Normalization* 12

First Normal Form 13
Second Normal Form 15
Third Normal Form 16
Circumstances Under When Normalization can be Avoided 18
Denormalization of Tables 19
Denormalizing First Normal Form to Unnormalized Tables 20
Denormalizing Second Normal Form to First Normal Form 21
Denormalizing Third Normal Form to Second Normal Form 22

Section-II: Setting up Oracle

4. *Oracle 9I Architecture* **24**

Oracle Physical File Structure 25
Oracle Memory Components 26
Oracle Background Processes 26
Oracle Instance 27
Oracle Database 27
Oracle Architecture Components - In Detail 27
Oracle Memory Components 27
Oracle Memory Components 28
Database Buffer Cache 29
Dirty Buffers 30
Redo Log Buffer 32
Shared Pool 33
Other Memory Structures 34
Server Background Processes 34
System Monitor (SMON) 34
Process Monitor (PMON) 35
Database Writer (DBWR) 35
Log Writer (LGWR) 36
Archiver (ARCH) 36
Checkpoint (CKPT) 36
Recoverer (RECO) 36
Dispatcher (Dnnn) 37
Lock (LCKn) 37
Server (Snnn) 37

5. *Tablespace in Oracle* **39**

Logical Structures of a Database 39
Tablespaces 39
The Oracle System Tablespace 39
Tablespace Usage 40
The Create Command for Tablespaces 41
Creating a Tablespace using SQL *Plus 45
Creating Tablespace through Enterprise Manager 47
Self Review Questions 54
Hands on Exercises 54

6. *Users, Roles and Privileges* **55**

Changing the Default Password for SYS 55
Activating/Deactivating the Oracle 9i Engine 59
Disabling Automatic Startup 59
Enabling a Service on Demand 63
Manually Enabling the Oracle 9i Services 63
Creating a DBA Login ID 64
Creating a User 70
Creating a User for Oracle 9i 70

Granting and Revoking Permissions 76
Granting Privileges Using the Grant Statement 76
Referencing a Table Belonging to Another User 77
Granting Privileges When a Grantee has been Given the Grant Privilege 77
Revoking Privileges Given 77
Revoking Permissions Using the Revoke Statement 78
Self Review Questions 78
Hands on Exercises 79
7. *Creating Database* **80**
Physical Database Structure 88
Database Files 88
Control Files 88
Data Files 88
Log Files 88
Answer to Self Questions 90
Solution to Hands on Exercises 91
Section - III: Setting up the Business Model
8. *A Business Model for Retail Banking* **93**
Banking Business Model Specifications 93
Saving Account (It's child processes described) 94
Savings Bank Transactions 94
Opening a Savings Bank Account (Details of the Process Flow) 94
Opening a Current Account (Detail of the Process Flow) 95
Fixed Deposits (It's Child Process Described) 96
Opening a Fixed Deposit (Details of the Process Flow) 97
Premature Discharge of a Fixed Deposit 98
Table Structure Principles 99
Actual Table Structures 99
Scanned Banking Model Forms 99
Savings Accounts Opening Form 99
Fixed Deposit Opening Form 100
Current Account Opening Form 101
The Bank Account Deposit Slip 104
The Withdrawal Slip 105
The Banks Cheque 105
9. *Project Planning for the Retail Banking Model* **107**
Table Definitions for Retail Banking 107
Branches of the Bank 107
Employees of the Bank 108
Customers of the Bank 109
Accounts Opened with the Bank 110
Account Opening Support Documents 112
Fixed Deposits with the Bank 113
Fixed Deposit Details 116

Banking Account Nominee Information 117
Bank Account or Fixed Deposit Identity Details 118
Bank Customers Address and Contact Information 119
Banking Transactions 121
Banking Transaction Details 122
Entity Relationship Diagram for Retail Banking 123
Tracking a Customer's or Nominee's Address and Contact Information 124
Employee Details 125
Nominee Details 125
Fixed Deposits 126
Banking Transactions 127
The Complete Entity Relationships for Accounts opening 128

Section - IV: Structured Query Language (SQL)

10. Interactive SQL Part - I ***130***

Table Fundamentals 130
Oracle Data Types 130
Basic Data Types 130
Comparison Between Oracle 8i/9i for Various Oracle Data Types 132
The Create Table Command 134
Rules for Creating Tables 134
A Brief Checklist When Creating Tables 135
Temporary Tables 135
Inserting Data Into Tables 136
Viewing Data in the Tables 137
All Rows and All Column 137
Filtering Table Data 137
Selected Columns and All Rows 139
Selected Rows and All Columns 139
Selected Columns and Selected Rows 140
Eliminating Duplicate Rows When Using a Select Statement 141
Sorting Data in a Table 142
Creating a Table Form a Table 143
Inserting Data into a Table from Another Table 144
Inserting of a Data Set into a Table from Another Table 144
Delete Operations 144
Removal of All Rows 145
Removal of Specific Row(s) 145
Removal of Specific Row(s) Based on the Data held by the Other Table 145
Updating the Contents of a Table 146
Updating All Rows 146
Updating Records Conditionality 146
Modifying the Structure of Tables 146
Adding New Columns 147
Dropping a Column from a Table 147
Restrictions on the Alter Table 147

Renaming Tables 148
Truncating Tables 148
Destroying Tables 148
Creating Synonyms 149
Dropping Synonyms 150
Examining Objects Created by a User 150
Finding Out the Tables Created by a User 150
Displaying the Table Structure 151
Self Review Questions 151
Hands on Exercises 152

11. Interactive SQL Part - II **155**

Data Constraints 155
Applying Data Constraints 155
Types of Data Constraints 156
I/O Constraints 156
The Primary Key Constraint 156
Primary Key Constraint Defined at Column Level 157
Primary Key Constraint Defined at Table Level 158
The Foreign Key (Self References) Constraint 159
Insert or Update Operation in the Foreign Key Table 159
Delete Operation on the Primary Key Table 159
Foreign Key Constraint Defined at the Column Level 160
Foreign Key Constraint Defined at the Table Level 160
Foreign Key Constraint Defined with on Delete Cascade 161
Foreign Key Constraint Defined with on Delete Set Null 162
Assigning User Defined Names to Constraints 163
The Unique Key Constraint 164
Unique Constraint Defined at the Column Level 165
Unique Constraint Defined at the Table Level 166
Business Rule Constraints 167
Column Level Constraints 167
Table Level Constraints 167
Null Value Concepts 168
Principles of Null Values 168
Difference between an Empty String and a Null Value 168
Not Null Constraint Defined at the Column Level 169
The Check Constraint 170
Check Constraint Defined at the Column Level 170
Check Constraint Defined at the Table Level 171
Restrictions on Check Constraints 172
Defining Different Constraints on a Table 173
The User_Constraints Table 173
Defining Integrity Constraints via the Alter Table Command 174
Dropping Integrity Constraints via the Alter Table Command 175
Default Value Concepts 175
Self Review Questions 176

Hands on Exercises 177

12. Interactive SQL Part - III 181

Computations done on Table Data 181
- Arithmetic Operators 181
- Renaming Columns Used with Expression Lists 182
- Logical Operators 183
- Range Searching 186
- Pattern Matching 188
  - The Use of the Like Predicate 188
- The Oracle Table - Dual 191
- SYSDATE 191

Oracle Functions 192
- Function_Name(argument1, argument2) 192
- Group Functions (Aggregate Functions) 192
- Scalar Functions (Single Row Functions) 192
- Aggregate Functions 192
- Numeric Functions 194
- String Functions 197
- Conversion Functions 202

Date Conversion Functions 203
Date Functions 204
- Manipulating Dates in SQL Using the Date() 206
  - To_Char 206
  - To_Date 207
- Special Date Formats Using To_Char Function 208
  - Use of TH in the To_Char() Function 209
  - Use of SP in the To_Char() Function 209
  - Use of SPTH in the To_Char() Function 210

Miscellaneous Functions 210
Self Review Questions 214
Hands on Exercises 215

13. Interactive SQL Part - IV 217

Grouping Data from Tables in SQL 217
- The Concept of Grouping 217
- Group by Clause 217
- Having Clause 219
- Determining Whether Values are Unique 221
- Group by Using the Rollup Operator 223
- Grouping by Using the Cube Operator 224

Subqueries 226
- Using sub-query in the From Clause 231
- Using Correlated Sub-queries 233
- Using Multi Column Subquery 234
- Using Sub-query in Case Expressions 234
- Using Subquery in an Order By Clause 236
- Using Exists/Not Exists Operator 236

Joins 238
Joining Multiple Tables (Equi Joins) 238
Inner Join 239
Adding an Additional Where Clause Condition 244
Outer Join 245
Cross Join 248
Guidelines For Creating Joins 250
Joining a Table to itself (Self Joins) 250
Concatenating Data From Table Columns 252
Using the Union, Intersect and Minus Clause 254
Union Clause 254
Union All Clause 257
Intersect Clause 259
Minus Clause 261
Self Review Questions 263
Hands on Exercises 264
Answer to Self Review Questions 264
Solutions to Hands on Exercises 266

Section - V: Advanced SQL

14. SQL Performance Tuning *277*

Indexes 277
Address Field in the Index 278
Duplicate / Unique Index 282
Creating of an Index 282
Creating Simple Index 282
Creating Composite Index 283
Creating of Unique Index 283
Reverse Key Indexes 284
Bitmap Indexes 285
Function Based Index 285
Key-Compressed Index 286
Dropping Indexes 286
Multiple Indexes on a Table 286
Instances When the Oracle Engine Uses an Index for Data Extraction 287
Instances When the Oracle Engine Does Not Use an Index for Data Extraction 287
Too Many Indexes - A Problem 287
Using Rowid to Delete Duplicate Rows From a Table 287
Inner Select Statement 289
Parent SQL Statement 289
Using Rownum in SQL Statements 290
Using Rownum to Limit Number of Rows in a Query 290
Views 291
Creating View 292
Renaming the Columns of a View 292
Selecting a Data Set from A View 293

Updating Views 293
Views Defined from Multiple Tables (When have been Created with a Referencing Clause) 294
Common Restrictions on Updateable Views 296
Destroy a View 296
Clusters 296
Sequences 297
Creating Sequences 298
Keywords and Parameters 298
Referencing a Sequence 299
Altering A Sequence 300
Dropping a Sequence 301
Snapshots 301
Creating a Snapshot 302
Altering a Snapshot 304
Dropping a Snapshot 305
Self Review Questions 305
Hands on Exercises 308

15. *Oracle Object Oriented Features* 309

Oracle 9i Database Flavours 309
Why should Objects be used? 309
Object Types 310
Nested Tables 311
Varying Arrays 311
Large Objects 312
References 312
Object Views 312
Features of Objects 312
Naming Conventions for Objects 313
A Common Object Example 313
The Structure of a Simple Object 314
Inserting Records into the Customer Table 317
Implementing Object Views 321
Why Use Object Views? 321
Using a Where Clause in Object Views 322
Benefits of Using Object Views 322
Manipulating Data via Object Views 323
Nested Tables 323
An Introduction 323
Implement a Nested Table 323
Variable Arrays 325
Creating a Varying Array 325
Describing the Varying Array 325
Data Manipulation 327
Referencing Objects 327
Examples for the Use of Ref 328

Self Review Questions 329
Hands on Exercises 331

16. Introduction to PL/SQL 333

Advantages of PL/SQL 333
The Generic PL/SQL Block 334
The Declare Section 334
The Begin Section 334
The Exception Section 334
The End Section 335
The PL/SQL Execution Environment 335
PL/SQL in the Oracle Engine 335
PL/SQL 335
The Character Set 335
Literals 336
PL/SQL Data Types 336
Variables 337
Constants 337
LOB Types 338
Logical Comparisons 339
Displaying User Messages on the VDU Screen 339
Comments 339
Control Structure 340
Conditional Control 340
Iterative Control 341
Sequential Control 344
Else 345
Self Review Questions 345

17. Cursors and Exceptions 348

What is a Cursor? 348
Types of Cursors 349
Implicit Cursor 349
Implicit Cursor Processing in Client Server Environment 349
Implicit Cursor Attribute 349
Explicit Cursor 352
The Functionality of Open, Fetch and Close Commands 352
Explicit Cursor Attributes 354
Cursor for Loops 358
Parameterized Cursors 360
Declaring a Parameterized Cursor 361
Opening a Parameterized Cursor and Passing Values to the Cursor 361
Exception Handling in PL/SQL 363
Oracle's Named Exception Handlers 365
User-Named Exception Handler 366
User Defined Exception Handlers (For I/O Validations) 367
User Defined Exception Handling (For Business Rule Validations) 370
Self Review Questions 372

Hands on Exercises 373

18. PL/SQL Database Objects 375

What are Procedures/Functions 375
Declarative Part 375
Executable Part 375
Exception Handling Part 375
Where Do Stored Procedures and Functions Reside? 376
How Does the Oracle Engine Create a Stored Procedure/Function? 376
How Does the Oracle Engine Execute Procedures/Functions? 376
Advantages of Using a Procedure or Function 376
Procedures Versus Functions 377
Creating Stored Procedure 377
Keywords and Parameters 377
Creating a Functions 378
Keywords and Parameters 378
Using a Function 379
Using a Procedure 381
Deleting a Stored Procedure or Function 384
Oracle Packages 384
Components of an Oracle Package 385
Why Use Package? 385
Package Specification 385
Creating Packages 389
Invoking a Package via the Oracle Engine 389
The Syntax for Dot Notation 390
Alterations to an Existing Package 391
Package Objects - Private V/S Public 391
Variables, Cursors and Constants 391
Package State 391
Package Dependency 391
Overloading Procedures and Functions 394
Overloading Built-In PL/SQL Functions and Procedures 396
Benefits of Overloading 397
Where to Overload Functions and Procedures 397
Restrictions on Overloading 398
Function or Procedure Overloading 400
Database Triggers 401
Introduction 401
Use of Database Triggers 401
Database Triggers V/S Procedures 402
Database Triggers V/S Declarative Integrity Constraints 402
How to Apply Database Triggers 402
Types of Triggers 403
Row Triggers 403
Statement Triggers 403
Before V/S After Triggers 403

Before Triggers 403
After Triggers 403
Combinations Triggers 404
Keywords and Parameters 404
Deleting a Triggers 406
Applications Using Database Triggers 406
Raise_Application_Error Procedure 412
Generating a Primary Key Using a Database Trigger 414
Introduction 414
Automatic Primary Key Generation 414
Generating Primary Key Using Sequences 414
Generating Primary Key Using the Max Function 415
Generating Primary Key Using a Lookup Table 416
DBMS_SQL 417
Processing of an SQL Sentence in the Oracle Engine 417
What is Parsing? 417
Opening a Cursor 419
What is Data Binding? 419
Defining a Column 419
Executing a Query and Fetching Data from the Underlying Tables into the Cursor 420
Positioning the Cursor on a Specific Row 420
Getting Values from the Specified Row 420
Processing of Data 420
Closing the Cursor 420
General Flow of Dynamic SQL 420
The Define_Column Procedure 423
Applications Using Dynamic SQL 425
Primary Key Validation 426
Data Definition Language Programs 427
Self Review Questions 429
Hands on Exercises 430

19. Import and Export of Data 432

An Overview 432
Using the Export Utility 432
Different Modes of Export 432
Different Levels of Export 433
Complete Exports 433
Cumulative Exports 433
Incremental Exports 433
Using the Import Utility 433
Different Modes of Import 433
Answer to Self Review Questions 434
Solution to Hands on Exercises 437

Section - VI: Appendix

A. Test Records for Retail Banking 444

Section - I

DATABASE CONCEPTS

1

Introduction To Database

A database can be defined as a collection of coherent, meaningful data. The phrase collection of coherent data needs to have a point of reference to be understood. A simple point of reference would be the example of a postal address, this would generally contain:

- A building name
- A flat number in the building (if it is co-op housing society rather than a bungalow)
- A road name
- An area name
- A state name
- A pincode
- A country name (This is optional, but necessary if the letter is destined to a foreign country)

To project on this further, multiple addresses kept together in one place, such as an address book, could be termed as a coherent collection of data. Thus the **address book** is a **database** and the **postal addresses** in the book, is the **data** that fills the database.

Introduction To DBMS

If now a telephone number were added to the address held in the address book the contours of the database will change. The database cannot be considered solely an Address database but it morphs to a Contact Information database. This is because a telephone number brings a new dimension to the address book quite unnecessary for a letter to be delivered to its destination. Hence, the addition of the telephone number changes the shape of the database.

Using this simple model several interesting things come alive. For a database to exist apparently the following must exist:

A coherent collection of data	The Addresses
An **object** that holds this coherent collection of data within it	The Address Book

This is a real world concept, (i.e. the world that human beings live in. With a little imagination multiple databases can be identified and mapped to real world models.

Real world databases
Recipes in a cook book

A coherent collection of data	A recipe and its ingredients
An **object** that holds this coherent collection of data within it	The cook book

Database
Telephone numbers added to the memory of a mobile phone

A coherent collection of data	Each telephone number and name combination
An **object** that holds this coherent collection of data within it	The mobile phone's internal memory

When a computer is used to create models as described above a few problem areas are encountered that must be addressed. Take the address database, in the real world there maybe areas, which have not yet been assigned a pincode. In other areas of the real world there could be post offices that will not accept a letter for delivery unless the envelope contains a legitimate pincode. Hence any **address database's** contour can change from one real world domain to another.

This is the first problem area that needs to be addressed when trying to model a real world database in a computer. A fixed, pre-created, database cannot be used because the very same database may have different contours in different real world domains.

To help resolve this issue, **D**ata**B**ase **M**anagement **S**ystem (i.e. DBMS) software has been created that will allow a programmer to structure a database that will model exactly to the collection of coherent (meaningful) data that belongs to a specific real world domain.

What is Database Management Systems (DBMS)

To be able to successfully design and maintain databases the following has to be done:

1. Identify which part of the world's data is of interest
2. Identify what specific objects in that part of the world's data are of interest
3. Identify a relationship between the objects

Hence, the objects, their attributes and the relationship between them (that are of interest to us) are stored in the database that is designed, built and populated with data for a specific purpose.

Software houses took up the challenge of designing systems that would **manage** data in such a database. These systems were called Database Management Systems (DBMS). DBMS is a system that allows inserting, updating, deleting and processing of data. Some of the DBMS developed by software houses were Oracle, MySQL, Postgre, MS SQL Server, M.S. Access, M.S. Visual Foxpro, and so on.

Benefits of DBMS

1. The quantum of redundant data within the data stored can be reduced
2. No inconsistent data
3. Stored data can be shared by a single or multiple users
4. Standards can be set and followed
5. Data integrity can be maintained. Data integrity refers to the problem of ensuring that database contains only accurate data
6. Security of data can be quite simply implemented
7. Data independence can be achieved, **i.e.** data and programs that manipulate the data are two different entities

Areas where DBMS Is Used

- A DBMS is used in many applications, spanning virtually the entire range of computer software
- A DBMS is the preferred method of data storage for large multiuser applications, where coordination between many users is needed
- Even individual users find them convenient and many electronic mail programs and personal organizers are based on standard database technology
- Software database drivers are available for most database platforms so that application software can use a common **A**pplication **P**rogramming **I**nterface (API) to retrieve the information stored in a various databases. Two commonly used DBMS APIs are ODBC and JDBC.

Types Of Database Systems

Conceptually, any DBMS user interface links to the keyboard and mouse in a computer system. This is the DBMS connection to the real world (i.e. the world in which the user exists). A user communicates with the DBMS user interface using these tools. Once the user interface has captured user input it has simply to pass this input to the DBMS engine running in memory for execution.

The DBMS engine analyses user input, if it cannot understand the user input an appropriate error message is returned by the DBMS engine to the VDU for the user to read. If it understands the user input then a complex set of processes begin in the computer's memory to fulfill whatever the user requested. The eventual output of this processing is displayed on the VDU for the user to see.

Each DBMS has its own way of communicating with its data storage tables and locating data requested for. There are **three** tried and tested **techniques** used by DBMS engines to work with their table data and respond to a user's data requests. They are:

- Hierarchic
- Network
- Relational

The hierarchic technique is obsolete. It is impossible to find a DBMS product that manipulates table data using this technique today.

The network technique is almost obsolete. It is exceedingly rare (if at all) to find a product that manipulates table data using the network technique.

The **R**elational **D**ata**B**ase **M**anagement **S**ystem (**RDBMS**) is the most robust, popular and commonly used technique today to manipulate table data.

What is A relational database management system (RDBMS)

A Relational Database Management System (RDBMS) is a database management system (DBMS) that is based on the relational model as introduced by Dr. Edgar F. Codd. Strictly speaking it should also satisfy Codd's 12 rules, but in practice there is no DBMS that satisfies **all** 12 rules. In fact, most successful DBMS that are considered to be relational violate the relational model in several important ways, including the Structured Query Language (SQL). However, most database practitioners and researchers use the term in a loose way such that most databases that support SQL are included.

Relational Database Management Systems (RDBMS) stores data in the form of related tables. RDBMS are powerful because they require few assumptions about how data is related or how it will be extracted from the database. As a result, the same database can be viewed in many different ways.

An important feature of relational systems is that a single database can be spread across several tables. This differs from flat-file databases, in which each database is self-contained in a single table.

The first released RDBMS that was a relatively faithful implementation of the relational model was the Multics Relational Data Store first sold in 1978. Others have been Berkeley Ingres, QUEL and IBM BS12.

Today, popular commercial RDBMS for large databases include Oracle, Microsoft SQL Server, Sybase SQL Server, and IBM's DB2. The most commonly used free RDBMS are MySQL, PostgreSQL.

Object Oriented DataBase

Traditional Applications

For over forty years the traditional DB systems were file system, hierarchical, network or relational based. Each DB system was designed for business applications like inventory, banking, manufacturing, airline reservation systems and so on. Each of these DB systems had a set of common features. The common features, used in commercial application development are:

- ❑ **Uniformity:** Each record in the database is of exactly the same size
- ❑ **Record Orientation:** Each field of the record is of a fixed length. (Hence the record is of a fixed length)
- ❑ **Small Data Items:** Each record is short
- ❑ **Atomic Fields:** There is no structure within a field
- ❑ **Short Transactions:** Transactions are completed within fractions of a second. There is no human interaction with a transaction during its execution
- ❑ **Static conceptual schemes:** The database schema is changed infrequently. Only simple changes are allowed, (e.g. in RDBMS: create tables, remove tables, add/remove columns to/from a table schema)

New Applications

In today's world, these kinds of DB systems would be hard pressed to cope. Today's data storage requires:

Engineering Databases: These include the storage of:

- ❑ Computer-Aided Design (CAD) data
- ❑ Computer-Aided Manufacturing (CAM) data
- ❑ Computer-Aided Engineering (CAE) data
- ❑ Computer-Integrated Manufacturing (CIM) data and so on

A CAD database stores data pertaining to an engineering design, including the components of the items being designed, the inter-relationship of components and old versions of designs.

Computer Aided Software Engineering (CASE)

A CASE database stores data required to assist software developers, including source code, dependencies between software modules, definitions and use of variables, the development history of the software system and so on.

Multimedia Databases

A multimedia database contains spatial data, such as audio or video data. Databases of this sort arise from geophysical data required by geographical information systems, voice mail systems and graphics applications.

Office Information Systems (OIS)

Office automation includes workstation-based tools for document creation and retrieval, tools for maintaining appointment calendars and so on. An OIS DB must allow queries pertaining to schedules, documents and contents of documents.

Hypertext Databases

Hypertext is text enriched with links that point to other documents, **e.g.** WWW. Hypertext documents. These documents may also be structured in specific ways that helps index them. Hypertext database must support the ability to retrieve documents based on links and to query documents based on their structure.

Expected DB Features For New Applications

Complex Objects: A complex object is an item that is viewed as a **single** object in the real world, but contains other objects (with an arbitrary complex internal structure). Often objects are stored hierarchically, representing the scope of their relationship. This leads to object-oriented Databases and nested relational databases.

Behavioral Data: Distinct objects may need to respond in different ways to the same command. For example, the deletion of certain records may require deleting other records in case for Master / Detail data relationships. In CAD and CASE applications the behavior of different objects in response to a given command (**i.e.** delete) may be very different. This capability is provided by methods of **O**bject **O**riented **D**ata**B**ases (OODBs) and by rules within **K**nowledge **B**ased (KB) systems.

Meta knowledge: General rules about the application rather than specific records, (**i.e.** information about data stored) form an important part of expert databases.

Long duration transactions: CAD and CASE applications involve human interaction with data. **What-If** modifications that the user may wish to **undo**, concurrent designer efforts that may lead to conflicts between active transactions and so on.

The Object-Oriented Data Model

A data model is a logical organization of real world objects (**i.e.** entities), constraints bound to them and relationships between them. A DB language is native syntax that can be used to create a data model. A DB system always implements a data model.

A core object-oriented data model consists of the following basic object-oriented concepts:

- ❑ **Object And Object Identifier:** Any real world entity is uniformly modeled as an object (associated with a **unique id**, used to pinpoint an object for its retrieval)

- **Attributes And Methods:** Every object has a **state** (**i.e.** a set of values for the attributes of the object) and a **behavior** (**i.e.** a set of methods which can set the state of an object). The state and behavior are encapsulated inside an object. They can be accessed or invoked from outside, only through explicit message passing
- A **Class** is a means of grouping objects, which share the same set of attributes and methods. An object must belong to only **one class** as an instance of that class. A class is similar to an abstract data type. A class **may also** be primitive (no attributes), **e.g.** integer, string, Boolean
- **Class Hierarchy And Inheritance:** Permits the derivation of a new class (*subclass*) from an existing class (*superclass*). The subclass inherits all the attributes and methods of the existing superclass **and** may have additional attributes and methods as well.

There are database management systems available today that answer all these specialized data storage needs, this breed of DBMS is called an OODBMS, **i.e.** an **O**bject **O**riented **D**atabase **M**anagement **S**ystem.

Dr. E. F. Codd's Rules For RDBMS

Dr. E. F. Codd is an IBM researcher who first developed the relational data model in 1970. In 1985, Dr. Codd published a list of 12 rules that define the ideal relational database and provide a guideline for the design of all relational database systems.

Dr. Codd has used the term **guideline** because till date no commercial relational database system fully conforms to all 12 rules. For a few years, scorecards were kept that rated each commercial product's conformity to Codd's rules. Today, the rules are not talked about as much but remain a goal for relational database design.

- **Rule 1: The Information Rule** - All data should be presented in table form
- **Rule 2: Guaranteed Access Rule** - All data should be accessible without ambiguity. This can be accomplished through a combination of the table name, primary key, and column name
- **Rule 3: Systematic Treatment of Null Values** - A field should be allowed to remain empty. This involves the support of a null value, which is distinct from an empty string or a number with a value of zero. Of course, this can't apply to primary keys. In addition, most database implementations support the concept of a not-null field constraint that prevents null values in a specific table column
- **Rule 4: Dynamic On-Line Catalog based on the Relational Model** - A relational database must provide access to its structure through the same tools that are used to access the data. This is usually accomplished by storing the structure definition within special system tables
- **Rule 5: Comprehensive Data Sublanguage Rule** - The database must support at least one clearly defined language that includes functionality for data definition, data manipulation, data integrity, and database transaction control. All commercial relational databases use forms of **standard** SQL (i.e. **S**tructured **Q**uery **L**anguage) as their supported comprehensive language
- **Rule 6: View Updating Rule** - Data can be presented in different logical combinations called views. Each view should support the same full range of data manipulation that has direct access to a table available. In practice, providing update and delete access to logical views is difficult and is not fully supported by any current database
- **Rule 7: High-level Insert, Update, and Delete** - Data can be retrieved from a relational database in sets constructed of data from multiple rows and/or multiple tables. This rule states that insert, update, and delete operations should be supported for any retrievable set rather than just for a single row in a single table

- **Rule 8: Physical Data Independence** - The user is isolated from the physical method of storing and retrieving information from the database. Changes can be made to the underlying architecture (hardware, disk storage methods) without affecting how the user accesses it
- **Rule 9: Logical Data Independence** - How data is viewed should not be changed when the logical structure (table's structure) of the database changes. This rule is particularly difficult to satisfy. Most databases rely on strong ties between the data viewed and the actual structure of the underlying tables
- **Rule 10: Integrity Independence** - The database language (like SQL) should support constraints on user input that maintain database integrity. This rule is not fully implemented by most major vendors. At a minimum, all databases do preserve two constraints through SQL. No component of a primary key can have a null value. If a foreign key is defined in one table, any value in it must exist as a primary key in another table.
- **Rule 11: Distribution Independence** - A user should be totally unaware of whether or not the database is distributed (whether parts of the database exist in multiple locations). A variety of reasons make this rule difficult to implement.
- **Rule 12: Non subversion Rule** - There should be no way to modify the database structure other than through the multiple row database language (like SQL). Most databases today support administrative tools that allow some direct manipulation of the data structure.

DBMS V/s RDBMS

DBMS	***RDBMS***
In DBMS relationship between two tables or files are maintained programmatically	In RDBMS relationship between two tables or files can be specified at the time of table creation
DBMS does not support Client/Server Architecture	Most of the RDBMS supports Client/Server Architecture
DBMS does not support Distributed databases	Most of the RDBMS supports Distributed databases
In DBMS there is no security of data	In RDBMS there are multiple levels of security 1. Logging in at O/S level 2. Command level (i.e. at RDBMS level) 3. Object level
Each table is given an extension in DBMS	Many tables are grouped in one database in RDBMS
DBMS may satisfy less than 7 to 8 rules of Dr. E F Codd	RDBMS usually satisfy more than 7 to 8 rules of Dr. E F Codd

Naming Conventions

DBMS	***RDBMS***
Field	Column, Attributes
Record	Row, Tuple, Entity
File	Table, Relation, Entity Class

Many of the databases will be small, with one or two tables. But as the databases become braver, tackling bigger projects, it will be noticed that the design of the tables is proving problematic. The SQL written starts to become unmanageable and data anomalies start to creep in. This means it is time to learn about database normalization, or the optimization of tables.

2

Data Models And Data Integrity

Data Models

A model is an abstraction process that hides superfluous information while highlighting details pertinent to the applications at hand. A data model is a mechanism that provides this abstraction for database applications. Data modeling is used for representing entities and their relationships in the database. It allows the conceptualization of the association between various entities and their attributes.

A number of models for data representation have been developed. Most data representation models provide mechanisms to structure data for entities being modeled and allow a set of operations to be defined on them. The models can also enforce a set of constraints to maintain the integrity of the data. These models differ in their method of representing associations amongst entities and attributes.

Data Models Classification

Data Models can be classified as file-based systems, traditional data models or semantic data models.

File-Based Systems Or Primitive Models

In this model, entities or objects are represented by records that are stored together in files. Relationships between objects are represented by using directories of various kinds.

Traditional Data Models

Traditional data models are the hierarchical, network and relational models. The hierarchical model has evolved from the file-based system and the network model is superset of the hierarchical model. The relational data model is based to the mathematical concept of a relation.

Semantic Data Models

This class of data models was influenced by semantic networks. Semantic networks were developed to organize and represent general knowledge. Semantic data models are able to express greater interdependencies among entities. These interdependencies consist of both inclusion and exclusion, enabling the models to represent the semantics of the data in the database.

Entity Relationship Model

The entity-relationship data model grew out of the exercise of using a commercially available DBMS to model an application database. Earlier commercial systems were based on the hierarchical or network approach. The Entity relationship model is generalization of these models. It allows representation of explicit constraints as well as relationships.

It is useful in the design and communication of a logical database model. In this model, objects of a similar structure are collected into an entity set. The relationship between entities is represented by a named E-R relationship.

A relationship is always established between two entities. Entities can have following types of relationship:

- One-to-One
- One-to-Many
- Many-to-Many

Relational Data Model

In this model, a **relation** (*table*) is the only construct required to represent an association among the attributes of an entity as well as relationships among different entities.

One of the main reasons for introducing this model was to increase the productivity of the application programmer by eliminating the need to change application programs when a change is made to the database. Users need not know the exact physical structure of a relation.

The relation is the only data structure used in a relational model to represent both, entities and the relationship between them. An entity can be mapped down to a table. Each column of the table would then correspond to an attribute of the entity.

Rows of the relation (*table*) are referred to as **tuples** of the relation and the **columns** as it's **attributes**. Each attribute of a relation (*table*) has a distinct name. The values for an attribute (or column) are drawn from a set of values known as a **domain**.

The domain of an attribute contains the set of values that the attribute may assume. In a relational model, no two rows of a relation are identical and the ordering of the rows is not significant.

The order of the data in the table is not significant and no order is implied when records are included in the relation. Similarly the physical details of storage (whether random, indexed or sequential organization) are no concern to the analyst. Relational tables show only logical relationship.

A relationship is represented, (as in the E-R model) by combining the primary keys of entities involved in a relation and it's attributes. The correspondence between two relations is implied by the data values of attributes in the relation defined on the common domains. Such abstractions are used in navigating through a relational database.

Network Data Model

The network data model was formalized in the late 1960s by the Database Task Group of the Conference on Data System Language (**DBTG/CODASYL**). The model conforming to the specifications is known as the DBTG data model.

The DBTG model uses two different data structures to represent database entities and relationships between the entities, namely record type and set type. A record type is used to represent an entity type. It is made up of number of data items that represent the attributes of the entity.

A set type is used to represent a direct relationship between two record types and the number record type. The set type is named and specifies that there is a one-to-many relationship between the owner and member record types. The set type can have more than one record type as it's member, but only one record type is allowed to be the owner in a given set type.

A database could have one or more occurrences of each of it's record and set type. An occurrence of a set type consists of an occurrence of the owner record type and any number of occurrences of each of it's member record types. A record type cannot be a number of two distinct occurrence of the same set type.

Each entity in an E-R diagram is represented by a logical record type with the same name. Data fields of the record represent the attributes of the entity.

In the network model, the relationships as well as the navigation through the database is predefined while creating a database. When relationships involving a weak entity set is converted to a network set, it is possible that several identical occurrences of the logical record type corresponding to weak entity could exist. These identical occurrences are distinguished by their membership in different occurrences of the sets.

Hierarchical Model

Like an organization chart or a family tree, a hierarchy is an ordered tree and is easy to understand.

Note

A tree may be defined as a set of nodes such that there is one specially designed node called the **root** (node) and the remaining nodes are partitioned into disjoint sets, each of which in turn is a tree, the **subtrees** of the root. If the relative order of the subtree is **significant**, the tree is an **ordered tree**.

In an hierarchical database, data is organized in a hierarchical or ordered tree structure and a database is a collection of such disjoint trees. The nodes of the tree represent record type. Each tree effectively represents a root record type and all of it's dependent record types.

An occurrence of a hierarchical tree type consists of one occurrence of the root record type along with zero or more occurrences of it's dependent subtree types. Each subtree in turn, is hierarchical and consists of a record type as it's root node.

In an hierarchical model, no dependent record can occur without its parent record occurrence. Furthermore, no dependent record occurrences may be connected to more than one parent record occurrences.

A hierarchical model can represent a one-to-many relationship between two entities where, these two entities are respectively parent and child. However, to represent many-to-many relationship requires duplication of one of the record types corresponding to one of the entities involved in this relationship.

Data Integrity

Database integrity is one of the core principals on which Relational databases were developed. The first lesson of learning SQL statements is usually the methods and commands for creating and implementing **integrity constraints** on tables.

Centralized control can also ensure that adequate checks are incorporated in the DBMS to provide Data Integrity. Data integrity means that the data contained in the database is both accurate and consistent. Data values being entered for storage could be checked to ensure that they fall within a specified range and are of correct format.

Another integrity check that **should be** incorporated in the database is to ensure that if there is a reference to certain object, that object **must exist**.

Implementing data integrity is done in the following ways:

- ❑ By creating constraints on specific columns of a table
- ❑ By maintaining data integrity through Application code

A nice secure way of maintaining data integrity is by implementing it at the Database level. Data integrity through application logic should be implemented only if one is very sure that all interaction with the data will be done via application code and **not** at the back-end database.

For example, an application developer can enforce data integrity rules through **Database Triggers**, but the difficulty in this kind of an approach is that a database trigger will not check the data that is **already present** in a table (A scenario where data integrity is being applied with retrospective effect).

Following are the five integrity constraint types and their categories:

Constraint	Category
Primary key	When set on columns, the Oracle engine will not allow any duplicate value and/or Null value to be entered in that column
Unique key	When set on columns, the Oracle engine will not allow any duplicate value to be entered in that column. However, it will allow the entry of **multiple** Null values.
Not null	When set on a column, the Oracle engine will not allow a Null value to be entered.
Check	When set on a column, check constraints will check and validate the data being entered against a business rule that is described in the check constraint.
Foreign key	When set on a column, the foreign key constraint will set up relation ship between two tables based on the primary key of the master table.

DBA's Role In Managing Data Integrity

From the DBA's perspective, Implementing integrity constraints on user data will also involve the task of managing different states in which integrity constraints are placed.

There are four states in which a constraint can be defined. These definitions are specified by way of commands or key words during the creation or alteration of a constraint.

- **DISABLE NOVALIDATE:** When this keyword is used while creating a constraint, the result is that constraint definition is stored in the data dictionary but neither the existing data nor the new data being entered is checked for any validations.
- **DISABLE VALIDATE:** When the constraint is set to this state, any modification to the constraint column/s are not allowed. In fact the constraint is put in this state only when a Non-Partitioned table is to be exchanged with a partitioned table.
- **ENABLE NOVALIDATE:** When any constraint is set to this state, the constraint will not check for the data that **already exists** in the table. Only new data being entered will be checked against the constraints.
- **ENABLE VALIDATE:** This is the **default state** of a constraint. When one creates a constraint **without any** of the above three key words, the constraint will be in this state. That means the constraint will check the data integrity for existing as well as new data being entered. This also means, while creating the constraint, if any data exists that violates the constraint condition, the constraint **will not be created at all**.

3

Normalization

Normalization is a process that helps analysts or database designers to design table structures for an application. The focus of normalization is to attempt to reduce **redundant** table data to the very minimum. Through the normalization process, the collection of data in a single table is replaced, by the same data being distributed over multiple tables with a specific relationship being setup between the tables. By this process RDBMS schema designers try their best to reduce redundant table data to the very minimum.

Note

 It is essential to remember that redundant data **cannot be reduced to zero** in any database management system.

Having said this, when the process of normalization is applied to table data and this data is spread across several associated tables (i.e. a specific relationship has been established between tables), it takes much longer to run a SQL query and retrieve user data from the set of tables.

Hence, often in a commercial application after 100% normalization is carried out across the master tables often the table structures are **de-normalized deliberately** to make SQL queries run faster. This means that in commercial applications there is often a trade off between redundant table data and the speed of query execution.

Normalization is carried out for the following reasons:

1. To structure the data between tables so that data maintenance is simplified
2. To allow data retrieval at optimal speed
3. To simplify data maintenance through updates, inserts and deletes
4. To reduce the need to restructure tables as new application requirements arise
5. To improve the quality of design for an application by the rationalization of table data

Normalization is a technique that:

1. Decomposes data into two-dimensional tables
2. Eliminates any relationships in which table data does fully depend upon the primary key of a record
3. Eliminates any relationship that contains transitive dependencies

A description of the three forms of Normalization follows.

First Normal Form

When a table is decomposed into two-dimensional tables with all repeating groups of data eliminated, the table data is said to be in its first normal form.

The repetitive portion of data belonging to the record is termed as repeating groups.

The following data will be taken as an example to understand the application of normalization to table data:

Project number	Project name	Employee number	Employee name	Rate category	Hourly rate
P001	Using MySQL On Linux	E001	Sharanam Shah	A	7000
		E002	Vaishali Shah	B	6500
		E006	Hansel Colaco	C	4500
P002	Using Star Office On Linux	E001	Sharanam Shah	A	7000
		E007	Chhaya Bankar	B	4000

In **EmpProj**, each project has a set of employees.

The above data after it is put through a table will look like:

Data held in a table structure:

Project number	Project name	Employee number	Employee name	Rate category	Hourly rate
P001	Using MySQL On Linux	E001	Sharanam Shah	A	7000
P001	Using MySL On Linux	E002	Vaishali Shah	B	6500
P001	Using MySQL On Linux	E006	Hansel Colaco	C	4500
P002	Using Star Office On Linux	E001	Sharanam Shah	A	7000
P002	Using Star Office On Linux	E007	Chhaya Bankar	B	4000

Table: EmpProj

Field	Key	Type
Project number	--	
Project name	--	
Employee number	--	1-n
Employee name	--	1-n
Rate category	--	1-n
Hourly rate	--	1-n

In the above data there are a few problems:

- ❑ The Project Name in the second record is misspelled. This can be solved by removing duplicates. Do this using normalization
- ❑ Data is repeated and thus occupies more space

A table is in 1st normal form if:

- ❑ There are no repeating groups
- ❑ All the key attributes are defined
- ❑ All attributes are dependent on a primary key

Note

 1-n indicates that there are many occurrences of this field - it is a repeating group.

Notice that the **project number** cannot be a primary key. It does not uniquely identify a row of data. In such a scenario the primary key must be a combination of **project number** and **employee number**. Together these two fields uniquely identify one row of data. This is because the same employee cannot be added more than once to a project.

Now even if the data is in table format, there are still some problems with it. The **Project Name** in the second record is **stored 3 times**! Besides the **waste of space**, there is another serious problem. The **Project Name** in the second record is **misspelled**. This can be solved by removing duplicates.

Imagine trying to recognize this error in a table with thousands of records. By using the table structure defined earlier, the chances of the data being corrupted increases drastically.

The solution is simply to take out the duplication.

This can be done as:

Look for partial dependencies. This means db columns that are dependent on a part of a key, and not the entire key. In the above example since both **project number** and **employee number** make up the key, look for db columns that are dependent only on project number or on employee number.

This should help identify two keys. **Project name** is dependent on **Project number** only, and the same applies to **employee name**, **hourly rate** and **rate category**, which are dependent on **employee number**.

This exercise has thus helped identifying repeating groups. So remove the repeating groups, and define the primary key.

To convert a table to its First Normal Form:

1. The unnormalized data in the first table is the entire table
2. A **key** that will uniquely identify each record should be assigned to the table. This key has to be unique because it should be capable of identifying any specific row from the table for extracting information for use. This key is called the table's **primary** key.

Table: EmpProj

Field	Key
Project number	Primary Key
Project name	- -
Employee number	Primary Key
Employee name	- -
Rate category	- -
Hourly rate	- -

This table is now in 1st normal form.

Second Normal Form

A table is said to be in its second normal form when each record in the table is in the first normal form and each column in the record is fully dependent on its primary key.

A table is in 2nd normal form if:

- It's in 1st normal form
- It includes no partial dependencies (where an attribute is dependent on only a part of a primary key)

The steps to convert a table to its Second Normal Form:

1. Find and remove fields that are related to the only part of the key
2. Group the removed items in the another table
3. Assign the new table with the key **i.e.** part of a whole **composite** key

Going through all the fields reveals the following:

- **Project name** is only dependent on **Project number**
- **Employee name**, **Rate category** and **Hourly rate** are dependent only on **Employee number**

Take these db columns out, and put it into a new table, consisting of the db columns that has the partial dependency, and the key it is dependent on. Since it is already identified that employee name, hourly rate and rate category as being dependent on employee number. The new table will consist of employee number as a key, and employee name, rate category and hourly rate as standard db columns.

This leads to the following 3 tables:

Table: EmpProj

Field	Key
Project number	Primary Key
Employee number	Primary Key

Data held in EmpProj:

Project number	Employee number
P001	E001
P001	E002
P001	E006
P002	E001
P002	E007

Table: Emp

Field	Key
Field	Key
Employee number	Primary Key
Employee name	--
Rate category	--
Hourly rate	--

Data held in Emp:

Employee number	Employee name	Rate category	Hourly rate
E001	Sharanam Shah	A	7000
E002	Vaishali Shah	B	6500
E006	Hansel Colaco	C	4500
E007	Chhaya Bankar	B	4000

Table: Proj

Field	Key
Project number	Primary Key
Project name	--

Data held in Proj:

Project number	Project name
P001	Using MySQL On Linux
P002	Using Star Office On Linux

<u>**The tables are now in 2nd normal form**</u>, but not yet in its 3rd normal form. Notice the reduction of duplication. The text "Using MySQL On Linux" is stored once only, not for each occurrence of an employee working on that project. The link is made through the key, the project number.

Third Normal Form

Table data is said to be in third normal format when all transitive dependencies are removed from this data.

The table is in 3rd normal form if:

- ❑ It's in 2nd normal form
- ❑ It contains no transitive dependencies (where a non-key attribute is dependent on another non-key attribute).

A general case of transitive dependencies is as follows:

A, B, C are three columns in table.

If C is related to B

If B is related to A

Then C is indirectly related to A

This is when transitive dependency exists.

The problem above is that **Chhaya Bankar** is paid an hourly rate of Rs. 4000, when she actually belongs to category B, and should be paid an hourly rate of Rs. 6500. This means once again data is stored redundantly. The hourly rate and the rate category relationship is being stored and repeated as required for each employee.

The solution, as before, is to remove this excess data into its own table.

This can be done as:

Look for transitive relationships, or relationships where a non-key attribute is dependent on another non-key relationship.

In this example, **Hourly rate**, while being in one sense dependent on **Employee number** is actually <u>dependent</u> on **Rate category.**

Remove it, and place it in a new table, with its actual key.

To convert such data to its third normal form remove this transitive dependency by splitting each relation in two separate relations. This means that data in columns A, B, C must be placed in three separate tables, which are linked using a foreign key.

Going through all the fields reveals the following:

- ❑ Employee table is the only one with more than one non-key attribute
- ❑ Employee name is not dependent on either Rate category or Hourly rate
- ❑ Hourly rate is dependent on Rate category

To convert the table into the third normal form remove and place these fields in a separate table, with the attribute it was dependent on as key, as follows:

This leads to the following 4 tables:

Table: EmpProj

Field	Key
Project number	Primary Key
Employee number	Primary Key

Table: Emp

Field	Key
Employee number	Primary Key
Employee name	--
Rate category	--

Table: Rate

Field	Key
Rate category	Primary Key
Hourly rate	--

Table: Proj

Field	Key
Project number	Primary Key
Project name	--

These tables are all now in their 3rd normal form, and ready to be implemented.

After this exercise it is now impossible to mistakenly assume rate category "B" is associated with an hourly rate of anything but Rs. 6500. These relationships are only stored in one place i.e. Rate table, where it can be ensured they are accurate.

There are other normal forms such as Boyce-Codd normal form, and 4th normal form, but these are very rarely used for business applications. In most cases, tables that are in their 3rd normal form already conform to these types of table formats anyway.

Circumstances under which Normalization can be avoided

There are situations when normalization can be avoided. This can be seen in the following table structure:

Table: Customer

Field	Key
Customer number	Primary Key
Customer name	--
Address	--
Pincode	
City	

Going through all the fields reveals the following:

- ❑ No repeating groups exists
- ❑ A primary key is defined

This proves that it is at least in 1st normal form

- ❑ There is only one key so partial dependencies do not exists

This proves that it is at least in 2nd normal form

- ❑ There are transitive dependencies

It seems that like City might be determined by Pincode, which is usually the case in most parts of the world, but there is no need to remove City, and place it in a separate table, with Pincode as the key.

Although this table is **not** technically in its 3rd normal format, removing this information is not worth it. Creating more tables increases the load slightly, slowing processing down. This is often counteracted by the reduction in table sizes, and redundant data. But in this case, where the City would almost always be referenced as part of the address, it isn't worth it. Normalization is just a helpful process that usually results in the most efficient table structure, and not a rule for database design.

Denormalization of Tables

Relational database table design efforts encompass both the conceptual and physical modeling levels of the three-schema architecture. Conceptual diagrams, either entity-relationship or object-oriented are a precursor to designing relational table structures. CASE tools will generate relational database tables at least to the third normal form (3NF) based on conceptual models, but have not advanced to the point that they produce table structures that guarantee acceptable levels of system processing performance.

As firms move away from the mainframe toward cheaper client-server platforms, managers face a different set of issues in the development of information systems. One critical issue is the need to continue to provide a satisfactory level of system performance, usually reflected by system response time, for mission critical, on-line, transaction processing systems.

A fully normalized database schema can fail to provide adequate system response time due to excessive table join operations. It is difficult to find formal guidance in the technical material that outlines approaches to **denormalizing** a database schema.

Denormalization must balance the need for good system response time with the need to maintain minimum redundant data, while avoiding the various anomalies or problems associated with denormalized table structures. Denormalization goes hand-in-hand with the detailed analysis of critical transactions through **view analysis**. View analysis must include the specification of primary and secondary access paths for tables that provide end-user views of the data in the tables. Additionally, denormalization should only be attempted under conditions that allow designers to collect detailed performance measurements for comparison with system performance requirements. Further, designers should only denormalize during the physical design phase, **never during conceptual modeling**.

Relational database theory provides guidelines for achieving an ideal representation of data and data relationships. Conversely, client-server systems require physical database design measures that optimize performance for specific target systems under less than ideal conditions. The final database schema must be adjusted for characteristics of the environment such as hardware, software, network and other application development and deployment framework constraints.

The following are the general guidelines to denormalization:

- ❑ Perform a detailed view analysis in order to identify situations where an excessive number of table joins appears to be required to produce a specific end-user table data view. While no hard rule exists for defining **excessive**, any view requiring more than three joins should be considered as a candidate for denormalization. Beyond this, system performance testing by simulating the production environment is necessary to **prove the need** for denormalization
- ❑ The designer should attempt to reduce the number of foreign keys in order to reduce index maintenance during insertions and deletions. Reducing foreign keys is closely related to reducing the number of relational tables
- ❑ The ease of data maintenance provided by normalized table structures must also be provided by the denormalized schema. Thus, a satisfactory approach would not require excessive programming code (triggers) to maintain data integrity and consistency

Denormalizing First Normal Form To Unnormalized Tables

Denormalization is a technique to move from higher to lower normal forms of database modeling in order to speed up database access.

There are more published formal guidelines for denormalizing first normal form than for any other normal form. This stems from the fact that repeating fields occur fairly often in business information systems. Therefore, designers and relational database theoreticians have been forced to come to grips with the issue. Consider a situation where a customer has several telephone numbers that must be tracked. The third normal form solution and the denormalized table structure is given below with telephone number (Phone1, Phone2, Phone3, ...) as a repeating field:

Third Normal Form:

Customer (CustomerId, CustomerName,...)

Cust_Phone (CustomerId, Phone)

Denormalized:

Customer (CustomerId, CustomerName, Phone1, Phone2, Phone3, ...)

In the denormalized solution, code must be written (or a screen designed) to enable any new telephone number to be stored in any of the three Phone fields. This is not a difficult task and can be easily accomplished with modern CASE tools. Still, this denormalized solution is usually only appropriate if one can guarantee that a customer will have a limited, finite, number of telephone numbers or if the firm makes a management decision not store more than "n" number of telephone numbers.

Both solutions provide good data retrieval of telephone numbers as indicated by the following SQL statements. The denormalized solution requires a simpler, smaller index structure for the CustomerId key field. The normalized solution would require at least two indices for the **Cust_Phone table**, one on the composite key to ensure uniqueness integrity and the other on the **CustomerId** field to provide a fast primary access path to records.

```
Select * from Cust_Phone where CustomerId = '8777';
Select * from Customer where CustomerId = '8777';
```

If the customer name is also required in the query, then the denormalized solution is superior as no table joins are involved.

```
Select * from Cust_Phone CP, Customer C where CP.CustomerId = '8777'
and CP.CustomerId = C.CustomerId;
```

The effort required to extract telephone numbers for a specific customer based on the customer name is also more difficult for the 3NF solution as a table join is required.

```
Select * from Cust_Phone CP, Customer C where C.CustomerName = 'Sharanam
Shah'
and CP.CustomerId = C.CustomerId;
```

If the telephone number fields represent different types of telephones, for example, a voice line, a dedicated fax line, and a dedicated modem line, then the appropriate table structures are:

Third Normal Form:

Customer (CustomerId, CustomerName, ...)

Cust_Phone (CustomerId, Phone)

Phone (Phone, PhoneType)

Denormalized:

Customer (CustomerId, CustomerName, VoicePhone, FaxPhone, ModemPhone, ...)

Again the denormalized solution is simpler for data storage and retrieval and as before, the only factor favoring a 3NF solution is the number of potential telephone numbers that an individual customer may have. The Phone table would be at least 30 to 50 percent the size of the Cust_Phone table. The decision to denormalize is most crucial when the Customer table is large in a client-server environment.

For example: One lakh customers, each having two or three telephone numbers. The join of Customer, Cust_Phone and Phone may be prohibitive in terms of processing efficiency.

Denormalizing Second Normal Form To First Normal Form

The well-known order entry modeling problem involving Customers, Orders and Items provides a realistic situation where denormalization is possible without significant data maintenance anomalies. Consider the following table structures.

Third Normal Form:

Customer (CustomerId, CustomerName,...)

OrderMaster (OrderId, OrderDate, DeliveryDate, Amount, CustomerId)

OrderDetails (OrderId, ItemId, QtyOrdered, OrderPrice)

ItemMaster (ItemId, ItemDescription, CurrentPrice)

The many-to-many relationship between the OrderMaster and ItemMaster entities represents a business transaction that occurs repeatedly over time. Further, such transactions, once complete are essentially **written in stone** since the transaction records would never be deleted. Even if an order is partially or fully deleted at the request of the customer, other tables not shown above will be used to record the deletion of an item or an order as a separate business transaction for archival (or audit trailing) purposes.

The OrderPrice field in the OrderDetails table represents the storage of data that is time-sensitive. The OrderPrice is stored in the OrderDetails table because this monetary value may differ from the monetary value in the CurrentPrice field of the Item table since item prices may change over time. While the OrderPrice field is functionally determined by the combination of ItemId and OrderDate, storing the OrderDate field in the OrderDetails table is not necessary, since the OrderPrice is recorded at the time that the transaction takes place. Therefore, while OrderDetails is not technically in 3NF, most designers would consider the above solution third normal form for all practical purposes. A true third normal form alternative solution would store price data in an ItemPriceHistory table.

In the proposed denormalized first normal form solution shown below (the Customer and OrderMaster tables remain unchanged) the ItemMaster.ItemDescription field is duplicated in the OrderDetails table. This solution violates second normal form since the ItemDescription field is fully determined by ItemId and is not determined by the full key (OrderId + ItemId). Again, this denormalized solution must be evaluated for the potential effect on data storage and retrieval.

Denormalized First Normal Form:

OrderDetails (OrderId, ItemId, QtyOrdered, OrderPrice, ItemDescription)

ItemMaster (ItemId, ItemDescription, CurrentPrice)

OrderDetails records for a given order are added to the appropriate tables at the time that an order is made. Since the OrderPrice for a given item is retrieved from the CurrentPrice field of the Item table at the time that the sale takes place, the additional processing required to retrieve and store the ItemDescription value in the OrderDetails table is negligible.

The additional expense of storing OrderDetails.ItemDescription must be weighed against the processing required to produce various end-user views of these data tables. Consider the production of a printed invoice. The third normal form solution requires joining four tables to produce an invoice view of the data. The denormalized first normal form solution requires only the Customer, OrderMaster and OrderDetails tables. Clearly, the OrderMaster table will be accessed by an indexed search based on the OrderId field. Similarly, the retrieval of records from the OrderDetails and ItemMaster tables may also be via indexes. The savings in processing time may offset the cost of extra storage.

Denormalizing Third Normal Form To Second Normal Form

An example for denormalizing from a 3NF to a 2NF solution can be found by extending the above example to include data for salespersons. The relationship between the Salesperson and OrderMaster entities is one-to-many (many orders can be processed by a single salesperson, but an order is normally associated with **one and only one** salesperson). The 3NF solution for the Salesperson and OrderMaster tables is given below, along with a denormalized 2NF solution.

Third Normal Form:

Salesperson (SalespersonId, SalespersonName,...)

OrderMaster (OrderId, OrderDate, DeliveryDate, Amount, SalespersonId)

Denormalized Second Normal Form:

Salesperson (SalespersonId, SalespersonName,...)

OrderMaster (OrderId, OrderDate, DeliveryDate, Amount, SalespersonId, SalespersonName)

Note that the SalespersonId in the OrderMaster table is a foreign key linking the OrderMaster and Salesperson tables. Denormalizing the table structures by duplicating the SalespersonName in the OrderMaster table results in a solution that is second normal form because the non-key SalespersonName field is determined by the non-key Salesperson field.

By using view analysis for a typical printed invoice or order form, it is discovered that most end-user views require printing of a salesperson's name, not their identification number on order invoices and order forms. Thus, the third normal form solution requires joining the Salesperson and OrderMaster two tables, in addition to the Customer and OrderDetails tables from the denormalized first normal form solution given earlier in order to meet processing requirements.

As before, a comparison of the third normal form solution and the denormalized second normal form solution reveals that the salesperson name could easily be recorded to the denormalized OrderMaster table at the time that the order transaction takes place. Once a sales transaction takes place, the probability of changing the salesperson credited with making the sales is very unlikely.

One should also question the need to maintain the consistency of data between the OrderMaster and Salesperson tables. In this situation, there is a requirement to support name changes for salespeople is very small and only occurs, for the most part, when a salesperson changes names due to marriage. Furthermore, the necessity to update the OrderMaster table in such a situation is a decision for management to make. An entirely conceivable notion is that such data maintenance activities may be ignored, since the important issue for salesperson's usually revolves around whether or not they get paid their commission, and the denormalized second normal form solution supports payroll activities as well as the production of standard end-user views of the database.

Denormalization requires thorough system testing to prove the effect that denormalized table structures have on processing efficiency. Furthermore, unseen adhoc data queries may be adversely affected by denormalized table structures. Denormalization must be accomplished in conjunction with a detailed analysis of the tables required to support various end-user views of the database. This analysis must include the identification of primary and secondary access paths to data.

Section - II

SETTING UP ORACLE

Oracle 9i Architecture

Today application developers spend a lot of time designing systems without fully understanding the RDBMS system that a particular commercial application uses for data storage.

This leads to a system, which may not be efficient. More often than not many developers try their level best at tweaking the front-end application developed but make little or no effort in tweaking the RDBMS system to boost application performance.

In order to improve the performance of an Oracle RDBMS system when mapped to any commercial application, it is essential to know Oracle Database architecture and design philosophy.

Improving the performance of the Oracle RDBMS system is dependent on a variety of factors and may differ on a case-to-case basis. The tuning of the Oracle RDBMS system is similar to a person wanting to cure people with diseases. A comparative analysis given below will make the concept clearer.

Table 4.1

Doctor	*Oracle DBA*
Study to be a doctor and get thorough grounding as a doctor.	Study the Oracle physical and Memory Architecture and be a DBA.
Apply acquired skills by looking at human health symptoms.	Apply acquired skills in recognizing areas in the Software system, which may not be performing well.
Link the symptoms to some disease	Link system weakness to its cause.
Provide a cure via medicine	Provide a cure via system re-configuration.

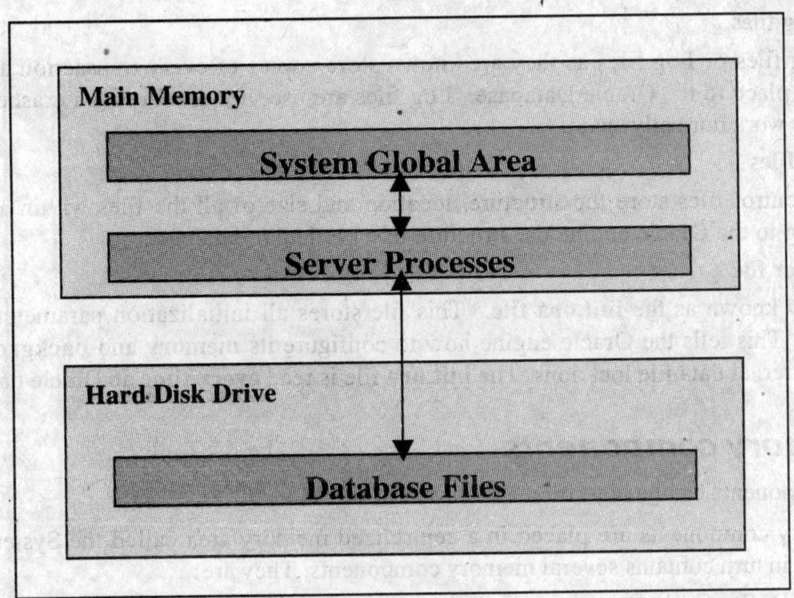

Diagram 4.1: Relation between Database files, the Oracle engine's processes and the Server's memory

Oracle Database Architecture consists of a combination of three main components.

- ❑ Oracle Memory Components
- ❑ Oracle Server Processes
- ❑ Oracle Physical Files

Oracle's memory components and Oracle's Server processes run in the **main memory** of the Windows NT server on which the Oracle engine is installed and run.

Oracle's physical files are all on the Windows NT server's hard disk drive from which their **instances** (copies off) are loaded in main memory.

These can be further categorized into separate sections as follows:

- ❑ Oracle Physical File structure
- ❑ Oracle Memory components
- ❑ Oracle Background processes
- ❑ Oracle Instance
- ❑ Oracle Database

Oracle Physical file Structure

The Physical file structure consists of the following categories of files:

1. **Data files**

   These are the files that actually store the physical data being added on the Oracle Database (tables) by different users.

2. **Redo Log files**

   Redo log files or Log files as they are known store copies of every transaction and log changes that take place to the Oracle Database. Log files are used for recovering a crashed database and making it work normally again.

3. **Control files**

   Oracle control files store the structure, location and size of all the files within a database, thus indicating to the Oracle engine the structure of a particular database.

4. **Parameter file**

   Popularly known as the **init.ora** file. This file stores all initialization parameters of an Oracle database. This tells the Oracle engine how to configure its **memory** and **background** processes and its external data file locations. The **init.ora** file is read **every time** an Oracle database instance is started.

Oracle Memory components

The Memory components can be classified as follows:

All Oracle memory components are placed in a centralized memory area called the **S**ystem **G**lobal **A**rea (**SGA**). The SGA in turn contains several memory components. They are:

- ❑ Database Buffer Cache
- ❑ Shared Pool Area - contains,
  - The Shared SQL Area (Library Cache)
  - The Data Dictionary Cache
  - The Control Structures
- ❑ Redo Log Buffer
- ❑ Sort Extent Pool

The SGA works using a read/ write manner. **i.e.** All user connections can read from the Oracle instance's SGA and can write back to the SGA after the execution of user processes. In addition, the SGA also contains information that is communicated between different processes such as table Locking information and so on.

Oracle Background Processes

There are background processes, which come into existence from the time a database instance is started. These processes constantly interact with memory components and the physical data files (on the hard disk) to maintain an explicit synchronization within the database and keep it functioning smoothly.

There are several background processes that are present when an Oracle instance runs in memory. Four of these processes must be compulsorily present at all times for an Oracle database instance function smoothly. These background processes are:

SMON – System Monitor

PMON – Process Monitor

DBWR – Database Writer

LGWR – Log Writer

Along with the above processes, other processes that activate from time to time are:

CKPT – Checkpoint

ARCH – Archiver

RECO – Recoverer

Oracle Instance

An Oracle instance is nothing but **a combination** of the Oracle engine, its SGA and four master background processes.

Oracle Database

An Oracle instance (in memory) is **conceptually** associated with an **open** database physically resident on the hard disk drive. The instance is combination of set of memory components and background processes which accesses and modifies user data held within an Oracle database.

Hence the Oracle database system consists of the Oracle engine, all its memory structures, background processes and the Logical and Physical structures of the database on the hard disk drive.

Oracle Architecture Components - In Detail

Oracle Memory Components

When Oracle 9i is invoked and the engine is loaded into the server's memory the first thing that the Oracle engine does is to reserve areas in memory in which to place vital Oracle 9i database information. These areas in memory are taken from the operating system and reserved for the exclusive use of Oracle 9i processes. The areas in memory thus reserved are called **memory structures**.

This is done because Oracle, just like any other RDBMS, requires having complete control of its own memory segments as this speeds up data processing. If user requests have to be routed to the operating system, which then processed the user request by appropriate memory segment mapping, the response time would be miserable. All RDBMS perform their own memory manipulation completely bypassing operating system processes normally used to manipulate memory segments.

Oracle 9i, being from the RDBMS family also takes this approach, hence when the Oracle engine is invoked the first thing that the engine takes care of is to extract from the operating system (through mutual handshaking routines) an appropriate quantity of memory segments in which to manage its own affairs.

Memory structures, from now on referred to as **memory components**, are further grouped by the functionality and size of each memory component. A memory component's basic task is to keep data in memory so that when a user issues a command to either read or modify the said data, it is always found in memory and can be quickly supplied to a user.

If the data requested by a user is not found in memory, Oracle server processes will have to search and locate the said data from the hard disk, hence data retrieval will be **much** longer (due to disk i/o) when compared to the data retrieved from its own preloaded memory components.

Take a simple example, if someone asks us for any information, which is held readily in our memory, such as our name and address, this will be supplied immediately.

On the other hand if some information such as old medical history details are requested (information which is **not readily** in our memory) we will have to search through the pages of several files to find the required information. It is this **search** and **find** operation that consumes time before the data becomes available.

This is exactly the same thing that happens when data that are not available in Oracle's memory components is requested for by a user.

- ❑ Oracle has to extract (stream) data from its hard disk into memory

- Once in memory the data is scanned for a match
- If a match is found the data is passed back to the user that requested it
- If a match is not found the process repeats until all the data held on the hard disk is scanned and an error message is returned to the user

All of the above obviously takes a large amount of time when compared to the time taken by the CPU to scan memory components and return appropriate data in response to a User request.

Hence the Oracle engine attempts to keep data in its memory components to help speed up the data manipulation process. The amount of data that can be kept in memory will depend on various factors:

- The quantity of physical memory available on the Server
- The size of each memory component and so on.

Note

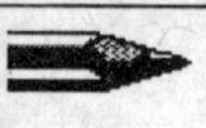

The size of each memory component is defined as one of the initialization parameters in the **init.ora** file.

Tip

When the Oracle engine (server) is started, Oracle allocates a memory area called the System Global Area (SGA) along with one or more background processes. The combination of memory structures and background processes is known as the Oracle instance.

Oracle Memory Components

The Oracle SGA (System Global Area)

The Oracle PGA (Program Global Area)

The **SGA** is made up of the following memory components. The (Database) Buffer cache takes the largest area within SGA followed by the Shared Pool Area, and Redo Log Buffers.

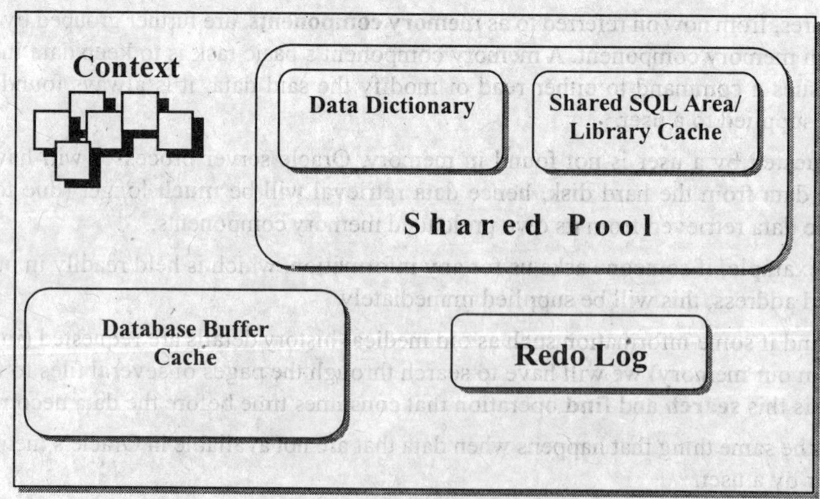

Diagram 4.2: System Global Area (SGA)

- ❑ The Buffer Cache
- ❑ The Shared Pool
- ❑ The Redo Log Buffers
- ❑ The Context Area

When the database is started, the Oracle engine displays SGA information as follows:

Total System Global Area	4505744 bytes
Fixed Size.	31344 bytes
Variable Size	4056608 bytes
Database Buffers	409600 bytes
Redo Buffers	8192 bytes

Note

The memory area taken over by the Oracle engine **is released** when the Oracle instance is shutdown. The data in the SGA is shared among the users connected to the database. Ideally the SGA must be as large as possible and store as much data as possible thus reducing read/ write operations to the hard disk.

Database Buffer Cache

Oracle stores its data in a physical file on the hard disk as a **data file**. A single data file on the hard disk is actually made up of several **data blocks**. The size of a single **Oracle** Data Block can be a multiple of the standard **Operating System data block** (which is usually 2048 bytes). The Oracle data block size is determined at the time of database creation.

The Database Buffer cache, which is the largest component within SGA, contains a copy of the data blocks belonging to a data file. Whenever a user accesses or modifies data, it is the **copy of the data blocks,** resident in the Database Buffer Cache that are actually being manipulated.

The database buffer cache stores the most recently used blocks of data. This way when a user queries the database the Oracle engine will first look in the Database Buffer Cache for data to satisfy the users request.

If the data requested by the user is found in the Database Buffer Cache it will be read directly from the buffer cache and returned to the user.

In case the data is not found in the Database Buffer Cache then Oracle Server processes reads additional data from the hard disk into the **SGA** and attempts to locate the user requested data. Once found, Oracle Server processes copy this data into the Database Buffer Cache from where it is dispatched to the user.

Although it is obvious that bigger the database buffer cache better the Oracle engine's performance, Oracle Corporation recommends the database buffer cache should not be larger than **one-fourth of total RAM**.

At startup, the Oracle engine reads the **INIT.ORA** file to determine the size of the **Database Buffer Cache**. The size of **Database Buffer Cache** can be calculated as

Size of the database buffers = database block size * database block buffers

In the **INIT.ORA** file:

The **DB_Block_Size** parameter specifies the size of a database block.

The **DB_Block_Buffers** parameter specifies the number of database blocks in the Database Buffer Cache area of SGA.

These parameters are represented in **INIT.ORA** as follows:

db_block_size = 2048

db_block_buffers = 200

Hence actually it is:

Size of the database buffer **Cache = DB_Block_Size * DB_Block_Buffers**

For example, if the **INIT.ORA** file is as follows:

DB_Block_Size = 2048

DB_Block_Buffers = 200

then,

Size of database buffers = 200 * 2048 bytes = 409600 bytes

Note

The size of the Database Buffers is displayed when the database is started or when the **show SGA** command is entered at the SVRMGR prompt.

SVRMGR>show SGA

Total System Global Area	4505744 bytes
Fixed Size	31344 bytes
Variable Size	4056608 bytes
Database Buffers	409600 bytes
Redo Buffers	8192 bytes

Oracle engine reads data from the hard disk to the Database Buffer Cache for the following reasons:

- ❑ There is a data read request from a user
- ❑ Modified or New data has to be inserted into a table

To optimize the reading and writing of data in the buffers, Oracle engine organizes the blocks in the database buffers into the following lists:

- ❑ The Dirty Buffer list
- ❑ Free buffers
- ❑ Buffers that are in use or pinned buffers.

Dirty Buffers

The Database Buffer Cache maintains two lists, one is **LRU List** and the second is **Dirty List** or **Changed Data List.**

The Database Buffer Cache works on a LRU Algorithm (**i.e.** A Least Recently Used mechanism). Data buffers that hold **modified** data are called **Dirty Buffers** or **Changed Buffers**. The **Dirty Buffer List** contains a list of all the **Dirty Buffers** that have **not been written** to the disk.

Note

As soon as a dirty buffer's contents have been flushed to hard disk the buffer is **flagged as clean** by the same Oracle engine process that flushed the buffer to the hard disk.

The Oracle engine uses a process called **Database Writer (DBWR)** to write data from these dirty buffers to the data files on the hard disk. This process is started when Oracle engine is started. The **DBWR** uses the **Least Recently Used Algorithm** to determine which Database Buffer has to be written to a data file on the hard disk.

When a user **commits** data, the data in the dirty buffers need to be written to a data file on the hard disk. Frequent data writes will result in large disk I/O slowing the system down appreciably. To minimize hard disk I/O, committed transactions are **not written immediately** to a data file on the hard disk.

The changes are held in the database buffer cache. As and when there is a request for more data buffers to write to the **least** used data buffers are flushed to the disk. The **event** of writing data from the dirty buffers to the data file on the hard disk is called a **Checkpoint.**

When the system is shut down normally, the Oracle engine will flush the remaining dirty buffers to the hard disk and then close the database instance.

Thus the data within the data file on the hard disk (**i.e.** a permanent representation of the data held in the Database Buffer Cache) will be an **exact copy** of the data held within the Database Buffer Cache at the time when the Oracle instance was shutdown. This ensures (guarantees) the integrity of table data.

Refer to diagram 4.3 for a graphical representation of the above.

Just in case the Oracle instance is shutdown **abnormally** (As would be in the case of a instance crashing) the data held in the data file on the hard disk **would not be an exact copy** of the data held in the Database Buffer Cache and thus the data in the database tables would **lack** data integrity.

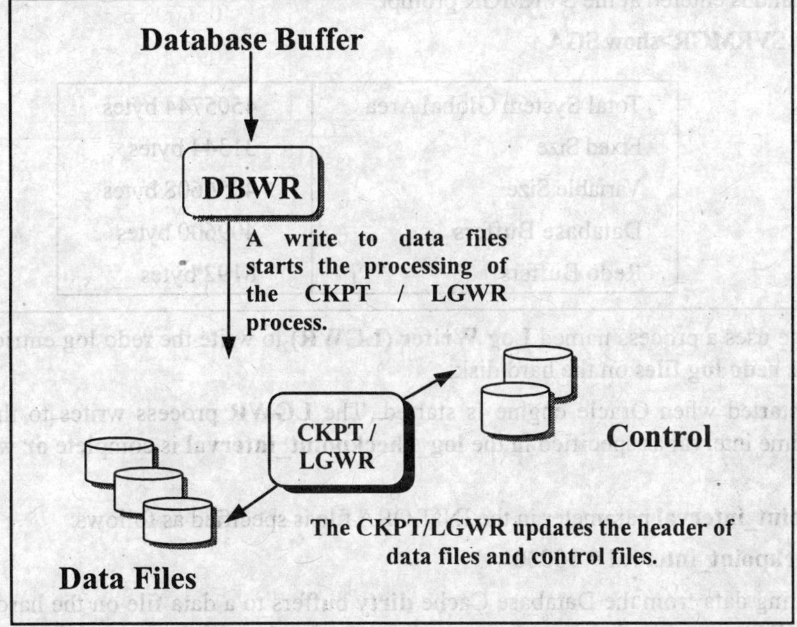

Diagram 4.3: Process of writing data to the data files

Redo Log Buffer

The Redo Log Buffer is a memory component within the SGA, which records all the changes made to the Database. Such as INSERT, UPDATE, DELETE, CREATE, ALTER and DROP. Redo Log buffers are written in a circular manner. Writing in this circular manner allows server process to write new data to the Redo Log Buffers. The **redo log buffer** entries are written to the online **redo log files** on the hard disk by a background process **LGWR** (Log Writer). Redo Log entries are used for recovery purposes.

Whenever there is a change in the Database Cache Buffer data, the Oracle engine saves the **before and after image of the data** until the transaction is either committed or rolled back.

The **before image** is a copy of the data before it was changed and the **after image** is the data after the change has taken place. Both these images are stored in a file called the **redo log file**.

Note

This file acts a guide to the DBWR process when modifying the underlying data files on the hard disk. This file tells the Oracle engine what changes to store permanently in its data files on the hard disk in the event of automatic crash recovery.

The **Log_buffers** parameter in the **INIT.ORA** file determines the amount of memory allocated for the redo log buffers by the Oracle instance when invoked. Log Buffers are specified in bytes. All changes made to a Database Buffer Cache are also recorded in the redo log buffers in memories.

For e.g.: Log_buffers = 8192

Note

The size of the Log Buffers is displayed when the database is started or when the show SGA command is entered at the SVRMGR prompt.

SVRMGR>show SGA

Total System Global Area	4505744 bytes
Fixed Size	31344 bytes
Variable Size	4056608 bytes
Database Buffers	409600 bytes
Redo Buffers	8192 bytes

The Oracle engine uses a process named **Log Writer (LGWR)** to write the redo log entries from the **redo log buffers** to the **redo log files** on the hard disk.

This process is started when Oracle engine is started. The **LGWR** process writes to the redo log files when either the time interval as specified in the **log_checkpoint_interval** is complete **or** when the redo log buffer is full.

The **log_checkpoint_interval** parameter in the INIT.ORA file is specified as follows:

log_checkpoint_interval = 10000

The event of writing data from the Database Cache **dirty** buffers to a data file on the hard disk is called a **Checkpoint (CKPT)**. The Checkpoint process updates the headers of the control files and the Database Cache Buffer files to reflect the latest **checkpoint**.

If for any reason the **CKPT** process is not enabled at instance startup, the **LGWR** process can also update the headers of the control files and the Database Cache Buffer files to reflect the latest **checkpoint**.

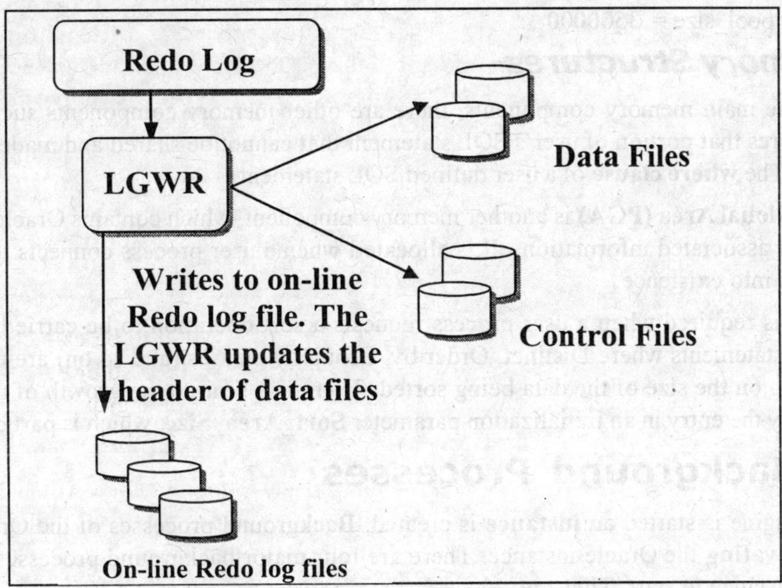

Diagram 4.4: Process of writing to the redo-log files

Shared Pool

The Shared Pool is an area in memory that the Oracle engine uses to store and manipulate data from the Oracle database held in the data file on the hard disk. The Shared Pool is also loaded with data extracted by user defined SQL statements from the data file on the hard disk.

The Shared Pool has two parts, the **Data Dictionary Cache** and the **Library Cache** or **Shared SQL Area**.

Data Dictionary Cache

Oracle engine stores all the information regarding the opened database **(i.e.** the Oracle instance) in its **Data Dictionary**. The Data Dictionary is a set of Oracle tables and views that store information about the logical and physical structure of the database as resident on its hard disk.

The Oracle engine, in order to reflect the status of the database correctly at all times automatically updates the Data Dictionary Tables and Views.

Shared SQL Area

When an SQL statement is executed against a database, the Oracle engine divides the statement into **Public/Shared** SQL information and **Private** SQL information. The Public SQL information is stored in the **Shared SQL Area**. The **Private SQL** information is stored in the **Private SQL Area**.

Shared SQL area is required to process user defined SQL statements submitted to the database. This way a single shared SQL area can be used to hold data required by multiple user defined SQL statements. This saves the reparsing time of an SQL statement that needs to access the **same table data** held in the Shared SQL area.

The **Shared_Pool_Size** parameter of the **INIT.ORA** file specifies the size of the Shared Pool in bytes as follows:

shared_pool_size = 3500000

Other Memory Structures

Apart from these main memory components, there are other memory components such as **Private SQL Area**, which stores that portion of user's SQL statement that cannot be shared and made part of the Shared SQL Area (**e.g.** The **where clause** of a user defined SQL statement).

The **Program Global Area (PGA)** is another memory component, which contains Oracle session variables, arrays and other associated information. It is allocated when a user process connects to the database and a session comes into existence.

The **Sort Area** is required when a user process requests a sort operation to be carried out on table data. These are SQL statements where Distinct, Order by, Group by clauses (and so on) are used. The sort area grows depending on the size of the data being sorted. There is a limit to the growth of the sort area's size. This is limited by the entry in an initialization parameter **Sort_Area_Size**, which is part of the **init.ora** file.

Server Background Processes

When Oracle engine is started an **instance** is created. Background processes of the Oracle engine play a vital role in **activating** the Oracle instance. There are four major background processes, which must start for the Oracle instance to start. They are:

- SMON
- PMON
- LGWR
- DBWR

Note

When an Oracle instance is instantiated in a server's memory the following process should be available:

- Process Monitor (PMON)
- System Monitor (SMON)
- Database Writer (DBWR)
- Log Writer (LGWR)
- Archiver (ARCH)
- Recoverer (RECO)
- Checkpoint (CKPT)
- Lock (LCKn)
- Dispatcher (Dnnn)
- Server Processes (Snnn)

System Monitor (SMON)

The System Monitor performs instance recovery at the startup of the Oracle instance.

SMON looks to see if changes recorded in the Redo Log Files are written to the database or not. If these changes are not written to the data files on the hard disk, it only means that the database was **not shutdown normally**.

SMON now updates the data files by **Rolling Forward** everything as specified in the Redo Logs. SMON writes all the completed or committed transactions to the data file on the hard disk and **Rolls Back** any uncommitted transactions.

It also performs cleanup operations. SMON is responsible for cleaning up temporary segments that are no longer in use. SMON also converts extents (portions of data files), which are **free** into one big contiguous larger extent.

Process Monitor (PMON)

The Process Monitor performs a memory clean up after any user processes die, fail, or crash. Cleaning up can include:

- Freeing up database locks
- Resetting the Oracle internal table that tracks active transactions
- Cleaning up Caches
- Removing the process id of the failed process from the list of active processes and so on.

In this way the Oracle engine continues to run even when user processes fail. The failure of user processes may be because of number of reasons ranging from failure of network connection, to users abruptly switching of their machines.

Without PMON, a user whose process has failed could **hold locked table data indefinitely**. For this reason, PMON is activated from time to time to check for failed processes and clean up memory components (segments) if any are found.

Database Writer (DBWR)

The Database Writer is responsible for writing of data to the data file on the hard disk **i.e.** data that is cached in the Database Cache Buffers.

The Oracle engine reads from the data files on the hard disk and caches this data in the Database Buffer Cache. This copy of data in the Database Buffer Cache is said to be **clean**, as an identical copy exists in the data files on the hard disk.

A user who now modifies the data in the Database Buffer Cache will cause the Database Buffer Cache to become **dirty**.

When the Database Buffer Cache dirty buffers are **equal to the numbers** specified in the **INIT.ORA** or the Database Buffer Cache **is full** and requires some free space to cache more data, the **DBWR** writes all the dirty buffers back to the data files on the hard disk and marks the Database Buffer Cache as **clean** once again.

When a read data request is placed on a data file on the hard disk and this data is cached in the Database Cache Buffer, it may happen that there **may not be enough free** Database Buffer Cache components (memory segments) available. An **LRU (Least Recently Used)** algorithm is used to determine which block of data can be flushed from the Data Buffer Cache to free up memory segments.

If the blocks, which are to be flushed, are dirty, the DBWR writes the information to the data files first and then flags the Data Buffer Cache block as clean (i.e. can be overwritten).

Log Writer (LGWR)

The Log Writer is responsible for physically writing data from the on-line Redo Log Buffers in memory to the Redo Log Files on the hard disk. The LGWR updates the headers of all data files when such a **checkpoint** occurs.

The LGWR writes to the Redo Log files if any one of the following conditions is true:

- ❑ A user process commits a transaction.
- ❑ Every three seconds by default
- ❑ When the redo log buffer is one third full
- ❑ When the DBWR process writes modified data buffers to disk

Archiver (ARCH)

The Archiver is an **optional** process and is started **only if** automatic archiving is turned **on**. This process takes log files, and copies them to an archive destination, which may be hard disk, tape or CD-ROM.

Checkpoint (CKPT)

Checkpoint is an event that occurs when the DBWR process writes all modified Database Buffer Cache information, including committed and uncommitted data in the SGA, to their respective data files on the hard disk.

Checkpoints are implemented for the following reasons:

- ❑ Checkpoints ensure that data segment blocks in memory that change frequently are written to data files at regular intervals.

Note

Because of the **LRU** algorithm used, a data segment that changes very frequently might not qualify it as least recently used block and thus **might never** be written to data file.

- ❑ Because all database changes up to the checkpoint have been recorded in the data files, redo log entries prior to the checkpoint are deleted. These entries no longer need to be applied to data files if instance recovery is required. Thus checkpoints help expedite instance recovery.

The checkpoint process is responsible for signaling to the DBWR at checkpoints thus updating all the data files and control files of the Oracle database on hard disk to indicate the most recent checkpoint. If the CKPT process is not present, LGWR process assumes the responsibilities of the CKPT process.

Note

Very busy Oracle engines with large number of data files may slow the system down if LGWR takes the responsibilities of the CKPT process.

Recoverer (RECO)

The Recoverer process is used by Oracle engine when installed with the **distributed processing option** active.

The distributed option allows one **Commit** command to update data in two or more locations, all as a **single atomic transaction**.

RECO ensures that all such updates, in such a distributed transaction, either commit together or rollback together. The Recoverer process at timed intervals tries to connect to remote databases and automatically completes a commit or rollback of the local portion of any pending distributed processing.

Dispatcher (Dnnn)

Dispatchers are server processes, which are present when the Oracle engine has been configured to run as **multi-threaded** server.

A Multi-Threaded server configuration allows many user processes to share server processes. Without the multi threaded server option, each user would require their own dedicated server process. At least one dispatcher process is created for every communication protocol in use (D000 ... Dnnn).

Each dispatcher process is responsible for routing requests from connected user processes and returning the responses back to the appropriate user processes.

Lock (LCKn)

Some hardware architectures like loosely coupled processors allow multiple computers to share access to data, software or peripheral devices. The Oracle engine with a **parallel server** option can take advantage of such architecture by running multiple instances that share a single physical database.

The Lock processes are used for inter-instance locking of a parallel Server with a **multiple instance** option. A maximum of ten lock processes from **LCK0** to **LCK9** are used for this purpose.

Server (Snnn)

Oracle engine creates server processes to handle requests from connected user processes.

A server process is in charge of communicating with the user process and interacting with the Oracle engine to carry out the request of the associated user process.

It is the server process that reads data from data files on the hard disk when a user process places a request and the data is **not found** in the SGA Database Buffer Cache.

Oracle architecture, depicting its many memory components (structures), and server processes is as shown in diagram 4.5.

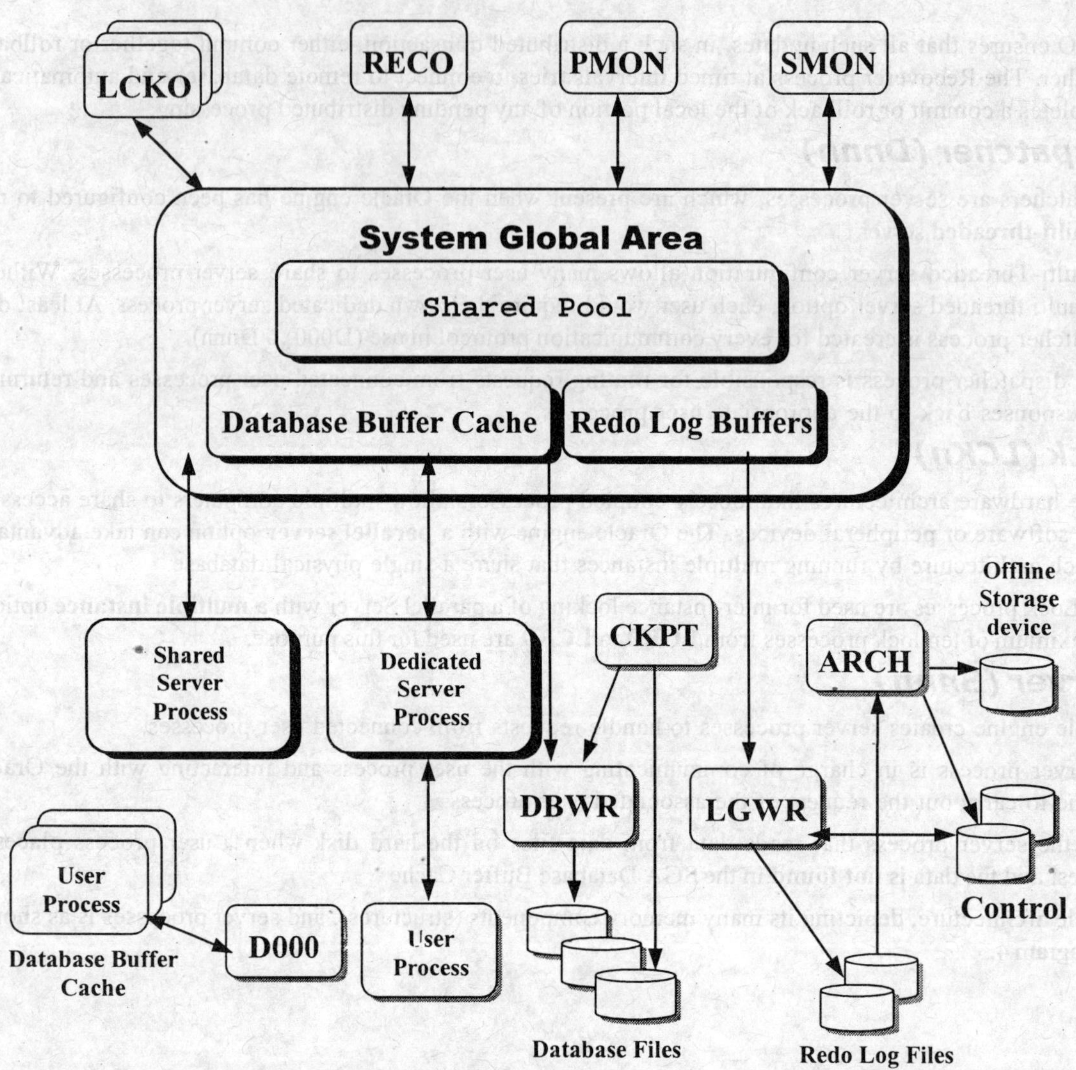

Diagram 4.5: Graphical Representation of the Oracle Internal Architecture

5

Tablespace in Oracle

Logical Structures Of a Database

An Oracle database comprises of a number of physical files called data files. These files are logically grouped together into an Oracle (logical) structure called a **Tablespace**.

Tablespaces

User data in an Oracle database is **logically** stored in tablespaces and **physically** stored in **data files**, which are bound to the corresponding tablespace.

Tablespaces are a mechanism or a means by which logical objects such as tables, indexes and views are mapped to a specific data file. Tablespaces are also used to group different types of (logical) database objects together.

A database administrator can use tablespaces to:

- ❑ Control hard disk or space allocation for database data
- ❑ Assign specific hard disk or space quotas for database users
- ❑ Control the availability of data by taking individual tablespaces online or offline
- ❑ Perform partial database backup or recovery operations
- ❑ Allocate data storage across multiple devices to improve performance

A database is made up of one or more tablespaces. Each tablespace is made up of one or more data files. The size of the tablespace can be determined as the sum of the sizes of all its data files. The sum of the size of all the tablespaces represents the storage capacity of the database.

Note

When any database is created, the Oracle engine creates a default tablespace named System within the database.

The Oracle System Tablespace

When installing Oracle for the very first time **or** when creating a new database using the **CREATE DATABASE** statement a **System** tablespace is automatically created within the new database schema. The System tablespace contains the Oracle data dictionary, which holds definitions of all Oracle objects within the database.

If no other tablespace exists within the database, **user objects**, (such as Tables, Views Indexes and so on) when created, will be stored in the **System** tablespace. This is because every user of an Oracle database must be bound to a tablespace so that there is a predefined place within which user objects can be stored.

Caution

When a user is created, in the absence of any other tablespace in the database, the user will be automatically bound to the System tablespace.

The storage of user objects in the **System** tablespace increases the likelihood of **space management problems,** which may destroy the tablespace and require it to be rebuilt.

Oracle **strongly recommends** that a separate tablespace be created within the database and users bound to this tablespace. This ensures that Oracle objects are kept completely isolated from user objects. A **separate tablespace** can be created (within the database) either using Oracle's GUI tools or SQL syntax.

Note

In **Oracle 7.1** and older versions, the System tablespace could be altered or rebuilt only by re-creating the Database.

This is the time, when user objects could be moved out of the System tablespace into a separate tablespace created by the Oracle **DBA**.

Tablespace Usage

Software projects generally require a large number of tables to capture and hold user data. When these tables are placed within the System tablespace, free space can be consumed very rapidly by the growth of user tables and their associated data.

If the rapid growth of user tables and data consumes the free space within the System tablespace then the Oracle engine will not have space to save any of its vital database information to the System tablespace. This will cause the System tablespace to get corrupted. Once the System tablespace corrupts, the Oracle database cannot be mounted when invoked and is thus damaged.

To protect the Oracle database and prevent this happening Oracle Corp. strongly recommends that User tables and all other User objects are kept in another Tablespace and not within the System tablespace.

Most software development teams will have an Oracle **D**ata**B**ase **A**dministrator (DBA) as part of the team. This individual is responsible for the day-to-day, smooth running of the Oracle database. It is generally the responsibility of the Oracle DBA to create a separate tablespace within the database to hold user objects. It is very rare (definitely not recommended) that users are given permission to create their own tablespaces.

Note

In the absence of a DBA login it may be necessary to manually create one. It is imperative that such login id's have a password to protect then and that the password is carefully preserved and changed regularly.

In the absence of a DBA login, the Sys or System logins can be used to create tablespaces. These logins are created by default when Oracle is being installed. Read the documentation for the default passwords assigned to them when the login id's were created.

The complete, detailed, SQL syntax for creating a tablespace along with examples follows.

The CREATE Command for TABLESPACES

All objects in Oracle database are stored in **tablespaces**, which is a unit of logical storage for an Oracle database. The **CREATE TABLESPACE** command allows creating a tablespace and one or more initial data files. It also allows specifying default storage parameters.

The **syntax for CREATE TABLESPACE** is a follows:

```
CREATE [TEMPORARY] TABLESPACE DATAFILE/TEMPFILE '<Path and Filename>'
     [AUTOEXTEND [OFF/ON NEXT <integer>[K/M]
               MAXSIZE [<integer>[K/M]/UNLIMITED] ] ]
     [LOGGING/NOLOGGING] [TEMPORARY/PERMANENT] [OFFLINE/ONLINE]
    DEFAULT STORAGE <storage_clause> [MINIMUM EXTENT <integer>[K/M]]
     [EXTENT MANAGEMENT [DIRECTORY/LOCAL
          [AUTOALLOCATE/UNIFORM [SIZE <integer>[K/M] ] ] ] ]
     [CHUNK <integer>] [NOCACHE]
```

The CREATE TABLESPACE command has the following keywords and parameters:

<table>
<tr><th>Attribute Name</th><th colspan="2">Description</th></tr>
<tr><td>TABLESPACE_NAME</td><td colspan="2">Name of the tablespace to be created.</td></tr>
<tr><td>DATAFILE</td><td colspan="2">Specifies the data file or files used to compose the tablespace.</td></tr>
<tr><td>MIMIMUMEXTENT</td><td colspan="2">Integer clause that controls free-space fragmentation in the tablespace by ensuring that every used and/or free extent size in a tablespace is a least as large as the integer and is a multiple of a integer.</td></tr>
<tr><td rowspan="7">AUTOEXTEND</td><td colspan="2">Enables or disables the automatic extension of the data files:</td></tr>
<tr><td>Options</td><td>Description</td></tr>
<tr><td>OFF</td><td>Disables AUTOEXTEND if set to 'ON'. NEXT and MAXSIZE are set to zero. To re-enable the feature after AUTOEXTEND is disabled, specify the values again for NEXT and MAXSIZE in additional ALTER TABLESPACE AUTOEXTEND commands.</td></tr>
<tr><td>ON</td><td>Enables AUTOEXTEND.</td></tr>
<tr><td>NEXT</td><td>Specifies disk space to allocate to the data file when more extents are required.</td></tr>
<tr><td>MAXSIZE</td><td>Specifies the maximum disk space allowed for allocation to the data file.</td></tr>
<tr><td>UNLIMITED</td><td>Allows the data file to have no limit on allocation of disk space</td></tr>
</table>

Caution

Be careful with **AUTOEXTEND** on all versions of Oracle 8 and Oracle 8i, because in versions of Oracle up to 8.1.7.1, the maximum block allocation for Oracle is 4,194,303 Oracle bocks. This limit on the number of blocks leads to a hard limit on the maximum size of an Oracle data file, which can be **silently** exceeded by **AUTOEXTEND**, causing data dictionary corruption.

Attribute Name	Description
LOGGING/ NOLOGGING	Specifies the default logging attributes of all tables, indexes and partitions within the tablespace. **LOGGING** is the default. If **NOLOGGING** is specified, no undo and redo logs are generated for operations that support the **NOLOGGING** option on the tables, indexes and partitions within the tablespace. The tablespace-level, logging attribute can be overridden by logging specifications at the table, index and partition level.
DEFAULT STORAGE	Specifies the default storage parameters for all objects created in the tablespace.
ONLINE	Makes the tablespace available immediately after creation to users who have been granted access to the tablespace.
OFFLINE	Makes the tablespace unavailable immediately after creation.

Note

By default, the tablespace is set to **ONLINE** and **LOGGING**.

Attribute Name	Description
PERMANENT	Specifies that the tablespace will be used to hold permanent objects. This is default.
TEMPORARY	Specifies that the tablespace will be used only to hold temporary objects.For example, Segments used by implicit sorts to handle ORDER BY clause.
EXTENT MANAGEMENT	Can be either **DICTIONARY** (the default) or **LOCAL**. If **LOCAL** management is specified, a bitmap located in the tablespace itself is used to manage extends reducing the load on the **FET$** and **UET$** data dictionary extent management tables and recursive SQL.**LOCAL** managed extents can either be **AUTOALLOCATED** or **UNIFORM**. If **UNIFORM**, the **SIZE** for each extent in **K** or **M** can be specified.
CHUNK	Specifies a multiple of the database block size up to **32K**. Used for specifying **LOB** storage area.
NOCACHE	Specifies that the objects within the tablespace should not be cached.

Caution

The concept of the **CREATE TEMPORARY TABLESPACE** command is new in **Oracle 9i**. This differs for a **CREATE TABLESPACE ... TEMPORARY**' command. As the former uses a **TEMPFILE**, while the latter uses a **DATAFILE**.

The **CREATE TABLESPACE ... TEMPORARY** type tablespace **can be** altered to hold **PERMANENT** objects, whereas a **CREATE TEMPORARY TABLESPACE** type tablespace **cannot** be altered.

The STORAGE clause and its options are as follows:

```
... STORAGE( [INITIAL <integer>[K/M]] [NEXT <integer>[K/M]]
    [MINEXTENTS <integer>] [MAXEXTENTS <integer>/UNLIMITED]
    [PCTINCREASE <integer>]
    [FREELISTS <integer>] [FREELIST GROUPS <integer>]
    [OPTIMAL <integer>[K/M]/NULL ]
    [BUFFER_POOL '<pool_name>' [DEFAULT] / [KEEP/RECYCLE] ]
) ...
```

The STORAGE clause has the following parameters:

Attribute Name	Description
INITIAL	Size in bytes of the initial extent of the object segment. The default value is the size of **5 data blocks**. The minimum value is the size of **2 data blocks** for **non-bitmapped segments** or **3 data blocks** for **bitmapped segments**, plus **one data block** for each **free list group** specified. The maximum value depends on the operation system. Oracle rounds values up to the next multiple of the data block size for values less than 5 data blocks, and it rounds up to the next multiple of 5 data blocks for values greater than 5 data blocks.
NEXT	Size for the next extent after **INITIAL** is used. The default is **5 blocks**, the minimum is **1 block** and the maximum is **4,095 MB**. This is the value that will be used for each new extent, if **PCTINCREASE** is set to **'0'**.
MINEXTENTS	Number of initial extents for the objects. Generally, except for rollback segments, it's set to **'1'**. If a large amount of space is required and if there's not enough contiguous space for the table sitting, using a smaller extent size and specifying several extents may solve the problem.
MAXEXTENTS	Largest number of extents allowed for object. This defaults to the maximum allowed for the block size, as of **version 7.3**. However, it is possible to set **MAXEXTENTS** to unlimited after **version 8**, allowing over **2 billion extents**. However, Oracle suggests **not** going over **4,000 extents** for a single object.

<table>
<tr><td>OPTIMAL</td><td colspan="2">Used only for rollback segments. Specifies the value to which a rollback segment will shrink after extending.</td></tr>
<tr><td>FREELISTS GROUPS</td><td colspan="2">Parameter that specifies the number of freelist groups to maintain for a table or index. This parameter is generally meaningful for only parallel server database and can't be specified unless a database is altered into parallel or share mode.</td></tr>
<tr><td>PCTINCREASE</td><td colspan="2">Specifies how much to grow each extent after the INITIAL and NEXT extents are used. A specification of 50 will grow each extent after NEXT by 50% for each subsequent extent. This means that for a table created with one INITIAL and a NEXT extent, any further extents will increase in size by 50% over the predecessors.In Oracle 7.2 and later versions, this parameter is applied only against the size of the previous extent. Increase this value if it is not known how much the table will grow, though significantly.The value of PCTINCREASE indicates a growth rate for subsequent extents. A tablespace with a default storage setting for PCTINCREASE of 0 will not be automatically coalesced by the SMON process.</td></tr>
<tr><td>FREELISTS</td><td colspan="2">For objects other than tablespaces, specifies the number of freelists for each of the freelist groups for the table, index or cluster. The minimum value is 1 and the maximum is block-size dependent.Before version 8.1.6, this could not be reset without re-creating the table. In 8.1.6 and greater, it can be reset dynamically if the COMPATIBLE initialization parameter is set to 8.1.6 at a minimum.</td></tr>
<tr><td rowspan="3">BUFFER_POOL <pool_name></td><td colspan="2">Specifies the area of the buffer pool where the object will be cached. The <pool_name> parameter corresponds to:</td></tr>
<tr><td>DEFAULT

KEEP

RECYCLE</td><td>The value assigned if no BUFFER_POOL parameter is specified
For objects that should not be rapidly aged out of the buffer pool.
For objects that should be rapidly aged out of the buffer pool.</td></tr>
<tr><td colspan="2">The KEEP and RECYCLE pools are sub-sections of the DEFAULT pools and must be configured in the initialization parameters BUFFER_POOL_KEEP and BUFFER_POOL_RECYCLE before being used.</td></tr>
</table>

Note

Once any tablespace is created it must be **Online** to be useable. The create tablespace syntax, by default, ensures that the Tablespace is placed online. Only when the tablespace is online can users bound to the tablespace use it for storing their objects.

*Creating A Tablespace Using SQL *Plus*

Start a session of **SQL Plus** by clicking on the **Start** button on the taskbar. Then select **All Programs →** **Oracle-OraHome → Application Development → SQL Plus**. Refer to diagram 5.1.

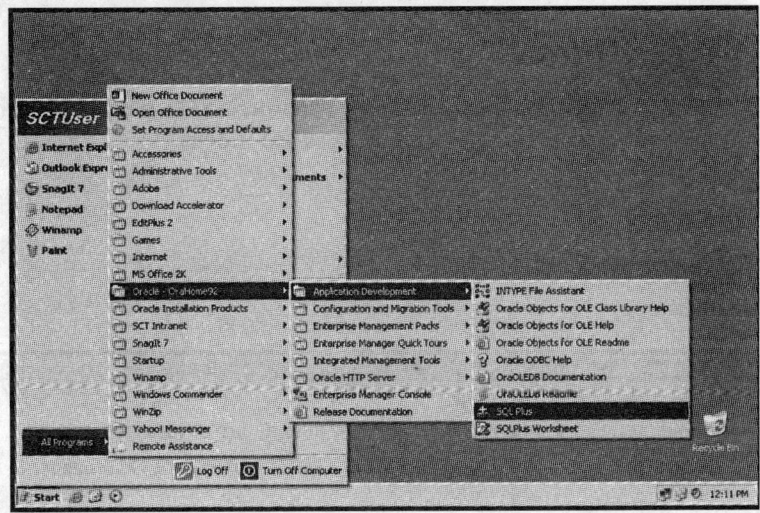

Diagram 5.1

Enter the **User Name** and **Password** in the fields appearing on the **Oracle Log On** dialog box. Refer to diagram 5.2. Click on **OK** to connect to Oracle database server.

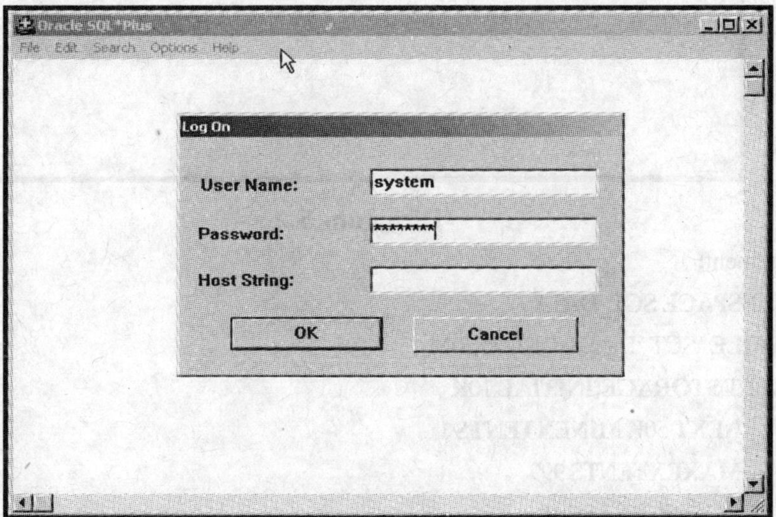

Diagram 5.2

After a successful SQL Login the **Oracle SQL * Plus** window will be visible as shown in diagram 5.3.

Example:

To create a tablespace named **SCT_Admin** connected to data file **sct_admin.dat** with a size of **10 MB**.

CREATE TABLESPACE SCT_Admin

DATAFILE 'sct_admin.dat' **SIZE** 10M

ONLINE;

Create a tablespace named **SCT_Data**. The name of the data file is **SCT_Data.dat** and the size is **20 MB**. The specification for the tablespace's storage parameters is as follows:

INITIAL EXTENT SIZE 10k

NEXT EXTENT SIZE 50k

MINEXTENTS 1 **MAXEXTENTS** 999

PCTINCREASE 10

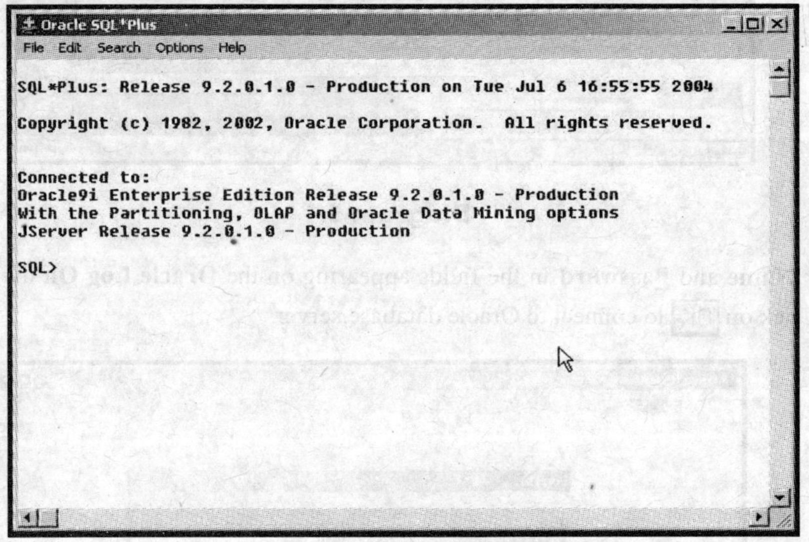

Diagram 5.2

Using SQL statement:

CREATE TABLESPACE SCT_DATA

DATAFILE 'SCT_Data.dat' **SIZE** 20M

DEFAULT STORAGE(INITIAL 10K

NEXT 50K **MINEXTENTS** 1

MAXEXTENTS 999

PCTINCREASE 10

) ONLINE;

When the above SQL commands are typed into Oracle SQL *Plus window the results are as shown in diagram 5.4.

```
Oracle SQL*Plus
File  Edit  Search  Options  Help

Connected to:
Oracle9i Enterprise Edition Release 9.2.0.1.0 - Production
With the Partitioning, OLAP and Oracle Data Mining options
JServer Release 9.2.0.1.0 - Production

SQL> CREATE TABLESPACE SCT_Admin
  2   DATAFILE 'sct_admin.dat' SIZE 10M ONLINE;

Tablespace created.

SQL> CREATE TABLESPACE SCT_DATA
  2   DATAFILE 'SCT_Data.dat'
  3   SIZE 20M DEFAULT STORAGE(
  4    INITIAL 10K NEXT 50K
  5    MINEXTENTS 1
  6    MAXEXTENTS 999
  7    PCTINCREASE 10
  8   )
  9   ONLINE;

Tablespace created.

SQL> |
```

Diagram 5.2

Creating Tablespace Through Enterprise Manager

The **Oracle Enterprise Manager Console** utility has been designed to assist Oracle DBA's in managing the Oracle 9i database. It is user-friendly due to its GUI and multiple features.

One of it's many features is its ability to create tablespaces. This reduces the need to remember the actual syntax to create a tablespace. This part of the material will deal with the creation of a tablespace through this tool available in **Oracle 9i - Enterprise Edition**.

Note

Starting Oracle 9i's Listener Service

If the **Startup** property for **Oracle9i - TNSListener** service has been set to manual, then it is necessary to manually activate the **Oracle9i - TNSListener** service.

Creating A Tablespace

Click on **Start**. Then select **All Programs à Oracle – OraHome92 à Enterprise Manager Console** to activate **Oracle Enterprise Manager Console**.

This will activate the **Oracle Enterprise Manager Login** dialog box. Select the option **Launch standalone** and click on the **OK** button.

In the **Oracle Enterprise Manager Console** window, select and expand the second node belonging to the **Global Database Name** specified during installation. This will display the **Database Connect Information** dialog box

In this dialog box enter the **Username** as **SYS** along with its appropriate **Password** and click on OK to continue.

When the node expands click on the (plus) sign besides the **Storage** node to expand it, as shown in diagram 5.5.

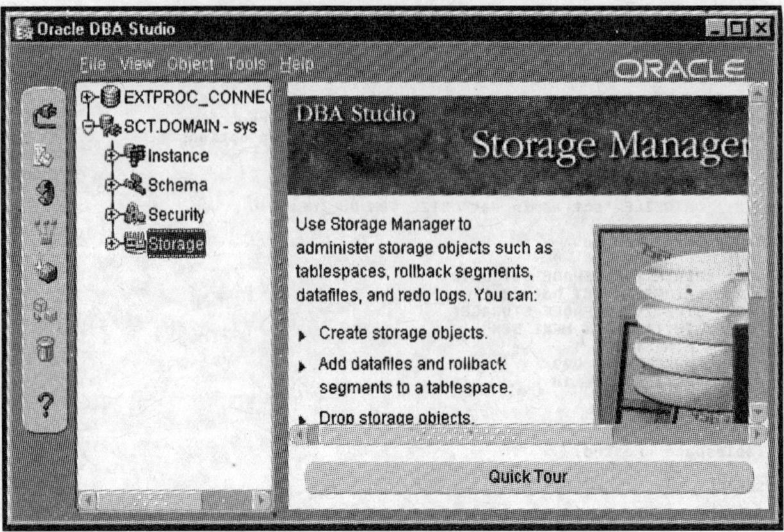

Diagram 5.5

When node expands, select the node **Tablespaces** below **Storage** to get a list of tablespaces created under Oracle 9i. Refer to diagram 5.6.

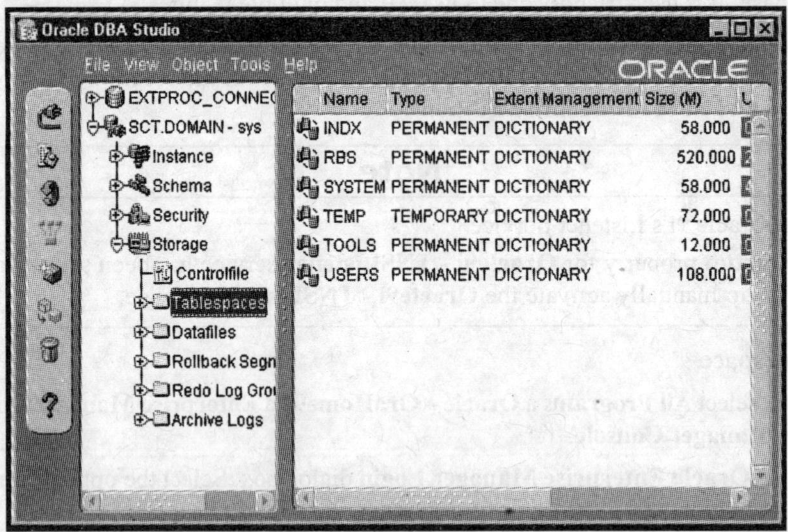

Diagram 5.6

Right click on the **Tablespaces** node to get a popup menu as shown in diagram 5.7.

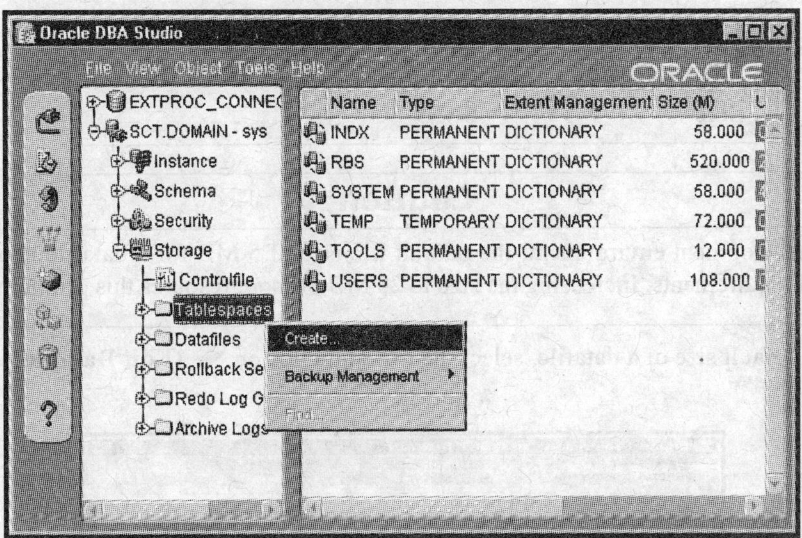

Diagram 5.7

Click on the **Create...** menu option to get the **Create Tablespace** dialog box as shown in diagram 5.8.

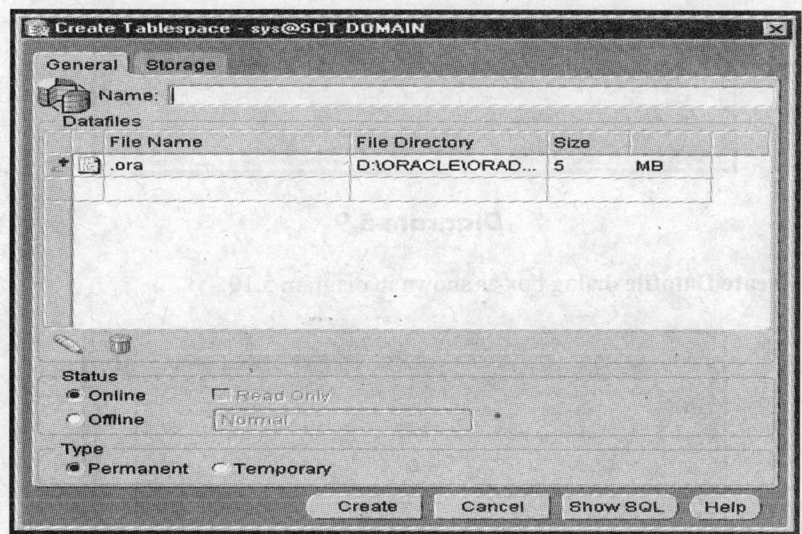

Diagram 5.8

Enter a **Name** for the new tablespace in the field provided. As a value is keyed into this field, the fields in the Datafiles section get auto-populated.

The **Datafiles** section contains values related to **datafiles** physical storage on the HDD. These values are the filename, path and size of a datafile.

The default values for a datafile, set in the **Datafiles** section are:

File Name	<Tablespace Name>**.ora**
File Directory	<Oracle Home>/ **ORADATA/**<SID>
Size	**5 MB**

Caution

In a development environment, the default file size of 5 MB for a datafile could be less than actual requirements. Increasing the size to 20 MB or more resolves this problem.

To change to the default size of a datafile, select the row and click on **(Edit Datafile)** icon as shown in diagram 5.9.

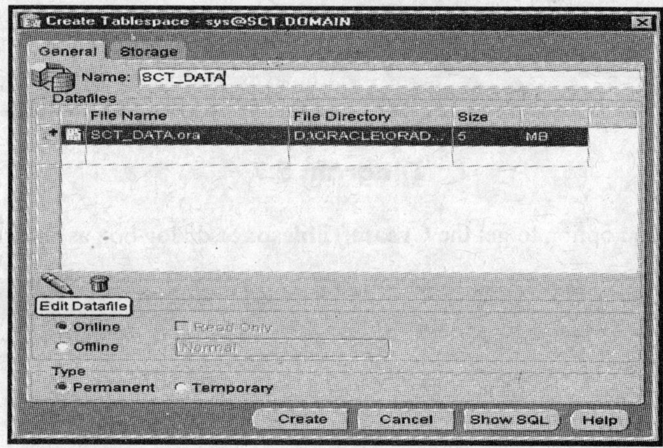

Diagram 5.9

This will open the **Create Datafile** dialog box as shown in diagram 5.10.

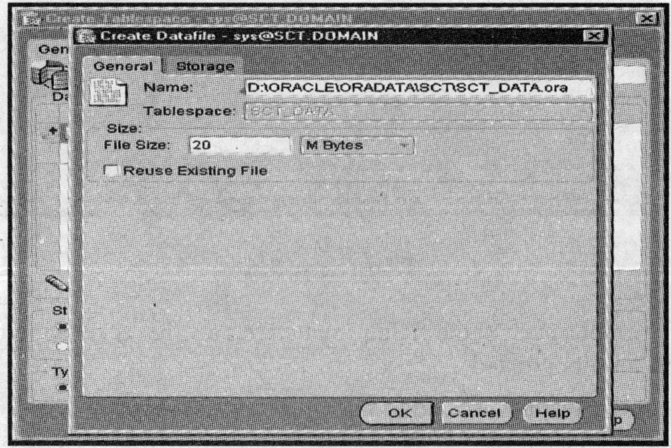

Diagram 5.10

Place appropriate values in File name, File directory and size. This provides appropriate values to parameters required by the **Create tablespace** UI.

Click on the **Storage** tab. In the tab sheet visible select the option that activates the datafile's **AUTOEXTEND** parameter. Then specify the values for the fields **Increment** and **Maximum Size**. Refer to diagram 5.11.

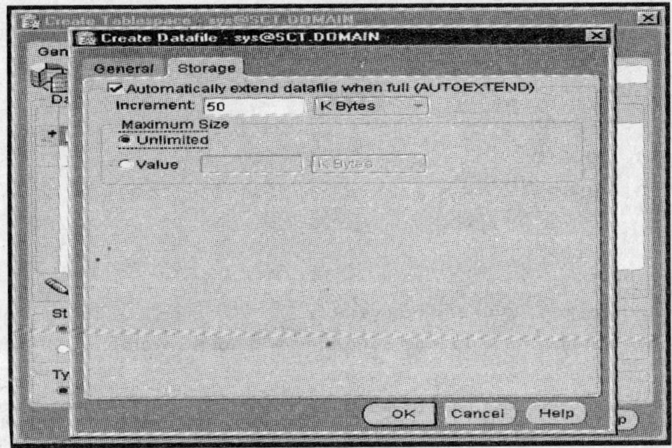

Diagram 5.11

Note

Multiple **Datafiles** can be added to a tablespace by clicking on the blank row in the **Datafiles** section. On being clicked, the blank row will automatically display default values. To change the default datafile name, overtype the contents of the **File Name** column.

Click on OK to close the **Create Datafile** dialog box and **return to the Create Tablespace** dialog box.

Once done click on the **Storage** tab for the **Create Tablespace** dialog box to get a display as shown in diagram 5.12.

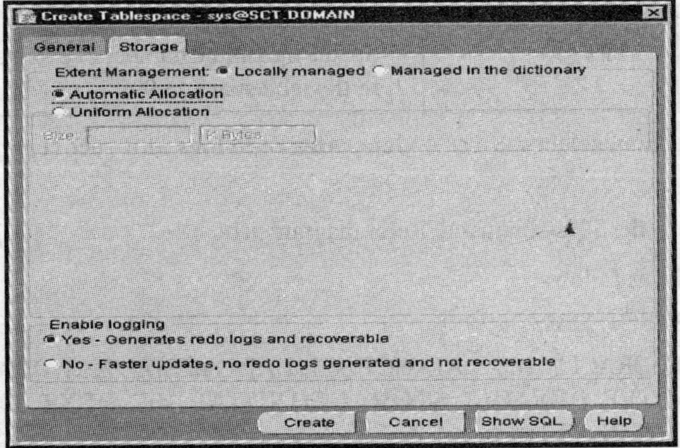

Diagram 5.12

Select the radio button **Managed in the dictionary**. A tab sheet will appear as shown in diagram 5.13.

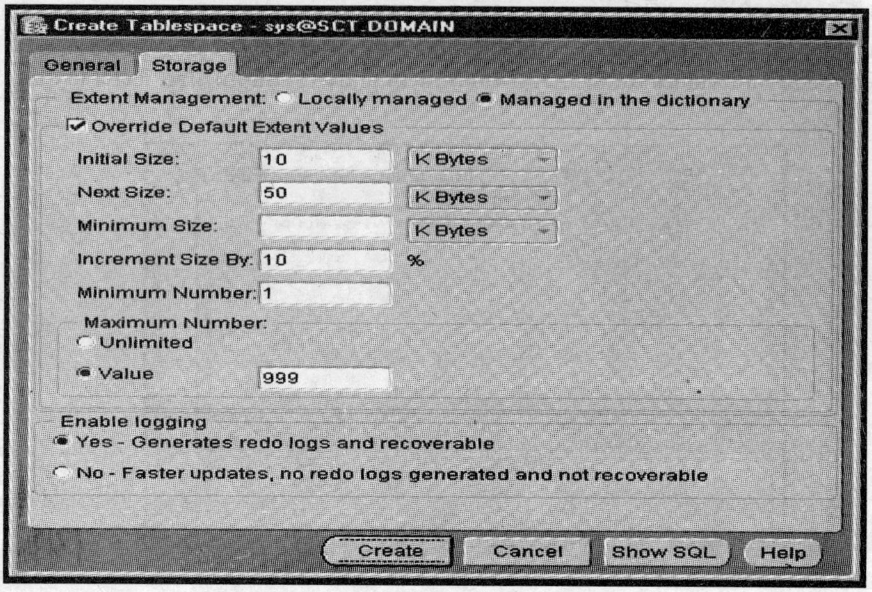

Diagram 5.13

Enter the values for the following fields:

Field Name	Value	Description
Initial Size	10 K Bytes	Set the initial extent of the objects in the tablespace to 10KB.
Next Size	50 K Bytes	Size for the next extent after **INITIAL** is used
Increment Size By	10%	Set the size for the next extent to increase by 10%.
Minimum Number	1	Set the minimum number of extents allowed for an object in the tablespace to 1.
Maximum Number	999	Set the maximum number of extents allowed for an object in the tablespace to 999.

In the **Enable logging** section, select the **Yes – Generates redo logs and recoverable** option to allow the creation of logs files.

Click on Show SQL to view the SQL command. Refer diagram 5.14.

The SQL Command will be as follows:

CREATE TABLESPACE "SCT_DATA"

LOGGING DATAFILE 'D:\ORACLE \ORADATA\SCT\SCT_DATA.ora' **SIZE** 20M **AUTOEXTEND ON NEXT** 50K **MAXSIZE** UNLIMITED **DEFAULT STORAGE(INITIAL** 10K **NEXT** 50K **MINEXTENTS** 1 **MAXEXTENTS** 999 **PCTINCREASE** 10)

Click on Create to execute the SQL Command generated by the **Create Tablespace** dialog box.

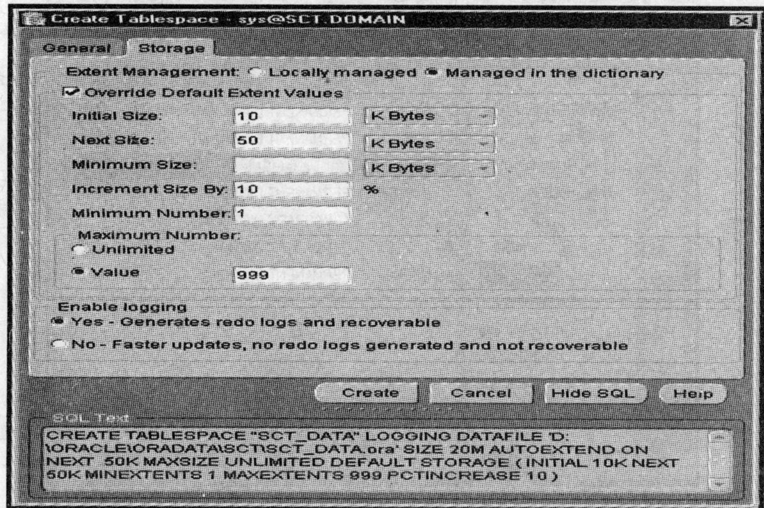

Diagram 5.14

When the new tablespace is created a message is displayed as shown in diagram 5.15.

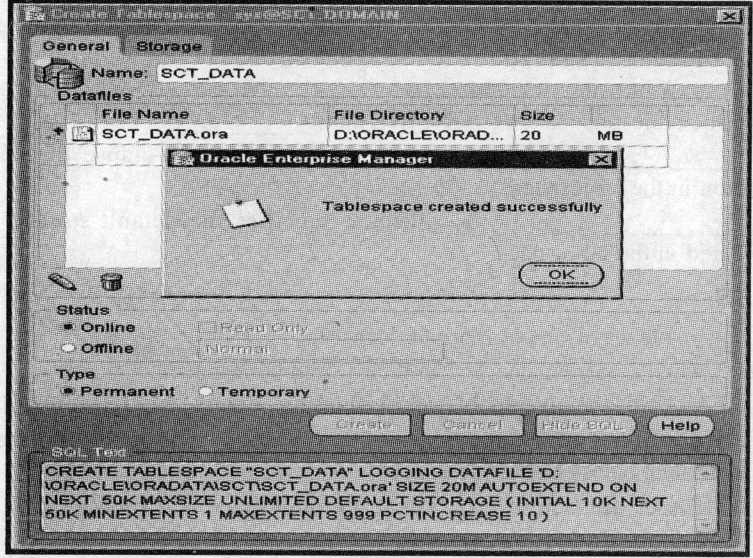

Diagram 5.15: Message indicating that the new tablespace is created.

Click on OK to continue. When the **Create Tablespace** dialog box automatically closes, the new tablespace will be listed with those previously created within the database. Refer to diagram 5.16.

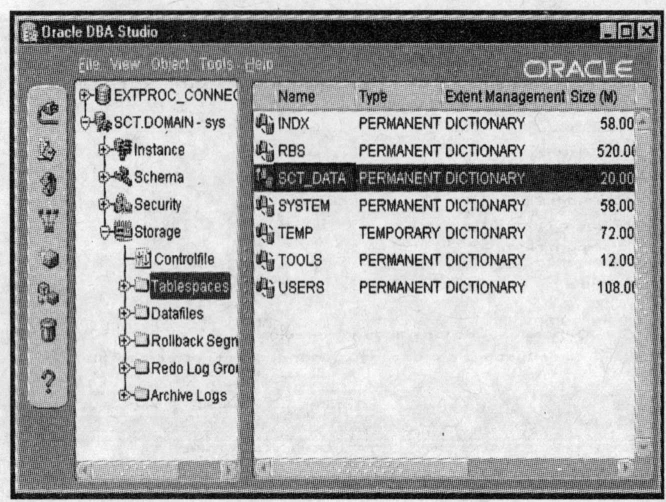

Diagram 5.16: New list of tablespace within the database.

Self Review Questions

Fill in the Blanks

1. The size of the tablespace can be determined as the _________ of the sizes of all its data files.
2. When any database is created, the Oracle engine creates a default tablespace named ___________ within the database.
3. By default, the tablespace is set to ONLINE and ____________.
4. The ____________________ attribute accepts the integer clause that controls free-space fragmentation in the tablespace.
5. The ___________ ___________ attribute specifies the default storage parameters for all objects created in the tablespace.

True or False

6. A database is made up of one or more tablespaces.
7. User objects when created are stored in the System tablespace.
8. The AUTOEXTEND attribute enables or disables the automatic extension of the data files.
9. The OFFLINE attribute makes the tablespace available immediately after creation to users who have been granted access to the tablespace.
10. The TEMPORARY attribute specifies that the tablespace will be used only to hold temporary objects.

Hands On Exercises

1. Using the SQL*PLUS tool, create a tablespace named **SCT_INVT**. The name of the data file will be **SCT_Invt.dat** and the size will be **25 MB**. The specification for the tablespace's storage parameters is as follows:
   INITIAL EXTENT SIZE 10k **NEXT EXTENT SIZE** 50k
   MINEXTENTS 1 **MAXEXTENTS** 499 **PCTINCREASE** 10
2. Using the SQL*PLUS tool, create a user bound to the **SCT_INVT** tablespace. The name of the Oracle user will be **DBA_INVTSYS** and will have a password of choice.

6

Users, Roles and Privileges

Changing the Default Password for SYS

Once Oracle 9i is installed on M.S. Windows, change the default passwords for Oracle logins, created during the installation process, using a utility called Enterprise Manager Console.

Invoke DBA Studio as follows:

Click on Start. Then select **All Programs → Oracle - OraHome92 → Enterprise Manager Console.**

This will activate the Oracle Enterprise Manager Console Login dialog box, which permits connecting to a specific Oracle resource. Refer to diagram 6.1.

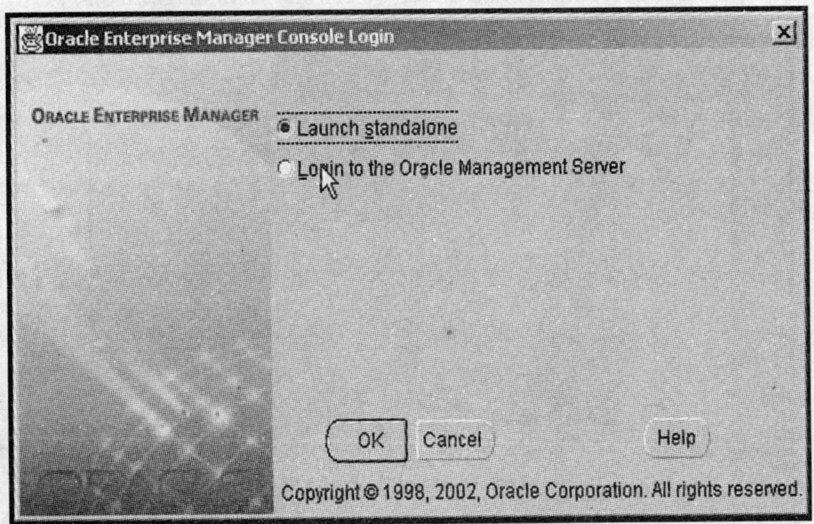

Diagram 6.1: The Oracle Enterprise Manager Login.

Select the Launch standalone radio button and click on OK.

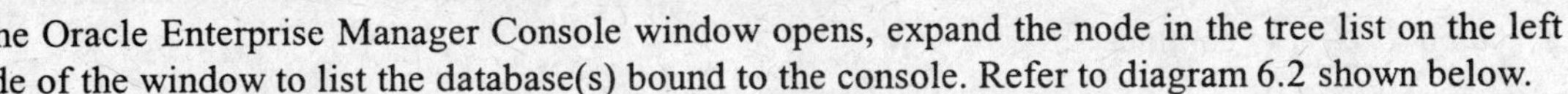

When the Oracle Enterprise Manager Console window opens, expand the node in the tree list on the left hand side of the window to list the database(s) bound to the console. Refer to diagram 6.2 shown below.

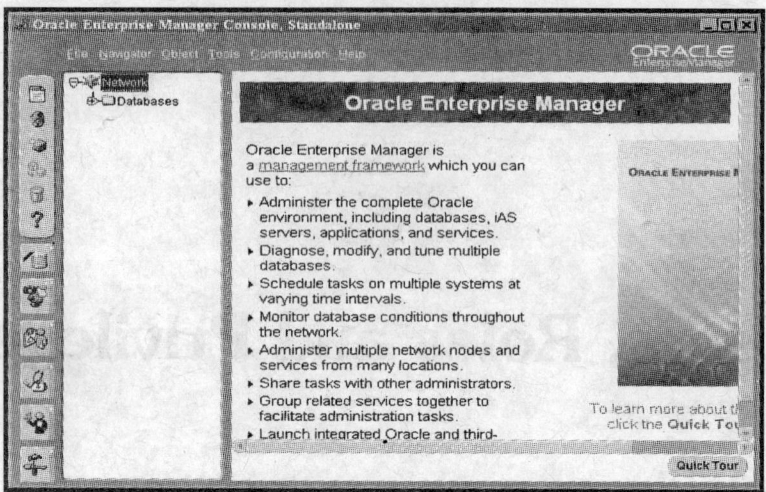

Diagram 6.2: The Oracle Enterprise Manager.

Note
The Global Database Name was set to SCT at the time the Oracle engine was installed.

Click on the  (plus) sign besides the node belonging to the Global Database Name and expand it. This will display the Database Connect Information dialog box as shown in diagram 6.3.

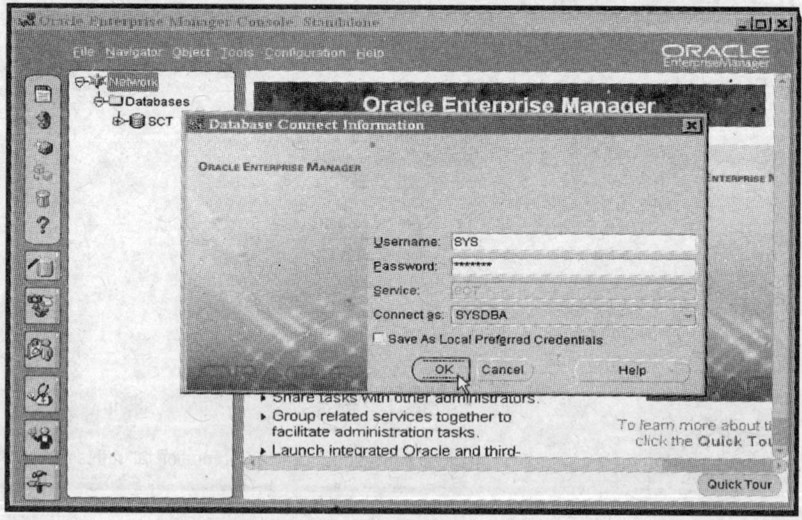

Diagram 6.3: The Database Connect Information dialog box.

In this dialog box enter the Username as sys and the Password as mentioned during the installation process. Click on OK to continue.

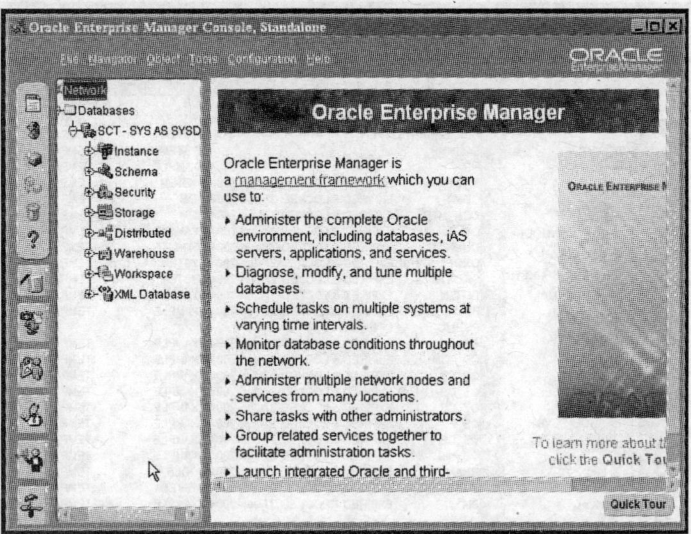

Diagram 6.4.1: Oracle 9i - Security.

When the node expands, the screen as shown in diagram 6.4.1 will appear.

Select the Security node and click on the ⊞ (plus) sign besides it to expand it. This will display the screen as shown in diagram 6.4.2.

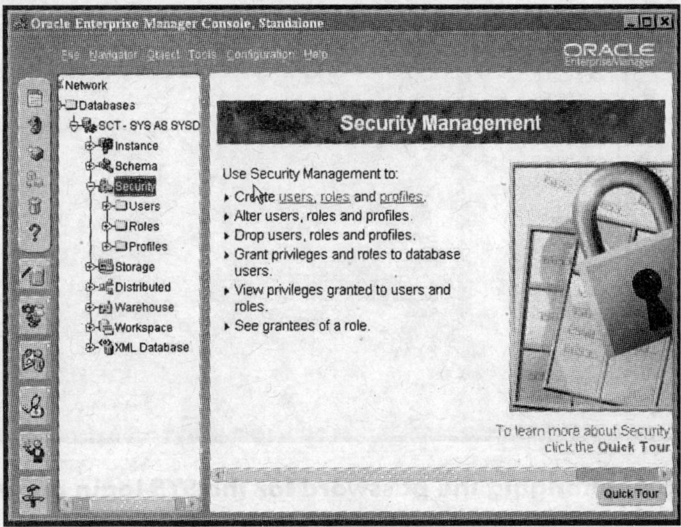

Diagram 6.4.2

Select the Users node and expand it by clicking on the ⊞ (plus) sign besides it. The Oracle Enterprise Manager window will display a list of users existing under Oracle 9i for the current database. Refer to diagram 6.5.

Select SYS under Users the screen as shown in diagram 6.6 appears.

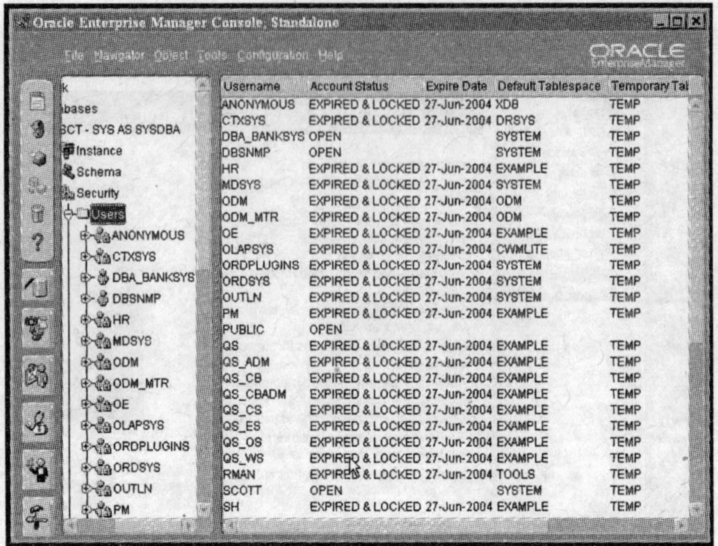

Username	Account Status	Expire Date	Default Tablespace	Temporary Tal
ANONYMOUS	EXPIRED & LOCKED	27-Jun-2004	XDB	TEMP
CTXSYS	EXPIRED & LOCKED	27-Jun-2004	DRSYS	TEMP
DBA_BANKSYS	OPEN		SYSTEM	TEMP
DBSNMP	OPEN		SYSTEM	TEMP
HR	EXPIRED & LOCKED	27-Jun-2004	EXAMPLE	TEMP
MDSYS	EXPIRED & LOCKED	27-Jun-2004	SYSTEM	TEMP
ODM	EXPIRED & LOCKED	27-Jun-2004	ODM	TEMP
ODM_MTR	EXPIRED & LOCKED	27-Jun-2004	ODM	TEMP
OE	EXPIRED & LOCKED	27-Jun-2004	EXAMPLE	TEMP
OLAPSYS	EXPIRED & LOCKED	27-Jun-2004	CWMLITE	TEMP
ORDPLUGINS	EXPIRED & LOCKED	27-Jun-2004	SYSTEM	TEMP
ORDSYS	EXPIRED & LOCKED	27-Jun-2004	SYSTEM	TEMP
OUTLN	EXPIRED & LOCKED	27-Jun-2004	SYSTEM	TEMP
PM	EXPIRED & LOCKED	27-Jun-2004	EXAMPLE	TEMP
PUBLIC	OPEN			
QS	EXPIRED & LOCKED	27-Jun-2004	EXAMPLE	TEMP
QS_ADM	EXPIRED & LOCKED	27-Jun-2004	EXAMPLE	TEMP
QS_CB	EXPIRED & LOCKED	27-Jun-2004	EXAMPLE	TEMP
QS_CBADM	EXPIRED & LOCKED	27-Jun-2004	EXAMPLE	TEMP
QS_CS	EXPIRED & LOCKED	27-Jun-2004	EXAMPLE	TEMP
QS_ES	EXPIRED & LOCKED	27-Jun-2004	EXAMPLE	TEMP
QS_OS	EXPIRED & LOCKED	27-Jun-2004	EXAMPLE	TEMP
QS_WS	EXPIRED & LOCKED	27-Jun-2004	EXAMPLE	TEMP
RMAN	EXPIRED & LOCKED	27-Jun-2004	TOOLS	TEMP
SCOTT	OPEN		SYSTEM	TEMP
SH	EXPIRED & LOCKED	27-Jun-2004	EXAMPLE	TEMP

Diagram 6.5: List of Users under Oracle 9i

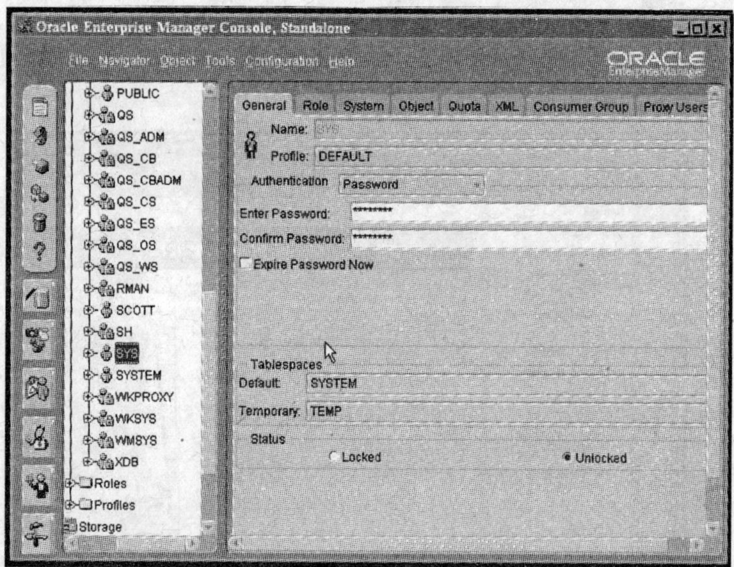

Diagram 6.6: Changing the password for the SYS login under Oracle 9i.

Replace the contents of the Enter Password and the Confirm Password fields with a new password for the SYS login.

On clicking Apply the contents of both fields will be cross-checked and the new password for the SYS login will be registered with the Oracle engine.

Activating/Deactivating the Oracle 9i Engine

During the installation process, the services of Oracle Database and its Listener are set to startup automatically, (i.e. when the computer is switched on). This causes computer resources (i.e. memory) to be occupied by these services, even though they may not be in use. This adds to the load on the computers CPU and can affect performance.

To avoid such resource blockage, disable the automatic start up of Oracle 9i. Oracle can be started on demand when required.

Disabling Automatic Startup

To disable Automatic Startup of Oracle 9i under Windows XP:

Click on Start. Then select Control Panel. When the Control Panel window will appear as shown in diagram 6.7, select the link named Performance and Maintenance. The Control Panel window will change to the Performance and Maintenance Window.

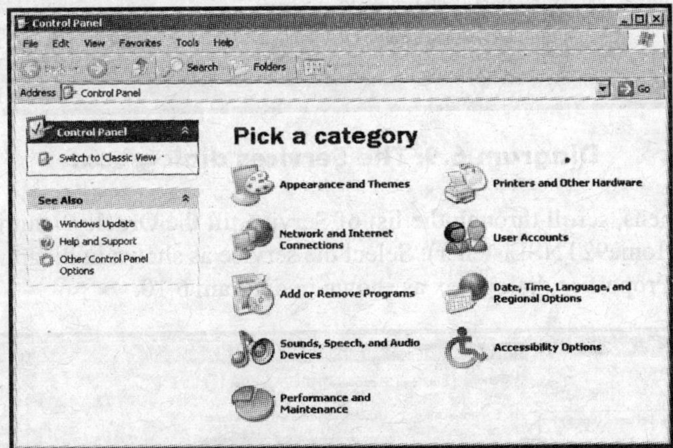

Diagram 6.7: The Control Panel window.

Select the option Administrators Tools to get a window as shown in diagram 6.8.

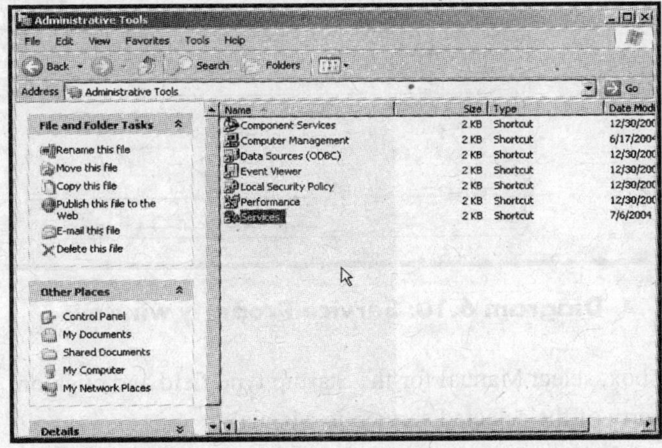

Diagram 6.8: The Administrators Tools window.

Double click on the Services icon to get the dialog box as shown in diagram 6.9.

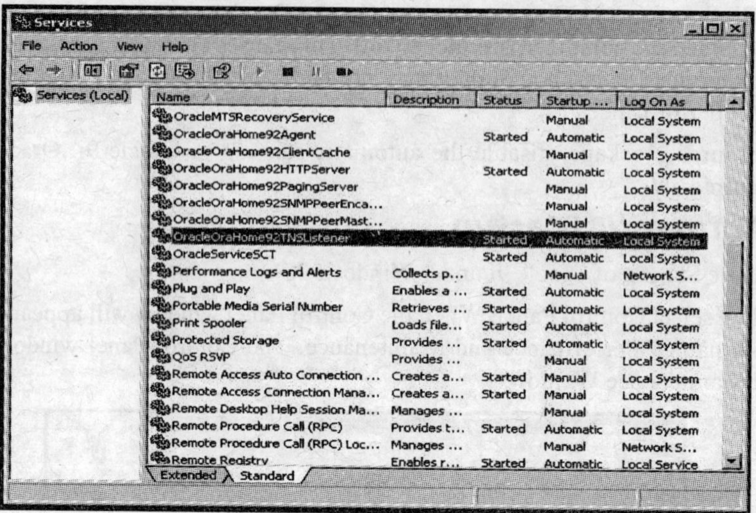

Diagram 6.9: The Services dialog box.

When the dialog box opens, scroll through the list of Service till the Oracle 9i automatic startup service is visible, (i.e. OracleOraHome92TNSListener). Select the service as shown in diagram 6.9. Double click the select option to get the Properties dialog box as shown in diagram 6.10.

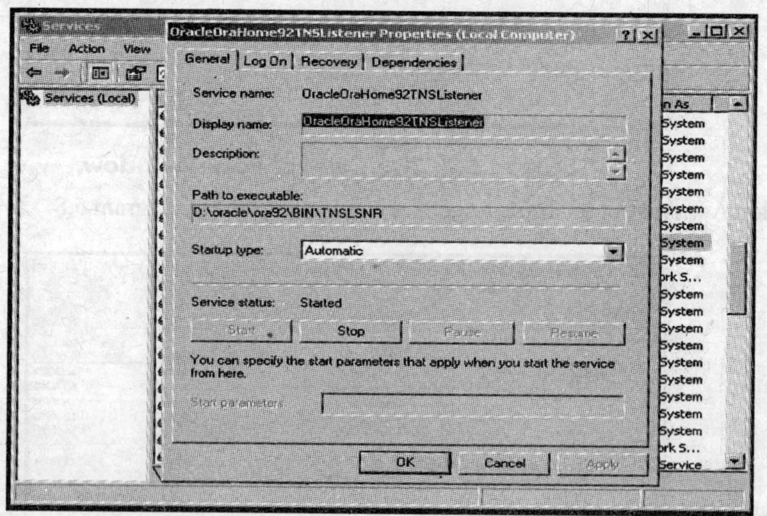

Diagram 6.10: Service Property window.

In the Properties dialog box, select Manual for the Startup type field and click on Apply. This will change the Startup property of the selected service to Manual.

In the Service status section, click on Stop. The progress dialog box as shown in diagram 6.11 appears.

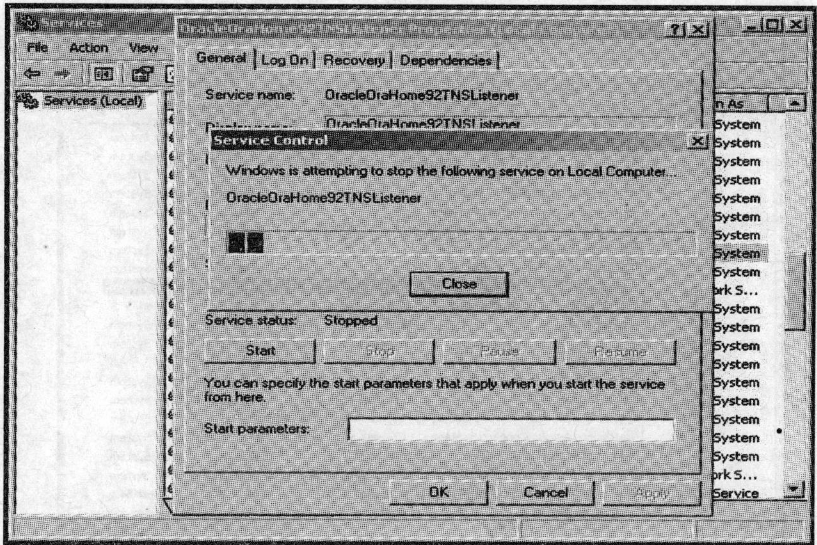

Diagram 6.11: Progress for stopping the service.

When the service is stopped the Status property for the selected service will be blank. Refer diagram 6.12.

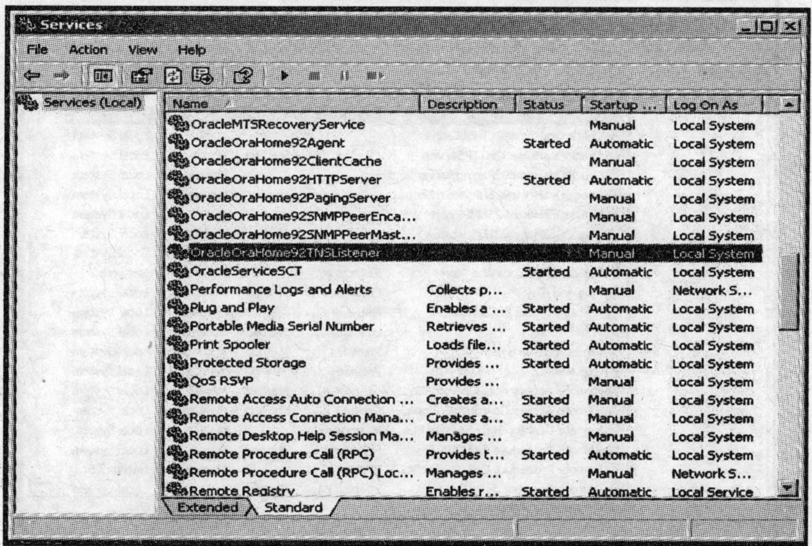

Diagram 6.12: Status changed for the service.

Select the next Oracle service whose startup is set to automatic and repeat the above steps.

When the automatic startup feature for all services belonging to Oracle 9i have been set to manual (i.e. disabled) the Service dialog box will appear as shown in diagrams 6.13 to 6.15.

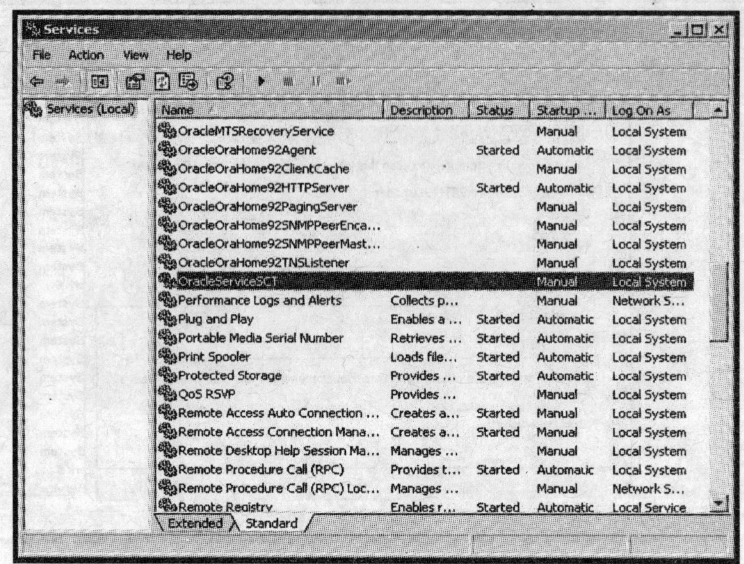

Diagram 6.13: Disabling Oracle SID.

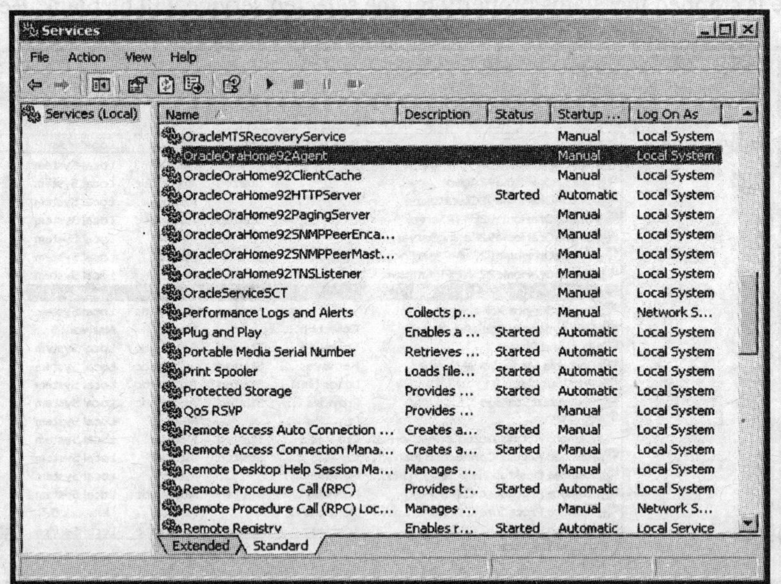

Diagram 6.14: Disabling Oracle Agent.

The services those are disabled includes:

- ❑ OracleOraHome92Agent
- ❑ OracleOraHome92HTTPService
- ❑ OracleService<SID>

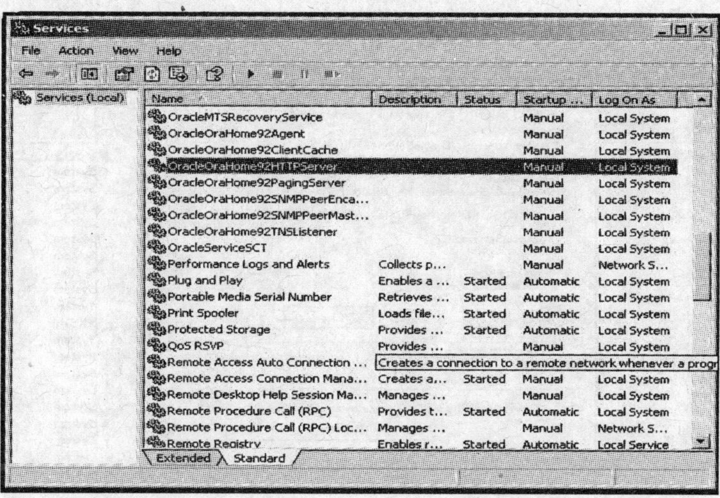

Diagram 6.15: Disabling Oracle HTTP Service.

Enabling A Service on Demand

To access the Oracle 9i database, it is necessary to have the Oracle Database Server running. It is only when the listener services and the Database service is running that Oracle resources such as Tables and Views and so on can be accessed.

Manually Enabling The Oracle 9i Services

Click on Start. Then select Settings à Control Panel.

When the Control Panel window open double click on the Services icon to get the Service dialog box. Scroll through the list of Service to select the Oracle Database Service (i.e. OracleServiceSCT). Double click the selected option, as shown in diagram 6.16. When the Properties dialog box appears, click Start to get the progress dialog box.

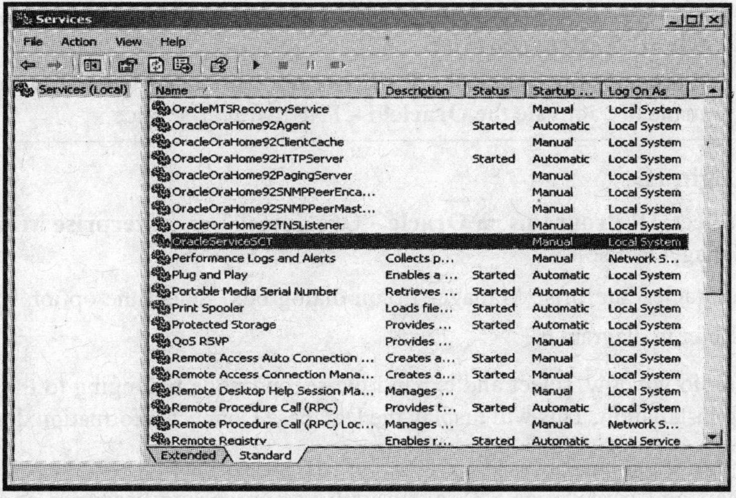

Diagram 6.16

A Progress dialog box indicating that the service will be started is displayed as shown in diagram 6.17.

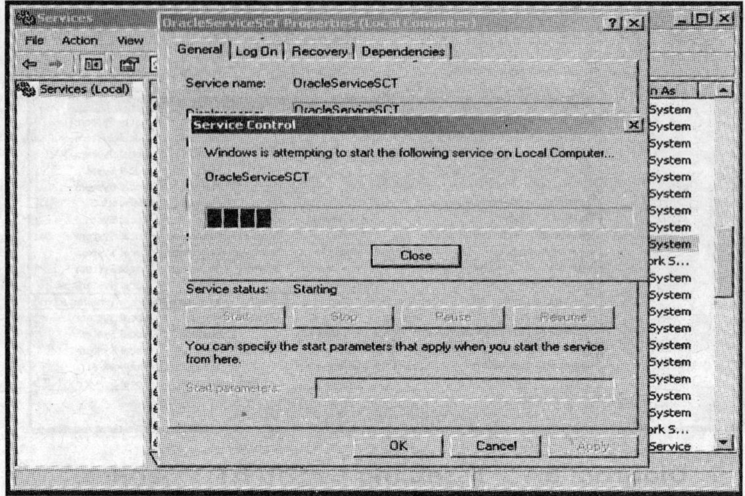

Diagram 6.17

Once the service has been activated, it continues to run in memory as long as it is not manually stopped or the computer is switched off. All other Oracle services must be activated in the similar manner when required.

Creating a DBA Login ID

If a DBA login ID does not exist then it has to be created manually. The following steps indicate how a DBA login ID is created and appropriate privileges given to the DBA login ID with a special focus on creating tablespaces.

Note

 **Starting Oracle 9i's Listener Service**

If the **Startup** property for **Oracle9i - TNSListener** service has been set to manual, then it is necessary to manually activate the **Oracle9i - TNSListener** service.

Creating A DBA Login ID

Click on Start. Then select **All Programs → Oracle - OraHome92 → Enterprise Manager** Console to activate Enterprise Manager Console.

This will activate the Oracle Enterprise Manager Login dialog box. Select the option Launch standalone and click on OK. Refer to diagram 6.1.

In the Oracle DBA Studio window, select and expand the second node belonging to the Global Database Name specified during installation. This will display the Database Connect Information dialog box as shown in diagram 6.3.

In this dialog box enter the Username as SYS along with its appropriate Password and click OK to continue.

When the node expands click on the ⊞ (plus) sign besides the Security node to expand it. Then expand the Users node by clicking on the ⊞ (plus) sign besides it to get a list of user existing under Oracle 9i for the current database. Refer to diagram 6.5.

Right click on the User node and select the Create... option from the popup menu, as shown in diagram 6.18.

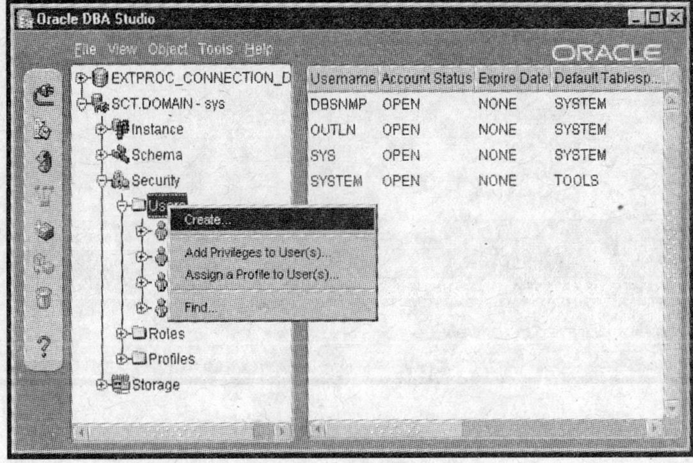

Diagram 6.18

This will open new window as shown in diagram 6.19. Enter DBA_SCT as the value of the Name field.

Make appropriate entries for the Enter Password and the Confirm Password fields. In the Tablespaces frame, select the Default tablespace as SYSTEM.

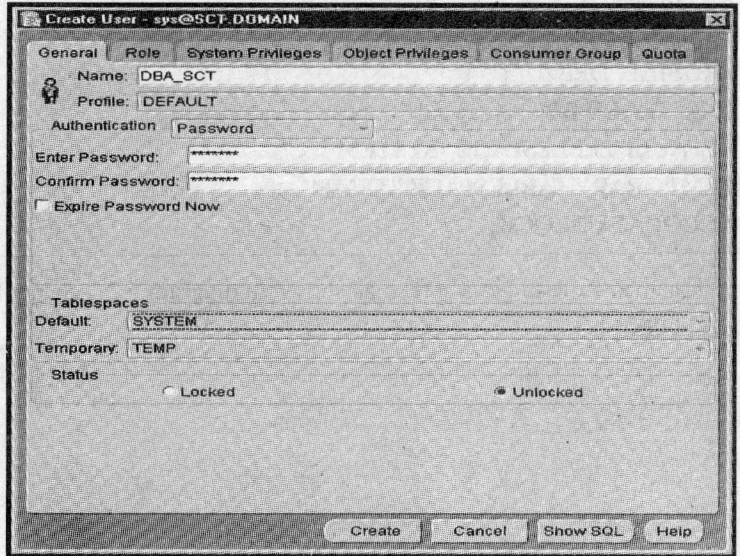

Diagram 6.19

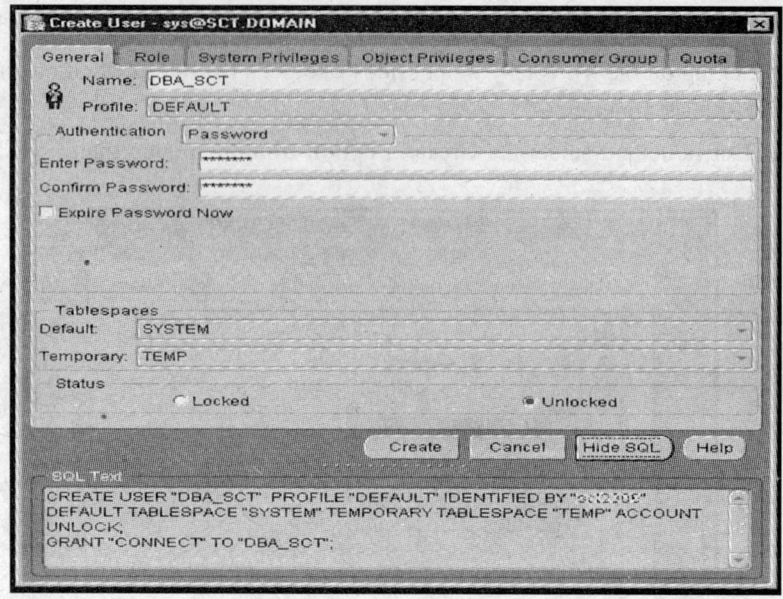

Diagram 6.20

Tip

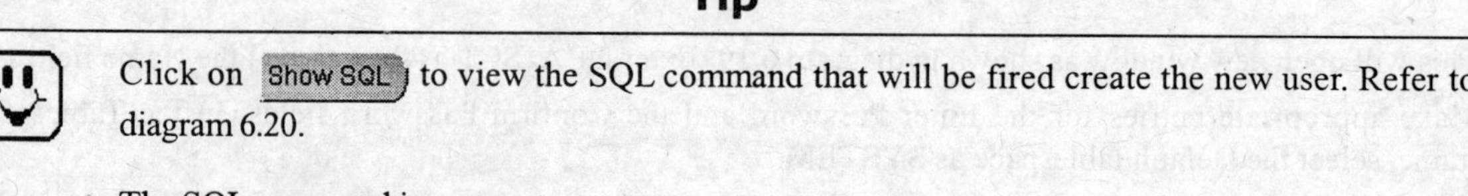

Click on Show SQL to view the SQL command that will be fired create the new user. Refer to diagram 6.20.

The SQL command is:

CREATE USER "DBA_SCT"
PROFILE "DEFAULT"
IDENTIFIED BY "<password>"
DEFAULT TABLESPACE "SYSTEM"
TEMPORARY TABLESPACE "TEMP"
ACCOUNT UNLOCK;

Click on the tab mark named Role to get a screen as shown in diagram 6.21. Select the role named DBA and click on to add the role.

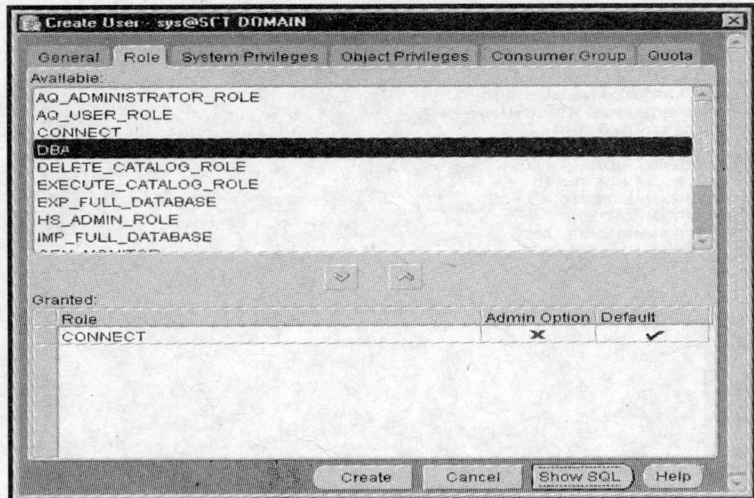

Diagram 6.21

After the new role is added, click on the cell below Admin Option to change the ✗ (cross) sign to the ✓ (check) sign. Refer to diagram 6.22.

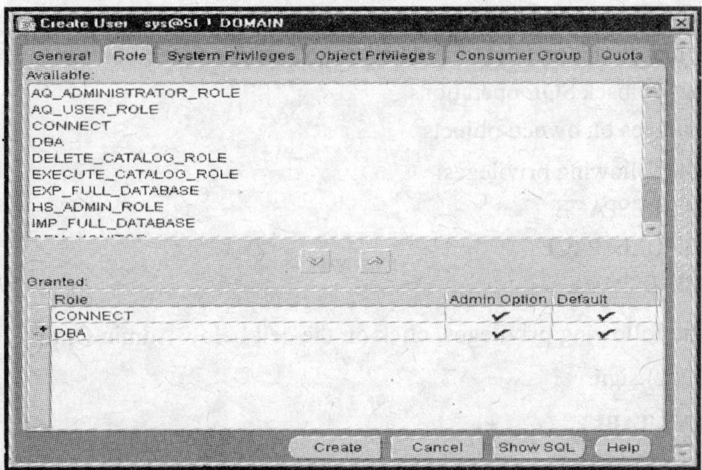

Diagram 6.22

The SQL command displayed on click of Show SQL will now have the following additional lines:

GRANT "CONNECT" **TO** "DBA_SCT"

WITH ADMIN OPTION;

GRANT "DBA" **TO** "DBA_SCT"

WITH ADMIN OPTION;

Click on the tab mark named System Privileges to get a screen as shown in diagram 6.23.

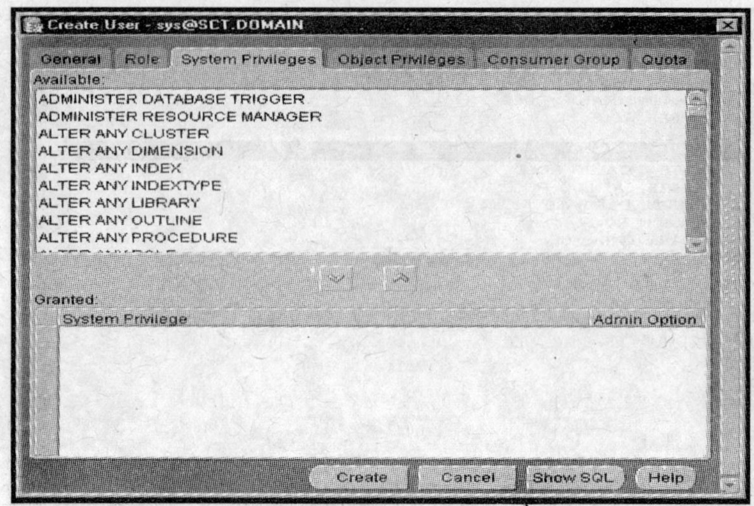

Diagram 6.23

Select from the list of System Privileges and click on [⌄] to add them.

Include privileges required to perform basic SQL operations like:

- ❑ Creating, modifying and deleting tables or views
- ❑ Inserting, modifying and deleting data within self created tables
- ❑ Commit or Rollback SQL operations
- ❑ Grant privileges on owned objects

Additionally, add the following privileges:

- ❑ ALTER TABLESPACE
- ❑ CREATE TABLESPACE
- ❑ DROP TABLESPACE

Then for each of the following privileges, click on the cell below Admin Option to change the ✘ (cross) sign to the ✔ (check) sign.

ALTER ANY TABLE

CREATE ANY TABLE

CREATE TABLE

DELETE ANY TABLE

DROP ANY TABLE

GRANT ANY PRIVILEGE

INSERT ANY TABLE

SELECT ANY TABLE

UPDATE ANY TABLE

The window will now appear as shown in diagram 6.24.

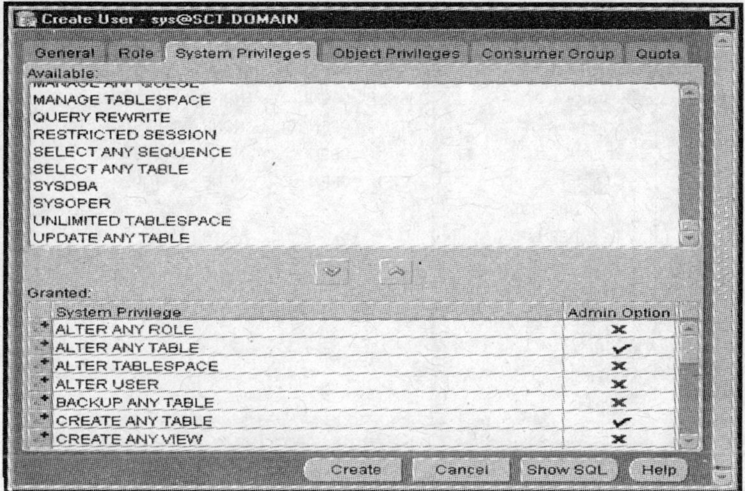

Diagram 6.24

Click Show SQL to view the additional lines of SQL commands.

Click on Create to create the new user with DBA rights. If the SQL command was successfully executed a message indicating the same will be displayed, as shown in diagram 6.25.

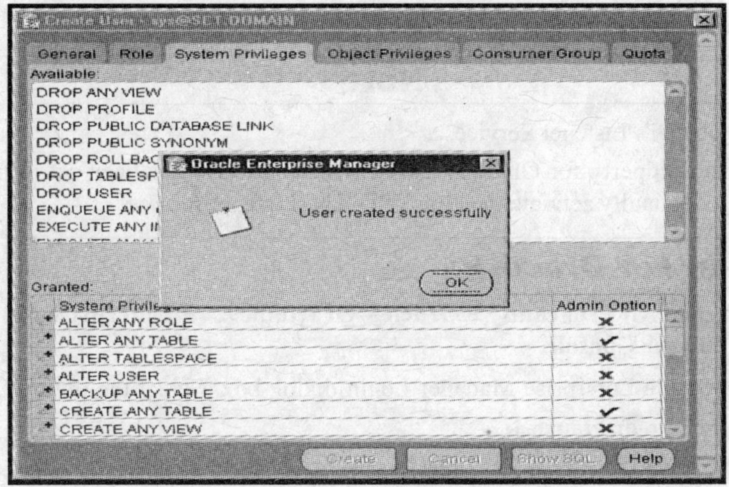

Diagram 6.25

Click on OK to continue.

The new user with DBA rights will be listed along with the other user for Oracle 8i, as shown in diagram 6.26.

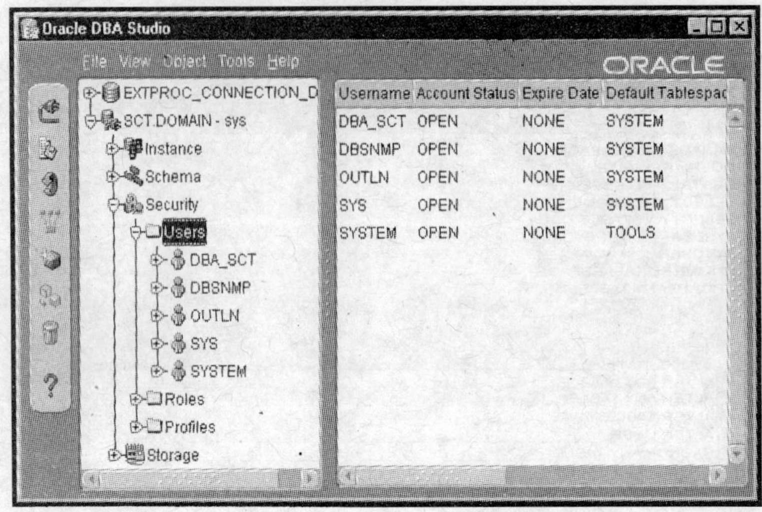

Diagram 6.26

Creating a User

The Database Administrator (DBA) can, use the Enterprise Manager Console utility to create new users who will use Oracle 9i resources. Users created by the DBA will have limited privileges, being restricted to creating and managing tables or views within a single tablespace.

The technique of creating a User, under Oracle 9i, is similar to creating the DBA. The difference is in the set of privileges assigned to a user.

Note

Starting Oracle 9i's Listener Service

If the Startup property for Oracle9i - TNSListener service has been set to manual, then it is necessary to manually activate the Oracle9i - TNSListener service.

Creating A User For Oracle 9i

Click on Start. Then select **All Programs → Oracle - OraHome92 → Enterprise Manager Console** to activate **Enterprise Manager Console.**

This will activate the Oracle Enterprise Manager Login dialog box. Select the option Launch standalone and click on OK. Refer to diagram 6.1

In the Enterprise Manager Console window, select and expand the second node belonging to the Global Database Name specified during installation. This will display the Database Connect Information dialog box as shown in diagram 6.27

In this dialog box enter the Username as DBA along with its Password and click OK to continue.

Diagram 6.7

When the node expands click on the (plus) sign besides the Security node to expand it. Then expand the Users node by clicking on the (plus) sign besides it to get a list of user existing under Oracle 8i for the current database. Refer to diagram 6.28.

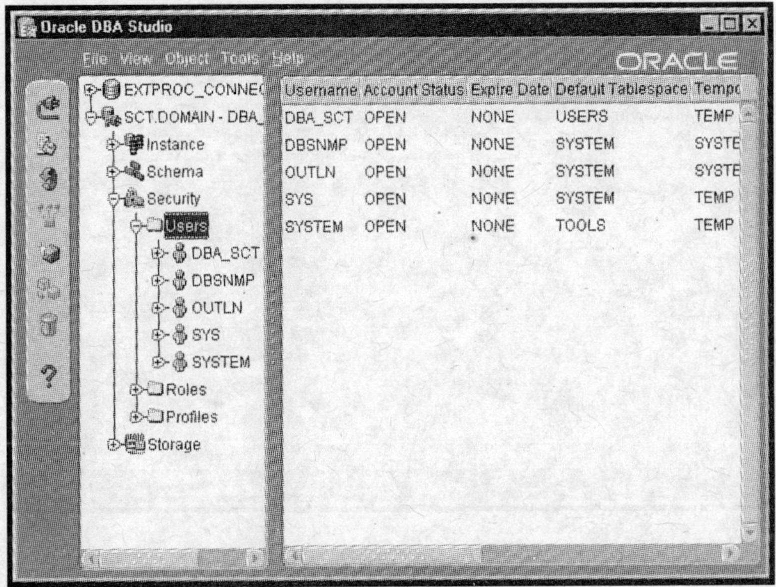

Diagram 6.28: List of Users within the database

Right click on the Users node and select the Create... option from the popup menu, as shown in diagram 6.29

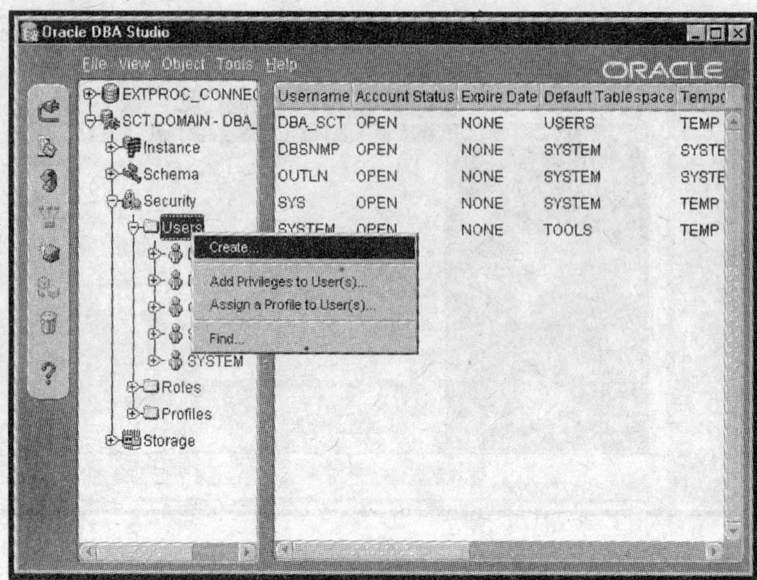

Diagram 6.29

This will open new window as shown in diagram 6.30. Enter an appropriate user name value in the Name field.

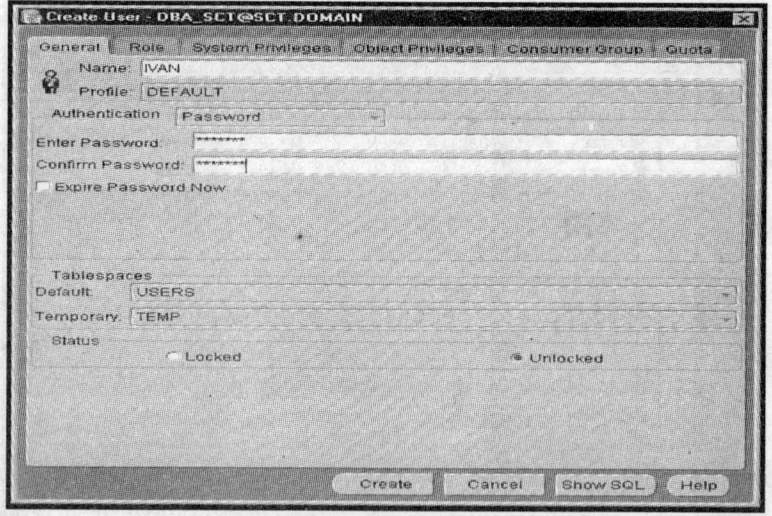

Diagram 6.30

Then appropriate values in the Enter Password and the Confirm Password fields.

In the Tablespaces frame, click on the Default field and select SCT_DATA for the popup menu. Refer to diagram 6.31.

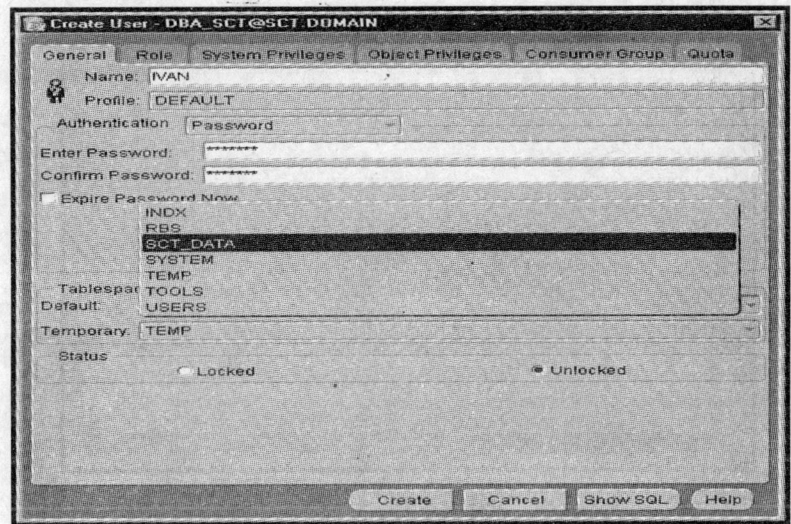

Diagram 6.31

Click on the tab mark named Role. A screen as shown in diagram 6.32 appears.

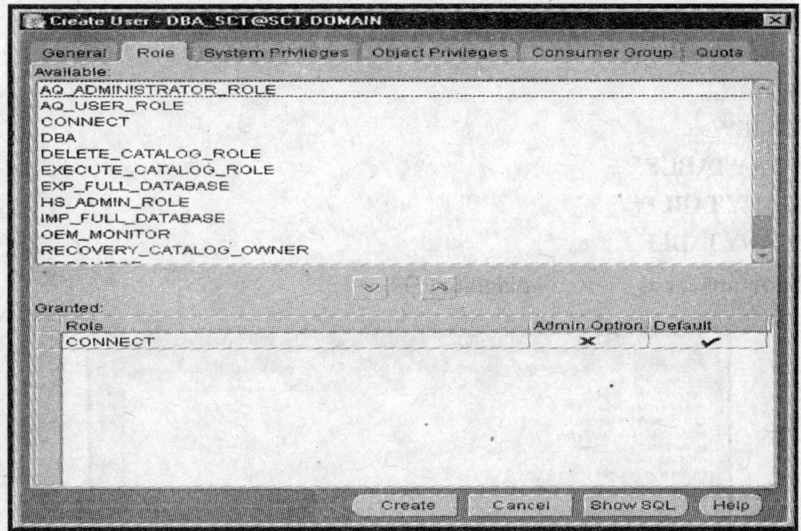

Diagram 6.32

Click on the cell below Admin Option to change the ✗ (cross) signs into ✓ (check) signs. Refer to diagram 6.33.

Click on the tab mark named System Privileges. Select from the list of System Privileges and click on [button] to add them.

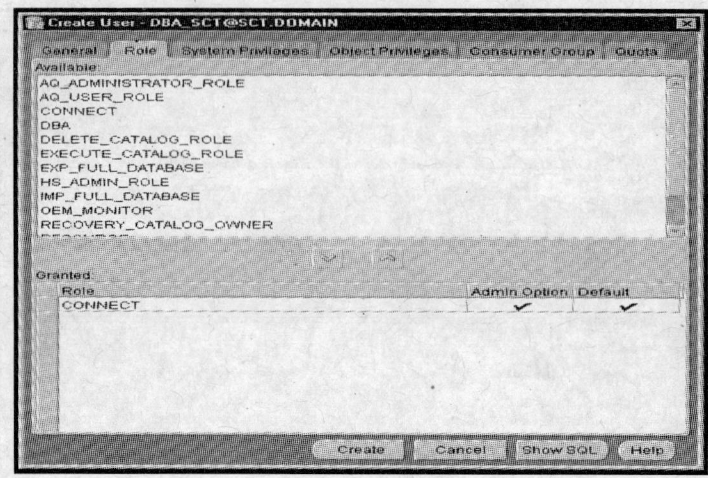

Diagram 6.33

Include privileges required by a user to performing basic SQL operations like:

- ❑ Creating, modifying and deleting tables or views
- ❑ Inserting, modifying and deleting data within self created tables
- ❑ Commit or Rollback SQL operations
- ❑ Grant privileges on owned objects

CREATE TABLE

CREATE VIEW

INSERT ANY TABLE

SELECT ANY TABLE

UPDATE ANY TABLE

The window will now appear as shown in diagram 6.34.

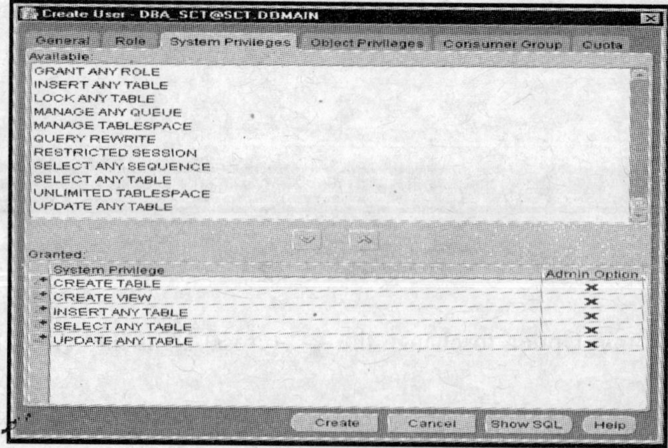

Diagram 6.34

The SQL command displayed on click of Show SQL will be as follows:

CREATE USER "IVAN"
PROFILE "DEFAULT"
IDENTIFIED BY "<password>"
DEFAULT TABLESPACE "SCT_DATA"
TEMPORARY TABLESPACE "TEMP"
ACCOUNT UNLOCK;
GRANT INSERT ANY TABLE TO "IVAN"
GRANT SELECT ANY TABLE TO "IVAN"
GRANT UPDATE ANY TABLE TO "IVAN"
GRANT CREATE VIEW TO "IVAN"
GRANT CREATE TABLE TO "IVAN"
GRANT "CONNECT" TO "IVAN" **WITH ADMIN OPTION;**

Click on Create to create the new user. If the SQL command was successfully executed a message indicating the same will be displayed, as shown in diagram 6.35.

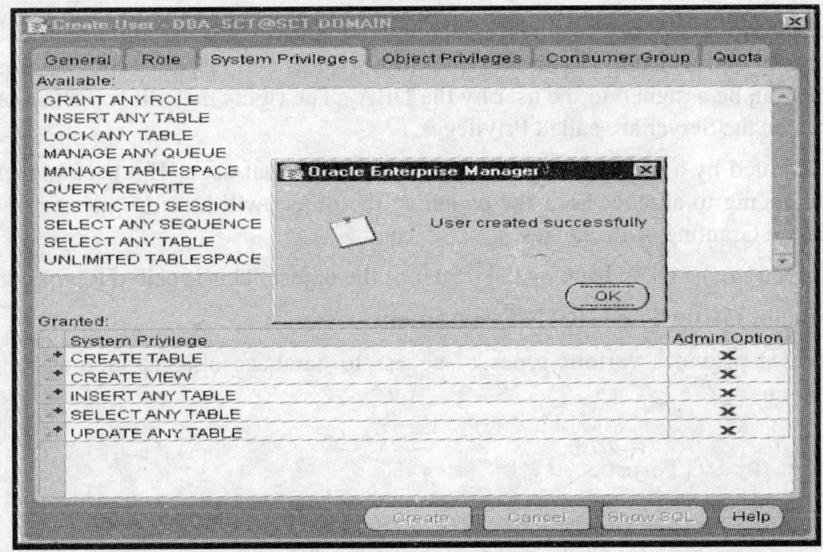

Diagram 6.35

Click on OK to continue.

The new user will be listed along with the other user for Oracle 9i, as shown in diagram 6.36.

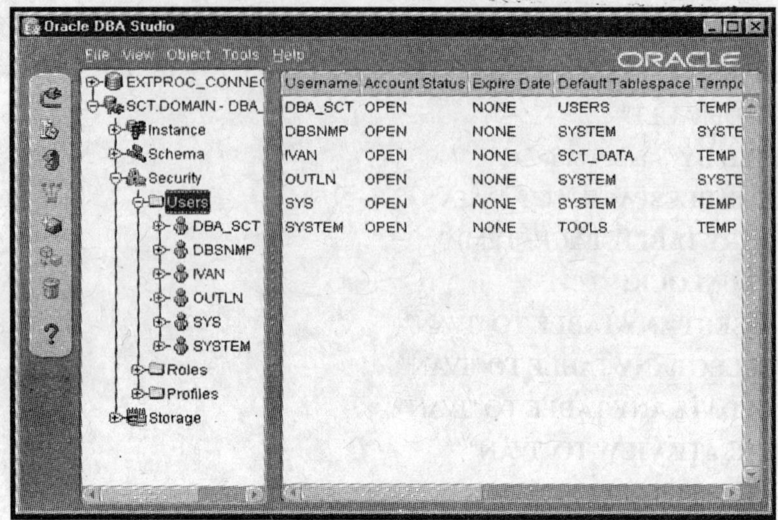

Diagram 6.36

Granting and Revoking Permissions

Oracle provides extensive security features in order to safeguard information stored in its tables from unauthorized viewing and damage. Depending on a user's status and responsibility, appropriate rights on Oracle's resources can be assigned to the user by the DBA. The rights that allow the use of some or all of Oracle's resources on the Server are called Privileges.

Objects that are created by a user are owned and controlled by that user. If a user wishes to access any of the objects belonging to another user, the owner of the object will have to give permissions for such access. This is called Granting of Privileges.

Privileges once given can be taken back by the owner of the object. This is called Revoking of Privileges.

Granting Privileges Using The GRANT Statement

The Grant statement provides various types of access to database objects such as tables, views and sequences and so on.

Syntax:

```
GRANT <Object Privileges>
      ON <ObjectName>
      TO <UserName>
            [WITH GRANT OPTION];
```

Object Privileges

Each object privilege that is granted authorizes the grantee to perform some operation on the object. A user can grant all the privileges or grant only specific object privileges.

The list of object privileges is as follows:

ALTER	Allows the grantee to change the table definition with the ALTER TABLE command
DELETE	Allows the grantee to remove the records from the table with the DELETE command

INDEX	Allows the grantee to create an index on the table with the CREATE INDEX command
INSERT	Allows the grantee to add records to the table with the INSERT command
SELECT	Allows the grantee to query the table with the SELECT command
UPDATE	Allows the grantee to modify the records in the tables with the UPDATE command

With Grant Option

The WITH GRANT OPTION allows the grantee to in turn grant object privileges to other users.

The examples that follow require users to be created prior granting permissions. To create the required users follow the steps as explained in the

Example 1:

Give the user Sharanam all data manipulation permissions on the table EMP_MSTR.

GRANT ALL ON EMP_MSTR **TO** Sharanam;

Example 2:

Give the user Hansel permission to only view and modify records in the table CUST_MSTR.

GRANT SELECT, UPDATE ON CUST_MSTR **TO** Hansel;

Example 3:

Give the user Ivan all data manipulation privileges on the table ACCT_MSTR along with an option to further grant permission on the ACCT_MSTR table to other users.

GRANT ALL ON ACCT_MSTR **TO** Ivan **WITH GRANT OPTION;**

Referencing A Table Belonging To Another User

Once a user has privileges to access another user's object(s), the user can access the table by prefixing the table with the name of the owner.

Example 4:

View the contents of the FD_MSTR table that belongs to **Sharanam.**

SELECT * FROM Sharanam.FD_MSTR;

Granting Privileges When A Grantee Has Been Given The GRANT Privilege

If the user wants to grant privileges to other users, the user must be the owner of the object or must be given the GRANT option by the owner of the object.

Example 5:

Give the user Chhaya permission to view records from the TRANS_MSTR table. The table originally belongs to the user Vaishali, who has granted you the privilege to pass on the privileges that you have to others using the GRANT privilege option.

GRANT SELECT ON Vaishali.TRANS_MSTR **TO** Chhaya;

Revoking Privileges Given

Privileges once given can be denied to a user using the REVOKE command. The object owner can revoke privileges granted to another user. A user of an object who is not the owner, but has been granted the GRANT privilege, has the power to REVOKE the privileges from a grantee.

Revoking Permissions Using The REVOKE Statement

The REVOKE statement is used to deny the grant given on an object.

Syntax:

```
REVOKE <Object Privileges>
      ON <ObjectName>
      FROM <UserName>;
```

Note

The revoke command is used to revoke object privileges that the user previously granted directly to the grantee.

The REVOKE command cannot be used to revoke the privileges granted through the operating system.

Example 6:

All privileges on the table NOMINEE_MSTR have been granted to Anil. Take back the Delete privilege on the table.

REVOKE DELETE ON NOMINEE_MSTR **FROM** Anil;

Example 7:

Take back all privileges on the table NOMINEE_MSTR from Anil.

REVOKE ALL ON NOMINEE_MSTR **FROM** Anil;

Example 8:

Rocky has the permission to view records from FDSLAB_MSTR. Take back this permission. Note that Alex is the original owner of FDSLAB_MSTR table.

REVOKE SELECT ON Alex.FDSLAB_MSTR **FROM** Rocky;

Self Review Questions

Fill in the Blanks

1. A database comprises of a number of physical files called ________________.
2. Data files are logically grouped together into an Oracle (logical) structure called a ____________.
3. LOCAL managed extents can either be ____________ or ____________.
4. The value of ________________ indicates a growth rate for subsequent extents.
5. ________________ specifies the number of freelist groups to maintain for a table or index.
6. The ____________ attribute specifies the area of the buffer pool where the object will be cached.
7. The rights that allow the use of some or all of Oracle's resources on the Server are called ________________.
8. Objects that are created by a user are owned and controlled by ________________.
9. The ____________ statement provides various types of access to database objects.
10. ____________ privilege allows the grantee to remove the records from the table.

11. __________ privilege allows the grantee to query the table.
12. The _________________________ allows the grantee to in turn grant object privileges to other users.
13. If the user wants to grant privileges to other users, the user must be the _______ of the object or must be given the __________ option by the owner of the object.
14. Privileges once given can be denied to a user using the ____________ command.
15. The REVOKE command cannot be used to revoke the privileges granted through the __________________________.

True or False

16. User data in an Oracle database is logically stored in data files.
17. The NOCACHE attribute is used for specifying LOB storage area.
18. The OPTIMAL attribute specifies the value to which a rollback segment will shrink after extending.
19. FREELISTS specifies the number of freelists for each of the freelist groups for the table, index or cluster including tablespaces.
20. Multiple Datafiles can be added to the table by typing the filename in the blank row provided within the table.
21. Objects that are created by a user are owned and controlled by that user.
22. Privileges once given cannot be taken back by the owner of the object.
23. Alter privilege allows the grantee to change the table definition.
24. Index privilege allows the grantee to create an index and modify table.
25. The WITH GRANT OPTION allows the grantee to in turn grant object privileges to other users.
26. If the user wants to grant privileges to other users, the user need not be the owner of the object.
27. If the user wants to grant privileges to other users, the user must be given the GRANT option by the owner of the object.
28. A user of an object who is not the owner, but has been granted the GRANT privilege, has the power to REVOKE the privileges from a grantee.
29. The REVOKE command can be used to revoke the privileges granted through the operating system.

Hands on Exercises

1. Using the SQL*PLUS tool, convert the user named DBA_INVTSYS into a super admin (Oracle DBA) for the SCT_INVT tablespace.
2. Give the user IVAN permission only to view records in the tables Sales_order and Sales_order_details, along with an option to further grant permission on these tables to other users.
3. Give the user IVAN all data manipulation privileges on the table Client_Master without an option to further grant permission on the Client_Master table to other users.
4. Take back all privileges given to the user IVAN on the table Client_Master.

Creating Database

Select Start → Programs → Oracle - OraHome92 → Configuration and Migration Tools → Database Configuration Assistant as shown in the following diagram 7.1.

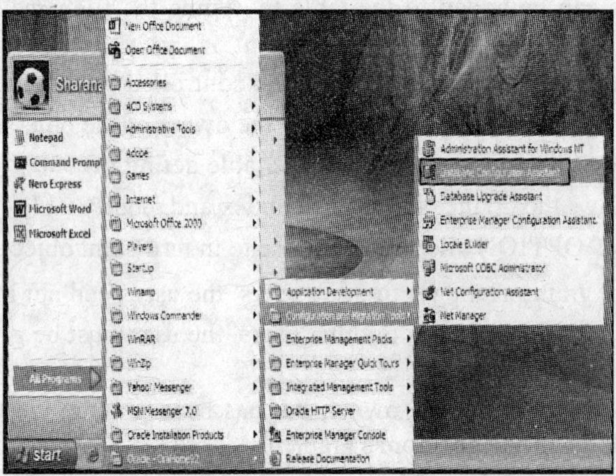

Diagram 7.1

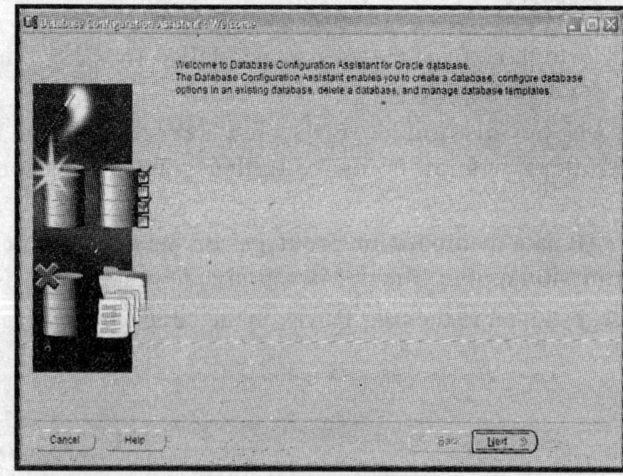

Diagram 7.2

The **Database Configuration Assistance: Welcome** dialog box appears as shown in diagram 7.2.

Click Next >. The **Database Configuration Assistance: Step 1 of 8 Operations** dialog box appears prompting for the selection of the operation to be performed. Refer to diagram 7.3.

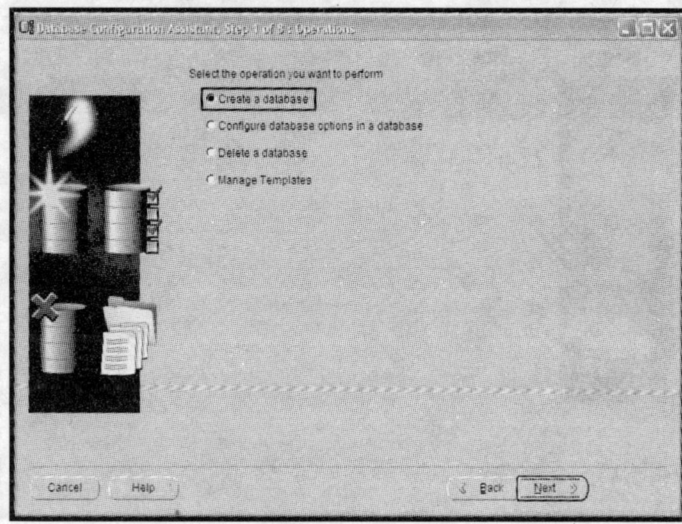

Diagram 7.3

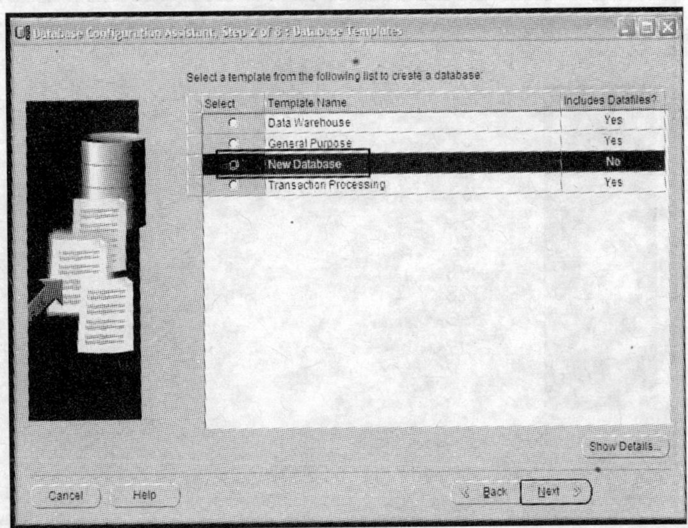

Diagram 7.4

Click Next >. The **Database Configuration Assistance: Step 2 of 8 Database Templates** dialog box appears prompting for the selection of the template to create a database. Select the third option i.**e. New Database**. Refer to diagram 7.4.

Click Next >. The **Database Configuration Assistance: Step 3 of 8 Database Identification** dialog box appears prompting for the **Global Database Name** and **SID**. In this material The Global Database name and SID is **ora1**. Refer to diagram 7.5.

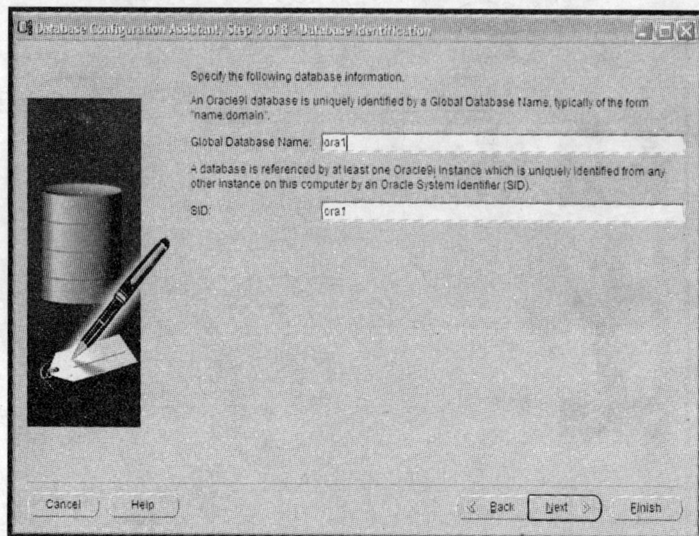

Diagram 7.5

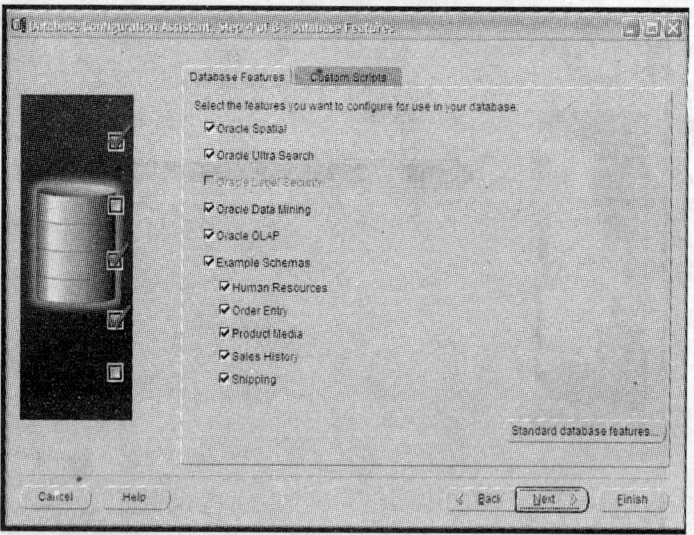

Diagram 7.6

Click Next >. The **Database Configuration Assistance: Step 4 of 8 Database Features** dialog box appears displaying the list of the database features. Refer to diagram 7.6.

Click Next >. The **Database Configuration Assistance: Step 5 of 8 Database Connection Options** dialog box appears prompting to select the type of mode needed for the database. Select the option **Dedicated Server Mode**. Refer to diagram 7.7.

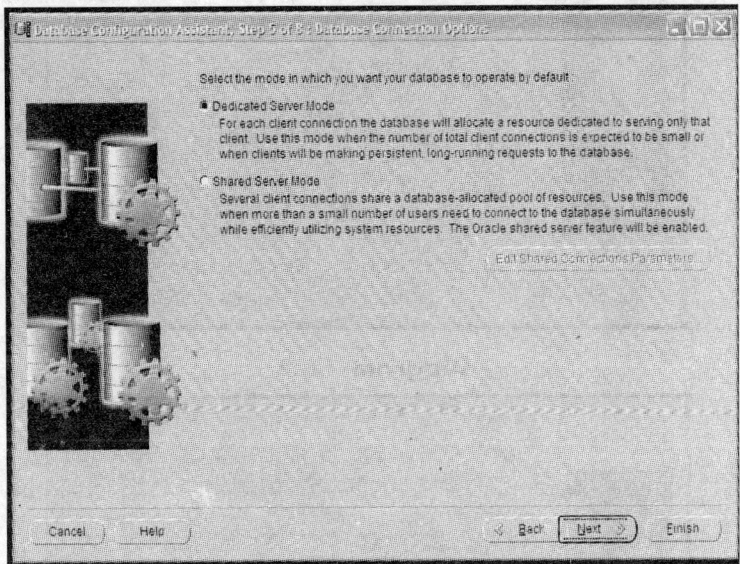

Diagram 7.7

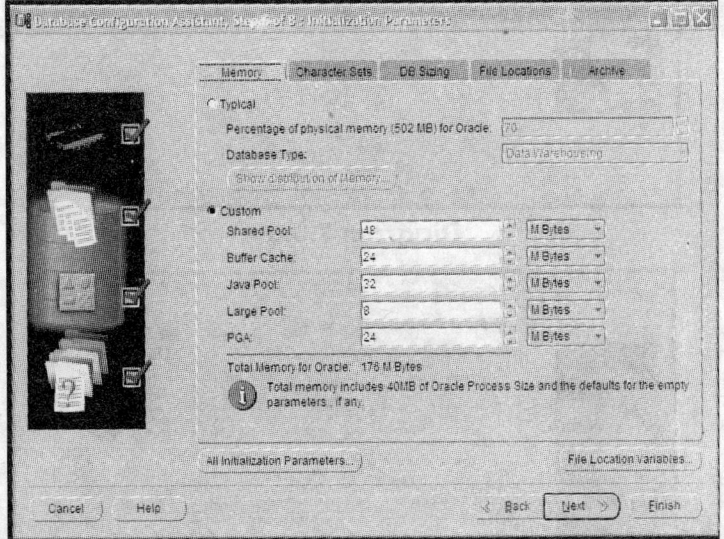

Diagram 7.8.1

Click Next >. The **Database Configuration Assistance: Step 6 of 8 Initialization Parameters** dialog box appears displaying the details like Memory, Character Set, DB Sizing, File Locations and Archive. Keep the settings as it is. Refer to diagrams 7.8.1 to 7.8.5.

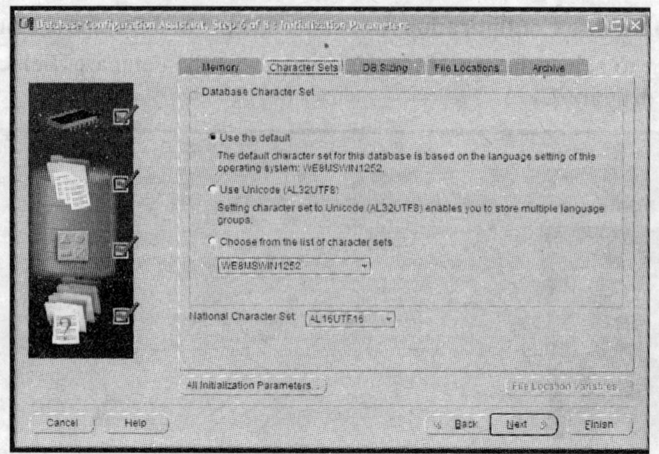

Diagram 7.8.2

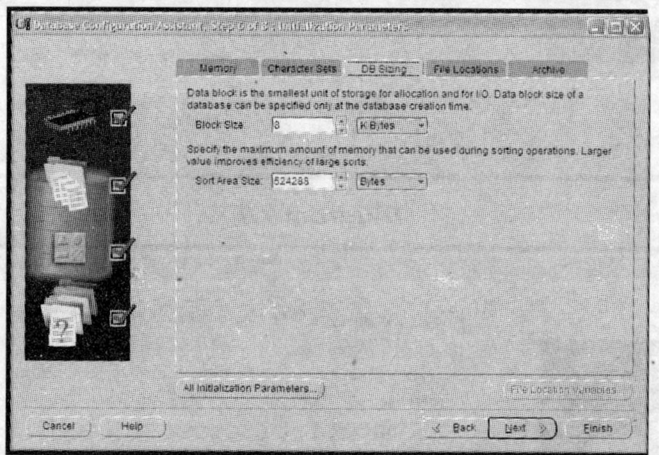

Diagram 7.8.3

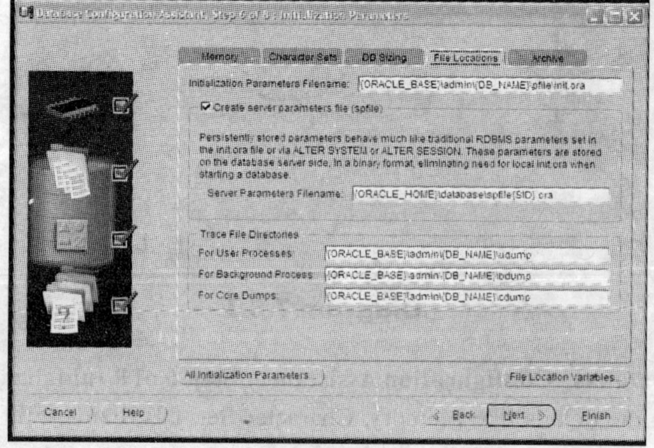

Diagram 7.8.4

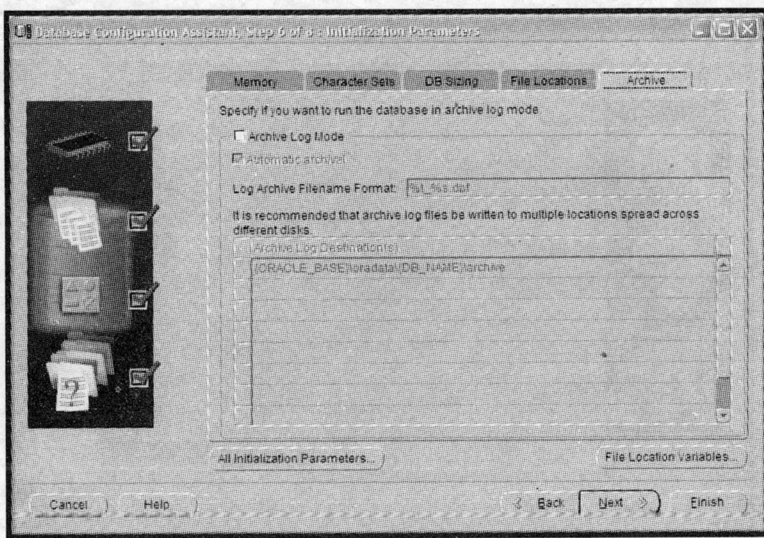

Diagram 7.8.5

Click [Next >]. The **Database Configuration Assistance: Step 7 of 8 Database Storage** dialog box appears wherein it allows changing and viewing the following objects: (Refer to diagrams 7.9)

- ❑ Controlfiles
- ❑ Tablespaces
- ❑ Datafiles
- ❑ Rollback Segments
- ❑ Redo Log Groups

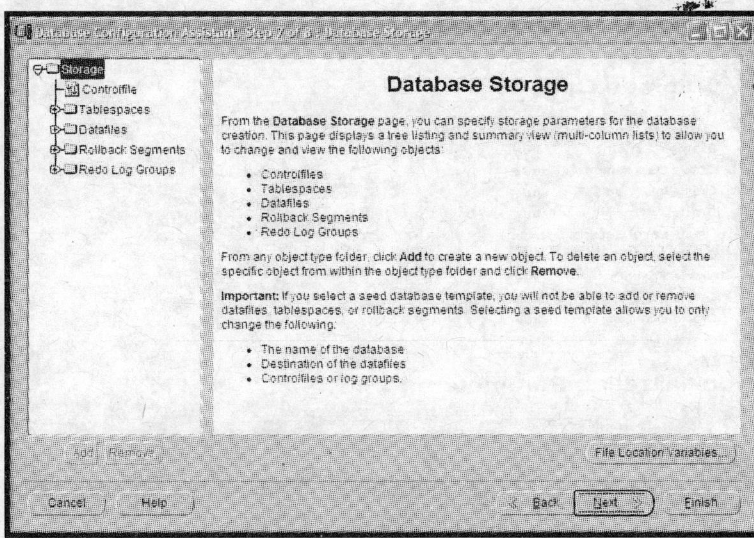

Diagram 7.9

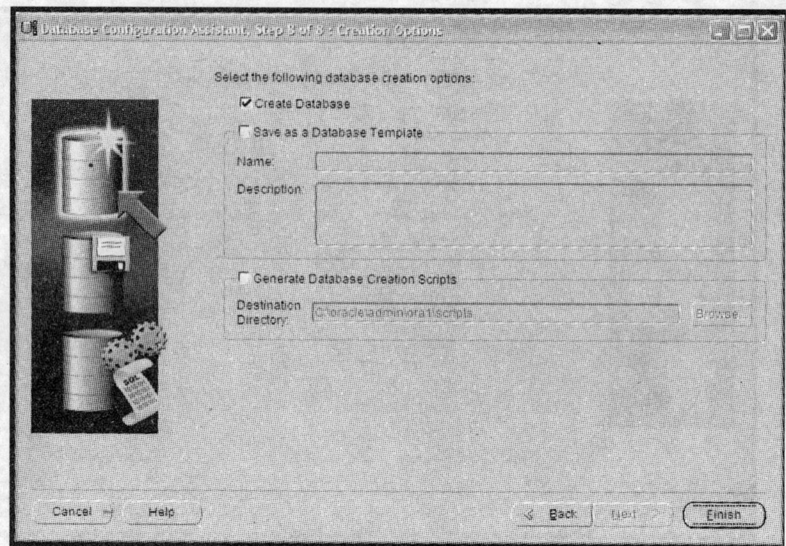

Diagram 7.10

Keep the settings as it is. Click [Next >>]. **The Database Configuration Assistance: Step 8 of 8 Creation Options** dialog box appears prompting for the selection of database creation options. Select the first option i.e. **Create Database**. Refer to diagrams 7.10.

Click [Finish]. The **Summary** dialog box appears displaying the details of the operations to be performed for the database named **ora1**. Refer to diagram 7.11.

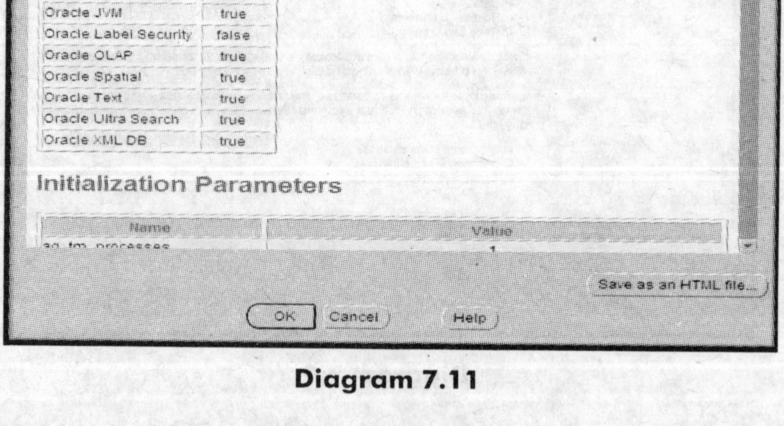

Summary

Following operation(s) will be performed:
Creation of database with db name "ora1".

Use this template to create a customized database.

Common Options

Option Name	Selected
Example Schemas	true
Oracle Data Mining	true
Oracle Intermedia	true
Oracle JVM	true
Oracle Label Security	false
Oracle OLAP	true
Oracle Spatial	true
Oracle Text	true
Oracle Ultra Search	true
Oracle XML DB	true

Initialization Parameters

Name	Value
aq_tm_processes	1

Save as an HTML file...

OK Cancel Help

Diagram 7.11

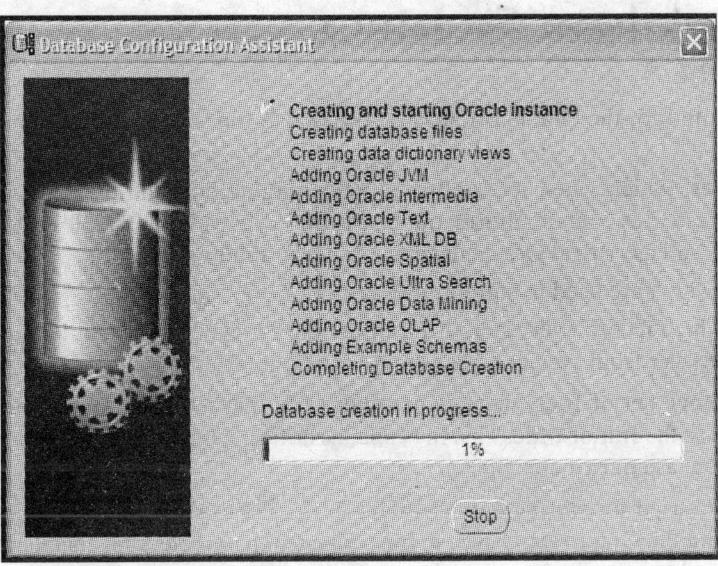

Diagram 7.12

Click [OK]. The **Database Configuration Assistant** dialog box appears displaying the list required for the creation of database. This will take a lot of time.

After the completion of the creating a database a dialog box appears prompting for the change of password for SYS and SYSTEM accounts in the new database. Refer to diagram 7.13.

Database Configuration Assistant

Database creation complete. Check the logfiles at C:\oracle\admin\ora1\create for details.

Database Information:
Global Database Name: ora1
System Identifier(SID): ora1
Server Parameters Filename: C:\oracle\ora92\database\spfileora1.ora

Change Passwords

For security reasons, you must specify a password for the SYS and SYSTEM accounts in the new database.

SYS Password: *******
Confirm SYS Password: *******
SYSTEM Password: *******
Confirm SYSTEM Password: *******

Note: All database accounts except SYS, SYSTEM, DBSNMP, and SCOTT are locked. Select the Password Management button to view a complete list of locked accounts or to manage the database accounts. From the Password Management window, unlock only the accounts you will use. Oracle Corporation strongly recommends changing the default passwords immediately after unlocking the account.

Password Management...

Exit

Diagram 7.13

Click [Exit] to exit from the Database Configuration Assistant dialog box.

Physical Database Structure

Database Files

All information required for the Oracle Database processes to run successfully is contained within a set of files. They are:

- **Control files**, which when read tell the Oracle engine how the database is to be structured in memory. These files contain information indicating where all the Oracle database related files may be found as well as critical Oracle database configuration information.
- **Data files**, which are used to store user data.
- **Log files**, which record every step in a transaction, for every transaction, thus enabling the Oracle engine to recover from system crashes to a very large extent.

In addition to the above set of files, there is one more file that is of extreme importance to the Oracle Database, it is known as the **Init.ora** file. This file contains critical, Oracle database, configuration information i.e. it is the Oracle database **parameter** file.

The init.ora file is not used for storing any user data. It is used to store information required by the CPU to set up and configure the Oracle Database engine's physical parameters for its memory management.

Understanding how these files work together in harmony provides the basis of the Oracle DBA's in managing an Oracle Database. Troubleshooting time (required to solve a database site's problem) depends directly on the DBA's understanding of these files.

Control Files

When the Oracle engine is started, a **very simple loader program** is initially invoked.

- This program needs to know
- The name of the last database used, so that it can be remounted at startup
- The location of all its database files
- The appropriate init.ora file to be read i.e. a complete database map.
- This Database Map is held in a binary file.

This **binary** file is the database **Control File**. A binary file is used to help speed up CPU interaction with the file. There is no interpretation environment used that will slow down the interaction between the CPU and the control file.

The Control file contains the physical media information required by the Oracle engine to open and manage its data files. It contains information such as:

- Database name
- Names and locations of data files and redo log files
- The time-stamp of database creation

When the database is being mounted in the server's memory, the Oracle instance **loader** program reads the **INIT.ORA** file to identify the location of the control file.

The **Control_Files** parameter in the **INIT.ORA** file specifies the control file name as follows:

Control_files = ORACLE:ORANW732\DATABASE\ctl1orcl.ora

The control file is then opened within the server's memory within a namespace created by the Oracle instance loader program.

Note

It is important that the control files are backed up regularly. In the event of the loss of this file an Oracle database instance cannot be started.

Data Files

Data files contain system as well as user data. The logical database structures such as tables, indexes and procedures and so on are stored in data files allocated to a database. A data file must be associated with only one database. One or more data files form a logical unit of database storage called a **Tablespace**.

For example, if the user executes

```
SELECT * FROM {table name};
```

The data file identified in (table name) is read. The content of this read operation is stored in the database buffer cache of the Oracle engine.

Data files are allocated a particular size that is denoted in KB or MB when being created for the first time by the DBA prior their use. Data files are grouped together by a logical object called a Tablespace.

Multiple data files **can be** bound to a Tablespace. However, a data file **cannot** be bound to **multiple** Tablespaces. A data file's size can be enlarged or shrunk by the DBA when required, depending on an application's need.

Log Files

1. On-line Redo Log Files

The singular purpose of the On-Line Redo log files is to help the Oracle engine to recover from system crashes without losing data. The On-Line Redo log files record all the changes made to the Database Buffer Cache. At regular intervals the contents of the On-Line Redo log files in the server's memory are flushed to the hard disk drive or some other permanent backup media.

In the event of a database server crash, modified data held within the Database Buffer Cache may not have been permanently written to a data file on the hard disk drive by the DBWR process, as the database server crashed prior the DBWR running.

When the server is restarted, the Oracle engine will automatically use the contents of the On-Line Redo log files, (permanently flushed to hard disk), to register the changes that occurred in the Database Buffer Cache and write these changes to a data file.

Tip

Obviously in any fixed, pre-determined time period, the number of times the DBWR process runs in a database server's memory is **much fewer** when compared to the number of times LGWR (the Log Writer process) process runs in same server's memory.

Hence the Re-Do Log files will always have the latest footprint of the Database Buffer Cache and can be effectively used for recovery.

The On-Line Redo log files have a fixed size as specified at the time of log file creation. The on-line redo log files are organized into **Log Groups**. Every Oracle database must include at least **two** Log Groups.

Each redo group includes **at least one redo log file**. The redo log files included in a group are called **Log Members**. Thus every database group must include at least **one Log Member**.

When the Oracle engine starts successfully, Oracle processes start recording transaction information in the first Log Group. When the first log group is full, Oracle process starts writing in the second Log Group and so on. After writing on all the Log Groups the Oracle engine starts re-writing in the first Log Group and the process iterates.

After a crash, when the Oracle engine is restarted, the Oracle instance obtains the changes from the redo log groups. These changes are then applied to the data in data files. Thus the Oracle instance attempts recovery and user data is not lost.

Note
 The process of applying the log file information to the data files and writing it on the disk is known as **Rolling Forward**.

Since the on-line redo log files play an important role in database recovery, multiple copies of the on-line redo log files should be maintained. Oracle engine allows creation of multiple redo log file members. Oracle engine writes the same transaction log information in each of the Redo Log Members. Thus Oracle engine maintains multiple copies of the transaction log in different Redo Log Files.

If the redo log group includes more than one redo log member, the Oracle engine uses the first Redo Log Member for database recovery.

2. Off-line redo log files / Archive log files

The on-line redo log files play an important role in Database recovery. But, if the numbers of redo log groups is less, the redo log group files are over written and thus the recovery information is lost.

The off-line redo log files are used to eliminate this problem. As and when Oracle engine processes switch from one Log Group to another, a copy of the last written Log file is made. The copies of Log files made by the Oracle engine are called **Off-Line Redo Log** files or **Archive log files**.

Answer To Self Review Questions

5. *Table Space in Oracle*

Fill in te Blanks

1. sum
2. System
3. LOGGING
4. MIMIMUM EXTENT
5. DEFAULT STORAGE

True or False

6. True
7. True
8. True
9. False
10. True

6. *Users, Roles and Privileges*

Fill in the Blanks

1. data files
2. Tablespace
3. AUTOALLOCATED or UNIFORM
4. PCTINCREASE
5. FREELISTS GROUPS

True or False

16. False
17. False
18. True
19. False
20. True

6. BUFFER_POOL
7. Privileges
8. that, user
9. Grant
10. Delete
11. Select
12. WITH GRANT OPTION
13. owner, GRANT
14. REVOKE
15. operating system

21. True
22. False
23. False
24. False
25. True
26. False
27. True
28. False
29. False

Solution To Hands On Exercises

5. *Table Space in Oracle*

1. SQL Statement for creating the tablespace:

```
CREATE TABLESPACE SCT_INVT
        DATAFILE 'SCT_Invt.dat'
        SIZE 25M DEFAULT STORAGE(
                INITIAL 10K NEXT 50K
                MINEXTENTS 1
                MAXEXTENTS 499
                PCTINCREASE 10
        )
        ONLINE;
```

2. SQL Statement for creating the user:

```
CREATE USER "DBA_INVTSYS"
        PROFILE "DEFAULT"
        IDENTIFIED BY "sct2306"
        DEFAULT TABLESPACE "SCT_INVT"
        TEMPORARY TABLESPACE "TEMP"
        ACCOUNT UNLOCK;
```

6. *Users, Roles and Privileges*

1. SQL Statement for granting the user permission of an Oracle DBA:

```
GRANT "DBA" TO "DBA_INVTSYS" WITH ADMIN OPTION;
```

2. **Giving the user IVAN permission only to view records in the tables Sales_order and** Sales_order_details, along with an option to further grant permission on these tables to other users.

GRANT SELECT ON Sales_Order **TO** IVAN **WITH GRANT OPTION;**

GRANT SELECT ON Sales_Order_Details **TO** IVAN **WITH GRANT OPTION;**

3. Giving the user IVAN all data manipulation privileges on the table Client_Master without an option to further grant permission on the Client_Master table to other users.

   GRANT ALL ON Client_Master **TO** IVAN;

4. Taking back all privileges given to the user IVAN on the table Client_Master.

   REVOKE ALL ON Client_Master **FROM** IVAN;

Section - III

SETTING UP THE BUSINESS MODEL

8

A Business Model For Retail Banking

Banking Business Model Specifications

Banking, like any other business model has a master business process (**i.e.** Retail Banking), which is supported by a number of sub processes. This concept is described in diagram 8.1.

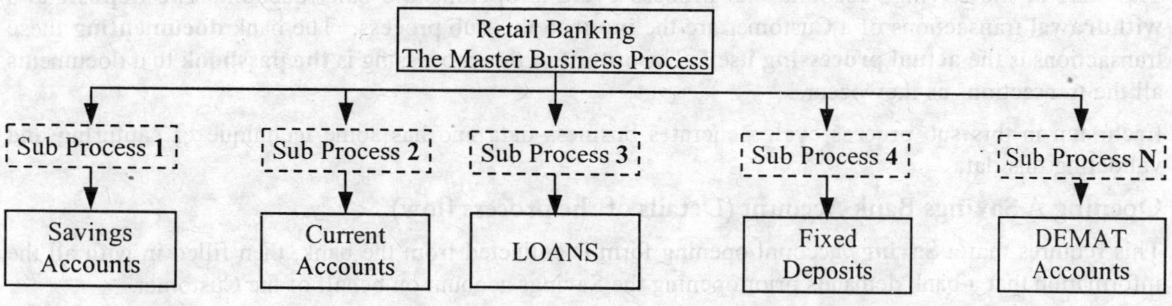

Diagram 8.1: The Retail Banking Business Model

To create a full-fledged, retail banking, commercial product, all the sub processes of the retail banking business model have to be fully computerized.

Each sub process described above, in turn has multiple child processes that work together in harmony for the sub process to be successful. This concept is described below.

Savings Account (It's child processes described)

- Collecting the account opening forms from the bank
- Getting support documents together to be submitted to the bank for opening the Savings account
- Submitting the documents to an account opening officer at the bank
- The documents submitted are verified and validated by the account opening officer at the bank
- Once acceptable, an unique account number is assigned to the Customers Savings account
- A cheque book, as well as cash and cheque deposit books, are given to the Customer by the bank
- The Savings account is opened. Banking transactions can now begin

Savings Bank Transactions

Saving bank transactions, both **deposits** and **withdrawals**, are at the heart of any Savings account. These transactions continue until the account is closed.

Each deposit or withdrawal, whether by **cheque**, **bank draft** or **cash** is documented by the bank. This documentation is available to the account holder in the form of a hand written **or** especially printed out **passbook or** a **computerized print out** that is universally accepted as the passbook.

This document (**i.e.** either the passbook or the computer printout) is accepted by all government authorities such as Income tax, Professional tax, Sales tax and so on, as **valid proof** of all transactions carried out by the account holder.

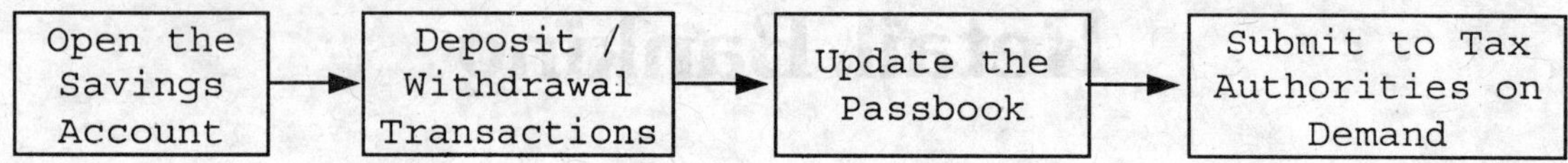

Diagram 8.2: The Savings Account sub process cycle.

The Savings bank account, sub process **cycle**, of a retail banking business model can be described as shown in diagram 8.2.

The start of the Savings account, sub process **cycle** is opening the bank account. The **deposit** and **withdrawal** transactions of a Customer are the **input** to this sub process. The bank **documenting** these transactions is the **actual processing** itself. The **output** of this processing is **the passbook** that documents all the transactions as they occur.

Each step in this sub process cycle generates business data and has some technique of capturing and validating this data.

Opening A Savings Bank Account (Details of the process flow)

This requires that a **Savings** account opening form is collected from the bank, then filled in with all the information that a bank demands prior opening the Savings account on behalf of the Customer.

Some of the information required by the bank prior account opening is:

- Customers Name
- Address
- Contact Information **i.e.** Residence, Office & Mobile telephone numbers

- ❑ Introducer's Name and Account number

And so on.

Additionally, a Customer must submit specific support documents along with the appropriately filled in Savings bank account opening form, to the bank. The documents are:

- ❑ A Xerox copy of the Customers Income Tax, **P**ermanent **A**ccount **N**umber

Or

- ❑ Form **60** providing supplemental taxation details
- ❑ A Xerox copy of the Customer's Ration card, or passport, or latest Electricity or Telephone bill needs to be submitted as address proof
- ❑ Two, colored passport sized photographs, of the Customer

Once these documents and support material is submitted to a bank they are checked by a bank employee. The bank employee **signs** and **dates** the application form, if everything submitted conforms exactly to the banks requirements.

The bank employee then passes these documents and their support material to the bank manager for perusal. The bank manager does a second validation check of all the material submitted. The bank manager then signs and dates the application form and issues the Savings account number, which from that day onwards is bound to the Customer until the account is closed.

A cheque book as well as withdrawal and deposit slip book is issued to the Customer.

The Savings bank account is opened ready for all transactions. The process of opening a Savings bank account is complete. Deposit and withdrawal transaction can commence.

Opening A Current Account (Details of the process flow)

This requires that a **Current** account opening form is collected from the bank, then filled in with all the information that a bank demands prior opening the Current account on behalf of the Customer.

Some of the information required by the bank prior account opening is:

- ❑ Company Name
- ❑ Full Postal Address
- ❑ Directors Contact Information **i.e.** Full postal Address, Residence, Office & Mobile telephone numbers
- ❑ Introducer's Name and Account number

And so on.

Additionally, a Customer must submit specific support documents, along with the appropriately filled in Current bank account opening form, to the bank. The documents are:

If the company is a Private or Public Limited company then:

- ❑ A copy of its Memorandum Of Understanding
- ❑ A letter with an **extract of a board meeting** where it is resolved to open a Current account with the bank

If the company is a proprietorship:

- ❑ A letter signed by the proprietor indicating a desire to open a Current account with the bank
- ❑ A Xerox copy of the company's Income Tax, **P**ermanent **A**ccount **N**umber

Or

- A form **60** providing supplemental taxation details
- Two, colored passport sized photographs, of each individual who will operate the account

Once these documents and support material is submitted to a bank they are checked by a bank employee. The bank employee **signs** and **dates** the application form, if everything submitted conforms exactly to the banks requirements.

The bank employee then passes these documents and their support material to the bank manager for perusal. The bank manager does a second validation check of all the material submitted. The bank manager then signs and dates the application form and issues the Current account number, which from that day onwards is bound to the company or proprietor until the account is closed.

A Cheque book as well as withdrawal and deposit books are issued.

The Current account is opened ready for all transactions. The process of opening a Current bank account is complete. Deposit and withdrawal transactions can commence.

It may appear that a Current account is exactly the same as a Savings account. While the account opening process may appear to be the same there are differences in the running of each account.

Some of the differences are:

- The monies deposited (and held) in a Savings account attract an annual interest of 4.5%
- The monies deposited into a Current account attract nothing. In fact, banks normally charge a customer to setup and run a Current account
- A bank normally has **R**eserve **B**ank Of **I**ndia (RBI) guidelines to follow which restricts the amount of money that can be withdrawn from a Saving bank account
- There are no such limitations on the withdrawal of money from a Current account
- There is always a minimum balance that has to be maintained in a savings and/or current account. However, the minimum balance to be maintained in a current account is **substantially larger** than the minimum balance that has to be maintained in a savings account

Having said all this, the way both the accounts **are operated** by their respective account holders is identical.

Money is **deposited** and money is **withdrawn**. There is simply a running check kept of all deposit and withdrawal transactions in each type of account. Money can be deposited by cash, cheque or bank draft (**i.e.** a bankers cheque). Money can be withdrawn by cash, cheque or bank draft (**i.e.** a bankers cheque).

The monthly statement of an account holder's transactions (i.e. deposits and withdrawals) is accepted by all government agencies such as Income Tax, Sales Tax and so on as proof that the transaction actually took place. This (as mentioned earlier) is the significance of running a Savings or Current account with a bank.

Fixed Deposits (It's child processes described)

Another banking product is **fixed deposits**. This product offers an attractive rate of return, on funds that are parked as fixed deposits with a bank.

There is a higher degree of safety of the principal amount and the interest thereon, when fixed deposits are used to generate additional funds when compared to placing the same funds in company stock. Retired people, (or anyone who wishes to hedge risk) normally opt for a fixed deposit with a bank to generate additional funds.

A fixed deposit, as the name suggests, is when funds are parked with a bank for a fixed, predetermined period. Most banks define the period during which the funds are locked in **time slabs**.

Table 8.1

Period of Fixed Deposit	Interest Rate Applicable
15 days and above to 30 days	5.00%
31 days and above upto 45 days	5.25%
45 days and above but less than 3 months	5.50%
3 months and above but less than 6 months	5.75%
6 months and above but less than 12 months	6.00%
12 months and above but less than 36 months	6.25%
36 months and above upto 120 months	6.50%

The rate of interest applicable to a fixed deposit is proportional to the period of lock in (i.e. longer the period of lock in the greater the interest rate applicable). Refer to table 8.1 as an example.

Bank Customers make a choice of the time slab and then instruct the bank the amount of funds that will be parked in the fixed deposit. Once the time slab and amount is finalized the bank will create a fixed deposit receipt and hand this over to the customer.

The fixed deposit receipt mentions, the period of lock in, the principal amount and the rate of interest applicable. When the period of lock in completes the customer surrenders the fixed deposit receipt and the bank pays back the principal amount together with the interest, which has accrued on the principal amount to the customer.

Opening A Fixed Deposit (Details of the process flow)

This requires a **F**ixed **D**eposit (FD) opening form be collected from the bank, then filled in with all the information that a bank demands prior issuing the fixed deposit receipt to the customer.

Some of the information required by bank prior issuing the FD receipt is:

- ❑ Customer Name
- ❑ Full Postal Address
- ❑ Contact Information (**i.e.** Residence, Office & Mobile telephone numbers)
- ❑ Introducer's Name and Account number (if available)

And so on.

Additionally, a Customer must submit specific support documents, along with the appropriately filled in fixed deposit opening form, to the bank. The documents are:

- ❑ A Xerox copy of the most recent Electricity bill, Telephone bill, Ration card or Passport to verify the postal address provided above
- ❑ A Xerox copy of the Customer's Income Tax, **Permanent Account Number**

Or

- ❑ A form **60** providing supplemental taxation details
- ❑ Three, colored passport sized photographs, of the customer

Once these documents and support material is submitted to a bank they are checked by a bank employee. The bank employee **signs** and **dates** the Fixed deposit opening form, if everything submitted conforms exactly to the banks requirements.

The bank employee then passes these documents and their support material to the bank manager for perusal. The bank manager does a second validation check of all the material submitted. The bank manager then signs and dates the fixed deposit opening form. This finalizes the fixed deposit opening form, data validation.

Once this is complete the bank manager issues instructions to a bank employee for the preparation of the fixed deposit receipt. This depends on whether the FD is being opened with cash, bank draft or cheque. If the FD is being opened by Cash or Bank Draft the FD receipt is issued immediately.

If the FD is being opened by a cheque **and** the bank account on which the cheque is drawn is external to the bank that is issuing the FD receipt, then the bank will wait until the cheque clears and only then issue the FD receipt.

Note

Since funds for the FD are being parked with the bank, the bank draft or cheque used to pay for the FD must be made in the (FD receipt issuing) banks name.

As soon as the funds are available with the bank the FD receipt is issued to the customer.

Once the FD receipt is issued to the customer, the customer has to wait until the lock in period mentioned on the FD receipt is over before encashing the FD.

To encash a FD the customer has to discharge the FD to the bank that issued it. This is done by the customer pasting a revenue stamp on the reverse of the FD receipt (at an appropriate place) signing on partly on the revenue stamp and partly on the reverse of the FD receipt.

The receipt is then handed over to the bank. The bank then immediately repays the principal amount mentioned on the receipt **and** the interest accrued based on the interest percentage mentioned on the FD receipt. Once this is done the current FD process is complete.

Premature Discharge Of A Fixed Deposit

Fixed deposits can be discharged prematurely. Irrespective of the completion date mentioned on the FD it can be discharged at any time. The penalty for premature discharge is bound to the rate of interest of the FD.

Generally, if a FD is prematurely terminated, the bank only pays **simple interest** on the funds parked in the FD.

Note

This banking project covers **only** the opening and running of Savings and Current accounts together with Fixed Deposits. Loans, DEMAT accounts and so on are not covered in this project.

Since only the Savings account, Current account and Fixed deposit business processes, of the banking business model, are being dealt with in this project the first order of the day is to go to the bank and collect all the **application forms** necessary used to initiate each of these business processes.

When collecting the application forms for each of these business processes, establish exactly what **additional support documents** have to be submitted by a customer (to the bank) to complete each business process.

Note

Given below are scanned images of bank documents, which are required by each banking business process being dealt with (**i.e.** Savings accounts, Current accounts and Fixed deposits). Refer to diagrams 8.3.1 to 8.8.

Table structures used to capture form data are designed based on the application forms for each banking business process.

Table Structuring Principles

Fundamentally, a **mother table** for each form is created by simply ensuring that there is a **column** in the table for **each data capture field** visible on the form.

Once the mother table has been structured, it is **normalized**. The mother table can then decompose into several master / detail tables (*if necessary*) to ensure that the **minimum** of redundant data is stored.

Once a mother table is decomposed into appropriate master / detail tables (appropriately normalized), these become **production tables** in which data captured by the applications forms is stored. Application forms **always** work against production tables.

Actual Table Structures

The structure of the **production tables** for the Savings account, Current account and Fixed deposit, business processes of a banking business model, are given immediately after the scanned images of bank documents.

Scanned Banking Model Forms

Savings Accounts Opening Form:

SICB

THE SOUTH INDIAN CO-OPERATIVE BANK LTD.

.... BRANCH

SAVING ACCOUNT OPENING FORM DATE : ________

S.F. No. ________ A/c. No. [ ]

Dear Sir,

Please open a Savings Account in my/our name/s in your Bank. I/We agree to comply with and be bound by the Bank rules and regulations prevailing now and as may be changed from time to time.

The account shall be operated by me/us.

☐ Singly ☐ Either or Survivor ☐ Jointly ☐ Anyone or Survivor

Please issue pass book.

Yours faithfully

FULL NAME/S OF ACCOUNT HOLDER/S	SPECIMEN SIGNATURES
1.	1.
2.	2.

Manager / Accountant Date :

Diagram 8.3.1: The Front Of The Savings Account Opening Form

FULL NAME/S, ADDRESSES OF ACCOUNT HOLDER/S

1. Name ____________________

Off. Address ____________________

____________________ Tel. : __________

Resi. Address ____________________

____________________ Tel. : __________

2. Name ____________________

Off. Address ____________________

____________________ Tel. : __________

Resi. Address ____________________

____________________ Tel. : __________

FULL NAME & ADDRESS OF INTRODUCER :

I know the applicant/s desirous of opening the A/c with you for __________ Years and recommend the same.

Introducer's Signature __________ Name of the Introducer __________

S.F.S.B./C. A/c. No. __________

Address ____________________

____________________ Tel. No. __________

Diagram 8.3.2: The Rear Of The Savings Account Opening Form

Fixed Deposit Opening Form:

THE SOUTH INDIAN CO-OP. BANK LTD., MUMBAI

FIXED DEPOSIT / REINVESTMENT CERTIFICATE	S. B. A/c. No.	C. A/c. No.	S. F. No.
I/We desire to invest a sum of Rs. ________ (Rupees ____________________) in your Bank as Fixed Deposit / Re-Investment Certificate for a period ________ at @________ p.a. We have read and understood the rules in respect of the said account and agree to be bound by them as now in force or any change that may be made therein from time to time. ____________________ Signature	INTRODUCED BY : Name : __________ Address : __________ __________ __________ A/c. No. ________ S. F. No. ________ INSTRUCTIONS		
FULL NAME (IN BLOCK LETTERS)	SPECIMEN SIGNATURE		
1.			
2.			
3.			
	____________________ Signature of the Officer		

Diagram 8.4.1: The Front Of The Fixed Deposit Form

THE SOUTH INDIAN CO-OP. BANK LTD.,
SICB
MUMBAI.

Name : ____________________

Address : ____________________

Occupation : ____________ Tel. No. : ____________

F. D. / R. I. C. No.	AMOUNT	DATE OF DEPOSIT	DATE OF EXPIRY	INTEREST RATE	PERIOD

Diagram 8.4.2: The Rear Of The Fixed Deposit Form

Current Account Opening Form:

CURRENT ACCOUNT OPENING FORM
For Partnerships/Limited Company/Trusts/Society, etc.

To,

The South Indian Co-operative Bank Ltd.
MUMBAI.
SICB

Account No. ________
Ledger/Folio ________
Date ________
Branch ________

Dear Sir,

I/We request you to open/continue a Current Deposit Account with your Bank, as per particulars given below. I/We have read and understood the rules in respect of Current Deposit A/c. and agree to be bound by them as now in force or to any change that may be made therein from time to time.

Name / Title of Account ____________________ (In Block Letters)

Address ____________________

Constitution ____________________

Occupation/Line of Business ____________________

Instructions for operation ____________________

Necessary documents are attached herewith (as per details given below)

____

I/We further declare that we have got no Account/Account with ____________ Bank(s) and do not enjoy / enjoy credit facilities with them, as per sheet attached.

Please supply a cheque book for my/our use and issue a Pass Book/note to send a statement of account every ____________

Yours faithfully

____

SPECIMEN SIGNATURES-CUM-INDEMNITY FOR COLLECTION OF BILL ETC.

I/we may have occation from time to time to handle your collection or negotiation of Cheques, Drafts or Bills of Exchange (with or without documents attached) and I/we hereby agree to your forwarding the same to your agents for the time being for collection or negotiation. In the event of your having no independent Collecting Agents at any centre. I/We hereby authorise you to send cheqes by mail directly to the drawee bank itself. I/We shall keep/hold you harmless, free from responsibility and indemnified by you in handling this business due to any cause whatsover including delay in transit presentation, payment or default by your agents.

In addition to your ordinary rights as holders of such cheques, Drafts or Bills of Exchange, you are authorised to accept in payment thereof a banker's cheque or banker's cheque payable in your station or at other places and in the event of such cheque or cheques not being paid on presentation to debit the amount to our account with all charges incurred thereon. I/We confirm that you can present Bills and receive the amount in respect thereof in accordance with the usage of the place where the Bills are made payable.
It is understood that these transactions are in all respects at our entire risk and responsibility.

Full Name **Specimen Signature**

Mr. ____________ will sign as ____________

Mr. ____________ will sign as ____________

Mr. ____________ will sign as ____________

Introduced by

Name ____________

Address ____________

Signature ____________

Signatures

Open the Account

Manager

Diagram 8.5.1: Page One Of The Current Account Opening Form

(A) FOR SOCIETIES CLUBS OR SIMILAR BODIES

In terms of the certified copy of the resolution of the Executive/Governing body of ______________________ dated____________ handed over to you separately, kindly authorise the operation on the accounts by Mr.______________ ______________________(designation) or by Mr. ______________________(designation) and counter signed by its Secretary or Mr.______________________(designation) and debit the amount hereof to the account.

Chairman/President Secretary

It is hereby confirmed and declared by me/us that I/We have no beneficial interest in the account referred to on the reverse hereof and it is understood that all money's herein or hereafter standing to the credit of this account will in the event of my/our death during the currency of account form no part or my/our estate and that account thereafter will be operated upon by my/our successor(s) in office for the time being.

(B) FOR PARTNERSHIP ACCOUNTS

We the undersigned beg to inform you that we are the only partners in the firm of ______________________ ______________________ and are jointly and severally responsible for the liabilities thereof. We shall advise you in writing of any change that may take place in the partnership and all the present partners will be liable to you jointly and severally on any obligation which may be standing in the firm's name in your books on the date of the receipt of such notice and until all such obligations shall have been liquidated.

We confirm that our partnership is registered not registered with the Registrar or Firms and is written/verbal.

I/We hereby jointly and severally free you from any liability for the funds and the securities if any, charged to or deposited in the account that may be withdrawn by the remaining partners after the death bankruptly or retirement of any partner(s) of our firm. We further hereby agree to indemnify you against all claims, actions and demands arising from such withdrawal of the funds and the securities by the remaining partners. We also agree and declare that this agreement shall be binding upon ourselves and our respective legal representatives and you will not be liable in any way for the operations on the account in the name of the firm by any one or more of us or for withdrawal of the funds and securities by any one or more of us or any survivors of us.

Signature

(D) FOR LIMITED COMPANY A/CS

Extracts or minutes of the meeting of the Board of Directors of ______________________

held at its registered office at ______________________ on ______________________

RESOLVED

(a) That an account in the name of the Company be opened with The South Indian Co-operative Bank Ltd. at............ and that Mr.______________________

(give name & designation)

★ and Mr.______________________

(give name & designation)

is/are authorised to do so and sign the necessary forms and documents thereafter.

(b) And that the bank be instructed to honour all cheques, promissory notes, and other orders drawn by and all bills accepted on behalf of the company whether such account be in credit or overdrawn, and to accept and credit to the account of the company all moneys deposited with or owing by bank on any account or accounts at any time or times kept or to be kept in the name of the company and the amount of all cheques, notes, bills other negotiable instruments, orders or receipt provided they are endorsed/signed by Mr. ______________________★ and Mr.______________________ for the time being of the company on behalf of the company and such signatures(s) shall be sufficient authority to bind the company in all transactions between the bank and the company including those specifically referred to herein.

Diagram 8.5.2: Page Two Of The Current Account Opening Form

(c) And that Mr. __________ ★and Mr. __________ be authorised to withdraw and deal with any of the company's securities or properties or documents of title thereto which may be deposited with the bank from time to time whether by way or security otherwise.

(d) And that Mr. __________ ★and Mr. __________ is/are authorised to acknowledge all types of debts and liabilities on behalf of the company.

(e) And that the bank be furnished with a copy of its memorandum and Articles of Association and a list of names and specimen signatures of the Directors and other officer (s) of the company authorised to sign on behalf of the company and be informed from time to time by a notice in writing under the hand of the Chairman of any changes which may take place therein and be entitled to act upon such notice until, the receipt of further notice under the hand of the Chairman.

(f) And that a copy of any resolution of the Board if purporting to be certified as correct by the Chairman of the meeting or by the Secretary of the company shall as between the bank and the company, be conclusive evidence of the resolution so certified

(g) And that this resolution be communicated to the bank and shall remain in force until notice in writing of its withdrawal or cancellation is given to the bank by the Chairman of the company.

Certified that the above is a correct copy of the resolution passed on __________ by the Board of Directors of __________ and that it has been entered in the usual course of business in the minitues book of the company and signed therein by the Chairman of the meeting/company and is in accordance with the memorandum of Articles of Association of the Company.

__________ __________
Chairman of the meeting

★ Delete one name if authority is to be vested in a single person.

Indicative Guidelines for filling up Current A/c. Opening Form

(1) List of Documents to be submitted according to the consititution in original (for inspection & return wherever applicable)

(a) For partnership Firm

(i) Partnership deed and/or copy of registration certificate.

(b) For Joint Stock Companies

(i) Copy of Memorandum and the Articles of Association.
(ii) Certificate of Incorporation.
(iii) Certificate of commencement of business/Registration Certificate.
(iv) Certified copy of a Resolution of Board of Directors regulating Conduct of such account (as per proforma given in this form)

(c) For Trust Accounts

(i) Trust Deed
(ii) Resolution of Trustees
(iii) List of Trustees

(d) For Clubs, Societies, Association & other similar bodies

(i) Constitution & bye-laws
(ii) Certificate of Registration
(iii) Resolution

(e) For HUF—Letter to be filled up

(2) The Account is to be introduced by a persons well-known to the bank such as an account-holder or share-holder

(3) **Instructions for Operation**
Please write the mode of operation of the account-viz, joint operation by all account-holders, Former or Survivor Either or Survivor, and the names of officials along with their designations [in case of incorporate body].

Diagram 8.5.3: Page Three Of The Current Account Opening Form

The Bank Account Deposit Slip:

THE SOUTH INDIAN CO-OP. BANK LTD.
SICB

Date 200

Wanted a FD / CC Share No. ....

....

In Favour of ....

the sum of Rupees ....
(In Words)

....

....

Cash / Cheque Rs. ....

Recd. by ....

PARTICULARS OF PAYMENT

By Cash (Notes)	Rs.	P.
x 1000		
x 500		
x 100		
x 50		
x 20		
x 10		
x 5		
Coins		
(By Cheque Details overleaf)		
TOTAL		

Recd. by ....

THE SOUTH INDIAN CO-OP. BANK LTD.
SICB

Voucher No. : Date :

Wanted a FD / CC Share No.

For Rs.

In Favour of : Rs.

Office Use

Officer APPLICANT'S SIGNATURE

Diagram 8.6.1: The Front Of The Pay In Slip

Particulars of Cheque

Drawee Bank / Branch	Cheque No.	Place	Amount Rs.	P.

Drawee Bank / Branch	Cheque No	Amount Rs	P.

Diagram 8.6.2: The Rear Of The Pay In Slip

Whether a Savings account, Current account or a Fixed deposit is being opened, each process begins with a customer depositing money with the bank. This is done via a **Pay In slip** as shown in diagrams 8.6.1 and 8.6.2. A Pay In slip is instrument that is used to document all customer **deposit transactions** with the bank.

For customer **withdrawals transactions** the bank provides a **Withdrawal slip** and a **Chequebook** to their customers. Refer to diagrams 8.7.1, 8.7.2 and 8.8.

Occasionally, account withdrawals (Savings or Current) can be done using a **Bank draft**.

The Banks Withdrawal Slip:

The South Indian Co-Operative Bank Ltd.
PASS BOOK MUST ACCOMPANY THIS WITHDRAWAL SLIP

________________ Branch

S.B A/c. No.

Date ________________

Pay self the sum of Rupees ________________________
(in words)

______________________________ Rs.

L.F. ______________

Entered by ____________

Vr.No.

Signature

Diagram 8.7.1: The Front Of The Withdrawal Slip

I authorise Shri/Smt. ______________________________

Whose signature is attested below to receive the payment of the amount mentioned

overleaf.

Signature of authorised Agent Depositor

Diagram 8.7.2: The Rear Of The Withdrawal Slip

The Banks Cheque:

In most cases the bank does not encourage its customers to withdraw money from an account using a withdrawal slip. Most banks prefer that a customer use a cheque for the withdrawal of money from any account. A sample of the bank's cheque is shown in diagram 8.8.

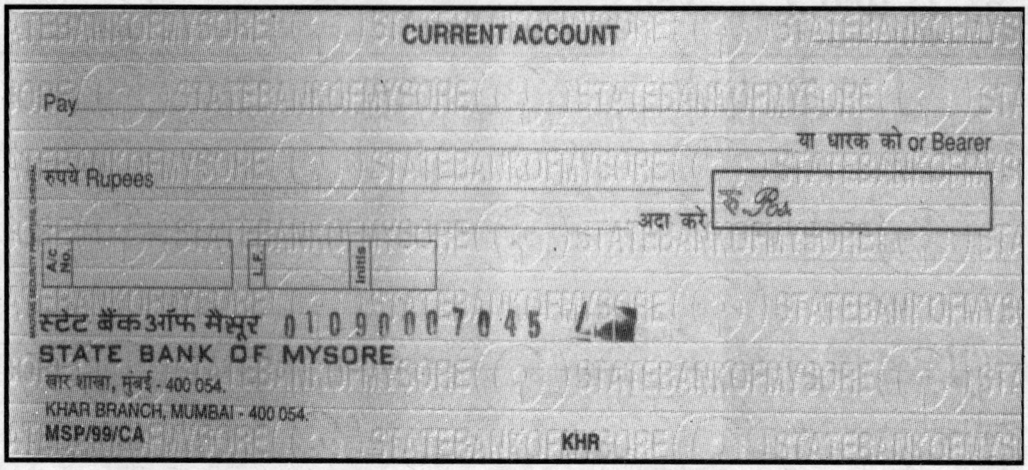

CURRENT ACCOUNT

Pay

या धारक को or Bearer

रुपये Rupees

अदा करें ₹ Rs.

A/C No. L.F. Initls

स्टेट बैंक ऑफ मैसूर 0 1 0 9 0 0 0 7 0 4 5

STATE BANK OF MYSORE

खार शाखा, मुंबई - 400 054.

KHAR BRANCH, MUMBAI - 400 054.

MSP/99/CA

KHR

Diagram 8.8: A Cheque Sample Issued By The Bank.

This completes all the paper forms used by the bank to carry out the business processes that this project has undertaken to computerize. Based on a study of the business data being captured by these forms table structures will be designed.

Table structure definitions now follow.

9

Project Planning For The Retail Banking Model

Based on the business model for Retail Banking presented in the previous chapter, the following table structures are identified.

Table Definitions FOR Retail Banking

Branches Of The Bank

Table Definition:

Table Name	**: BRANCH_MSTR**
Primary Key	: BRANCH_MSTR.BRANCH_NO
Foreign Key	: - -

Column Definition:

Column Name	Data Type	Width	Allow Null	Default
BRANCH_NO	VarChar2	10		
NAME	VarChar2	25		

Table Description:

Column Name	Description
BRANCH_NO	A system generated number auto posted to this table column
NAME	Branch location

Explanation:

The BRANCH_MSTR table stores the Unique ID Number and location of different branches of the bank.

Employees Of The Bank

Table Definition:

Table Name	**: EMP_MSTR**
Primary Key	: EMP_MSTR.EMP_NO
Foreign Key	:EMP_MSTR.BRANCH_NO à BRANCH_MSTR.BRANCH_NO

Column Definition:

Column Name	Data Type	Width	Allow Null	Default
EMP_NO	VarChar2	10		
BRANCH_NO	VarChar2	10		
FNAME	VarChar2	25		
MNAME	VarChar2	25		
LNAME	VarChar2	25		
DEPT	VarChar2	30		
DESIG	VarChar2	30		
MNGR_NO	VarChar2	10		

Table Description:

Column Name	Description
EMP_NO	A system generated number auto posted to this table column
BRANCH_NO	A unique branch Id number This value must be present in the BRANCH_MSTR table

The **EMP_MSTR** table structure details continued:

Table Description:

Column Name	Description
FNAME	First name of a bank employee
MNAME	Middle name of a bank employee
LNAME	Last name of a bank employee
DEPT	Bank employee's department
DESIG	Bank employee's official designation
MNGR_NO	Employer Id number of the manager to whom the employee reportsThis value must be present in the EMP_MSTR table

Explanation:

The EMP_MSTR table stores bank employee information (*across all branches*).

Each branch of the bank will access this repository as though it was local to the branch. This requires that each branch be connected to the central repository via a WAN, which has excellent bandwidth.

The WAN is expected to have a consistent 512 kpbs bandwidth to start with using dedicated ISDN lines. Once more than 10 branches go live, this bandwidth will be quickly ramped up to GB size with failsafe and Server redundancy built-in to ensure 24/7 operations for the bank.

This means that, a Savings account or Current account opened at one branch can be accessed at any other branch as though it were local to the branch. Thus cash, bank draft or cheque transactions can be carried out for a customer at any branch of the bank.

Additionally, fixed deposits can be opened at any branch. Any branch employee can verify the fixed deposit opening transaction. Finally the fixed deposit receipt can be issued from any branch convenient to the customer. If required the fixed deposit itself can be transferred to any branch on instructions from the customer. A truly open, multi user, multi location, retail banking.

Customers Of The Bank

Table Definition:

Table Name	**: CUST_MSTR**
Primary Key	: CUST_MSTR.CUST_NO
Foreign Key	: - -

Column Definition:

Column Name	Data Type	Width	Allow Null	Default
CUST_NO	VarChar2	10		
FNAME	VarChar2	25		
MNAME	VarChar2	25		
LNAME	VarChar2	25		
DOB_INC	Date/Time			
OCCUP	VarChar2	25		
PHOTOGRAPH	VarChar2	25		
SIGNATURE	VarChar2	25		
PANCOPY	VarChar2	1		
FORM60	VarChar2	1		

The **CUST_MSTR** table structure details continued:

Table Description:

Column Name	Description
CUST_NO	A system generated number auto posted to this table column
FNAME	Customer's first name
MNAME	Customer's middle name
LNAME	Customer's last name
DOB_INC	Customer's date of birth (for individuals) or data of incorporation (for organizations)
OCCUP	Customer's occupation or line of business
PHOTOGRAPH	Location to customer's scanned photograph (for individuals only)
SIGNATURE	Location to customer's scanned signature (for individuals only)
PANCOPY	Holds **Y** if a copy of PAN card has been submitted
FORM60	Holds **Y** if the Form 60 has been submitted

Explanation:

The CUST_MSTR stores customer information collected once, when a customer opens a new account or creates a fixed deposit with the bank.

Accounts Opened With The Bank

Table Definition:

Table Name	**: CUST_MSTR**
Primary Key	: ACCT_MSTR.ACCT_NO
Foreign Key	: ACCT_MSTR.BRANCH_NO →BRANCH_MSTR.BRANCH_NO: ACCT_MSTR.INTRO_CUST_NO → CUST_MSTR.CUST_NO: ACCT_MSTR.INTRO_ACCT_NO → ACCT_MSTR.ACCT_NO: ACCT_MSTR.CORP_CUST_NO → CUST_MSTR.CUST_NO: ACCT_MSTR.VERI_EMP_NO → EMP_MSTR.EMP_NO

Column Definition:

Column Name	Data Type	Width	Allow Null	Default
ACCT_NO	VarChar2	10		
SF_NO	VarChar2	10		
LF_NO	VarChar2	10		
BRANCH_NO	VarChar2	10		
INTRO_CUST_NO	VarChar2	10		
INTRO_ACCT_NO	VarChar2	10		

INTRO_SIGN	VarChar2	1		
TYPE	VarChar2	2		
OPR_MODE	VarChar2	2		
CUR_ACCT_TYPE	VarChar2	4		
TITLE	VarChar2	30		
CORP_CUST_NO	VarChar2	10		
APLNDT	Date			
OPNDT	Date			
VERI_EMP_NO	VarChar2	10		
VERI_SIGN	VarChar2	1		

The **ACCT_MSTR** table structure details continued:

Column Name	Data Type	Width	Allow Null	Default
MANAGER_SIGN	VarChar2	1		
CURBAL	Number	8, 2		0
STATUS	VarChar2	1		A

Table Description:

Column Name	Description
ACCT_NO	A system generated number auto posted to this table column
SF_NO	Holds the account's S. F. number
LF_NO	Holds the account's Ledger / Folio number
BRANCH_NO	This value must be present in BRANCH_MSTR table
INTRO_CUST_NO	Introducers, customer identity number This value must be present in the CUST_MSTR table
INTRO_ACCT_NO	Introducers, bank account numberThis value must be present in the ACCT_MSTR table
INTRO_SIGN	Holds **Y** if the introducer's has signed the account opening, application form
TYPE	Can hold the values: **CA** - Current Account, **SB** - Savings Bank Account
OPR_MODE	Can hold the values: **SI** for singly operated account **ES** for account operated by either or survivor **JO** for jointly operated account **AS** account operated by anyone or survivor

CUR_ACCT_TYPE	Can hold the values: **ØS** for Individuals/Savings Bank Account **1C** for Propriety/Sole Trading Concerns **2C** for Partnership Concerns **3C** for Hindu Undivided Family Businesses **4C** for Limited Companies **5C** for Trust Accounts**6C** for Clubs/Societies **7C** for Legislative Bodies
TITLE	Holds an account name in those cases where an organization has opened the account
CORP_CUST_NO	Customer number of the Corporate account holderThis value must be present in the CUST_MSTR table
APLNDT	The date of submission of the account opening application form
OPNDT	The date on which the account was actually opened
VERI_EMP_NO	The employee ID number of the bank officer who physically verified the customers application formThis value must be present in the EMP_MSTR table
VERI_SIGN	Holds **Y** if the bank official who verified the application form has signed and dated the form
MANAGER_SIGN	Holds **Y** if the bank branch manager has signed and dated the form
CURBAL	Holds the current balance of an account
STATUS	Can hold the following values: **A** for active accounts **S** for suspended accounts **T** for terminated accounts

The **ACCT_MSTR** table structure details continued:

Explanation:

The ACCT_MSTR table stores all the details of opening any type of account, whether Savings or Current, with the bank. This information is largely one time information gathered and registered with the bank when an account is opened for the first time. Additionally, this table holds the current, real time, balance held in a specific account.

Account Opening Support Documents

Table Definition:

Table Name	**: SPRT_DOC**
Primary Key	: SPRT_DOC.ACCT_CODE
Foreign Key	: - -

Column Definition:

Column Name	Data Type	Width	Allow Null	Default
ACCT_CODE	VarChar2	4		
TYPE	VarChar2	30		
DOCS	VarChar2	75		

Table Description:

Column Name	Description
ACCT_CODE	Can hold the values: **ØS** for Individuals/Savings Bank Account **1C** for Propriety/Sole Trading Concerns **2C** for Partnership Concerns**3C** for Hindu Undivided Family Businesses
ACCT_CODE	Also, can hold the values: **4C** for Limited Companies **5C** for Trust Accounts **6C** for Clubs/Societies **7C** for Legislative Bodies
TYPE	Describes the organization type
DOCS	Stores document(s) required by the bank for verification prior account opening

Explanation:

The SPRT_DOC table stores information related to the documents submitted to the bank via which a customer's details, written in the application form, are verified and supported.

Different support documents must be submitted to the bank depending upon whether an **individual** or an **organization** is opening the account, **or** fixed deposit.

Fixed Deposits With The Bank

Table Definition:

Table Name	: FD_MSTR
Primary Key	: FD_MSTR.FD_SER_NO
Foreign Key	: FD_MSTR.BRANCH_NO à BRANCH_MSTR.BRANCH_NO : FD_MSTR.INTRO_CUST_NO à CUST_MSTR.CUST_NO : FD_MSTR.INTRO_ACCT_NO à ACCT_MSTR.ACCT_NO : FD_MSTR.ACCT_NO à ACCT_MSTR.ACCT_NO : FD_MSTR.CORP_CUST_NO à CUST_MSTR.CUST_NO : FD_MSTR.VERI_EMP_NO à EMP_MSTR.EMP_NO

The **FD_MSTR** table structure details continued:

Column Definition:

Column Name	Data Type	Width	Allow Null	Default
FD_SER_NO	VarChar2	10		
SF_NO	VarChar2	10		
BRANCH_NO	VarChar2	10		
INTRO_CUST_NO	VarChar2	10		
INTRO_ACCT_NO	VarChar2	10		
INTRO_SIGN	VarChar2	1		
ACCT_NO	VarChar2	10		
TITLE	VarChar3	30		
CORP_CUST_NO	VarChar2	10		
CORP_CNST_TYPE	VarChar2	4		
VERI_EMP_NO	VarChar2	10		
VERI_SIGN	VarChar2	1		
MANAGER_SIGN	VarChar2	1		

Table Description:

Column Name	Description
FD_SER_NO	A system generated number auto posted to this table column
SF_NO	Holds the account's S. F. number
BRANCH_NO	This value must be present in the BRANCH_MSTR table
INTRO_CUST_NO	Customer number of the Introducer (*Optional*)This value must be present in the CUST_MSTR table
INTRO_ACCT_NO	Introducer's bank account number. (*Optional*)This value must be present in the ACCT_MSTR table
INTRO_SIGN	Holds **Y** if the introducer has signed the fixed deposit opening application form (*Optional*)
ACCT_NO	Bank Account number (if any) held by the F. D. holder(s)This value must be present in the ACCT_MSTR table
TITLE	Holds an account name in those cases where an organization has opened the account
CORP_CUST_NO	Customer number of the Corporate account holder. (**Foreign Key:** Should be present in CUST_MSTR table)
CORP_CNST_TYPE	Can hold the values: **ØS** for Individuals/Savings Bank Account **1C** for Propriety/Sole Trading Concerns **2C** for Partnership Concerns

	3C for Hindu Undivided Family Businesses **4C** for Limited Companies **5C** for Trust Accounts **6C** for Clubs/Societies **7C** for Legislative Bodies
VERI_EMP_NO	Employee ID number of the bank officer who physically verified the account application form. This value must be present in the EMP_MSTR table
VERI_SIGN	Holds **Y** if the above verifier has signed the form
MANAGER_SIGN	Holds **Y** if the bank manager has signed the form

The **FD_MSTR** table structure details continued:

Explanation:

The FD_MSTR table stores all the details of **opening** a fixed deposit with the bank. This information is one time information gathered and stored when a customer opens a fixed deposit with the bank.

Table Definition:

Table Name	**: FDSLAB_MSTR**
Primary Key	: FDSLAB_MSTR.FDSLAB_NO
Foreign Key	: - -

Column Definition:

Column Name	Data Type	Width	Allow Null	Default
FDSLAB_NO	Number	2		
MINPERIOD	Number	5		
MAXPERIOD	Number	5		
INTRATE	Number	5, 2		

Table Description:

Column Name	Description
FDSLAB_NO	A system generated number auto posted to this table column
MINPERIOD	Minimum period in months
MAXPERIOD	Maximum period in months
INTRATE	Rate of Interest charged on the Deposit

Explanation:

The FDSLAB_MSTR is a **lookup** table that stores details of the interest payable on a fixed deposit bound to specific time slabs.

Fixed Deposit Details

Table Definition:

Table Name	: **FD_DTLS**
Primary Key	: FD_DTLS.FD_NO
Foreign Key	: FD_DTLS.FD_SER_NO → FD_MSTR.FD_SER_NO : FD_DTLS.PAYTO_ACCTNO → ACCT_MSTR.ACCT_NO

Column Definition:

Column Name	Data Type	Width	Allow Null	Default
FD_SER_NO	VarChar2	10		
FD_NO	VarChar2	10		
TYPE	VarChar2	1		
PAYTO_ACCTNO	VarChar2	10		
PERIOD	Number	5		
OPNDT	Date			
DUEDT	Date			
AMT	Number	8, 2		
DUEAMT	Number	8, 2		
INTRATE	Number	8, 2		
STATUS	VarChar2	1		A
AUTO_RENEWAL	VarChar2	1		

The **FD_DTLS** table structure details continued:

Table Description:

Column Name	Description
FD_SER_NO	This value must be present in the FD_MSTR table
FD_NO	Unique Identity Number for each fixed depositA system generated number auto posted to this table column
TYPE	Can hold the values: **S** of standard fixed deposits **R** for recursive fixed deposits
PAYTO_ACCTNO	Account number to which the F.D. amount should be transferred on maturity (*Optional*) This value must be present in the ACCT_MSTR table
PERIOD	Period of the fixed deposit in days
OPNDT	The date on which the fixed deposit is opened

DUEDT	The maturity date of the fixed deposit
AMT	Principle amount for the fixed deposit
DUEAMT	Amount due when the fixed deposit matures
INTRATE	The rate of interest applicable to the fixed deposit
STATUS	Can hold the values: **A** for active **C** for Cancelled **M** for Matured
AUTO_RENEWAL	Holds **Y** if the F. D. should be automatically renewed on maturity

Explanation:

The FD_DTLS table stores specific and complete details of every fixed deposit **receipt** issued to a bank customer.

The fixed deposit, banking business model, sub process, involves three tables. FD_MSTR, FD_SLAB and FD_DTLS.

- The table FD_MSTR stores all the information bound to the documentation of a fixed deposit being opened with the bank.
- The table FD_SLAB is a lookup table. This table stores information about the rate of interest payable on a fixed deposit based on the period of time that the money is locked with the bank.
- The table FD_DTLS stores information about every fixed deposit receipt issued by the bank to a customer.

When the fixed deposit receipt is being printed out from the FD_DTLS tables, the FD_SLAB table is referenced and the appropriate rate of interest is printed on the FD receipt. Additionally, the FD_DTLS table also stores a flag indicating the status of all fixed deposits created with the bank. An FD status could be A, C or M. A = Active, C = Cancelled, M = Matured.

Bank Account Nominee Information

Table Definition:

Table Name	**: NOMINEE_MSTR**
Primary Key	: NOMINEE_MSTR.NOMINEE_NO
Foreign Key	: NOMINEE_MSTR.ACCT_FD_NO → ACCT_MSTR.ACCT_NO **OR** NOMINEE_MSTR.ACCT_FD_NO → FD_MSTR.FD_SER_NO

The **NOMINEE_MSTR** table structure details continued:

Column Name	Data Type	Width	Allow Null	Default
NOMINEE_NO	VarChar2	10		
ACCT_FD_NO	VarChar2	10		
NAME	VarChar2	75		
DOB	Date			
RELATIONSHIP	VarChar2	25		

Table Description:

Column Name	Description
NOMINEE_NO	Unique Identity Number for each nomineeA system generated number auto posted to this table column
ACCT_FD_NO	Identifies the account or F.D. to which the individual is a nomineeThis should be present in either ACCT_MSTR table **or** FD_MSTR table
NAME	The name of the nominee
DOB	The date of birth of the nominee
RELATIONSHIP	The nominee's relationship with the account or F.D. holder(s)

Explanation:

The NOMINEE_MSTR table stores account or fixed deposit, nominee information. Nominees can be set for Savings accounts, Current accounts and Fixed deposits.

Bank Account Or Fixed Deposit Identity Details

Table Definition:

Table Name	**: ACCT_FD_CUST_DTLS**
Primary Key	**: - -**
Foreign Key	: ACCT_FD_CUST_DTLS.ACCT_FD_NO → ACCT_MSTR.ACCT_NO **OR** ACCT_FD_CUST_DTLS.ACCT_FD_NO → FD_MSTR.FD_SER_NO : ACCT_FD_CUST_DTLS.CUST_NO → CUST_MSTR.CUST_NO

Column Definition:

Column Name	Data Type	Width	Allow Null	Default
ACCT_FD_NO	VarChar2	10		
CUST_NO	VarChar2	10		

Table Description:

Column Name	Description
ACCT_FD_NO	Identifies the account / F.D. to which the customer is bound. This value must be present in either ACCT_MSTR table or FD_MSTR table
CUST_NO	Customer number associated with an account / F.D. This value must be present in the CUST_MSTR table

Explanation:

The ACCT_FD_CUST_DTLS table stores a list of bank accounts or fixed deposit identity numbers. Each Savings or Current account and fixed deposit identity number will have a customer number bound to it.

The contents of this table allow the linking of a Savings account, Current account or Fixed deposit with a specific **customer** and **contact** information.

The **ACCT_FD_CUST_DTLS** table structure details continued:

Without this table, a **one to many** relationship, cannot be maintained between Current accounts, Savings accounts and Fixed deposits with multiple customers.

All contact information such as a **multiple** postal addresses together with **multiple** telephone, mobile and pager numbers and/or Email addresses and Web Site URLs can be bound to specific Savings accounts, Current accounts and Fixed deposits due to the contents of the ACCT_FD_CUST_DTLS table.

Bank Customers Address And Contact Information

Table Definition:

Table Name	**: ADDR_DTLS**
Primary Key	: ADDR_DTLS.ADDR_NO
Foreign Key	: ADDR_DTLS.CODE_NO → CUST_MSTR.CUST_NO **OR** ADDR_DTLS.CODE_NO → NOMINEE_MSTR.NOMINEE_NO **OR** ADDR_DTLS.CODE_NO → BRANCH_MSTR.BRANCH_NO **OR** ADDR_DTLS.CODE_NO → EMP_MSTR.EMP_NO

Column Definition:

Column Name	Data Type	Width	Allow Null	Default
ADDR_NO	Number	6		
CODE_NO	VarChar2	10		
ADDR_TYPE	VarChar2	1		
ADDR1	VarChar2	50		
ADDR2	VarChar2	50		
CITY	VarChar2	25		
STATE	VarChar2	25		
PINCODE	VarChar2	6		

Table Description:

Column Name	Description
ADDR_NO	A system generated number auto posted to this table column
CODE_NO	Identifies a person or organization to whom the address belongs Should be present in either BRANCH_MSTR table, CUST_MSTR table, EMP_MSTR table or NOMINEE_MSTR table

ADDR_TYPE	Can hold the values: **C** for Current Residential address **N** for Native place **i.e.** Permanent Residential address, **H** for Head Office or **B** for Branch
Addr1	Postal Address (House number & Name, Road name)
Addr2	Postal address (Locality & area)
City	Postal address (City name)
State	Postal address (State name)
Pincode	Postal address (Pin code)

Explanation:

The ADDR_DTLS table stores multiple postal addresses of customers who have either Savings accounts, Current accounts or Fixed deposits with the bank.

Table Definition:

Table Name	**: CNTC_DTLS**
Primary Key	**: - -**
Foreign Key	: CNTC_DTLS.ADDR_NO → ADDR_DTLS.ADDR_NO : CNTC_DTLS.CODE_NO → CUST_MSTR.CUST_NO **OR** CNTC_DTLS.CODE_NO → NOMINEE_MSTR.NOMINEE_NO **OR** CNTC_DTLS.CODE_NO → BRANCH_MSTR.BRANCH_NO **OR** CNTC_DTLS.CODE_NO → EMP_MSTR.EMP_NO

Column Definition:

Column Name	Data Type	Width	Allow Null	Default
ADDR_NO	Number	6		
CODE_NO	VarChar2	10		
CNCT_TYPE	VarChar2	1		
CNCT_DATA	VarChar2	75		

Table Description:

Column Name	Description
ADDR_NO	This value must be present in the ADDR_DTLS table
CODE_NO	Identifies the person or organization to whom the address belongsShould be present in either BRANCH_MSTR table, CUST_MSTR table, EMP_MSTR table or NOMINEE_MSTR table

CNCT_TYPE	Can hold the values: **R** for Residence telephone number **O** for Office telephone number **M** for Mobile telephone number **P** for Pager number **E** for Email address **F** for Fax number **W** for Website's URL
CNCT_DATA	Actual contact details of a client, **i.e.** A telephone, mobile, Fax, pager number, Email address or Web site URL

Explanation:

The CNTC_DTLS table stores complete contact information for a bank's branch employees, customers, or nominees to any account or fixed deposit. There can be multiple contact details for each.

The tables ADDR_DTLS and CNTC_DTLS are common to the system. They hold the complete Postal address and Residence, Office, Mobile, Pager, Fax, Email and Web site URLs (if any) of all the banks branch employees, customers and their nominees.

Banking Transactions

Table Definition:

Table Name	**: TRANS_MSTR**
Primary Key	: TRANS_MSTR.TRANS_NO
Foreign Key	: TRANS_MSTR.ACCT_NO à ACCT_MSTR.ACCT_NO

The **TRANS_MSTR** table structure continued:

Column Definition:

Column Name	Data Type	Width	Allow Null	Default
TRANS_NO	VarChar2	10		
ACCT_NO	VarChar2	6		
DT	Date			
TYPE	VarChar2	1		
PARTICULAR	VarChar2	30		
DR_CR	VarChar2	1		
AMT	Number	8,2		
BALANCE	Number	8,2		

Table Description:

Column Name	Description
TRANS_NO	A system generated number auto posted to this table column
ACCT_NO	This value must be present in the ACCT_MSTR table
DT	Transaction date
TYPE	Can hold the values: **B** for Cheque transaction **C** for Cash transaction or **D** for Demand Draft transaction
PARTICULAR	Short summary for the transaction
DR_CR	Transaction type (**D** - Deposit or **W** - Withdrawal)
AMT	The amount of the transaction
BALANCE	A calculated, real time, balance held in the account

Explanation:

The TRANS_MSTR table stores the daily transactions of deposits or withdrawals carried out by all customers of the bank.

Banking Transaction Details

Table Definition:

Table Name	**: TRANS_DTLS**
Primary Key	: - -
Foreign Key	: TRANS_DTLS.TRANS_NO à TRANS_MSTR.TRANS_NO

Column Definition:

Column Name	Data Type	Width	Allow Null	Default
TRANS_NO	VarChar2	10	No	
INST_NO	Number	6	No	
INST_DT	Date		No	
PAYTO	VarChar2	30	No	
INST_CLR_DT	Date		No	
BANK_NAME	VarChar2	35	No	
BRANCH_NAME	VarChar2	25	No	
PAIDFROM	VarChar2	10	No	

The **TRANS_DTLS** table structure continued:

Table Description:

Column Name	Description
TRANS_NO	This value must be present in the TRANS_MSTR table
INST_NO	Instrument number (**i.e.** Cheque number)
INST_DT	Instrument date (**i.e.** Cheque date)
PAYTO	The name to whom the cheque is made out to
INST_CLR_DT	Date on which an instrument (**i.e.** Cheque) deposited with the bank is cleared by the bank on which it was drawn
BANK_NAME	Name of the drawee bank
BRANCH_NAME	Branch of the drawee bank
PAIDFROM	The Account number at the bank on which the cheque is drawn

Explanation:

The TRANS_DTLS table stores the daily cheque transactions carried out by the bank's customers. The information in the TRANS_MSTR and TRANS_DTLS tables are combined to obtain the entries to be written / printed in a customer's passbook **or** computerized passbook.

Entity Relationship Diagram For Retail Banking

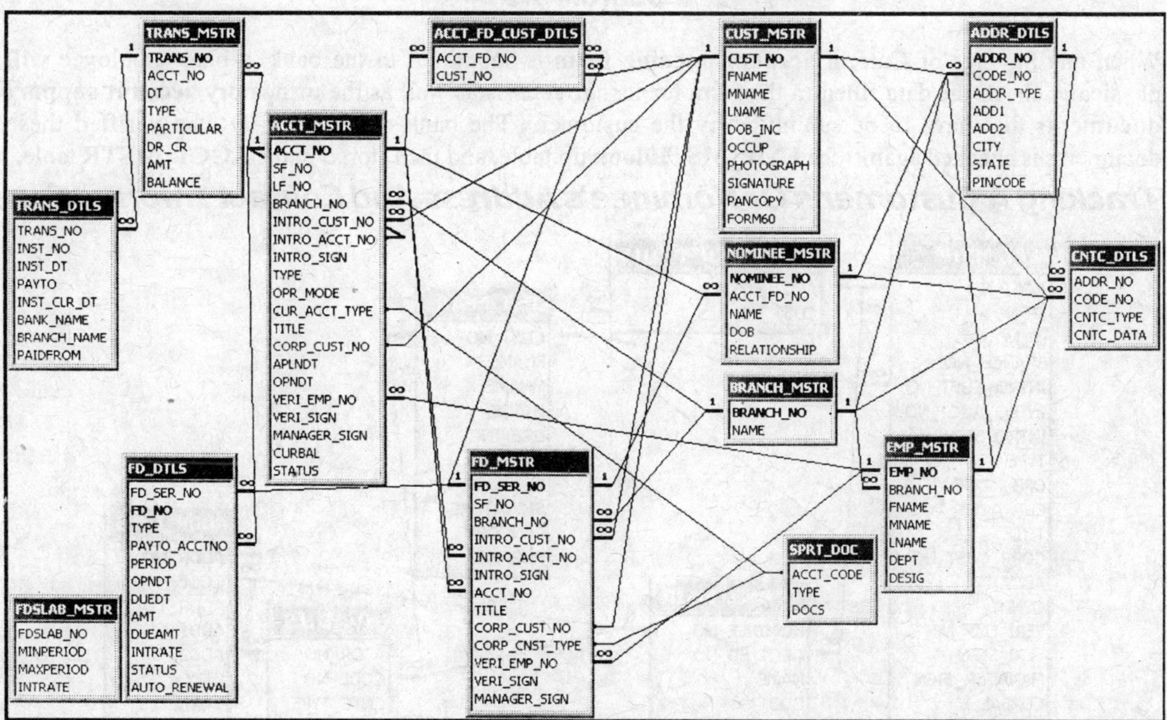

Diagram 9.1

The above diagram, attempts to give a visual representation of the entity relationship between various tables required under the project. The symbols '1' and 'oo' indicate a **one-to-many** relationship.

The **ACCT_MSTR** table references the **BRANCH_MSTR** and **EMP_MSTR** tables. Refer to diagram 9.2.

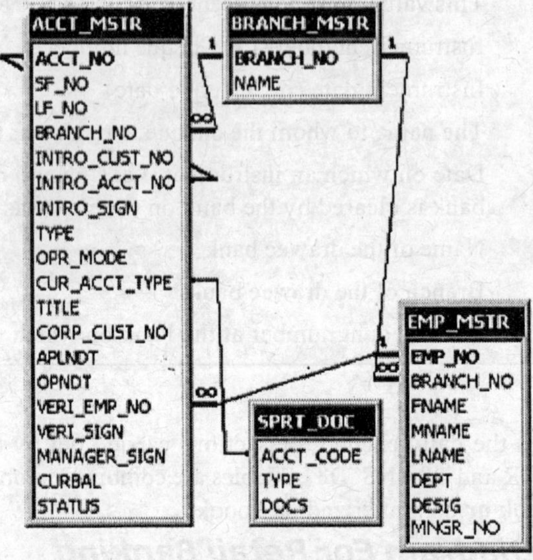

Dagram 9.2

When any Savings or Current **account opening form** is submitted to the bank, a bank employee will physically check the data filled in the form for its correctness as well as the mandatory **account support documents** that have to be submitted by the customer. The bank employee's ID who verified these documents is checked against the **EMP_MSTR look up** table, and then stored in the **ACCT_MSTR** table.

Tracking A Customer's Or Nominee's Address And Contact Information

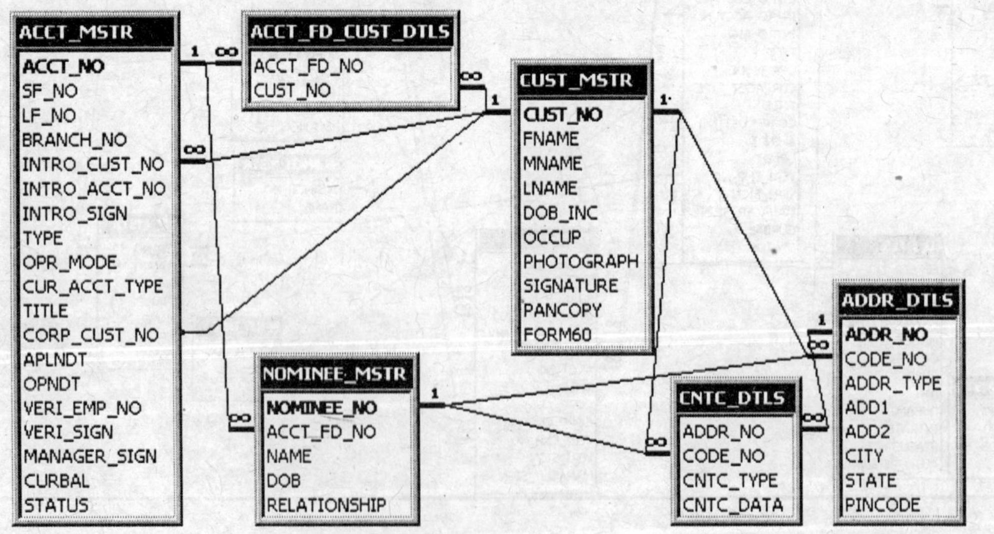

Diagram 9.3

When a customer opens an account with the bank **or** creates a fixed deposit, the customers and their nominee's full postal address and contact information needs to be stored in the retail banking system. The tables that store such information are **CUST_MSTR, NOMINEE_MSTR, ADDR_DTLS** and **CNTC_DTLS**.

The CUST_MSTR table is bound to the ACCT_MSTR table via the column **ACCT_FD_NO** in the **ACCT_FD_CUST_DTLS** table, which stores the value held in ACCT_MSTR.ACCT_NO. The NOMINEE_MSTR table is bound to the ACCT_MSTR table via the column **ACCT_FD_NO**, which stores the value held in ACCT_MSTR.ACCT_NO. The ADDR_DTLS and the CNTC_DTLS tables are bound to the ACCT_MSTR and the NOMINEE_MSTR / CUST_MSTR tables via the column **CODE_NO**.

This column will hold either the value held in CUST_MSTR.CUST_NO **or** the value held in NOMINEE_MSTR.NOMINEE.NO.

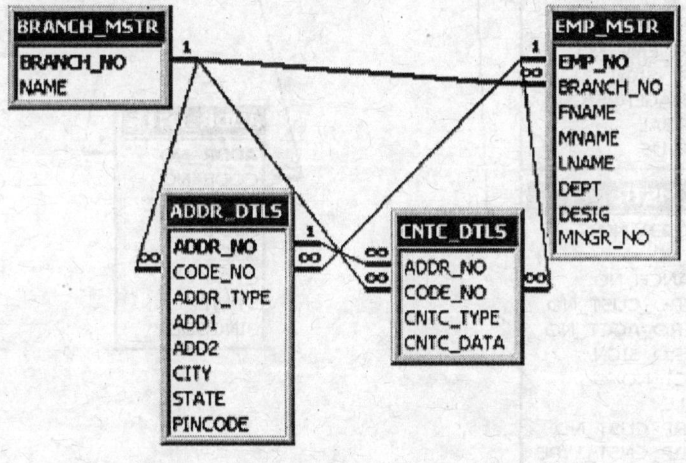

Diagram 9.4

Employee Details

ADDR_DTLS and **CNTC_DTLS** are common lookup tables used across the system for storing the contact information of Branches, Employees, Customers, and Nominees. The column **CODE_NO** in these tables will hold BRANCH_NO, EMP_NO, CUST_NO or NOMINEE_NO thus binding address and contact information to any of the four.

Nominee Details

Nominees can be setup for Savings or Current accounts as well as Fixed Deposits. Nominee information is stored in the **NOMINEE_MSTR** table. This table is bound to the **ACT_MSTR** and/or the **FD_MSTR** via the **ACCT_FD_NO** column. This column can hold either an account number or a fixed deposit number.

A nominee's address and contact information is stored in the tables **ADDR_DTLS** and **CNTC_DTLS** where the value held in **NOMINEE_NO** is stored in their **CODE_NO** columns.

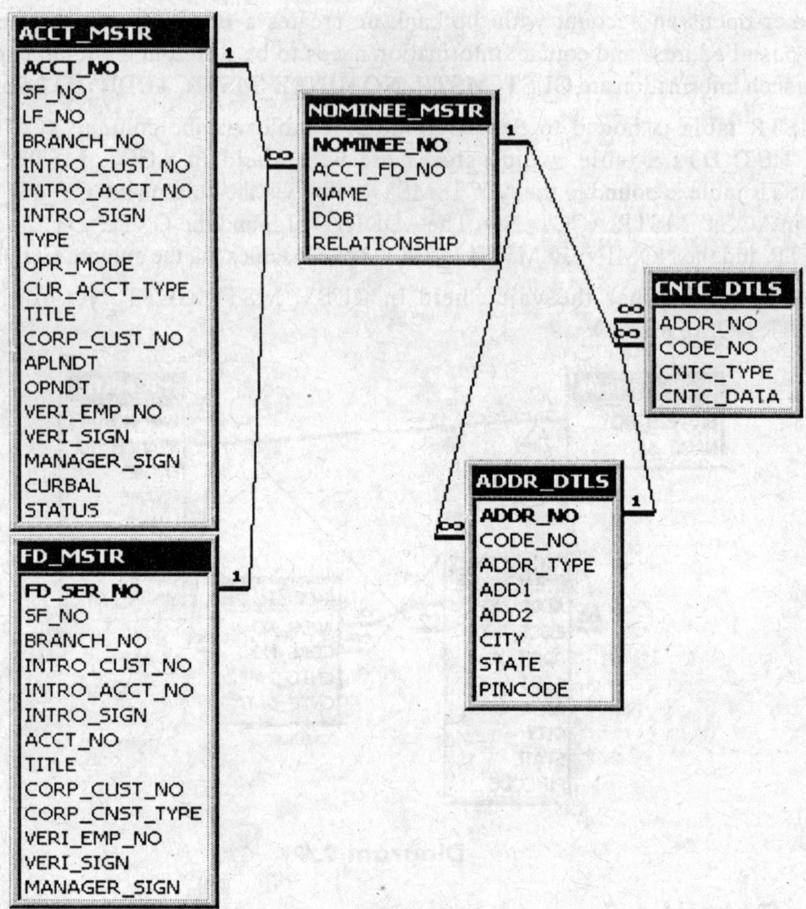

Diagram 9.5

Fixed Deposits

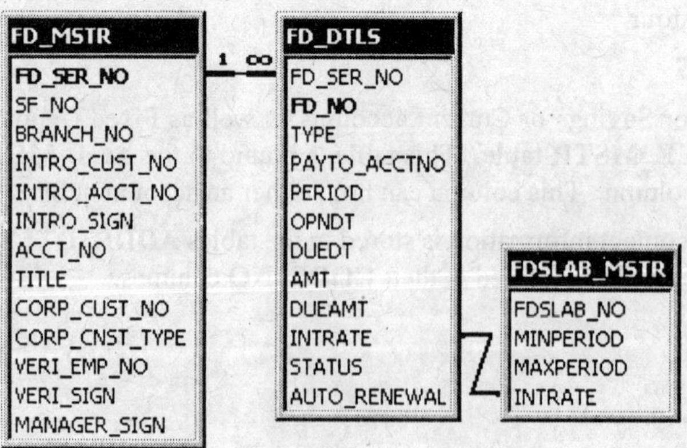

Diagram 9.6

When creating fixed deposits with the bank there are two sets of information to be captured and stored. The table **FD_MSTR** stores information about the bank application documentation that leads to the issue of a fixed deposit receipt. The table **FD_DTLS** stores the details of the fixed deposit.

Fixed deposits are created for a specific time duration called a slab. Depending upon this time slab an interest rate will be applied to the fixed deposit. Whenever a fixed deposit is being created, the interest rate applicable to the deposit is obtained from the **FDSLAB_MSTR** lookup table.

Information printed on the fixed deposit receipt is taken from the FD_DTLS table. The fixed deposit receipt, which is the output of this sub system, is a combination of a **fixed template** and **dynamic information** obtained from the FD_DTLS table.

The table FD_MSTR also references several other look up tables they are, ACCT_MSTR, CUST_MSTR, EMP_MSTR:

- FD_MSTR.BRANCH_NO references BRANCH_MSTR.BRANCH_NO
- FD_MSTR.INTRO_CUST_NO references CUST_MSTR.CUST_NO

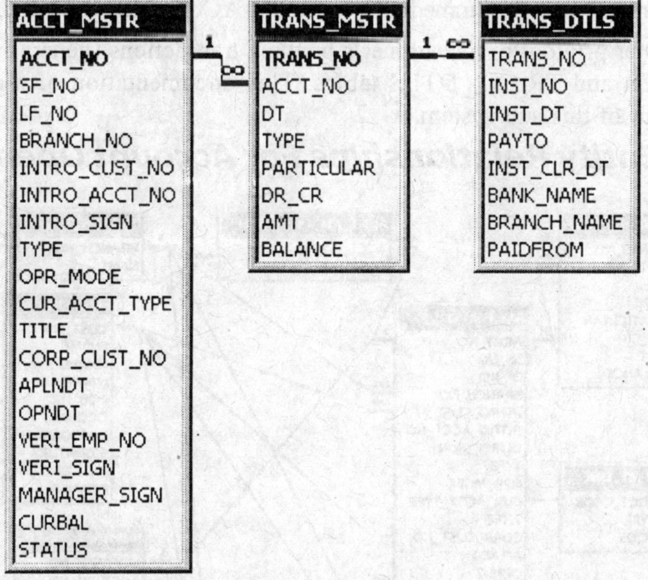

Diagram 9.7

FD_MSTR.INTRO_ACCT_NO references ACCT_MSTR.ACCT_NO

- FD_MSTR.ACCT_NO references ACCT_MSTR.ACCT_NO
- FD_MSTR.CORP_CUST_NO references CUST_MSTR.CUST_NO
- FD_MSTR.VERI_EMP_NO references EMP_MSTR.EMPNO

Banking Transactions

The transactions of both Savings and Current accounts are identical. Transactions documented in this retail banking are either deposits or withdrawals. Transactions can be done via Cash, Bank draft or Cheque.

Transactions

Transactions must occur for a specific Account. Hence, the table TRANS_MSTR references ACCT_MSTR.ACCT_NO.

Transactions (**i.e.** Deposits or Withdrawals) can be Cash, Bank draft or Cheque. This information is stored in TRANS_MSTR.TYPE.

If the transaction is via Bank draft or Cheque their details are stored in:

TRANS_DTLS.INST_NO

TRANS_DTLS.INST_DT

TRANS_DTLS.BANK_NAME

The type of transaction (i.e. whether a Deposit or Withdrawal) is stored in TRANS_MSRT.DR_CR.

The transaction amount and the running balance of the account are stored in TRANS_MSTR.AMT and TRANS_MSTR.BALANCE respectively.

Once calculated, the running balance is immediately posted to ACCT_MSTR.CURBAL.

The passbook or computer printout of a customer's banking transactions (generally month wise) is taken from the TRANS_MSTR and TRANS_DTLS tables. This documentation of a customer's day-to-day transactions is the output of this sub system.

The Complete Entity Relationships For Account Opening

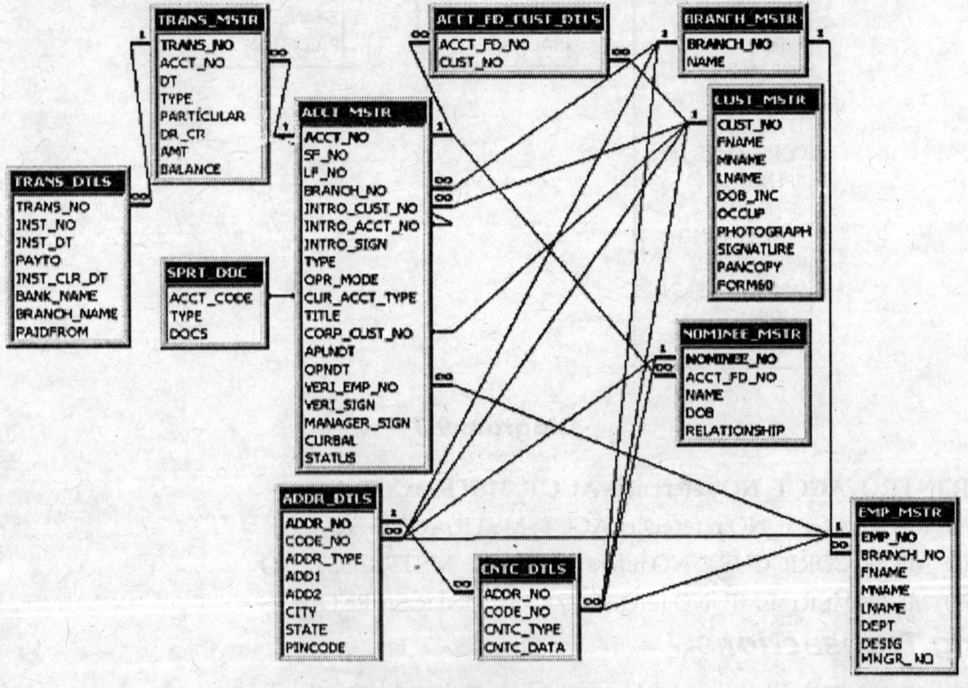

Diagram 9.8

The Complete Entity Relationships For Fixed Deposit Creation

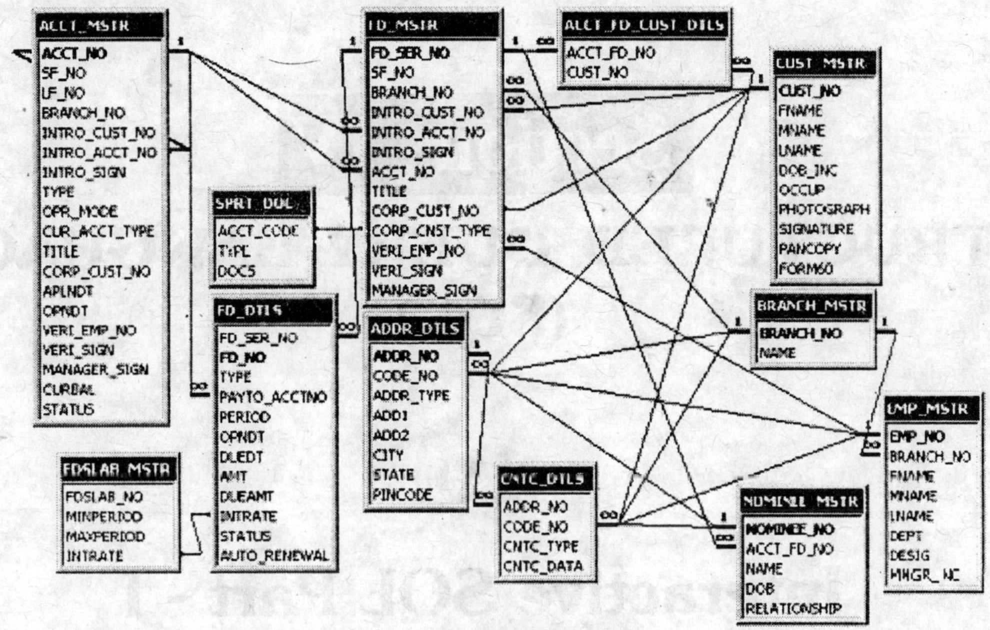

Diagram 9.9

Note

 Refer to the Appendix A of this book for the **test data** bound to tables of the **Retail Banking**.

Section - IV

STRUCTURED QUERY LANGUAGE (SQL)

10

Interactive SQL Part - I

Table fundamentals

A **table** is database object that holds user data. The simplest analogy is to think of a table as a spreadsheet. The cells of the spreadsheet equate to the columns of a table having a specific **data type** associated with them. If the spreadsheet cell has a number data type associated with it, then storing letters (**i.e.** characters) in the same cell is not allowed. The same logic is applied to a table's column. Each column of the table will have a specific data type bound to it. Oracle ensures that only data, which is identical to the data type of the column, will be stored within the column.

Oracle Data Types

Basic Data Types

Data types come in several forms and sizes, allowing the programmer to create tables suited to the scope of the project. The decisions made in choosing proper data types greatly influence the performance of a database, so it is wise to have a detailed understanding of these concepts.

Oracle is capable of many of the data types that even the novice programmer has probably already been exposed to. Refer to table 10.1 for some of the more commonly used include:

Table 10.1

Data Type	Description
CHAR(size)	This data type is used to store character strings values of fixed length. The size in brackets determines the number of characters the cell can hold. The maximum number of characters (i.e. the size) this data type can hold is 255

	characters. The data held is right-padded with spaces to whatever length specified.For example: In case of **Name CHAR(60)**, if the data held in the variable Name is only 20 characters in length, then the entry will be padded with 40 characters worth of spaces. These spaces will be removed when the value is retrieved though. These entries will be sorted and compared by ORACLE in case-insensitive fashions unless the BINARY keyword is associated with it.The BINARY attribute means that column values are sorted and compared in case-sensitive fashion using the underlying character code values rather then a lexical ordering. BINARY doesn't affect how the column is stored or retrieved.
VARCHAR (size) / VARCHAR2(size)	This data type is used to store variable length alphanumeric data. It is a more flexible form of the CHAR data type. The maximum this data type can hold upto 4000 characters. One difference between this data type and the CHAR data type is ORACLE compares VARCHAR values using non-padded comparison semantics i.e. the inserted values will not be padded with spaces. It also represents data of type String, yet stores this data in variable length format. VARCHAR can hold **1** to **255** characters. VARCHAR is usually a wiser choice than CHAR, due to it's variable length format characteristic. But, keep in mind, that CHAR is much faster than VARCHAR, sometimes up to **50%**.
DATE	This data type is used to represent date and time. The standard format is DD-MON-YY as in 21-JUN-04. To enter dates other than the standard format, use the appropriate functions. DateTime stores date in the 24-hour format. By default, the time in a date field is 12:00:00 am, if no time portion is specified. The default date for a date field is the first day of the current month. Valid dates range from January 1, 4712 B.C. to December 31, 4712 A.D.
NUMBER (P, S)	The NUMBER data type is used to store numbers (fixed or floating point). Numbers of virtually any magnitude maybe stored up to 38 digits of precision. Valid values are 0, and positive and negative numbers with magnitude 1.0E-130 to 9.9…E125. Numbers may be expressed in two ways: first, with the numbers 0 to 9, the signs + and -, and a decimal point (.); second, in scientific notation, such as, 1.85E3 for 1850. The precision (P), determines the maximum length of the data, whereas the scale (S), determines the number of places to the right of the decimal. If scale is omitted then the default is zero. If precision is omitted, values are stored with their original precision upto the maximum of 38 digits.
LONG	This data type is used to store variable length character strings containing upto 2 GB. LONG data can be used to store arrays of binary data in ASCII format. Only one LONG value can be defined per table. LONG values cannot be used in subqueries, functions, expressions, where clauses or indexes and the normal character functions such as SUBSTR cannot be applied to LONG values. A table containing a LONG value cannot be clustered.
RAW/ LONG RAW	The RAW /LONG RAW data types are used to store binary data, such as digitized picture or image. Data loaded into columns of these data types are stored without any further conversion. RAW data type can have a maximum length of 255 bytes. LONG RAW data type can contain up to 2 GB. Values stored in columns having LONG RAW data type cannot be indexed.

Comparison Between Oracle 8i/9i For Various Oracle Data Types

Table 10.2

Data Type	Oracle 8i	Oracle 9i	Explanation
dec(p, s)	The maximum precision is 38 digits.	The maximum precision is 38 digits.	Where *p* is the precision and *s* is the scale. For example, dec(3,1) is a number that has 2 digits before the decimal and 1 digit after the decimal.
decimal(p, s)	The maximum precision is 38 digits.	The maximum precision is 38 digits.	Where *p* is the precision and *s* is the scale. For example, decimal(3,1) is a number that has 2 digits before the decimal and 1 digit after the decimal.
double precision float int integer real smallint			
numeric(p, s)	The maximum precision is 38 digits.	The maximum precision is 38 digits.	Where *p* is the precision and *s* is the scale. For example, numeric(7,2) is a number that has 5 digits before the decimal and 2 digits after the decimal.
number(p, s)	The maximum precision is 38 digits.	The maximum precision is 38 digits.	Where *p* is the precision and *s* is the scale. For example, number(7,2) is a number that has 5 digits before the decimal and 2 digits after the decimal.
char (size)	Up to 32767 bytes in PLSQL. Up to 2000 bytes in Oracle 8i.	Up to 32767 bytes in PLSQL. Up to 2000 bytes in Oracle 9i.	Where *size* is the number of characters to store. Fixed-length strings. Space padded.
varchar2 (size)	Up to 32767 bytes in PLSQL. Up to 4000 bytes in Oracle 8i.	Up to 32767 bytes in PLSQL. Up to 4000 bytes in Oracle 9i.	Where *size* is the number of characters to store. Variable-length strings.
long	Up to 2 giga bytes.	Up to 2 giga bytes.	Variable-length strings. (backward compatible)
raw	Up to 32767 bytes in PLSQL. Up to 2000 bytes in Oracle 8i.	Up to 32767 bytes in PLSQL. Up to 2000 bytes in Oracle 9i.	Variable-length binary strings

long raw	Up to 2 giga bytes.	Up to 2 giga bytes.	Variable-length binary strings. (backward compatible)
date	A date between Jan 1, 4712 BC and Dec 31, 9999 AD.	A date between Jan 1, 4712 BC and Dec 31, 9999 AD.	
timestamp *fractional seconds* (*precision*)	Not supported in Oracle 8i.	*fractional seconds precision* must be a number between 0 and 9. (default is 6)	Includes year, month, day, hour, minute, and seconds. For example:timestamp(6)
timestamp (*fractional seconds precision*) with time zone	Not supported in Oracle 8i.	*fractional seconds precision* must be a number between 0 and 9. (default is 6)	Includes year, month, day, hour, minute, and seconds; with a time zone displacement value. For example:timestamp(5) with time zone
timestamp (*fractional seconds precision*) with local time zone	Not supported in Oracle 8i.	*fractional seconds precision* must be a number between 0 and 9. (default is 6)	Includes year, month, day, hour, minute, and seconds; with a time zone expressed as the session time zone. For example:timestamp(4) with local time zone
interval year (*year precision*) to month	Not supported in Oracle 8i.	*year precision* must be a number between 0 and 9. (default is 2)	Time period stored in years and months. For example: interval year(4) to month
urowid [size]	Up to 2000 bytes.	Up to 2000 bytes.	Universal rowid. Where *size* is optional.
interval day (*day precision*) to second (*fractional seconds precision*)	Not supported in Oracle 8i.	*day precision* must be a number between 0 and 9. (default is 2) *fractional seconds precision* must be a number between 0 and 9. (default is 6)	Time period stored in days, hours, minutes, and seconds. For example:interval day(2) to second(6)
rowid	The format of the rowid is: BBBBBBB.RRRR. FFFFF Where BBBBBBB is the block in the database file; RRRR is the row	The format of the rowid is: BBBBBBB.RRRR. FFFFF Where BBBBBBB is the block in the database file; RRRR is the row	Fixed-length binary data. Every record in the database has a physical address or rowid.

	in the block; FFFFF is the database file.	in the block; FFFFF is the database file.	
boolean	Valid in PLSQL, but this datatype does not exist in Oracle 8i.	Valid in PLSQL, but this datatype does not exist in Oracle 9i.	
nchar (size)	Up to 32767 bytes in PLSQL. Up to 2000 bytes in Oracle 8i	Up to 32767 bytes in PLSQL. Up to 2000 bytes in Oracle 9i.	Where *size* is the number of characters to store. Fixed-length NLS string
nvarchar2 (size)	Up to 32767 bytes in PLSQL. Up to 4000 bytes in Oracle 8i.	Up to 32767 bytes in PLSQL. Up to 4000 bytes in Oracle 9i.	Where *size* is the number of characters to store. Variable-length NLS string
bfile	Up to 4 gigabytes.	Up to 4 gigabytes.	File locators that point to a read-only binary object outside of the database
blob	Up to 4 gigabytes.	Up to 4 gigabytes.	LOB locators that point to a large binary object within the database
clob	Up to 4 gigabytes.	Up to 4 gigabytes.	LOB locators that point to a large character object within the database
nclob	Up to 4 gigabytes.	Up to 4 gigabytes.	LOB locators that point to a large NLS character object within the database

Prior using a table to store user data it needs to be created. Table creation is done using the **Create Table** syntax. When Oracle creates a table in response to a create table command, it stores table structure information within its Data Dictionary.

The CREATE TABLE Command

The **CREATE TABLE** command defines each column of the table uniquely. Each column has a minimum of three attributes, a name, datatype and size (**i.e.** column width). Each table column definition is a single clause in the create table syntax. Each table column definition is separated from the other by a comma. Finally, the SQL statement is terminated with a semi colon.

Rules For Creating Tables

1. A name can have maximum upto 30 characters
2. Alphabets from A-Z, a-z and numbers from 0-9 are allowed
3. A name should begin with an alphabet
4. The use of the special character like _ is allowed and also recommended. (Special characters like $, # are allowed **only in Oracle**).
5. SQL reserved words **not** allowed. For Example: create, select, and so on.

Syntax:

```
CREATE TABLE <TableName>
```

```
(<ColumnName1> <DataType>(<size>), <ColumnName2>
    <DataType>(<Size>));
```

Note

 Each column must have a datatype. The column should either be defined as null or not null and if this value is left blank, the database assumes "null" as the default.

A Brief Checklist When Creating Tables

The following provides a small checklist for the issues that need to be considered before creating a table:

- ❑ What are the attributes of the rows to be stored?
- ❑ What are the data types of the attributes?
- ❑ Should varchar2 be used instead of char?
- ❑ Which columns should be used to build the primary key?
- ❑ Which columns do (not) allow null values? Which columns do / do not, allow duplicates?
- ❑ Are there default values for certain columns that **also** allow null values?

Example:

Create the **BRANCH_MSTR** table as shown in the **Chapter 6** along with the structure for other table belonging to the **Bank System.**

```
CREATE TABLE "DBA_BANKSYS"."BRANCH_MSTR"(
    "BRANCH_NO" VARCHAR2(10),
    "NAME" VARCHAR2(25));
```

Output:

```
Table created.
```

Note

 All table columns belong to a **single record**. Therefore all the table column definitions are enclosed within parenthesis.

Temporary Tables

In addition to permanent tables, Oracle can create temporary tables to hold session-private data that exists only for the duration of a transaction or session.

The **CREATE GLOBAL TEMPORARY TABLE** statement creates a temporary table that can be transaction-specific or session-specific.

For transaction-specific temporary tables, data exists for the duration of the transaction.

For session-specific temporary tables, data exists for the duration of the session.

Temporary tables have following features:

- ❑ Data in a temporary table is private to the session
- ❑ Each session can only see and modify its own data
- ❑ DML locks are not acquired on the data of the temporary tables

- ❑ The LOCK statement has no effect on a temporary table, because each session has its own private data
- ❑ A TRUNCATE statement issued on a session-specific temporary table truncates data in its own session

Tip

The TRUNCATE statement does not truncate the data of other sessions that are using the same table.

- ❑ DML statements on temporary tables do not generate redo logs for the data changes

Tip

Undo logs for the data and redo logs for the undo logs are generated.

- ❑ Data from the temporary table is automatically dropped in the case of session termination, either when the user logs off or when the session terminates abnormally such as during a session or instance failure
- ❑ Indexes can be created on temporary tables using the CREATE INDEX statement

Tip

Indexes created on temporary tables are also temporary, and the data in the index has the same session or transaction scope as the data in the temporary table.

- ❑ Views can also be created that can access both temporary and permanent tables
- ❑ Triggers can be created on temporary tables

Syntax:

1. Creating a Session-Specific Temporary Table
```
CREATE GLOBAL TEMPORARY TABLE ... [ON COMMIT PRESERVE ROWS]
```
2. Creating a Transaction-Specific Temporary Table
```
CREATE GLOBAL TEMPORARY TABLE ... [ON COMMIT DELETE ROWS]
```

Example:

CREATE GLOBAL TEMPORARY TABLE Temp_Transactions
    ON COMMIT PRESERVE ROWS
    AS SELECT ACCT_NO "Account No.", DT "Date", Type, DR_CR "Mode", AMT "Amount"
    FROM TRANS_MSTR;

Inserting Data Into Tables

Once a table is created, the most natural thing to do is load this table with data to be manipulated later.

When inserting a single row of data into the table, the insert operation:

- ❑ Creates a new row (empty) in the database table
- ❑ Loads the values passed (by the SQL insert) into the columns specified

Syntax:

```
INSERT INTO <tablename> (<columnname1>, <columnname2>)
      VALUES (<expression>, <expression2>);
```

Example:

Insert the values into the BRANCH_MSTR table (For values refer to 6th chapter under Test Records)

INSERT INTO BRANCH_MSTR (BRANCH_NO, NAME) **VALUES**('B1', 'Vile Parle (HO)');

INSERT INTO BRANCH_MSTR (BRANCH_NO, NAME) **VALUES**('B2', 'Andheri');

INSERT INTO BRANCH_MSTR (BRANCH_NO, NAME) **VALUES**('B3', 'Churchgate');

INSERT INTO BRANCH_MSTR (BRANCH_NO, NAME) **VALUES**('B4', 'Sion');

INSERT INTO BRANCH_MSTR (BRANCH_NO, NAME) **VALUES**('B5', 'Borivali');

INSERT INTO BRANCH_MSTR (BRANCH_NO, NAME) **VALUES**('B6', 'Matunga');

Output for each of the above INSERT INTO statements:

```
1 row created.
```

Tip

Character expressions placed within the **INSERT INTO** statement must be enclosed in **single quotes** (').

In the **INSERT INTO** SQL sentence, table columns and values have a one to one relationship, (**i.e.** the first value described is inserted into the first column, and the second value described is inserted into the second column and so on).

Hence, in an **INSERT INTO** SQL sentence if there are exactly the same numbers of values as there are columns and the values are sequenced in exactly in accordance with the data type of the table columns, there is **no need** to indicate the column names.

However, if there are less values being described than there are columns in the table then it is **mandatory** to indicate **both** the table **column name** and its corresponding **value** in the **INSERT INTO** SQL sentence.

In the absence of mapping a table column name to a value in the **INSERT INTO** SQL sentence, the Oracle engine will not know which columns to insert the data into. This will generally cause a loss of data integrity. Then the data held within the table will be largely useless.

Viewing Data Data in the Tables

Once data has been inserted into a table, the next most logical operation would be to view what has been inserted. The **SELECT** SQL verb is used to achieve this. The SELECT command is used to retrieve rows selected from one or more tables.

All Rows And All Columns

In order to view global table data the **syntax** is:

```
SELECT <ColumnName 1> TO <ColumnName N> FROM TableName;
```

Note

 Here, **ColumnName1 to ColumnName N** represents table column names.

Syntax:

```
SELECT * FROM <TableName>;
```

Example:

Show all employee numbers, first name, middle name and last name who work in the bank.

```
SELECT EMP_NO, FNAME, MNAME, LNAME FROM EMP_MSTR;
```

Output:

EMP_NO	FNAME	MNAME	LNAME
E1	Ivan	Nelson	Bayross
E2	Amit		Desai
E3	Maya	Mahima	Joshi
E4	Peter	Iyer	Joseph
E5	Mandhar	Dilip	Dalvi
E6	Sonal	Abdul	Khan
E7	Anil	Ashutosh	Kambli
E8	Seema	P.	Apte
E9	Vikram	Vilas	Randive
E10	Anjali	Sameer	Pathak

10 rows selected.

Example:

Show all the details related to the Fixed Deposit Slab

SELECT * FROM FDSLAB_MSTR;

Output:

FDSLAB_NO	MINPERIOD	MAXPERIOD	INTRATE
1	1	30	5
2	31	92	5.5
3	93	183	6
4	184	365	6.5
5	366	731	7.5
6	732	1097	8.5
7	1098	1829	10

7 rows selected.

Tip

When data from all rows and columns from the table are to be viewed the syntax of the SELECT statement will be: **SELECT * FROM <TableName>;**

Oracle allows the use of the Meta character asterisk (*), this is expanded by Oracle to mean all rows and all columns in the table.

The Oracle Server parses and compiles the SQL query, executes it, and retrieves data from all rows/columns from the table.

Filtering Table Data

While viewing data from a table it is rare that **all the data** from the table will be required **each time**. Hence, SQL provides a method of filtering table data that is not required.

The ways of filtering table data are:

- ❑ Selected columns and all rows
- ❑ Selected rows and all columns
- ❑ Selected columns and selected rows

Selected Columns And All Rows

The retrieval of specific columns from a table can be done as shown below:

Syntax:

```
SELECT <ColumnName1>, <ColumnName2> FROM <TableName>;
```

Example:

Show the first name and the last name of the bank employees

SELECT FNAME, LNAME **FROM** EMP_MSTR;

Output:

FNAME	LNAME
Ivan	Bayross
Amit	Desai
Maya	Joshi
Peter	Joseph
Mandhar	Dalvi
Sonal	Khan
Anil	Kambli
Seema	Apte
Vikram	Randive
Anjali	Pathak

10 rows selected.

Selected Rows And All Columns

If information of a particular client is to be retrieved from a table, its retrieval must be based on a **specific condition**.

The SELECT statement used until now displayed all rows. This is because there was no condition set that informed Oracle about how to choose a specific set of rows (**or** a specific row) from any table. Oracle provides the option of using a **WHERE Clause** in an SQL query to apply a filter on the rows retrieved.

When a where clause is added to the SQL query, the Oracle engine compares each record in the table with the condition specified in the where clause. The Oracle engine displays only those records that satisfy the specified condition.

Syntax:

```
SELECT * FROM <TableName> WHERE <Condition>;
```

Here, **<Condition>** is always quantified as **<ColumnName = Value>**

Example:

Display the branch details of the branch named Vile Parle (HO)

SELECT * FROM BRANCH_MSTR **WHERE** NAME = 'Vile Parle (HO)';

Output:

BRANCH_NO	NAME
B1	Vile Parle (HO)

Note

When specifying a condition in the **where clause** all standard operators such as logical, arithmetic, predicates and so on, can be used.

Selected Columns And Selected Rows

To view a specific set of rows and columns from a table the syntax will be as follows:

Syntax:

```
SELECT <ColumnName1>, <ColumnName2> FROM <TableName>
       WHERE <Condition>;
```

Example:

List the savings bank account numbers and the branch to which they belong.

SELECT ACCT_NO, BRANCH_NO **FROM** ACCT_MSTR **WHERE** TYPE = 'SB';

Output:

ACCT_NO	BRANCH_NO
SB1	B1
SB3	B1
SB5	B6
SB6	B4
SB8	B2
SB9	B4

7 rows selected.

Eliminating Duplicate Rows When Using A Select Statement

A table could hold duplicate rows. In such a case, to view only unique rows the distinct clause can be used.

The DISTINCT clause allows removing duplicates from the result set. The DISTINCT clause can only be used with select statements.

The **DISTINCT** clause scans through the values of the column/s specified and displays only unique values from amongst them.

Syntax:

```
SELECT DISTINCT <ColumnName1>, <ColumnName2> FROM <TableName>;
```

The **SELECT DISTINCT** * SQL syntax scans through **entire rows**, and eliminates rows that have exactly the same contents in each column.

Syntax:

```
SELECT DISTINCT * FROM <TableName>;
```

Example:

Show different types of occupations of the bank customers by eliminating the repeated occupations

SELECT DISTINCT OCCUP **FROM** CUST_MSTR;

Output:

OCCUP

Business

Community Welfare

Executive

Information Technology

Retail Business

Self Employed

Service

7 rows selected.

First insert one more record in the table **BRANCH_MSTR** so as to see the output for the next query example.

INSERT INTO BRANCH_MSTR (BRANCH_NO, NAME) **VALUES**('B6', 'Matunga');

Example:

Show only unique branch details.

SELECT DISTINCT * FROM BRANCH_MSTR;

The following output shows the entry for B6 only once even though entered twice in the table.

Output:

BRANCH_NO	NAME
B1	Vile Parle (HO)
B2	Andheri
B3	Churchgate
B4	Sion
B5	Borivali
B6	Matunga

6 rows selected.

Sorting Data In A Table

Oracle allows data from a table to be viewed in a sorted order. The rows retrieved from the table will be sorted in either **ascending** or **descending** order depending on the condition specified in the **SELECT** sentence. The syntax for viewing data in a sorted order is as follows:

Syntax:

```
SELECT * FROM <TableName>
         ORDER BY <ColumnName1>, <ColumnName2> <[Sort Order]>;
```

The ORDER BY clause sorts the result set based on the columns specified. The ORDER BY clause can only be used in SELECT statements.

Example:

Show details of the branch according to the branch's name.

SELECT * FROM BRANCH_MSTR **ORDER BY** NAME;

Output:

BRANCH_NO	NAME
B2	Andheri
B5	Borivali
B3	Churchgate
B6	Matunga
B6	Matunga
B4	Sion
B1	Vile Parle (HO)

7 rows selected.

Tip

For viewing data in descending sorted order the word **DESC** must be mentioned **after** the column name and before the semi colon in the **order by** clause. In case there is no mention of the sort order, the Oracle engine sorts in **ascending order by default**.

Example:

Show the details of the branch according to the branch's name in descending order.

SELECT * FROM BRANCH_MSTR **ORDER BY** NAME **DESC;**

Output:

BRANCH_NO	NAME
B1	Vile Parle (HO)
B4	Sion
B6	Matunga
B6	Matunga
B3	Churchgate
B5	Borivali
B2	Andheri

7 rows selected.

Creating A Table From A Table

Syntax:

```
CREATE TABLE <TableName> (<ColumnName>, < ColumnName>)
        AS SELECT <ColumnName>, <ColumnName> FROM <TableName>
```

Example:

Create a table named ACCT_DTLS having three fields i.e. ACCT_NO, BRANCH_NO and CURBAL from the source table named ACCT_MSTR and rename the field CURBAL to BALANCE.

CREATE TABLE ACCT_DTLS (ACCT_NO, BRANCH_NO, BALANCE)

AS SELECT ACCT_NO, BRANCH_NO, CURBAL **FROM** ACCT_MSTR;

Output:

```
Table created.
```

Note

 If the Source Table **Acct_Mstr** was populated with records then the target table **Acct_Dtls** will also be populated with the same.

The **Source** table is the table identified in the **SELECT** section of this SQL sentence. The **Target** table is one identified in the **CREATE** section of this SQL sentence. This SQL sentence populates the Target table with data from the Source table.

To create a Target table without the records from the source table (i.e. create the structure only), the select statement must have a **WHERE clause**. The **WHERE clause** must specify a condition that **cannot** be satisfied.

This means the **SELECT** statement in the CREATE TABLE definition **will not retrieve** any rows from the source table, it will just retrieve the table structure thus the target table will be created empty.

Example:

Create a table named ACCT_DTLS having three fields i.e. ACCT_NO, BRANCH_NO and CURBAL from the source table named ACCT_MSTR and rename the field CURBAL to BALANCE. The table ACCT_DTLS should not be populated with any records.

CREATE TABLE ACCT_DTLS (ACCT_NO, BRANCH_NO, BALANCE)
    AS SELECT ACCT_NO, BRANCH_NO, CURBAL **FROM** ACCT_MSTR **WHERE 1=2;**

Output:

```
Table created.
```

Inserting Data Into A Table From Another Table

In addition to inserting data one row at a time into a table, it is quite possible to populate a table with data that already exists in another table. The syntax for doing so is as follows:

Syntax:

```
INSERT INTO <TableName>
        SELECT <ColumnName 1>, <ColumnName N> FROM <TableName>;
```

Example:

Insert data in the table ACCT_DTLS using the table ACCT_MSTR as a source of data.

INSERT INTO ACCT_DTLS **SELECT** ACCT_NO, BRANCH_NO, CurBal **FROM** ACCT_MSTR;

Output:

```
10 rows created.
```

Insertion Of A Data Set Into A Table From Another Table

Syntax:

```
INSERT INTO <TableName> SELECT <ColumnName 1>, <ColumnName N>
        FROM <TableName> WHERE <Condition>;
```

Example:

Insert only the savings bank accounts details in the target table ACCT_DTLS.

INSERT INTO ACCT_DTLS **SELECT** ACCT_NO, BRANCH_NO, CurBal **FROM** ACCT_MSTR
    WHERE ACCT_NO **LIKE** 'SB%';

Output:

```
6 rows created.
```

Delete Operations

The DELETE command deletes rows from the table that satisfies the condition provided by its where clause, **and** returns the number of records deleted.

Caution

If a DELETE statement without a WHERE clause is issued then, all rows are deleted.

The verb **DELETE** in SQL is used to remove either:

- ❑ All the rows from a table

OR

- ❑ A set of rows from a table

Removal Of All Rows

Syntax:

```
DELETE FROM <TableName>;
```

Example:

Empty the ACCT_DTLS table

DELETE FROM ACCT_DTLS;

Output:

```
16 rows deleted.
```

Removal Of Specific Row(s)

Syntax:

```
DELETE FROM <TableName> WHERE <Condition>;
```

Example:

Remove only the savings bank accounts details from the ACCT_DTLS table.

DELETE FROM ACCT_DTLS **WHERE** ACCT_NO **LIKE** 'SB%';

Output:

```
6 rows deleted.
```

Removal Of Specific Row(s) Based On The Data Held By The Other Table

Sometimes it is desired to delete records in one table based on values in another table. Since it is not possible to list more than one table in the FROM clause while performing a delete, the EXISTS clause can be used.

Example:

Remove the address details of the customer named **Ivan**.

DELETE FROM ADDR_DTLS **WHERE EXISTS(SELECT** FNAME **FROM** CUST_MSTR
    WHERE CUST_MSTR.CUST_NO = ADDR_DTLS.CODE_NO
        AND CUST_MSTR.FNAME = 'Ivan');

Output:

```
1 row deleted.
```

Explanation:

This will delete all records in the ADDR_DTLS table where there is a record in the CUST_MSTR table whose FNAME is Ivan, and the CUST_NO field belonging to the table CUST_MSTR is the same as the CODE_NO belonging to the table ADDR_DTLS.

Updating The Contents Of A Table

The **UPDATE** command is used to change or modify data values in a table.

The verb update in SQL is used to either update:

- All the rows from a table

OR

- A select set of rows from a table

Updating All Rows

The **UPDATE** statement updates columns in the existing table's rows with new values. The **SET** clause indicates which column data should be modified and the new values that they should hold. The **WHERE** clause, if given, specifies which rows should be updated. Otherwise, **all** table rows are updated.

Syntax:

```
UPDATE <TableName>
    SET <ColumnName1> = <Expression1>, <ColumnName2> =
    <Expression2>;
```

Example:

Update the address details by changing its city name to Bombay

UPDATE ADDR_DTLS **SET** City = 'Bombay';

Output:

44 rows updated.

Updating Records Conditionally

Syntax:

```
UPDATE <TableName>
    SET <ColumnName1> = <Expression1>, <ColumnName2> =
    <Expression2>
        WHERE <Condition>;
```

Example:

Update the branch details by changing the Vile Parle (HO) to head office.

UPDATE BRANCH_MSTR **SET** NAME = 'Head Office'

WHERE NAME = 'Vile Parle (HO)';

Output:

```
1 row updated.
```

Modifying The Structure Of Tables

The structure of a table can be modified by using the **ALTER TABLE** command. **ALTER TABLE** allows **changing the structure of an existing table**. With **ALTER TABLE** it is possible to **add** or **delete** columns, **create** or **destroy** indexes, **change the data type** of existing columns, or **rename columns** or the **table** itself.

ALTER TABLE works by making a temporary copy of the original table. The alteration is performed on the copy, then the original table is deleted and the new one is renamed. While **ALTER TABLE** is executing, the original table is still readable by users of Oracle.

Updates and **writes** to the table are **stalled** until the new table is ready, and then are automatically redirected to the new table **without any failed updates**.

Note

 To use **ALTER TABLE**, the **ALTER**, **INSERT**, and **CREATE** privileges for the table are required.

Adding New Columns

Syntax:

```
ALTER  TABLE  <TableName>
     ADD(<NewColumnName>  <Datatype>  (<Size>),
          <NewColumnName>  <Datatype>  (<Size>)...);
```

Example:

Enter a new field called City in the table BRANCH_MSTR.

ALTER TABLE BRANCH_MSTR **ADD** (CITY VARCHAR2(25));

Output:

```
Table altered.
```

Dropping A Column From A Table

Syntax:

```
ALTER  TABLE  <TableName>  DROP  COLUMN  <ColumnName>;
```

Example:

Drop the column city from the BRANCH_MSTR table.

ALTER TABLE BRANCH_MSTR **DROP COLUMN** CITY;

Output:

```
Table altered.
```

Modifying Existing Columns

Syntax:

```
ALTER  TABLE  <TableName>
          MODIFY  (<ColumnName>  <NewDatatype>(<NewSize>));
```

Example:

Alter the BRANCH_MSTR table to allow the NAME field to hold maximum of 30 characters

ALTER TABLE BRANCH_MSTR **MODIFY** (NAME VARCHAR2(30));

Output:

```
Table altered.
```

Restrictions on the ALTER TABLE

The following tasks **cannot** be performed when using the **ALTER TABLE** clause:

- ❑ Change the name of the table
- ❑ Change the name of the column
- ❑ Decrease the size of a column if table data exists

Renaming Tables

Oracle allows renaming of tables. The rename operation is done **atomically**, which means that **no other thread** can access any of the tables while the rename process is running.

Note

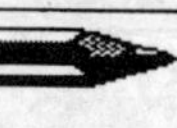

To rename a table the ALTER and DROP privileges on the original table, and the CREATE and INSERT privileges on the new table are required.

To rename a table, the syntax is

Syntax:

```
RENAME <TableName> TO <NewTableName>
```

Example:

Change the name of branches table to branch table

RENAME BRANCH_MSTR **TO** BRANCHES;

Output:

```
Table renamed.
```

Truncating Tables

TRUNCATE TABLE empties a table completely. Logically, this is equivalent to a **DELETE** statement that deletes all rows, but there are practical differences under some circumstances.

TRUNCATE TABLE differs from **DELETE** in the following ways:

- ❑ Truncate operations drop and re-create the table, which is much faster than deleting rows one by one
- ❑ Truncate operations are not transaction-safe (i.e. an error will occur if an active transaction or an active table lock exists)
- ❑ The number of deleted rows are not returned

Syntax:

```
TRUNCATE TABLE <TableName>;
```

Example:

Truncate the table BRANCH_MSTR

TRUNCATE TABLE BRANCH_MSTR;

Output:

```
Table truncated.
```

Destroying Tables

Sometimes tables within a particular database become obsolete and need to be discarded. In such situation using the DROP TABLE statement with the table name can destroy a specific table.

Syntax:

```
DROP TABLE <TableName>;
```

Caution

If a table is dropped all records held within it are lost and cannot be recovered.

Example:

Remove the table BRANCH_MSTR along with the data held.

DROP TABLE BRANCH_MSTR;

Output:

```
Table dropped.
```

Creating Synonyms

A synonym is an alternative name for objects such as tables, views, sequences, stored procedures, and other database objects.

Syntax:

```
CREATE [OR REPLACE] [PUBLIC] SYNONYM [SCHEMA .]
    SYNONYM_NAME FOR [SCHEMA .]
    OBJECT_NAME [@ DBLINK];
```

In the syntax,

- ❑ The **OR** replace phrase allows to recreate the synonym (if it already exists) without having to issue a DROP synonym command.
- ❑ The **PUBLIC** phrase means that the synonym is a public synonym and is accessible to all users. Remember though that the user must first have the appropriate privileges to the object to use the synonym.
- ❑ The **SCHEMA** phrase is the appropriate schema. If this phrase is omitted, Oracle assumes that a reference is made to the user's own schema.
- ❑ The **OBJECT_NAME** phrase is the name of the object for which you are creating the synonym. It can be one of the following:
  - Table
  - Package
  - View
  - Materialized View
  - Sequence
  - Java Class Schema Object
  - Stored Procedure
  - User-Defined Object
  - Function
  - Synonym

Example:

Create a synonym to a table named EMP held by the user SCOTT.

CREATE PUBLIC SYNONYM EMPLOYEES **FOR** SCOTT.EMP;

Output:

```
Synonym created.
```

Explanation:

Now, users of other schemas can reference the table EMP, which is now called as EMPLOYEES without having to prefix the table name with the schema named SCOTT. For example:

SELECT * FROM EMPLOYEES;

Dropping Synonyms

Syntax:

```
DROP [PUBLIC] SYNONYM [SCHEMA.]SYNONYM_NAME [FORCE];
```

In the syntax,

- ❑ The **PUBLIC** phrase allows to drop a public synonym. If public is specified, then there is no need to specify a schema.
- ❑ The **FORCE** phrase will force Oracle to drop the synonym even if it has dependencies. It is probably not a good idea to use the force phrase as it can cause invalidation of Oracle objects

Example:

Drop the public synonym named EMPLOYEES

DROP PUBLIC SYNONYM EMPLOYEES;

Output:

```
Synonym dropped.
```

Examining Objects Created By A User

Finding Out The Table/s Created By A User

The command shown below is used to determine the tables to which a user has access. The tables created under the **currently selected** tablespace are displayed.

Example:

SELECT * FROM TAB;

Output:

TNAME	TABTYPE	CLUSTERID
ACCT_FD_CUST_DTLS	TABLE	
ACCT_MSTR	TABLE	
ADDR_DTLS	TABLE	
BRANCH_MSTR	TABLE	
CNTC_DTLS	TABLE	
CUST_MSTR	TABLE	
EMP_MSTR	TABLE	
FDSLAB_MSTR	TABLE	
FD_DTLS	TABLE	
FD_MSTR	TABLE	
NOMINEE_MSTR	TABLE	
SPRT_DOC	TABLE	
TRANS_DTLS	TABLE	
TRANS_MSTR	TABLE	

14 rows selected.

Displaying The Table Structure

To display information about the columns defined in a table use the following syntax

Syntax:

```
DESCRIBE <TableName>;
```

This command displays the column names, the data types and the special attributes connected to the table.

Example:

Show the table structure of table BRANCH_MSTR

DESCRIBE BRANCH_MSTR;

Output:

Name	Null?	Type
BRANCH_NO		VARCHAR2(10)
NAME		VARCHAR2(25)

Self Review Questions

Fill in the Blaks

1. A ____________ is a database object that holds user data.
2. Table creation is done using the ______________________ syntax.
3. Character expressions placed within the insert into statement must be enclosed in ____________ quotes.
4. Oracle provides the option of using a __________ __________ in an SQL query to apply a filter on the rows retrieved.
5. The ___________ ___________ SQL syntax scans through the values of the column/s specified and displays only unique values from amongst them.
6. The SQL sentence populates the __________ table with data from the _________ table.
7. The name of the column cannot be changed using the __________ __________ clause.
8. The ____________ command is used to change or modify data values in a table.
9. All table columns belong to a __________ _________.

True or False

10. If a spreadsheet has a number data type associated with, then it can store characters as well.
11. Each table column definition is separated from the other by a colon.
12. All table columns belong to a single record.
13. In the insert into SQL sentence table columns and values have a one to many relationship.
14. The SELECT DISTINCT SQL syntax scans through entire rows, and eliminates rows that have exactly the same contents in each column.
15. When specifying a condition in the where clause only logical standard operators can be used.
16. Oracle allows data from a table to be viewed in a sorted order.

17. In order to view the data in descending sorted order the word 'desc' must be mentioned after the column name and before the semi colon in the order by clause.
18. The MODIFY command is used to change or modify data values in a table.
19. The name of the table cannot be changed using the ALTER TABLE clause.

Hands On Exercises

1. Create the tables described below:

Table Name:	CLIENT_MASTER
Description:	Used to store client information.

Column Name	Data Type	Size	Default	Attributes
CLIENTNO	Varchar2	6		
NAME	Varchar2	20		
ADDRESS1	Varchar2	30		
ADDRESS2	Varchar2	30		
CITY	Varchar2	15		
PINCODE	Number	8		
STATE	Varchar2	15		
BALDUE	Number	10,2		

Table Name:	PRODUCT_MASTER
Description:	Used to store product information.

Column Name	Data Type	Size	Default	Attributes
PRODUCTNO	Varchar2	6		
DESCRIPTION	Varchar2	15		
PROFITPERCENT	Number	4,2		
UNITMEASURE	Varchar2	10		
QTYONHAND	Number	8		
REORDERLVL	Number	8		
SELLPRICE	Number	8,2		
COSTPRICE	Number	8,2		

Table Name:	SALESMAN_MASTER
Description:	Used to store salesman information working for the company.

Column Name	**Data Type**	**Size**	**Default**	**Attributes**
SALESMANNO	Varchar2	6		
SALESMANNAME	Varchar2	20		
ADDRESS1	Varchar2	30		
ADDRESS2	Varchar2	30		
CITY	Varchar2	20		
PINCODE	Number	8		
STATE	Varchar2	20		
SALAMT	Number	8,2		
TGTTOGET	Number	6,2		
YTDSALES	Number	6,2		
REMARKS	Varchar2	60		

2. Insert the following data into their respective tables:

(a) Data for **CLIENT_MASTER** table:

ClientNo	**Name**	**City**	**Pincode**	**State**	**BalDue**
C00001	Ivan Bayross	Mumbai	400054	Maharashtra	15000
C00002	Mamta Muzumdar	Madras	780001	Tamil Nadu	0
C00003	Chhaya Bankar	Mumbai	400057	Maharashtra	5000
C00004	Ashwini Joshi	Bangalore	560001	Karnataka	0
C00005	Hansel Colaco	Mumbai	400060	Maharashtra	2000
C00006	Deepak Sharma	Mangalore	560050	Karnataka	0

(b) Data for **PRODUCT_MASTER** table:

ProductNo	**Description**	**Profit Percent**	**Unit Measure**	**QtyOn Hand**	**Reorder Lvl**	**Sell Price**	**Cost Price**
P00001	T-Shirts	5	Piece	200	50	350	250
P0345 350		Shirts	6	Piece	150	50	500
P06734	Cotton Jeans	5	Piece	100	20	600	450
P07865	Jeans	5	Piece	100	20	750	500
P07868	Trousers	2	Piece	150	50	850	550
P07885	Pull Overs	2.5	Piece	80	30	700	450
P07965	Denim Shirts	4	Piece	100	40	350	250
P07975	Lycra Tops	5	Piece	70	30	300	175
P08865	Skirts	5	Piece	75	30	450	300

(c) Data for **SALESMAN_MASTER** table:

SalesmanNo	Name	Address1	Address2	City	PinCode	State
S00001	Aman	A/14	Worli	Mumbai	400002	Maharashtra
S00002	Omkar	65	Nariman	Mumbai	400001	Maharashtra
S00003	Raj	P-7	Bandra	Mumbai	400032	Maharashtra
S00004	Ashish	A/5	Juhu	Mumbai	400044	Maharashtra

SalesmanNo	SalAmt	TgtToGet	YtdSales	Remarks
S00001	3000	100	50	Good
S00002	3000	200	100	Good
S00003	3000	200	100	Good
S00004	3500	200	150	Good

3. Exercise on retrieving records from a table
   a. Find out the names of all the clients.
   b. Retrieve the entire contents of the Client_Master table.
   c. Retrieve the list of names, city and the sate of all the clients.
   d. List the various products available from the Product_Master table.
   e. List all the clients who are located in Mumbai.
   f. Find the names of salesmen who have a salary equal to Rs.3000.
4. Exercise on updating records in a table
   a. Change the city of ClientNo 'C00005' to 'Bangalore'.
   b. Change the BalDue of ClientNo 'C00001' to Rs. 1000.
   c. Change the cost price of 'Trousers' to Rs. 950.00.
   d. Change the city of the salesman to Pune.
5. Exercise on deleting records in a table
   a. Delete all salesmen from the Salesman_Master whose salaries are equal to Rs. 3500.
   b. Delete all products from Product_Master where the quantity on hand is equal to 100.
   c. Delete from Client_Master where the column state holds the value 'Tamil Nadu'.
6. Exercise on altering the table structure
   a. Add a column called 'Telephone' of data type 'number' and size ='10' to the Client_Master table.
   b. Change the size of SellPrice column in Product_Master to 10,2.
7. Exercise on deleting the table structure along with the data
   a. Destroy the table Client_Master along with its data.
8. Exercise on renaming the table
   a. Change the name of the Salesman_Master table to sman_mast.

11

Interactive SQL Part - II

Data Constraints

All businesses of the world run on business data being gathered, stored and analyzed. Business managers determine a set of business rules that must be applied to their data prior to it being stored in the database/ table to ensure its integrity.

For instance, no employee in the sales department can have a salary of less than Rs.1000/-.

Such rules have to be enforced on data stored. Only data, which satisfies the conditions set, should be stored for future analysis. If the data gathered fails to satisfy the conditions set, it must be rejected. This ensures that the data stored in a table will be valid, and have integrity.

Business rules that are applied to data are completely **System dependent**. The rules applied to data gathered and processed by a **Savings bank system** will be very different, to the business rules applied to data gathered and processed by an **Inventory system**, which in turn will be very different, to the business rules applied to data gathered and processed by a **Personnel management system**.

Business rules, which are enforced on data being stored in a table, are called **Constraints**. Constraints, **super control** the data being entered into a table for permanent storage.

To understand the concept of data constraints, several tables will be created and different types of constraints will be applied to table columns **or** the table itself. The set of tables are described below. Appropriate examples of data constraints are bound to these tables.

Applying Data Constraints

Oracle permits data constraints to be attached to table columns via SQL syntax that checks data for integrity prior storage. Once data constraints are part of a table column construct, the Oracle database engine checks the data being entered into a table column against the data constraints. If the data passes this check, it is stored in the table column, else the data is rejected. Even if a single column of the record being entered into the table fails a constraint, the **entire record is rejected and not stored in the table**.

Both the **Create Table** and **Alter Table** SQL verbs can be used to write SQL sentences that attach constraints (i.e. Business / System rules) to a table column.

Caution

Until now tables created in this material have **not** had any data constraints attached to their table columns. Hence the tables have **not** been given any instructions to filter what is being stored in the table. This situation **can** and **does**, result in erroneous data being stored in the table.

Once a constraint is attached to a table column, any SQL **INSERT** or **UPDATE** statement automatically causes these constraints to be applied to data prior it is being inserted into the table column for storage.

Note

Oracle also permits applying data constraints at **Table level**. More on table level constraints later in this material.

Types Of Data Constraints

There are two types of data constraints that can be applied to data being inserted into a Oracle table. One type of constraint is called an **I/O** constraint (input / output). This data constraint determines the speed at which data can be inserted or extracted from a Oracle table. The other type of constraint is called a **business rule** constraint.

I/O Constraints

The input/output data constraints are further divided into **two** distinctly different constraints.

The PRIMARY KEY Constraint

A primary key is one or more column(s) in a table used to uniquely identify **each row** in the table. None of the fields that are part of the primary key can contain a null value. A table can have only one primary key.

A **primary key column** in a table has special attributes:

- ❑ It defines the column, as a mandatory column (**i.e.** the column cannot be left blank). As the NOT NULL attribute is active
- ❑ The data held across the column MUST be UNIQUE

A single column primary key is called a **Simple** key. A multicolumn primary key is called a **Composite** primary key. The only function of a primary key in a table is to **uniquely identify a row**. When a record cannot be uniquely identified using a value in a simple key, a composite key must be defined. A primary key can be defined in either a **CREATE TABLE** statement or an **ALTER TABLE** statement.

For example, a **SALES_ORDER_DETAILS** table will hold multiple records that are sales orders. Each such sales order will have multiple products that have been ordered. Standard business rules do not allow multiple entries for the same product. However, multiple orders will definitely have multiple entries of the same product.

Under these circumstances, the only way to uniquely identify a row in the **SALES_ORDER_DETAILS** table is via a composite primary key, consisting of **ORDER_NO** and **PRODUCT_NO**. Thus the combination of order number and product number will uniquely identify a row.

Features of Primary key

1. Primary key is a column or a set of columns that uniquely identifies a row. Its main purpose is the **Record Uniqueness**

2. Primary key will not allow duplicate values
3. Primary key will also not allow null values
4. Primary key is not compulsory but it is recommended
5. Primary key helps to identify one record from another record and also helps in relating tables with one another
6. Primary key cannot be LONG or LONG RAW data type
7. Only one Primary key is allowed per table
8. Unique Index is created automatically if there is a Primary key
9. One table can combine upto 16 columns in a Composite Primary key

PRIMARY KEY Constraint Defined At Column Level

Syntax:

```
<ColumnName> <Datatype>(<Size>) PRIMARY KEY
```

Example:

Drop the CUST_MSTR table, if it already exists. Create a table CUST_MSTR such that the contents of the column CUST_NO is unique and not null.

DROP TABLE CUST_MSTR;

CREATE TABLE CUST_MSTR (

"CUST_NO" VARCHAR2(10) **PRIMARY KEY**,

"FNAME" VARCHAR2(25), "MNAME" VARCHAR2(25),

"LNAME" VARCHAR2(25), "DOB_INC" DATE,

"OCCUP" VARCHAR2(25), "PHOTOGRAPH" VARCHAR2(25),

"SIGNATURE" VARCHAR2(25), "PANCOPY" VARCHAR2(1),

"FORM60" VARCHAR2(1));

Output:

```
Table created.
```

For testing purpose, execute the following **INSERT INTO** statement:

INSERT INTO CUST_MSTR (CUST_NO, FNAME, MNAME, LNAME, DOB_INC, OCCUP, PHOTOGRAPH, SIGNATURE, PANCOPY, FORM60)

VALUES('C1', 'Ivan', 'Nelson', 'Bayross', '25-JUN-1952', 'Self Employed', 'D:/ClntPht/C1.gif', 'D:/ClntSgnt/C1.gif', 'Y', 'Y');

Output:

```
1 row created.
```

To verify whether the Primary Key Constraint is functional, reissue the same **INSERT INTO** statement. The result is the following error:

Output:

```
INSERT INTO CUST_MSTR (CUST_NO, FNAME, MNAME, LNAME, DOB_INC, OCCUP,
PHOTOGRAPH, SIGNATURE, PANCOPY,
*
ERROR at line 1:
```

```
ORA-00001: unique constraint (DBA_BANKSYS.SYS_C003009) violated
```

PRIMARY KEY Constraint Defined At Table Level

Syntax:

```
PRIMARY KEY (<ColumnName>, <ColumnName>)
```

Example:

Drop the FD_MSTR table, if it already exists. Create a table FD_MSTR where there is a composite primary key mapped to the columns FD_SER_NO and CORP_CUST_NO.

Since this constraint spans across columns, it must be described at table level.

DROP TABLE FD_MSTR;

CREATE TABLE "DBA_BANKSYS"."FD_MSTR"(
    "FD_SER_NO" VARCHAR2(10), "SF_NO" VARCHAR2(10),
    "BRANCH_NO" VARCHAR2(10), "INTRO_CUST_NO" VARCHAR2(10),
    "INTRO_ACCT_NO" VARCHAR2(10), "INTRO_SIGN" VARCHAR2(1),
    "ACCT_NO" VARCHAR2(10), "TITLE" VARCHAR2(30),
    "CORP_CUST_NO" VARCHAR2(10), "CORP_CNST_TYPE" VARCHAR(4),
    "VERI_EMP_NO" VARCHAR2(10), "VERI_SIGN" VARCHAR2(1),
    "MANAGER_SIGN" VARCHAR2(1), **PRIMARY KEY(**FD_SER_NO, CORP_CUST_NO**));**

Output:

```
Table created.
```

For testing purpose, execute the following **INSERT INTO** statement:

INSERT INTO FD_MSTR (FD_SER_NO, SF_NO, BRANCH_NO, ACCT_NO, TITLE, CORP_CUST_NO, CORP_CNST_TYPE, INTRO_CUST_NO, INTRO_ACCT_NO, INTRO_SIGN, VERI_EMP_NO, VERI_SIGN, MANAGER_SIGN**)**

VALUES ('FS1', 'SF-0011', 'B1', 'CA2', 'Uttam Stores', 'O11', '1C', null, null, 'N', 'E1', 'Y', 'Y'**);**

Output:

1 row created.

To verify whether the Composite Primary Key Constraint is functional, reissue the same **INSERT INTO** statement. The result is the following error:

Output:

```
INSERT INTO FD_MSTR (FD_SER_NO, SF_NO, BRANCH_NO, ACCT_NO, TITLE,
CORP_CUST_NO, CORP_CNST_TYPE, INTR
*
ERROR at line 1:
ORA-00001: unique constraint (DBA_BANKSYS.SYS_C003010) violated
```

Now, simply modify the INSERT INTO statement as show below, to allow the record to pass the composite primary key constraint:

INSERT INTO FD_MSTR (FD_SER_NO, SF_NO, BRANCH_NO, ACCT_NO, TITLE, CORP_CUST_NO, CORP_CNST_TYPE, INTRO_CUST_NO, INTRO_ACCT_NO, INTRO_SIGN, VERI_EMP_NO, VERI_SIGN, MANAGER_SIGN**)**

VALUES ('FS2', 'SF-0012', 'B1', 'CA4', 'Sun''s Pvt. Ltd.', 'C12', '4C', null, null, 'N', 'E1', 'Y', 'Y');

Output:

```
1 row created.
```

The Foreign Key (Self Reference) Constraint

Foreign keys represent relationships between tables. A foreign key is a column (or a group of columns) whose values are derived from the **primary key** or **unique key** of some other table.

The table in which the foreign key is defined is called a **Foreign table** or **Detail table**. The table that defines the **primary** or **unique** key and is referenced by the **foreign key** is called the **Primary table** or **Master table**. A Foreign key can be defined in either a CREATE TABLE statement or an ALTER TABLE statement

The master table can be referenced in the foreign key definition by using the clause **REFERENCES TableName.ColumnName** when defining the foreign key, column attributes, in the detail table.

Features of Foreign Keys

1. Foreign key is a column(s) that references a column(s) of a table and it can be the same table also
2. Parent that is being referenced has to be unique or Primary key
3. Child may have duplicates and nulls but unless it is specified
4. Foreign key constraint can be specified on child but not on parent
5. Parent record can be delete provided no child record exist
6. Master table cannot be updated if child record exist

This constraint establishes a relationship between records (i.e. column data) across a Master and a Detail table. This relationship ensures:

- ❑ Records cannot be **inserted** into a **detail table** if corresponding records in the master table do not exist
- ❑ Records of the master **table** cannot be **deleted** if corresponding records in the detail table actually exist

Insert Or Update Operation In The Foreign Key Table

The existence of a foreign key implies that the table with the foreign key is **related** to the master table from which the foreign key is derived. A foreign key must have a corresponding primary key or unique key value in the master table.

For example a personnel information system includes two tables (i.e. department and employee). An employee cannot belong to a department that does not exist. Thus the department number specified in the employee table must be present in the department table.

Delete Operation On The Primary Key Table

Oracle **displays an error message** when a record in the master table is deleted and corresponding records exists in a detail table and **prevents the delete operation** from going through.

Note

The default behavior of the foreign key can be changed, by using the **ON DELETE CASCADE** option. When the **ON DELETE CASCADE** option is specified in the foreign key definition, if a record is deleted in the master table, all corresponding records in the detail table along with the record in the master table will be deleted.

Principles of **Foreign Key/References** constraint:

- Rejects an **INSERT** or **UPDATE** of a value, if a corresponding value does not currently exist in the master key table
- If the **ON DELETE CASCADE** option is set, a **DELETE** operation in the master table will trigger a **DELETE** operation for corresponding records **in all** detail tables
- If the **ON DELETE SET NULL** option is set, a **DELETE** operation in the master table will set the value held by the foreign key of the detail tables to null
- **Rejects a DELETE** from the Master table if **corresponding records** in the DETAIL table **exist**
- Must reference a **PRIMARY KEY** or **UNIQUE** column(s) in primary table
- Requires that the **FOREIGN KEY** column(s) and the **CONSTRAINT** column(s) have **matching** data types
- Can reference the same table named in the **CREATE TABLE** statement

FOREIGN KEY Constraint Defined At The Column Level

Syntax:

```
<ColumnName>  <DataType>(<Size>)
      REFERENCES  <TableName>  [(<ColumnName>)]
             [ON  DELETE  CASCADE]
```

Example:

Drop the table EMP_MSTR, if it already exists. Create a table EMP_MSTR with its primary as EMP_NO referencing the foreign key BRANCH_NO in the BRANCH_MSTR table.

DROP TABLE EMP_MSTR;

CREATE TABLE "DBA_BANKSYS"."EMP_MSTR"(

"EMP_NO" VARCHAR2(10) **PRIMARY KEY**,

"BRANCH_NO" VARCHAR2(10) **REFERENCES** BRANCH_MSTR,

"FNAME" VARCHAR2(25), "MNAME" VARCHAR2(25),

"LNAME" VARCHAR2(25), "DEPT" VARCHAR2(30),

"DESIG" VARCHAR2(30));

Output:

```
Table created.
```

The **REFERENCES** key word points to the table **BRANCH_MSTR**. The table **BRANCH_MSTR** has the column **BRANCH_NO** as its primary key column. Since no column is specified in the foreign key definition, Oracle applies an automatic (default) link to the primary key column i.e. **BRANCH_NO** of the table **BRANCH_MSTR**.

The foreign key definition is specified as

```
"BRANCH_NO"  VARCHAR2(10)  REFERENCES  BRANCH_MSTR
```

FOREIGN KEY Constraint Defined At The Table Level

Syntax:

```
FOREIGN  KEY  (<ColumnName>  [,<ColumnName>]  )
      REFERENCES  <TableName>  [(<ColumnName>,<ColumnName>)
```

Example:

Drop the table ACCT_FD_CUST_DTLS, if it already exists. Create a table ACCT_FD_CUST_DTLS with CUST_NO as foreign key referencing column CUST_NO in the CUST_MSTR table

DROP TABLE ACCT_FD_CUST_DTLS;

CREATE TABLE "DBA_BANKSYS"."ACCT_FD_CUST_DTLS"(

"ACCT_FD_NO" VARCHAR2(10), "CUST_NO" VARCHAR2(10),

FOREIGN KEY (CUST_NO) **REFERENCES** CUST_MSTR(CUST_NO));

Output:

```
Table created.
```

FOREIGN KEY Constraint Defined With ON DELETE CASCADE

Example:

Drop the table FD_MSTR, if it already exists. Create a table FD_MSTR with its primary key as FD_SER_NO.

Drop the table FD_DTLS, if it already exists. Create a table FD_DTLS with its foreign key as FD_SER_NO with the ON DELETE CASCADE option. The foreign key is FD_SER_NO and is available as a primary key column named FD_SER_NO in the FD_MSTR table.

Insert some records into both the tables.

DROP TABLE FD_MSTR;

CREATE TABLE "DBA_BANKSYS"."FD_MSTR"(

"FD_SER_NO" VARCHAR2(10) **PRIMARY KEY**,

"SF_NO" VARCHAR2(10), "BRANCH_NO" VARCHAR2(10),

"INTRO_CUST_NO" VARCHAR2(10), "INTRO_ACCT_NO" VARCHAR2(10),

"INTRO_SIGN" VARCHAR2(1), "ACCT_NO" VARCHAR2(10),

"TITLE" VARCHAR2(30), "CORP_CUST_NO" VARCHAR2(10),

"CORP_CNST_TYPE" VARCHAR(4), "VERI_EMP_NO" VARCHAR2(10),

"VERI_SIGN" VARCHAR2(1), "MANAGER_SIGN" VARCHAR2(1));

Output:

```
Table created.
```

DROP TABLE FD_DTLS;

CREATE TABLE "DBA_BANKSYS"."FD_DTLS"(

"FD_SER_NO" VARCHAR2(10), "FD_NO" VARCHAR2(10),

"TYPE" VARCHAR2(1), "PAYTO_ACCTNO" VARCHAR2(10),

"PERIOD" NUMBER(5), "OPNDT" DATE,

"DUEDT" DATE, "AMT" NUMBER(8,2),

"DUEAMT" NUMBER(8,2), "INTRATE" NUMBER(3),

"STATUS" VARCHAR2(1) DEFAULT 'A', "AUTO_RENEWAL" VARCHAR2(1) ,

CONSTRAINT f_FDSerNoKey

```
FOREIGN KEY (FD_SER_NO) REFERENCES FD_MSTR(FD_SER_NO)
ON DELETE CASCADE);
```

Output:

```
Table created.
```

Now delete a record from the FD_MSTR table as:

DELETE FROM FD_MSTR **WHERE** FD_SER_NO = 'FS1';

Output:

```
1 row deleted.
```

Query the table FD_DTLS for records:

SELECT * FROM FD_DTLS;

Notice the deletion of the records belonging to **FS1**.

Explanation:

In this example, a primary key is created in the FD_MSTR table. It consists of only **one field** i.e. FD_SER_NO field. Then a foreign key is created in the FD_DTLS table that references the FD_MSTR table based on the contents of the FD_SER_NO field.

Because of the **cascade delete**, when a record in the FD_MSTR table is deleted, all records in the FD_DTLS table will also be deleted that have the same FD_SER_NO value.

FOREIGN KEY Constraint Defined With ON DELETE SET NULL:

A FOREIGN key with a **SET NULL ON DELETE** means that if a record in the parent table is deleted, then the corresponding records in the child table will have the foreign key fields set to **null**. The records in the child table **will not** be deleted.

A FOREIGN key with a **SET NULL ON DELETE** can be defined in either a CREATE TABLE statement or an ALTER TABLE statement.

Example:

Drop the table FD_MSTR, if it already exists. Create a table FD_MSTR with its primary key as FD_SER_NO.

Drop the table FD_DTLS, if it already exists. Create a table FD_DTLS with its foreign key as FD_SER_NO with the ON DELETE SET NULL option. The foreign key is FD_SER_NO and is available as a primary key column named FD_SER_NO in the FD_MSTR table.

Insert some records into both the tables.

```
DROP TABLE FD_MSTR;
CREATE TABLE "DBA_BANKSYS"."FD_MSTR"(
    "FD_SER_NO" VARCHAR2(10) PRIMARY KEY, "SF_NO" VARCHAR2(10),
    "BRANCH_NO" VARCHAR2(10), "INTRO_CUST_NO" VARCHAR2(10),
    "INTRO_ACCT_NO" VARCHAR2(10), "INTRO_SIGN" VARCHAR2(1),
    "ACCT_NO" VARCHAR2(10), "TITLE" VARCHAR2(30), "CORP_CUST_NO" VARCHAR2(10),
    "CORP_CNST_TYPE" VARCHAR(4), "VERI_EMP_NO" VARCHAR2(10),
    "VERI_SIGN" VARCHAR2(1), "MANAGER_SIGN" VARCHAR2(1));
```

Output:

```
Table created.
```

DROP TABLE FD_DTLS;

CREATE TABLE "DBA_BANKSYS"."FD_DTLS"(
"FD_SER_NO" VARCHAR2(10), "FD_NO" VARCHAR2(10), "TYPE" VARCHAR2(1),
"PAYTO_ACCTNO" VARCHAR2(10), "PERIOD" NUMBER(5), "OPNDT" DATE,
"DUEDT" DATE, "AMT" NUMBER(8,2), "DUEAMT" NUMBER(8,2), "INTRATE" NUMBER(3),
"STATUS" VARCHAR2(1) DEFAULT 'A', "AUTO_RENEWAL" VARCHAR2(1) ,
CONSTRAINT f_FDSerNoKey
FOREIGN KEY (FD_SER_NO) **REFERENCES** FD_MSTR(FD_SER_NO)
ON DELETE SET NULL);

Output:

```
Table created.
```

Now delete a record from the FD_MSTR table as:

DELETE FROM FD_MSTR **WHERE** FD_SER_NO = 'FS1';

Output:

```
1 row deleted.
```

Query the table FD_DTLS for records:

SELECT * FROM FD_DTLS;

Notice the value held by the field FD_SER_NO.

Explanation:

In this example, a primary key is created in the FD_MSTR table. It consists of only one field i.e. FD_SER_NO field. Then a foreign key is created in the FD_DTLS table that references the FD_MSTR table based on the FD_SER_NO field.

Because of the **cascade set null**, when a record in the FD_MSTR table is deleted, all corresponding records in the FD_DTLS table will have the FD_SER_NO values set to **null**.

Assigning User Defined Names To Constraints

When constraints are defined, Oracle assigns a **unique name** to each constraint. The convention used by Oracle is

SYS_Cn

where **n** is a **numeric value** that makes the constraint name **unique**.

Constraints can be given a unique user-defined name along with the constraint definition. A constraint can then, be dropped by referring to the constraint by its name. Under these circumstances a user-defined constraint name becomes very convenient.

User named constraints simplifies the task of dropping constraints. A constraint can be given a user-defined name by preceding the constraint definition with the reserved word **CONSTRAINT** and a **user-defined name**.

Syntax:

CONSTRAINT <Constraint Name> <Constraint Definition>

Example:

Drop the CUST_MSTR table, if it already exists. Create a table CUST_MSTR with a primary key constraint on the column CUST_NO and also define its constraint name.

```
DROP TABLE CUST_MSTR;
CREATE TABLE CUST_MSTR (
    "CUST_NO" VARCHAR2(10) CONSTRAINT p_CUSTKey PRIMARY KEY,
    "FNAME" VARCHAR2(25), "MNAME" VARCHAR2(25),
    "LNAME" VARCHAR2(25), "DOB_INC" DATE,
    "OCCUP" VARCHAR2(25), "PHOTOGRAPH" VARCHAR2(25),
    "SIGNATURE" VARCHAR2(25), "PANCOPY" VARCHAR2(1),
    "FORM60" VARCHAR2(1));
```

Output:

```
Table created.
```

Example:

Drop the table EMP_MSTR, if it already exists. Create a table EMP_MSTR with its foreign key as BRANCH_NO. The foreign key is BRANCH_NO available and as a primary key in the BRANCH_MSTR table. Also define the name of the foreign key.

```
DROP TABLE EMP_MSTR;
CREATE TABLE "DBA_BANKSYS"."EMP_MSTR"(
    "EMP_NO" VARCHAR2(10), "BRANCH_NO" VARCHAR2(10),
    "FNAME" VARCHAR2(25), "MNAME" VARCHAR2(25),
    "LNAME" VARCHAR2(25), "DEPT" VARCHAR2(30),
    "DESIG" VARCHAR2(30),
    CONSTRAINT f_BranchKey
        FOREIGN KEY (BRANCH_NO) REFERENCES BRANCH_MSTR);
```

Output:

```
Table created.
```

The Unique Key Constraint

The **Unique** column constraint **permits multiple entries** of NULL into the column. These NULL values are clubbed at the top of the column in the order in which they were entered into the table. This is **the essential difference** between the Primary Key and the Unique constraints when applied to table column(s).

Key point about Unique Constraint:

1. Unique key will not allow duplicate values
2. Unique index is created automatically
3. A table can have more than one Unique key which is not possible in Primary key

4. Unique key can combine upto 16 columns in a Composite Unique key
5. Unique key can not be LONG or LONG RAW data type

UNIQUE Constraint Defined At The Column Level

Syntax:

```
<ColumnName>  <Datatype>(<Size>)  UNIQUE
```

Example:

Drop the CUST_MSTR table, if it already exists. Create a table CUST_MSTR such that the contents of the column CUST_NO are unique across the entire column.

DROP TABLE CUST_MSTR;

CREATE TABLE CUST_MSTR **(**

"CUST_NO" VARCHAR2(10) **UNIQUE**, "FNAME" VARCHAR2(25), "MNAME" VARCHAR2(25), "LNAME" VARCHAR2(25), "DOB_INC" DATE, "OCCUP" VARCHAR2(25), "PHOTOGRAPH" VARCHAR2(25), "SIGNATURE" VARCHAR2(25), "PANCOPY" VARCHAR2(1), "FORM60" VARCHAR2(1)**)**;

Output:

```
Table created.
```

For testing the Unique constraint execute the following INSERT INTO statements:

INSERT INTO CUST_MSTR (CUST_NO, FNAME, MNAME, LNAME, DOB_INC, OCCUP, PHOTOGRAPH, SIGNATURE, PANCOPY, FORM60**)**

VALUES('C1', 'Ivan', 'Nelson', 'Bayross', '25-JUN-1952', 'Self Employed', 'D:/ClntPht/C1.gif', 'D:/ClntSgnt/C1.gif', 'Y', 'Y'**)**;

INSERT INTO CUST_MSTR (CUST_NO, FNAME, MNAME, LNAME, DOB_INC, OCCUP, PHOTOGRAPH, SIGNATURE, PANCOPY, FORM60**)**

VALUES('C1', 'Chriselle', 'Ivan', 'Bayross', '29-OCT-1982', 'Service', 'D:/ClntPht/C2.gif', 'D:/ClntSgnt/C2.gif', 'N', 'Y'**)**;

INSERT INTO CUST_MSTR (CUST_NO, FNAME, MNAME, LNAME, DOB_INC, OCCUP, PHOTOGRAPH, SIGNATURE, PANCOPY, FORM60**)**

VALUES('C2', 'Mamta', 'Arvind', 'Muzumdar', '28-AUG-1975', 'Service', 'D:/ClntPht/C3.gif', 'D:/ClntSgnt/C3.gif', 'Y', 'Y'**)**;

Output:

The first INSERT INTO statement will execute without any errors as show below:

```
1 row created.
```

When the second INSERT INTO statement is executed an errors occurs as show below:

```
INSERT INTO CUST_MSTR (CUST_NO, FNAME, MNAME, LNAME, DOB_INC, OCCUP,
PHOTOGRAPH, SIGNATURE, PANCOPY,
*
ERROR at line 1:
ORA-00001: unique constraint (DBA_BANKSYS.SYS_C003007) violated
```

The third INSERT INTO statement rectifies this and the result is as show below:

```
1 row created.
```

When a SELECT statement is executed on the Client_Master table the records reterived are:

SELECT CUST_NO, FNAME, MNAME, LNAME **FROM** CUST_MSTR;

Output:

CUST_NO	FNAME	MNAME	LNAME
C1	Ivan	Nelson	Bayross
C2	Mamta	Arvind	Muzumdar

UNIQUE Constraint Defined At The Table Level

Syntax:

```
CREATE TABLE TableName
    (<ColumnName1> <Datatype>(<Size>), <ColumnName2>
    <Datatype>(<Size>),
        UNIQUE (<ColumnName1>, <ColumnName2>));
```

Example:

Drop the CUST_MSTR table, if it already exists. Create a table CUST_MSTR such that the contents of the column CUST_NO are unique across the entire column.

DROP TABLE CUST_MSTR;

CREATE TABLE CUST_MSTR (

"CUST_NO" VARCHAR2(10), "FNAME" VARCHAR2(25),

"MNAME" VARCHAR2(25), "LNAME" VARCHAR2(25),

"DOB_INC" DATE, "OCCUP" VARCHAR2(25),

"PHOTOGRAPH" VARCHAR2(25), "SIGNATURE" VARCHAR2(25),

"PANCOPY" VARCHAR2(1), "FORM60" VARCHAR2(1),

UNIQUE(CUST_NO));

Output:

```
Table created.
```

In the case of the table level unique constraints, the result for the following INSERT INTO statement will remain the same as explained earlier.

INSERT INTO CUST_MSTR (CUST_NO, FNAME, MNAME, LNAME, DOB_INC, OCCUP, PHOTOGRAPH, SIGNATURE, PANCOPY, FORM60)

VALUES('C1', 'Ivan', 'Nelson', 'Bayross', '25-JUN-1952', 'Self Employed', 'D:/ClntPht/C1.gif', D:/ClntSgnt/C1.gif', 'Y', 'Y');

INSERT INTO CUST_MSTR (CUST_NO, FNAME, MNAME, LNAME, DOB_INC, OCCUP, PHOTOGRAPH, SIGNATURE, PANCOPY, FORM60)

VALUES('C1', 'Chriselle', 'Ivan', 'Bayross', '29-OCT-1982', 'Service', 'D:/ClntPht/C2.gif', 'D:/ClntSgnt/C2.gif', 'N', 'Y');

INSERT INTO CUST_MSTR (CUST_NO, FNAME, MNAME, LNAME, DOB_INC, OCCUP, PHOTOGRAPH, SIGNATURE, PANCOPY, FORM60)
VALUES('C2', 'Mamta', 'Arvind', 'Muzumdar', '28-AUG-1975', 'Service', 'D:/ClntPht/C3.gif', 'D:/ClntSgnt/C3.gif', 'Y', 'Y');

Business Rule Constraints

Oracle allows the application of **business rules** to table columns. Business managers determine business rules, they vary from system to system as mentioned earlier. These rules are applied to data, **prior** the data is being inserted into table columns. This ensures that the data (**records**) in the table have integrity.

For example, the rule that no employee in the company shall get a salary less than Rs.1000/- is a business rule. This means that no cell in the **salary** column of the employee table should hold a **value** less than 1000. If an attempt is made, to insert a value less than 1000 into the salary column, the database engine rejects the entire record automatically.

Business rules can be implemented in Oracle by using **CHECK** constraints. Check Constraints can be bound to a **column** or a **table** using the **CREATE TABLE** or **ALTER TABLE** command.

Business rule validation checks are performed when any table **write** operation is carried out. Any insert or update statement causes the relevant Check constraint to be evaluated. The Check constraint must be satisfied for the write operation to succeed. Thus **Check constraints** ensure the integrity of the data in tables.

Conceptually, data constraints are connected to a column, by the Oracle engine, as **flags**. Whenever, an attempt is made to load the column with data, the Oracle engine observes the flag and recognizes the presence of a constraint. The Oracle engine then retrieves the Check constraint definition and then applies the Check constraint definition, to the data being loaded into the table column. If the data being entered into a column fails any of the data constraint checks, the **entire** record is rejected. The Oracle engine will then flash an appropriate **error message**.

Oracle allows programmers to define constraints at:

- Column Level
- Table Level

Column Level Constraints

If data constraints are defined as an attribute of a column definition when creating or altering a table structure, they are **column level constraints.**

> **Caution**
>
> 
>
> Column level constraints are applied to the **current column**. The current column is the column that immediately **precedes** the constraint (**i.e.** they are local to a specific column). A column level constraint **cannot** be applied if the data constraint spans **across multiple columns** in a table.

Table Level Constraints

If data constraints are defined **after defining all table column attributes** when creating or altering a table structure, it is a **table level constraint**.

Note

 A table level constraint **must** be applied if the data constraint **spans across multiple columns** in a table.

Constraints are stored as a part of the global table definition by the Oracle engine in its **system tables.** The SQL syntax used to attach the constraint will change depending upon whether it is a column level or table level constraint.

NULL Value Concepts

Often there may be records in a table that do not have values for every field. This could be because the information is not available at the time of data entry or because the field is not applicable in every case. If the column was created as **NULLABLE**, Oracle will place a NULL value in the column in the **absence** of a user-defined value.

A NULL value is **different from** a blank or a zero. A **NULL value** can be inserted into **columns** of **any data type**.

Principles Of NULL Values

- Setting a NULL value is appropriate when the actual value is unknown, or when a value would not be meaningful
- A NULL value is **not equivalent** to a value of **zero** if the data type is **number** and is not equivalent to **spaces** if the data type is **character**
- A NULL value will evaluate to NULL in any expression (**e.g.** NULL multiplied by 10 is NULL)
- NULL value can be inserted into columns of **any data type**
- If the column has a NULL value, Oracle ignores any UNIQUE, FOREIGN KEY, CHECK constraints that may be attached to the column

Difference Between An Empty String And A NULL Value

Oracle has changed its rules about empty strings and null values in newer versions of Oracle. Now, an empty string is treated as a null value in Oracle.

To understand this go through the following example:

Example:

Drop the BRANCH_MSTR table, if it already exists. Create a table BRANCH_MSTR such that the contents of the column CUST_NO are unique across the entire column.

DROP TABLE BRANCH_MSTR;

CREATE TABLE BRANCH_MSTR **(**
"BRANCH_NO" VARCHAR2(10), "NAME" VARCHAR2(25));

Output:

```
Table created.
```

Next, insert two records into this table.

INSERT INTO BRANCH_MSTR (BRANCH_NO, NAME) VALUES('B1', null);

Output:

```
1 row created.
```

INSERT INTO BRANCH_MSTR (BRANCH_NO, NAME) **VALUES**('B2', '');

Output:

```
1 row created.
```

The first statement inserts a record with a branch name that is null, while the second statement inserts a record with an empty string as a branch name.

Now, retrieve all rows with a branch name that is an empty string value as follows:

SELECT * FROM BRANCH_MSTR **WHERE** NAME = '';

When this statement is executed, it is expected to retrieve the row that was inserted above. But instead, this statement will not retrieve any records at all.

Now, try retrieving all rows where the branch name contains a null value:

SELECT * FROM BRANCH_MSTR **WHERE** NAME **IS NULL;**

When this statement is executed, both rows are retrieved. This is because Oracle has now changed its rules so that empty strings behave as null values.

It is also important to note that the null value is unique. Usual operands such as =, <, > and so on cannot be used on a null value. Instead, the IS NULL and IS NOT NULL conditions have to be used.

NOT NULL Constraint Defined At The Column Level

In addition to Primary key and Foreign Key, Oracle has **NOT NULL** as column constraint. The **NOT NULL** column constraint ensures that a table column cannot be left empty.

When a column is defined as **not null**, then that column becomes a **mandatory** column. It implies that a value must be entered into the column if the record is to be accepted for storage in the table.

Syntax:

```
<ColumnName> <Datatype>(<Size>) NOT NULL
```

Example:

Drop the table CUST_MSTR, if already exists and then create it again making Date of Birth field not null. Refer to the details of table in chapter 6

```
CREATE TABLE "DBA_BANKSYS"."CUST_MSTR"(
    "CUST_NO" VARCHAR2(10), "FNAME" VARCHAR2(25),
    "MNAME" VARCHAR2(25), "LNAME" VARCHAR2(25),
    "DOB_INC" DATE NOT NULL, "OCCUP" VARCHAR2(25),
    "PHOTOGRAPH" VARCHAR2(25), "SIGNATURE" VARCHAR2(25),
    "PANCOPY" VARCHAR2(1), "FORM60" VARCHAR2(1));
```

Output:

```
Table created.
```

Note

 A The **NOT NULL** constraint can only be applied at column level.

Execute the following INSERT INTO statements to verify whether mandatory field constraints are applied:

INSERT INTO CUST_MSTR (CUST_NO, FNAME, MNAME, LNAME, DOB_INC, OCCUP, PHOTOGRAPH, SIGNATURE, PANCOPY, FORM60)

VALUES('O14', null, null, null, null, 'Retail Business', null, null, 'N', 'Y');

Output:

```
INSERT INTO CUST_MSTR (CUST_NO, FNAME, MNAME, LNAME, DOB_INC, OCCUP,
PHOTOGRAPH, SIGNATURE, PANCOPY,
*
ERROR at line 1:
ORA-01400: cannot insert NULL into ("DBA_BANKSYS"."CUST_MSTR"."DOB_INC")
```

The above **error** message confirms that the mandatory field constraints are applied successfully.

Caution

The **NOT NULL** constraint can only be applied at column level. Although **NOT NULL** can be applied as a **CHECK** constraint, Oracle Corp recommends that this should **not be done**.

The CHECK Constraint

Business Rule validations can be applied to a table column by using **CHECK** constraint. **CHECK** constraints must be specified as a logical expression that evaluates either to **TRUE** or **FALSE**.

Note

A **CHECK** constraint takes substantially longer to execute as compared to NOT NULL, PRIMARY KEY, FOREIGN KEY or UNIQUE. Thus CHECK constraints must be avoided if the constraint can be defined using the Not Null, Primary key or Foreign key constraint.

CHECK constraint defined at the column level:

Syntax:

```
<ColumnName> <Datatype>(<Size>) CHECK (<Logical Expression>)
```

Example:

Drop the table CUST_MSTR, if already exists. Create a table **CUST_MSTR** with the following check constraints:

- Data values being inserted into the column **CUST_NO** must start with the capital letter **C**
- Data values being inserted into the column **FNAME, MNAME and LNAME** should be in **upper case** only

CREATE TABLE CUST_MSTR("CUST_NO" VARCHAR2(10) CHECK(CUST_NO LIKE 'C%'),

"FNAME" VARCHAR2(25) **CHECK** (FNAME = UPPER(FNAME)),

"MNAME" VARCHAR2(25) **CHECK** (MNAME = UPPER(MNAME)),

"LNAME" VARCHAR2(25) **CHECK** (LNAME = UPPER(LNAME)), "DOB_INC" DATE,

"OCCUP" VARCHAR2(25), "PHOTOGRAPH" VARCHAR2(25), "SIGNATURE" VARCHAR2(25),

"PANCOPY" VARCHAR2(1), "FORM60" VARCHAR2(1));

Output:

```
Table created.
```

CHECK Constraint Defined At The Table Level:

Syntax:

```
CHECK (<Logical Expression>)
```

Example:

Drop the table CUST_MSTR, if already exists. Create a table **CUST_MSTR** with the following check constraints:

- Data values being inserted into the column **CUST_NO** must start with the capital letter **C**
- Data values being inserted into the column **FNAME, MNAME and LNAME** should be in **upper case** only

```
CREATE TABLE CUST_MSTR("CUST_NO" VARCHAR2(10), "FNAME" VARCHAR2(25),
    "MNAME" VARCHAR2(25), "LNAME" VARCHAR2(25), "DOB_INC" DATE,
    "OCCUP" VARCHAR2(25), "PHOTOGRAPH" VARCHAR2(25), "SIGNATURE" VARCHAR2(25),
    "PANCOPY" VARCHAR2(1), "FORM60" VARCHAR2(1),
    CHECK (CUST_NO LIKE 'C%'), CHECK (FNAME = UPPER(FNAME)),
    CHECK (MNAME = UPPER(MNAME)), CHECK (LNAME = UPPER(LNAME)));
```

Output:

```
Table created.
```

Execute the following INSERT INTO statements to verify whether check constraints are applied:

```
INSERT INTO CUST_MSTR (CUST_NO, FNAME, MNAME, LNAME, DOB_INC, OCCUP,
PHOTOGRAPH, SIGNATURE, PANCOPY, FORM60)
    VALUES('O14', 'SHARANAM', 'CHAITANYA', 'SHAH', '03-Jan-1981', 'Business', null, null, 'N',
'Y');
```

Output:

```
INSERT INTO CUST_MSTR (CUST_NO, FNAME, MNAME, LNAME, DOB_INC, OCCUP,
PHOTOGRAPH, SIGNATURE, PANCOPY,
*
ERROR at line 1:
ORA-02290: check constraint (DBA_BANKSYS.SYS_C003055) violated
```

```
INSERT INTO CUST_MSTR (CUST_NO, FNAME, MNAME, LNAME, DOB_INC, OCCUP,
PHOTOGRAPH, SIGNATURE, PANCOPY, FORM60)
    VALUES('C14', 'sharanam', 'CHAITANYA', 'SHAH', '03-Jan-1981', 'Business', null, null, 'N', 'Y');
```

Output:

```
INSERT INTO CUST_MSTR (CUST_NO, FNAME, MNAME, LNAME, DOB_INC, OCCUP,
PHOTOGRAPH, SIGNATURE, PANCOPY,
*
ERROR at line 1:
ORA-02290: check constraint (DBA_BANKSYS.SYS_C003056) violated
```

INSERT INTO CUST_MSTR (CUST_NO, FNAME, MNAME, LNAME, DOB_INC, OCCUP, PHOTOGRAPH, SIGNATURE, PANCOPY, FORM60)

VALUES('C14', 'SHARANAM', '**Chaitanya**', 'SHAH', '03-Jan-1981', 'Business', null, null, 'N', 'Y');

Output:

```
INSERT INTO CUST_MSTR (CUST_NO, FNAME, MNAME, LNAME, DOB_INC, OCCUP,
PHOTOGRAPH, SIGNATURE, PANCOPY,
*
ERROR at line 1:
ORA-02290: check constraint (DBA_BANKSYS.SYS_C003057) violated
```

INSERT INTO CUST_MSTR (CUST_NO, FNAME, MNAME, LNAME, DOB_INC, OCCUP, PHOTOGRAPH, SIGNATURE, PANCOPY, FORM60)

VALUES('C14', 'SHARANAM', 'CHAITANYA', '**sHAh**', '03-Jan-1981', 'Business', null, null, 'N', 'Y');

Output:

```
INSERT INTO CUST_MSTR (CUST_NO, FNAME, MNAME, LNAME, DOB_INC, OCCUP,
PHOTOGRAPH, SIGNATURE, PANCOPY,
*
ERROR at line 1:
ORA-02290: check constraint (DBA_BANKSYS.SYS_C003058) violated
```

The above **error** messages confirm that the check constraints are applied successfully.

When using **CHECK** constraints, consider the ANSI / ISO standard, which states that a CHECK constraint is violated only if the condition evaluates to **False**. A check constraint is not violated if the condition evaluates to **True**.

Note

If the expression in a check constraint does not return a **true / false**, the value is **Indeterminate** or **Unknown.** Unknown values do not violate a check constraint condition. For example, consider the following CHECK constraint for SellPrice column in the Product_Master table:

CHECK (SellPrice > 0)

At first glance, this rule may be interpreted as "do not allow a row in the **Product_Master** table unless **the Sellprice** is greater than 0". However, note that if a row is inserted with a **null SellPrice**, the row **does not violate** the CHECK constraint because the entire check condition is evaluated as **unknown**.

In this particular case, prevent such violations by placing the **not null** integrity constraint along with the check constraint on **SellPrice** column of the table **Product_Master**.

Restrictions On CHECK Constraints

A **CHECK** integrity constraint requires that a condition be **true** or **unknown** for the row to be processed. If an SQL statement causes the condition to evaluate to **false**, an appropriate error message is displayed and processing stops.

A **CHECK** constraint has the following limitations:

- The condition must be a **Boolean** expression that can be evaluated using the values in the row being inserted or updated.
- The condition cannot contain **subqueries** or **sequences**.
- The condition cannot include the SYSDATE, UID, USER or USERENV SQL functions.

Defining Different Constraints On A Table

Example:

Drop the table FD_MSTR, if already exists. Create FD_MSTR table where

- The FD_SER_NO is a primary key to this table
- The BRANCH_NO is the foreign key referencing the table BRANCH_MSTR
- The CORP_CUST_NO is the foreign key referencing the table CUST_MSTR
- The VERI_EMP_NO is a foreign key referencing the table EMP_MSTR
- The CORP_CNST_TYPE will hold wither of the following values:
  ØS, 1C, 2C, 3C, 4C, 5C, 6C, 7C indicating different types of companies

```
CREATE TABLE "DBA_BANKSYS"."FD_MSTR"("FD_SER_NO" VARCHAR2(10),
    "SF_NO" VARCHAR2(10), "BRANCH_NO" VARCHAR2(10), "INTRO_CUST_NO"
    VARCHAR2(10),
    "INTRO_ACCT_NO" VARCHAR2(10), "INTRO_SIGN" VARCHAR2(1),
    "ACCT_NO" VARCHAR2(10), "TITLE" VARCHAR2(30), "CORP_CUST_NO" VARCHAR2(10),
    "CORP_CNST_TYPE" VARCHAR(4), "VERI_EMP_NO" VARCHAR2(10),
    "VERI_SIGN" VARCHAR2(1), "MANAGER_SIGN" VARCHAR2(1),
    CONSTRAINT PK PRIMARY KEY (FD_SER_NO, CORP_CUST_NO),
    CONSTRAINT FK_BR FOREIGN KEY (BRANCH_NO) REFERENCES BRANCH_MSTR,
    CONSTRAINT FK_CU FOREIGN KEY (CORP_CUST_NO) REFERENCES CUST_MSTR,
    CONSTRAINT FK_EM FOREIGN KEY (VERI_EMP_NO) REFERENCES EMP_MSTR,
    CONSTRAINT CHK CHECK (CORP_CNST_TYPE IN ('ØS', '1C', '2C', '3C', '4C', '5C', '6C', '7C')));
```

Output:

```
Table created.
```

THE USER_CONSTRAINTS TABLE

A table can be created with multiple constraints attached to its columns. If a user wishes to see the table structure along with its constraints, Oracle provides the **DESCRIBE <TableName>** command.

This command displays only the column names, data type, size and the NOT NULL constraint. The information about the other constraints that may be attached to the table columns such as the PRIMARY KEY, FOREIGN KEY, and so on, is not available using the DESCRIBE verb.

Oracle stores such information in a table called **USER_CONSTRAINTS**. Querying **USER_CONSTRAINTS** provides information bound to the names of all the constraints on the table. **USER_CONSTRAINTS** comprises of multiple columns, some of which are described below:

USER_CONSTRAINTS Table:

Column Name	Description
OWNER	The owner of the constraint.
CONSTRAINT_NAME	The name of the constraint
TABLE_NAME	The name of the table associated with the constraint
CONSTRAINT_TYPE	The type of constraint: **P**: Primary Key Constraint **R**: Foreign Key Constraint **U**: Unique Constraint **C**: Check Constraint
SEARCH_CONDITION	The search condition used (for CHECK Constraints)
R_OWNER	The owner of the table referenced by the FOREIGN KEY constraints
R_CONSTRAINT_NAME	The name of the constraint referenced by a FOREIGN KEY constraint.

Example:

View the constraints of the table CUST_MSTR

```
SELECT OWNER, CONSTRAINT_NAME, CONSTRAINT_TYPE FROM USER_CONSTRAINTS
    WHERE TABLE_NAME = 'CUST_MSTR';
```

Output:

OWNER	CONSTRAINT_NAME	CONSTRAINT_TYPE
DBA_BANKSYS	SYS_C003027	C
DBA_BANKSYS	SYS_C003028	C
DBA_BANKSYS	SYS_C003029	C
DBA_BANKSYS	SYS_C003030	C

Defining Integrity Constraints Via The Alter Table Command

Integrity constraints can be defined using the **constraint** clause, in the **ALTER TABLE** command.

Note

 Oracle **will not allow** constraints defined using the **ALTER TABLE**, to be applied to the table if data previously placed in the table **violates such constraints**.

If a Primary key constraint was being applied to a table in retrospect and the column has duplicate values in it, the Primary key constraint **will not** be set to that column.

The following examples show the definitions of several integrity constraints:

Example:

Alter the table EMP_MSTR by adding a primary key on the column EMP_NO.

ALTER TABLE EMP_MSTR **ADD PRIMARY KEY** (EMP_NO);

Output:

```
Table altered.
```

Example:

Add FOREIGN KEY constraint on the column **VERI_EMP_NO** belonging to the table **FD_MSTR**, which references the table **EMP_MSTR**. Modify column **MANAGER_SIGN** to include the **NOT NULL** constraint

ALTER TABLE FD_MSTR **ADD CONSTRAINT** F_EmpKey **FOREIGN KEY**(VERI_EMP_NO)
REFERENCES EMP_MSTR **MODIFY**(MANAGER_SIGN **NOT NULL**);

Output:

```
Table altered.
```

Dropping Integrity Constraints Via The ALTER TABLE Command

Integrity constraint can be dropped if the rule that it enforces is no longer **true** or if the constraint is no longer **needed**. Drop the constraint using the **ALTER TABLE** command with the **DROP** clause. The following examples illustrate the dropping of integrity constraints:

Example:

Drop the PRIMARY KEY constraint from EMP_MSTR.

ALTER TABLE EMP_MSTR **DROP PRIMARY KEY;**

Output:

```
Table altered.
```

Example:

Drop FOREIGN KEY constraint on column VERI_EMP_NO in table FD_MSTR

ALTER TABLE FD_MSTR **DROP CONSTRAINT F_EmpKey;**

Output:

```
Table altered.
```

Note

 Dropping UNIQUE and PRIMARY KEY constraints **also drops all** associated indexes.

Default Value Concepts

At the time of table creation a **default value** can be assigned to a column. When a record is loaded into the table, and the column is left empty, the Oracle engine will automatically load this column with the default value specified. The data type of the default value should match the data type of the column. The **DEFAULT** clause can be used to specify a default value for a column.

Syntax:

```
<ColumnName> <Datatype>(<Size>) DEFAULT <Value>;
```

Example:

Create ACCT_MSTR table where the column CURBAL is the number and by default it should be zero. The other column STATUS is a varchar2 and by default it should have character **A**. (Refer to table definitions in the chapter 6)

```
CREATE TABLE "DBA_BANKSYS"."ACCT_MSTR"("ACCT_NO" VARCHAR2(10),
    "SF_NO" VARCHAR2(10), "LF_NO" VARCHAR2(10), "BRANCH_NO" VARCHAR2(10),
    "INTRO_CUST_NO" VARCHAR2(10), "INTRO_ACCT_NO" VARCHAR2(10),
    "INTRO_SIGN" VARCHAR2(1), "TYPE" VARCHAR2(2), "OPR_MODE" VARCHAR2(2),
    "CUR_ACCT_TYPE" VARCHAR2(4), "TITLE" VARCHAR2(30),
    "CORP_CUST_NO" VARCHAR2(10), "APLNDT" DATE, "OPNDT" DATE,
    "VERI_EMP_NO" VARCHAR2(10), "VERI_SIGN" VARCHAR2(1),
    "MANAGER_SIGN" VARCHAR2(1), "CURBAL" NUMBER(8, 2) DEFAULT 0,
    "STATUS" VARCHAR2(1) DEFAULT 'A');
```

Output:

```
Table created.
```

Note

- The data type of the default value should match the data type of the column
- Character and date values will be specified in single quotes
- If a column level constraint is defined on the column with a default value, the default value clause must precede the constraint definition

Thus the syntax will be:

```
<ColumnName> <Datatype>(<Size>) DEFAULT <Value>
<constraint definition>
```

Self Review Questions

Fill in the Blanks

1. Business rules, which are enforced on data being stored in a table, are called ___________.
2. If the column was created as ___________ Oracle will place a NULL value in the column in the absence of a user-defined value.
3. When a column is defined as not null, then that column becomes a ___________ column.
4. The ___________ constraint can only be applied at column level.
5. A ___________ value can be inserted into the columns of any data type.
6. A single column primary key is called a ___________ key.
7. The data held across the primary key column must be ___________.
8. ___________ keys represent relationships between tables.
9. The table in which the foreign key is defined is called a Foreign table or ___________ table.
10. The default behavior of the foreign key can be changed by using the ___________ option.

11. ___________ constraints must be specified as a logical expression that evaluates either to TRUE or FALSE.
12. In a CHECK constraint the condition must be a ___________ expression that can be evaluated using the values in the row being inserted or updated.
13. _____________ constraints can be defined using the constraint clause, in the ALTER TABLE command.
14. Dropping UNIQUE and PRIMARY KEY constraints also drops all associated ___________.

True or False

15. Business rules that have to be applied to data are completely System dependent.
16. Constraints super control the data being entered into a table for temporary storage.
17. A NULL value is equivalent to a value of zero.
18. Setting a NULL value is appropriate when the actual value is unknown.
19. A table cannot contain multiple unique keys.
20. Oracle ignores any UNIQUE, FOREIGN KEY, CHECK constraints on a NULL value.
21. A primary key column in a table is an optional column.
22. Standard business rules do not allow multiple entries for the same product.
23. The master table can be referenced in the foreign key definition by using the clause REFERENCES tablename.columname when defining the foreign key.
24. A CHECK constraint consists of subqueries and sequences.
25. The USER_CONSTRAINTS command displays only the column names, data type, size and the NOT NULL constraint.
26. Drop the constraint using the DROP TABLE command with the DELETE clause.
27. At the time of table creation a default value can be assigned to a column.
28. If a column level constraint is defined on the column with a default value, the default value clause must precede the constraint definition.

Hands On Exercises

1. Create the tables described below:

Table Name:	**CLIENT_MASTER**
Description:	Used to store client information.

Column Name	Data Type	Size	Default	Attributes
CLIENTNO	Varchar2	6		Primary Key / first letter must start with 'C'
NAME	Varchar2	20		Not Null
ADDRESS1	Varchar2	30		

Details for **CLIENT_MASTER** table continued.

Column Name	Data Type	Size	Default	Attributes
Column Name	Data Type	Size	Default	Attributes
ADDRESS2	Varchar2	30		
CITY	Varchar2	15		
PINCODE	Number	8		
STATE	Varchar2	15		
BALDUE	Number	10,2		

Table Name:	PRODUCT_MASTER
Description:	Used to store product information.

Column Name	Data Type	Size	Default	Attributes
PRODUCTNO	Varchar2	6		Primary Key / first letter must start with 'P'
DESCRIPTION	Varchar2	15		Not Null
PROFITPERCENT	Number	4,2		Not Null
UNITMEASURE	Varchar2	10		Not Null
QTYONHAND	Number	8		Not Null
REORDERLVL	Number	8		Not Null
SELLPRICE	Number	8,2		Not Null, Cannot be 0
COSTPRICE	Number	8,2		Not Null, Cannot be 0

Table Name:	SALESMAN_MASTER
Description:	Used to store salesman information working for the company.

Column Name	Data Type	Size	Default	Attributes
SALESMANNO	Varchar2	6		Primary Key / first letter
must start with 'S'				
SALESMANNAME	Varchar2	20		Not Null
ADDRESS1	Varchar2	30		Not Null
ADDRESS2	Varchar2	30		
CITY	Varchar2	20		
PINCODE	Number	8		
STATE	Varchar2	20		
SALAMT	Number	8,2		Not Null, Cannot be 0
TGTTOGET	Number	6,2		Not Null, Cannot be 0
YTDSALES	Number	6,2		Not Null
REMARKS	Varchar2	60		

Table Name:	**SALES_ORDER**
Description:	Used to store client's orders.

Column Name	Data Type	Size	Default	Attributes
ORDERNO	Varchar2	6		Primary Key / first letter must start with 'O'
CLIENTNO	Varchar2	6		Foreign Key references ClientNo of Client_Master table
ORDERDATE	Date			Not Null
DELYADDR	Varchar2	25		
SALESMANNO	Varchar2	6		Foreign Key references SalesmanNo of Salesman_Master table
DELYTYPE	Char	1	F	Delivery: part (P) / full (F)
BILLYN	Char	1		
DELYDATE	Date			Cannot be less than Order_Date
ORDERSTATUS	Varchar2	10		Values ('In Process', 'Fulfilled', 'BackOrder', 'Cancelled')

Table Name:	**SALES_ORDER_DETAILS**
Description:	Used to store client's orders with details of each product ordered.

Column Name	Data Type	Size	Default	Attributes
ORDERNO	Varchar2	6		Foreign Key references OrderNo of Sales_Order table
PRODUCTNO	Varchar2	6		Foreign Key references ProductNo of Product_Master table
QTYORDERED	Number	8		
QTYDISP	Number	8		
PRODUCTRATE	Number	10,2		

2. Insert the following data into their respective tables:
   a. Re-insert the data generated for tables CLIENT_MASTER, PRODUCT_MASTER, and SALESMAN_MASTER. Refer to hands-on exercised for **Chapter 07:Interactive SQL-Part I**.

(a) Data for Sales_Order table:

OrderNo	ClientNo	OrderDate	SalesmanNo	DelyType	BillYN	DelyDate	OrderStatus
O19001	C00001	12-June-04	S00001	F	N	20-July-02	In Process
O19002	C00002	25-June-04	S00002	P	N	27-June-02	Cancelled
O46865	C00003	18-Feb-04	S00003	F	Y	20-Feb-02	Fulfilled
O19003	C00001	03-Apr-04	S00001	F	Y	07-Apr-02	Fulfilled
O46866	C00004	20-May-04	S00002	P	N	22-May-02	Cancelled
O19008	C00005	24-May-04	S00004	F	N	26-July-02	In Process

(b) Data for Sales_Order_Details table:

OrderNo	ProductNo	QtyOrdered	QtyDisp	ProductRate
O19001	P00001	4	4	525
O19001	P07965	2	1	8400
O19001	P07885	2	1	5250
O19002	P00001	10	0	525
O46865	P07868	3	3	3150
O46865	P07885	3	1	5250
O46865	P00001	10	10	525
O46865	P0345	4	4	1050
O19003	P03453	2	2	1050
O19003	P06734	1	1	12000
O46866	P07965	1	0	8400
O46866	P07975	1	0	1050
O19008	P00001	10	5	525
O19008	P07975	5	3	1050

12

Interactive SQL Part - III

Computations Done on Table Data

None of the techniques used till now allows display of data from a table after some arithmetic has been done with it.

Computations may include displaying an employee's name and the employee's salary from the Employee_Master table along with the **annual salary** of the employee (**i.e.** Salary*12). The arithmetic (Salary * 12) is an example of table data arithmetic.

Arithmetic and logical operators give a new dimension to SQL sentences.

Arithmetic Operators

Oracle allows arithmetic operators to be used while viewing records from a table or while performing Data Manipulation operations such as Insert, Update and Delete. These are:

+	Addition	*	Multiplication
-	Subtraction	**	Exponentiation
/	Division	()	Enclosed operation

Example:

List the fixed deposits held by the customers and also show what will be the amount payable by the bank if the fixed deposits are cancelled by the **end of the day**.

Synopsis:

Tables:	FD_DTLS
Columns:	FD_NO, TYPE, PERIOD, OPNDT, DUEDT, AMT, INTRATE, DUEAMT
Technique:	**Functions:** ROUND(), **Operators:** *, -, /, **Clauses:** WHERE, **Others:** SYSDATE

Solution:

```
SELECT FD_NO, TYPE, PERIOD, OPNDT, DUEDT, AMT, INTRATE, DUEAMT,
        ROUND(AMT + (AMT * ROUND(SYSDATE – OPNDT)/365 * (INTRATE/100)), 2)
    FROM FD_DTLS WHERE DUEDT > SYSDATE;
```

Output:

FD_NO	TYPE	PERIOD	OPNDT	DUEDT	AMT	INTRATE	DUEAMT
ROUND(AMT+(AMT*ROUND(SYSDATE-OPNDT)/365*(INTRATE/100)),2)							
F6	S	732	19-JUL-03	20-JUL-05	5000	9	5902.47
						5429.04	
F7	S	366	27-JUL-03	27-JUL-04	5000	8	5401.1
						5372.6	

Explanation:

Here, **ROUND(AMT + (AMT * ROUND(SYSDATE – OPNDT)/365 * (INTRATE/100)),2)** is **not** a column in the table **FD_DTLS**. However, the arithmetic specified is done on the contents of the columns **AMT, OPNDT and INTRATE** of the table **FD_DTLS** and displayed in the output of the query.

By default, the Oracle engine will use the column names of the table **FD_DTLS** as column headers when displaying column output on the VDU screen.

Since there are no columns with the arithmetic expression applied on the table **FD_DTLS**, the Oracle engine performs the required arithmetic and uses the **formula** as the **default** column header when displaying output as seen above.

Renaming Columns Used With Expression Lists

Rename the default output column names with an **alias**, when required.

Syntax:

```
SELECT <ColumnName> <AliasName>, <ColumnName> <AliasName>
    FROM <TableName>;
```

Example:

List the fixed deposits held by the customers and also show what will be the amount received if the fixed deposits are cancelled on the same day. Use Alias to rename the calculative column to **Pre-Maturity Amount**.

Synopsis:

Tables:	FD_DTLS
Columns:	FD_NO, TYPE, PERIOD, OPNDT, DUEDT, AMT, INTRATE, DUEAMT
Technique:	**Functions:** ROUND(), **Operators:** *, -, /, **Clauses:** WHERE, **Others:** ALIAS, SYSDATE

Solution:

SELECT FD_NO, TYPE, PERIOD, OPNDT, DUEDT, AMT, INTRATE, DUEAMT,
ROUND(AMT + (AMT * **ROUND(SYSDATE** - OPNDT)/365 * (INTRATE/100)), 2) "PreMaturity Amount"
FROM FD_DTLS **WHERE** DUEDT > **SysDate;**

Output:

FD_NO	TYPE	PERIOD	OPNDT	DUEDT	AMT	INTRATE	DUEAMT
Pre Maturity Amount							
F6 5429.04	S	732	19-JUL-03	20-JUL-05	5000	9	5902.47
F7 5372.6	S	366	27-JUL-03	27-JUL-04	5000	8	5401.1

Explanation:

Here, **ROUND(AMT + (AMT * ROUND(SYSDATE – OPNDT)/365 * (INTRATE/100)),2)** is renamed to alias "Pre-Maturity Amount".

Logical Operators

Logical operators that can be used in SQL sentences are:

The AND Operator:

The AND operator allows creating an SQL statement based on two or more conditions being met. It can be used in any valid SQL statement such as select, insert, update, or delete. The AND operator requires that each condition must be met for the record to be included in the result set.

The Oracle engine will process all rows in a table and display the result only when **all** of the conditions specified using the **AND** operator are satisfied.

Example:

Display all those transactions performed today for amount ranging between 500 and 5000 **both inclusive**.

Synopsis:

Tables:	TRANS_MSTR
Columns:	All Columns
Technique:	**Functions:** TO_CHAR(), **Operators:** AND, **Clauses:** WHERE, **Others:** SYSDATE

Solution:

SELECT * FROM TRANS_MSTR **WHERE** AMT >= 500 **AND** AMT <= 5000
AND TO_CHAR(DT, 'DD/MM/YYYY') = **TO_CHAR(SYSDATE,** 'DD/MM/YYYY');

Output:

TRANS_NO	ACCT_NO	DT	TYPE	PARTICULAR	DR_CR	AMT	BALANCE
T7	CA7	14-MAR-2004	B	Initial Payment	D	2000	2000

Explanation:

Here, the AND operator is used to compare the value held in the amount field with a constant. Only those transactions carried out today, that satisfy this comparison, are shown. This is done by comparing transaction dates with the current date after converting them to characters.

The OR Operator:

The OR condition allows creating an SQL statement where records are returned when any one of the conditions are met. It can be used in any valid SQL statement such as select, insert, update, or delete. The OR condition requires that any of the conditions must be met for the record to be included in the result set.

The Oracle engine will process all rows in a table and display the result only when **any of** the conditions specified using the **OR** operator is satisfied.

Example:

Display the customers whose belong to Information Technology or are self-employed.

Synopsis:

Tables:	CUST_MSTR, ADDR_DTLS
Columns:	CUST_NO, FNAME, MNAME, LNAME
Technique:	**Operators:** LIKE, AND, OR, **Clauses:** WHERE, **Others:** CONCAT

Solution:

```
SELECT CUST_NO, FNAME || ' ' || MNAME || ' ' || LNAME "Customers"
    FROM CUST_MSTR, ADDR_DTLS
        WHERE CUST_MSTR.CUST_NO = ADDR_DTLS.CODE_NO
            AND (OCCUP = 'Information Technology' OR OCCUP = 'Self Employed')
            AND CUST_NO LIKE 'C%';
```

Output:

CUST_NO	Customers
C1	Ivan Nelson Bayross
C10	Namita S. Kanade
C7	Anil Arun Dhone

Explanation:

Here, the **OR** operator is used to compare the value held in the **OCCUP** field. If the comparison condition is satisfied then only those customers who belong to Information Technology or are self-employed are shown. The **LIKE** operator is used to avoid display of those rows held in the **CUST_MSTR** table, which identify corporates.

Combining the AND and OR Operator:

The **AND** and **OR** conditions can be combined in a single SQL statement. It can be used in any valid SQL statement such as select, insert, update, or delete.

When combining these conditions, it is important to use brackets so that the database knows what order to evaluate each condition.

The Oracle engine will process all rows in a table and display the result only when **all** of the conditions specified using the **AND** operator are satisfied and when **any of** the conditions specified using the **OR** operator are satisfied.

Example:

Display all the customers whose **last name** is **Bayross** and are **less than 25** yrs old **or** all those customers who are **more than 25** but **less than 50** yrs old.

Synopsis:

Tables:	CUST_MSTR, ADDR_DTLS
Columns:	CUST_NO, FNAME, MNAME, LNAME
Technique:	**Operators:** LIKE, AND, OR, **Clauses:** WHERE, **Others:** CONCATENATE

Solution:

```
SELECT CUST_NO, FNAME || ' ' || MNAME || ' ' || LNAME "Customers",
    ROUND((SYSDATE - DOB_INC)/365) "Age" FROM CUST_MSTR
  WHERE (ROUND((SYSDATE - DOB_INC)/365) < 25 AND LNAME='Bayross')
    OR (ROUND((SYSDATE - DOB_INC)/365) > 25
      AND ROUND((SYSDATE - DOB_INC)/365) < 50) AND CUST_NO LIKE 'C%';
```

Output:

CUST_NO	Customers	Age
C2	Chriselle Ivan Bayross	22
C3	Mamta Arvind Muzumdar	29
C4	Chhaya Sudhakar Bankar	28
C5	Ashwini Dilip Joshi	26
C8	Alex Austin Fernandes	42
C10	Namita S. Kanade	26

6 rows selected.

Explanation:

This would return all the records where the value calculated by the arithmetic expression **i.e.** age is less than 25 and the value held in the field **LNAME** is **Bayross**. This will also return those records where the value calculated by the arithmetic expression **i.e.** age is more than 25 but less than 50. The brackets determine what order the **AND / OR** conditions are evaluated in.

The NOT Operator:

The Oracle engine will process all rows in a table and display only those records that **do not** satisfy the condition specified.

Example:

List the accounts details of those accounts which are **neither** Singly and **nor** Joint Accounts.

Synopsis:

Tables:	CUST_MSTR, ADDR_DTLS
Tables:	ACCT_MSTR
Columns:	ACCT_NO, TYPE, OPR_MODE, OPNDT, CURBAL, STATUS
Technique:	**Operators:** NOT, OR, **Clauses:** WHERE

Solution:

SELECT ACCT_NO, TYPE, OPR_MODE, OPNDT, CURBAL, STATUS
FROM ACCT_MSTR **WHERE NOT** (OPR_MODE = 'SI' **OR** OPR_MODE = 'JO');

Output:

ACCT_NO	TYPE	OPR_MODE	OPNDT	CURBAL	STATUS
CA4	CA	AS	05-FEB-03	2000	A
SB6	SB	ES	27-FEB-03	500	A
CA7	CA	AS	14-MAR-03	2000	A
CA10	CA	AS	19-APR-03	2000	A

Explanation:

The Oracle engine **will not** display rows from the ACCT_MSTR table where the value of the field **OPR_MODE** is either **SI** (Single) or **JO** (Joint). This means that all those records, which satisfy the condition specified using the NOT operator, will not be shown.

Range Searching

In order to select data that is within a range of values, the **BETWEEN** operator is used. The **BETWEEN** operator allows the selection of rows that contain values within a specified lower and upper limit. The range coded after the word **BETWEEN** is **inclusive**.

The lower value must be coded first. The two values in between the range must be linked with the keyword **AND**. The **BETWEEN** operator can be used with both character and numeric data types. However, the data types cannot be mixed **i.e.** the lower value of a range of values from a character column and the other from a numeric column.

Example:

List the transactions performed in months of January to March.

Synopsis:

Tables:	TRANS_MSTR
Columns:	All Columns
Technique:	**Functions:** TO_CHAR(), **Operators:** BETWEEN, **Clauses:** WHERE

Solution:

SELECT * FROM TRANS_MSTR **WHERE TO_CHAR**(DT, 'MM') **BETWEEN** 01 **AND** 03;

Equivalent to:

SELECT * FROM TRANS_MSTR
WHERE TO_CHAR(DT, 'MM') >= 01 **AND TO_CHAR**(DT, 'MM') <= 03;

Output:

TRANS_NO	ACCT_NO	DT	TYPE	PARTICULAR	DR_CR	AMT	BALANCE
T1	SB1	05-JAN-03	C	Initial Payment	D	500	500
T2	CA2	10-JAN-03	C	Initial Payment	D	2000	2000
T3	SB3	22-JAN-03	C	Initial Payment	D	500	500
T4	CA4	05-FEB-03	B	Initial Payment	D	2000	2000
T5	SB5	15-FEB-03	B	Initial Payment	D	500	500
T6	SB6	27-FEB-03	C	Initial Payment	D	500	500
T7	CA7	14-MAR-03	B	Initial Payment	D	2000	2000
T8	SB8	29-MAR-03	C	Initial Payment	D	500	500

8 rows selected.

Explanation:

The above select will retrieve all those records from the ACCT_MSTR table where the value held in the DT field is between 01 and 03 (both values inclusive). This is done using TO_CHAR() function which extracts the month value from the DT field. This is then compared using the AND operator.

Example:

List all the accounts, which have not been accessed in the fourth quarter of the financial year.

Synopsis:

Tables:	TRANS_MSTR
Columns:	ACCT_NO
Technique:	**Functions:** TO_CHAR(),**Operators:** NOT, BETWEEN, **Clauses:** WHERE

Solution:

SELECT DISTINCT
FROM TRANS_MSTR
WHERE TO_CHAR(DT, 'MM') **NOT BETWEEN 01** AND **04;**

Output:

```
ACCT_NO
SB9
```

Explanation:

The above select will retrieve all those records from the ACCT_MSTR table where the value held in the DT field is not between 01 and 04 (both values inclusive). This is done using TO_CHAR() function which extracts the month value from the DT field and then compares them using the not and the between operator.

Pattern Matching

The use of the LIKE predicate

The comparison operators discussed so far have compared one value, exactly to one other value. Such precision may not always be desired or necessary. For this purpose Oracle provides the **LIKE** predicate.

The **LIKE** predicate allows comparison of one string value with another string value, which is not identical. This is achieved by using wildcard characters. Two wildcard characters that are available are:

For character data types:

- % allows to match any string of any length (including zero length)
- _ allows to match on a single character

Example:

List the customers whose names begin with the letters 'Ch'.

Synopsis:

Tables:	CUST_MSTR
Columns:	FNAME, LNAME, DOB_INC
Technique:	**Operators:** LIKE, **Clauses:** WHERE, **Others:** ALIAS

Solution:

```
SELECT FNAME, LNAME, DOB_INC "BIRTHDATE", OCCUP FROM CUST_MSTR
        WHERE FNAME LIKE 'Ch%';
```

Output:

FNAME	LNAME	Birthday	OCCUP
Chriselle	Bayross	29-OCT-82	Service
Chhaya	Bankar	06-OCT-76	Service

Explanation:

In the above example, all those records where the value held in the field FNAME begins with **Ch** are displayed. The **%** indicates that any number of characters can follow the letters **Ch**.

Example:

List the customers whose names have the second character as **a** or **s**.

Synopsis:

Tables:	CUST_MSTR
Columns:	FNAME, LNAME, DOB_INC
Technique:	**Operators:** LIKE, **Clauses:** WHERE, **Others:** ALIAS

Solution:

```
SELECT FNAME, LNAME, DOB_INC "Birthday", OCCUP FROM CUST_MSTR
```

WHERE FNAME **LIKE** '_a%' **OR** FNAME **LIKE** '_s%';

Output:

FNAME	LNAME	Birthday	OCCUP
Mamta	Muzumdar	28-AUG-75	Service
Ashwini	Joshi	20-NOV-78	Business
Hansel	Colaco	01-JAN-82	Service
Ashwini	Apte	19-APR-79	Service
Namita	Kanade	10-JUN-78	Self Employed

Explanation:

In the above example, all those records where the value held in the field FNAME contains the second character as **a** or **s** are displayed. The **_a** and **_s** indicates that only one character can precede the character a or s. The **%** indicates that any number of characters can follow the letters **Ch**.

Example:

List the customers whose names begin with the letters **Iv** and it is a four letter word.

Synopsis:

Tables:	CUST_MSTR
Columns:	FNAME, LNAME, DOB_INC
Technique:	**Operators:** LIKE, **Clauses:** WHERE, **Others:** ALIAS

Solution:

SELECT FNAME, LNAME, DOB_INC "Birthday", OCCUP **FROM** CUST_MSTR
WHERE FNAME **LIKE** 'Iv__'; **(i.e. two underscore characters)**

Output:

FNAME	LNAME	Birthday	OCCUP
Ivan	Bayross	25-JUN-52	Self Employed

Explanation:

In the above example, all those records where the value held in the field FNAME begins with **Iv** are displayed. The __ **(i.e. two underscore characters)** indicates that only two characters can follow the letters **Iv**. This means the whole word will only be four characters.

The IN and NOT IN predicates:

The arithmetic operator **(=)** compares a single value to another single value. In case a value needs to be compared to a list of values then the **IN** predicate is used. The IN predicate helps reduce the need to use multiple OR conditions

Example:

List the customer details of the customers named Hansel, Mamta, Namita and Aruna.

Synopsis:

Tables:	CUST_MSTR
Columns:	FNAME, LNAME, DOB_INC
Technique:	**Operators:** IN, **Clauses:** WHERE, **Others:** ALIAS

Solution:

```
SELECT FNAME, LNAME, DOB_INC "birthday", OCCUP FROM CUST_MSTR
    WHERE FNAME IN('Hansel', 'Mamta', 'Namita', 'Aruna');
```

Output:

FNAME	LNAME	Birthday	OCCUP
Mamta	Muzumdar	28-AUG-75	Service
Hansel	Colaco	01-JAN-82	Service
Namita	Kanade	10-JUN-78	Self Employed

Explanation:

The above example, displays all those records where the FNAME field holds any one of the four specified values.

The **NOT IN** predicate is the opposite of the IN predicate. This will select all the rows where values **do not** match the values in the list.

Example:

List the customer details of the customers other then Hansel, Mamta, Namita and Aruna.

Synopsis:

Tables:	CUST_MSTR
Columns:	FNAME, LNAME, DOB_INC
Technique:	**Operators:** NOT, IN, **Clauses:** WHERE, **Others:** ALIAS

Solution:

```
SELECT FNAME, LNAME, DOB_INC "Birthday", OCCUP FROM CUST_MSTR
    WHERE FNAME NOT IN('Hansel', 'Mamta', 'Namita', 'Aruna');
```

Output:

FNAME	LNAME	Birthday	OCCUP
Ivan	Bayross	25-JUN-52	Self Employed
Chriselle	Bayross	29-OCT-82	Service
Chhaya	Bankar	06-OCT-76	Service
Ashwini	Joshi	20-NOV-78	Business
Anil	Dhone	12-OCT-83	Self Employed
Alex	Fernandes	30-SEP-62	Executive
Ashwini	Apte	19-APR-79	Service

7 rows selected.

Explanation:

In the above example by just changing the predicate to **NOT IN** the Select statement will now retrieve all the rows where the FNAME is **not in** the values specified. In other words, information about customers whose names are **not Hansel, Mamta, Namita, Aruna** will be displayed.

The Oracle Table - DUAL

DUAL is a table owned by SYS. SYS owns the data dictionary, and DUAL is part of the data dictionary. Dual is a small Oracle worktable, which consists of only one row and one column, and contains the value **x** in that column. Besides arithmetic calculations, it also supports **date** retrieval and it's formatting.

Often a simple calculation needs to be done, for example, 2*2. The only SQL verb to cause an output to be written to a VDU screen is **SELECT**. However, a SELECT must have a table name in its FROM clause, otherwise the SELECT **fails**.

When an arithmetic exercise is to be performed such as 2*2 or 4/2 and so on, there is no table being referenced, only **numeric literals** are being used.

To facilitate such calculations via a SELECT, Oracle provides a **dummy** table called **DUAL**, against which SELECT statements that are required to manipulate numeric literals can be fired, and appropriate output obtained.

The structure of the dual table if viewed is as follows:

DESC DUAL;

Output:

NAME	Null?	TYPE
Dummy		VARCHAR2(1)

If the dual table is queried for records the output is as follows:

SELECT * FROM DUAL;

Output:

```
D
X
```

Example:

SELECT 2*2 FROM DUAL;

Output:

```
2*2
4
```

SYSDATE

SYSDATE is a pseudo column that contains the current date and time. It requires no arguments when selected from the table DUAL and returns the current date.

Example:

SELECT SYSDATE FROM DUAL;

Output:

```
SYSDATE
01-JUL-04
```

Oracle Functions

Oracle Functions serve the purpose of manipulating data items and returning a result. Functions are also capable of accepting user-supplied variables or constants and operating on them. Such variables or constants are called **arguments**. Any number of arguments (**or** no arguments at all) can be passed to a function in the following format:

Function_Name(argument1, argument2,..)

Oracle Functions can be clubbed together depending upon whether they operate on a single row or a group of rows retrieved from a table. Accordingly, functions can be classified as follows:

Group Functions (Aggregate Functions)

Functions that act on a **set of values** are called **Group Functions**. For example, **SUM**, is a function, which calculates the total set of numbers. A group function returns a single result row for a group of queried rows.

Scalar Functions (Single Row Functions)

Functions that act on **only one value** at a time are called **Scalar Functions**. For example, **LENGTH,** is a function, which calculates the length of one particular string value. A single row function returns one result for every row of a queried table or view.

Single row functions can be further grouped together by the data type of their arguments and return values. For example, **LENGTH** relates to the **String** Data type. Functions can be classified corresponding to different data types as:

String Functions: For String *Data type*

Numeric Functions: For **Number** Data type

Conversion Functions: For **Conversion** of one Data type to another.

Date Functions: For **Date** Data type

Aggregate Functions

AVG: Returns an average value of '**n**', **ignoring** null values in a column.

Syntax:

```
AVG ([<DISTINCT>|<ALL>] <n>)
```

Example:

SELECT AVG(CURBAL) "Average Balance" **FROM** ACCT_MSTR;

Output:

```
Average Balance
           1100
```

Note

In the above SELECT statement, **AVG** function is used to calculate the average balance of all accounts branch wise. The selected column is renamed as **Average Balance** in the output.

MIN: Returns a minimum value of **expr**.

Syntax:

```
MIN([<DISTINCT>|<ALL>]  <expr>)
```

Example:

SELECT MIN(CURBAL) "Minimum Balance" **FROM** ACCT_MSTR;

Output:

```
Minimum Balance
            500
```

COUNT(expr): Returns the number of rows where **expr** is not null.

Syntax:

```
COUNT([<DISTINCT>|<ALL>]  <expr>)
```

Example:

SELECT COUNT(ACCT_NO) "No. Of Accounts" **FROM** ACCT_MSTR;

Output:

```
No. Of Accounts
            10
```

COUNT(*): Returns the number of rows in the table, including duplicates and those with nulls.

Syntax:

```
COUNT(*)
```

Example:

SELECT COUNT(*) "No. Of Records" **FROM** ACCT_MSTR;

Output:

```
No. of Records
            10
```

MAX: Returns the maximum value of **expr**.

Syntax:

```
MAX([<DISTINCT>|<ALL>]  <expr>)
```

Example:

SELECT MAX(CURBAL) "Maximum Balance" **FROM** ACCT_MSTR;

Output:

```
Maximum Balance
            2000
```

SUM: Returns the sum of the values of **'n'**.

Syntax:

```
SUM([<DISTINCT>|<ALL>]  <n>)
```

Example:

SELECT SUM(CURBAL) "Total Balance" **FROM** ACCT_MSTR;

Output:

```
Total Balance
      11000
```

Numeric Functions

ABS: Returns the absolute value of **'n'**.

Syntax:

```
ABS(n)
```

Example:

SELECT ABS(-15) "Absolute" **FROM DUAL;**

Output:

```
Absolute
      15
```

POWER: Returns **m** raised to the **n**th power. **n** must be an integer, else an error is returned.

Syntax:

```
POWER(m,n)
```

Example:

SELECT POWER(3,2) "Raised" **FROM DUAL;**

Output:

```
Raised
      9
```

ROUND: Returns **n**, rounded to **m** places to the right of a decimal point. If **m** is omitted, **n** is rounded to **0** places. **m** can be negative to round off digits to the left of the decimal point. **m** must be an integer.

Syntax:

```
ROUND(n[,m])
```

Example:

SELECT ROUND(15.19,1) "Round" **FROM DUAL;**

Output:

```
Round
15.2
```

SQRT: Returns square root of **n**. If **n**<0, NULL. SQRT returns a **real** result.

Syntax:

```
SQRT(n)
```

Example:

SELECT SQRT(25) "Square Root" **FROM DUAL;**

Output:

```
Square Root
        5
```

EXP: Returns e raised to the **nth** power, where **e = 2.71828183**.

Syntax:

```
EXP(n)
```

Example:

SELECT EXP(5) "Exponent" **FROM DUAL;**

Output:

```
Exponent
148.413159
```

EXTRACT: Returns a value extracted from a date or an interval value. A DATE can be used only to extract YEAR, MONTH, and DAY, while a timestamp with a time zone datatype can be used only to extract TIMEZONE_HOUR and TIMEZONE_MINUTE.

Syntax:

```
EXTRACT( {year | month | day | hour | minute | second |
timezone_hour | timezone_minute | timezone_region |
timezone_abbr}
    FROM { date_value | interval_value } )
```

Example:

SELECT EXTRACT(YEAR FROM DATE '2004-07-02') "Year",
EXTRACT(MONTH FROM SYSDATE) "Month" **FROM DUAL;**

Output:

Year	Month
2004	7

GREATEST: Returns the greatest value in a list of expressions.

Syntax:

```
GREATEST(expr1, expr2, ... expr_n)
```

where, **expr1**, **expr2**, … **expr_n** are expressions that are evaluated by the greatest function.

Example:

SELECT GREATEST(4, 5, 17) "Num", **GREATEST**('4', '5', '17') "Text" **FROM DUAL;**

Output:

Num	Text
17	5

LEAST: Returns the least value in a list of expressions.

Syntax:

```
LEAST(expr1, expr2, ... expr_n)
```

where, **expr1**, **expr2**, … **expr_n** are expressions that are evaluated by the least function.

Example:

SELECT LEAST(4, 5, 17) "Num", **LEAST**('4', '5', '17') "Text" **FROM DUAL;**

Output:

Num	Text
4	17

Note

In the **GREATEST()** and **LEAST()** function if the datatypes of the expressions are different, all expressions will be converted to whatever is datatype of the first expression in the list. If the comparison is based on a character comparison, one character is considered greater than another if it has a higher character set value.

MOD: Returns the remainder of a first number divided by second number passed a parameter. If the second number is zero, the result is the same as the first number.

Syntax:

```
MOD(m, n)
```

Example:

SELECT MOD(15, 7) "Mod1", **MOD**(15.7, 7) "Mod2" **FROM DUAL;**

Output:

Mod1	Mod2
1	1.7

TRUNC: Returns a number truncated to a certain number of decimal places. The decimal place value must be an integer. If this parameter is omitted, the TRUNC function will truncate the number to 0 decimal places.

Syntax:

```
TRUNC(number, [decimal_places])
```

Example:

SELECT TRUNC(125.815, 1) "Trunc1", **TRUNC**(125.815, -2) "Trunc2" **FROM DUAL;**

Output:

Trunc1	Trunc2
125.8	100

FLOOR: Returns the largest integer value that is equal to or less than a number.

Syntax:

```
FLOOR(n)
```

Example:

SELECT FLOOR(24.8) "Flr1", **FLOOR**(13.15) "Flr2" **FROM DUAL;**

Output:

Flr1	Flr2
24	13

CEIL: Returns the smallest integer value that is greater than or equal to a number.

Syntax:

```
CEIL(n)
```

Example:

SELECT CEIL(24.8) "Ceil1",CEIL(13.15) "Ceil2" FROM DUAL;

Output:

Ceil1	Ceil2
25	14

Note

Several other Numeric functions are available in Oracle. These include the following:

- **ACOS(), ASIN(), ATAN(), ATAN2(),**
- **COS(), COSH(), SIN(), SINH(), TAN(), TANH(),**
- **COVAR_POP(), COVAR_SAMP(), VAR_POP(), VAR_SAMP(),**
- **CORR(), SIGN()**

String Functions

LOWER: Returns char, with all letters in lowercase.

Syntax:

```
LOWER(char)
```

Example:

SELECT LOWER('IVAN BAYROSS') "Lower" FROM DUAL;

Output:

```
Lower
ivan bayross
```

INITCAP: Returns a string with the first letter of each word in **upper case.**

Syntax:

```
INITCAP(char)
```

Example:

SELECT INITCAP('IVAN BAYROSS') "Title Case" FROM DUAL;

Output:

```
Title Case
```

```
Ivan Bayross
```

UPPER: Returns char, with all letters forced to uppercase.

Syntax:

```
UPPER (char)
```

Example:

SELECT UPPER('Ms. Carol') "Capitalised" **FROM DUAL;**

Output:

```
Capitalised
MS. CAROL
```

SUBSTR: Returns a portion of characters, beginning at character **m,** and going upto character **n.** If **n** is omitted, the result returned is upto the last character in the string. The first position of char is **1.**

Syntax:

```
SUBSTR(<string>, <start_position>, [<length>])
```

where, **string** is the source string.

start_position is the position for extraction. The first position in the string is always 1.

length is the number of characters to extract.

Example:

SELECT SUBSTR('SECURE',3,4) "Substring" **FROM DUAL;**

Output:

```
Substring
CURE
```

ASCII: Returns the NUMBER code that represents the specified character. If more than one character is entered, the function will return the value for the first character and ignore all of the characters after the first.

Syntax:

```
ASCII(<single_character>)
```

where, **single_character** is the specified character to retrieve the NUMBER code for.

Example:

SELECT ASCII('a') "ASCII1", **ASCII**('A') "ASCII2" **FROM DUAL;**

Output:

ASCII1	ASCII2
97	65

COMPOSE: Returns a Unicode string. It can be a **char, varchar2, nchar, nvarchar2, clob,** or **nclob.**

Syntax:

```
COMPOSE(<single>)
```

Below is a listing of **unistring** values that can be combined with other characters in the compose function.

Unistring Value	Resulting character
UNISTR('\0300')	grave accent (`)
UNISTR('\0301')	acute accent (')
UNISTR('\0302')	circumflex (^)
UNISTR('\0303')	tilde (~)
UNISTR('\0308')	umlaut (¨)

Example:

SELECT COMPOSE('a' || **UNISTR**('\0301')) "Composed" **FROM DUAL;**

Output:

```
Composed
á
```

DECOMPOSE: Accepts a string and returns a Unicode string.

Syntax:

```
DECOMPOSE(<single>)
```

Example

SELECT DECOMPOSE(COMPOSE('a' || **UNISTR**('\0301'))) "Decomposed" **FROM DUAL;**

Output:

```
Decomposed
a´
```

INSTR: Returns the location of a substring in a string.

Syntax:

```
INSTR(<string1>, <string2>, [<start_position>], [<nth_appearance>])
```

where, **string1** is the string to search.

string2 is the substring to search for in string1.

start_position is the position in **string1** where the search will start. If omitted, it defaults to 1. The first position in the string is 1. If the **start_position** is negative, the function counts back **start_position** number of characters from the end of **string1** and then searches towards the beginning of **string1**.

nth_appearance is the **nth** appearance of **string2**. If omiited, it defaults to 1.

Example:

SELECT INSTR('SCT on the net', 't') "Instr1", **INSTR**('SCT on the net', 't', 1, 2) "Instr2" **FROM DUAL;**

Output:

Instr1	Instr2
8	14

TRANSLATE: Replaces a sequence of characters in a string with another set of characters. However, it replaces a single character at a time. For example, it will replace the 1st character in the string_to_replace with the 1st character in the replacement_string. Then it will replace the 2nd character in the string_to_replace with the 2nd character in the replacement_string, and so on.

Syntax:

```
TRANSLATE(<string1>, <string_to_replace>,
<replacement_string>)
```

where, **string1** is the string to replace a sequence of characters with another set of characters.

string_to_replace is the string that will be searched for in string1.

All characters in the **string_to_replace** will be replaced with the corresponding character in the **replacement_string**.

Example:

SELECT TRANSLATE('1sct523', '123', '7a9'**)** "Change" **FROM DUAL;**

Output:

```
Change
7sct5a9
```

LENGTH: Returns the length of a word.

Syntax:

```
LENGTH(word)
```

Example:

SELECT LENGTH('SHARANAM'**)** "Length" **FROM DUAL;**

Output:

```
Length
     8
```

LTRIM: Removes characters from the left of char with initial characters removed upto the first character not in set.

Syntax:

```
LTRIM(char[,set])
```

Example:

SELECT LTRIM('NISHA','N'**)** "LTRIM" **FROM DUAL;**

Output:

```
LTRIM
ISHA
```

RTRIM: Returns char, with final characters removed after the last character not in the set. '**set**' is optional, it defaults to spaces.

Syntax:

```
RTRIM (char,[set])
```

Example:

SELECT RTRIM('SUNILA','A'**)** "RTRIM" **FROM DUAL;**

Output:

```
RTRIM
SUNIL
```

TRIM: Removes all specified characters either from the beginning or the ending of a string.

Syntax:

```
TRIM( [leading | trailing | both [<trim_character> FROM ]
] <string1> )
```

where, **leading** - remove **trim_string** from the front of **string1**.

trailing - remove **trim_string** from the end of **string1**.

both - remove **trim_string** from the front and end of **string1**.

If none of the above option is chosen, the **TRIM** function will remove **trim_string** from both the front and end of **string1**.

trim_character is the character that will be removed from string1. If this parameter is omitted, the trim function will remove all leading and trailing spaces from string1.

string1 is the string to trim.

Example 1:

SELECT TRIM(' Hansel ') "Trim both sides" **FROM DUAL;**

Output:

```
Trim both sides
Hansel
```

Example 2:

SELECT TRIM(LEADING 'x' **FROM** 'xxxHanselxxx') "Remove prefixes" **FROM DUAL;**

Output:

```
Remove prefixes
Hanselxxx
```

Example 3:

SELECT TRIM(BOTH 'x' **FROM** 'xxxHanselxxx') "Remove prefixes N suffixes" **FROM DUAL;**

Output:

```
Remove prefixes N suffixes
Hansel
```

Example 4:

SELECT TRIM(BOTH '1' **FROM** '123Hansel12111') "Remove string" **FROM DUAL;**

Output:

```
Remove string
23Hansel12
```

LPAD: Returns **char1**, left-padded to length **n** with the sequence of characters specified in **char2**. If **char2** is not specified Oracle uses blanks by default.

Syntax:

```
LPAD(char1,n [,char2])
```

Example:

SELECT LPAD('Page 1',10,'*') "LPAD" **FROM DUAL;**

Output:

```
LPAD
****Page1
```

RPAD: Returns **char1**, right-padded to length **n** with the characters specified in **char2**. If **char2** is not specified, Oracle uses blanks by default.

Syntax:

```
RPAD(char1,n[,char2])
```

Example:

SELECT RPAD(FNAME,10,'x') "RPAD Example" **FROM** CUST_MSTR
WHERE FNAME = 'Ivan';

Output:

```
RPAD Example
Ivanxxxxxx
```

VSIZE: Returns the number of bytes in the internal representation of an expression.

Syntax:

```
VSIZE(<expression>)
```

Example:

SELECT VSIZE('SCT on the net') "Size" **FROM DUAL;**

Output:

```
Size
14
```

Conversion Functions

TO_NUMBER: Converts **char**, a **CHARACTER** value expressing a number, to a NUMBER datatype.

Syntax:

```
TO_NUMBER(char)
```

Example:

UPDATE ACCT_MSTR **SET** Curbal = Curbal + **TO_NUMBER(SUBSTR**('$100',2,3));

Output:

```
10 rows updated.
```

Note

 Here, the value 100 will be added to every accounts current balance in the Acct_Mstr table.

TO_CHAR (number conversion): Converts a value of a **NUMBER** datatype to a **character** datatype, using the optional format string. TO_CHAR() accepts a number (**n**) and a numeric format (**fmt**) in which the number has to appear. If **fmt** is omitted, **n** is converted to a char value exactly long enough to hold all significant digits.

Syntax:

```
TO_CHAR  (n[,fmt])
```

Example:

SELECT TO_CHAR(17145, '$099,999') "Char" **FROM DUAL;**

Output:

```
Char
$017,145
```

TO_CHAR (date conversion): Converts a value of a **DATE** datatype to **CHAR** value. TO_CHAR() accepts a date, as well as the format (fmt) in which the date has to appear. **fmt** must be a date format. If **fmt** is omitted, the **date** is converted to a character value using the default date format, **i.e.** "DD-MON-YY".

Syntax:

```
TO_CHAR(date[,fmt])
```

Example:

SELECT TO_CHAR(DT, 'Month DD, YYYY') "New Date Format" **FROM** Trans_Mstr
WHERE Trans_No = 'T1';

Output:

```
New Date Format
January   05, 2003
```

Date Conversion Functions

The DATE data type is used to store date and time information. The DATE data type has special properties associated with it. It stores information about century, year, month, day, hour, minute and second for each date value.

The value in the column of a DATE data type, **is always** stored in a specific **default** format. This default format is 'DD-MON-YY HH:MI:SS'. Hence, when a date has to be inserted in a date field, its value has to be specified in the same format. Additionally, values of DATE columns are always displayed in the **default** format when **retrieved** from the table.

If data from a date column has to be viewed in any other format other than the default format, Oracle provides the **TO_DATE** function that can be used to specify the required format.

The same function can also be used for storing a date into a DATE field in a particular format (other than default). This can be done by specifying the date value, along with the format in which it is to be inserted. The TO_DATE() function also allows part insertion of a DATE value into a column, for example, only the day and month portion of the date value.

To enter the time portion of a date, the TO_DATE function must be used with a **format mask** indicating the time portion.

TO_DATE: Converts a character field to a date field.

Syntax:

```
TO_DATE(char  [,  fmt])
```

Example:

INSERT INTO CUST_MSTR(CUST_NO, FNAME, MNAME, LNAME, DOB_INC)

VALUES('C1', 'Ivan', 'Nelson', 'Bayross',

TO_DATE('25-JUN-1952 10:55 A.M.', 'DD-MON-YY HH:MI A.M.'));

Output:

```
1 rows created.
```

Date Functions

To manipulate and extract values from the date column of a table Oracle provides some date functions. These are discussed below:

ADD_MONTHS: Returns date after adding the number of months specified in the function.

Syntax:

```
ADD_MONTHS(d,n)
```

Example:

SELECT ADD_MONTHS(SYSDATE, 4) "Add Months" FROM DUAL;

Output:

```
Add Months
01-NOV-04
```

LAST_DAY: Returns the last date of the month specified with the function.

Syntax:

LAST_DAY(d)

Example:

SELECT SYSDATE, LAST_DAY(SYSDATE) "LastDay" FROM DUAL;

Output:

SYSDATE	LastDay
01-JUL-04	31-JUL-04

MONTHS_BETWEEN: Returns number of months between **d1** and **d2**.

Syntax:

```
MONTHS_BETWEEN(d1, d2)
```

Example:

SELECT MONTHS_BETWEEN('02-FEB-92', '02-JAN-92') "Months" FROM DUAL;

Output:

```
Months
     1
```

NEXT_DAY: Returns the date of the first weekday named by **char** that is after the date named by **date**. **char** must be a day of the week.

Syntax:

```
NEXT_DAY(date, char)
```

Example:

SELECT NEXT_DAY('06-JULY-02', 'Saturday') "NEXT DAY" **FROM DUAL;**

Output:

```
NEXT_DAY
13-July-02
```

ROUND: Returns a date rounded to a specific unit of measure. If the second parameter is omitted, the **ROUND** function will round the date to the nearest day.

Syntax:

```
ROUND(date, [format])
```

Below are the valid format parameters:

Unit	Format parameters	Rounding Rule
Year	SYYYY, YYYY, YEAR, SYEAR, YYY, YY, Y	Rounds up on July 1st
ISO Year	IYYY, IY, I	
Quarter	Q	Rounds up on the 16th day of the second month of the quarter
Month	MONTH, MON, MM, RM	Rounds up on the 16th day of the month
Week	WW	Same day of the week as the first day of the year
IW	IW	Same day of the week as the first day of the ISO year
W	W	Same day of the week as the first day of the month
Day	DDD, DD, J	
Hour	HH, HH12, HH24	
Start day of the week	DAY, DY, D	
Minute	MI	

Example:

SELECT ROUND(TO_DATE('01-JUL-04'), 'YYYY') "Year" **FROM DUAL;**

Output:

```
Year
01-JAN-05
```

NEW_TIME: Returns the date after converting it from **time zone1** to a date in **time zone2**.

Syntax:

```
NEW_TIME(date, zone1, zone2)
```

Value	Description	Value	Description
AST	Atlantic Standard Time	ADT	Atlantic Daylight Time
BST	Bering Standard Time	BDT	Bering Daylight Time
CST	Central Standard Time	CDT	Central Daylight Time
EST	Eastern Standard Time	EDT	Eastern Daylight Time
GMT	Greenwich Mean Time	HST	Alaska-Hawaii Standard Time
HDT	Alaska-Hawaii Daylight Time	MST	Mountain Standard Time
MDT	Mountain Daylight Time	NST	Newfoundland Standard Time
PST	Pacific Standard Time	PDT	Pacific Daylight Time
YST	Yukon Standard Time	YDT	Yukon Daylight Time

Example:

The following example converts an Atlantic Standard Time into a Mountain Standard Time:

SELECT NEW_TIME(TO_DATE('2004/07/01 01:45', 'yyyy/mm/dd HH24:MI'), 'AST', 'MST') "MST"
FROM DUAL;

Output:

```
MST
30-JUN-04
```

Note

Several other Date function are available in Oracle. These include the following:

- **DbTimeZone(), SessionTimeZone(), SysTimestamp(), Tz_Offset()**

The above Oracle date functions are **just a few** selected from the many date functions that are built into Oracle. These Oracle functions are commonly used in commercial application development.

Manupulating Dates in SQL Using the Date()

A column of data type **Date** is always displayed in a default format, which is **'DD-MON-YY'**. If this default format is not used when entering data into a column of the **date** data type, Oracle **rejects the data** and returns an error message.

If a **date** has to be retrieved or inserted into a table in a format **other than** the default one, Oracle provides the **TO_CHAR** and **TO_DATE** functions to do this.

TO_CHAR

The TO_CHAR function facilitates the retrieval of data in a format different from the default format. It can also extract a part of the date, i.e. the date, month, or the year from the date value and use it for sorting or grouping of data according to the date, month, or year.

Syntax:

```
TO_CHAR(<date value> [,<fmt>])
```

where **date value** stands for the date and **fmt** is the specified format in which date is to be displayed.

Example:

SELECT TO_CHAR(SYSDATE, 'DD-MM-YY') **FROM DUAL;**

Output:

```
TO_CHAR(
01-07-04
```

TO_DATE

TO_DATE converts a **char** value into a **date** value. It allows a user to insert date into a date column in any required format, by specifying the **character** value of the date to be inserted and its format.

Syntax:

```
TO_DATE(<char value>[,<fmt>])
```

where **char value** stands for the value to be inserted in the date column, and **fmt** is a date format in which the 'char value' is specified.

Example:

SELECT TO_DATE ('06/07/02', 'DD/MM/YY') **FROM DUAL;**

Output:

```
TO_DATE('
06-JUL-02
```

Example:

List the transaction details in order of the months for account no. **SB9**. The **Transaction Date** should be displayed in **'DD/MM/YY'** format.

Synopsis:

Tables:	TRANS_MSTR
Columns:	TRANS_NO, ACCT_NO, DT, PARTICULAR, DR_CR, AMT, BALANCE
Technique:	**Functions:** TO_CHAR(), **Clauses:** WHERE, ORDER BY

Solution:

SELECT TRANS_NO, ACCT_NO, TO_CHAR(DT, 'DD/MM/YY') "Transaction Date",
PARTICULAR, DR_CR, AMT, BALANCE
FROM TRANS_MSTR **WHERE** ACCT_NO = 'SB9' **ORDER BY TO_CHAR**(DT, 'MM');

Output:

TRANS_NO	**ACCT_NO**	**Transaction Date**	**PARTICULAR**	**DR_CR**	**AMT**	**BALANCE**
T9	SB9	05/04/03	Initial Payment	D	500	500
T10	SB9	15/04/03	CLR-204907	D	3000	3500
T11	SB9	17/04/03	Self	W	2500	1000
T13	SB9	05/06/03	CLR-204908	D	3000	4000
TRANS_NO	ACCT_NO	Transaction Date	PARTICULAR	DR_CR	AMT	BALANCE
T14	SB9	27/06/03	Self	W	2500	1500

Explanation:

Here the value held in the DT field is formatted using the TO_CHAR() function to display the date in the **DD/MM/YY** format. The ordering of the output data set is based on the "**MONTH**" segment of the data in the column DT. This is done using the **TO_CHAR()** function, in the order by clause, extracting only the "**MONTH**" segment of the DT to sort on.

Example:

Insert the following data in the table CUST_MSTR, wherein the time component has to be stored along with the date in the column DOB_INC.

Cust_No	Fname	Lname	Dob_Inc
C100	Sharanam	Shah	03/Jan/1981 12:23:00

INSERT INTO CUST_MSTR (CUST_NO, FNAME, LNAME, DOB_INC)
VALUES('C100', 'Sharanam', 'Shah', **TO_DATE**('03/Jan/1981 12:23:00', 'DD/MON/YY hh:mi:ss'));

Output:

```
1 row created.
```

Special Date Formats Using TO_CHAR function

Sometimes, the date value is required to be displayed in special formats, for example, instead of 03-JAN-81, displays the date as 03rd of January, 1981. For this, Oracle provides **special attributes**, which can be used in the format specified with the **TO_CHAR** and **TO_DATE** functions. The significance and use of these characters are explained in the examples below.

All three examples below are based on the CUST_MSTR table

The query is as follows:

SELECT CUST_NO, FNAME, LNAME, DOB_INC
FROM CUST_MSTR **WHERE** CUST_NO **LIKE** 'C_';

Output:

CUST_NO	FNAME	LNAME	DOB_INC
C1	Ivan	Bayross	25-JUN-52
C2	Chriselle	Bayross	29-OCT-82
C3	Mamta	Muzumdar	28-AUG-75
C4	Chhaya	Bankar	06-OCT-76
C5	Ashwini	Joshi	20-NOV-78
C6	Hansel	Colaco	01-JAN-82
C7	Anil	Dhone	12-OCT-83
C8	Alex	Fernandes	30-SEP-62
C9	Ashwini	Apte	19-APR-79

9 rows selected.

Variations in this output can be achieved as follows:

❑ *Use of TH in the TO_CHAR() function:*

DDTH places TH, RD, ND for the date (DD), for example, 2ND, 3RD, 08TH etc

SELECT CUST_NO, FNAME, LNAME, **TO_CHAR(**DOB_INC, 'DDTH-MON-YY'**)** "DOB_DDTH"
    FROM CUST_MSTR **WHERE** CUST_NO **LIKE** 'C_';

Output:

CUST_NO	FNAME	LNAME	DOB_DDTH
C1	Ivan	Bayross	25TH-JUN-52
C2	Chriselle	Bayross	29TH-OCT-82
C3	Mamta	Muzumdar	28TH-AUG-75
C4	Chhaya	Bankar	06TH-OCT-76
C5	Ashwini	Joshi	20TH-NOV-78
C6	Hansel	Colaco	01ST-JAN-82
C7	Anil	Dhone	12TH-OCT-83
C8	Alex	Fernandes	30TH-SEP-62
C9	Ashwini	Apte	19TH-APR-79

9 rows selected.

❑ *Use of SP in the TO_CHAR() function*

DDSP indicates that the date (DD) must be displayed by spelling the date such as ONE, TWELVE etc.

SELECT CUST_NO, FNAME, LNAME, **TO_CHAR(**DOB_INC, 'DDSP'**)** "DOB_DDSP"
    FROM CUST_MSTR **WHERE** CUST_NO **LIKE** 'C_';

Output:

CUST_NO	FNAME	LNAME	DOB_DDSP
C1	Ivan	Bayross	TWENTY-FIVE
C2	Chriselle	Bayross	TWENTY-NINE
C3	Mamta	Muzumdar	TWENTY-EIGHT
C4	Chhaya	Bankar	SIX
C5	Ashwini	Joshi	TWENTY
C6	Hansel	Colaco	ONE
C7	Anil	Dhone	TWELVE
C8	Alex	Fernandes	THIRTY
C9	Ashwini	Apte	NINETEEN

9 rows selected.

❑ *Use of 'SPTH' in the to_char function*

SPTH displays the date (DD) with **th** added to the spelling fourteen**th**, twelf**th**.

SELECT CUST_NO, FNAME, LNAME, **TO_CHAR**(DOB_INC, 'DDSPTH') "DOB_DDSPTH"
    FROM CUST_MSTR **WHERE** CUST_NO **LIKE** 'C_';

Output:

CUST_NO	FNAME	LNAME	DOB_DDSPTH
C1	Ivan	Bayross	TWENTY-FIFTH
C2	Chriselle	Bayross	TWENTY-NINTH
C3	Mamta	Muzumdar	TWENTY-EIGHTH
C4	Chhaya	Bankar	SIXTH
C5	Ashwini	Joshi	TWENTIETH
C6	Hansel	Colaco	FIRST
C7	Anil	Dhone	TWELFTH
C8	Alex	Fernandes	THIRTIETH
C9	Ashwini	Apte	NINETEENTH

9 rows selected.

Miscellaneous Functions

UID: This function returns an integer value corresponding to the UserID of the user currently logged in.

Syntax:

```
UID  [INTO  <variable>]
```

where, **variable** will now contain the id number for the user's session.

Example:

SELECT UID FROM DUAL;

Output:

```
UID
61
```

USER: This function returns the **user name** of the user who has logged in. The value returned is in varchar2 data type.

Syntax:

```
USER
```

Example:

SELECT USER FROM DUAL;

Output:

```
    USER
DBA_BANKSYS
```

SYS_CONTEXT: Can be used to retrieve information about Oracle's environment.

Syntax:

```
SYS_CONTEXT (<namespace>, <parameter>, [<length>])
```

where, **namespace** is an Oracle namespace that has already been created. If the **namespace** of **USERENV** is used, attributes describing the current Oracle session can be returned.

parameter is a valid attribute that has been set using the DBMS_SESSION.set_context procedure.

length is the length of the return value in bytes. If this parameter is omitted or if an invalid entry is provided, the **SYS_CONTEXT** function will default to **256 bytes**.

The valid parameters for the namespace called **USERENV** are as follows:

Parameter	Explanation	Return Length
AUDITED_CURSORID	Returns the cursor ID of the SQL that triggered the audit	N/A
AUTHENTICATION_DATA	Authentication data	256
AUTHENTICATION_TYPE	Describes how the user was authenticated. Can be one of the following values: Database, OS, Network, or Proxy	30
BG_JOB_ID	If the session was established by an Oracle background process, this parameter will return the Job ID. Otherwise, it will return NULL.	30
CLIENT_IDENTIFIER	Returns the client identifier (global context)	64
CLIENT_INFO	User session information	64
CURRENT_SCHEMA	Returns the default schema used in the current schema	30
CURRENT_SQL	Returns the SQL that triggered the audit event	64
CURRENT_USER	Name of the current user	30
CURRENT_USERID	Userid of the current user	30
DB_NAME	Name of the database from the DB_NAME initialization parameter	30
ENTRYID	Available auditing entry identifier	30
EXTERNAL_NAME	External of the database user	256
HOST	Name of the host machine from which the client has connected	54
CURRENT_SCHEMAID	Returns the identifier of the default schema used in the current schema	30
DB_DOMAIN	Domain of the database from the DB_DOMAIN initialization parameter	256
FG_JOB_ID	If the session was established by a client foreground process, this parameter will return the Job ID. Otherwise, it will return NULL.	30
GLOBAL_CONTEXT_MEMORY	The number used in the System Global Area by the globally accessed context	N/A

INSTANCE	The identifier number of the current instance	30
IP_ADDRESS	IP address of the machine from which the client has connected	30
ISDBA	Returns TRUE if the user has DBA privileges. Otherwise, it will return FALSE.	30
LANG	The ISO abbreviate for the language	62
LANGUAGE	The language, territory, and character of the session. In the following format: language_territory.characterset	52
NETWORK_PROTOCOL	Network protocol used	256
NLS_CALENDAR	The calendar of the current session	62
NLS_CURRENCY	The currency of the current session	62
NLS_DATE_FORMAT	The date format for the current session	62
NLS_DATE_LANGUAGE	The language used for dates	62
NLS_SORT	BINARY or the linguistic sort basis	62
NLS_TERRITORY	The territory of the current session	62
OS_USER	The OS username for the user logged in	30
PROXY_USER	The name of the user who opened the current session on behalf of SESSION_USER	30
PROXY_USERID	The identifier of the user who opened the current session on behalf of SESSION_USER	30
SESSION_USER	The database user name of the user logged in	30
SESSION_USERID	The database identifier of the user logged in	30
SESSIONID	The identifier of the auditing session	30
TERMINAL	The OS identifier of the current session	10

Example:

SELECT SYS_CONTEXT('USERENV', 'NLS_DATE_FORMAT') "SysContext" **FROM DUAL;**

Output:

```
SysContext
DD-MON-RR
```

USERENV: Can be used to retrieve information about the current Oracle session. Although this function still exists in Oracle for backwards compatibility, it is recommended that the **SYS_CONTEXT** function is used instead.

Syntax:

```
USERENV(<parameter>)
```

where, **parameter** is the value to return from the current Oracle session.

The possible values are:

Parameter	Explanation
CLIENT_INFO	Returns user session information stored using the DBMS_APPLICATION_INFO package
ENTRYID	Available auditing entry identifier
INSTANCE	The identifier number of the current instance
ISDBA	Returns TRUE if the user has DBA privileges. Otherwise, it will return FALSE.
LANG	The ISO abbreviate for the language
LANGUAGE	The language, territory, and character of the session. In the following format:language_territory.characterset
SESSIONID	The identifier of the auditing session
TERMINAL	The OS identifier of the current session

Example:

SELECT USERENV('LANGUAGE') **FROM DUAL;**

Output:

```
USERENV('LANGUAGE')
AMERICAN_AMERICA.WE8MSWIN1252
```

COALESCE: Returns the first non-null expression in the list. If all expressions evaluate to null, then the **coalesce** function will return null.

Syntax:

```
COALESCE(<expr1>, <expr2>, ... <expr_n>)
```

Example:

SELECT COALESCE(FNAME, CUST_NO**) Customers FROM** CUST_MSTR;

The above coalesce statement is equivalent to the following IF-THEN-ELSE statement:

```
IF FNAME IS NOT NULL THEN
    Customers := FNAME;
ELSIF CUST_NO IS NOT NULL THEN
    Customers := CUST_NO;
ELSE
    Customers := NULL;
END IF;
```

Output:

```
CUSTOMERS
Ivan
Chriselle
Mamta
Chhaya
Ashwini
Hansel
```

```
Anil
Alex
Ashwini
Namita
O11
O12
O13
O14
```

Explanation:

In the above example, Oracle will display the first name i.e. the value held in the field FNAME if first name field holds a value. If does not hold a value, then Oracle will move on to the next column in the **COALESCE** function and display the value held in the next column i.e. CUST_NO if it hold a value.

In case the second column also does not hold a value, then Oracle will display null as an output.

Self Review Questions

Fill in the Blanks

1. The Oracle engine will process all rows in a table and display the result only when any of the conditions specified using the _________ operator are satisfied.
2. The ___________ predicate allows for a comparison of one string value with another string value, which is not identical.
3. For character datatypes the __________ sign matches any string.
4. __________ is a small Oracle worktable, which consists of only one row and one column, and contains the value x in that column.
5. Functions that act on a set of values are called as _________ _________.
6. Variables or constants accepting by functions are called __________.
7. The ___________ function returns a string with the first letter of each word in upper case.
8. The _________ function removes characters from the left of char with initial characters removed upto the first character not in set.
9. _________ returns the string passed as a parameter after right padding it to a specified length.
10. The ____________ function converts char, a CHARACTER value expressing a number, to a NUMBER datatype.
11. The ____________ function converts a value of a DATE datatype to CHAR value.
12. The ____________ function returns number of months between two dates.
13. The ________ function returns an integer value corresponding to the UserID of the user currently logged in.

True or False

14. The Oracle engine will process all rows in a table and display the result only when none of the conditions specified using the NOT operator are satisfied.
15. In order to select data that is within a range of values, the IN BETWEEN operator is used.
16. For character datatypes the percent sign matches any single character.
17. COUNT(expr) function returns the number of rows where expr is not null.

18. ROOT function returns square root of a numeric value.
19. The second parameter in the ROUND function specifies the number of digits after the decimal point.
20. The LOWER function returns char, with all letters in lowercase.
21. The UPPER function returns a string with the first letter of each word in upper case.
22. The LENGTH function returns the length of a word.
23. The LTRIM returns char, with final characters removed after the last character not in the set. 'set' is optional, it defaults to spaces.
24. LPAD returns the string passed as a parameter after left padding it to a specified length.
25. The TO_CHAR (date conversion) converts a value of a NUMBER datatype to a character datatype, using the optional format string.
26. The DATE data type is used to store date and time information.
27. The TO_DATE() function also disallows part insertion of a DATE value into a column.
28. The ADD_MONTHS function returns date after adding the number of months specified in the function.
29. The TO-DATE function allows a user to insert date into a date column in any required format, by specifying the character value of the date to be inserted and its format.

Hands On Exercises

Using the tables created previously generate the SQL statements for the operations mentioned below. The tables in user are as follows:

a. Client_Master
b. Product_Master
c. Salesman_Master
d. Sales_Order
e. Sales_Order_Details

1. Perform the following computations on table data:
   a. List the names of all clients having 'a' as the second letter in their names.
   b. List the clients who stay in a city whose First letter is 'M'.
   c. List all clients who stay in 'Bangalore' or 'Mangalore'
   d. List all clients whose BalDue is greater than value 10000.
   e. List all information from the Sales_Order table for orders placed in the month of June.
   f. List the order information for ClientNo 'C00001' and 'C00002'.
   g. List products whose selling price is greater than 500 and less than or equal to 750.
   h. List products whose selling price is more than 500. Calculate a new selling price as, original selling price * .15. Rename the new column in the output of the above query as new_price.
   i. List the names, city and state of clients who are not in the state of 'Maharashtra'.
   j. Count the total number of orders.
   k. Calculate the average price of all the products.

l. Determine the maximum and minimum product prices. Rename the output as max_price and min_price respectively.

m. Count the number of products having price less than or equal to 500.

n. List all the products whose QtyOnHand is less than reorder level.

2. Exercise on Date Manipulation:

a. List the order number and day on which clients placed their order.

b. List the month (in alphabets) and date when the orders must be delivered.

c. List the OrderDate in the format 'DD-Month-YY'. e.g. 12-February-02.

d. List the date, 15 days after today's date.

13

Interactive SQL Part - IV

Grouping Data From Tables in SQL

The Concept Of Grouping

Till now, all SQL **SELECT** statements have:

- Retrieved all the rows from tables
- Retrieved selected rows from tables with the use of a **WHERE** clause, which returns only those rows that meet the conditions specified
- Retrieved unique rows from the table, with the use of **DISTINCT** clause
- Retrieved rows in the sorted order **i.e.** ascending or descending order, as specified, with the use of **ORDER BY** clause.

Other than the above clauses, there are two other clauses, which facilitate selective retrieval of rows. These are the **GROUP BY** and **HAVING** clauses. These are parallel to the **order by** and **where** clause, except that they act on record sets, and **not on** individual records.

Group by Clause

The **GROUP BY** clause is another section of the **select** statement. This optional clause tells Oracle to group rows based on distinct values that exist for **specified columns.** The GROUP BY clause creates a data set, containing several sets of records **grouped together** based on a condition.

Syntax:

```
SELECT <ColumnName1>, <ColumnName2>, <ColumnNameN>,
    AGGREGATE_FUNCTION (<Expression>)
    FROM TableName WHERE <Condition>
        GROUP BY <ColumnName1>, <ColumnName2>, <ColumnNameN>;
```

Example:

Find out how many employees are there in each branch.

Synopsis:

Tables:	EMP_MSTR
Columns:	BRANCH_NO, EMP_NO
Technique:	**Functions:** COUNT(), **Clauses:** GROUP BY, **Others:** Alias

Solution:

SELECT BRANCH_NO "Branch No.", **COUNT**(EMP_NO) "No. Of Employees"
FROM EMP_MSTR **GROUP BY** BRANCH_NO;

Output:

Branch No.	No. Of Employees
B1	2
B2	2
B3	2
B4	2
B6	2

Explanation:

In the above example, the data that has to be retrieved is available in the **EMP_MSTR** table. Since the **number of employees** per branch is required, the records need to be **grouped** on the basis of field **BRANCH_NO** and then the **COUNT()** function must be applied to the field **EMP_NO** which calculates the number of employees on a per branch basis.

Example:

Find out the total number of (Current and Savings Bank) accounts verified by each employee.

Synopsis:

Tables:	ACCT_MSTR
Columns:	VERI_EMP_NO, ACCT_NO
Technique:	**Functions:** COUNT(), **Clauses:** GROUP BY, **Others:** Alias

Solution:

SELECT VERI_EMP_NO "Emp. No.", **COUNT**(ACCT_NO) "No. Of A/Cs Verified"
FROM ACCT_MSTR **GROUP BY** VERI_EMP_NO;

Output:

Emp. No.	No. Of A/Cs Verified
E1	7
E4	8

Explanation:

In the above example, the data that has to be retrieved is available in the **ACCT_MSTR** table. Since the **number of accounts verified** per employee is required, the records need to be **grouped** on the basis of field **VERI_EMP_NO** and then the **COUNT()** function is applied to the field **ACCT_NO** which calculates the number of accounts verified per employee.

Example:

Find out the total number of accounts segregated on the basis of account type per branch.

Synopsis:

Tables:	ACCT_MSTR
Columns:	BRANCH_NO, TYPE, ACCT_NO
Technique:	**Functions:** COUNT(), **Clauses:** GROUP BY, **Others:** Alias

Solution:

SELECT BRANCH_NO "Branch No.", TYPE "A/C Type", **COUNT(**ACCT_NO) "No. Of A/Cs"
FROM ACCT_MSTR **GROUP BY** BRANCH_NO, TYPE;

Output:

Branch No.	A/C Type	No. Of A/Cs
B1	CA	1
B1	SB	2
B2	CA	2
B2	SB	1
B3	SB	2
B4	SB	2
B5	CA	2
B6	CA	1
B6	SB	2

9 rows selected.

Explanation:

In the above example, the data that has to be retrieved is available in the **ACCT_MSTR** table. Since the **number of accounts** based on the account type per branch is required, the records need to be **grouped** on the basis of two fields i.e. **BRANCH_NO** and within it **TYPE** and then the **COUNT()** function is applied to the field **ACCT_NO** which calculates the number of accounts of a particular type in a particular branch.

HAVING Clause

The **HAVING** clause can be used in conjunction with the **GROUP BY** clause. **HAVING** imposes a condition on the **GROUP BY** clause, which further filters the groups created by the **GROUP BY** clause. Each column specification specified in the **HAVING** clause must occur within a statistical function or must occur in the list of columns named in the **GROUP BY** clause.

Example:

Find out the customers having more than one account in the bank.

Synopsis:

Tables:	ACCT_FD_CUST_DTLS
Columns:	CUST_NO, ACCT_FD_NO
Technique:	**Functions:** COUNT(), **Operators:** LIKE, OR, **Clauses:** GROUP BY ... HAVING, **Others:** Alias

Solution:

```
SELECT CUST_NO, COUNT(ACCT_FD_NO) "No. Of A/Cs Held" FROM ACCT_FD_CUST_DTLS
    WHERE ACCT_FD_NO LIKE 'CA%' OR ACCT_FD_NO LIKE 'SB%'
        GROUP BY CUST_NO HAVING COUNT(ACCT_FD_NO)>1;
```

Output:

CUST_NO	No. Of A/Cs Held
C1	4
C10	2
C2	2
C3	3
C4	6
C5	3
C9	2

7 rows selected.

Explanation:

In the above example, the data that has to be retrieved is available in the Accounts-F.D.-Customers link table (i.e. **ACCT_FD_CUST_DTLS**). This table holds data related to accounts as well as fixed deposits. Since, only the data related to accounts is required there is a need to **filter** the data. This is done using the LIKE operator, which will only retrieve the records related to Current and Savings Bank Accounts (i.e. value held in the **ACCT_FD_NO** field beginning with **CA** or **SB**). The **Count()** function is applied to the field **ACCT_FD_NO** which will now hold only the filtered values i.e. either **CA__** or **SB__**. This filtered information is then **grouped** on the basis of Customer Number (i.e. the **CUST_NO** field). Since only those customers who hold more than one account are to be retrieved, the **HAVING** clause is used to finally filter the data to retain only those records where the value calculated using the **COUNT()** function is **greater than 1**.

Example:

Find out the number of accounts opened at a branch after **03rd January 2003, only** if the number of accounts opened after 03rd January 2003 **exceeds 1**.

Synopsis:

Tables:	ACCT_MSTR
Columns:	BRANCH_NO, ACCT_NO
Technique:	**Functions:** COUNT(),TO_CHAR(), **Operators:** LIKE, **Clauses:** GROUP BY ... HAVING, **Others:** Alias

Solution:

```
SELECT BRANCH_NO, COUNT(ACCT_NO) "No. Of A/Cs Activated"
    FROM ACCT_MSTR WHERE TO_CHAR(OPNDT, 'DD-MM-YYYY') > '03-01-2003'
        GROUP BY BRANCH_NO HAVING COUNT(ACCT_NO) > 1;
```

Output:

BRANCH_NO	No. Of A/Cs Activated
B1	3
B2	3
B3	2
B4	2
B5	2
B6	3

6 rows selected.

Explanation:

In the above example, the data that has to be retrieved is available in the ACCT_MSTR table. This table holds data related to all the accounts that have been activated under a particular branch. Since, only the data related to a particular date is required there is a need to **filter** the data. This is done using the **WHERE** clause and the **TO_CHAR()** function which converts the date to character format and makes it available for comparison with the date **'3rd January 2003'**, which will only retrieve the accounts opened after that date. (i.e. value held in the **OPNDT** field is greater than **'3rd January 2003'**). The **Count()** function is applied to the field **ACCT_NO** which will now hold only the filtered values i.e. those accounts which were activated after **'3rd January 2003'**. This filtered information is then **grouped** on the basis of Branch Number (i.e. the **BRANCH_NO** field). Since only those records that have the count of account numbers **more than 1** are to be retrieved, the **HAVING** clause is used to finally filter the data to retain only those records where the value calculated using the **COUNT()** function is **greater than 1**.

Rules For Group By and Having Clause

- Columns listed in the select statement have to be listed in the GROUP BY clause
- Columns listed in the GROUP BY clause need not be listed in the SELECT statement
- Only group functions can be used in the HAVING clause
- The group functions listed in the having clause need not be listed in the SELECT statement

Determining Whether Values Are Unique

The **HAVING** clause can be used to find unique values in situations to which DISTINCT does not apply.

The **DISTINCT** clause eliminates duplicates, but does not show which values actually were duplicated in the original data. The **HAVING** clause can identify which values were unique or non-unique.

Example:

List customer numbers, which are associated with only one account (or Fixed deposit) in the bank. (Unique Entries Only)

Synopsis:

Tables:	ACCT_FD_CUST_DTLS
Columns:	CUST_NO, ACCT_FD_NO
Technique:	**Functions:** COUNT(), **Clauses:** GROUP BY ... HAVING, **Others:** Alias

Solution:

SELECT CUST_NO, **COUNT**(ACCT_FD_NO) "No. Of A/Cs Or FDs Held"
    FROM ACCT_FD_CUST_DTLS **GROUP BY** CUST_NO **HAVING COUNT**(ACCT_FD_NO) = 1;

Output:

CUST_NO	No. Of A/Cs Or FDs Held
C7	1

Explanation:

In the above example, the data that has to be retrieved is available in the Accounts-F.D.-Customers link table (i.e. **ACCT_FD_CUST_DTLS**). This table holds data related to accounts as wells as fixed deposits. The **Count()** function is applied to the field **ACCT_FD_NO** which will hold the number of accounts or fixed deposits held by a particular customer. This information is then **grouped** on the basis of Customer Number (i.e. the **CUST_NO** field). Since only those customers who hold **only one** account or fixed deposit are to be retrieved, the **HAVING** clause is used to finally filter the data to retain only those records where the value calculated using the **COUNT()** function is **equal to 1**.

Example:

List the customer numbers associated with **more** than one account (or Fixed deposits). (Non-Unique Entries)

Synopsis:

Tables:	ACCT_FD_CUST_DTLS
Columns:	CUST_NO, ACCT_FD_NO
Technique:	**Functions:** COUNT(), **Clauses:** GROUP BY ... HAVING, **Others:** Alias

Solution:

SELECT CUST_NO, **COUNT**(ACCT_FD_NO) "No. Of A/Cs or FDs Held"
    FROM ACCT_FD_CUST_DTLS **GROUP BY** CUST_NO **HAVING COUNT**(ACCT_FD_NO) > 1;

Output:

CUST_NO	No. Of A/Cs Or FDs Held
C1	4
C10	3
C2	3
C3	4
C4	7
C5	6
C6	2
C8	2
C9	3

9 rows selected.

Explanation:

In the above example, the data that has to be retrieved is available in the Accounts-F.D.-Customers link table (i.e. **ACCT_FD_CUST_DTLS**).

This table holds data related to accounts as wells as fixed deposits. The **COUNT()** function is applied to the field **ACCT_FD_NO** which will hold the number of accounts or fixed deposits held by a particular customer. This information is then **grouped** on the basis of Customer Number (i.e. the **CUST_NO** field). Since only those customers who hold more than one account or fixed deposit are to be retrieved, the **HAVING** clause is used to finally filter the data to retain only those records where the value calculated using the **COUNT()** function is **greater than 1**.

Group By Using The ROLLUP Operator

The ROLLUP operator is used to calculate aggregates and super aggregates for expressions within a GROUP BY statement. Report writers usually use this operator to extract statistics and/or summaries from a result set.

Example:

Create a report on the fixed deposits accounts available in the bank, providing the **amount** and the **due amount** per fixed deposit (per FD_NO in the FD_DTLS table) and per slot (per FD_SER_NO in the FD_MSTR table) of fixed deposit held by the customer.

Synopsis:

Tables:	FD_MSTR
Columns:	FD_SER_NO, FD_NO, AMT, DUEAMT
Technique:	**Functions:** SUM(), **Operators:** ROLLUP(), **Clauses:** GROUP BY

Solution:

SELECT FD_SER_NO, FD_NO, **SUM(AMT), SUM(DUEAMT)**

FROM FD_DTLS **GROUP BY ROLLUP** (FD_SER_NO, FD_NO);

Output:

FD_SER_NO	FD_NO	AMT	DUEAMT
FS1	F1	15000	16050
FS1	F2	5000	5350
FS1		20000	21400
FS2	F3	10000	10802.19
FS2	F4	10000	10802.19
FS2		20000	21604.38
FS3	F5	2000	2060.16
FS3		2000	2060.16
FS4	F6	5000	5902.47
FS4		5000	5902.47
FS5	F7	15000	16203.3
FS5		15000	16203.3
		62000	***67170.31***

13 rows selected.

Explanation:

In the above example, the data that has to be retrieved is available in the **FD_DTLS** table. This table holds data related to individual fixed deposits (i.e. per FD_NO) **held within a fixed deposit slot (i.e. per FD_SER_NO in the FD_MSTR table).** The **SUM()** function is applied on the field **AMT** and **DUEAMT** which will hold the sum of amount and due amount per FD with a slot. This information is then **grouped** on the basis of **FD_SER_NO** and **FD_NO** using the **ROLLUP** operator.

The **ROLLUP** operator is used to display the amount and due amount per fixed deposit (i.e. per FD_NO) and the total amount and total due amount per fixed deposit slot (i.e. per FD_SER_NO).

The ROLLUP operator first calculates the standard aggregate values for the groups specified in the group by clause (**SUM** of **AMT** and **DUEAMT** for each fixed deposit i.e. per **FD_NO**) then creates higher level subtotals, moving from right to left through the list of grouping columns (**SUM** of **AMT** and **DUEAMT** for each fixed deposit slot i.e. per **FD_SER_NO**).

Grouping By Using The CUBE Operator

The **CUBE** operator can be applied to all aggregates functions like **AVG()**, **SUM()**, **MAX()**, **MIN()** and **COUNT()** within a **GROUP BY** statement. This operator is usually used by, report writers to extract cross-tabular reports from a result set. CUBE produces subtotals for all possible combinations of groupings specified in the **GROUP BY** clause along with a grand total as against the ROLLUP operator which produces only a fraction of possible subtotal combinations.

Example:

Find out the Balance of the account holders on per account and per branch basis along with a grand total.

Synopsis:

Tables:	ACCT_MSTR
Columns:	BRANCH_NO, ACCT_NO, CURBAL
Technique:	**Functions:** SUM(), **Operators:** CUBE(), **Clauses:** GROUP BY

Solution:

```
SELECT BRANCH_NO, ACCT_NO, SUM(CURBAL) FROM ACCT_MSTR
        GROUP BY CUBE (BRANCH_NO, ACCT_NO);
```

Output:

BRANCH_NO	ACCT_NO	SUM(CURBAL)
		88500
	CA2	3000
	CA4	12000
	CA7	22000
	SB1	500
	SB3	500
	SB5	500
	SB6	500
	SB8	500
	SB9	500
	CA10	32000
	CA12	5000
	CA14	10000
	SB11	500
	SB13	500
	SB15	500
B1		23000
B1	CA7	22000
B1	SB1	500
B1	SB11	500
B2		8500
B2	CA2	3000
B2	SB8	500
B2	CA12	5000
B3		1000

B3	SB3	500
B3	SB13	500
B4		1000
B4	SB6	500
B4	SB9	500
B5		22000
B5	CA4	12000
B5	CA14	10000
B6		33000
B6	SB5	500
B6	CA10	32000
B6	SB15	500

37 rows selected.

Explanation:

In the above example, the data that has to be retrieved is available in the **ACCT_MSTR** table. This table holds data related to savings and current accounts held by the bank. The **SUM()** function is applied to the field **CURBAL** which will hold the sum of balance per account. This information is then **grouped** on the basis of **BRANCH_NO** and **ACCT_NO** using the **CUBE** operator.

The balance of every account within a branch is displayed using the group by clause. The **CUBE** operator is used to display the **balance per account**, the **total balance** held in **each branch** of the bank, the total balance per account irrespective of the branch and the total balance held in all branches of the bank irrespective of the accounts held.

The **CUBE** operator first calculates the standard aggregate values for the groups specified in the group by clause (Sum of **CURBAL** for each account) then creates higher level subtotals, moving from right to left through the list of grouping columns (Sum of **CURBAL** for each branch). Additionally the **CUBE** operator displays the total balance per account irrespective of branch and the total balance of all the branches irrespective of the accounts held.

Subqueries

A **subquery** is a form of an SQL statement that appears inside another SQL statement. It is also termed as **nested query**. The statement containing a subquery is called a **parent** statement. The parent statement uses the rows (i.e. the result set) returned by the subquery.

It can be used for the following:

- ❑ To insert records in a target table
- ❑ To create tables and insert records in the table created
- ❑ To update records in a target table
- ❑ To create views
- ❑ To provide values for **conditions** in WHERE, HAVING, IN and so on used with SELECT, UPDATE, and DELETE statements

Example:

Retrieve the address of a customer named 'Ivan Bayross'.

Synopsis:

Tables:	CUST_MSTR, ADDR_DTLS
Columns:	CUST_MSTR: CUST_NO, FNAME, LNAMEADDR_DTLS: CODE_NO, ADDR1, ADDR2, CITY, STATE, PINCODE
Technique:	**Sub-Queries, Operators:** IN, **Clauses:** WHERE, **Other:** Concat (||)

Solution:

```
SELECT CODE_NO "Cust. No.", ADDR1 || ' ' || ADDR2 || ' ' || CITY || ', ' || STATE || ', ' || PINCODE
"Address"
    FROM ADDR_DTLS WHERE CODE_NO IN(SELECT CUST_NO FROM CUST_MSTR
        WHERE FNAME = 'Ivan' AND LNAME = 'Bayross');
```

Output:

Cust. No.	**Address**
C1	F-12, Diamond Palace, West Avenue, North Avenue, Santacruz (West), Mumbai, Maharashtra, 400056

Explanation:

In the above example, the data that has to be retrieved is available in the **ADDR_DTLS** table, which holds the address for customer named **'Ivan Bayross'**. This table holds all the address details identified by the customer number i.e. **CODE_NO**. However, the **ADDR_DTLS** table does not contain the field, which holds the customer's name, which is required to make a comparison.

The Customers Name is available in the **CUST_MSTR** table where each customer is identified by a unique number (i.e. **CUST_NO**). So it is required to access the table **CUST_MSTR** and retrieve the **CUST_NO** based on which a comparison can be made with the **CODE_NO** field held in the table **ADDR_DTLS**.

Using the **CUST_NO** retrieved from the **CUST_MSTR** table, it is now possible to retrieve the address(es) from the **ADDR_DTLS** table by finding a matching value in the **CODE_NO** field in that table.

This type of processing can be done elegantly using a subquery.

In the above solution the sub-query is as follows:

```
SELECT CUST_NO FROM CUST_MSTR
    WHERE FNAME = 'IVAN' AND LNAME = 'BAYROSS';
```

The target table will be as follows:

Output:

```
CUST_NO
C1
```

The outer sub-query output will simplify the solution as shown below:

```
SELECT CODE_NO "Cust. No.", ADDR1 || ' ' || ADDR2 || ' ' || CITY || ', ' || STATE || ', ' || PINCODE
"Address" FROM ADDR_DTLS WHERE CODE_NO IN('C1');
```

When the above SQL query is executed the resulting output is equivalent to the desired output of the SQL query using two levels of Sub-queries.

Example:

Find the customers who do not have bank branches in their vicinity.

Synopsis:

Tables:	CUST_MSTR, ADDR_DTLS
Columns:	CUST_MSTR: CUST_NO, FNAME, LNAMEADDR_DTLS: CODE_NO, PINCODE
Technique:	**Sub-Queries, Operators:** IN, **Clauses:** WHERE, **Other:** Concat (||)

Solution:

```
SELECT (FNAME || ' ' || LNAME) "Customer" FROM CUST_MSTR
        WHERE CUST_NO IN(SELECT CODE_NO FROM ADDR_DTLS
                WHERE CODE_NO LIKE 'C%' AND PINCODE NOT IN(SELECT PINCODE
                FROM ADDR_DTLS WHERE CODE_NO LIKE 'B%'));
```

Output:

```
Customer
Ivan Bayross
Namita Kanade
Chriselle Bayross
Mamta Muzumdar
Chhaya Bankar
Ashwini Joshi
Hansel Colaco
Anil Dhone
Alex Fernandes
Ashwini Apte
10 rows selected.
```

Explanation:

In the above example, the data that has to be retrieved is available in the **CUST_MSTR**, which holds the Customer details. The **CUST_MSTR** table will only provide all the customer names but to retrieve only those customers who do not have any bank branches in their vicinity, one more tables will be involved that is **ADDR_DTLS** table, which holds the branch as well as customer addresses. This table holds all the address details identified by the branch / customer number i.e. **CODE_NO**. This table will help comparing the value held in the **PINCODE** field belonging to the customer addresses with the ones of bank branch addresses.

To understand the solution the query mentioned above needs to be simplified. The inner most sub-queries should be handled first and then proceeded outwards.

The **first step** is to identify the vicinities in which the branches are located. This is done by extracting the **PINCODE** from the address details table (i.e. **ADDR_DTLS**) for all entries belonging to the branches. The SQL query for this will be as follows:

SELECT PINCODE **FROM** ADDR_DTLS **WHERE** CODE_NO **LIKE** 'B%'

The target table will be as follows:

Output:

```
PINCODE
400057
400058
400004
400045
400078
110004
6 rows selected.
```

The resulting output simplifies the solution as shown below:

SELECT (FNAME || ' ' || LNAME) "Customer" **FROM** CUST_MSTR
WHERE CUST_NO **IN(SELECT** CODE_NO **FROM** ADDR_DTLS
WHERE CODE_NO **LIKE** 'C%' **AND** PINCODE **NOT IN**('400057', '400058',
'400004', '400045', '400078', '110004'));

The **second step** is to identify the customers who are not resident near a branch. To do this the customer numbers (i.e. **CODE_NO**) have to be retrieved from the Address details table (i.e. **ADDR_DTLS**). The SQL query for this will be as follows:

SELECT CODE_NO **FROM** ADDR_DTLS **WHERE** CODE_NO **LIKE** 'C%'
AND PINCODE **NOT IN**('400057', '400058', '400004', '400045', '400078', '110004')

The target table will be as follows:

Output:

```
CODE_NO
C1
C2
C3
C4
C5
C6
C7
C8
C9
C10
10 rows selected.
```

The outer sub-query output will simplify the solution as shown below:

SELECT (FName || ' ' || LName) "Customer" **FROM** Cust_Mstr
WHERE Cust_No **IN**('C1', 'C2', 'C3', 'C4', 'C5', 'C6', 'C7', 'C8', 'C9', 'C10');

When the above SQL query is executed the resulting output is equivalent to the desired output of the SQL query using two levels of Sub-queries.

Example:

List customers holding Fixed Deposits in the bank of amount more than 5,000.

Synopsis:

Tables:	CUST_MSTR, ACCT_FD_CUST_DTLS, FD_DTLS
Columns:	CUST_MSTR: CUST_NO, FNAME, LNAMEACCT_FD_CUST_DTLS: CUST_NO, ACCT_FD_NOFD_DTLS: FD_SER_NO, AMT
Technique:	**Sub-Queries, Operators:** IN() **Clauses:** WHERE, **Other:** Concat (||)

Solution:

SELECT (FNAME || ' ' || LNAME) "Customer" **FROM** CUST_MSTR **WHERE** CUST_NO
IN(SELECT CUST_NO **FROM** ACCT_FD_CUST_DTLS **WHERE** ACCT_FD_NO
IN(SELECT FD_SER_NO **FROM** FD_DTLS **WHERE** AMT > 5000));

Output:

```
Customer
Chriselle Bayross
Mamta Muzumdar
Chhaya Bankar
Ashwini Joshi
```

Explanation:

In the above example, the data that has to be retrieved is available in the **CUST_MSTR**, which holds the Customer details. The **CUST_MSTR** table will only provide all the customer names but to retrieve only those customers who hold fixed deposits of amount exceeding Rs.5000, two more tables will be involved that is **ACCT_FD_DTLS** and **FD_DTLS.** The **ACCT_FD_DTLS** acts as a link between the **CUST_MSTR** and **FD_DTLS** table and hold details identified by the **ACCT_FD_NO** field. The **FD_DTLS** table actually hold all the details related to the fixed deposits held by the customers in a bank identified by the **FD_SER_NO** field.

To understand the solution the query mentioned above needs to be simplified. The inner most sub-queries should be handled first and then proceeded outwards.

The **first step** is to identify the fixed deposits of amount more than 5000. This is done by extracting the value held by the **FD_SER_NO** field from the fixed deposits details table (i.e. **FD_DTLS**). The SQL query for this will be as follows:

SELECT FD_SER_NO **FROM** FD_DTLS **WHERE** AMT > 5000

The target table will be as follows:

Output:

```
FD_SER_NO
FS1
FS2
FS2
FS5
```

The data retrieved by the above **SELECT** statement will be passed to the outer sub-query as in:

```
SELECT (FNAME || ' ' || LNAME) "Customer" FROM CUST_MSTR WHERE CUST_NO
    IN(SELECT CUST_NO FROM ACCT_FD_CUST_DTLS WHERE ACCT_FD_NO
        IN('FS1', 'FS2', 'FS2', 'FS5'));
```

The **second step** is to identify the customer numbers who hold these FDs i.e. ('FS1', 'FS2', 'FS2', 'FS5'). To do this the customer numbers (i.e. **CUST_NO**) have to be retrieved from the Account FD details table (i.e. **ACCT_FD_DTLS**). The SQL query for this will be as follows:

```
SELECT CUST_NO FROM ACCT_FD_CUST_DTLS
    WHERE ACCT_FD_NO IN('FS1', 'FS2', 'FS2', 'FS5')
```

The target table will be as follows:

Output:

```
CUST_NO
C2
C3
C4
C5
C5
C5
6 rows selected.
```

The outer sub-query output will simplify the solution as shown below:

```
SELECT (FNAME || ' ' || LNAME) "Customer" FROM CUST_MSTR
    WHERE CUST_NO IN('C2', 'C3', 'C4', 'C5', 'C5', 'C5');
```

When the above SQL query is executed the resulting output is equivalent to the desired output of the SQL query using two levels of Sub-queries.

Using Sub-query In The FROM Clause

A subquery can be used in the **FROM** clause of the **SELECT** statement. The concept of using a subquery in the **FROM** clause of the **SELECT** statement is called an **inline view**. A subquery in the **FROM** clause of the **SELECT** statement defines a **data source** from that particular **Select** statement.

Example:

List accounts along with the current balance, the branch to which it belongs and the average balance of that branch, having a balance more than the average balance of the branch, to which the account belongs.

Synopsis:

Tables:	ACCT_MSTR
Columns:	ACCT_NO, CURBAL, BRANCH_NO
Technique:	**Sub-Queries, Join, Functions:** AVG(), **Clauses:** WHERE, GROUP BY

Solution:

```
SELECT A.ACCT_NO, A.CURBAL, A.BRANCH_NO, B.AVGBAL
    FROM ACCT_MSTR A, (SELECT BRANCH_NO, AVG(CURBAL) AVGBAL FROM ACCT_MSTR
        GROUP BY BRANCH_NO) B
```

WHERE A.BRANCH_NO = **B**.BRANCH_NO **AND A**.CURBAL > **B**.AVGBAL;

Output:

ACCT_NO	CURBAL	BRANCH_NO	AVGBAL
CA7	22000	B1	7666.67
CA2	3000	B2	2833.33
CA12	5000	B2	2833.33
CA4	12000	B5	11000
CA10	32000	B6	11000

Explanation:

In the above example, the data that has to be retrieved is available in the **ACCT_MSTR**, which holds the accounts held by the bank. The output requirements are the **account number**, the **current balance** of that account, the **branch** to which that account belongs and the **average balance** of that branch.The first three requirements can be retrieved from the **ACCT_MSTR** table.

The average of the balance on a per branch basis requires use of another select query and a group by clause. This means a sub query can be used, but in this case, the sub query will return a value, which will be a part of the output. Since this query is going to act as a source of data it is placed in the **FROM** clause of the outer query and given an alias **B**. Finally to produce the output a join is used to get the data on the basis of the outer query i.e. (**A**.BRANCH_NO = **B**.BRANCH_NO) followed by a **WHERE** clause which actually filters the data before producing the output.

To understand the solution the query mentioned above needs to be simplified. The inner most sub-queries should be handled first and then continued outwards.

The **first step** is to identify the branch numbers and their average balance. This is done by, extracting the value held by the **BRANCH_NO** field from the **BRANCH_MSTR** table. The SQL query for this will be as follows:

SELECT BRANCH_NO, **AVG**(CURBAL) AVGBAL **FROM** ACCT_MSTR
GROUP BY BRANCH_NO

The target table will be as follows:

Output:

BRANCH_NO	AVGBAL
B1	7666.67
B2	2833.33
B3	500
B4	500
B5	11000
B6	11000

6 rows selected.

The **second step** is to associate the data returned by the inner query with the outer. This is done by binding the Sub-query with the **FROM** clause and using join. The output shown above is treated as an individual (temporary) table. This new table is referred as **B**, the alias name specified in the main **SELECT** statement.

The **third step** is to filter the data to output only those records where the current balance is more then the average balance of the branch to which they belong This is done using a **WHERE** clause i.e.(**A.**CURBAL > **B.**AVGBAL)

Finally, the **SELECT** statement is executed as a JOIN i.e. (**WHERE A.**BRANCH_NO = **B.**BRANCH_NO). This is explained in greater depth later in this chapter.

Using Correlated Sub-queries

A sub-query becomes correlated when the subquery references a column from a table in the parent query. A correlated subquery is evaluated once for each row processed by the parent statement, which can be any of SELECT, DELETE or UPDATE.

A correlated subquery is one way of reading every row in a table and comparing values in each row against related data. It is used whenever a subquery must return a different result for each candidate row considered by the parent query.

Example:

List accounts along with the current balance and the branch to which it belongs, having a balance more than the average balance of the branch, to which the account belongs.

Synopsis:

Tables:	ACCT_MSTR
Columns:	ACCT_NO, CURBAL, BRANCH_NO
Technique:	**Sub-Queries, Join, Functions:** AVG(), **Clauses:** WHERE

Solution:

```
SELECT ACCT_NO, CURBAL, BRANCH_NO FROM ACCT_MSTR A
    WHERE CURBAL > (SELECT AVG(CURBAL) FROM ACCT_MSTR
        WHERE BRANCH_NO = A.BRANCH_NO);
```

Output:

ACCT_NO	CURBAL	BRANCH_NO
CA2	3000	B2
CA4	12000	B5
CA7	22000	B1
CA10	32000	B6
CA12	5000	B2

Explanation:

In the above example, the data that has to be retrieved is available in the **ACCT_MSTR**, which holds the accounts held by the bank. The output requirements are the **account number**, the **current balance** of that account, the **branch** to which that account belongs. These requirements can be retrieved from the **ACCT_MSTR** table. However the average balance on a per branch basis requires use of another select query.

This means a correlated sub query can be used. The correlated sub-query specifically computes the average balance of each branch. Since both the queries (i.e. Outer and the Inner) use **ACCT_MSTR** table an alias is allotted to the table in the outer query. It is because of this **alias** the inner query is able to distinguish the inner column from the outer column.

Using Multi Column Subquery

Example:

Find out all the customers having same names as the employees.

Synopsis:

Tables:	CUST_MSTR, EMP_MSTR
Columns:	CUST_MSTR: FNAME, LNAME, EMP_MSTR: FNAME, LNAME
Technique:	**Sub_Queries, Operators:** IN, **Clauses:** WHERE

Solution:

```
SELECT FNAME, LNAME FROM CUST_MSTR
    WHERE (FNAME, LNAME) IN(SELECT FNAME, LNAME FROM EMP_MSTR);
```

Output:

FNAME	LNAME
Ivan	Bayross

Explanation:

In the above example, each row of the outer query is compared to the values from the inner query (Multi Row and Multi Column). This means that the values of **FNAME** and **LNAME** from the outer query are compared with **FNAME** and **LNAME** values retrieved by the inner query.

Using Sub-query in CASE Expressions

Example:

List the account numbers along with the transaction date, transaction type **i.e.** whether it's a deposit or withdrawal, the mode of transaction **i.e.** Cash or Cheque and the amount of transaction.

Synopsis:

Tables:	TRANS_MSTR, TRANS_DTLS
Columns:	TRANS_MSTR: ACCT_NO, DT, DR_CR, TRANS_NO, AMT, TRANS_DTLS: TRANS_NO
Technique:	**Operators:** IN, **Clauses:** CASE WHEN ... THEN

Solution:

SELECT ACCT_NO, DT, DR_CR, (**CASE WHEN** TRANS_NO **IN(SELECT** TRANS_NO **FROM** TRANS_DTLS) **THEN** 'Cheque' **ELSE** 'Cash' **END)** "Mode", AMT **FROM** TRANS_MSTR;

Output:

ACCT_NO	DT	DR_CR	Mode	AMT
SB1	05-NOV-03	D	Cash	500
CA2	10-NOV-03	D	Cash	2000
CA2	13-NOV-03	D	Cash	3000
SB3	22-NOV-03	D	Cash	500
CA2	10-DEC-03	W	Cash	2000
CA4	05-DEC-03	D	Cheque	2000
SB5	15-DEC-03	D	Cheque	500
SB6	27-DEC-03	D	Cash	500
CA7	14-JAN-04	D	Cheque	2000
SB8	29-JAN-04	D	Cash	500
SB9	05-FEB-04	D	Cash	500
SB9	15-FEB-04	D	Cheque	3000
SB9	17-FEB-04	W	Cash	2500
CA10	19-FEB-04	D	Cheque	2000
SB9	05-APR-04	D	Cheque	3000
SB9	27-APR-04	W	Cash	2500
SB11	05-MAR-04	D	Cash	500
CA12	10-MAR-04	D	Cash	2000
SB13	22-MAR-04	D	Cash	500
CA14	05-APR-04	D	Cheque	2000

20 rows selected.

Explanation:

In the above example, the inner query will return a value (i.e. if a record exists in the **TRANS_DTLS** table then the transaction is done via a Cheque). Based on the value returned the outer query will display the Transaction mode as either Cheque or Cash.

Using Subquery In An ORDER BY clause

Example:

List the employees of the bank in the order of the branch names at which they are employed.

Synopsis:

Tables:	EMP_MSTR,
Columns:	EMP_MSTR: EMP_NO, FNAME, LNAME, DEPT
Technique:	**Clauses:** ORDER BY **Others:** Alias, Concat (||)

Solution:

```
SELECT EMP_NO, (FNAME || ' ' || LNAME) "Name", DEPT FROM EMP_MSTR E
    ORDER BY (SELECT NAME FROM BRANCH_MSTR B
        WHERE E.BRANCH_NO = B.BRANCH_NO);
```

Output:

EMP_NO	Name	DEPT
E2	Amit Desai	Loans And Financing
E9	Vikram Randive	Marketing
E3	Maya Joshi	Client Servicing
E8	Seema Apte	Client Servicing
E6	Sonal Khan	Administration
E10	Anjali Pathak	Administration
E5	Mandhar Dalvi	Marketing
E7	Anil Kambli	Marketing
E1	Ivan Bayross	Administration
E4	Peter Joseph	Loans And Financing

10 rows selected.

Explanation:

In the above example, the output needs to be ordered on the basis of branch names in which they are employed. The Data required is available in the **EMP_MSTR** table. Since the output needs to be ordered on the basis of branch names, which are available in the **BRANCH_MSTR** table, there is a need of a separate query, which can return the branch names from the **BRANCH_MSTR** table to which the employees belong. Based on the values returned from the inner query the output produced by the outer query will be ordered. This is done, by placing the inner query, in the **ORDER BY** clause and further correlated with the outer query on the basis of the **BRANCH_NO** being **the common field** in the tables **EMP_MSTR** and **BRANCH_MSTR**.

Using EXISTS / NOT EXISTS Operator

The **EXISTS** operator is usually used with correlated subqueries. This operator enables to test whether a value retrieved by the outer query exists in the results set of the values retrieved by the inner query. If the subquery returns at least one row, the operator returns **TRUE**. If the value does not exist, it returns **FALSE**.

The **EXISTS** operator ensures that the search in the inner query terminates when at least one match is found.

Similarly, the **NOT EXISTS** operator enables to test whether a value retrieved by the outer query is not a part of the result set of the values retrieved by the inner query.

Example:

List employees who have verified at least one account.

Synopsis:

Tables:	EMP_MSTR, ACCT_MSTR
Columns:	EMP_MSTR: EMP_NO, FNAME, LNAME, ACCT_MSTR: VERI_EMP_NO
Technique:	**Operators:** EXISTS(), **Clauses:** WHERE

Solution:

```
SELECT EMP_NO, FNAME, LNAME FROM EMP_MSTR E WHERE EXISTS(SELECT 'SCT'
    FROM ACCT_MSTR WHERE VERI_EMP_NO = E.EMP_NO);
```

Output:

EMP_NO	FNAME	LNAME
E1	Ivan	Bayross
E4	Peter	Joseph

Explanation:

In the above example, the inner query is correlated with the outer query via the **EMP_NO** field. As soon as the search in the inner query retrieves at least one match, i.e. **VERI_EMP_NO = E.EMP_NO**, the search is terminated. This means that the inner query stops it's processing and the outer query then produces the output. In the case of the inner query there is no need to return a specific value, hence a constant **'SCT'** is used instead. This is useful in terms of performance as it will be faster to select a constant than a column.

Example:

List those branches, which don't have employees yet.

Synopsis:

Tables:	BRANCH_MSTR, EMP_MSTR
Columns:	BRANCH_MSTR: BRANCH_NO, NAME, LNAME, EMP_MSTR: BRANCH_NO
Technique:	**Operators:** NOT, EXISTS(); **Clauses:** WHERE; **Others:** Alias

Solution:

```
SELECT BRANCH_NO, NAME FROM BRANCH_MSTR B WHERE NOT EXISTS(SELECT 'SCT'
    FROM EMP_MSTR WHERE BRANCH_NO = B.BRANCH_NO);
```

Output:

BRANCH_NO	NAME
B5	Borivali

Explanation:

In the above example, the inner query is correlated with the outer query via the **BRANCH_NO** field. Since the **NOT EXISTS** operator is used, if the inner query retrieves no rows at all i.e. the condition **BRANCH_NO = B.BRANCH_NO** fails, the outer query produces the output. This means after the inner query stops it's processing, the outer query sends the output based on the operator used. In the case of the inner query there is no need to return a specific value, hence a constant **'SCT'** is used instead. This is useful in terms of performance as it will be faster to select a constant than a column.

JOINS

Joining Multiple Tables (Equi Joins)

Sometimes it is necessary to work with multiple tables as though they were a single entity. Then a single SQL sentence can manipulate data from all the tables. **Joins** are used to achieve this. Tables are joined on columns that have the same **data type** and **data width** in the tables.

Tables in a database can be related to each other with keys. A primary key is a column with a unique value for each row. The purpose is to bind data together, across tables, without repeating all of the data in every table.

The JOIN operator specifies how to relate tables in the query.

Types of JOIN:

- ❑ INNER
- ❑ OUTER (LEFT, RIGHT, FULL)
- ❑ CROSS

INNER JOIN: Inner joins are also known as **Equi Joins**. There are the most common joins used in SQL*Plus. They are know as equi joins because the where statement generally compares two columns from two tables with the equivalence operator =. This type of join is by far the most commonly used. In fact, many systems use this type as the default join. This type of join can be used in situations where selecting only those rows that have values in common in the columns specified in the ON clause, is required. In short, the INNER JOIN returns all rows from both tables where there is a match

OUTER JOIN: Outer joins are similar to inner joins, but give a bit more flexibility when selecting data from related tables. This type of join can be used in situations where it is desired, to select all rows from the table on the left (or right, or both) regardless of whether the other table has values in common and (usually) enter NULL where data is missing.

CROSS JOIN: A cross join returns what's known as a Cartesian product. This means that the join combines every row from the left table with every row in the right table. As can be imagined, sometimes this join produces a mess, but under the right circumstances, it can be very useful. This type of join can be used in situations where it is desired, to select all possible combinations of rows and columns from both tables. This kind of join is usually not preferred as it may run for a very long time and produce a huge result set that may not be useful.

Syntax:

```
ANSI-style
SELECT <ColumnName1>, <ColumnName2>, <ColumnName N> FROM <TableName1>
    INNER JOIN <TableName2>
        ON <TableName1>.<ColumnName1>=<TableName2>.<ColumnName2>
            WHERE <Condition>
        ORDER BY <ColumnName1>, <ColumnName2>, <ColumnNameN>
Theta-style
SELECT <ColumnName1>, <ColumnName2>, <ColumnNameN>
    FROM <TableName1>,<TableName2>
    WHERE <TableName1>.<ColumnName1> = <TableName2>.<ColumnName2>
        AND <Condition>
        ORDER BY <ColumnName1>, <ColumnName2>, <ColumnNameN>
```

In the above syntax:

- ❑ **ColumnName1** in **TableName1** is usually that table's **Primary Key**
- ❑ **ColumnName2** in **TableName2** is a **Foreign Key** in that table
- ❑ **ColumnName1** and **ColumnName2** must have the **same Data Type** and for certain data types, the same size

Inner Join

Example:

List the employee details along with branch names to which they belong.

Synopsis:

<table>
<tr><td>Tables:</td><td>EMP_MSTR, BRANCH_MSTR</td></tr>
<tr><td>Columns:</td><td>EMP_MSTR: EMP_NO, FNAME, MNAME, LNAME, DEPT, DESIG, BRANCH_NOBRANCH_MSTR: NAME, BRANCH_NO</td></tr>
<tr><td>Technique:</td><td>Join: INNER JOIN ... ON, SIMPLE, Clauses: WHERE, Others: Concat (||)</td></tr>
</table>

Solution 1 (Ansi-style):

SELECT E.EMP_NO, (**E.**FNAME || ‘ ’ || **E.**MNAME || ‘ ’ || **E.**LNAME) “Name”, **B.**NAME “Branch”, **E.**DEPT, **E.**DESIG

FROM EMP_MSTR **E INNER JOIN** BRANCH_MSTR **B**

ON B.BRANCH_NO = **E.**BRANCH_NO;

Solution 2 (Theta-style):

SELECT E.EMP_NO, (**E.**FNAME || ‘ ’ || **E.**MNAME || ‘ ’ || **E.**LNAME) “Name”, **B.**NAME “Branch”, **E.**DEPT, **E.**DESIG

FROM EMP_MSTR **E**, BRANCH_MSTR **B WHERE B.**BRANCH_NO = **E.**BRANCH_NO;

Output:

EMP_NO	Name	Branch	DEPT	DESIG
E1	Ivan Nelson Bayross	Vile Parle (HO)	Administration	Managing Director
E4	Peter Iyer Joseph	Vile Parle (HO)	Loans And Financing	Clerk
E2	Amit Desai	Andheri	Loans And Financing	Finance Manager
E9	Vikram Vilas Randive	Andheri	Marketing	Sales Asst.
E3	Maya Mahima Joshi	Churchgate	Client Servicing	Sales Manager
E8	Seema P. Apte	Churchgate	Client Servicing	Clerk
E5	Mandhar Dilip Dalvi	Mahim	Marketing	Marketing Manager
E7	Anil Ashutosh Kambli	Mahim	Marketing	Sales Asst.
E6	Sonal Abdul Khan	Darya Ganj	Administration	Admin. Executive
E10	Anjali Sameer Pathak	Darya Ganj	Administration	HR Manager

10 rows selected.

Explanation:

In the above example, in the **EMP_MSTR** table, the **EMP_NO** column is the **primary key**, meaning that no two rows can have the same **EMP_NO**. The **EMP_NO** distinguishes two persons even if they have the same name. The data required in this example is available in two tables i.e. **EMP_MSTR** and **BRANCH_MSTR**. This is because branch names are going to be a part of the output but are not available in the **EMP_MSTR** table.

Notice that:

- The **EMP_NO** column is the primary key of the **EMP_MSTR** table
- The **BRANCH_NO** column is the primary key of the **BRANCH_MSTR** table
- The **BRANCH_NO** column in the **EMP_MSTR** table is used to refer to the branches in the **BRANCH_MSTR** table without using their names

On the basis of the reference available in the **EMP_MSTR** table i.e. the **BRANCH_NO** field its possible to link to the **BRANCH_MSTR** table and fetch the Branch names for display. This is easily possible with the use of inner join based on the condition (**B.**BRANCH_NO = **E.**BRANCH_NO).

Note

If the columnnames on which the **join** is to be specified are the same in each table reference the columns using **TableName.ColumnName**.

Example:

List the customers along with their multiple address details.

Synopsis:

Tables:	CUST_MSTR, ADDR_DTLS
Columns:	CUST_MSTR: CUST_NO, FNAME, MNAME, LNAMEADDR_DTLS: CODE_NO, ADDR1, ADDR2, CITY, STATE, PINCODE
Technique:	**Join:** INNER JOIN ... ON, SIMPLE, **Clauses:** WHERE **Others:** Concat (‖)

Solution 1 (Ansi-style):

```
SELECT C.CUST_NO, (C.FNAME || ' ' || C.MNAME || ' ' || C.LNAME) "Customer", (A.ADDR1 || ' ' ||
A.ADDR2 || ' ' || A.CITY || ', ' || A.STATE || ', ' || A.PINCODE) "Address"
    FROM CUST_MSTR C INNER JOIN ADDR_DTLS A ON C.CUST_NO = A.CODE_NO
    WHERE C.CUST_NO LIKE 'C%' ORDER BY C.CUST_NO;
```

Solution 2 (Theta-style):

```
SELECT C.CUST_NO, (C.FNAME || ' ' || C.MNAME || ' ' || C.LNAME) "Customer", (A.ADDR1 || ' ' ||
A.ADDR2 || ' ' || A.CITY || ', ' || A.STATE || ', ' || A.PINCODE) "Address"
    FROM CUST_MSTR C, ADDR_DTLS A WHERE C.CUST_NO = A.CODE_NO
        AND C.CUST_NO LIKE 'C%' ORDER BY C.CUST_NO;
```

Output:

CUST_NO	Customer	Address
C1	Ivan Nelson Bayross	F-12, Diamond Palace, West Avenue, North Avenue, Santacruz (West), Mumbai, Maharashtra, 400056
C10	Namita S. Kanade	B-10, Makarand Society, Cadal Road, Mahim, Mumbai, Maharashtra, 400016
C2	Chriselle Ivan Bayross	F-12, Silver Stream, Santacruz (East), Mumbai, Maharashtra, 400056
C3	Mamta Arvind Muzumdar	Magesh Prasad, Saraswati Baug, Jogeshwari(E), Mumbai, Maharashtra, 400060
C4	Chhaya Sudhakar Bankar	4, Sampada, Kataria Road, Mahim, Mumbai, Maharashtra, 400016
C5	Ashwini Dilip Joshi	104, Vikram Apts. Bhagat Lane, Shivaji Park, Mahim, Mumbai, Maharashtra, 400016
C6	Hansel I. Colaco	12, Radha Kunj, N.C Kelkar Road, Dadar, Mumbai, Maharashtra, 400028
C6	Hansel I. Colaco	203/A, Prachi Apmt., Andheri (East), Mumbai, Maharashtra, 400058
C7	Anil Arun Dhone	A/14, Shanti Society, Mogal Lane, Mahim, Mumbai, Maharashtra, 400016
C8	Alex Austin Fernandes	5, Vagdevi, Senapati Bapat Rd., Dadar, Mumbai, Maharashtra, 400016
C9	Ashwini Shankar Apte	A-10 Nutan Vaishali, Shivaji Park, Mahim, Mumbai, Maharashtra, 400016

11 rows selected.

Explanation:

In the above example, the data required is available in two tables i.e. CUST_MSTR and ADDR_DTLS. Both the tables are linked via a common field. This is because the data is spread across the tables based on a normalization schema.

Notice that:

- ❑ The **CUST_NO** column is the primary key of the **CUST_MSTR** table
- ❑ The **ADDR_DTLS** is a table that holds the address details of customers.

  In **ADDR_DTLS** table:

  - **ADDR_NO** column is the primary key of that table.
  - **CODE_NO** column is used to refer to the customers in the **CUST_MSTR** table via the **CUST_NO** column

To retrieve the data required, both the tables have to linked on the basis of a common column using joins as follows:

- ❑ **C.**CUST_NO = **A.**CODE_NO

This means the CUST_NO field of CUST_MSTR table is joined with CODE_NO field of the ADDR_DTLS table

Now since both the tables are linked using a join, data can be retrieved as if they are all in one table using the alias as:

C.CUST_NO, (**C.**FNAME || ' ' || **C.**MNAME || ' ' || **C.**LNAME) "Customer", (**A.**ADDR1 || ' ' || **A.**ADDR2 || ' ' || **A.**CITY || ', ' || **A.**STATE || ', ' || **A.**PINCODE) "Address"

Finally the output is ordered on the basis of Customers.

Example:

List the Customers along with the account details associated with them.

Synopsis:

Tables:	CUST_MSTR, ACCT_MSTR, ACCT_FD_CUST_DTLS, BRANCH_MSTR
Columns:	ACCT_FD_CUST_DTLS: ACCT_FD_NO, CUST_NOCUST_MSTR: CUST_NO, FNAME, MNAME, LNAMEACCT_MSTR: ACCT_NO, BRANCH_NO, CURBALBRANCH_MSTR: NAME, BRANCH_NO
Technique:	**Join:** INNER JOIN ... ON, **Operators:** ||**Join:** SIMPLE, **Operators:** ||, **Clauses:** WHERE

Solution 1 (Ansi-style):

```
SELECT C.CUST_NO, (C.FNAME || ' ' || C.MNAME || ' ' || C.LNAME) "Customer", A.ACCT_NO, B.NAME
"Branch", A.CURBAL
    FROM CUST_MSTR C INNER JOIN ACCT_FD_CUST_DTLS L
        ON C.CUST_NO = L.CUST_NO INNER JOIN ACCT_MSTR A
        ON L.ACCT_FD_NO = A.ACCT_NO INNER JOIN BRANCH_MSTR B
        ON A.BRANCH_NO = B.BRANCH_NO ORDER BY C.CUST_NO, A.ACCT_NO;
```

Solution 2 (Theta-style):

SELECT C.CUST_NO, (**C.**FNAME || ' ' || **C.**MNAME || ' ' || **C.**LNAME) "Customer", **A.**ACCT_NO, **B.**NAME "Branch", **A.**CURBAL
FROM CUST_MSTR **C**, ACCT_FD_CUST_DTLS **L**, ACCT_MSTR **A**, BRANCH_MSTR **B**
WHERE C.CUST_NO = **L.**CUST_NO **AND L.**ACCT_FD_NO = **A.**ACCT_NO
AND A.BRANCH_NO = **B.**BRANCH_NO **ORDER BY C.**CUST_NO, **A.**ACCT_NO;

Output:

CUST_NO	Customer	ACCT_NO	Branch	CURBAL
C1	Ivan Nelson Bayross	SB1	Vile Parle (HO)	500
C1	Ivan Nelson Bayross	SB11	Vile Parle (HO)	500
C1	Ivan Nelson Bayross	SB15	Darya Ganj	500
C1	Ivan Nelson Bayross	SB5	Darya Ganj	500
C10	Namita S. Kanade	CA10	Darya Ganj	32000
C10	Namita S. Kanade	SB9	Mahim	500
C2	Chriselle Ivan Bayross	CA12	Andheri	5000
C2	Chriselle Ivan Bayross	CA2	Andheri	3000
C3	Mamta Arvind Muzumdar	CA12	Andheri	5000
C3	Mamta Arvind Muzumdar	CA2	Andheri	3000
C3	Mamta Arvind Muzumdar	SB9	Mahim	500
C4	Chhaya Sudhakar Bankar	CA14	Borivali	10000
C4	Chhaya Sudhakar Bankar	CA4	Borivali	12000
C4	Chhaya Sudhakar Bankar	SB13	Churchgate	500
C4	Chhaya Sudhakar Bankar	SB15	Darya Ganj	500
C4	Chhaya Sudhakar Bankar	SB3	Churchgate	500
C4	Chhaya Sudhakar Bankar	SB5	Darya Ganj	500
C5	Ashwini Dilip Joshi	CA14	Borivali	10000
C5	Ashwini Dilip Joshi	CA4	Borivali	12000
C5	Ashwini Dilip Joshi	SB6	Mahim	500
C6	Hansel I. Colaco	CA7	Vile Parle (HO)	22000
C7	Anil Arun Dhone	SB6	Mahim	500
C8	Alex Austin Fernandes	CA7	Vile Parle (HO)	22000
C9	Ashwini Shankar Apte	CA10	Darya Ganj	32000
C9	Ashwini Shankar Apte	SB8	Andheri	500

25 rows selected.

Explanation:

In the above example, the data required is available in four tables i.e. CUST_MSTR, ACCT_FD_CUST_DTLS, ACCT_MSTR and BRANCH_MSTR. All the four tables are linked via some field in the other table. This is because the data is spread across the tables based on a normalization scheme.

Notice that:

- The **CUST_NO** column is the primary key of the **CUST_MSTR** table
- The **ACCT_NO** column is the primary key of the **ACCT_MSTR** table
- The **ACCT_FD_CUST_DTLS** is a link table between the CUST_MSTR and the ACCT_MSTR table. This table holds information related to which accounts belong to which customers.

  In **ACCT_FD_CUST_DTLS** table:
  - The **ACCT_FD_NO** column is used to refer to the accounts in the **ACCT_MSTR** table via the **ACCT_NO** column
  - The **CUST_NO** column is used to refer to the customers in the **CUST_MSTR** table via the **CUST_NO** column
- The **BRANCH_NO** column is the primary key of the **BRANCH_MSTR** table

To retrieve the data required, all the four tables have to linked on the basis of common columns using joins as follows:

- **C.**CUST_NO = **L.**CUST_NO

  This means the CUST_NO field of CUST_MSTR table is joined with CUST_NO field of the ACCT_FD_CUST_DTLS table
- **L.**ACCT_FD_NO = **A.**ACCT_NO

  This means the ACCT_FD_NO field of ACCT_FD_CUST_DTLS table is joined with ACCT_NO field of the ACCT_MSTR table
- **A.**BRANCH_NO = **B.**BRANCH_NO

  This means the BRANCH_NO field of ACCT_MSTR table is joined with BRANCH_NO field of the BRANCH_MSTR table

Now since the tables are linked using a join, data can be retrieved as if they are all in one table using the alias as:

C.CUST_NO, (**C.**FNAME || ' ' || **C.**MNAME || ' ' || **C.**LNAME) "Customer", **A.**ACCT_NO, **B.**NAME "Branch", **A.**CURBAL

Finally the output is ordered on the basis of Customers and within Customer, Account numbers.

Adding An Additional WHERE Clause Condition

Example:

List the employee details of only those employees who belong to the Administration department along with branch names to which they belong.

Synopsis:

Tables:	EMP_MSTR, BRANCH_MSTR
Columns:	EMP_MSTR: EMP_NO, FNAME, MNAME, LNAME, DEPT, DESIG, BRANCH_NOBRANCH_MSTR: NAME, BRANCH_NO
Technique:	**Join:** INNER JOIN ... ON, **Clauses:** WHERE, **Others:** Alias

Solution:

SELECT E.EMP_NO, (**E.**FNAME || ' ' || **E.**MNAME || ' ' || **E.**LNAME) "Name", **B.**NAME "Branch", **E.**DEPT, **E.**DESIG
FROM EMP_MSTR **E INNER JOIN** BRANCH_MSTR **B ON B.**BRANCH_NO = **E.**BRANCH_NO
WHERE E.DEPT = 'Administration';

Output:

EMP_NO	Name	Branch	DEPT	DESIG
E1	Ivan Nelson Bayross	Vile Parle (HO)	Administration	Managing Director
E6	Sonal Abdul Khan	Darya Ganj	Administration	Admin. Executive
E10	Anjali Sameer Pathak	Darya Ganj	Administration	HR Manager

Explanation:

In the above example, the data required is available in two tables i.e. EMP_MSTR and BRANCH_MSTR. Both the tables are linked via a common field. This is because the data is spread across the tables based on a normalization schema.

Notice that:

- ❑ The **EMP_NO** column is the primary key of the **EMP_MSTR** table
- ❑ The **BRANCH_NO** column is used to refer to the branch names in the BRANCH_MSTR table via the BRANCH_NO column
- ❑ The **BRANCH_NO** column is the primary key of the **BRANCH_MSTR** table

To retrieve the data required, both the tables have to linked on the basis of a common column using joins as follows:

- ❑ **B.**BRANCH_NO = **E.**BRANCH_NO

  This means the BRANCH_NO field of BRANCH_MSTR table is joined with BRANCH_NO field of the EMP_MSTR table

Now since both the tables are linked using a join, data can be retrieved as if they are all in one table using the alias as:

E.EMP_NO, (**E.**FNAME || ' ' || **E.**MNAME || ' ' || **E.**LNAME) "Name", **B.**NAME "Branch", **E.**DEPT, **E.**DESIG

Finally the output is filtered to display only those employees belonging to the administration department using WHERE clause as:

E.DEPT = 'Administration'

Outer Join

Example:

List the employee details along with the contact details (if any) Using Left Outer Join.

Synopsis:

Tables:	EMP_MSTR, CNTC_DTLS
Columns:	EMP_MSTR: EMP_NO, FNAME, LNAME, DEPTCNTC_DTLS: CODE_NO, CNTC_TYPE, CNTC_DATA
Technique:	**Join:** LEFT JOIN ... ON, **Clauses:** WHERE **Others:** Alias, Concat (||)

Solution 1 (Ansi-style):

```
SELECT (E.FNAME || ' ' || E.LNAME) "Name", E.DEPT, C.CNTC_TYPE, C.CNTC_DATA
    FROM EMP_MSTR E LEFT JOIN CNTC_DTLS C ON E.EMP_NO = C.CODE_NO;
```

Solution 2 (Theta-style):

```
SELECT (E.FNAME || ' ' || E.LNAME) "Name", E.DEPT, C.CNTC_TYPE, C.CNTC_DATA
    FROM EMP_MSTR E, CNTC_DTLS C WHERE E.EMP_NO = C.CODE_NO(+);
```

Output:

Name	DEPT	CNTC_TYPE	CNTC_DATA
Amit Desai	Loans And Financing	R	28883779
Maya Joshi	Client Servicing	R	28377634
Peter Joseph	Loans And Financing	R	26323560
Mandhar Dalvi	Marketing	R	26793231
Sonal Khan	Administration	R	28085654
Anil Kambli	Marketing	R	24442342
Seema Apte	Client Servicing	R	24365672
Vikram Randive	Marketing	R	24327349
Anjali Pathak	Administration	R	24302579
Ivan Bayross	**Administration**		

10 rows selected.

Explanation:

In the above example, the data required is all the employee details along with their contact details **if any**. This means all the employee details have to be listed even though their corresponding contact information is not present. The data is available in two tables i.e. EMP_MSTR and CNTC_DTLS

In such a situation, the **LEFT JOIN** can be used which returns all the rows from the first table (i.e. EMP_MSTR), even if there are no matches in the second table (CNTC_DTLS). This means, if there are employees in **EMP_MSTR** that do not have any contacts in **CNTC_DTLS**, those rows will also be listed. Notice the keyword **LEFT JOIN** in the first solution (Ansi-style) and the **(+)** in the second solution (Theta-style). This indicates that all rows from the first table i.e. EMP_MSTR will be displayed even though there exists no matching rows in the second table i.e. CNTC_DTLS.

Notice that:

- ❑ The **EMP_NO** column is the primary key of the **EMP_MSTR** table
- ❑ The **CNTC_DTLS** is a table that holds the contact details of employees.

  In **CNTC_DTLS** table:

  - **ADDR_NO** column is used to refer to the addresses in the ADDR_DTLS table via the ADDR_NO column.
  - **CODE_NO** column is used to refer to the employees in the **EMP_MSTR** table via the **EMP_NO** column

To retrieve the data required, both the tables have to linked on the basis of common columns using joins as follows:

- ❑ **E.EMP_NO = C.CODE_NO**
  This means the EMP_NO field of EMP_MSTR table is joined with CODE_NO field of the CNTC_DTLS table

Example:

List the employee details along with the contact details (if any) Using Right Outer Join.

Synopsis:

Tables:	EMP_MSTR, CNTC_DTLS
Columns:	EMP_MSTR: EMP_NO, FNAME, LNAME, DEPTCNTC_DTLS: CODE_NO, CNTC_TYPE, CNTC_DATA
Technique:	**Join:** RIGHT JOIN ... ON, **Clauses:** WHERE

Solution 1 (Ansi-style):

```
SELECT E.FNAME, E.LNAME, E.DEPT, C.CNTC_TYPE, C.CNTC_DATA FROM CNTC_DTLS C
    RIGHT JOIN EMP_MSTR E ON C.CODE_NO = E.EMP_NO;
```

Solution 2 (Theta-style):

```
SELECT E.FNAME, E.LNAME, E.DEPT, C.CNTC_TYPE, C.CNTC_DATA
    FROM CNTC_DTLS C, EMP_MSTR E WHERE C.CODE_NO(+) = E.EMP_NO;
```

Output:

FNAME	LNAME	DEPT	CNTC_TYPE	CNTC_DATA
Ivan	Bayross	Administration	R	26045953
Anjali	Pathak	Administration	R	24302579
Amit	Desai	Loans And Financing	R	28883779
Maya	Joshi	Client Servicing	R	28377634
Peter	Joseph	Loans And Financing	R	26323560
Mandhar	Dalvi	Marketing	R	26793231
Sonal	Khan	Administration	R	28085654
Anil	Kambli	Marketing	R	24442342
Seema	Apte	Client Servicing	R	24365672
Vikram	Randive	Marketing	R	24327349

10 rows selected.

Explanation:

In the above example, the data required is all the employee details along with their contact details **if any**. But in this case **RIGHT JOIN** is being used. This means all the employee details have to be listed even though their corresponding contact information is not present. The data is available in two tables i.e. EMP_MSTR and CNTC_DTLS

Since the **RIGHT JOIN** returns all the rows from the second table even if there are no matches in the first table. The first table in the FROM clause will have to be **CNTC_DTLS** and the second table **EMP_MSTR**. This means, if there are employees in **EMP_MSTR** that do not have any contacts in **CNTC_DTLS**, those rows will also be listed. Notice the keyword **RIGHT JOIN** in the first solution (Ansi-style) and the (+) in the second solution (Theta-style). This indicates that all rows from the second table i.e. EMP_MSTR will be displayed even though there exists no matching rows in the first table i.e. CNTC_DTLS.

Notice that:

- ❑ The **EMP_NO** column is the primary key of the **EMP_MSTR** table
- ❑ The **CNTC_DTLS** is a table that holds the contact details of employees.

  In **CNTC_DTLS** table:

  - **ADDR_NO** column is used to refer to the addresses in the ADDR_DTLS table via the ADDR_NO column.
  - **CODE_NO** column is used to refer to the employees in the **EMP_MSTR** table via the **EMP_NO** column

To retrieve the data required, both the tables have to linked on the basis of common columns using joins as follows:

- ❑ **C.**CODE_NO = **E.**EMP_NO

  This means the CODE_NO field of CNTC_DTLS table is joined with EMP_NO field of the EMP_MSTR table

Cross Join

Suppose it is desired to combine each deposit amount with a Fixed Deposits Interest Slab table so as to analyze each deposit amount at each interest rate and their minimum and maximum periods. This is elegantly done using a cross join.

Example:

Create a report using **cross join** that will display the maturity amounts for pre-defined deposits, based on the Minimum and Maximum periods fixed / time deposits. Ensure that a temporary table called TMP_FD_AMT stores the amounts for pre-defined deposits in the FD_AMT column.

Synopsis:

Tables:	TMP_FD_AMT, FDSLAB_MSTR
Columns:	TMP_FD_AMT: FD_AMT, FDSLAB_MSTR: MINPERIOD, MAXPERIOD, INTRATE
Technique:	**Join:** CROSS JOIN, **Operators:** (*), (/)

Prior executing the SQL statement a table called TMP_FD_AMT has to be created and filled in with some sample data.

CREATE TABLE "DBA_BANKSYS"."TMP_FD_AMT"("FD_AMT" **NUMBER**(6));

Insert Statements for the table TMP_FD_AMT:

INSERT INTO TMP_FD_AMT (FD_AMT) **VALUES**(5000);

```
INSERT INTO TMP_FD_AMT (FD_AMT) VALUES(10000);
INSERT INTO TMP_FD_AMT (FD_AMT) VALUES(15000);
INSERT INTO TMP_FD_AMT (FD_AMT) VALUES(20000);
INSERT INTO TMP_FD_AMT (FD_AMT) VALUES(25000);
INSERT INTO TMP_FD_AMT (FD_AMT) VALUES(30000);
INSERT INTO TMP_FD_AMT (FD_AMT) VALUES(40000);
INSERT INTO TMP_FD_AMT (FD_AMT) VALUES(50000);
```

Solution:

```
SELECT T.FD_AMT, S.MINPERIOD, S.MAXPERIOD, S.INTRATE,
        ROUND(T.FD_AMT + (T.FD_AMT * (S.INTRATE/100) * (S.MINPERIOD/365)))
            "Amt. Min. Period",
        ROUND(T.FD_AMT + (T.FD_AMT * (S.INTRATE/100) * (S.MAXPERIOD/365)))
            "Amt. Max. Period"
        FROM FDSLAB_MSTR S CROSS JOIN TMP_FD_AMT T;
```

Output:

FD_AMT	MINPERIOD	MAXPERIOD	INTRATE	Amt. Min. Period	Amt. Max. Period
5000	1	30	5	5001	5021
5000	31	92	5.5	5023	5069
5000	93	183	6	5076	5050
...					
20000	31	92	5.5	20093	20277
20000	93	183	6	20306	20602
20000	184	365	6.5	20655	21300
20000	366	731	7.5	21504	23004
...					
50000	184	365	6.5	51638	53250
50000	366	731	7.5	53760	57510
50000	732	1097	8.5	58523	62773
50000	1098	1829	10	65041	75055

56 rows selected.

Explanation:

In the above example, the data required is available in two tables i.e. TMP_FD_AMT and FDSLAB_MSTR. In the table TMP_FD_AMT, there exists, the deposit amounts. In the second table FDSLAB_MSTR, there exists a list of fixed deposits slabs comprising of minimum and maximum periods and the interest rates applicable for those periods.

The output is required in the form of a report, which will display calculation based on the FDSLAB_MSTR table for each row held in the TMP_FD_AMT. In such a situation, a CROSS JOIN can be used which will combine each record from the left table with that of the right table. In this example a cross join will combine each deposit amount (i.e. FD_AMT) from the TMP_FD_AMT table with each slab i.e. each record in the FDSLAB_MSTR table after applying some calculations. Using Cross Join, a matrix between the temporary table named TMP_FD_AMT table and the FDSLAB_MSTR table can be created.

The above SELECT statement creates a record for each deposit amount with the calculated maturity amount based on the interest rates and the minimum and maximum periods. The results are known as a Cartesian product, which combines every record in the left table i.e. FDSLAB_MSTR with every record in the right table i.e. TMP_FD_AMT.

Oracle versions **prior to 9i** don't support an explicit cross join, but the same results can be obtained by using the following statement:

```
SELECT T.FD_AMT, S.MINPERIOD, S.MAXPERIOD, S.INTRATE,
        ROUND(T.FD_AMT + (T.FD_AMT * (S.INTRATE/100) * (S.MINPERIOD/365)))
                "Amt. Min. Period",
        ROUND(T.FD_AMT + (T.FD_AMT * (S.INTRATE/100) * (S.MAXPERIOD/365)))
                "Amt. Max. Period"
        FROM FDSLAB_MSTR S, TMP_FD_AMT T;
```

Guidelines for Creating Joins

- When writing a select statement that joins tables, precede the column name with the table name for clarity
- If the same column name appears in more than one table, the column name must be prefixed with the table name
- The WHERE clause, is the most critical clause in a join select statement. Always make sure to include the WHERE clause

Joining A Table To Itself (Self Joins)

In some situations, it is necessary to join a table to itself, as though joining two separate tables. This is referred to as a **self-join**. In a self-join, two rows from the same table combine to form a result row.

To join a table to itself, **two** copies of the very same table have to be opened in memory. Hence in the **FROM** clause, the table name needs to be mentioned twice. Since the table names are the same, the second table will overwrite the first table and in effect, result in only one table being in memory. This is because a table name is translated into a specific memory location. To avoid this, each table is opened using an alias. Now these table aliases will cause two identical tables to be opened in different memory locations. This will result in two identical tables to be physically present in the computer's memory.

Using the table alias names these two identical tables can be joined.

```
FROM <TableName> [<Alias1>], <TableName> [<Alias2>] ....
```

Example:

Retrieve the names of the employees and the names of their respective managers from the employee table.

Synopsis:

Tables:	EMP_MNGR
Columns:	FNAME
Technique:	**Joins:** SELF, **Clauses**: WHERE **Others:** Alias

Solution:

```
SELECT EMP.FNAME "Employee", MNGR.FNAME "Manager"
    FROM EMP_MSTR EMP, EMP_MSTR MNGR
        WHERE EMP.MNGR_NO = MNGR.EMP_NO;
```

Note

In this query, the **EMP_MSTR** table is treated as two separate tables named **EMP** and **MNGR**, using the table **alias** feature of SQL.

Output:

Employee	Manager
Peter	Amit
Sonal	Ivan
Anil	Mandhar
Seema	Maya
Vikram	Anil
Anjali	Ivan

6 rows selected.

Explanation:

In the above example, the data required are all the employees and the names of their respective managers to whom they report. This data is available in the table **EMP_MSTR**. The EMP_MSTR table holds the employee number, their names and the manager numbers who in turn are employees in the same table.

The table EMP_MSTR holds the following data:

Emp_No	Fname	Lname	Mngr_No
E1	Ivan	Bayross	
E2	Amit	Desai	
E3	Maya	Joshi	
E4	**Peter**	**Joseph**	**E2**
E5	Mandhar	Dalvi	
E6	**Sonal**	**Khan**	**E1**
E7	**Anil**	**Kambli**	**E5**
E8	**Seema**	**Apte**	**E3**
E9	**Vikram**	**Randive**	**E7**
E10	**Anjali**	**Pathak**	**E1**

As can be seen from the data above employees named **Peter** having employee number **E4** reports to a manager (employee) named **Amit** having employee number **E2**.

Similarly, employees numbered **E6, E7, E8, E9, E10** report to managers (employees) numbered **E1, E5, E3, E7, E1** respectively.

This means:

- ❑ The **EMP_NO** column is the primary key of the **EMP_MSTR** table
- ❑ The **MNGR_NO** column is used to refer to the Employee details in the same table i.e. **EMP_MSTR** via the **EMP_NO** column

This simply means that MNGR_NO is a foreign key mapping to the EMP_NO which is the primary key of the table.

From the data available in the EMP_MSTR table seen above, it is possible to extract the manager number to which the employee reports, but in order to extract the manager name i.e. the employee's name (since the manager is also an employee) a reference to the same table EMP_MSTR has to be made. This can be done using a SELF JOIN i.e. making a copy of the same table EMP_MSTR and then referring to the columns to get the employee name against the manager number.

To form a copy of the same table alias have to be used in the FROM clause as:

FROM EMP_MSTR **EMP**, EMP_MSTR **MNGR**

Here the **EMP** is the **first copy** of the table **EMP_MSTR** and **MNGR** is the **second copy** of the table **EMP_MSTR**.

To retrieve the data required, both the copies of the same tables have to linked on the basis of common columns using joins as follows:

- ❑ **EMP.**MNGR_NO = **MNGR.**EMP_NO

  This means the MNGR_NO field of EMP_MSTR table (First Copy: EMP) is joined with EMP_NO field of the EMP_MSTR (Second Copy: MNGR) table

Concatenating Data From TABLE Columns

Example:

Create an English sentence, by joining predetermined string values with column data retrieved from the **ACCT_MSTR** table.

The string literals are:

Account No.	was introduced by Customer No.	At Branch No.

The columns are:

ACCT_NO	INTRO_CUST_NO	BRANCH_NO

Synopsis:

Tables:	ACCT_MSTR
Columns:	ACCT_NO, INTRO_CUST_NO, BRANCH_NO
Technique:	**Other:** Concat (||)

Solution:

```
SELECT 'ACCOUNT NO. ' || ACCT_NO || ' WAS INTRODUCED BY CUSTOMER NO. '
    || INTRO_CUST_NO || ' AT BRANCH NO. ' || BRANCH_NO FROM ACCT_MSTR;
```

Problem:

Since the above SELECT cannot find an appropriate column header to print on the VDU screen, the SELECT uses the **formula (i.e.** the entire SELECT content) as the column header as described below.

Output:

```
'ACCOUNTNO.'||ACCT_NO||'WASINTRODUCEDBYCUSTOMERNO.'||INTRO_CUST_NO
||'ATBRANCHNO.
ACCOUNT NO. SB1 WAS INTRODUCED BY CUSTOMER NO. C1 AT BRANCH NO. B1
ACCOUNT NO. CA2 WAS INTRODUCED BY CUSTOMER NO. C1 AT BRANCH NO. B2
ACCOUNT NO. SB3 WAS INTRODUCED BY CUSTOMER NO. C4 AT BRANCH NO. B3
ACCOUNT NO. CA4 WAS INTRODUCED BY CUSTOMER NO. C4 AT BRANCH NO. B5
ACCOUNT NO. SB5 WAS INTRODUCED BY CUSTOMER NO. C1 AT BRANCH NO. B6
ACCOUNT NO. SB6 WAS INTRODUCED BY CUSTOMER NO. C5 AT BRANCH NO. B4
ACCOUNT NO. CA7 WAS INTRODUCED BY CUSTOMER NO. C8 AT BRANCH NO. B1
ACCOUNT NO. SB8 WAS INTRODUCED BY CUSTOMER NO. C9 AT BRANCH NO. B2
ACCOUNT NO. SB9 WAS INTRODUCED BY CUSTOMER NO. C10 AT BRANCH NO. B4
ACCOUNT NO. CA10 WAS INTRODUCED BY CUSTOMER NO. C10 AT BRANCH NO. B6
ACCOUNT NO. SB11 WAS INTRODUCED BY CUSTOMER NO. C1 AT BRANCH NO. B1
ACCOUNT NO. CA12 WAS INTRODUCED BY CUSTOMER NO. C1 AT BRANCH NO. B2
ACCOUNT NO. SB13 WAS INTRODUCED BY CUSTOMER NO. C4 AT BRANCH NO. B3
ACCOUNT NO. CA14 WAS INTRODUCED BY CUSTOMER NO. C4 AT BRANCH NO. B5
ACCOUNT NO. SB15 WAS INTRODUCED BY CUSTOMER NO. C1 AT BRANCH NO. B6
15 rows selected.
```

To avoid a data header that appears meaningless, use an **alias** as shown below:

```
SELECT 'ACCOUNT NO. ' || ACCT_NO || ' WAS INTRODUCED BY CUSTOMER NO. '
    || INTRO_CUST_NO || ' AT BRANCH NO. ' || BRANCH_NO "Accounts Opened"
    FROM ACCT_MSTR;
```

Output:

```
Accounts Opened
ACCOUNT NO. SB1 WAS INTRODUCED BY CUSTOMER NO. C1 AT BRANCH NO. B1
ACCOUNT NO. CA2 WAS INTRODUCED BY CUSTOMER NO. C1 AT BRANCH NO. B2
ACCOUNT NO. SB3 WAS INTRODUCED BY CUSTOMER NO. C4 AT BRANCH NO. B3
ACCOUNT NO. CA4 WAS INTRODUCED BY CUSTOMER NO. C4 AT BRANCH NO. B5
ACCOUNT NO. SB5 WAS INTRODUCED BY CUSTOMER NO. C1 AT BRANCH NO. B6
ACCOUNT NO. SB6 WAS INTRODUCED BY CUSTOMER NO. C5 AT BRANCH NO. B4
ACCOUNT NO. CA7 WAS INTRODUCED BY CUSTOMER NO. C8 AT BRANCH NO. B1
ACCOUNT NO. SB8 WAS INTRODUCED BY CUSTOMER NO. C9 AT BRANCH NO. B2
ACCOUNT NO. SB9 WAS INTRODUCED BY CUSTOMER NO. C10 AT BRANCH NO. B4
ACCOUNT NO. CA10 WAS INTRODUCED BY CUSTOMER NO. C10 AT BRANCH NO. B6
ACCOUNT NO. SB11 WAS INTRODUCED BY CUSTOMER NO. C1 AT BRANCH NO. B1
ACCOUNT NO. CA12 WAS INTRODUCED BY CUSTOMER NO. C1 AT BRANCH NO. B2
ACCOUNT NO. SB13 WAS INTRODUCED BY CUSTOMER NO. C4 AT BRANCH NO. B3
ACCOUNT NO. CA14 WAS INTRODUCED BY CUSTOMER NO. C4 AT BRANCH NO. B5
ACCOUNT NO. SB15 WAS INTRODUCED BY CUSTOMER NO. C1 AT BRANCH NO. B6
15 rows selected.
```

Using the Union, Intersect and Minus Clause

Union Clause

Multiple queries can be put together and their output can be combined using the **union** clause. The **Union** clause merges the output of two or more queries into a single set of rows and columns.

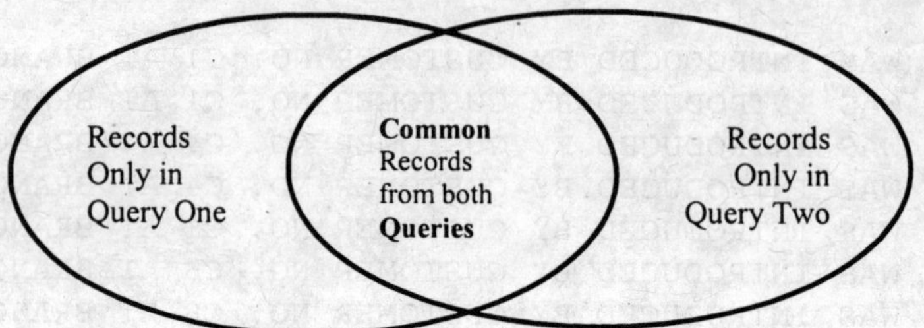

Diagram 13.1: Output of the Union Clause.

Note

The output of both the queries will be as displayed above. The final output of the union clause will be: **Output** = Records from query one + records from query two +
A single set of records, common in both queries.

While working with the UNION clause the following pointers should be considered:

- The number of columns and the data types of the columns being selected must be identical in all the **SELECT** statement used in the query. The names of the columns need not be identical.
- **UNION** operates over all of the columns being selected.
- **NULL** values are not ignored during duplicate checking.
- The **IN** operator has a higher precedence than the **UNION** operator.
- By default, the output is sorted in ascending order of the first column of the **SELECT** clause.

Example:

Retrieve the names of all the customers and employees residing in the city of **Mumbai**.

Synopsis:

Tables:	CUST_NO, FNAME, LNAME
Columns:	CUST_MSTR, EMP_MSTR, ADDR_DTLS
Technique:	**Operators:** LIKE, **Clauses:** WHERE, UNION, **Others:** Alias

Solution:

```
SELECT CUST_NO "ID", FNAME || ' ' || LNAME "Customers / Employees"
    FROM CUST_MSTR, ADDR_DTLS
        WHERE CUST_MSTR.CUST_NO = ADDR_DTLS.CODE_NO
            AND ADDR_DTLS.CITY = 'Mumbai' AND ADDR_DTLS.CODE_NO LIKE 'C%'
```

UNION

SELECT EMP_NO "ID", FNAME || ' ' || LNAME "Customers / Employees"
FROM EMP_MSTR, ADDR_DTLS
WHERE EMP_MSTR.EMP_NO = ADDR_DTLS.CODE_NO
AND ADDR_DTLS.CITY = 'Mumbai' **AND** ADDR_DTLS.CODE_NO **LIKE** 'E%';

Explanation:

Oracle executes the queries as follows:

The first query in the **UNION** example is as follows:

SELECT CUST_NO "ID", FNAME || ' ' || LNAME "Customers / Employees"
FROM CUST_MSTR, ADDR_DTLS
WHERE CUST_MSTR.CUST_NO = ADDR_DTLS.CODE_NO
AND ADDR_DTLS.CITY = 'Mumbai' **AND** ADDR_DTLS.CODE_NO **LIKE** 'C%';

The target table will be as follows:

ID	Customers / Employees
C1	Ivan Bayross
C10	Namita Kanade
C2	Chriselle Bayross
C3	Mamta Muzumdar
C4	Chhaya Bankar
C5	Ashwini Joshi
C6	Hansel Colaco
C7	Anil Dhone
C8	Alex Fernandes
C9	Ashwini Apte

10 rows selected.

SELECT EMP_NO "ID", FNAME || ' ' || LNAME "Customers / Employees"
FROM EMP_MSTR, ADDR_DTLS **WHERE** EMP_MSTR.EMP_NO = ADDR_DTLS.CODE_NO
AND ADDR_DTLS.CITY = 'Mumbai' **AND** ADDR_DTLS.CODE_NO **LIKE** 'E%';

The target table will be as follows:

ID	Customers / Employees
E1	Ivan Bayross
E2	Amit Desai
E3	Maya Joshi
E4	Peter Joseph
ID	Customers / Employees

E5	Mandhar Dalvi
E6	Sonal Khan
E7	Anil Kambli
E8	Seema Apte
E9	Vikram Randive

9 rows selected.

The **UNION** clause picks up the common records as well as the individual records in both queries. Thus, the output after applying the **UNION** clause will be:

Output:

ID	Customers / Employees
C1	Ivan Bayross
C10	Namita Kanade
C2	Chriselle Bayross
C3	Mamta Muzumdar
C4	Chhaya Bankar
C5	Ashwini Joshi
C6	Hansel Colaco
C7	Anil Dhone
C8	Alex Fernandes
C9	Ashwini Apte
E1	Ivan Bayross
E2	Amit Desai
E3	Maya Joshi
E4	Peter Joseph
E5	Mandhar Dalvi
E6	Sonal Khan
E7	Anil Kambli
E8	Seema Apte
E9	Vikram Randive

19 rows selected.

Note

 The alias assigned to the first query will be applied in the final output even though an alias has been assigned to the second query it is not applicable.

The Restrictions on using a union are as follows:

- Number of columns in all the queries should be the same
- The data type of the columns in each query must be same
- Unions cannot be used in subqueries
- Aggregate functions cannot be used with union clause

Union ALL Clause

Multiple queries can be put together and their output can be combined using the **union all** clause. The **Union all** clause merges the output of two or more queries into a single set of rows and columns without eliminating duplicates from the output.

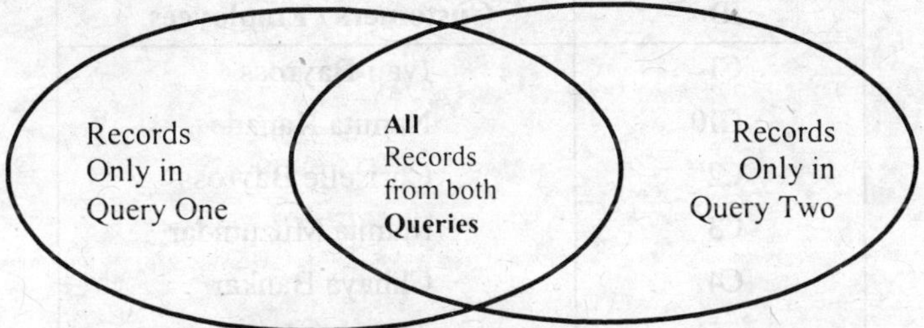

Diagram 13.2: Output of the Union All Clause.

Note
 The output of both the queries will be as displayed above. The final output of the union all clause will be: **Output** = Records from query one + records from query two.

Example:

Retrieve the names of all the customers and employees residing in the city of **Mumbai (Allow Duplicates)**.

Synopsis:

Tables:	CUST_NO, FNAME, LNAME
Columns:	CUST_MSTR, EMP_MSTR, ADDR_DTLS
Technique:	**Operators:** LIKE, **Clauses:** WHERE, UNION ALL, **Others:** Alias

Solution:

```
SELECT CUST_NO "ID", FNAME || ' ' || LNAME "Customers / Employees"
    FROM CUST_MSTR, ADDR_DTLS
        WHERE CUST_MSTR.CUST_NO = ADDR_DTLS.CODE_NO
            AND ADDR_DTLS.CITY = 'Mumbai' AND ADDR_DTLS.CODE_NO LIKE 'C%'
UNION ALL
SELECT EMP_NO "ID", FNAME || ' ' || LNAME "Customers / Employees"
    FROM EMP_MSTR, ADDR_DTLS
        WHERE EMP_MSTR.EMP_NO = ADDR_DTLS.CODE_NO
            AND ADDR_DTLS.CITY = 'Mumbai' AND ADDR_DTLS.CODE_NO LIKE 'E%';
```

Explanation:

Oracle executes the queries as follows:

The first query in the **UNION** example is as follows:

SELECT CUST_NO "ID", FNAME || ' ' || LNAME "Customers / Employees"
FROM CUST_MSTR, ADDR_DTLS
WHERE CUST_MSTR.CUST_NO = ADDR_DTLS.CODE_NO
AND ADDR_DTLS.CITY = 'Mumbai' **AND** ADDR_DTLS.CODE_NO **LIKE** 'C%';

The target table will be as follows:

ID	Customers / Employees
C1	Ivan Bayross
C10	Namita Kanade
C2	Chriselle Bayross
C3	Mamta Muzumdar
C4	Chhaya Bankar
C5	Ashwini Joshi
C6	Hansel Colaco
C7	Anil Dhone
C8	Alex Fernandes
C9	Ashwini Apte

10 rows selected.

SELECT EMP_NO "ID", FNAME || ' ' || LNAME "Customers / Employees"
FROM EMP_MSTR, ADDR_DTLS **WHERE** EMP_MSTR.EMP_NO = ADDR_DTLS.CODE_NO
AND ADDR_DTLS.CITY = 'Mumbai' **AND** ADDR_DTLS.CODE_NO **LIKE** 'E%';

The target table will be as follows:

ID	Customers / Employees
E1	Ivan Bayross
E2	Amit Desai
E3	Maya Joshi
E4	Peter Joseph
E5	Mandhar Dalvi
E6	Sonal Khan
E7	Anil Kambli
E8	Seema Apte
E9	Vikram Randive

9 rows selected.

The **UNION ALL** clause picks up all the records from both the queries. Thus, the output after applying the **UNION ALL** clause will be:

Output:

ID	Customers / Employees
C1	Ivan Bayross
C10	Namita Kanade
C2	Chriselle Bayross
C3	Mamta Muzumdar
C4	Chhaya Bankar
C5	Ashwini Joshi
C6	Hansel Colaco
C7	Anil Dhone
C8	Alex Fernandes
C9	Ashwini Apte
E1	Ivan Bayross
E2	Amit Desai
E3	Maya Joshi
E4	Peter Joseph
E5	Mandhar Dalvi
E6	Sonal Khan
E7	Anil Kambli
E8	Seema Apte
E9	Vikram Randive

19 rows selected.

Intersect Clause

Multiple queries can be put together and their output combined using the intersect clause. The **Intersect** clause outputs only rows produced by **both** the queries intersected **i.e.** the output in an Intersect clause will include only those rows that are retrieved common to both the queries.

Diagram 13.3: Output of the Intersect clause.

Note
 The output of both the queries will be as displayed above. The final output of the Intersect clause will be: **Output** = A single set of records which are common in both queries.

While working with the INTERSECT clause the following pointers should be considered:

- ❑ The number of columns and the data types of the columns being selected by the **SELECT** statement in the queries must be identical in all the **SELECT** statements used in the query. The names of the columns need not be identical.
- ❑ Reversing the order of the intersected tables does not alter the result.
- ❑ **INTERSECT** does not ignore **NULL** values.

Example:

Retrieve the customers holding accounts as well as fixed deposits in a bank.

Synopsis:

Tables:	ACCT_FD_CUST_DTLS
Columns:	CUST_NO
Technique:	**Operators:** LIKE, **Clauses:** WHERE, INTERSECT

Solution:

SELECT DISTINCT CUST_NO **FROM** ACCT_FD_CUST_DTLS The target table will be as follows:

```
CUST_NO
C1
C10
C2
C3
C4
C5
C6
C7
C8
C9
10 rows selected.
```

WHERE ACCT_FD_NO
    LIKE 'CA%' **OR** ACCT_FD_NO **LIKE** 'SB%'
INTERSECT
SELECT DISTINCT CUST_NO **FROM** ACCT_FD_CUST_DTLS
    WHERE ACCT_FD_NO **LIKE** 'FS%';

Explanation:

Oracle executes the queries as follows:

The first query in the **INTERSECT** example is as follows:

```
SELECT DISTINCT CUST_NO FROM ACCT_FD_CUST_DTLS
    WHERE ACCT_FD_NO LIKE 'CA%'
        OR ACCT_FD_NO LIKE 'SB%';
```

The target table will be as follows:

```
CUST_NO
C10
C2
C3
C4
C5
C6
C8
C9
8 rows selected.
```

The second query in the INTERSECT example is as follows:

```
SELECT DISTINCT CUST_NO FROM ACCT_FD_CUST_DTLS
    WHERE ACCT_FD_NO LIKE 'FS%';
```

Output:

```
CUST_NO
C10
C2
C3
C4
C5
C6
C8
C9
8 rows selected.
```

The **INTERSECT** clause picks up records that are common in both queries. Thus, the output after applying the INTERSECT clause will be as shown in the output.

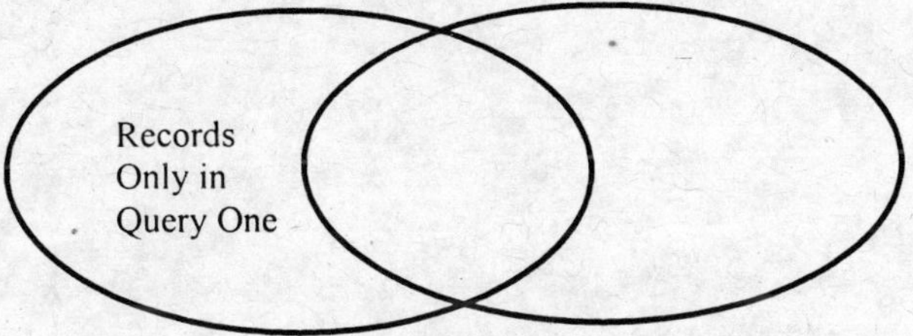

Diagram 13.4: Output of the Minus clause.

Minus Clause

Multiple queries can be put together and their output combined using the minus clause. The **Minus** clause outputs the rows produced by the first query, after **filtering** the rows retrieved by the second query.

Note
 The output of both the queries will be as displayed above. The final output of the minus clause will be: **Output** = Records only in query one

While working with the MINUS clause the following pointers should be considered:

- The number of columns and the data types of the columns being selected by the **SELECT** statement in the queries must be identical in all the **SELECT** statements used in the query. The names of the columns need not be identical.
- All on the columns in the **WHERE** clause must be in the **SELECT** clause for the **MINUS** operator to work.

Example:

Retrieve the customers holding accounts but not holding any fixed deposits in a bank.

Synopsis:

Tables:	ACCT_FD_CUST_DTLS
Columns:	CUST_NO
Technique:	**Operators:** LIKE, **Clauses:** WHERE, MINUS

Solution:

```
SELECT DISTINCT CUST_NO FROM ACCT_FD_CUST_DTLS
    WHERE ACCT_FD_NO LIKE 'CA%' OR ACCT_FD_NO LIKE 'SB%'
MINUS
SELECT DISTINCT CUST_NO FROM ACCT_FD_CUST_DTLS
    WHERE ACCT_FD_NO LIKE 'FS%';
```

The target table will be as follows:

```
CUST_NO
C1
C10
C2
C3
C4
C5
C6
C7
C8
C9
10 rows selected.
```

Explanation:

Oracle executes the queries as follows:

The first query in the **INTERSECT** example is as follows:

```
SELECT DISTINCT CUST_NO FROM ACCT_FD_CUST_DTLS
    WHERE ACCT_FD_NO LIKE 'CA%'
        OR ACCT_FD_NO LIKE 'SB%';
```

The second query in the **INTERSECT** example is as follows:

```
SELECT DISTINCT CUST_NO FROM ACCT_FD_CUST_DTLS
    WHERE ACCT_FD_NO LIKE 'FS%';
```

The target table will be as follows:

```
CUST_NO
C10
C2
C3
C4
C5
C6
C8
C9
8 rows selected.
```

The **MINUS** clause picks up records in the first query after filtering the records retrieved by the second query. Thus, the output after applying the MINUS clause will be as shown below.

Output:

```
CUST_NO
C1
C7
```

Self Review Questions

Fill in the Blanks

1. The ______________ clause is another section of the select statement.
2. The ____________ clause imposes a condition on the GROUP BY clause
3. A ____________ is a form of an SQL statement that appears inside another SQL statement.
4. A subquery is also termed as __________ query.
5. The concept of joining multiple tables is called ____________.
6. The __________ clause merges the output of two or more queries into a single set of rows and columns.
7. Multiple queries can be put together and their output combined using the ___________ clause.

True or False

8. The HAVING CLAUSE is an optional clause which tells Oracle to group rows based on distinct values that exist for specified columns.
9. The statement containing a subquery is called a parent statement.
10. Joining a table to itself is called Equi join.
11. If a select statement is defined as a subquery, the innermost select statement gets executed first.
12. In the union clause multiple queries can be put together but their outputs cannot be combined.

13. Unions can be used in subqueries.
14. The Intersect clause outputs only rows produced by both the queries intersected.
15. The Minus clause outputs the rows produced by the first query, before filtering the rows retrieved by the second query.

Hands On Exercises

1. Exercises on using Having and Group By Clauses:
   a. Print the description and total qty sold for each product.
   b. Find the value of each product sold.
   c. Calculate the average qty sold for each client that has a maximum order value of 15000.00.
   d. Find out the total of all the billed orders for the month of June.
2. Exercises on Joins and Correlation:
   a. Find out the products, which have been sold to 'Ivan Bayross'.
   b. Find out the products and their quantities that will have to be delivered in the current month.
   c. List the ProductNo and description of constantly sold (i.e. rapidly moving) products.
   d. Find the names of clients who have purchased 'Trousers'.
   e. List the products and orders from customers who have ordered less than 5 units of 'Pull Overs'.
   f. Find the products and their quantities for the orders placed by 'Ivan Bayross' and 'Mamta Muzumdar'.
   g. Find the products and their quantities for the orders placed by ClientNo 'C00001' and 'C00002'.
3. Exercise on Sub-queries:
   a. Find the ProductNo and description of non-moving products i.e. products not being sold.
   b. List the customer Name, Address1, Address2, City and PinCode for the client who has placed order no 'O19001'.
   c. List the client names that have placed orders before the month of May'02.
   d. List if the product 'Lycra Top' has been ordered by any client and print the Client_no, Name to whom it was sold.
   e. List the names of clients who have placed orders worth Rs. 10000 or more.

Answer To Self Review Questions

10. Interactive SQL: PART – I

Fill in the Blanks		True or False	
1.	table	10.	False
2.	Create Table	11.	False
3.	single	12.	True
4.	Where Clause	13.	False
5.	SELECT DISTINCT	14.	True

6.	Target, Source	15.	False
7.	ALTER TABLE	16.	True
8.	UPDATE	17.	True
9.	single record	18.	False
19.	True		

11. Interactive SQL: PART – II

	Fill in the Blanks		**True or False**
1.	Constraints	15.	True
2.	NULLABLE	16.	False
3.	mandatory	17.	False
4.	NOT NULL	18.	True
5.	NULL	19.	False
6.	Simple	20.	True
7.	UNIQUE	21.	False
8.	Foreign	22.	True
9.	Detail	23.	True
10.	ON DELETE CASCADE	24.	False
11.	CHECK	25.	True
12.	Boolean	26.	False
13.	Integrity	27.	True
14.	indexes	28.	True

12. Interactive SQL: PART – III

	Fill in the Blanks		**True or False**
1.	OR	14.	True
2.	LIKE	15.	False
3.	percent	16.	False
4.	Dual	17.	True
5.	Group Functions	18.	False
6.	arguments	19.	True
7.	INITCAP	20.	True
8.	LTRIM	21.	False
9.	RPAD	22.	True
10.	TO_NUMBER	23.	False
11.	TO_CHAR (date conversion)	24.	True
12.	MONTHS_BETWEEN	25.	False

13. Uid
26. True
27. False
28. True
29. True

13. Interactive SQL: Part – IV

Fill in the Blanks

1. GROUP BY
2. HAVING
3. subquery
4. nested
5. Equi Joins
6. Union
7. intersect

True or False

8. False
9. True
10. False
11. True
12. False
13. False
14. True
15. False

Solution To Hands On Exercises

10. Interactive PART - I

1. **SQL Statement for creating the tables:**

(a) **Table Name:** CLIENT_MASTER

```
CREATE TABLE CLIENT_MASTER(CLIENTNO varchar2(6), NAME varchar2(20),
        ADDRESS1 varchar2(30), ADDRESS2 varchar2(30), CITY varchar2(15),
        PINCODE number(8), STATE varchar2(15), BALDUE number(10,2));
```

(b) **Table Name:** PRODUCT_MASTER

```
CREATE TABLE PRODUCT_MASTER(PRODUCTNO varchar2(6), DESCRIPTION varchar2(15),
        PROFITPERCENT number(4,2), UNITMEASURE varchar2(10), QTYONHAND number(8),
        REORDERLVL number(8), SELLPRICE number(8,2), COSTPRICE number(8,2));
```

(c) **Table Name:** SALESMAN_MASTER

```
CREATE TABLE SALESMAN_MASTER(SALESMANNO varchar2(6),
        SALESMANNAME varchar2(20), ADDRESS1 varchar2(30), ADDRESS2 varchar2(30),
        CITY varchar2(20), PINCODE number(8), STATE varchar2(20), SALAMT number(8,2),
        TGTTOGET number(6,2), YTDSALES number(6,2), REMARKS varchar2(60));
```

2. **SQL Statement for inserting into their respective tables:**

(a) Data for **CLIENT_MASTER** table:

```
INSERT INTO Client_Master (ClientNo, Name, City, PinCode, State, BalDue)
        VALUES ('C00001', 'Ivan Bayross', 'Mumbai', 400054, 'Maharashtra', 15000);
INSERT INTO Client_Master (ClientNo, Name, City, PinCode, State, BalDue)
```

```
        VALUES ('C00002', 'Mamta Muzumdar', 'Madras", 780001, 'Tamil Nadu', 0);
INSERT INTO Client_Master (ClientNo, Name, City, Pincode, State, BalDue)
        VALUES ('C00003', 'Chhaya Bankar', 'Mumbai', 400057, 'Maharashtra', 5000);
INSERT INTO Client_Master (ClientNo, Name, City, PinCode, State, BalDue)
        VALUES ('C00004', 'Ashwini Joshi', 'Bangalore', 560001, 'Karnataka', 0);
INSERT INTO Client_Master (ClientNo, Name, City, PinCode, State, BalDue)
        VALUES ('C00005', 'Hansel Colaco', 'Mumbai', 400060, 'Maharashtra', 2000);
INSERT INTO Client_Master (ClientNo, Name, City, PinCode, State, BalDue)
        VALUES ('C00006', 'Deepak Sharma', 'Mangalore', 560050, 'Karnataka', 0);
```

(b) Data for **PRODUCT_MASTER** table

```
INSERT INTO Product_Master VALUES ('P00001', 'T-Shirts', 5, 'Piece', 200, 50, 350, 250);
INSERT INTO Product_Master VALUES ('P03453', 'Shirts', 6, 'Piece', 150, 50, 500, 350);
INSERT INTO Product_Master VALUES ('P06734', 'Cotton Jeans', 5, 'Piece', 100, 20, 600, 450);
INSERT INTO Product_Master VALUES ('P07865', 'Jeans', 5, 'Piece', 100, 20, 750, 500);
INSERT INTO Product_Master VALUES ('P07868', 'Trousers', 2, 'Piece', 150, 50, 850, 550);
INSERT INTO Product_Master VALUES ('P07885', 'Pull Overs', 2.5, 'Piece', 80, 30, 700, 450);
INSERT INTO Product_Master VALUES ('P07965', 'Denim Shirts', 4, 'Piece', 100, 40, 350, 250);
INSERT INTO Product_Master VALUES ('P07975', 'Lycra Tops', 5, 'Piece', 70, 30, 300, 175);
INSERT INTO Product_Master VALUES ('P08865', 'Skirts', 5, 'Piece', 75, 30, 450, 300);
```

(c) Data for **SALESMAN_MASTER** table

```
INSERT INTO Salesman_Master VALUES ('S00001', 'Aman', 'A/14', 'Worli', 'Mumbai', 400002,
'Maharashtra', 3000, 100, 50, 'Good');
INSERT INTO Salesman_Master VALUES ('S00002', 'Omkar', '65', 'Nariman', 'Mumbai', 400001,
'Maharashtra', 3000, 200, 100, 'Good');
INSERT INTO Salesman_Master VALUES ('S00003', 'Raj', 'P-7', 'Bandra', 'Mumbai', 400032,
'Maharashtra', 3000, 200, 100, 'Good');
INSERT INTO Salesman_Master VALUES ('S00004', 'Ashish', 'A/5', 'Juhu', 'Bombay', 400044,
'Maharashtra', 3500, 200. 150, 'Good');
```

3. SQL Statement for retrieving records from a table:

(a) Find out the names of all the clients.

```
SELECT Name FROM Client_Master;
```

(b) Retrieve the entire contents of the Client_Master table.

```
SELECT * FROM Client_Master;
```

(c) Retrieve the list of names, city and the sate of all the clients.

```
SELECT Name, City, State FROM Client_Master;
```

(d) List the various products available from the Product_Master table.

SELECT Description FROM Product_Master;

(e) List all the clients who are located in Mumbai.

SELECT * FROM Client_Master WHERE City = 'Mumbai';

(f) Find the names of salesmen who have a salary equal to Rs.3000.

SELECT Salesman_name FROM Salesman_Master WHERE SalAmt = 3000;

4. SQL Statement for updating records in a table:

(a) Change the city of ClientNo 'C00005' to 'Bangalore'.

UPDATE Client_Master SET City = 'Bangalore' WHERE ClientNo = 'C00005';

(b) Change the BalDue of ClientNo 'C00001' to Rs. 1000.

UPDATE Client_Master SET BalDue = 1000 WHERE Client_no = 'C00001';

(c) Change the cost price of 'Trousers' to Rs. 950.00.

UPDATE Product_Master SET CostPrice = 950.00 WHERE Description = 'Trousers';

(d) Change the city of the salesman to Pune.

UPDATE Client_Master SET City = 'Pune';

5. SQL Statement for deleting records in a table:

(a) Delete all salesmen from the Salesman_Master whose salaries are equal to Rs. 3500.

DELETE FROM Salesman_Master WHERE SalAmt = 3500;

(b) Delete all products from Product_Master where the quantity on hand is equal to 100.

DELETE FROM Product_Master WHERE QtyOnHand = 100;

(c) Delete from Client_Master where the column state holds the value 'Tamil Nadu'.

DELETE FROM Client_Master WHERE State = 'Tamil Nadu';

6. SQL Statement for altering the table structure:

(a) Add a column called 'Telephone' of data type 'number' and size ='10' to the Client_Master table.

ALTER TABLE Client_Master ADD (Telephone number(10));

(b) Change the size of SellPrice column in Product_Master to 10,2.

ALTER TABLE Product_Master MODIFY (SellPrice number(10,2));

7. SQL Statement for deleting the table structure along with the data:

(a) Destroy the table Client_Master along with its data.

DROP TABLE Client_Master;

8. SQL Statement for renaming the table:

(a) Change the name of the Salesman_Master table to sman_mast.

RENAME Salesman_Master TO sman_mast;

11. Interactive SQL PART - II

1. SQL Statement for creating the tables:

Note

Before, executing the CREATE TABLE with the Data Constraints ensure that the tables with similar names do not exist within the database. Executing the following SQL commands will eliminate the problem of existing tables.

```
DROP TABLE IF EXISTS SALES_ORDER_DETAILS;
DROP TABLE IF EXISTS SALES_ORDER;
DROP TABLE IF EXISTS SALESMAN_MASTER;
DROP TABLE IF EXISTS PRODUCT_MASTER;
DROP TABLE IF EXISTS CLIENT_MASTER;
```

(a) **Table Name:** CLIENT_MASTER

```
CREATE TABLE CLIENT_MASTER(CLIENTNO varchar2(6) PRIMARY KEY,
    NAME varchar2(20) NOT NULL, ADDRESS1 varchar2(30), ADDRESS2 varchar2(30),
    CITY varchar2(15), PINCODE number(8), STATE varchar2(15), BALDUE number(10,2),
    CONSTRAINT ck_client CHECK (CLIENTNO like 'C%'));
```

(b) **Table Name:** PRODUCT_MASTER

```
CREATE TABLE PRODUCT_MASTER(PRODUCTNO varchar2(6) PRIMARY KEY,
    DESCRIPTION varchar2(15) NOT NULL, PROFITPERCENT number(4,2) NOT NULL,
    UNITMEASURE varchar2(10) NOT NULL, QTYONHAND number(8) NOT NULL,
    REORDERLVL number(8) NOT NULL, SELLPRICE number(8,2) NOT NULL,
    COSTPRICE number(8,2) NOT NULL,
    CONSTRAINT ck_product CHECK (PRODUCTNO like 'P%'),
    CONSTRAINT ck_sell CHECK (SELLPRICE <> 0),
    CONSTRAINT ck_cost CHECK (COSTPRICE <> 0));
```

(c) **Table Name:** SALESMAN_MASTER

```
CREATE TABLE SALESMAN_MASTER(SALESMANNO varchar2(6) PRIMARY KEY,
    SALESMANNAME varchar2(20) NOT NULL, ADDRESS1 varchar2(30) NOT NULL,
    Address2 varchar2(30), CITY varchar2(20), PINCODE number(8), State varchar2(20),
    SALAMT number(8,2) NOT NULL, TGTTOGET number(6,2) NOT NULL,
    YTDSALES number(6,2) NOT NULL, REMARKS varchar2(60),
    CONSTRAINT ck_salesman CHECK (SALESMANNO like 'S%'),
    CONSTRAINT ck_sal CHECK (SALAMT <> 0),
    CONSTRAINT ck_target CHECK (TGTTOGET <> 0));
```

(d) **Table Name:** SALES_ORDER

```
CREATE TABLE SALES_ORDER(ORDERNO varchar2(6) PRIMARY KEY,
    CLIENTNO varchar2(6) REFERENCES CLIENT_MASTER, ORDERDATE date,
```

```
DELYADDR varchar2(25), SALESMANNO varchar2(6) REFERENCES
SALESMAN_MASTER,
DELYTYPE char(1) DEFAULT 'F', BILLEDYN char(1), DELYDATE date,
ORDERSTATUS varchar2(10), CONSTRAINT ck_order CHECK (ORDERNO like 'O%'),
CONSTRAINT ck_dely_type CHECK (DELYTYPE IN ('P', 'F')),
CONSTRAINT ck_ord_status
      CHECK(ORDERSTATUS IN ('In Process', 'Fulfilled', 'Backorder', 'Cancelled')));
```

(e) **Table Name:** SALES_ORDER_DETAILS

```
CREATE TABLE SALES_ORDER_DETAILS(
      ORDERNO varchar2(6) REFERENCES SALES_ORDER,
      PRODUCTNO varchar2(6) REFERENCES PRODUCT_MASTER,
      QTYORDERED number(8), QTYDISP number(8), PRODUCTRATE number(10,2),
      PRIMARY KEY (ORDERNO, PRODUCTNO));
```

2. SQL Statement for inserting data into their respective tables:

(a) Data for **CLIENT_MASTER** table:

```
INSERT INTO Client_Master (ClientNo, Name, City, PinCode, State, BalDue)
      VALUES ('C00001', 'Ivan Bayross', 'Mumbai', 400054, 'Maharashtra', 15000);
INSERT INTO Client_Master (ClientNo, Name, City, PinCode, State, BalDue)
      VALUES ('C00002', 'Mamta Muzumdar', 'Madras'', 780001, 'Tamil Nadu', 0);
INSERT INTO Client_Master (ClientNo, Name, City, Pincode, State, BalDue)
      VALUES ('C00003', 'Chhaya Bankar', 'Mumbai', 400057, 'Maharashtra', 5000);
INSERT INTO Client_Master (ClientNo, Name, City, PinCode, State, BalDue)
      VALUES ('C00004', 'Ashwini Joshi', 'Bangalore', 560001, 'Karnataka', 0);
INSERT INTO Client_Master (ClientNo, Name, City, PinCode, State, BalDue)
      VALUES ('C00005', 'Hansel Colaco', 'Mumbai', 400060, 'Maharashtra', 2000);
INSERT INTO Client_Master (ClientNo, Name, City, PinCode, State, BalDue)
      VALUES ('C00006', 'Deepak Sharma', 'Mangalore', 560050, 'Karnataka', 0);
```

(b) Data for **PRODUCT_MASTER** table

```
INSERT INTO Product_Master VALUES ('P00001', 'T-Shirts', 5, 'Piece', 200, 50, 350, 250);
INSERT INTO Product_Master VALUES ('P03453', 'Shirts', 6, 'Piece', 150, 50, 500, 350);
INSERT INTO Product_Master VALUES ('P06734', 'Cotton Jeans', 5, 'Piece', 100, 20, 600, 450);
INSERT INTO Product_Master VALUES ('P07865', 'Jeans', 5, 'Piece', 100, 20, 750, 500);
INSERT INTO Product_Master VALUES ('P07868', 'Trousers', 2, 'Piece', 150, 50, 850, 550);
INSERT INTO Product_Master VALUES ('P07885', 'Pull Overs', 2.5, 'Piece', 80, 30, 700, 450);
INSERT INTO Product_Master VALUES ('P07965', 'Denim Shirts', 4, 'Piece', 100, 40, 350, 250);
INSERT INTO Product_Master VALUES ('P07975', 'Lycra Tops', 5, 'Piece', 70, 30, 300, 175);
```

INSERT INTO Product_Master VALUES ('P08865', 'Skirts', 5, 'Piece', 75, 30, 450, 300);

(c) Data for **SALESMAN_MASTER** table

INSERT INTO Salesman_Master VALUES ('S00001', 'Aman', 'A/14', 'Worli', 'Mumbai', 400002, 'Maharashtra', 3000, 100, 50, 'Good');

INSERT INTO Salesman_Master VALUES ('S00002', 'Omkar', '65', 'Nariman', 'Mumbai', 400001, 'Maharashtra', 3000, 200, 100, 'Good');

INSERT INTO Salesman_Master VALUES ('S00003', 'Raj', 'P-7', 'Bandra', 'Mumbai', 400032, 'Maharashtra', 3000, 200, 100, 'Good');

INSERT INTO Salesman_Master VALUES ('S00004', 'Ashish', 'A/5', 'Juhu', 'Bombay', 400044, 'Maharashtra', 3500, 200, 150, 'Good');

(d) Data for **SALES_ORDER** table

INSERT INTO Sales_Order (OrderNo, OrderDate, ClientNo, DelyType, BilledYn, SalesmanNo, DelyDate, OrderStatus) VALUES('O19001', '12-june-02', 'C00001', 'F', ' N', 'S00001', '20-july-02', 'In Process');

INSERT INTO Sales_Order (OrderNo, OrderDate, ClientNo, DelyType, BilledYn, SalesmanNo, DelyDate, OrderStatus) VALUES('O19002', '25-june-02', 'C00002', 'P', ' N', 'S00002', '27-july-02', 'Cancelled');

INSERT INTO Sales_Order (OrderNo, OrderDate, ClientNo, DelyType, BilledYn, SalesmanNo, DelyDate, OrderStatus) VALUES('O19003', '18-feb-02', 'C00003', 'F', ' Y', 'S00003', '20-feb-02', 'Fulfilled');

INSERT INTO Sales_Order (OrderNo, OrderDate, ClientNo, DelyType, BilledYn, SalesmanNo, DelyDate, OrderStatus) VALUES('O19003', '03-apr-02', 'C00001', 'F', 'Y', 'S00001', '07-apr-02', 'Fulfilled');

INSERT INTO Sales_Order (OrderNo, OrderDate, ClientNo, DelyType, BilledYn, SalesmanNo, DelyDate, OrderStatus) VALUES('O46866', '20-may-02', 'C00004', 'P', 'N', 'S00002', '22-may-02', 'Cancelled');

INSERT INTO Sales_Order (OrderNo, OrderDate, ClientNo, DelyType, BilledYn, SalesmanNo, DelyDate, OrderStatus) VALUES('O19008', '24-may-02', 'C00005', 'F', 'N', 'S00004', '26-july-96', 'In Process');

(e) Data for **SALES_ORDER_DETAILS** table

INSERT INTO Sales_Order_Details (OrderNo, ProductNo, QtyOrdered, QtyDisp, ProductRate)
VALUES('O19001', 'P00001', 4, 4, 525);

INSERT INTO Sales_Order_Details (OrderNo, ProductNo, QtyOrdered, QtyDisp, ProductRate)
VALUES('O19001', 'P07965', 2, 1, 8400);

INSERT INTO Sales_Order_Details (OrderNo, ProductNo, QtyOrdered, QtyDisp, ProductRate)
VALUES('O19001', 'P07885', 2, 1, 5250);

INSERT INTO Sales_Order_Details (OrderNo, ProductNo, QtyOrdered, QtyDisp, ProductRate)
VALUES('O19002', 'P00001', 10, 0, 525);

INSERT INTO Sales_Order_Details (OrderNo, ProductNo, QtyOrdered, QtyDisp, ProductRate)

```
    VALUES('O46865', 'P07868', 3, 3, 3150);
INSERT INTO Sales_Order_Details (OrderNo, ProductNo, QtyOrdered, QtyDisp, ProductRate)
    VALUES('O46865', 'P07885', 3, 1, 5250);
INSERT INTO Sales_Order_Details (OrderNo, ProductNo, QtyOrdered, QtyDisp, ProductRate)
    VALUES('O46865', 'P00001', 10, 10, 525);
INSERT INTO Sales_Order_Details (OrderNo, ProductNo, QtyOrdered, QtyDisp, ProductRate)
    VALUES('O46865', 'P03453', 4, 4, 1050);
INSERT INTO Sales_Order_Details (OrderNo, ProductNo, QtyOrdered, QtyDisp, ProductRate)
    VALUES('O19003', 'P03453', 2, 2, 1050);
INSERT INTO Sales_Order_Details (OrderNo, ProductNo, QtyOrdered, QtyDisp, ProductRate)
    VALUES('O19003', 'P06734', 1, 1, 12000);
INSERT INTO Sales_Order_Details (OrderNo, ProductNo, QtyOrdered, QtyDisp, ProductRate)
    VALUES('O46866', 'P07965', 1, 0, 8400);
INSERT INTO Sales_Order_Details (OrderNo, ProductNo, QtyOrdered, QtyDisp, ProductRate)
    VALUES('O46866', 'P07975', 1, 0, 1050);
INSERT INTO Sales_Order_Details (OrderNo, ProductNo, QtyOrdered, QtyDisp, ProductRate)
    VALUES('O19008', 'P00001', 10, 5, 525);
INSERT INTO Sales_Order_Details (OrderNo, ProductNo, QtyOrdered, QtyDisp, ProductRate)
    VALUES('O19008', 'P07975', 5, 3, 1050);
```

12. *InteractiveSQL PART - III*

1. **Generate SQL Statements to perform the following computations on table data:**

a. Listing of the names of all clients having 'a' as the second letter in their names.

SELECT Name FROM Client_Master WHERE Name like '_a%';

b. Listing of clients who stay in a city whose first letter is 'M'

SELECT ClientNo, Name FROM Client_Master WHERE City LIKE 'M%';

c. List all clients who stay in 'Bangalore' or 'Mangalore'

SELECT ClientNo, Name FROM Client_Master WHERE City IN('Bangalore', 'Mangalore');

d. List all clients whose BalDue is greater than value 10000.

SELECT ClientNo, Name FROM Client_Master WHERE Baldue > 10000;

e. Print the information from Sales_Order table for orders placed in the month of June.

SELECT * FROM Sales_Order WHERE TO_CHAR(OrderDate,'MON') = 'JUN';

f. Displaying the order information of ClientNo 'C00001' and 'C00002'.

SELECT * FROM Sales_Order WHERE ClientNo IN('C00001', 'C00002');

g. List products whose selling price is greater than 500 and less than or equal to 750.

SELECT ProductNo, Description FROM Product_Master WHERE SellPrice > 500 and SellPrice < 750;

h. Listing of products whose selling price is more than 500 with the new selling price calculated as original selling price plus 15%.

SELECT ProductNo, Description, SellPrice, SellPrice*15 new_price FROM Product_Master
WHERE SellPrice > 500;

i. Listing of names, city and state of clients who are not in the state of 'Maharashtra'.

SELECT Name, City, State FROM Client_Master WHERE State NOT IN('Maharashtra');

j. Count the total number of orders.

SELECT COUNT(OrderNo) 'No. Of Order' FROM Sales_Order;

k. Calculating the average price of all the products.

SELECT AVG(SellPrice) FROM Product_Master;

l. Determining the maximum and minimum price for the product prices.

SELECT MAX(SellPrice) max_price, MIN(SellPrice) min_price FROM Product_Master;

m. Count the number of products having price greater than or equal to 500.

SELECT COUNT(ProductNo) FROM Product_Master WHERE SellPrice <= 1500;

n. Find all the products whose QtyOnHand is less than reorder level.

SELECT ProductNo, Description FROM Product_Master WHERE QtyOnHand < ReorderLvl;

2. SQL Statements for Date Manipulation:

a. Display the order number and day on which clients placed their order.

SELECT OrderNo, TO_CHAR(OrderDate, 'day') FROM Sales_Order;

b. Display the month (in alphabets) and date when the order must be delivered.

SELECT TO_CHAR(DelyDate, 'month'), DelyDate FROM Sales_Order
ORDER BY TO_CHAR(DelyDate, 'month');

c. List the OrderDate in the format 'DD-Month-YY'. e.g. 12-February-02.

SELECT TO_CHAR(Orderdate, 'DD-Month-YY') FROM Sales_Order;

d. Find the date, 15 days after today's date.

SELECT SYSDATE + 15 FROM DUAL;

13. *Interactive SQL PART - IV*

1. SQL statements for using Having and Group By Clauses:

a. Printing the description and total quantity sold for each product.

SELECT description, SUM(QtyDisp) FROM Product_Master, Sales_Order_Details
WHERE Product_Master.ProductNo = Sales_Order_Details.ProductNo
GROUP BY Description;

b. Finding the value of each product sold.

SELECT Sales_Order_Details.ProductNo, Product_Master.Description,
SUM(Sales_Order_Details.QtyDisp * Sales_Order_Details.ProductRate) 'Sales Per Product'

```
FROM Sales_Order_Details, Product_Master
    WHERE Product_Master.ProductNo = Sales_Order_Details.ProductNo
    GROUP BY Sales_Order_Details.ProductNo, Product_Master.Description;
```

c. Calculating the average quantity sold for each client that has a maximum order value of 15000.00.

```
SELECT CM.ClientNo, CM.Name, AVG(SOD.QtyDisp) 'Avg. Sales'
    FROM Sales_Order_Details SOD, Sales_Order SO, Client_Master CM
        WHERE CM.ClientNo = SO.ClientNo AND SO.OrderNo = SOD.OrderNo
    GROUP BY CM.ClientNo, Name HAVING MAX(SOD.QtyOrdered * SOD.ProductRate) >
    15000;
```

d. Finding out the total of all the billed orders for the month of June.

```
SELECT SO.OrderNo, SO.OrderDate, SUM(SOD.QtyOrdered * SOD.ProductRate) 'Order Billed'
    FROM Sales_Order SO, Sales_Order_Details SOD WHERE SOD.OrderNo = SO.OrderNo
    AND SO.Billed = 'Y' AND to_char(OrderDate, 'MON') = 'Jun' GROUP BY SO.OrderNo;
```

2. **Exercises on Joins and Correlation:**

a. Find out the products, which have been sold to 'Ivan Bayross'.

```
SELECT SOD.ProductNo, PM.Description
    FROM Sales_Order_Details SOD, Sales_Order SO, Product_Master PM, Client_Master
    CM
        WHERE PM.ProductNo = SOD.ProductNo AND SO.OrderNo = SOD.OrderNo
            AND CM.ClientNo = SO.ClientNo AND CM.Name = 'Ivan Bayross';
```

b. Finding out the products and their quantities that will have to be delivered in the current month.

```
SELECT SOD.ProductNo, PM.Description, SUM(SOD.QtyOrdered)
    FROM Sales_Order_Details SOD, Sales_Order SO, Product_Master PM
        WHERE PM.ProductNo = SOD.ProductNo AND SO.OrderNo = SOD.OrderNo
            AND TO_CHAR(DelyDate, 'MON-YY') = TO_CHAR(SYSDATE,
            'MON-YY')
        GROUP BY SOD.ProductNo, PM.Description;
```

c. Listing the ProductNo and description of constantly sold (i.e. rapidly moving) products.

```
SELECT DISTINCT Product_Master.ProductNo, Description
    FROM Sales_Order_Details, Product_Master
        WHERE Product_Master.ProductNo =Sales_Order_Details.ProductNo;
```

d. Finding the names of clients who have purchased 'Trousers'.

```
SELECT DISTINCT Sales_Order.ClientNo, Client_Master.Name
    FROM Sales_Order_Details, Sales_Order, Product_Master, Client_Master
        WHERE Product_Master.ProductNo = Sales_Order_Details.ProductNo
            AND Sales_Order.OrderNo = Sales_Order_Details.OrderNo
```

```
AND Client_Master.ClientNo = Sales_Order.ClientNo
AND Description = 'Trousers';
```

e. Listing the products and orders from customers who have ordered less than 5 units of 'Pull Overs'.

```
SELECT Sales_Order_Details.ProductNo, Sales_Order_Details.OrderNo
    FROM Sales_Order_Details, Sales_Order, Product_Master
        WHERE Sales_Order.OrderNo = Sales_Order_Details.OrderNo
        AND Product_Master.ProductNo = Sales_Order_Details.ProductNo
        AND Sales_Order_Details.QtyOrdered < 5 AND Product_Master.Description =
        'Pull Overs';
```

f. Finding the products and their quantities for the orders placed by 'Ivan Bayross' and 'Mamta Muzumdar'.

```
SELECT SOD.ProductNo, PM.Description, SUM(QtyOrdered) 'Units Ordered'
    FROM Sales_Order_Details SOD, Sales_Order SO, Product_Master PM, Client_Master
    CM
        WHERE SO.OrderNo = SOD.OrderNo AND PM.ProductNo = SOD.ProductNo
            AND CM.ClientNo = SO.ClientNo
            AND (CM.Name = 'Ivan Bayross' OR CM.Name = 'Mamta Muzumdar')
        GROUP BY SOD.ProductNo, PM.Description;
```

g. Finding the products and their quantities for the orders placed by ClientNo 'C00001' and 'C00002'.

```
SELECT SO.ClientNo, SOD.ProductNo, PM.Description, SUM(QtyOrdered) 'Units Ordered'
    FROM Sales_Order SO, Sales_Order_Details SOD, Product_Master PM, Client_Master
    CM
        WHERE SO.OrderNo = SOD.OrderNo AND SOD.ProductNo = PM.ProductNo
            AND SO.ClientNo = CM.ClientNo
        GROUP BY SO.ClientNo, SOD.ProductNo, PM.Description
            HAVING SO.ClientNo = 'C00001' OR SO.ClientNo='C00002';
```

3. SQL statements for exercises on Sub-queries:

a. Finding the non-moving products i.e. products not being sold.

```
SELECT ProductNo, Description FROM Product_Master
    WHERE ProductNo NOT IN(SELECT ProductNo FROM Sales_Order_Details);
```

b. Finding the name and complete address for the customer who has placed Order number 'O19001'.

```
SELECT Name ,Address1, Address2, City, State, PinCode FROM Client_Master
    WHERE ClientNo IN(SELECT ClientNo FROM Sales_Order WHERE OrderNo = 'O19001');
```

c. Finding the clients who have placed orders before the month of May'02.

```
SELECT ClientNo, Name FROM Client_Master WHERE ClientNo IN(SELECT ClientNo
    FROM Sales_Order WHERE TO_CHAR(OrderDate, 'MON,YY') < 'MAY,02');
```

d. Find out if the product 'Lycra Tops' has been ordered by any client and print the ClientNo, Name to whom it was sold.

```
SELECT ClientNo, Name FROM Client_Master WHERE ClientNo
    IN(SELECT ClientNo FROM Sales_Order WHERE OrderNo IN(SELECT OrderNo
        FROM Sales_Order_Details WHERE ProductNo IN(SELECT ProductNo
            FROM Product_Master WHERE Description = 'Lycra Tops')));
```

e. Find the names of clients who have placed orders worth Rs. 10000 or more.

```
SELECT Name FROM Client_Master WHERE ClientNo IN(SELECT ClientNo FROM Sales_Order
    WHERE OrderNo IN(SELECT OrderNo FROM Sales_Order_Details
        WHERE (QtyOrdered * ProductRate) >= 10000));
```

Section-V

ADVANCE SQL

14

SQL Performance Tuning

Indexes

When a **SELECT** statement is fired to search for a particular record, the Oracle engine must first locate the table on the hard disk. The Oracle engine reads system information and finds the start location of a table's records on the current storage media. The Oracle engine then performs a sequential search to locate records that match user-defined criteria as specified in the **SELECT**.

For example, to locate all the accounts introduced by customer **C1** held in the **ACCT_MSTR** table, the Oracle engine must first locate the **ACCT_MSTR** table and then perform a table level, sequential search, on the **INTRO_CUST_NO** column seeking a value equal to C1.

Records in the **ACCT_MSTR** table are stored in the order in which they are keyed. Thus to get all accounts where **INTRO_CUST_NO** is equal to C1 the Oracle engine must search the **entire** table column.

Indexing a table is an **access strategy**, that is, a way to sort and search records in the table. Indexes are essential to improve the speed with which record(s) can be located and retrieved from a table.

Note

 An index is an ordered list of the contents of a column, (or a group of columns) of a table.

Indexing involves forming a two dimensional matrix completely independent of the table on which the index is being created. This two dimensional matrix will have a **single column**, which will hold sorted data, extracted from the table column(s) on which the index is created.

Another column called the **address field** identifies the location of the record in the Oracle database.

When data is inserted in the table, the Oracle engine automatically inserts the data value in the index. For every data value held in the index the Oracle engine inserts a unique **ROWID** value. This is done for every data value inserted into the index, without exception. This **ROWID** indicates exactly where the record is stored in the table.

Hence once the appropriate index data values have been located, the Oracle engine locates an associated record in the table using the **ROWID** found in the table.

The records in the index are sorted in the ascending order of the index column(s).

If the SELECT statement has a **WHERE** clause bound to a table column that is indexed, the Oracle engine will **scan the index** sequentially looking for a match of the search criteria **rather than** the table column itself. The sequential search is done using an ASCII compare routine to scan the columns of an index.

Since the data is sorted on the indexed column(s), the sequential search ends as soon as the Oracle engine reads an index data value that **does not meet** the search criteria.

Address Field In The Index

Each table in an Oracle database internally has a pseudocolumn named ROWID. This pseudocolumn is not evident when listing the structure of a table by executing a **SELECT** * statement, or a **DESCRIBE** statement using SQL*Plus, nor does the pseudocolumn take up space in the table. However, each row's address can be retrieved with a SQL query using the reserved word ROWID as a column name as:

SELECT *ROWID*, ACCT_NO **FROM** ACCT_MSTR;

Output:

ROWID	ACCT_NO
AAAHdpAABAAAMWCAAA	SB1
AAAHdpAABAAAMWCAAB	CA2
AAAHdpAABAAAMWCAAC	SB3
AAAHdpAABAAAMWCAAD	CA4
AAAHdpAABAAAMWCAAE	SB5
AAAHdpAABAAAMWCAAF	SB6
AAAHdpAABAAAMWCAAG	CA7
AAAHdpAABAAAMWCAAH	SB8
AAAHdpAABAAAMWCAAI	SB9
AAAHdpAABAAAMWCAAJ	CA10

10 rows selected.

The value of the pseudocolumn **ROWID** cannot be set or deleted using the **INSERT** or **UPDATE** statements. Oracle uses the **ROWID** values in the pseudocolumn ROWID internally for the construction of indexes. ROWIDs can be referenced like other table columns in **SELECT statements** and **WHERE clauses**, but cannot be stored in the database.

The address field of an index is called **ROWID**. **ROWID** is an internally generated and maintained value, which **uniquely** identifies a record. The information in the **ROWID** column provides the Oracle engine the location of the table and a specific record in the Oracle database.

Oracle uses ROWIDs internally for the construction of indexes. Each key in an index is associated with a ROWID that points to the associated row's address for fast access.

Users and application developers can also use ROWIDs for the following functions:

- ❑ Rowids are the fastest means of accessing particular rows
- ❑ Rowids can be used to see how a table is organized
- ❑ Rowids are unique identifiers for rows in a given table

A ROWID datatype are of two formats:

- ❑ **Extended:** The extended ROWID format supports tablespace-relative data block addresses and efficiently identifies rows in partitioned tables and indexes as well as nonpartitioned tables and indexes. Tables and indexes created by an Oracle8i or higher server always have extended ROWIDs
- ❑ **Restricted:** A restricted ROWID format is also available for backward compatibility with applications developed with Oracle7 or earlier releases

The **ROWID** format used by Oracle for **Restricted format** is as follows:

```
BBBBBBB.RRRR.FFFF
```

where, **FFFF** is a unique number given by the Oracle engine to each **Data File**. Data files are the files used by the Oracle engine to store user data.

For example, a database can be a collection of data files as follows:

Data File Name	Data File Number	Size of the Data Files
Sysorcl.ora	1	10 MB
Temporcl.ora	2	5 MB
Sctstaff.ora	3	30 MB
Sctstudent.ora	4	30 MB

Each data file is given a unique number at the time of data file creation. The Oracle engine uses this number to identify the data file in which, sets of table records are stored.

Each data file is further divided into **Data Blocks** and each block is given a unique number. The unique number assigned to the first data block in a data file is **0**. Thus block number can be used to identify the data block in which a record is stored. **BBBBBBB** is the block number in which the record is stored.

Each data block can store one or more **Records**. Thus each record in the data block is given a unique record number. The unique record number assigned to the first record in each data block is 0. Thus record number can be used to identify a record stored in a block. **RRRR** is a unique record number.

Each time a record is inserted into the table, Oracle locates free space in the **Data Blocks** in the data files. Oracle then inserts a record in the table and makes an entry in the index. The entry made in the index consists of table data combined with the Oracle engine created **ROWID** for the table record.

Thus, in a **restricted** format, data in an index will be represented as follows:

Data Field	Address Field
SB1	00000440.0000.0003
CA2	00000440.0001.0003
SB3	00000440.0002.0003
CA4	00000441.0000.0003
SB5	00000441.0001.0003

The **ROWID** format used by Oracle for **Extended format** is as follows:

OOOOOOFFFBBBBBBRRR

where,

OOOOOO is the data object number that identifies the database segment (**i.e. AAAHdp** in the example below). Schema objects in the same segment, such as a cluster of tables, will have the same data object number.

FFF is the TABLESPACE-relative datafile number of the datafile that contains the row (**i.e. AAB** in the example below).

BBBBBB is the data block that contains the row (**i.e. AAAMWC** in the example below). Block numbers are relative to their datafile, not tablespace. Therefore, two rows with identical block numbers could reside in two different datafiles of the same tablespace.

RRR is the row in the block (**i.e. AAA** in the example below).

Thus, in an **extended** format, data in an index will be represented as follows:

Data Field	Address Field
SB1	AAAHdpAABAAAMWCAAA
CA2	AAAHdpAABAAAMWCAAB
SB3	AAAHdpAABAAAMWCAAC
CA4	AAAHdpAABAAAMWCAAD
SB5	AAAHdpAABAAAMWCAAE

To retrieve data from an Oracle table at the fastest possible speed, the Oracle engine requires a **Search Criteria** (**i.e.** the value to look for in the index).

Since the data in the index is sorted, the sequential search ends as soon as the Oracle engine reads an index data value that does not meet the search criteria. Thus, Oracle engine need not search the entire indexed column. This sharply reduces data retrieval time.

Once the data value in an index is located, the address field in an index specifies a **ROWID** which points to a data file, block and the record number directly. Thus the time taken by the Oracle engine to locate table data on the hard disk is reduced and data retrieval time is vastly improved.

Example:

Show all those account number along with the account opening date verified by the employee **E1**. There is no index on the field VERI_EMP_NO created for the ACCT_MSTR table.

Solution:

SELECT ACCT_NO, OPNDT, VERI_EMP_NO **FROM** ACCT_MSTR
    WHERE VERI_EMP_NO = 'E1';

Output:

ACCT_NO	OPNDT	VERI_EMP_NO
SB1	05-NOV-03	E1
CA2	10-NOV-03	E1
SB5	15-DEC-03	E1
SB8	29-JAN-04	E1
SB11	10-MAR-04	E1
CA12	10-MAR-04	E1
SB15	15-APR-04	E1

Explanation:

When the above select statement is executed, since an index is not created on the **VERI_EMP_NO** column, the Oracle engine will scan the Oracle system information to locate the table in the data file. The Oracle engine will then perform a sequential search to retrieve records that match the search criteria (**i.e.** VERI_EMP_NO = E1) by comparing the value in the search criteria with the value in the **VERI_EMP_NO** column from the first record to the last record in the table.

Example:

Show all those account number along with the account opening date verified by the employee **E1**. There is an index on the field VERI_EMP_NO created for the ACCT_MSTR table.

Since an index exists on the **VERI_EMP_NO** column of the **ACCT_MSTR** table, the index data will be represented as follows:

Index Name: **idxVeriEmpNo**

VERI_EMP_NO	ROWID	VERI_EMP_NO	ROWID
E1	AAAHeeAABAAAMWCAAA	E1	AAAHeeAABAAAMWCAAB
E4	AAAHeeAABAAAMWCAAC	E4	AAAHeeAABAAAMWCAAD
E1	AAAHeeAABAAAMWCAAE	E4	AAAHeeAABAAAMWCAAF
E4	AAAHeeAABAAAMWCAAG	E1	AAAHeeAABAAAMWCAAH
E4	AAAHeeAABAAAMWCAAI	E4	AAAHeeAABAAAMWCAAJ
E1	AAAHeeAABAAAMWCAAK	E1	AAAHeeAABAAAMWCAAL
E4	AAAHeeAABAAAMWCAAM	E4	AAAHeeAABAAAMWCAAN
E1	AAAHeeAABAAAMWCAAO		

Note

 The index is in the **ascending** order of VERI_EMP_NO. The addresses have been assigned a data object number, a datafile number, a data block numbers and a row number in the **order of creation.**

Solution:

SELECT ACCT_NO, OPNDT, VERI_EMP_NO **FROM** ACCT_MSTR
    WHERE VERI_EMP_NO = 'E1';

When the above select statement is executed, since an index is created on **VERI_EMP_NO** column, the Oracle engine will scan the index to search for a specific data value (**i.e.** VERI_EMP_NO = E1). The Oracle engine will then perform a sequential search to retrieve records that match the search criteria (**i.e.** VERI_EMP_NO = E1). When **E2** is read, the Oracle engine stops further retrieval from the index.

For the seven records retrieved, the Oracle engine locates the address of the table records from the **ROWID** field and retrieves records stored at the specified address.

Output:

VERI_EMP_NO	ROWID
El	AAAHeeAABAAAMWCAAA
El	AAAHeeAABAAAMWCAAB
El	AAAHeeAABAAAMWCAAE
El	AAAHeeAABAAAMWCAAH
El	AAAHeeAABAAAMWCAAK
El	AAAHeeAABAAAMWCAAL
El	AAAHeeAABAAAMWCAAO

The **Rowid** in the current example indicates that the records with VERI_EMP_NO E1 are located in **data object** numbered **AAAHee** having **datafile** numbered **AAB**, **data block** numbered **AAAMW** and the **rows** number as **AA_**.

Thus data retrieval from a table by using an index is much faster than data retrieval from the table where indexes are not defined.

Duplicate / Unique Index

Oracle allows the creation of two types of indexes. These are:

- Indexes that **allow** duplicate values for the indexed columns **i.e. Duplicate Index**
- Indexes that **deny** duplicate values for the indexed columns **i.e. Unique Index**

Creation Of An Index

An index can be created on one or more columns. Based on the number of columns included in the index, an index can be:

- Simple Index
- Composite Index

Creating Simple Index

An index created on a single column of a table is called a **Simple Index**. The syntax for creating simple index that allows duplicate values is as described.

Syntax:

```
CREATE INDEX <IndexName> ON <TableName> (<ColumnName>);
```

Example:

Create a simple index on **VERI_EMP_NO** column of the **ACCT_MSTR** table.

Solution:

CREATE INDEX idxVeriEmpNo **ON** ACCT_MSTR (VERI_EMP_NO);

Output:

```
Index created.
```

Creating Composite Index

An index created on more than one column is called a **Composite Index**. The syntax for creating a composite index that allows duplicate values is:

Syntax:

```
CREATE INDEX <IndexName>
      ON <TableName> (<ColumnName1>, <ColumnName2>);
```

Example:

Create a composite index on the **TRANS_MSTR** table on columns **TRANS_NO** and **ACCT_NO**

Solution:

CREATE INDEX idxTransAcctNo **ON** TRANS_MSTR (TRANS_NO, ACCT_NO);

Output:

```
Index created.
```

Note

 The indexes in the above examples do not enforce uniqueness **i.e.** the columns included in the index can hold duplicate values. To create unique index, the keyword **UNIQUE** should be included in the **Create Index** command.

Creation of Unique Index

A unique index can also be created on one or more columns. If an index is created on a single column, it is called a **Simple Unique Index**. The syntax for creating a simple unique index is as follows:

Syntax:

```
CREATE UNIQUE INDEX <IndexName> ON <TableName>
(<ColumnName>);
```

If an index is created on more than one column, it is called a **Composite Unique Index**. The syntax for creating a composite unique index is as follows:

Syntax:

```
CREATE UNIQUE  INDEX <IndexName>
      ON <TableName> (<ColumnName>, <ColumnName>);
```

Example:

Create a unique index on **CUST_NO** column of the **CUST_MSTR** table.

Solution:

CREATE UNIQUE INDEX idx_CustNo **ON** CUST_MSTR (CUST_NO);

Output:

```
Index created.
```

Note

 When the user defines a primary key or a unique key constraint at table or column level, the Oracle engine automatically creates a **unique index** on the primary key or unique key column(s).

Reverse Key Indexes

Creating a reverse key index, when compared to a simple index, reverses each byte of the column being indexed while keeping the column order. Such an arrangement can help avoid performance degradation in indexes where modifications to the index are concentrated on a small set of blocks. By reversing the keys of the index, the insertions become distributed all over the index.

For example, the column value is stored in an index as shown below:

In normal index	In reverse index
C1	1C
C2	2C
C3	3C
C4	4C

Here, column values are stored in a normal index. Then the rows will be stored together in one block as the values are almost the same for all rows. When the same column is indexed in reverse mode then the column values will be stored in different blocks as the starting value differs.

Using the key arrangement eliminates the ability to run an index range-scanning query on the index. As lexically adjacent keys are not stored next to each other in a reverse key index, only fetch-by-key or full-index (table) scans can be performed.

Under some circumstances, using a reverse-key index can make an application run faster.

Syntax:

```
CREATE  INDEX  <IndexName>
        ON  <TableName>  (<ColumnName>)  REVERSE
```

Example:

Create a reverse index on **CUST_NO** column of the **CUST_MSTR** table.

Solution:

CREATE INDEX idx_CustNo **ON** CUST_MSTR (CUST_NO) **REVERSE;**

Output:

```
Index created.
```

A reverse key index can be rebuilt into a normal index using the keywords **REBUILD NOREVERSE**.

Syntax:

```
ALTER  INDEX  <IndexName>  REBUILD  NOREVERSE;
```

Example:

Modify the reverse index just created to a normal index on **CUST_NO** column of the **CUST_MSTR** table.

ALTER INDEX idx_CustNo **REBUILD NOREVERSE;**

Note
A normal index **cannot** be rebuilt as a reverse key index.

Bitmap Indexes

The advantages of using bitmap indexes are greatest for low cardinality columns **i.e.** columns in which the number of distinct values is small compared to the number of rows in the table. If the values in a column are repeated more than a hundred times, the column is a candidate for a bitmap index. For example, in a table with one million rows, rows with 10,000 distinct values are candidates for a bitmap index.

Syntax:

```
CREATE BITMAP INDEX <IndexName> ON <TableName>
(<ColumnName>);
```

Example:

Create a bitmap index on **TRANS_NO** column of the **TRANS_MSTR** table.

CREATE BITMAP INDEX bitidx_TransNo **ON** TRANS_DTLS (TRANS_NO);

Output:

```
Index created.
```

Bitmap indexing provides the following benefits:

- ❑ Reduced response time for large classes of ad hoc queries
- ❑ A substantial reduction of space usage compared to other indexing techniques
- ❑ Dramatic performance gains even on very low end hardware

Fully indexing a large table with a normal index can be prohibitively expensive in terms of space since the index can be several times larger than the data in the table. Bitmap indexes are typically only a fraction of the size of the indexed data in the table.

In adhoc queries or similar situations, bitmap indexes can dramatically improve query performance. AND and OR conditions in the **WHERE** clause of a query can be quickly resolved by performing the corresponding Boolean operations directly on the bitmaps before converting the resulting bitmap to rowids. If the resulting number of rows is small, the query can be answered very quickly without resorting to a full scan of the table.

Function Based Index

A column's index **will not** be used when the same column is expressed in an arithmetic expression or function in the **WHERE** clause.

To facilitate such an operation Oracle **allows** creating indexes based on a function or expression mapped to one or more columns in a table. Function based indexes are very useful when the **where clause** contains functions or expressions to evaluate a query.

The function used for building the index can be an arithmetic expression or an expression that contains a PL/SQL function, package function, or SQL function. The expression **cannot contain** any aggregate functions. A function-based index cannot be created on a LOB column, REF, nested table column or the object type contains a LOB, REF, or nested table.

Syntax:

```
CREATE INDEX <IndexName> ON <TableName>
(<Function>(<ColumnName>));
```

Example:

Create an index on the function **UPPER** used on **FNAME** column of the **CUST_MSTR** table.

CREATE INDEX idx_Name **ON** CUST_MSTR **(UPPER(**FNAME**));**

Output:

```
Index created.
```

Key-Compressed Index

Key compression breaks an index key into a prefix and a suffix entry. Compression is achieved by sharing the prefix entries among all the suffix entries in an index block. This sharing can lead to huge savings in space, allowing more keys to be stored per index block.

Key compression can be useful when in a non-unique index the ROWID is appended to make the key unique. When key compression is used, the duplicate key will be stored as a prefix entry on the index block without the ROWID. The remaining rows will be suffix entries consisting of only the ROWID.

Syntax:

```
CREATE INDEX <IndexName> ON <TableName>
    (<ColumnName1>, <ColumnName2>, ...) COMPRESS 1
```

For unique indexes, the valid range of prefix length values is from 1 to the number of key columns minus 1. The default prefix length is the number of key columns minus 1.

For non-unique indexes, the valid range of prefix length values is from 1 to the number of key columns. The default prefix length is the number of key columns.

Dropping Indexes

Indexes associated with the tables can be removed by using the **DROP INDEX** command.

Syntax:

```
DROP INDEX <indexname>;
```

Example:

Remove index **idx_CustNo** created for the table **CUST_MSTR.**

DROP INDEX idx_CustNo;

Note

When a table, which has associated indexes (unique or non-unique), is dropped, the Oracle engine automatically drops all the associated indexes as well.

Multiple Indexes On A Table

The Oracle engine allows creation of multiple indexes on each table. The Oracle engine prepares a **query plan** to decide on the index that must be used for specific data retrieval based on the **WHERE clause** or the **ORDER BY clause** specified in the SELECT statement.

Whenever a SELECT statement is executed, the Oracle engine prepares a query plan that identifies the data retrieval method. The query plan (among other information) holds the name of the table from which data will be retrieved and the name of the index that must be used for data retrieval.

Note
If a SELECT statement is fired without a where clause and without an order by clause the Oracle engine **does not** use the indexes created on the table for data extraction.

- If a where clause or an ORDER BY clause is specified, the Oracle engine uses the index created on a column on which the where clause or the order by clause is specified
- If there is no index for the column specified in the WHERE clause or the ORDER BY clause is not created, data is retrieved without using indexes

Instances When The Oracle Engine Uses An Index For Data Extraction

- A SELECT statement with WHERE clause specified on the column on which an index exists
- A SELECT statement with ORDER BY clause specified on the column on which an index exists

Instances When The Oracle Engine Does Not Use An Index For Data Extraction

- A SELECT statement without search criteria and order by clause
- A SELECT statement with WHERE clause specified on the column on which an index is not defined
- A SELECT statement with ORDER BY clause specified on the column on which an index is not defined

Too Many Indexes - A Problem

Each time a record is inserted into the table:

- The Oracle engine locates free space in the blocks in the data files
- Then inserts a record in all the indexes associated with the table
- The index entries are sorted in the ascending order as well

If too many indexes are created on a table the Oracle engine will take longer to insert a record in a table since index processing must be done for each record that is inserted, updated or deleted.

Thus while indexes speeds up data retrieval, data insertion slows down considerably. A balance must be maintained such that only columns that are frequently used for data retrieval (**i.e.** querying the table) are indexed.

Using ROWID to delete duplicate rows from a table

Retaining one row in table, while deleting all other duplicate rows, is quite an interesting exercise. If the delete statement contains a WHERE clause based on **EMP_NO** then **all rows** in the table will be deleted immediately.

For example, if the data in the **EMP_MSTR** table is:

EMP_NO	FNAME	DEPT
E1	Ivan	Administration
E1	Ivan	Administration
E1	Ivan	Administration
E2	Amit	Loans And Financing
E3	Maya	Client Servicing

EMP_NO	FNAME	DEPT
E4	Peter	Loans And Financing
E5	Mandhar	Marketing
E6	Sonal	Administration
E7	Anil	Marketing
E8	Seema	Client Servicing
E9	Vikram	Marketing
E10	Anjali	Administration

And a delete statement is executed as:

DELETE FROM EMP_Master **WHERE** EMP_NO **IN**('E1' , 'E2', 'E3');

All records with EMP_NO E1, E2 or E3 will be deleted immediately.

However, what is required is that the Oracle engine **must retain one record** and delete all other duplicate records. To retain one record, the where clause must be defined on the column that **uniquely** identifies each record.

As seen earlier, even if user enters duplicate records, the Oracle engine will assign a unique **rowid** value that points to a record within a block, in the data file, for each record entered by the user.

A specific record in a table will be stored within a block in the data file. Each record in a block is given a unique record number. Thus at any time the value in the rowid column will always be unique.

A DELETE statement must be written such that the WHERE clause is defined using the **rowid** column. The values for the WHERE clause in the DELETE statement must be identified by using a SELECT statement that retrieves the rowid of the first row in each set of duplicate records in the table.

Then when a WHERE clause is specified in the DELETE statement with the **NOT IN** operator it deletes all duplicate rows but isolates one row in each set.

A **subquery** is an SQL statement that extracts values from table columns using a SELECT statement and passes these values as input to another SQL statement. The SELECT statement is called **Inner SQL statement** and the SQL statement to which the values of the select statement are passed is called **Parent SQL statement**. The parent SQL statement can be an INSERT, UPDATE, DELETE, SELECT or CREATE TABLE statement.

The Oracle engine executes the inner SELECT statement and then processes the parent SQL statement based on the values retrieved by the inner SELECT statement.

Inner Select Statement

To create a record set of identical records from a table, the records must be grouped on all the columns in the table by using a GROUP BY clause in the SELECT statement.

A SELECT statement will then retrieve the ROWID of the first row in each set of duplicate records. The first row in each set can be extracted by using the **MIN** function that returns the minimum value from a set of values. Thus the select statement will be:

SELECT MIN(ROWID) FROM EMP_MSTR **GROUP BY** EMP_NO, FNAME, DEPT ….

Parent SQL Statement

In the current example the Parent SQL statement will be a DELETE statement that will delete the records based on the ROWID fetched by the Inner SQL statement.

The query used to delete duplicate rows will be:

Example:

```
DELETE FROM EMP_MSTR WHERE ROWID NOT IN(SELECT MIN(ROWID)
    FROM EMP_MSTR GROUP BY EMP_NO, FNAME, DEPT);
```

When the inner SELECT statement is executed, data is grouped on all the columns of the table and the **MIN** function returns the minimum ROWID in the group. Thus the output held in memory will be as follows:

ROWID	EMP_NO	FNAME	DEPT
AAAHebAABAAAMVqAAA	E1	Ivan	Administration
AAAHebAABAAAMVqAAB	E2	Amit	Loans And Financing
AAAHebAABAAAMVqAAC	E3	Maya	Client Servicing
AAAHebAABAAAMVqAAD	E4	Peter	Loans And Financing
AAAHebAABAAAMVqAAE	E5	Mandhar	Marketing
AAAHebAABAAAMVqAAF	E6	Sonal	Administration
AAAHebAABAAAMVqAAG	E7	Anil	Marketing
AAAHebAABAAAMVqAAH	E8	Seema	Client Servicing
AAAHebAABAAAMVqAAI	E9	Vikram	Marketing
AAAHebAABAAAMVqAAJ	E10	Anjali	Administration

The Oracle engine after the execution of the inner SELECT statement replaces the SELECT statement with the minimum ROWID for each group as retrieved by the SELECT statement. Thus the delete statement will be changed to:

```
DELETE FROM EMP_MSTR WHERE ROWID NOT IN('AAAHebAABAAAMVqAAA',
    'AAAHebAABAAAMVqAAB', 'AAAHebAABAAAMVqAAC',
'AAAHebAABAAAMVqAAD',
    'AAAHebAABAAAMVqAAE', 'AAAHebAABAAAMVqAAF',
'AAAHebAABAAAMVqAAG',
    'AAAHebAABAAAMVqAAH', 'AAAHebAABAAAMVqAAI',
'AAAHebAABAAAMVqAAJ');
```

Thus all records with rowid other than those in the list specified above are deleted.

If a select statement is executed on the **EMP_MSTR** table after such a delete operation, the Oracle engine displays the following output for the query.

SELECT EMP_NO, FNAME, DEPT **FROM** EMP_MSTR;

Output:

EMP_NO	FNAME	DEPT
E1	Ivan	Administration
E2	Amit	Loans And Financing
E3	Maya	Client Servicing
E4	Peter	Loans And Financing
E5	Mandhar	Marketing
E6	Sonal	Administration
E7	Anil	Marketing
E8	Seema	Client Servicing
E9	Vikram	Marketing
E10	Anjali	Administration

Using this technique, duplicate records can be deleted from the table while maintaining one record in the table for reference.

Using ROWNUM In SQL Statements

For each row returned by a query, the **ROWNUM** pseudo column returns a number indicating the order in which Oracle engine selects the row from a table or set of joined rows. The first row selected has a **ROWNUM** of **1**, the second has **2**, and so on.

Using ROWNUM To Limit Number Of Rows In A Query

ROWNUM can be used to limit the number of rows retrieved.

Example:

Retrieve first three rows from the BRANCH_MSTR table using ROWNUM

Table Name: BRANCH_MSTR

BRANCH_NO	NAME	BRANCH_NO	NAME
B1	Vile Parle (HO)	B2	Andheri
B3	Churchgate	B4	Mahim
B5	Borivali	B6	Darya Ganj

SELECT ROWNUM, BRANCH_NO, NAME **FROM** BRANCH_MSTR **WHERE ROWNUM** < 4;

Output:

ROWNUM	BRANCH_NO	NAME
1	B1	Vile Parle (HO)
2	B2	Andheri
3	B3	Churchgate

Caution

The Oracle engine assigns a **ROWNUM** value to each row as it is retrieved, before rows are sorted on the column(s) in the ORDER BY clause. The order in which data is retrieved is dependent upon the indexes created on the table.

If an index is created on the column(s) used in the order by clause, the Oracle engine uses the index to retrieve data in a sorted order. Thus the ROWNUM will be in the order of the rows retrieved from the index.

If an index is not created on the column(s) used in the order by clause, the Oracle engine will retrieve data from the table in the order of data insertion and thus an ORDER BY clause does not affect the ROWNUM of each row.

VIEWS

After a table is created and populated with data, it may become necessary to prevent all users from accessing all columns of a table, for data security reasons. This would mean creating several tables having the appropriate number of columns and assigning specific users to each table, as required. This will answer data security requirements very well but will give rise to a great deal of redundant data being resident in tables, in the database.

To reduce **redundant data** to the minimum possible, Oracle allows the creation of an object called a **View**. A View is mapped, to a SELECT sentence. The table on which the view is based is described in the FROM clause of the SELECT statement. The SELECT clause consists of a sub-set of the columns of the table. Thus a View, which is mapped to a table, will in effect have a sub-set of the actual columns of the table from which it is built. This technique offers a simple, effective way of hiding columns of a table.

An interesting fact about a View is that it is stored only as a definition in Oracle's system catalog. When a reference is made to a View, its definition is scanned, the base table is opened and the View created on top of the base table. Hence, a view holds no data at all, until a specific call to the view is made. This reduces redundant data on the HDD to a very large extent. When a View is used to manipulate table data, the underlying base table will be completely invisible. This will give the level of data security required.

The Oracle engine treats a View just as though it was a base table. Hence a View can be queried exactly as though it was a base table. However, a query fired on a view will run slower than a query fired on a base table. This is because the View definition has to be retrieved from Oracle's system catalog, the base table has to be identified and opened in memory and then the View has to be constructed on top of the base table, suitably masking table columns. Only then will the query actually execute and return the active data set.

Some Views are used only for looking at table data. Other Views can be used to Insert, Update and Delete table data as well as View data. If a View is used to only look at table data and nothing else the View is called a **Read-Only** View. A View that is used to look at table data as well as Insert, Update and Delete table data is called an **Updateable** View.

The reasons why views are created are:

- When Data security is required
- When Data redundancy is to be kept to the minimum while maintaining data security

Lets spend some time in learning how a View is:

- Created
- Used for only viewing and / or manipulating table data (**i.e.** a read-only or updateable view)
- Destroyed

Views can be either simple or complex.

- A Simple view selects from one table. A Complex view selects from one or more tables
- A Simple view does not contain functions but Complex views contain functions
- DML can be performed on Simple views but not always on Complex views

Creating View

Syntax:

```
CREATE VIEW <ViewName> AS
    SELECT <ColumnName1>, <ColumnName2> FROM <TableName>
        WHERE <ColumnName> = <Expression List>;
        GROUP BY <Grouping Criteria> HAVING <Predicate>
```

Note

The ORDER BY clause **cannot** be used while creating a view.

Example:

Create a view called Customers on the CUST_MSTR table.

CREATE VIEW vw_Customers **AS SELECT * FROM** CUST_MSTR;

Note

The columns of the table are related to the view using a **one-to-one** relationship.

Example:

Create a view called Employees on the **EMP_MSTR** table.

CREATE VIEW vw_Employees **AS** SELECT FNAME, MNAME, LNAME, DEPT
FROM EMP_MSTR;

This creates a view by the name of **vw_Employees** based on the table **EMP_MSTR**.

Renaming The Columns Of A View

The columns of the view can take on different names from the table columns, if required.

Example:

CREATE VIEW vw_Transactions **AS**
    SELECT ACCT_NO "Account No.", DT "Date", Type, DR_CR "Mode", AMT "Amount"
        FROM TRANS_MSTR;

Selecting A Data Set From A View

Once a view has been created, it can be queried exactly like a base table.

Syntax:

```
SELECT <ColumnName1>,<ColumnName2> FROM <ViewName>;
```

Note

 Instead of a **table** name in the FROM clause, a **view** name is used. The SELECT statement can have all the clauses like WHERE, ORDER BY etc.

Example:

SELECT FNAME, LNAME, DEPT **FROM** vw_Employees
    WHERE DEPT IN('Marketing', 'Loans And Financing');

Updateable Views

Views can also be used for data manipulation (**i.e.** the user can perform the Insert, Update and Delete operations). Views on which data manipulation can be done are called **Updateable Views**. When an **updateable view name** is given in an Insert Update, or Delete SQL statement, modifications to data in the view will be immediately passed to the underlying table.

For a view to be updateable, it should meet the following criteria:

- ❑ Views defined from Single table
- ❑ If the user wants to **INSERT** records with the help of a view, then the PRIMARY KEY column(s) and **all** the NOT NULL columns must be included in the view
- ❑ The user can **UPDATE, DELETE** records with the help of a view even if the PRIMARY KEY column and NOT NULL column(s) **are excluded** from the view definition

Example:

Table Name: NOMINEE_MSTR

Column Name	Data Type	Width	Attributes
NOMINEE_NO	VarChar2	10	Primary key
ACCT_FD_NO	VarChar2	10	Not Null
NAME	VarChar2	75	Not Null
DOB	Date		
RELATIONSHIP	VarChar2	25	

CREATE VIEW vw_Nominees **AS**
    SELECT NOMINEE_NO, ACCT_FD_NO, NAME **FROM** NOMINEE_MSTR;

When an INSERT operation is performed using the view:

INSERT INTO vw_Nominees **VALUES(**'N100', 'SB432', 'Sharanam');

Oracle returns the following message:

```
1 row created
```

When a MODIFY operation is performed using the view:

UPDATE vw_Nominees **SET** NAME = 'Vaishali' **WHERE** NAME='Sharanam';

Oracle returns the following message:

```
1 row updated.
```

When a DELETE operation is performed using the view

DELETE FROM vw_Nominees **WHERE** NAME = 'Vaishali';

Oracle returns the following message:

```
1 row deleted.
```

A view can be created from more than one table. For the purpose of creating the View these tables will be linked by a **join** specified in the **WHERE clause** of the View definition.

The behavior of the View will vary for Insert, Update, Delete and Select table operations depending upon the following:

- ❑ Whether the tables were created using a Referencing clause
- ❑ Whether the tables were created without any Referencing clause and are actually standalone tables not related in any way

Views Defined From Multiple Tables (Which Have No Referencing Clause)

If a view is created from multiple tables, which were not created using a **Referencing clause** (**i.e.** No logical linkage exists between the tables), then though the PRIMARY Key Column(s) as well as the NOT NULL columns are included in the View definition the view's behavior will be as follows:

The INSERT, UPDATE or DELETE operation is **not allowed**. If attempted, Oracle displays the following error message:

For insert/modify:

ORA –01779: cannot modify a column, which maps to a non key-preserved table.

For delete:

ORA –01752: cannot delete from view without exactly one key-preserved table.

Views Defined From Multiple Tables (Which Have Been Created With A Referencing Clause)

If a view is created from multiple tables, which were created using a **Referencing clause** (i.e. a logical linkage exists between the tables), then though the **PRIMARY Key** Column(s) as well as the **NOT NULL** columns are included in the View definition, the view's behavior will be as follows:

- ❑ An **INSERT** operation is not allowed
- ❑ The **DELETE** or **MODIFY** operations **do not** affect the Master table
- ❑ The view can be used to **MODIFY** the columns of the **detail table** included in the view

If a **DELETE** operation is executed on the view, the corresponding records from the **detail table** will be deleted.

Example:

Table Name: BRANCH_MSTR

Column Name	Data Type	Size	Attributes
BRANCH_NO	VarChar2	10	Primary Key / First letter must be 'B'
NAME	VarChar2	25	

Table Name: ADDR_DTLS

Column Name	Data Type	Size	Attributes
ADDR_NO	Number	6	Primary Key
CODE_NO	VarChar2	10	Foreign Key references BRANCH_NO of the BRANCH_MSTR table.
ADDR_TYPE	VarChar2	1	Can hold the values: **H** for Head Office or **B** for Branch
ADDR1	VarChar2	50	
ADDR2	VarChar2	50	
CITY	VarChar2	25	
STATE	VarChar2	25	
PINCODE	VarChar2	6	

Syntax for creating a Master/Detail View

CREATE VIEW vw_Branch **AS**

SELECT BRANCH_NO, NAME, ADDR_TYPE, ADDR1, ADDR2, CITY, STATE, PINCODE

FROM BRANCH_MSTR, ADDR_DTS

WHERE ADDR_DTLS.CODE_NO = BRANCH_MSTR.BRANCH_NO;

When an INSERT operation is performed using the view

INSERT INTO vw_Branch VALUES('B7', 'Dahisar', 'B', 'Vertex Plaza, Shop 4,', 'Western Express Highway, Dahisar (East),', 'Mumbai', 'Maharashtra', '400078'**);**

Oracle returns the following error message:

ORA-01776: cannot modify more than one base table through a join view

When a MODIFY operation is performed using the view

UPDATE vw_Branch SET PINCODE = '400079' **WHERE** BRANCH_NO = 'B5';

Oracle returns the following message:

```
1 row updated.
```

When a DELETE operation is performed using the view

SQL> DELETE FROM vw_Branch WHERE BRANCH_NO = 'B5';

Oracle returns the following message:

```
1 row deleted.
```

Common Restrictions On Updateable Views

The following condition holds true irrespective of the view being created from a single table or multiple tables.

For the view to be updateable the view definition must not include:

- Aggregate functions
- DISTINCT, GROUP BY or HAVING clause
- Sub-queries
- Constants, Strings or Value Expressions like Sell_price * 1.05
- UNION, INTERSECT or MINUS clause
- If a view is defined from another view, the second view should be updateable

If the user tries to perform any of INSERT, UPDATE, DELETE operation, on a view, which is created from a non-updateable view Oracle returns the following error message

For insert/modify/delete

ORA-01732: data manipulation operation not legal on this view

Destroying A View

The **DROP VIEW** command is used to remove a view from the database.

Syntax:

```
DROP VIEW <ViewName>;
```

Example:

Remove the view **vw_Branch** from the database.

DROP VIEW vw_Branch;

Clusters

Clustering is an important concept for improving Oracle performance. Whenever the database is accessed, any reduction in input / output (**i.e.** I/O) always helps in improving it's throughput and overall performance. The concept of a **cluster** is where member records are stored **physically** near parent records. For Oracle, clusters can be used to define common, one-to-many access paths, and the member rows can be stored on the same database block as their owner row.

Clusters are used to store data from different tables in the **same physical data blocks**. They are appropriate to use if the records from those tables are frequently queried together. By storing them in the same data blocks, the number of database block **reads** needed to fulfill such queries decreases, thereby improving performance.

Note

Clusters may have a negative performance impact on the data manipulation transactions and on queries that only reference one of the tables in the cluster.

Because of their unique structure, clustered tables have different storage requirements from nonclustered tables. Each cluster stores the table's data, as well as maintains the cluster index that is used to sort table data.

The Cluster Key

The columns within the cluster index are called the **cluster key (i.e.** the set of columns that the tables in the cluster have in common). Since the cluster key columns determine the physical placement of rows within the cluster, the cluster key is usually the foreign key of one table that references the primary key of another table in the cluster.

After the cluster has been created, the cluster index is created on the cluster key columns. After the cluster key index has been created, data can be entered into the tables stored in the cluster. As rows are inserted, the database will store a cluster key and its associated rows in each of the cluster's blocks.

Syntax:

```
CREATE CLUSTER <ClusterName> (<Column> <DataType>
      [, <Column> <DataType>] . . .) [<Other Options>];
```

The cluster name follows the table naming conventions, also column and datatype is the name and datatype used as the cluster key. The column name may be same as one of the columns of a table or it may be any other valid name.

Example:

CREATE CLUSTER "DBA_BANKSYS"."BRANCH_INFO"("BRANCH_NO" **VARCHAR2(10)**);

CREATE TABLE "DBA_BANKSYS"."BRANCH_MSTR"(
"BRANCH_NO" **VARCHAR2(10) PRIMARY KEY,** "NAME" **VARCHAR2(25)**)
CLUSTER BRANCH_INFO(BRANCH_NO);

CREATE TABLE "DBA_BANKSYS"."ADDR_DTLS"(
"ADDR_NO" **NUMBER(6) PRIMARY KEY**, "CODE_NO" **VARCHAR2(10)**,
"ADDR_TYPE" **VARCHAR2(1)**, "ADDR1" **VARCHAR2(50)**,
"ADDR2" **VARCHAR2(50)**, "CITY" **VARCHAR2(25)**,
"STATE" **VARCHAR2(25)**, "PINCODE" **VARCHAR2(6)**);
CLUSTER BRANCH_INFO(BRANCH_NO);

Following are the advantages of Clusters:

- ❑ Disk I/O is reduced and access time improves for joins of clustered tables.
- ❑ In a cluster, a cluster key value is the value of the cluster key columns for a particular row. Each cluster key value is stored only once each in the cluster and the cluster index, no matter how many rows of different tables contain the value.
- ❑ Since all rows in clustered tables use the same columns as the common primary key, the columns are stored only once for all tables, yielding some storage benefit.

Following are the disadvantages of Clusters:

- ❑ Clusters can reduce the performance of INSERT statements as compared with storing a table separately with its own index.
- ❑ Columns that are updated often are not good candidates for the cluster key.

Sequences

The quickest way to retrieve data from a table is to have a column in the table whose data uniquely identifies a row. By using this column and a specific value, in the **WHERE** condition of a **SELECT** sentence the Oracle engine will be able to identify and retrieve the row the fastest.

To achieve this, a constraint is attached to a specific column in the table that ensures that the column is never left empty and that the data values in the column are unique. Since human beings do data entry, it is quite likely that a duplicate value could be entered, which violates this constraint and the entire row is rejected.

If the value entered into this column is **computer generated** it will always fulfill the unique constraint and the row will always be accepted for storage.

Oracle provides an object called a **Sequence** that can generate numeric values. The value generated can have a maximum of 38 digits. A sequence can be defined to:

- ❑ Generate numbers in ascending or descending order
- ❑ Provide intervals between numbers
- ❑ Caching of sequence numbers in memory to speed up their availability

A sequence is an independent object and can be used with any table that requires its output.

Creating Sequences

The minimum information required for generating numbers using a sequence is:

- ❑ The starting number
- ❑ The maximum number that can be generated by a sequence
- ❑ The increment value for generating the next number.

This information is provided to Oracle at the time of sequence creation.

Syntax:

```
CREATE SEQUENCE <SequenceName>
     [INCREMENT BY <IntegerValue>
     START WITH <IntegerValue>
     MAXVALUE <IntegerValue> / NOMAXVALUE
     MINVALUE <integervalue> / NOMINVALUE
     CYCLE / NOCYCLE
     CACHE <IntegerValue> / NOCACHE
     ORDER / NOORDER]
```

Note

 Sequence is always given a name so that it can be referenced later when required.

Keywords And Parameters

INCREMENT BY: Specifies the interval between sequence numbers. It can be any positive or negative value but not zero. If this clause is omitted, the default value is 1.

MINVALUE: Specifies the sequence minimum value.

NOMINVALUE: Specifies a minimum value of 1 for an ascending sequence and -(10)^26 for a descending sequence.

MAXVALUE: Specifies the maximum value that a sequence can generate.

NOMAXVALUE: Specifies a maximum of 10^27 for an ascending sequence or -1 for a descending sequence. This is the default clause.

START WITH: Specifies the first sequence number to be generated. The default for an ascending sequence is the sequence minimum value (1) and for a descending sequence, it is the maximum value (-1).

CYCLE: Specifies that the sequence continues to generate repeat values after reaching either its maximum value.

NOCYCLE: Specifies that a sequence cannot generate more values after reaching the maximum value.

CACHE: Specifies how many values of a sequence Oracle pre-allocates and keeps in memory for faster access. The minimum value for this parameter is **two.**

NOCACHE: Specifies that values of a sequence are not pre-allocated.

Note

 If the CACHE / NOCACHE clause is omitted ORACLE caches 20 sequence numbers by default.

ORDER: This guarantees that sequence numbers are generated in the order of request. This is only necessary if using Parallel Server in Parallel mode option. In exclusive mode option, a sequence always generates numbers in order.

NOORDER: This does not guarantee sequence numbers are generated in order of request. This is only necessary if you are using Parallel Server in Parallel mode option. If the ORDER/NOORDER clause is omitted, a sequence takes the NOORDER clause by default.

Note

 The ORDER, NOORDER Clause has no significance, if Oracle is configured with Single Server option.

Example:

Create a sequence by the name **ADDR_SEQ**, which will generate numbers from 1 upto 9999 in **ascending** order with an interval of 1. The sequence must restart from the number 1 after generating number 999.

CREATE SEQUENCE ADDR_SEQ **INCREMENT BY** 1 **START WITH** 1
MINVALUE 1 **MAXVALUE** 999 **CYCLE;**

Referencing A Sequence

Once a sequence is created SQL can be used to view the values held in its cache. To simply view sequence value use a SELECT sentence as described below:

```
SELECT <SequenceName>.NextVal FROM DUAL;
```

This will display the next value held in the cache on the VDU screen. Every time **nextval** references a sequence its output is automatically incremented from the old value to the new value ready for use.

The example below explains how to access a sequence and use its generated value in the INSERT statement.

Example:

Insert values for ADDR_TYPE, ADDR1, ADDR2, CITY, STATE and PINCODE in the **ADDR_DTLS** table. The **ADDR_SEQ** sequence must be used to generate ADDR_NO and CODE_NO must be a value held in the BRANCH_NO column of the BRANCH_MSTR table.

Table Name: ADDR_DTLS

Column Name	Data Type	Size	Attributes
ADDR_NO	Number	6	Primary Key
CODE_NO	VarChar2	10	Foreign Key references BRANCH_NO of the BRANCH_MSTR table.
ADDR_TYPE	VarChar2	1	Can hold the values: **H** for Head Office or **B** for Branch
ADDR1	VarChar2	50	
ADDR2	VarChar2	50	
CITY	VarChar2	25	
STATE	VarChar2	25	
PINCODE	VarChar2	6	

INSERT INTO ADDR_DTLS (ADDR_NO, CODE_NO, ADDR_TYPE, ADDR1, ADDR2, CITY, STATE, PINCODE) **VALUES(ADDR_SEQ.NextVal,** 'B5', 'B', 'Vertex Plaza, Shop 4,', 'Western Express Highway, Dahisar (East),', 'Mumbai', 'Maharashtra', '400078');

To reference the current value of a sequence:

```
SELECT <SequenceName>.CurrVal FROM DUAL;
```

This is a method a numeric value generated by the system, using a sequence can be used to insert values into a primary key column.

The most commonly used technique in commercial application development is to concatenate a sequence-generated value with a user-entered value.

The ADDR_NO stored in the **ADDR_DTLS** table, can be a concatenation of the month and year from the system date and the number generated by the sequence ADDR_SEQ. For example ADDR_NO 01041 is generated with 01 (month in number format), 04 (year in number format) and 1(a sequence generated value).

To help keep the sequence-generated number from becoming too large, each time either the month (or year) changes the sequence can be reset.

The sequence can be reset at the end of each month. If the company generated 50 addresses are keyed in for the month of January 2004, the ADDR_DTLS will start with 01041 upto 010450. Again when the month changes to February and as the sequence is reset, the numbering will start with 02041, 02042 and so on.

Using this simple technique of resetting the sequence at the end of each month and concatenating the sequence with the system date, unique values can be generated for the ADDR_NO column and reduce the size of the number generated by the sequence.

Example:

INSERT INTO ADDR_DTLS (ADDR_NO, CODE_NO, ADDR_TYPE, ADDR1, ADDR2, CITY, STATE, PINCODE) **VALUES(TO_CHAR(SYSDATE, 'MMYY) || TO_CHAR(ADDR_SEQ.NextVal),** 'B5', 'B', 'Vertex Plaza, Shop 4,', 'Western Express Highway, Dahisar (East),', 'Mumbai', 'Maharashtra', '400078');

Altering A Sequence

A sequence once created can be altered. This is achieved by using the **ALTER SEQUENCE** statement.

Syntax:

```
ALTER SEQUENCE <SequenceName>
      [INCREMENT BY <IntegerValue> MAXVALUE <IntegerValue>
      / NOMAXVALUE
      MINVALUE <IntegerValue> / NOMINVALUE CYCLE / NOCYCLE
      CACHE <IntegerValue> / NOCACHE ORDER / NOORDER]
```

Note

 The **START** value of the sequence cannot be altered.

Example:

Change the Cache value of the sequence ADDR_SEQ to 30 and interval between two numbers as 2.

ALTER SEQUENCE ADDR_SEQ **INCREMENT BY** 2 **CACHE** 30;

Dropping A Sequence

The DROP SEQUENCE **command is used to remove the sequence from the database.**

Syntax:

```
DROP SEQUENCE <SequenceName>;
```

Example:

Destroy the sequence **ADDR_SEQ**.

DROP SEQUENCE ADDR_SEQ;

Snapshots

A snapshot is a recent **copy** of a table from database or in some cases, a subset of rows/columns of a table. The SQL statement that creates and subsequently maintains a snapshot normally reads data from a database residing on the server. A snapshot is created on the destination system with the **create snapshot** SQL command. The **remote table** is immediately defined and populated from the **master** table.

In a distributed computing environment, the snapshots are defined considering the following reasons:

- Response time improves when a local read-only copy of a table exists – this can be many times faster than reading data directly from a remote database.
- Once a snapshot is built on a remote database, if the node containing the data from which the snapshot is built is not available, the snapshot can be used without the need to access the unavailable database.

The query that creates the snapshot closely resembles the code used to create a view. The secret to keep a snapshot up to date is the specification of it's **refresh interval**. When defining a snapshot, the DBA specifies this interval, and Oracle 8i from then on automatically manages the propagation of data from the table(s) upon which the snapshot is built.

Snapshots are used to dynamically replicate data between distributed databases. The master table will be updateable but the snapshots can be either read-only or updateable. Read-only snapshots are the most common types of snapshots implemented. There are two types of snapshots available i.e. complex snapshots and simple snapshots.

In a simple snapshot, each row is based on a single row in a single remote table. A row in a complex snapshot may be based on more than one row in a remote table, such as via a **group by** operation or on the result of a **multi-table join**. Simple snapshots are thus a subset of the snapshots that can be created.

Creating A Snapshot

Snapshots can be simple or complex. A simple snapshot consists pf either single table or a simple SELECT of rows from a single table. A complex snapshot consists of joined tables, views, or grouped and complex SELECT statements queries.

Syntax:

```
CREATE SNAPSHOT <SnapshotName>
ALTER SNAPSHOT <SnapshotName>
    [<schema>]
    [   [PCTFREE <Integer>] [PCTUSED <Integer>] [INITRANS
    <Integer>]
        [MAXTRANS <Integer>] [TABLESPACE <Tablespace>]
        [STORAGE <StorageClause>]
    /   [CLUSTER <Cluster> (<Column1>[,<Column2>, ...])]
    ]
    [USING
        [INDEX
            [PCTFREE <Integer>] [PCTUSED <Integer>]
            [INITRANS <Integer>] [MAXTRANS <Integer>]
        ]
        [DEFAULT ROLLBACK SEGMENT
            [MASTER <RollbackSegment>/LOCAL]
        ]
    ]
    [REFRESH [FAST/COMPLETE/FORCE]
        [START WITH <Date>] [NEXT <Date>]
        [WITH [PRIMARY KEY/ROWID]]
    ]
    AS <SubQuery>
    [FOR UPDATE]
```

The keywords and parameters for the CREATE SNAPSHOT are as follows:

- **schema** - Contains the snapshot. If not specified, Oracle creates the snapshot in user's schema.
- **snapshot** - Specifies the name of the snapshot to be created. Oracle chooses names for the table, views and index used to maintain the snapshot by adding a prefix and suffix to the snapshot name. To limit these names to 30 bytes and allow them to contain the entire snapshot name, limit your snapshot names to 19 bytes.
- **PCTFREE, PCTUSED, INITRANS, and MAXTRANS** - Establish values for the specified parameters for the internal table Oracle uses to maintain the snapshot's data.
- **TABLESPACE** - Specifies the tablespace in which the snapshot is to be created. If user omits this option, Oracle creates the snapshot in the default tablespace of the owner of the snapshot's schema.
- **STORAGE** - Establishes storage characteristics for the table Oracle uses to maintain the snapshot's data.

- **CLUSTER** - Creates the snapshot as part of the specified cluster. Because a clustered snapshot uses the cluster's space allocation, **do not use** the **PCTFREE**, **PCTUSED**, **INITRANS**, **MAXTRANS**, **TABLESPACE**, or **STORAGE** parameters with the CLUSTER option.
- **USING INDEX** - Specifies parameters for the index Oracle creates to maintain the snapshot. User can choose the values of the **INITRANS**, **MAXTRANS**, **TABLESPACE**, **STORAGE**, and **PCTFREE** parameters. For the **PCTFREE**, **PCTUSED**, **INITRAANS**, and **MAXTRANS** parameters, specify the default storage and transaction attributes for the snapshot.
- **ROLLBACK SEGMENT** - Specifies the local snapshot and/or remote master rollback segments to be used during snapshot refresh.
- **DEFAULT** - Specifies that Oracle will choose which rollback segment to use.
- **MASTER** - Specifies the rollback segment to be used at the remote master for the individual snapshot.
- **LOCAL** - Specifies the rollback segment to be used for the local refresh group that contains the snapshot. If user does not specify **MASTER** or **LOCAL**, Oracle uses **LOCAL by default**. If user does not specify rollback segment, Oracle chooses the rollback segment to be used automatically. If user specifies **DEFAULT**, user **cannot specify rollback** segment.
- **REFRESH** - Specifies how and when Oracle automatically refreshes the snapshot.
- **FAST** - Specifies a fast refresh or one using only the updated data stored in the snapshot log associated with the master table.
- **COMPLETE** - Specifies a complete refresh or one that re-executes the snapshot's query.
- **FORCE** - Specifies a fast refresh, if one is possible, or complete refresh, if a fast refresh is not possible. Oracle decides whether a fast refresh is possible at refresh time. If user omits the **FAST**, **COMPLETE**, and **FORCE** options, Oracle uses FORCE by default.
- **START WITH** - Specifies a date expression for the first automatic refresh time.
- **NEXT** - Specifies a date expression for calculating the interval between automatic refreshes. Both the **START WITH** and **NEXT** values must evaluate to a time in the future. If user omits the **START WITH** value, Oracle determines the first automatic refresh time by evaluating the **NEXT** expression when a user creates the snapshot. If a user specifies a START WITH value but omits the **NEXT** value, Oracle refreshes the snapshot only once. If a user omits both the **START WITH** and **NEXT** values, or if you omit the **REFRESH** clause entirely, Oracle does not automatically refresh the snapshot.
- **WITH PRIMARY KEY** - Specifies that primary key snapshots are to be created. These snapshots allow snapshot master tabies to be reorganized without impacting the snapshot's ability to continue to fast refresh. A user can also define primary key snapshots as simple snapshots with subqueries.
- **WITH ROWID** - Specifies that **ROWID** snapshots are to be created. These snapshots provide backward compatibility with Oracle Release 7.0 masters. If a user omits both **WITH PRIMARY KEY** and **WITH ROWID**, Oracle creates primary key snapshots by default.
- **FOR UPDATE** - Allows a simple snapshot to be updated. When used in conjunction with the replication option, these updates will be propagated to the master.
- **AS <subquery>** - Specifies the snapshot query. When a user creates the snapshot, Oracle executes this query and places the results in the snapshot. The select list can contain up to 1,000 expressions. The syntax of a snapshot query is described with the syntax description of a subquery. The syntax of a snapshot query is subject to the same restrictions as a view query. For a list of these restrictions, see the **CREATE VIEW** command.

Example:

Following code creates a snapshot of **EMP_MSTR** table in the default tablespace i.e. System

```
CREATE SNAPSHOT NEW_EMP
    PCTFREE 10 PCTUSED 70 TABLESPACE System
    STORAGE (INITIAL 50K NEXT 50K PCTINCREASE 0)
    REFRESH START WITH ROUND(SYSDATE + 7) + 2/24
        NEXT NEXT_DATE(TRUNC(SYSDATE, 'MONDAY') + 2/24
    AS SELECT * FROM EMP_MSTR;
```

Altering A Snapshot

A snapshot is altered using ALTER SNAPSHOT command. Usually storage and space usage parameters, types and frequency of refresh are altered.

Syntax:

```
ALTER SNAPSHOT <SnapshotName>
      [<Schema>]
      [     [PCTFREE <Integer>] [PCTUSED <Integer>]
            [INITRANS <Integer>] [MAXTRANS <Integer>]
            [TABLESPACE <Tablespace>] [STORAGE
            <StorageClause>]
      /     [CLUSTER <Cluster> (<Column1>[,<Column2>, ...])]
      ]
      [USING
            [INDEX
                  [PCTFREE <Integer>] [PCTUSED <Integer>]
                  [INITRANS <Integer>] [MAXTRANS <Integer>]
            ]
            [DEFAULT ROLLBACK SEGMENT
                  [MASTER <rollback segment>/LOCAL]
            ]
      ]
      [REFRESH [FAST/COMPLETE/FORCE]
            [START WITH <date>] [NEXT <date>] [WITH PRIMARY
            KEY]
      ]
```

The parameters for ALTER SNAPSHOT are as follows:

- ❑ **Schema - is the schema in which to store the log. If not specified, this will default to the user's own schema.**
- ❑ **<Table>** - is the table name to create the snapshot log for.
- ❑ **PCTFREE, PCTUSED, INITRANS,** and **MAXTRANS** – are the values for these creation parameters to use for the created log file.
- ❑ **STORAGE** - is a standard storage clause.
- ❑ **REFRESH** - specifies the refresh mode:
- ❑ **FAST** - uses a **SNAPSHOT LOG**. It is the default mode.

- **COMPLETE** - re-performs the sub-query and is the only valid mode for a complex snapshot.
- **FORCE** - causes the system to first try a **FAST**, and if this is not possible, then a **COMPLETE**.
- **START WITH** - specifies the date for the first refresh.
- **NEXT** - specifies either a date or a time interval for the next refresh of the snapshot. **START WITH** and **NEXT** values are used to determine the refresh cycle for the snapshot. If just **START WITH** is specified, only the initial refresh is done. If both are specified, the first is done on the **START WITH** date, and the **NEXT** is evaluated against the **START WITH** to determine future refreshes. If just the **NEXT** value is specified, if computers based on the date the snapshot is created. If neither is specified, the snapshot is not automatically refreshed.

Dropping A Snapshot

A snapshot is dropped using DROP SNAPSHOT command.

Syntax:

```
DROP SNAPSHOT <SnapshotName>
```

Example:

DROP SNAPSHOT New_Client

Note

When a snapshot is dropped, if it has a snapshot log associated with, only the rows required for maintaining that snapshot are dropped. Dropping a master table upon which a snapshot is based does not drop the snapshot. Any subsequent refreshes however, will fail.

Self Review Questions

Fill in the Blaks

1. ____________ a table is an access strategy, that is, a way to sort and search records in the table.
2. Indexing involves forming a __________ dimensional matrix completely independent of the table on which the index is being created.
3. The address field of an index is called __________.
4. Each data file is further divided into __________ and each block is given a unique number.
5. An index that allows duplicate values for the indexed columns is called __________ indexes.
6. An index created on a single column of a table is called __________ Index.
7. An index created on more than one column it is called __________ Index.
8. If an index is created on more than one column it is called __________ Index.
9. A reverse key index can be rebuilt into a normal index using the keywords __________ __________.
10. ____________ indexes are typically only a fraction of the size of the indexed data in the table.
11. An index is ____________ prefixed if it is partitioned on the left prefix of the index columns.
12. In case of a __________ Index, the index cannot be split or merged separately.
13. Querying ______________ will provide details on columns on which the user's indexes are created.

14. A ____________ is an SQL statement that extracts values from table columns using a SELECT statement and passes these values as input to another SQL statement.
15. The SQL statement to which the values of the select statement are passed is called ____________ statement.
16. To reduce redundant data to the minimum possible, an object is created called a ____________.
17. A View that is used to Look at table data as well as Insert, Update and Delete table data is called an ____________ View.
18. The concept of a ____________ is where member records are stored physically near parent records.
19. The columns within the cluster index are called the ____________.
20. ____________ that are updated often are not good candidates for the cluster key.
21. The ____________ parameter specifies the interval between sequence numbers.
22. The ____________ parameter specifies a minimum value of 1 for an ascending sequence and -(10)^26 for a descending sequence.
23. The ____________ parameter specifies the maximum value that a sequence can generate.
24. The ____________ parameter specifies that values of a sequence are not pre-allocated.
25. In Snapshots ____________ ____________ improves when a local read-only copy of a table exists.
26. A ____________ snapshot consists of joined tables, views, or grouped and complex SELECT statements queries.
27. A ____________ snapshot consists pf either single table or a simple SELECT of rows from a single table.
28. The ____________ parameter establishes storage characteristics for the table Oracle uses to maintain the snapshot's data.
29. The ____________ parameter creates the snapshot as part of the specified cluster.
30. The ____________ parameter specifies the local snapshot and/or remote master rollback segments to be used during snapshot refresh.
31. The ____________ parameter specifies the rollback segment to be used at the remote master for the individual snapshot.
32. In a CREATE SNAPSHOT the ____________ parameter specifies a fast refresh, if one is possible, or complete refresh, is a fast refresh is not possible.
33. In a CREATE SNAPSHOT the ____________ parameter specifies that ROWID snapshots are to be created.
34. A user can also define primary key snapshots as simple snapshots with ____________.
35. A snapshot is altered using ____________ command.
36. In ALTER SNAPSHOT the ____________ parameter re-performs the subquery and is the only valid mode for a complex snapshot.

True or False

37. Indexes adversely affect the speed at which the records are retrieved.
38. An index is an ordered list of the contents of a row, (or a group of rows) of a table.
39. ROWID is an internally generated and maintained, binary value, which identifies a record.
40. Each data block can store only one Record.
41. Data files are the files used by the Oracle engine to store user data.

42. Indexes that deny duplicate values for the indexed columns are called Unique Indexes.
43. An index cannot be created on more than one column.
44. Each data file is given an unique number at the time of data file creation.
45. If an index is created on a single column it is called Single Unique Index.
46. To create unique index, the keyword UNIQUE should be included in the Create Index command.
47. A normal index can be rebuilt as a reverse key index.
48. In adhoc queries or similar situations, bitmap indexes adversely affect the performance of queries.
49. A column's index will not be used when the same column is expressed in an arithmetic expression or function in the WHERE clause.
50. The expression cannot contain any aggregate functions.
51. When key compression is used, the duplicate key will be stored as a suffix entry on the index block.
52. It is not possible to manipulate index partitions.
53. Querying USER_INDEXES will provide details on INDEXES that the user has created.
54. Indexes associated with the tables can be removed by using the DELETE INDEX command.
55. Indexes speeds up data retrieval.
56. The SELECT statement is called Parent SQL statement.
57. The order in which data is retrieved is dependent upon the indexes created on the table.
58. The ORDER BY clause cannot be used while creating a view.
59. The DELETE or MODIFY operations affect the Master table.
60. Clusters are used to store data from different tables in the same physical data blocks.
61. Clusters can reduce the performance of UPDATE statements as compared with storing a table separately with its own index.
62. The INCREMENT BY parameter can be any positive or negative value or zero.
63. The MINVALUE specifies the sequence minimum value.
64. The CYCLE parameter specifies that the sequence continues to generate repeat values after reaching its minimum value.
65. The NOMAXVALUE parameter specifies a maximum of 10^27 for an ascending sequence or -1 for a descending sequence.
66. The NOCYCLE keyword specifies that a sequence can generate more values after reaching the maximum value.
67. Snapshots are used to dynamically replicate data between distributed databases.
68. PCTFREE parameter for the CREATE SNAPSHOT establishes values for the specified parameters for the internal table Oracle uses to maintain the snapshot's data.
69. The DEFAULT parameter specifies the rollback segment to be used at the remote master for the individual snapshot.
70. If a user omits both WITH PRIMARY KEY and WITH ROWID, Oracle creates primary key snapshots by default.
71. In a CREATE SNAPSHOT the DATE parameter specifies a date expression for the first automatic refresh time.

72. In ALTER SNAPSHOT the FORCE parameter causes the system to first try a FAST, and if this is not possible, then a COMPLETE.

Hands On Exercises

1. Write appropriate SQL statements for the following:
   (a) Create a simple index idx_Prod on product cost price from the Product_Master table.
   (b) Create a sequence inv_seq with the following parameters, increment by 3, cycle, cache 4 and which will generate the numbers from 1 to 9999 in ascending order.
   (c) Create view on OrderNo, OrderDate, OrderStatus of the Sales_Order table and ProductNo,ProductRate and QtyOrdered of Sales_Order_Details.

15

Oracle Object Oriented Features

Oracle 9i Database Flavours

An upgrade to Oracle 9i, immediately means that for developers there are three different **flavors** of ORACLE available:

Relational	The traditional ORACLE relational database (RDBMS)
Object-relational	The traditional ORACLE relational database, extended to include Objectoriented concepts and structures such as abstract datatype, nested tables, and varying arrays
Object-oriented	An object-oriented database whose design is based solely on ObjectOriented Analysis and Design principles

Oracle provides full support for all three different implementations i.e. Relational, Objectrelational, and objectoriented. Regardless of the method chosen, there should first be a familiarity, with the functions and features of the core ORACLE relational database. Even if OO capabilities are used, the functions and datatypes available in Oracle, as well as its programming languages (SQL and PL/SQL) should be known.

Why Should Objects Be Used?

Objects reduce complexity by giving an intuitive way of representing complex data and its relations.

Besides simplifying the interaction with data, objects may help in other ways. Examples of benefits that come from using OO features are:

- **Object reuse:** If OO code is written, the chances of reusing previously written code modules are increased. Similarly, if OO database objects are created the chances that these database objects will be reused is increased
- **Standards adherence:** If database objects are built using standards, then the chances they will be reused increase exponentially. If multiple applications or tables use the same set of database objects, then a de facto standard for applications or tables is being created

For example, if a standard datatype is created and used for all addresses, then all the addresses in the database will use the same internal format.

The cost of using objects are chiefly the added complexity of the system and the time it takes to learn how to implement OO features. The basics of extending the Oracle RDBMS to include OO capabilities build easily upon the relational model. The short time required to develop and use abstract datatypes is a good gauge to the time required for learning Oracle's OO features.

Objects have data, and objects have **methods** for interacting with data. Thus a combination of data and methods makes up an object. **For example**, in an employee list there is a standard for the structure of an address, it starts with a person's name, followed by a street name, city name, state name and zip code. When a new person is added to the list the same procedure is followed. Methods for **address** could include:

Add_Person ()	For adding a person to the list
Update_Person ()	For updating a person's entry
Remove_Person ()	For deleting a person from the list

Methods do not have to manipulate data only, they can report on data. They can perform functions on data and return the result of the function to the user. **For example**, if worker's birth dates are stored, then an Age method could be used to calculate and report a worker's current age.

This sort of information is quite valuable when trying to understand whether the workforce is aging, especially when new skills training is about to commence.

Object Types

Oracle supports many different types of objects. In the following sections, major object types are described.

Abstract Datatype

Abstract datatype is a datatype that consists of one or more subtypes. Rather than being constrained to the standard Oracle data type of NUMBER, DATE, and VARCHAR2, the abstract data type can more accurately describe data.

For example, an abstract data type for an **address** may consist of the following columns:

Street	VARCHAR2 (50)
City	VARCHAR2 (25)
State	VARCHAR2 (25)
Zip	NUMBER

When a table that uses address information is created, a column that uses the abstract datatype for **address** could be created. This will contain the Street, City, State and Zip columns that are part of the abstract data type.

Example:

```
CREATE TYPE ADDRESS_TY AS OBJECT(
        STREET VARCHAR2(50), CITY VARCHAR2(25), STATE VARCHAR2(25), ZIP NUMBER);
```

Output:

```
Type created.
```

Abstract data types can be nested and can contain references to other abstract data types.

Example:

```
CREATE TYPE PERSON_TY AS OBJECT(
        NAME VARCHAR2(25), ADDRESS ADDRESS_TY);
```

Output:

```
Type created.
```

The benefits listed earlier for objects, such as reuse and standards adherence is realized from using the abstract data type. When an abstract datatype is created, a standard for the representation of abstract data elements (like addresses, people or companies) is created.

If the same abstract datatype is used in multiple places, then the same logical data is represented in the same manner in each place.

The reuse of the abstract datatype leads to the enforcement of standard representation for the data to which it is bound.

An abstract datatype can be used to create an **object table**. In an object table, the columns of the table map to the columns of an abstract datatype.

Nested Tables

A nested table is a table within a table. A nested table is a collection of rows, represented as a column within the main table. For each record within the main table, the nested table may contain multiple rows. In one sense, it's a way of storing a one-to-many relationship within one table.

Consider a table that contained information about departments, in which each department may have many projects in progress at any one time. In a strictly relational model, two separate tables would be created:

- ❑ DEPARTMENT
- ❑ PROJECT

Nested tables allow storing the information about projects within the DEPARTMENT table. The project table records can be accessed directly via the DEPARTMENT table, without the need to perform a join.

The ability to select data without traversing joins makes data access easier. Even if methods for accessing nested data are not defined. Department and Project data have clearly been associated.

In a strictly relational model, the association between the DEPARTMENT and PROJECT tables would be accomplished via a foreign key.

Varying Arrays

A varying array is a set of objects, each with the same datatype. The size of the array is limited when it is created.

Note

 When a table is created with a varying array, the array is a nested table with a **limited** set of rows.

Varying arrays, also known as **VARRAYS**, allows storing repeating attributes in tables. **For example**, suppose there is a PROJECT table, and projects having workers assigned to them.

A project can have many workers, and a worker can work on multiple projects. In a strictly relational implementation, a PROJECT table, a WORKER table, and an intersection table PROJECT_WORKER would be created that stores the relationships between them.

Varying arrays can be used to store the worker names in the PROJECT table. If projects are limited to ten workers or fewer, a varying array with a limit of ten entries can be created. The datatype for the varying arrays will be whatever datatype is appropriate for the worker name values.

The varying array can then be populated, so that for each project the names of all of the project's workers can be selected without querying the WORKER table.

Large Objects

A large object, or LOB, is capable of storing large volumes of data. The LOB datatypes available are BLOB, CLOB, NCLOB, and BFILE.

- The BLOB datatype is used for binary data, and can extend to 4GB in length.
- The CLOB datatype stores character data and can store data up to 4GB in length.
- The NCLOB datatype is used to store CLOB data for multibyte character sets.
- The data for BLOB, CLOB, and NCLOB datatype is stored inside the database. Thus, there can be a single row in the database that is over 4GB in length.

The fourth LOB datatype, BFILE, is a pointer to an external file. The files referenced by BFILEs exist at operating system level. The database only maintains a pointer to the file. The size of the external file is limited only by the operating system. Since the data is stored outside the database, ORACLE does not maintain concurrency or integrity of the data.

Multiple LOBs per table can be used. For example, there can be a table with a CLOB column and two BLOB columns. This is an improvement over the LONG datatype, as there can be one LONG per table. ORACLE provides a number of functions and procedures, which can be used to manipulate and select LOB data.

References

Nested tables and varying arrays are embedded objects. They are physically embedded within another object. Another type of object, called referenced objects, are **physically separate** from the objects that refer to them. References (also known as REFs) are essentially pointers to row objects. A **row object** is different from a **column object**. An example of a column object would be a varying array, it is an object that is treated as a column in a table. A row object, on the other hand, **always** represents a row.

References are typically among the **last OO features** implemented when migrating a relational database to an object-relational or pure **OO** one.

Object Views

Object views allow adding OO concepts **on top** of existing relational tables. For example, an abstract datatype can be created based on an existing table definition. Thus, object views give the benefits of relational table storage and OO structures. Object views allow the development of OO features within a relational database, a kind of bridge between the relational and OO worlds.

Note
 Before using object views, there should be a familiarity with the abstract datatype.

Features of Objects

An object has a name, a standard representation, and a standard collection of operations that affect it. The operations that affect an object are called methods. Thus, an abstract datatype has a name, a standard representation, and defined methods for accessing data. All objects that use the abstract datatype will share the same structure, methods, and representation **i.e.** Abstract datatype model a class of data within the database.

Abstract data types are part of an OO concept called **abstraction,** the conceptual existence of **classes** within a database. As noted earlier, the abstract data type may be nested. It is not necessary to create physical tables at each level of abstraction instead, the structural existence of the abstract types are sufficient.

The methods attached to each level of abstraction may be called from higher levels of abstraction. **For example**, the ADDRESS data type's methods can be accessed during a call to a PERSON datatype.

During the creation of objects, they **inherit** the structure of the data elements they descend from.

For example, if **address** is a class of data, then **PERSON_TY**, the person name and the corresponding **address** would inherent the structural definitions of address.

From a data perspective, nested abstract data type inherits the representations of their **parents**. The ability to create hierarchies of abstract datatype is available from Oracle 8.1 onwards.

Naming Conventions For Objects

When working with OO the following rules should be enforced:

1. Table and column names will be **singular** (such as EMPLOYEE, Name, and State)
2. Abstract datatype names will be singular nouns with a **_TY** suffix (such as PERSON_TY or ADDRESS_TY)
3. Table and Datatype names will always be **uppercase** (such as EMPLOYEE or PERSON_TY)
4. Column names will always be **lower case** (such as state and start_date)
5. Object view names will be singular nouns with a **_OV** suffix (such as PERSON_OV or ADDRESS_OV)
6. Nested table names will be plural nouns with a **_NT** suffix (such as WORKERS_NT)
7. Varying array names will be plural nouns with a **_VA** suffix (such as WORKERS_VA)

The name of an object should consist of two parts, the core object name and the suffix. The core object name should follow naming standards, the suffixes help to identify the type of object.

A Common Object Example

Let's consider a common object found in most systems, **addresses**. Addresses are maintained and selected. The addresses of workers follow a standard format. The street name, city name, state name and zip code can be used as the basis of an abstract datatype for addresses. Use the create type command to create an abstract datatype.

Example:

```
CREATE TYPE ADDRESS_TY AS OBJECT(
        STREET VARCHAR2 (50), CITY VARCHAR2 (25), STATE VARCHAR2 (25), ZIP NUMBER);
```

Output:

```
Type created.
```

The **CREATE TYPE** command is an interesting command in Oracle. What the command in the above example says is **create** an abstract datatype named ADDRESS_TY. It will be represented as having four attributes, named Street, City, State, and Zip, using a defined datatype and length for each attribute.

So far, no methods have been created for the abstract data type but as soon as it is declared and created Oracle8i/9i automatically and internally creates appropriate methods.

Note

Within the **CREATE TYPE** command, note the **as object** clause. The **as object** clause explicitly identifies ADDRESS_TY as an OO implementation.

Now that the ADDRESS_TY datatype exists, it can be used within other datatypes. **For example**, the creation of a standard datatype required for people. People have names and addresses. Therefore the following abstract data type can be created:

Example:

```
CREATE TYPE PERSON_TY AS OBJECT(
        NAME VARCHAR2 (25), ADDRESS ADDRESS_TY);
```

Output:

```
Type created.
```

First, the abstract datatype was given a name PERSON_TY and identified as an object via the **as object** clause. Then, two columns were defined.

The line:

- (NAME VARCHAR2 (25),: Defines the first column of PERSON_TY's representation
- ADDRESS ADDRESS_TY); : Defines the second column of PERSON_TY's representation

The second column, Address, uses the ADDRESS_TY abstract datatype previously created. The columns within ADDRESS_TY, (according to the ADDRESS_TY definition) are as follows:

- (STREET VARCHAR2 (50), : Defines the first column of ADDRESS_TY's representation
- CITY VARCHAR2 (25), : Defines the second column of ADDRESS_TY's representation
- STATE VARCHAR2 (25), : Defines the third column of ADDRESS_TY's representation
- ZIP NUMBER); : Defines the forth column of ADDRESS_TY's representation

So, a PERSON_TY entry will have a Name, Street, City, State, and Zip columns because one of its columns is explicitly bound to the **ADDRESS_TY** abstract type.

Just imagine how this capability to define and reuse abstract data types can simplify data representation within a database. **For example**, a Street column is seldom used by itself, it is almost always used as part of an address. Abstract datatype allows the joining of these elements together and dealing with the whole address instead of its parts like Street and other columns that constitute the address.

The PERSON_TY datatype can be now used to create an OO based table.

The Structure Of A Simple Object

Data **cannot be inserted** into PERSON_TY. The reason is straightforward, a datatype describes data, it **does not** store data. To store data, **a table** that uses this datatype has to be created. Only then will it be possible to store data in that table, formatted for the datatype specified.

The following command creates a table named CUSTOMER. A customer has a Customer_ID and all the attributes of a person (via the PERSON_TY datatype).

Example:

```
CREATE TABLE CUSTOMER(
        CUSTOMER_ID NUMBER, PERSON PERSON_TY);
```

Output:

```
Type created.
```

Example:

The following command is used to retrieve CUSTOMER table's column definition.

DESC CUSTOMER;

Output:

Name	Null?	Type
CUSTOMER_ID		NUMBER
PERSON		PERSON_TY

The Person column is shown by the **DESCRIBE** command to be defined by a **named TYPE.**

The **DESCRIBE** command does not show the structure of the **TYPE** associated with the Person column. To see that information, there is a need to query the data dictionary directly.

Example:

DESC PERSON_TY;

Output:

Name	Null?	Type
Name	Null?	Type
NAME		VARCHAR2(25)
ADDRESS		ADDRESS_TY

Example:

DESC ADDRESS_TY;

Output:

Name	Null?	Type
STREET		VARCHAR2(50)
CITY		VARCHAR2(25)
STATE		VARCHAR2(25)
ZIP		NUMBER

Note

The data dictionary is a series of tables and views that contain information about **structures** and **users** in the database. The data dictionary can be queried for information about database objects that are owned or on which access rights have been granted.

Example:

The **USER_TAB_COLUMNS** data dictionary view can be queried to see the datatype associated with each column in the CUSTOMER table:

```
SELECT COLUMN_NAME, DATA_TYPE FROM USER_TAB_COLUMNS
    WHERE TABLE_NAME = 'CUSTOMER';
```

Output:

COLUMN_NAME	DATA_TYPE
CUSTOMER_ID	NUMBER
PERSON	PERSON_TY

Note

USER_TAB_COLUMNS lists detailed Information about columns within the tables and views owned by a user. The query output shows that the Person column of the CUSTOMER table has been defined using the PERSON_TY datatype. Further explanation of the data dictionary is necessary to see the construction of the PERSON_TY datatype. The columns of an abstract datatype are referred to as its attributes. Within the data dictionary, the USER_TYPE_ATTRS view displays information about the attributes of a user's abstract datatype.

Example:

In the following query, the name, length, and datatype are selected for each of the attributes within the PERSON_TY datatype.

```
SELECT ATTR_NAME, LENGTH, ATTR_TYPE_NAME FROM USER_TYPE_ATTRS
    WHERE TYPE_NAME = 'PERSON_TY';
```

Output:

ATTR_NAME	LENGTH	ATTR_TYPE_NAME
NAME	25	VARCHAR2
ADDRESS		ADDRESS_TY

The query output shows that the PERSON_TY type consists of a Name column (defined as a VARCHAR2 column with a length of 25) and an Address column (defined using the ADDRESS_TY type).

Example:

Query USER_TYPE_ATTRS again to see the attributes of the ADDRESS_TY datatype:

```
SELECT ATTR_NAME, LENGTH, ATTR_TYPE_NAME FROM USER_TYPE_ATTRS
    WHERE TYPE_NAME = 'ADDRESS_TY';
```

Output:

ATTR_NAME	LENGTH	ATTR_TYPE_NAME
ATTR_NAME	LENGTH	ATTR_TYPE_NAME
STREET	50	VARCHAR2
CITY	25	VARCHAR2
STATE	25	VARCHAR2
ZIP		NUMBER

Note

Often there will be no need to **completely decompose** the types that constitute a table. If the need arises queries can be used as shown in this section to **drill down** through the layers of abstraction. Once the structures of each of the abstract Datatype used by the table are known, records can be inserted into it.

Note

ALL_TAB_COLUMNS and ALL_TYPE_ATTRS in place of USER_COLUMNS and USER_TYPE_ATTRS can be queried if the tables and types are not owned and the information has to be found out. The ALL_TAB_COLUMNS and ALL_TYPE_ATTRS views show all of the columns and attributes for the tables and types that you either own or have been granted access to. Both ALL_TAB_COLUMNS and ALL_TYPE_ATTRS contain an Owner column that identifies the table or type's owner.

Inserting Records Into The CUSTOMER TABLE

Oracle creates methods, called constructor methods, for data management when an abstract datatype is created. A constructor method is a program that is named after the datatype. Its parameters are the **names of the attributes** defined for the datatype. When records are to be inserted into a table created from abstract datatypes, constructor methods can be used.

For example, the CUSTOMER table uses the PERSON_TY datatype, and the PERSON_TY datatype uses the ADDRESS_TY abstract datatype. In order to insert a record into the CUSTOMER table, a record using the PERSON_TY and ADDRESS_TY datatype needs to be inserted. To insert records using this datatype, the use of the constructor methods for the abstract datatype is required.

Example:

In the following example, a record is inserted into CUSTOMER using the constructor methods for the PERSON_TY and ADDRESS_TY abstract data types. The constructor methods for these abstract data types are shown in bold in the example. They have the same names as the data type:

INSERT INTO CUSTOMER **VALUES(**1, **PERSON_TY(**'Sharanam',
  ADDRESS_TY('Dadar', 'Mumbai', 'Maharashtra', 400016**)));**

Output:

```
1 row created.
```

The insert command provides the values to be inserted as a row in the **CUSTOMER** table. The values provided must match the columns in the table.

In this example, a CUSTOMER_ID value of 1 is specified. Next, the values for the Person column are inserted, using the **PERSON_TY** constructor method (shown in bold). Within the PERSON_TY datatype, a Name is specified, and then the ADDRESS_TY constructor method (shown in bold and underlined) is used to insert the Address values.

So, for the record inserted in the example, the Name value is **Sharanam**, and the Street value is **Dadar**. Note that the parameters for the constructor method are in the **exact same order** as the attributes of the datatype.

A second record can be inserted into CUSTOMER, using the exact same format for the calls to the constructor methods:

```
INSERT INTO CUSTOMER VALUES(2,      PERSON_TY ('Vaishali',
        ADDRESS_TY ('Balgovinddas Rd', 'Mumbai', 'Maharashtra', 400016)));
```

The second record has now been inserted into the customer table. The use of constructor methods are needed when manipulating records in tables that use an abstract datatype.

Selecting From An Abstract Datatype:

Example:

If the selection of CUSTOMER_ID values from CUSTOMER is required, that column can simply be queried from the table.

```
SELECT CUSTOMER_ID FROM CUSTOMER;
```

Output:

```
CUSTOMER_ID
1
2
```

Querying the CUSTOMER_ID values is straightforward, since that column is a normal datatype within the CUSTOMER table. When all of the columns of the CUSTOMER table are queried, the complexity of the abstract datatype is revealed.

Example:

```
SELECT * FROM CUSTOMER;
```

Output:

CUSTOMER_ID
PERSON(NAME, ADDRESS(STREET, CITY, STATE, ZIP))
1
PERSON_TY('Sharanam', ADDRESS_TY('Dadar', 'Mumbai', 'Maharashtra', 400016))
2
PERSON_TY('Vaishali', ADDRESS_TY('Balgovinddas Rd', 'Mumbai', 'Maharashtra', 400016))

The output shows that CUSTOMER_ID is a column within CUSTOMER, and that the PERSON column uses an abstract datatype. The column name for the Person column shows the names of the abstract datatype used and the nesting of the **ADDRESS_TY** datatype within the **PERSON_TY** datatype.

Example:

SELECT CUSTOMER_ID, CLIENT.PERSON.NAME **FROM** CUSTOMER **CLIENT;**

Notice the column syntax for the Name column:

CLIENT.PERSON.NAME

Note

 Refer to the structure of the customer table shown earlier.

As a column name, **CLIENT.PERSON.NAME** points to the Name attribute within the PERSON_TY datatype. The format for the column name is:

TABLEALIAS.COLUMN.ATTRIBUTE

Output:

CUSTOMER_ID	PERSON.NAME
1	Praveen
2	Mita

Note

 During, **INSERTS**, the name of the **datatype** is needed (actually, the name of the constructor method is needed, which is the same as the name of the datatype). During **SELECTS**, the name of the **column** is used.

What if the **selection** of the Street values from the CUSTOMER table is needed?

The **STREET** column is part of the ADDRESS_TY datatype, which in turn is part of the PERSON_TY datatype. To select this data, extend the Column. Attribute format to include the nested type. The format will be:

TABLEALIAS.COLUMN.COLUMN.ATTRIBUTE

Example:

To select the STREET attribute of the ADDRESS attribute within the PERSON column, the query will be:

SELECT CLIENT.PERSON.ADDRESS.STREET **FROM** CUSTOMER **CLIENT;**

Output:

```
PERSON.ADDRESS.STREET
Dadar
Balgovinddas Rd
```

The syntax SELECT **CLIENT.PERSON.ADDRESS.STREET** tells Oracle exactly how and where to find the Street attribute.

Caution

 If an abstract datatype is used, neither **INSERT** nor **SELECT** values for the abstract datatype attributes can be done **without knowing** the exact structure of the attributes.

For example, the CUSTOMER table's **city** values cannot be selected unless it is known that **city** is part of the Address attribute, and Address is part of the Person column. A column's values **cannot be inserted** or **updated** unless the datatype is known and the nesting of datatypes needed to reach it.

What if reference to the City column is required as part of a **where** clause?

As in prior examples, City can be referred to as part of the Address attribute, nested within the Person column.

Example:

```
SELECT CLIENT.PERSON.NAME, CLIENT.PERSON.ADDRESS.CITY
    FROM CUSTOMER CLIENT
        WHERE CLIENT.PERSON.ADDRESS.CITY LIKE 'M%';
```

Output:

PERSON.NAME	PERSON.ADDRESS.CITY
Sharanam	Mumbai
Vaishali	Mumbai

When updating data within an abstract datatype, refer to its attributes via the Column.Attributes syntax shown in the preceding examples.

Example:

To change the **CITY** value for customers who live in Mumbai execute the following **UPDATE** statement:

```
UPDATE CUSTOMER CLIENT SET CLIENT.PERSON.ADDRESS.CITY = 'Bombay'
    WHERE CLIENT.PERSON.ADDRESS.CITY = 'Mumbai';
```

Output:

```
2 rows updated.
```

Oracle will use the **WHERE** clause to find the right records to update, and the **SET** clause to set the new values for the row's **CITY** columns.

As shown in these examples, using an abstract datatype simplifies the representation of the data but may complicate the way in which it is queried and worked with. The benefits of abstract datatype need to be weighed (more intuitive representation of the data) against the potential increase in complexity of data access and manipulation.

When deleting data within an abstract datatype, refer to its attributes via the COLUMN.ATTRIBUTES syntax shown in the preceding examples.

For example, to delete the record for the customers who live in **Dadar**, execute the following **delete** statement:

Example:

```
DELETE FROM CUSTOMER CLIENT WHERE CLIENT.PERSON.ADDRESS.STREET = 'Dadar';
```

Oracle will use the **where** clause to find the right records to delete.

Output:

```
1 row deleted.
```

Implementing Object Views

When implementing object-relational database applications, the relational database design methods are first used. After the database design is properly normalized, groups of columns that can be represented by an abstract datatype are looked for. Abstract datatypes are created for these groups of columns. Then tables can be created based on the abstract datatypes.

Thus as in the previous example, the order of operations is as follows:

1. Create the **ADDRESS_TY** datatype
2. Create the **PERSON_TY** datatype, using the **ADDRESS_TY** datatype
3. Create the **CUSTOMER** table, using the **PERSON_TY** datatype

Why Use Object Views?

What if tables already exist?

What if a relational database application is already created and existing and **object-relational** concepts are to be implemented in the application **without rebuilding** and recreating the entire application?

The need would be the ability to overlay **Object-Oriented** (OO) structures, such as abstract datatypes, on existing relational tables. Oracle provides **object views** as a means for doing exactly this.

If the **CUSTOMER** table already existed, the **ADDRESS_TY** and **PERSON_TY** datatypes could be created, and object views could be used to relate them to the **CUSTOMER** table. In the **following example**, the **CUSTOMER** table is created as a relational table, using only the Oracle8i/9i standard datatypes:

```
CREATE TABLE CUSTOMER(
    CUSTOMER_ID NUMBER PRIMARY KEY, NAME VARCHAR2 (25),
    STREET VARCHAR2 (50), CITY VARCHAR2 (25), STATE VARCHAR2 (25), ZIP NUMBER);
```

If another table or application that stores information about people and addresses is required, **ADDRESS_TY** can be created and applied to the CUSTOMER table as well.

Example:

With the CUSTOMER table already created (and possibly containing data), the abstract datatypes should be created. First, create ADDRESS_TY.

Note

 The following example assumes that the **ADDRESS_TY** and **PERSON_TY** datatypes **do not** already exist in the current schema.

```
CREATE OR REPLACE TYPE ADDRESS_TY AS OBJECT(
    STREET VARCHAR2 (50), CITY VARCHAR2 (25), STATE VARCHAR2 (25), ZIP NUMBER);
```

Next, create **PERSON_TY** that uses **ADDRESS_TY:**

```
CREATE OR REPLACE TYPE PERSON_TY AS OBJECT(
    NAME VARCHAR2 (25), ADDRESS ADDRESS_TY);
```

Next, create **CUSTOMER_TY** that uses **PERSON_TY:**

```
CREATE OR REPLACE TYPE CUSTOMER_TY AS OBJECT(
    CUSTOMER_ID NUMBER, PERSON PERSON_TY);
```

In the following example, the **CUSTOMER_OV** is created to display customer columns.

```
CREATE OR REPLACE VIEW CUSTOMER_OV (CUSTOMER_ID, PERSON) AS
    SELECT CUSTOMER_ID, PERSON_TY (NAME, ADDRESS_TY (STREET, CITY, STATE, ZIP))
    FROM CUSTOMER;
INSERT INTO CUSTOMER VALUES(1, 'Sharanam', 'Dadar', 'Mumbai', 'Maharashtra', 400016);
INSERT INTO CUSTOMER
    VALUES(2, 'Vaishali', 'Balgovinddas Rd', 'Mumbai', 'Maharashtra',400016);
INSERT INTO CUSTOMER VALUES(3, 'Hansel', 'Darya Rd', 'Ahemdabad', 'Gujarat', 300042);
```

Using A Where Clause In Object Views

Example:

A **WHERE** clause can also be used in the query that forms the basis of the object view. In the following example, the **CUSTOMER_OV** is modified to include a where clause that limits the object view to only displaying the customer values for which the state column holds the value **Maharashtra**.

```
CREATE OR REPLACE VIEW CUSTOMER_OV (CUSTOMER_ID, PERSON) AS
    SELECT CUSTOMER_ID, PERSON_TY (NAME, ADDRESS_TY (STREET, CITY, STATE, ZIP))
    FROM CUSTOMER WHERE STATE = 'Maharashtra';
```

Note

When the object view **CUSTOMER_OV** is created, the **Where** clause of the view's base query does not refer to the abstract datatype. Instead, it refers directly to the column in the **CUSTOMER** table.

For example, The **Where** clause refers directly to the **STATE** column because the query refers directly to the columns in the **CUSTOMER** table i.e. a relational table that is not based on any abstract data-types.

For creating object views based on existing relational tables, the order of operation is:

1. Create the **CUSTOMER** table
2. Create the **ADDRESS_TY** datatype
3. Create the **PERSON_TY** datatype, using the **ADDRESS_TY** datatype
4. Create the **CUSTOMER_TY** datatype, using the **PERSON_TY** datatype
5. Create the **CUSTOMER_OV** object view, using the defined datatypes

Benefits of using Object Views

The main benefits to using object views are:

1. They allow creation of abstract datatypes within tables that already exist. Since the same abstract datatypes can be used in multiple tables within an application, an application's adherence to standard representation of data and the ability to reuse existing objects can be improved.
2. Object views allow two different ways to enter data i.e. a table can be treated as a relational table or an object table.

Manipulating Data Via Object Views

Data in the customer table can be inserted or updated via CUSTOMER_OV the object view, or the customer table can be updated directly. Treating **CUSTOMER** as just a table, data insertion can be performed via a normal SQL Insert command, as shown in the following example:

Example:

INSERT INTO CUSTOMER **VALUES(**4, 'Silicon Chip Technologies', 'A/5 Jay Chambers', 'Vile Parle (E)', 'Maharashtra', 400057**);**

This Insert command inserts a single record into the CUSTOMER table. Even though an object view has been created on the table, the CUSTOMER table can still be treated as a regular relational table.

Since the object view has been created on the CUSTOMER table, data can be inserted into CUSTOMER via the constructor methods used by the view.

The example shown in the following listing inserts a single record into the **CUSTOMER_OV** object view using the CUSTOMER_TY, PERSON_TY, and ADDRESS_TY constructor methods:

Example:

INSERT INTO CUSTOMER_OV **VALUES(**5, PERSON_TY **(**'Jasper International',
ADDRESS_TY **(**'A/7 Jay Chambers', 'Vile Parle (E)', 'Maharashtra', 400057**)));**

Since either method can be used to insert values into the CUSTOMER_OV object view, the manner in which the application performs data manipulation can be standardized. If the inserts are all based on abstract datatypes, then the same kind of code for inserts can be used, whether the abstract datatypes were created **before** or **after** the table.

Nested Tables

An Introduction

Oracle 8i/9i allows specifying a special object type known as **Nested Table**, or **tables-within-tables** type. This type is used when the number of dependent instances of the type is large or unknown. An example of this is the dependent attribute of an employee object.

Implement A Nested Table

Example:

1. For creating **TYPE** ADDRESS_TY:

   CREATE OR REPLACE TYPE ADDRESS_TY **AS OBJECT(**
   STREET **VARCHAR2(**50**)**, CITY **VARCHAR2(**25**)**, STATE **VARCHAR2(**25**)**, ZIP **NUMBER);**

2. For creating **TYPE** NAME_TY:

   CREATE OR REPLACE TYPE NAME_TY **AS OBJECT(**
   NAME **VARCHAR2(**25**)**, ADDRESS **ADDRESS_TY);**

3. For creating **TYPE** DEPENDENT_TY:

   CREATE OR REPLACE TYPE DEPENDENT_TY **AS OBJECT(**
   RELATION **VARCHAR2(**15**)**, NAME **NAME_TY**, AGE **NUMBER);**

4. For creating a **NESTED TABLE:**

CREATE OR REPLACE TYPE DEPENDENT_LIST **AS TABLE OF** DEPENDENT_TY;

5. For creating **TYPE** EMPLOYEE_INFO_TY:

```
CREATE OR REPLACE TYPE EMPLOYEE_INFO_TY AS OBJECT(
        EMPLOYEE_ID NUMBER(5), NAME NAME_TY, SALARY NUMBER(10,2),
        DEPT_ID NUMBER(5), DEPENDENTS DEPENDENT_LIST);
```

6. For creating the **TABLE** EMPLOYEE_INFO of the **TYPE** EMPLOYEE_INFO_TY:

```
CREATE TABLE EMPLOYEE_INFO OF EMPLOYEE_INFO_TY
        OIDINDEX OID_EMPLOYEE_INFO
                NESTED TABLE DEPENDENTS STORE AS DEPENDENTS_TY;
```

Note

The store table for the nested table type is specified. The store table will take on the default storage attributes of the master table's tablespace.

1. Inserting values in the nested table:

```
INSERT INTO EMPLOYEE_INFO EMP VALUES(1, NAME_TY('Sharanam',
        ADDRESS_TY('JAY Chambers', 'VILE PARLE', 'MUMBAI', 400057)),8000,10,
        DEPENDENT_LIST(
                DEPENDENT_TY('Sister', NAME_TY('Stuti',
                        ADDRESS_TY('Balgovinddas RD', 'Dadar', 'Mumbai', 400016)), 19),
                DEPENDENT_TY('Mother', NAME_TY('Gopi',
                        ADDRESS_TY('Balgovinddas RD', 'Dadar', 'Mumbai', 400016)), 40),
                DEPENDENT_TY('Father', NAME_TY('Chaitanya',
                        ADDRESS_TY('Balgovinddas RD', 'Dadar', 'Mumbai', 400016)), 42)));
```

2. Inserting only detail table values in the nested table:

```
INSERT INTO THE (SELECT DEPENDENTS FROM EMPLOYEE_INFO) DEPENDS
        VALUES(DEPENDENT_TY('Friend', NAME_TY('Vaishali',
                ADDRESS_TY('Balgovinddas Rd', 'Dadar', 'Mumbai', 400016)),23));
INSERT INTO THE (SELECT DEPENDENTS FROM employee_info) DEPENDS
        VALUES(DEPENDENT_TY('Colleague', NAME_TY('Hansel',
                ADDRESS_TY('Subhash Rd', :Parle', 'Mumbai', 400057)), 22));
```

3. Updating values of a child record in the nested table:

```
UPDATE THE (SELECT DEPENDENTS FROM EMPLOYEE_INFO) DEPENDS
        SET DEPENDS.RELATION = 'Wife' WHERE DEPENDS.RELATION = 'Friend';
```

4. Deleting values of a child record in the nested table:

```
DELETE THE (SELECT DEPENDENTS FROM EMPLOYEE_INFO) DEPENDS
        WHERE DEPENDS.RELATION = 'Colleague';
```

Variable Arrays

A varying array allows the storing of repeating attributes of a record in a single row. For example, consider a table that stores company information such as the **company name** and **address**. One company can have multiple addresses.

Example:

CREATE TABLE COMPANY_INFO(NAME **VARCHAR2**(50), ADDRESS **VARCHAR2**(1000));

Since one company can have multiple addresses, the company name will have to be repeated for all the addresses it has, though the name will be same for all the different records.

Note

Varying arrays are collectors that allow repetition of **only** those column values that change, potentially saving storage space. Varying arrays can be used to accurately represent **one-to-many** relationships where the maximum number of elements on the **many** side of the relationship is known and where the order of these elements is important.

Creating A Varying Array

A varying array can be created based on either an abstract datatype or one of Oracle's standard datatypes (such as NUMBER). When using varying arrays, the datatypes can consist of only one column. If multiple columns need to be used in an array, consider using nested tables.

The **COMPANY_ADDRESS_TY** abstract datatype has one attribute, **ADDRESS**. To use this datatype as part of a varying array in the **COMPANY_INFO** table, a decision needs to be made on the maximum number of addresses per company. For this example, assume that no more than **three addresses** per company will be stored.

To create the varying array, use the **AS VARRAY( )** clause of the **CREATE TYPE** command.

Example:

CREATE TYPE COMPANY_ADDRESS_TY **AS VARRAY**(3) **OF VARCHAR2**(1000);

This statement creates a **VARRAY** type called **COMPANY_ADDRESS_TY**, which can hold a maximum of **3 elements** of data-type **VARCHAR2**(1000), i.e. 3 entries per record, each storing address information for the company.

Now that the varying array COMPANY_ADDRESS_TY is created, this can be used as part of the creation of either a table or an abstract datatype.

Example:

CREATE TABLE COMPANY_INFO(
    COMPANY_NAME **VARCHAR2**(50), ADDRESS **COMPANY_ADDRESS_TY**);

This SQL statement creates a table called COMPANY_INFO, which contains an embedded object called ADDRESS that is a VARRAY of type COMPANY_ADDRESS_TY.

Describing the Varying Array

The COMPANY_INFO table will contain one record for each company, even if that company has multiple addresses. The multiple addresses will be stored in the address column, using the COMPANY_ADDRESS_TY varying array.

Note

 ORACLE stores the varying array data internally using the RAW datatype.

Example:

DESC COMPANY_INFO;

Output:

Name	Null?	Type
COMPANY_NAME		VARCHAR2 (50)
ADDRESS		COMPANY_ADDRESS_TY

The USER_TAB_COLUMNS data dictionary view is used to see information about the structure of the Address column:

Example:

SELECT COLUMN_NAME, DATA_TYPE **FROM** USER_TAB_COLUMNS
WHERE TABLE_NAME = 'COMPANY_INFO';

Output:

COLUMN NAME	DATA TYPE
COMPANY_NAME	VARCHAR2
ADDRESS	COMPANY_ADDRESS_TY

From the **USER_TAB_COLUMNS** output, it is seen that the address column uses the COMPANY_ADDRESS_TY varying array as its datatype.

The USER_TYPES data dictionary view can be queried to see the datatype COMPANY_ADDRESS_TY as:

Example:

SELECT TYPECODE, ATTRIBUTES **FROM** USER_TYPES
WHERE TYPE_NAME = 'COMPANY_ADDRESS_TY';

Output:

TYPECODE	ATTRIBUTES
COLLECTION	0

The USER_TYPE output shows that COMPANY_ADDRESS_TY A is a collector, with no attributes.

USER_COLL_TYPES

The USER_COLL_TYPES data dictionary view can be queried to see the characteristics of the Varying array, including the upper limit to the number of entries it can contain per record and the abstract datatype on which it is based.

The USER_COLL_TYPES data dictionary view can be queried to see the data type COMPANY_ADDRESS_TY as:

Example:

SELECT TYPE_NAME, COLL_TYPE, UPPER_BOUND **FROM** USER_COLL_TYPES
WHERE TYPE_NAME = 'COMPANY_ADDRESS_TY';

Output:

TYPE_NAME	COLL_TYPE	UPPER_BOUND
COMPANY_ADDRESS_TY	VARYING ARRAY	3

Data Manipulation

Data can be inserted into the table in the following way:

Example:

INSERT INTO COMPANY_INFO **VALUES**('Silicon Chip Technologies',
COMPANY_ADDRESS_TY('A/5 Jay Chambers, Service Road, Vile Parle (E), Mumbai 57', **NULL**, **NULL**));

INSERT INTO COMPANY_INFO **VALUES**('Jasper International',
COMPANY_ADDRESS_TY('S.D.F II, Seepz, Andheri(E), Mumbai', 'ABBA House, MIDC, Andheri (E), Mumbai', 'Emmar Commercial Complex, A/5-407, S.V. Road, Borivli(W)'));

Notice that each Insert statement uses the system-generated constructor for the VARRAY called **COMPANY_ADDRESS_TY**. Also, the first insert statement only inserts one address of data but two of the VARRAY elements are null, the second inserts three values for address.

Referencing Objects

The Referencing Object (**REFs** data type) is something that is new to Oracle. This data type acts as a **pointer** to an object. A REF can also be used in a manner similar to a foreign key in a RDBMS. A **REF** is used primarily to store an object identifier, and to allow the user to select that object.

REF's establish relationship between two object tables, much the same way as a primary-key/foreign-key relationship in relational tables. Relational tables however, have difficulty, if more than one table is needed in a primary-key/foreign-key relationship related to a single table. **For example**, an ADDRESS table, that stores addresses from several entities. The use of **REFs** eliminates this problem, because an unscoped REF can refer to any accessible object table.

A **SCOPE** clause in a definition forces a set of **REFs** for a given column to be confined to a single object table. There can be only one **REF** clause for a given **REF** column. **REF** scope can be set at either the column or table level.

REF values can be stored with or without a **ROWID**. Storing a **REF** with a **ROWID** speeds de-referencing operations, but takes more space. If **WITH ROWID** is not specified with the **REF** clause, the default is to not store **ROWIDs** with the **REF** values. **SCOPE** clauses prevent dangling references, as they will not allow **REF** values unless the corresponding entries in the **SCOPE** table is present.

REF columns can be added to nested tables with the **ALTER TABLE** command.

A call to a **REF** returns the **OID** of the object instance. An **OID** is a 128-byte base-64 number, which isn't very useful except as a handle to the object instance. To get the value stored in the instance that is referred to by a **REF**, the **DEREF** routine is used. **DEREF** returns values in the object instance referenced by a specific **REF** value.

Examples For The Use Of REF

1. For creating a TYPE object:

   CREATE TYPE DEPT_TY **AS OBJECT(**
   DNAME **VARCHAR2(100)**, ADDRESS **VARCHAR2(200));**

Output:

```
Type created.
```

2. For creating a TABLE object using the above TYPE object:

   CREATE TABLE DEPT **OF** DEPT_TY;

Output:

```
Type created.
```

3. For creating a TABLE object that references to the TYPE object and also specifies the SCOPE:

   CREATE TABLE EMP(
   ENAME VARCHAR2(100), ENUMBER **NUMBER**, EDEPT **REF DEPT_TY SCOPE IS** DEPT);

Output:

```
Type created.
```

4. For inserting values in the DEPT table:

   INSERT INTO DEPT **VALUES(DEPT_TY(**'Sales', '501 Baliga Street'));

   INSERT INTO DEPT **VALUES(DEPT_TY(**'Accounts', '84 Darya Ganj'));

Output:

```
1 row created.
1 row created.
```

5. For viewing the DEPT table:

   SELECT * FROM DEPT;

Output:

DNAME	ADDRESS
Sales	501 Baliga Street
Accounts	84 Darya Ganj

6. For viewing the REF from the DEPT table:

   SELECT REF(D) **FROM** DEPT D;

Output:

D
0000280209A656BEEF11D1AD5B0060972CFBA8A656BEEE11B811D1AD5B0060972CFBA8008000C10000
0000280209A656BEEF11D1AD5B0060972CFBA8A656BEEE11B811D1AD5B0060972CFBA8008000C10001

7. For inserting a row into the EMP table for an employee in Sales department:

   INSERT INTO EMP **SELECT** 'Nirmal Pandey', 1, REF(d) **FROM** DEPT D

   WHERE D.DNAME = 'Sales';

Output:

```
1 row created.
```

8. For viewing records from the EMP table:

   SELECT * FROM EMP;

Output:

ENAME	ENUMBER	EDEPT
Nirmal Pandey	1	000220208A656BEEF11B811D1AD5B0060972CFBA 8A656 BEEE11D1AD5B0060972CFBA8

9. For viewing the ENAME, ENUMBER and the details of EDEPT column of the EMP table using the DEREF routine:

   SELECT ENAME, ENUMBER, **DEREF** (EDEPT) **FROM** EMP;

Output:

ENAME	ENUMBER	DEREF (EDEPT) (DNAME, ADDRESS)
Nirmal Pandey	1	DEPT_T ('Sales', '501 Baliga Street')

Self Review Questions

Fill in the Blanks

1. ____________ reduce complexity by giving an intuitive way of representing complex data and its relations.
2. If database objects are built using ____________, then the chances they will be reused increase exponentially.
3. If multiple applications or tables use the same set of database objects, then a ____________ standard for applications or tables is being created.
4. A combination of data and methods makes up an ____________.
5. ____________ datatype is a datatype that consists of one or more subtypes.
6. When an abstract datatype is created, a ____________ for the representation of abstract data elements (like addresses, people or companies) is created.
7. A ____________ table is a collection of rows, represented as a column within the main table.
8. Varying arrays, also known as ____________, allows storing repeating attributes in tables.

9. A large object, or __________, is capable of storing large volumes of data.
10. The __________ datatype stores character data and can store data up to 4GB in length.
11. The fourth LOB datatype, __________, is a pointer to an external file.
12. A __________ array is a set of objects, each with the same datatype.
13. __________ are essentially pointers to row objects.
14. __________ views allow adding OO concepts on top of existing relational tables.
15. The operations that affect an object are called __________.
16. The __________ dictionary can be queried for information about database objects that are owned or on which access rights have been granted.
17. The columns of an abstract datatype are referred to as its __________.
18. Oracle creates methods, called __________ methods, for data management when an abstract datatype is created.
19. A __________ clause in a definition forces a set of REFs for a given column to be confined to a single object table.
20. REF values can be stored with or without a __________.
21. A call to a REF returns the __________ of the object instance.

True or False

22. If OO database objects are created the chances that the database objects being reused is decreased.
23. Even if a standard datatype is created and used for all addresses, all the addresses in the database will use the different internal formats.
24. Objects have data, and objects have methods for interacting with data.
25. Abstract data types cannot be nested and cannot contain references to other abstract data types.
26. An abstract datatype cannot be used to create an object table.
27. In an object table, the columns of the table map to the columns of an abstract datatype.
28. A nested table is a table within a table.
29. The size of the array is not limited when it is created.
30. The NCLOB datatype is used to store CLOB data for multibyte character sets.
31. Nested tables and varying arrays are not embedded objects.
32. When a table is created with a varying array, the array is a nested table with a limited set of rows.
33. The data for BLOB, CLOB, and NCLOB datatype is stored outside the database.
34. A row object is the same as a column object.
35. Object views allow the development of OO features within a relational database.
36. Abstract data types are part of an OO concept called abstraction.
37. It is necessary to create physical tables at each level of abstraction.
38. A datatype describes data, it does not store data.
39. A constructor method is a program that is named before the datatype.
40. When implementing object-relational database applications, the relational database design methods are first used.
41. When using varying arrays, the datatypes can consist of only one column.
42. REF columns can be added to nested tables with the MODIFY TABLE command.

Hands On Exercises

1. **Create type Address_Ty consisting of the following columns:**

Type Name: Address_Ty

Column Name	Data Type	Size
Address1	Varchar2	30
Address2	Varchar2	30
City	Varchar2	20
PinCode	Number	8
State	Varchar2	15

2. **Create the tables described below:**

Table Name:	SALESMAN_MASTER			
Description:	Used to store information about products..			
Column Name	**Data Type**	**Size**	**Default**	**Attributes**
SalesmanNo	Varchar2	6		
SalesmanName	Varchar2	20		
Address	Address_Ty			
SalAmt	Number	8,2		
SaleTrgt	Number	6,2		
SaleAchvd	Number	6,2		
Remarks	Varchar2	60		

3. **Insert the following data into their respective tables**

(a) Data for **SALESMAN_MASTER** table:

SalesmanNo	Name	Address1	Address2	City	PinCode	State
S00001	Aman	A/14	Worli	Mumbai	400002	Maharashtra
S00002	Omkar	65	Nariman	Mumbai	400001	Maharashtra
S00003	Raj	P-7	Bandra	Mumbai	400032	Maharashtra
S00004	Ashish	A/5	Juhu	Mumbai	400044	Maharashtra

SalesmanNo	SalAmt	TgtToGet	YtdSales	Remarks
S00001	3000	100	50	Good
S00002	3000	200	100	Good
S00003	3000	200	100	Good
S00004	3500	200	150	Good

4. Exercise on retrieving records from a table

(a) Retrieve the list of city and state from Salesman_Master

(b) Change the **city** value for salesman who live in Bombay to Chennai

(c) Delete the record for the salesman who live in **Chennai**

5. Create type objects as described below:

(a) Create type Dependent_Ty consisting of the following columns

Type Name: Dependent_Ty

Column Name	Data Type	Size
Relation	varchar2	15
Age	Number	

(b) Create nested table Dependent_List consisting of Dependent_Ty

(c) Create type Salesman_info_ty with the following columns

Type Name: Salesman_info_ty

Column Name	Data Type	Size
Id	Number	5
Name	Varchar2	20
Dependents	Dependent_List	

(d) Create the TABLE Salesman_info of the TYPE Salesman_info_ty

16

Introduction To PL/SQL

Though SQL is the natural language of the DBA, it suffers from various inherent **disadvantages**, when used as a conventional programming language.

1. SQL does not have any **procedural capabilities** i.e. SQL does not provide the programming techniques of condition checking, looping and branching that is vital for data testing before its permanent storage
2. SQL statements are passed to the Oracle Engine **one** at a time. Each time an SQL statement is executed, a call is made to the engine's resources. This adds to the traffic on the network, thereby decreasing the speed of data processing, especially in a multi-user environment
3. While processing an SQL sentence if an error occurs, the Oracle engine displays its own error messages. SQL has no facility for programmed handling of errors that arise during the manipulation of data

Although SQL is a very powerful tool, its set of disadvantages prevent, it from being a fully structured programming language. For a fully structured programming language, Oracle provides **PL/SQL**.

As the name suggests, PL/SQL is a **superset** of SQL. PL/SQL is a block-structured language that enables developers to combine the power of SQL with procedural statements. PL/SQL bridges the gap between database technology and procedural programming languages.

Advantages Of PL/SQL

1. PL/SQL is development tool that not only supports SQL data manipulation but also provides facilities of conditional checking, branching and looping
2. PL/SQL sends an **entire block** of SQL statements to the Oracle engine all in one go. Communication between the program block and the Oracle engine reduces considerably, reducing network traffic. Since the Oracle engine got the SQL statements as a single block, it processes this code much faster than if it got the code one sentence at a time. There is a definite improvement in the performance time of the Oracle engine. As an entire block of SQL code is passed to the Oracle engine at one time for execution, all changes made to the data in the table are **done** or **undone**, in one go
3. PL/SQL also permits dealing with errors as required, and facilitates displaying user-friendly messages, when errors are encountered
4. PL/SQL allows declaration and use of variables in blocks of code. These variables can be used to store intermediate results of a query for later processing, or calculate values and insert them into

an Oracle table later. PL/SQL variables can be used anywhere, either in SQL statements or in PL/SQL blocks

5. Via PL/SQL, all sorts of calculations can be done quickly and efficiently without the use of the Oracle engine. This considerably improves transaction performance
6. Applications written in PL/SQL are portable to any computer hardware and operating system, where Oracle is operational. Hence, PL/SQL code blocks written for a DOS version of Oracle will run on its Linux / UNIX version, **without** any modifications at all

The Generic PL/SQL Block

Every programming environment allows the creation of structured, logical blocks of code that describe processes, which have to be applied to data. Once these blocks are passed to the environment, the processes described are applied to data, suitable data manipulation takes place, and useful output is obtained.

PL/SQL permits the creation of structured logical blocks of code that describe processes, which have to be applied to data. A single PL/SQL code block consists of a set of SQL statements, clubbed together, and passed to the Oracle engine entirely. This block has to be logically grouped together for the engine to recognize it as a singular code block. A PL/SQL block has a definite structure, which can be divided into sections. The sections of a PL/SQL block are:

- ❑ The Declare section,
- ❑ The Master Begin and End section that **also** (optionally) **contains** an Exception section.

Each of these is explained below:

The Declare Section

Code blocks start with a declaration section, in which, memory variables and other Oracle objects can be declared, and if required initialized. Once declared, they can be used in SQL statements for data manipulation.

The Begin Section

It consists of a set of SQL **and** PL/SQL statements, which describe processes that have to be applied to table data. Actual data manipulation, retrieval, looping and branching constructs are specified in this section.

The Exception Section

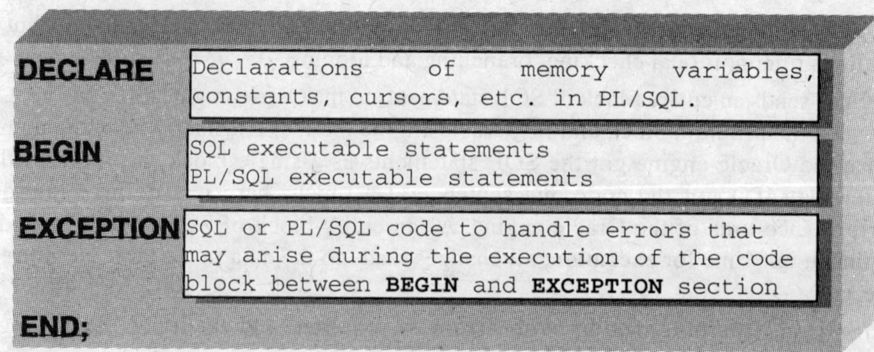

Diagram 16.1: The PL/SQL block structure.

This section deals with handling of errors that arise during execution of the data manipulation statements, which make up the PL/SQL code block. Errors can arise due to syntax, logic and/or validation rule violation.

The End Section

This marks the end of a PL/SQL block.

A PL/SQL code block can be diagrammatically represented as follows:

The PL/SQL Execution Environment

Wherever PL/SQL technology is required (**i.e.** in the RDBMS core or in its tools), the PL/SQL engine accepts any valid PL/SQL block as input.

PL/SQL In The Oracle Engine

The PL/SQL engine resides in the Oracle engine, the Oracle engine can process not only single SQL statements but also entire PL/SQL blocks.

These blocks are sent to the PL/SQL engine, where procedural statements are executed and SQL statements are sent to the SQL executor in the Oracle engine. Since the PL/SQL engine resides in the Oracle engine, this is an efficient and swift operation.

The call to the Oracle engine needs to be made only once to execute any number of SQL statements, if these SQL sentences are bundled inside a PL/SQL block.

Diagram 15.2 gives an idea of how these statements are executed and how convenient it is to bundle SQL code within a PL/SQL block. Since the Oracle engine is called only once for each block, the speed of SQL statement execution is vastly enhanced, when compared to the Oracle engine being called once for each SQL sentence.

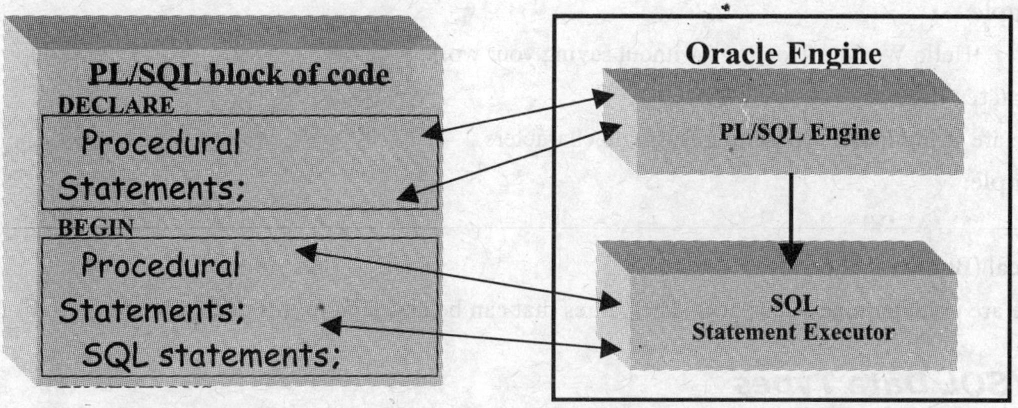

Diagram 16.2: The PL/SQL Execution Environment.

PL/SQL

The Character Set

The basic character set includes the following:

- ❑ Uppercase alphabets { **A - Z** }

- Lowercase alphabets { **a - z** }
- Numerals { **0 - 9** }
- Symbols **( ) + - * / < > = ! ; : . ' @ % , " # $ ^ & _ \ { } ? [ ]**

Words used in a PL/SQL block are called **Lexical Units**. Blank spaces can be freely inserted between lexical units in a PL/SQL block. The blank spaces have no effect on the PL/SQL block.

The ordinary symbols used in PL/SQL blocks are:

```
( )  +  -  *  /  <  >  =  ;  %  '  "  [ ]  :
```

Compound symbols used in PL/SQL blocks are:

```
< >   !=   ~=   ^=   <=   >=   :=   **   ..   ||  <<  >>
```

Literals

A literal is a numeric value or a character string used to represent itself.

Numeric Literal

These can be either integers or floats. If a float is being represented, then the integer part must be separated from the float part by a period.

Example:

25, 6.34, 7g2, 25e-03, .1, 1., 1.e4, +17, -5

String Literal

These are represented by one or more legal characters and must be enclosed within single quotes. The single quote character can be represented, by **writing it twice** in a string literal. This is **definitely not** the same as a double quote.

Example:

'Hello World', 'Don''t go without saving your work'

Character Literal

These are string literals consisting of single characters.

Example:

'*', 'A', 'Y'

Logical (Boolean) Literal

These are predetermined constants. The values that can be assigned to this data type are: TRUE, FALSE, NULL

PL/SQL Data Types

Both PL/SQL and Oracle have their foundations in SQL. Most PL/SQL data types are native to Oracle's data dictionary. Hence, there is a very easy integration of PL/SQL code with the Oracle Engine.

The default data types that can be declared in PL/SQL are **number** (for storing numeric data), **char** (for storing character data), **date** (for storing date and time data), **boolean** (for storing TRUE, FALSE or NULL). **number**, **char** and **date** data types can have NULL values.

The **%TYPE** attribute provides for further integration. PL/SQL can use the **%TYPE** attribute to declare variables based on definitions of columns in a table. Hence, if a column's attributes change, the variable's attributes will change as well. This provides for data independence, reduces maintenance costs, and allows programs to adapt to changes made to the table.

%TYPE declares a variable or constant to have the same data type as that of a previously defined variable or of a column in a table or in a view. When referencing a table, a user may name the table and the column, or name the owner, the table and the column.

NOT NULL causes creation of a variable or a constant that **cannot** be assigned a null value. If an attempt is made to assign the value NULL to a variable or a constant that has been assigned a **NOT NULL** constraint, Oracle senses the exception condition automatically and an internal error is returned.

Note

As soon as a variable or constant has been declared as NOT NULL, it must be assigned a value. Hence every variable or constant declared as NOT NULL **needs** to be followed by a PL/SQL expression that loads a value into the variable or constant.

Variables

Variables in PL/SQL blocks are **named** variables. A variable name must begin with a character and can be followed by a maximum of 29 other characters.

Reserved words cannot be used as variable names **unless** enclosed within double quotes. Variables must be separated from each other by at least one space or by a punctuation mark.

Case is insignificant when declaring variable names. A space cannot be used in a variable name. A variable of any data type either native to the Oracle Engine such as number, char, date, and so on or native to PL/SQL such as Boolean (i.e. logical variable content) can be declared.

Assigning Values to Variables

The assigning of a value to a variable can be done in two ways:

- Using the assignment operator := (i.e. a colon followed by an equal to sign).
- Selecting or fetching table data values into variables.

Note

An interesting point to note here is that if PL/SQL code blocks are used for loading and calculating variables, the power of the Oracle Engine is not used. This frees up the Oracle engine for other work and considerably improves response time.

Constants

Declaring a constant is similar to declaring a variable except that the keyword **constant** must be added to the variable name **and** a value assigned immediately. Thereafter, no further assignments to the constant are possible, while the constant is **within** the scope of the PL/SQL block.

Raw

Raw types are used to store **binary** data. Character variables are automatically converted between character sets by Oracle, if necessary. These are similar to char variables, except that they are not converted between character sets. It is used to store fixed length binary data. The maximum length of a raw variable is 32,767 bytes. However, the maximum length of a database raw column is 255 bytes.

Long raw is similar to long data, except that PL/SQL will not convert between character sets. The maximum length of a long raw variable is 32,760 bytes. The maximum length of a long raw column is 2 GB.

Rowid

This data type is the same as the database **ROWID** pseudo-column type. It can hold a rowid, which can be considered as a unique key for every row in the database. Rowids are stored internally as a fixed length binary quantity, whose actual fixed length varies depending on the operating system.

Various **DBMS_ROWID** functions are used to extract information about the ROWID pseudo-column. **Extended** and **Restricted** are two rowid formats. **Restricted** is used mostly to be backward compatible with previous versions of Oracle. The **Extended** format takes advantage of new Oracle features.

The **DBMS_ROWID** package has several procedures and functions to interpret the ROWIDs of records. The following table shows the **DBMS_ROWID** functions:

FUNCTION	DESCRIPTION
ROWID_VERIFY	Verifies if the ROWID can be extended; 0 = can be converted to extended format; 1 = cannot be converted to extended format
ROWID_TYPE	0 = ROWID, 1 = Extended
ROWID_BLOCK_NUMBER	The block number that contains the record; 1 = Extended ROWID
ROWID_OBJECT	The object number of the object that contains the record.
ROWID_RELATIVE_FNO	The relative file number contains the record.
ROWID_ROW_NUMBER	The row number of the record.
ROWID_TO_ABSOLUTE_FNO	The absolute file number; user need to input rowid_val, schema, and object; the absolute file number is returned.
ROWID_TO_EXTENDED	Converts the ROWID from Restricted to Extended; user need to input restr_rowid, schema, object; the extended number is returned.
ROWID_TO_RESTRICTED	Converts the ROWID from Extended to Restricted.

ROWID is a pseudo-column that has a unique value associated with each record of the database.

The **DBMS_ROWID** package is created by the

ORACLE_HOME/RDBMS/ADMIN/DBMSUTIL.SQL script.

This script is automatically run when the Oracle instance is created.

LOB Types

A company may decide that some comments about each of its vendors must be stored along with their details. This must be stored along with all the other details that they have on a particular vendor. This can be done in Oracle with the help of LOB types.

The LOB types are used to store large objects. A large object can be either a binary or a character value upto 4 GB in size. Large objects can contain unstructured data, which is accessed more efficiently than long or long raw data, with fewer restrictions. LOB types are manipulated using the **DBMS_LOB** package. There are four types of LOBs:

- **BLOB (Binary LOB)** - This stores unstructured binary data upto 4 GB in length. A blob could contain video or picture information.

- **CLOB (Character LOB)** - This stores single byte characters upto 4 GB in length. This might be used to store documents.
- **BFILE (Binary File)** - This stores a pointer to read only binary data stored as an external file outside the database.

Of these LOBs, **BFILE** is an **external** to the database. Internal objects store a **locator** in the Large Object column of a table. **Locator** is a pointer that specifies the actual location of LOB stored outside the database. The LOB locator for **BFILE** is a pointer to the location of the binary file stored by the operating system. The **DBMS_LOB** package is used to manipulate LOBs. Oracle supports data integrity and concurrency for all the LOBs except **BFILE** as the data is stored outside the database.

Storage for LOB data

The area required to store the LOB data can be specified at the time of creation of the table that includes the LOB column. The create table command has a storage clause that specifies the storage characteristics for the table.

Syntax:

```
CREATE TABLE <TableName> (<ColumnName> <Datatype> <Size()>,
        <ColumnName> <Datatype> <Size()>, <ColumnName> CLOB,…);
```

Logical Comparisons

PL/SQL supports the comparison between variables and constants in SQL and PL/SQL statements. These comparisons, often called **Boolean expressions**, generally consist of simple expressions separated by relational operators (<, >, =, < >, >=, <=) that can be connected by logical operators (AND, OR, NOT). A Boolean expression will always evaluate to **TRUE, FALSE** or **NULL**.

Displaying User Messages On The VDU Screen

Programming tools require a method through which messages can be displayed on the VDU screen.

DBMS_OUTPUT is a package that includes a number of procedures and functions that accumulate information in a buffer so that it can be retrieved later. These functions can also be used to display messages.

PUT_LINE puts a piece of information in the package buffer followed by an end-of-line marker. It can also be used to display a message. **PUT_LINE** expects a single parameter of character data type. If used to display a message, it is the **message** string.

To diṣplay messages, the **SERVEROUTPUT** should be set to **ON**. **SERVEROUTPUT** is a SQL *PLUS environment parameter that displays the information passed as a parameter to the **PUT_LINE** function.

Syntax:

```
SET SERVEROUTPUT [ON/OFF]
```

Comments

A comment can have two forms, as:

- The comment line begins with a double hyphen (—). The entire line will be treated as a comment.
- The comment line begins with a slash followed by an asterisk (/*) till the occurrence of an asterisk followed by a slash (*/). All lines within are treated as comments. This form of specifying comments can be used to span across multiple lines. This technique can also be used to enclose a section of a PL/SQL block that temporarily needs to be isolated and ignored.

Control Structure

The flow of control statements can be classified into the following categories:

- Conditional Control
- Iterative Control
- Sequential Control

Conditional Control

PL/SQL allows the use of an **IF** statement to control the execution of a block of code. In PL/SQL, the **IF - THEN - ELSIF - ELSE - END IF** construct in code blocks allow specifying certain conditions under which a specific block of code should be executed.

Syntax:

```
    IF <Condition> THEN
        <Action>
    ELSIF <Condition> THEN
        <Action>
    ELSE
        <Action>
    END IF;
```

Example:

Write a PL/SQL code block that will accept an account number from the user, check if the users balance is less than the minimum balance, only then deduct Rs.100/- from the balance. The process is fired on the ACCT_MSTR table.

```
DECLARE
/* Declaration of memory variables and constants to be used in the
Execution section.*/
    mCUR_BAL  number(11,2);
    mACCT_NO varchar2(7);
    mFINE number(4) := 100;
    mMIN_BAL constant number(7,2) := 5000.00;
BEGIN
/* Accept the Account number from the user*/
    mACCT_NO := &mACCT_NO;
/* Retrieving the current balance from the ACCT_MSTR table where the
ACCT_NO in the table is equal to the mACCT_NO entered by the user.*/
    SELECT CURBAL INTO mCUR_BAL FROM ACCT_MSTR WHERE ACCT_NO=
mACCT_NO;
/* Checking if the resultant balance is less than the minimum balance
of Rs.5000. If the condition is satisfied an amount of Rs.100 is deducted
as a fine from the current balance of the corresponding ACCT_NO.*/
    IF mCUR_BAL < mMIN_BAL THEN
        UPDATE ACCT_MSTR SET CURBAL = CURBAL - mFINE
            WHERE ACCT_NO = mACCT_NO;
    END IF;
END;
```

Output:

```
Enter value for macct_no: 'SB9'
old  11:   mACCT_NO := &mACCT_NO;
new  11:   mACCT_NO := 'SB9';

PL/SQL procedure successfully completed.
```

Iterative Control

Iterative control indicates the ability to repeat or skip sections of a code block. A **loop** marks a sequence of statements that has to be repeated. The keyword **loop** has to be placed before the first statement in the sequence of statements to be repeated, while the keyword **end loop** is placed immediately after the last statement in the sequence. Once a loop begins to execute, it will **go on forever**. Hence a conditional statement that controls the number of times a loop is executed **always accompanies** loops.

PL/SQL supports the following structures for iterative control:

Simple Loop

In simple loop, the key word **loop** should be placed before the first statement in the sequence and the keyword **end loop** should be written at the end of the sequence to end the loop.

Syntax:

```
Loop
    <Sequence of statements>
End loop;
```

Example:

Create a simple loop such that a message is displayed when a loop exceeds a particular value.

```
DECLARE
    i number := 0;
BEGIN
    LOOP
        i := i + 2;
        EXIT WHEN i > 10;
    END LOOP;
    dbms_output.put_line('Loop exited as the value of i has reached '
    || to_char(i));
END;
```

Output:

```
Loop exited as the value of i has reached 12
PL/SQL procedure successfully completed.
```

The WHILE loop

Syntax:

```
WHILE <Condition>
LOOP
    <Action>
END LOOP;
```

Example:

Write a PL/SQL code block to calculate the area of a circle for a value of radius varying from 3 to 7. Store the radius and the corresponding values of calculated area in an empty table named **Areas**, consisting of two columns **Radius** and **Area**.

Table Name: Areas

RADIUS	AREA

Create the table AREAS as:

CREATE TABLE AREAS (RADIUS NUMBER(5), AREA NUMBER(14,2));

```
DECLARE
/* Declaration of memory variables and constants to be used in the
Execution section.*/
      pi constant number(4,2) := 3.14 ;
      radius number(5);
      area number(14,2);
BEGIN
/* Initialize the radius to 3, since calculations are required for
radius 3 to 7 */
      radius := 3;

/* Set a loop so that it fires till the radius value reaches 7 */
      WHILE RADIUS <= 7
      LOOP
      /* Area calculation for a circle */
            area := pi * power(radius,2);
      /* Insert the value for the radius and its corresponding area
      calculated in the table */
            INSERT INTO areas     VALUES (radius, area);

      /* Increment the value of the variable radius by 1 */
            radius := radius + 1;
      END  LOOP;
END;
```

The above PL/SQL code block initializes a variable **radius** to hold the value of 3. The area calculations are required for the radius between 3 and 7. The value for area is calculated first with radius 3, and the radius and area are inserted into the table **Areas**. Now, the variable holding the value of radius is incremented by 1, i.e. it now holds the value 4. Since the code is held within a loop structure, the code continues to fire till the radius value reaches 7. Each time the value of radius and area is inserted into the areas table.

After the loop is completed the table will now hold the following:

Table Name: Areas

RADIUS	AREA
3	28.26
4	50.24
5	78.5
6	113.04
7	153.86

The FOR Loop

Syntax:

```
FOR variable IN [REVERSE] start..end
LOOP
     <Action>
END LOOP;
```

Note

 The **variable** in the For Loop need not be declared. Also the increment value cannot be specified. The For Loop variable is **always incremented** by **1**.

Example:

Write a PL/SQL block of code for inverting a number 5639 to 9365.

```
DECLARE
/* Declaration of memory variables and constants to be used in the
Execution section.*/
    given_number varchar(5) := '5639';
    str_length number(2);
    inverted_number varchar(5);
BEGIN
/* Store the length of the given number */
    str_length := length(given_number);
/* Initialize the loop such that it repeats for the number of times
equal to the length of the given number. Also, since the number is
required to be inverted, the loop should consider the last number first
and store it i.e. in reverse order */
    FOR cntr IN REVERSE 1..str_length
    /* Variables used as counter in the for loop need not be declared
    i.e. cntr declaration is not required */
    LOOP
    /* The last digit of the number is obtained using the substr
    function, and stored in a variable, while retaining the previous
    digit stored in the variable*/
```

```
        inverted_number := inverted_number || substr(given_number, cntr, 1);
    END LOOP;
/* Display the initial number, as well as the inverted number, which is
stored in the variable on screen */
    dbms_output.put_line ('The Given number is ' || given_number );
    dbms_output.put_line ('The Inverted number is'||inverted_number);
END;
```

Output:

```
    The Given number is 5639
    The Inverted number is 9365
```

The above PL/SQL code block stores the given number as well its length in two variables. Since the FOR loop is set to repeat till the length of the number is reached and in reverse order, the loop will fire 4 times beginning from the last digit i.e. **9**. This digit is obtained using the function **SUBSTR**, and stored in a variable. The loop now fires again to fetch and store the second last digit of the given number. This is appended to the last digit stored previously. This repeats till each digit of the number is obtained and stored.

Sequential Control

The GOTO Statement

The **GOTO** statement changes the **flow of control** within a PL/SQL block. This statement allows execution of a section of code, which is not in the normal flow of control. The entry point into such a block of code is marked using the tags **<<userdefined name>>**. The **GOTO** statement can then make use of this user-defined name to jump into that block of code for execution.

Syntax:

```
    GOTO <codeblock name>;
```

Example:

Write a PL/SQL block of code to achieve the following: If there are no transactions taken place in the last 365 days then mark the account status as **inactive**, and then record the account number, the opening date and the type of account in the **INACTV_ACCT_MSTR** table.

Table Name: INACTV_ACCT_MSTR

ACCT_NO	OPNDT	TYPE

Create the table INACTV_ACCT_MSTR as:

CREATE TABLE INACTV_ACCT_MSTR **(**

ACCT_NO **VARCHAR2(10)**, OPNDT **DATE**, TYPE **VARCHAR2(2))**;

```
DECLARE
/* Declaration of memory variables and constants to be used in the
Execution section.*/
    mACCT_NO VARCHAR2(10);
    mANS VARCHAR2(3);
    mOPNDT DATE;
```

```
    mTYPE VARCHAR2(2);
BEGIN
/* Accept the Account number from the user*/
    mACCT_NO := &mACCT_NO;
/* Fetch the account number into a variable */
    SELECT 'YES' INTO mANS FROM TRANS_MSTR WHERE ACCT_NO = mACCT_NO
        GROUP BY ACCT_NO HAVING MAX(SYSDATE - DT) >365;

/* If there are no transactions taken place in last 365 days the execution
control is transferred to a user labelled section of code, labelled as
mark_status in this example. */
    IF mANS = 'YES' THEN
        GOTO mark_status;
    ELSE
    dbms_output.put_line('Account number: ' || mACCT_NO || 'is active');
    END IF;

/* A labelled section of code which updates the STATUS of account
number held in the ACCT_MSTR table. Further the ACCT_NO, OPNDT and the
TYPE are inserted in to the table INACTV_ACCT_MSTR. */
    << mark_status>>
    UPDATE ACCT_MSTR SET STATUS = 'I' WHERE ACCT_NO = mACCT_NO;
    SELECT OPNDT, TYPE INTO mOPNDT, mTYPE
        FROM ACCT_MSTR WHERE ACCT_NO = mACCT_NO;
    INSERT INTO INACTV_ACCT_MSTR (ACCT_NO, OPNDT,TYPE)
        VALUES (mACCT_NO, mOPNDT, mTYPE);
    dbms_output.put_line(' Account number: '|| mACCT_NO || 'is marked
    as inactive');
END;
```

The PL/SQL code first fetches the Account number from the user into a variable **mACCT_NO**. It then verifies using an SQL statement, whether any transactions are performed within **last 365 days**.

If they are, then a message stating **"Account Number ____ is active"** is displayed.

But if there are no transactions performed in the last 365 days (i.e. 1 year) then a value **"YES"** is stored in a variable named **mANS**.

Based on the value held in this variable the **ACCT_MSTR table** is **updated** by setting the value held in the field **STATUS** to **I**.

This is followed by an insert statement, which inserts the account number the opening date and the type of that account in the **INACTV_ACCT_MSTR** table.

Finally a message stating **"Account Number ____ is marked as inactive"** is displayed.

Self Review Questions

Fill in the Blanks

1. Each time an SQL statement is executed, a ____________ is made to the engine's resources.

2. PL/SQL is a ________________ language.
3. Code blocks start with a __________ section.
4. The __________ section deals with handling of errors that arise during execution of the data manipulation statements, which make up the PL/SQL code block.
5. The ________ section marks the end of a PL/SQL block.
6. Words used in a PL/SQL block are called ________ _________.
7. A __________ is a numeric value or a character string used to represent itself.
8. In a numeric literal, if a float is being represented, then the integer part must be separated from the float part by a ________.
9. __________ literals can be either integers or floats.
10. The __________ attribute is used to declare variables based on definitions of columns in a table.
11. Raw types are used to store __________ data.
12. The maximum length of a long raw column is ________.
13. _________ are stored internally as a fixed length binary quantity, whose actual fixed length varies depending on the operating system.
14. The ______________ function verifies the block number that contains the record.
15. The ____________________ function verifies the absolute file number.
16. __________ data type stores unstructured binary data upto 4GB in length.
17. Internal objects store a __________ in the Large Object column of a table.
18. _________ is a pointer that specifies the actual location of LOB stored outside the database.
19. ___________ puts a piece of information in the package buffer followed by an end-of-line marker.
20. The _______________ function converts the ROWID from extended to restricted.
21. A ________ marks a sequence of statements that has to be repeated.
22. The _________ statement changes the flow of control within a PL/SQL block.

True or Fals

23. SQL does not provide the programming techniques of conditional checking.
24. Multiple SQL statements are passed to the Oracle Engine at a time.
25. SQL has facility for programmed handling of errors that arise during manipulation of data.
26. A PL/SQL block has a definite structure which can be divided into sections.
27. Actual data manipulation, retrieval, looping and branching constructs are specified in the declare section.
28. Blank spaces can be freely inserted between lexical units in a PL/SQL block.
29. TRUE, FALSE, NULL cannot be assigned to Logical literals.
30. NOT NULL causes creation of a variable or a constant that cannot have a null value.
31. The String literals should not be enclosed within single quotes.
32. Reserved words can be used as variable names in PL/SQL.
33. The ROWID_TO_EXTENDED function converts the ROWID from restricted to extended
34. Raw is used to store ASCII data.
35. The ROWID_VERIFY function verifies if the ROWID can be extended.
36. The CLOB (Character LOB) data type stores single byte characters upto 4GB in length.

37. DBMS_PROC is a package that includes a number of procedures and functions that accumulate information in a buffer so that it can be retrieved later.
38. The DBMS_LOB package is used to manipulate LOBs.
39. The comment line begins with an asterisk followed by a slash.
40. The keyword loop has to be placed after the first statement in the sequence of statements to be repeated.
41. The variable in the FOR loop should always be declared.

17

Cursors and Exceptions

What is a Cursor?

The Oracle Engine uses a work area for its internal processing in order to execute an SQL statement. This work area is private to SQL's operations and is called a **Cursor**.

The data that is stored in the cursor is called the **Active Data Set**. Conceptually, the size of the cursor in memory is the size required to hold the number of rows in the **Active Data Set**. The actual size, however, is determined by the Oracle engine's built in memory management capabilities and the amount of RAM available. Oracle has a pre-defined area in main memory set aside, within which cursors are opened. Hence the cursor's size will be limited by the size of this pre-defined area.

The values retrieved from a table are held in a cursor opened in memory by the Oracle Engine. This data is then transferred to the client machine via the network. In order to hold this data, a cursor is opened at the client end. If the number of rows returned by the Oracle engine is more than the area available in the cursor opened on the client, the cursor data and the retrieved data is swapped between the operating system's swap area and RAM.

Example:

When a user fires a select statement as:

SELECT EMP_NO, FNAME, DEPT **FROM** EMP_MSTR **WHERE** BRANCH_NO = 'B1';

The resultant data set in the cursor opened at the Server end is displayed as under:

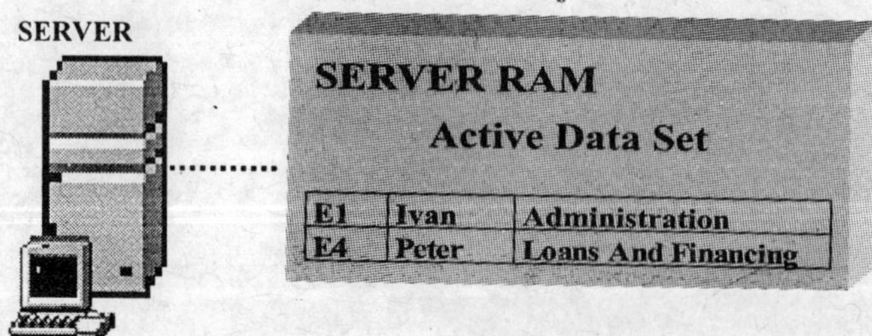

Diagram 17.1: Contents of a cursor.

When a cursor is loaded with multiple rows via a query the Oracle engine opens and maintains a row pointer. Depending on user's requests to view data the row pointer will be relocated within the cursor's

Active Data Set. Additionally Oracle also maintains multiple cursor variables. The values held in these variables indicate the status of the processing being done by the cursor.

Types Of Cursors

Cursors are classified depending on the circumstances under which they are opened. If the Oracle engine opened a cursor for its internal processing it is known as an **Implicit Cursor**. A cursor can also be opened for processing data through a PL/SQL block, on demand. Such a user-defined cursor is known as an **Explicit Cursor**.

General Cursor Attributes:

When the Oracle engine creates an Implicit or Explicit cursor, cursor control variables are also created to control the execution of the cursor. These are a set of four system variables, which keep track of the Current status of a cursor. These cursor variables can be accessed and used in a PL/SQL code block.

Both Implicit and Explicit cursors have four attributes. They are described below:

Attribute Name	Description
%ISOPEN	Returns TRUE if cursor is open, FALSE otherwise.
%FOUND	Returns TRUE if record was fetched successfully, FALSE otherwise.
%NOTFOUND	Returns TRUE if record was not fetched successfully, FALSE otherwise.
%ROWCOUNT	Returns number of records processed from the cursor.

Implicit Cursor

The Oracle engine implicitly opens a cursor on the Server to process each SQL statement. Since the implicit cursor is opened and managed by the Oracle engine internally, the function of reserving an area in memory, populating this area with appropriate data, processing the data in the memory area, releasing the memory area when the processing is complete is taken care of by the Oracle engine. The resultant data is then passed to the client machine via the network. A cursor is then opened in memory on the client machine to hold the rows returned by the Oracle engine. The number of rows held in the cursor on the client is managed by the client's operating system and it's swap area.

Implicit cursor attributes can be used to access information about the status of the last insert, update, delete or single-row select statements. This can be done by preceding the implicit cursor attribute with the cursor name (i.e. SQL). The values of the cursor attributes always refer to the most recently executed SQL statement, wherever the statement appears. If an attribute value is to be saved for later use, it must be assigned to a (boolean) memory variable.

Implicit Cursor Processing in Client Server Environment

Implicit Cursor Attributes

Attribute Name	Description
%ISOPEN	The Oracle engine automatically opens and closes the SQL cursor after executing its associated select, insert, update or delete SQL statement has been processed in case of implicit cursors. Thus the **SQL%ISOPEN** attribute of an implicit cursor cannot be referenced outside of its SQL statement. As a result, **SQL%ISOPEN** always evaluates to **FALSE.**

%FOUND	Evaluates to **TRUE**, if an insert, update or delete affected one or more rows, or a single-row select returned one or more rows. Otherwise, it evaluates to **FALSE**. The syntax for accessing this attribute is **SQL%FOUND**
%NOTFOUND	Is the logical opposite of **%FOUND**. It evaluates to **TRUE**, if an insert, update or delete affected no rows, or a single-row select returns no rows. Otherwise, it evaluates to FALSE. The syntax for accessing this attribute is **SQL%NOTFOUND**
%ROWCOUNT	Returns the number of rows affected by an insert, update or delete, or select into statement. The syntax for accessing this attribute is **SQL%ROWCOUNT**

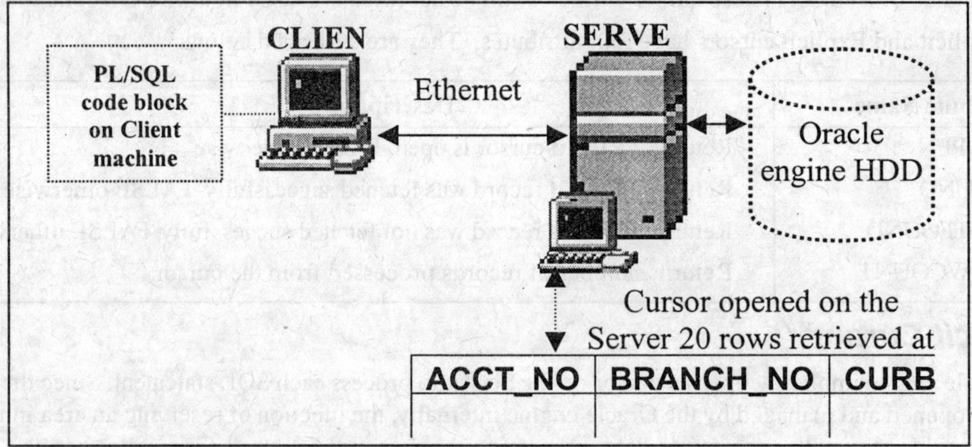

Diagram 17.2: Client Server and Cursor processing.

Example:

The bank manager has decided to transfer employees across branches. Write a PL/SQL block to accept an employee number and the branch number followed by updating the branch number of that employee to which he belongs appropriately. Display an appropriate message using SQL%FOUND based on the existence of the record in the EMP_MSTR table. Display an appropriate message using SQL%NOTFOUND based on the non-existence of the record in the EMP_MSTR table.

```
BEGIN
    UPDATE EMP_MSTR SET BRANCH_NO = &BRANCH_NO WHERE EMP_NO = &EMP_NO;
    IF SQL%FOUND THEN
        dbms_output.put_line('Employee Successfully Transferred');
    END IF;
    IF SQL%NOTFOUND THEN
        dbms_output.put_line('Employee Number does not Exist');
    END IF;
```

END;

Output:

```
Enter value for branch_no: 'B4'
old   2:  UPDATE EMP_MSTR SET BRANCH_NO = &BRANCH_NO
new   2:  UPDATE EMP_MSTR SET BRANCH_NO = 'B4'
Enter value for emp_no: 'E1'
old   3:    WHERE EMP_NO = &EMP_NO;
new   3:    WHERE EMP_NO = 'E1';
Employee Successfully Transferred

PL/SQL procedure successfully completed.
```

Note

 Both SQL%FOUND and SQL%NOTFOUND attributes evaluate to NULL until they are set by an implicit or explicit cursor operation.

Example:

For SQL%ROWCOUNT

The bank manager of **Darya Ganj** branch decides to activate all those accounts, which were previously marked as inactive for performing no transactions in last 365 days. Write a PL/SQL block to update the status of accounts. Display an appropriate message based on the number of rows affected by the update fired.

```
DECLARE
    Rows_Affected char(4);
BEGIN
    UPDATE ACCT_MSTR SET STATUS = 'A' WHERE STATUS = 'S' AND
          BRANCH_NO IN(SELECT BRANCH_NO FROM BRANCH_MSTR
                WHERE NAME = 'Darya Ganj');
    Rows_Affected := TO_CHAR(SQL%ROWCOUNT);

    IF SQL%ROWCOUNT > 0 THEN
          dbms_output.put_line(Rows_Affected || ' Account(s) Activated
          Successfully');
    ELSE
          dbms_output.put_line('Currently there exist no Inactive
          Accounts in the Darya Ganj Branch');
    END IF;
END;
```

Output:

```
2  Account(s) Activated Successfully
PL/SQL procedure successfully completed.
```

Explicit Cursor

When individual records in a table have to be processed inside a PL/SQL code block a cursor is used. This cursor will be declared and mapped to an SQL query in the Declare Section of the PL/SQL block and used within its Executable Section. A cursor thus created and used is known as an Explicit Cursor.

Explicit Cursor Management

The steps involved in using an explicit cursor and manipulating data in its active set are:

- Declare a cursor mapped to a SQL select statement that retrieves data for processing
- Open the cursor
- Fetch data from the cursor one row at a time into memory variables
- Process the data held in the memory variables as required using a loop
- Exit from the loop after processing is complete
- Close the cursor

Cursor Declaration

A cursor is defined in the declarative part of a PL/SQL block. This is done by naming the cursor and mapping it to a query. When a cursor is declared, the Oracle engine is informed that a cursor of the said name needs to be opened. The declaration is only an intimation. There is no memory allocation at this point in time. The three commands used to control the cursor subsequently are open, fetch and close.

The Functionality Of Open, Fetch And Close Commands

Initialization of a cursor takes place via the open statement, this:

- Defines a private SQL area named after the cursor name
- Executes a query associated with the cursor
- Retrieves table data and populates the named private SQL area in memory i.e. creates the Active Data Set
- Sets the cursor row pointer in the Active Data Set to the first record

A fetch statement then moves the data held in the Active Data Set into memory variables. Data held in the memory variables can be processed as desired.

The fetch statement is placed inside a Loop … End Loop construct, which causes the data to be fetched into the memory variables and processed until all the rows in the Active Data Set are processed. The fetch loop then exits. The exiting of the fetch loop is user controlled.

After the fetch loop exits, the cursor must be closed with the close statement. This will release the memory occupied by the cursor and its Active Data Set. A PL/SQL block is necessary to declare a cursor and create an Active Data Set. The cursor name is used to reference the Active Data Set held within the cursor.

Syntax:

```
CURSOR CursorName IS SELECT statement;
```

Opening A Cursor

Opening a cursor executes the query and creates the active set that contains all rows, which meet the query search criteria. An open statement retrieves records from a database table and places the records in the cursor (i.e. named private SQL area in memory). A cursor is opened in the Server's memory.

Syntax:

```
OPEN CursorName;
```

The working of the Client Tool and Oracle Engine when an explicit cursor is opened using the OPEN command is represented diagrammatically below:

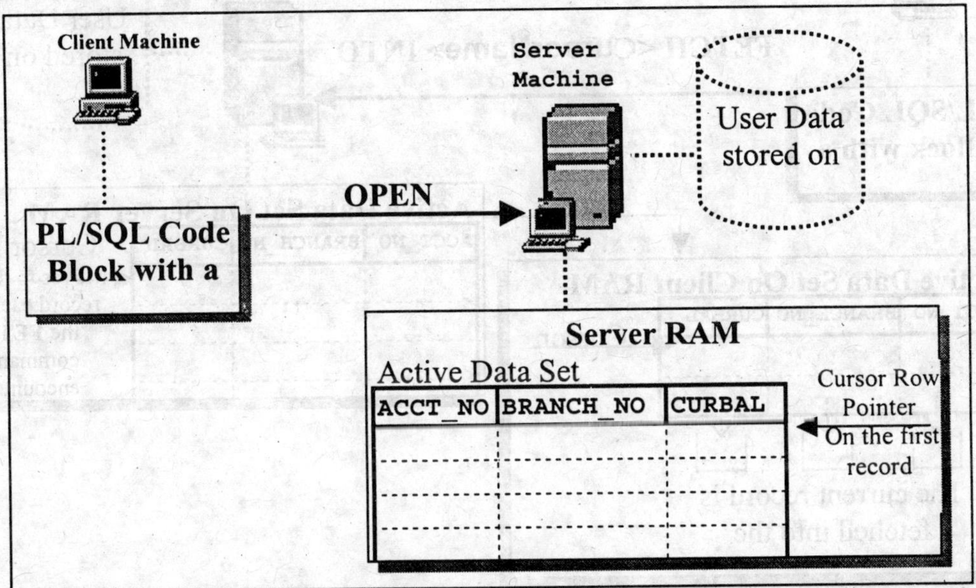

Diagram 17.3: Processing of OPEN CURSOR command in the Oracle Engine

Fetching A Record From The Cursor

The fetch statement retrieves the rows from the active set opened in the Server into memory variables declared in the PL/SQL code block on the client one row at a time. The memory variables are opened on the client machine. Each time a fetch is executed, the cursor pointer is advanced to the next row in the Active Data Set.

A standard loop structure (Loop-End Loop) is used to fetch records from the cursor into memory variables one row at a time.

Syntax:

```
FETCH CursorName INTO Variable1, Variable2, ...;
```

Note

There must be a memory variable for each column value of the Active Data Set. Data types must match. These variables will be declared in the DECLARE section of the PL/SQL block.

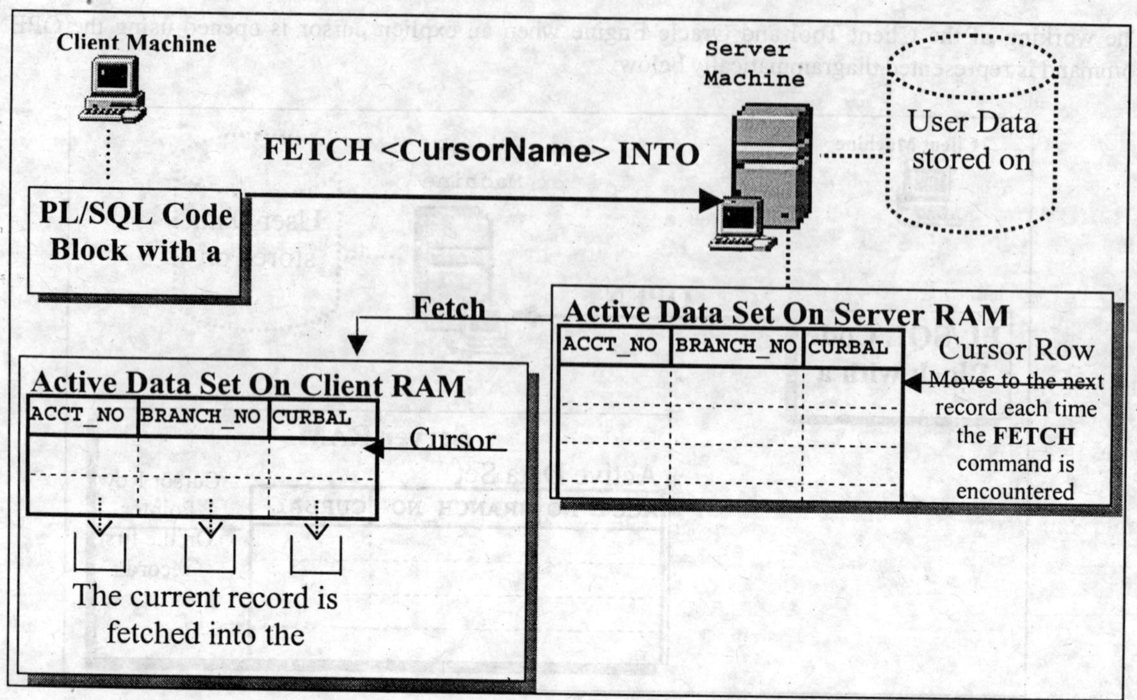

Diagram 17.4: Processing of FETCH command in the Oracle Engine

Closing A Cursor

The close statement disables the cursor and the active set becomes undefined. This will release the memory occupied by the cursor and its Data Set both on the Client and on the Server.

Syntax:

```
CLOSE CursorName;
```

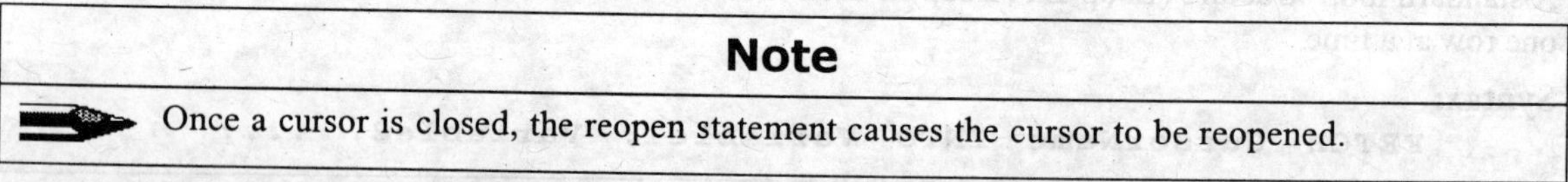

Note

Once a cursor is closed, the reopen statement causes the cursor to be reopened.

Explicit Cursor Attributes

Similar to the cursor attributes in case of implicit cursors, four attributes are associated with explicit cursors. The attributes can be used in a PL/SQL code block for processing of data or exiting. The cursor name is appended to the attribute name when referencing the attribute.

Attribute Name	Description
%FOUND	Evaluates to TRUE, if the last fetch succeeded because a row was available; or to FALSE, if the last fetch failed because no more rows were available. The syntax for accessing this attribute is CursorName**%FOUND.**
%NOTFOUND	Is the logical opposite of %FOUND. It evaluates to TRUE, if the last fetch has failed because no more rows were available; or to FALSE, if the last

	fetch returned a row. The syntax for accessing this attribute is CursorName**%NOTFOUND**.
%ISOPEN	Evaluates to TRUE, if an explicit cursor is open; or to FALSE, if it is closed. The syntax for accessing this attribute is CursorName**%ISOPEN**.
%ROWCOUNT	Returns the number of rows fetched from the active set. It is set to zero when the cursor is opened. The syntax for accessing this attribute is CursorName**%ROWCOUNT**.

Example:

The bank manager has decided to mark all those accounts as inactive (I) on which there are no transactions performed in the last 365 days. Whenever any such update takes place, a record for the same is maintained in the INACTV_ACCT_MSTR table comprising of the account number, the opening date and the type of account. Write a PL/SQL block to do the same.

Table Name: INACTV_ACCT_MSTR

ACCT_NO	OPNDT	TYPE

Create the table INACTV_ACCT_MSTR as:

CREATE TABLE INACTV_ACCT_MSTR (
ACCT_NO **VARCHAR2**(10), OPNDT DATE, TYPE **VARCHAR2**(2));

```
DECLARE
/* Declaration of the cursor named Crsr_NoTrans. The active data set
will include the account numbers and status of all the accounts held in
the ACCT_MSTR table. */
      CURSOR Crsr_NoTrans  IS
            SELECT ACCT_NO, STATUS, OPNDT, TYPE FROM ACCT_MSTR
                  WHERE ACCT_NO IN (SELECT ACCT_NO FROM TRANS_MSTR
                        GROUP BY ACCT_NO HAVING MAX(SYSDATE - DT)
                        >365);
/* Declaration of memory variable that holds data fetched from the
cursor. */
      str_ACCT_NO  ACCT_MSTR.ACCT_NO%type;
      str_STATUS  ACCT_MSTR.STATUS%type;
      dt_OPNDT  ACCT_MSTR.OPNDT%type;
      str_TYPE  ACCT_MSTR.TYPE%type;
BEGIN
      OPEN Crsr_NoTrans;
/* If the cursor is open continue with the data processing else display
an appropriate error message. */
      IF Crsr_NoTrans%ISOPEN  THEN
            LOOP
                  FETCH Crsr_NoTrans INTO str_ACCT_NO, str_STATUS,
                  dt_OPNDT, str_TYPE;
```

```
                EXIT WHEN Crsr_NoTrans%NOTFOUND;
                IF Crsr_NoTrans%FOUND THEN
                /* Updating status to 'S' and inserting each record
                into the INACTV_ACCT_MSTR table to keep track of
                the accounts marked as inactive. */
                    UPDATE ACCT_MSTR SET STATUS = 'S' WHERE ACCT_NO
                    = str_ACCT_NO;

                /* Inserting a record in the INACTV_ACCT_MSTR table. */
                    INSERT INTO INACTV_ACCT_MSTR
                        VALUES(str_ACCT_NO, dt_OPNDT, str_TYPE);
                END IF;
            END LOOP;
        /* Make the changes permanent. */
            COMMIT;
        ELSE
            dbms_output.put_line ('Unable to open Cursor');
        END IF;
/* Close cursor Crsr_NoTrans. */
        CLOSE Crsr_NoTrans;
END;
```

The above PL/SQL code marks all those accounts as inactive (S) on which there are no transactions performed in the last 365 days. To do this an Explicit cursor named Crsr_NoTrans is declared using the following query:

SELECT ACCT_NO, STATUS, OPNDT, TYPE **FROM** ACCT_MSTR
WHERE ACCT_NO **IN (SELECT** ACCT_NO **FROM** TRANS_MSTR
GROUP BY ACCT_NO **HAVING MAX**(SYSDATE - DT) >365);

The above query will retrieve account numbers, their status, the date on which the account was opened and the type of account. This information will be retrieved based on the following query:

SELECT ACCT_NO **FROM** TRANS_MSTR **GROUP BY** ACCT_NO
HAVING MAX(SYSDATE - DT) >365

This query is responsible to retrieve only those account numbers from the TRANS_MSTR table where the difference between the current date and the date on which the last transaction was performed is more than 365 days i.e. one year. This means a concept of Subquery is applied here.

Since the above query will retrieve more than one value the following variables are declared to hold them.

str_ACCT_NO ACCT_MSTR.ACCT_NO%**type**;

str_STATUS ACCT_MSTR.STATUS%**type**;

dt_OPNDT ACCT_MSTR.OPNDT%**type**;

str_TYPE ACCT_MSTR.TYPE%**type**;

Note

 The %type here means that the data type of these variables will be as that from the table.

Since the above query may return more than one row a loop is created which is responsible to:

- ❑ Fetch the data retrieved by the cursor into the variable
- ❑ Check if any data is retrieved
  - Update the STATUS field of the ACCT_MSTR table to reflect the inactivity
  - Insert a record in the INACTV_ACCT_MSTR table to reflect the updation
- ❑ Repeat the above steps until the data retrieval process is complete.

Finally a COMMIT is fired to make the changes permanent

Example:

Write a PL/SQL block that will display the customer name, the fixed deposit number and the fixed deposit amount of the first 5 customers holding the highest amount in fixed deposits.

```
DECLARE
      CURSOR Crsr_HiFD IS SELECT FNAME || ' ' || LNAME, FD_NO, AMT
            FROM CUST_MSTR C, ACCT_FD_CUST_DTLS A, FD_DTLS F
                  WHERE C.CUST_NO = A.CUST_NO AND A.ACCT_FD_NO =
                  F.FD_SER_NO
                        ORDER BY AMT Desc;
      str_NAME VARCHAR2(50);
      str_FD_NO FD_DTLS.FD_NO%type;
      num_AMT FD_DTLS.AMT%type;

BEGIN
      OPEN Crsr_HiFD;
      dbms_output.Put_line (' Name                         FD No.   Amount');
      dbms_output.Put_line (' --------------- --------- ----------');

      LOOP
            FETCH Crsr_HiFD INTO str_NAME, str_FD_NO, num_AMT;
            EXIT WHEN (Crsr_HiFD%ROWCOUNT - 1) = 5 or
            Crsr_HiFD%NOTFOUND;
            dbms_output.Put_line(str_NAME || '    ' || str_FD_NO || '
            ' || num_AMT);
      END LOOP;
END;
```

Output:

Name	FD No.	Amount
Chriselle Bayross	F1	15000
Mamta Muzumdar	F1	15000
Ashwini Joshi	F7	15000
Chhaya Bankar	F3	10000
Chhaya Bankar	F4	10000

PL/SQL procedure successfully completed.

The above PL/SQL code displays the customer name, the fixed deposit number and the fixed deposit amount of the first 5 customers holding the highest amount in a fixed deposit. To do this an Explicit cursor named Crsr_HiFD is declared using the following query:

```
SELECT FNAME || ' ' || LNAME, FD_NO, AMT
    FROM CUST_MSTR C, ACCT_FD_CUST_DTLS A, FD_DTLS F
        WHERE C.CUST_NO = A.CUST_NO AND A.ACCT_FD_NO = F.FD_SER_NO
        ORDER BY AMT Desc;
```

The above query will retrieve the customer name (Concatenating the first name and the last name), fixed deposit numbers and the amount of the fixed deposit. This information is available in CUST_MSTR, ACCT_FD_CUST_DTLS, FD_DTLS tables.

To retrieve the data required, both the tables have to linked on the basis of common columns using joins as follows:

- ❑ C.CUST_NO = A.CUST_NO: This means the CUST_NO field of CUST_MSTR table is joined with CUST_NO field of the ACCT_FD_CUST_DTLS table
- ❑ A.ACCT_FD_NO = F.FD_SER_NO: This means the ACCT_FD_NO field of ACCT_FD_CUST_DTLS table is joined with FD_SER_NO field of the FD_DTLS table

Since this query is responsible to retrieve only the first 5 customers holding the highest amount of fixed deposit, the ORDER BY clause is used to switch the order of display to DESCENDING.

Since the above query will retrieve more than one value the following variables are declared to hold them.

str_NAME VARCHAR2(50);

str_FD_NO FD_DTLS.FD_NO%**type**;

num_AMT FD_DTLS.AMT%**type**;

Note

 The %type here means that the data type of these variables will be as that from the table.

Since the above query may return more than one row a loop is created which is responsible to:

- ❑ Fetch the data retrieved by the cursor into the variable
- ❑ Repeat the above steps until the number of records retrieved becomes 5 (i.e. Crsr_HiFD%ROWCOUNT - 1) or the data retrieval process completes (i.e. Crsr_HiFD%NOTFOUND) whichever earlier.

Cursor for Loops

Another technique commonly used to control the Loop…End Loop within a PL/SQL block is the FOR variable IN value construct. This is an example of a machine defined loop exit i.e. when all the values in the FOR construct are exhausted looping stops.

Syntax:

```
FOR memory variable IN CursorName
```

Here, the verb FOR automatically creates the memory variable of the %rowtype. Each record in the opened cursor becomes a value for the memory variable of the %rowtype.

The FOR verb ensures that a row from the cursor is loaded in the declared memory variable and the loop executes once. This goes on until all the rows of the cursor have been loaded into the memory variable. After this the loop stops.

A cursor for loop automatically does the following:

- ❑ Implicitly declares its loop index as a %rowtype record
- ❑ Opens a cursor
- ❑ Fetches a row from the cursor for each loop iteration
- ❑ Closes the cursor when all rows have been processed

A cursor can be closed even when an exit or a goto statement is used to leave the loop prematurely, or if an exception is raised inside the loop.

Example:

The bank manager has decided to mark all those accounts as inactive (I) on which there are no transactions performed in the last 365 days. Whenever any such update takes place, a record for the same is maintained in the INACTV_ACCT_MSTR table comprising of the account number, the opening date and the type of account. Write a PL/SQL block to do the same.

Table Name: INACTV_ACCT_MSTR

ACCT_NO	OPNDT	TYPE

Create the table INACTV_ACCT_MSTR as:

CREATE TABLE INACTV_ACCT_MSTR(

ACCT_NO **VARCHAR2**(10), OPNDT **DATE,** TYPE **VARCHAR2**(2));

```
DECLARE
/* Declaration of the cursor named Crsr_NoTrans. The active data set
will include the account numbers and status of all the accounts held in
the ACCT_MSTR table. */
      CURSOR Crsr_NoTrans IS
      SELECT ACCT_NO, STATUS, OPNDT, TYPE FROM ACCT_MSTR
            WHERE ACCT_NO IN (SELECT ACCT_NO FROM TRANS_MSTR
                  GROUP BY ACCT_NO HAVING MAX(SYSDATE - DT) >365);

BEGIN
/* Use of a cursor FOR LOOP. */
      FOR NoTrans_Rec IN Crsr_NoTrans
      LOOP
      /* Updating status to 'S' and inserting each record into the
      INACTV_ACCT_MSTR table to keep track of the accounts marked as
      inactive. */
            UPDATE ACCT_MSTR SET STATUS = 'S' WHERE ACCT_NO =
            NoTrans_Rec.ACCT_NO;

      /* Inserting a record in the INACTV_ACCT_MSTR table. */
```

```
            INSERT INTO INACTV_ACCT_MSTR
                   VALUES (NoTrans_Rec.ACCT_NO, NoTrans_Rec.OPNDT,
                   NoTrans_Rec.TYPE);
      END LOOP;
      COMMIT ;
END;
```

Output:

PL/SQL procedure successfully completed.

The above PL/SQL code marks all those accounts as inactive (I) on which there are no transactions performed in the last 365 days. To do this an Explicit cursor named Crsr_NoTrans is declared using the following query:

SELECT ACCT_NO, STATUS, OPNDT, TYPE **FROM** ACCT_MSTR
WHERE ACCT_NO **IN (SELECT** ACCT_NO **FROM** TRANS_MSTR
GROUP BY ACCT_NO **HAVING MAX**(SYSDATE - DT) >365);

The above query will retrieve account numbers, their status, the date on which the account was opened and the type of account. This information will be retrieved based on the following query:

SELECT ACCT_NO FROM TRANS_MSTR GROUP BY ACCT_NO
HAVING MAX(SYSDATE - DT) >365

This query is responsible to retrieve only those account numbers from the TRANS_MSTR table where the difference between the current date and the date on which the last transaction was performed is more than 365 days i.e. one year. This means a concept of Subquery is applied here.

Since a FOR LOOP is used in the process there is no need to declare any variable.

The FOR NoTrans_Rec IN Crsr_NoTrans here means an implicit declaration of memory variables, as a %rowtype record, required for the data retrieval process is undertaken.

The FOR LOOP is responsible to:

- Automatically fetch the data retrieved by the cursor into the NoTrans_Rec record set
- The sequence of statements inside the loop is executed once for every row that is fetched, i.e. check if any data is retrieved
  - Update the STATUS field of the ACCT_MSTR table to reflect the inactivity
  - Insert a record in the INACTV_ACCT_MSTR table to reflect the updation
- Automatically repeat the above steps until the data retrieval process is complete.
- The cursor closes automatically when all the records in the cursor have been processed. This is because there are no more rows left to load into NoTrans_Rec. This situation is sensed by the FOR verb which, causes the loop to exit.

Finally a COMMIT is fired to make the changes permanent

Parameterized Cursors

Till now, all the cursors that have been declared and used fetch a pre-determined set of records. Records, which satisfy conditions, set in the WHERE clause of the SELECT statement mapped to the cursor. In other words, the criterion on which the Active Data Set is determined is hard coded and never changes.

Commercial applications require that the query, which, defines the cursor, be generic and the data that is retrieved from the table be allowed to change according to need.

Oracle recognizes this and permits the creation of parameterized cursors for use. The contents of a parameterized cursor will constantly change depending upon the value passed to its parameter.

Since the cursor accepts user-defined values into its parameters, thus changing the Result set extracted, it is called as Parameterized Cursor.

Declaring A Parameterized Cursor

Syntax:

```
CURSOR CursorName (VariableName Datatype) IS <SELECT
statement...>
```

Opening A Parameterized Cursor And Passing Values To The Cursor

Syntax:

```
OPEN CursorName (Value / Variable / Expression )
```

Note

 The scope of cursor parameters is local to that cursor, which means that they can be referenced only within the query declared in the cursor declaration. Each parameter in the declaration must have a corresponding value in the open statement.

Example:

Write a PL/SQL block of code that will merge the data available in the newly created table NEW_BRANCHES with the data available in the table BRANCH_MSTR. If the data in the first table already exist in the second table then that data should be skipped.

```
CREATE TABLE NEW_BRANCHES(
    BRANCH_NO VARCHAR2(10),
    NAME VARCHAR2(25));

INSERT INTO NEW_BRANCHES (BRANCH_NO, NAME) VALUES('B4', 'Mahim');
INSERT INTO NEW_BRANCHES (BRANCH_NO, NAME) VALUES('B5', 'Borivali');
INSERT INTO NEW_BRANCHES (BRANCH_NO, NAME) VALUES('B6', 'Darya Ganj');
INSERT INTO NEW_BRANCHES (BRANCH_NO, NAME) VALUES('B7', 'Thane');
INSERT INTO NEW_BRANCHES (BRANCH_NO, NAME) VALUES('B8', 'Mulund');
INSERT INTO NEW_BRANCHES (BRANCH_NO, NAME) VALUES('B9', 'Chembur');
INSERT INTO NEW_BRANCHES (BRANCH_NO, NAME) VALUES('B10', 'Khar');
```

```
DECLARE
/*Cursor Crsr_Branch_Mstr retrieves all records of NEW_BRANCHES table.*/
    CURSOR Crsr_Branch_Mstr IS SELECT * FROM NEW_BRANCHES;
/* Cursor Crsr_Branch_Chk accepts the value of NAME from the current
row of cursor Crsr_Branch_Mstr. */
```

```
    CURSOR Crsr_Branch_Chk (str_BRANCH_NAME varchar2) IS
          SELECT BRANCH_NO FROM BRANCH_MSTR WHERE NAME =
          str_BRANCH_NAME;

/* Variables that hold data from the cursor Crsr_Branch_Mstr. */
    str_BRANCH_NO BRANCH_MSTR.BRANCH_NO%type;
    str_BRANCH_NAME BRANCH_MSTR.NAME%type;

/* Variable that hold data from the cursor Crsr_Branch_Chk. */
    mast_ins_view VARCHAR2(10);
BEGIN
/* Open the Crsr_Branch_Mstr cursor. */
    OPEN Crsr_Branch_Mstr;
    LOOP
    /* Fetch the records from the Crsr_Branch_Mstr cursor. */
          FETCH Crsr_Branch_Mstr INTO str_BRANCH_NO, str_BRANCH_NAME;
          EXIT WHEN Crsr_Branch_Mstr%NOTFOUND;
    /* Open the Crsr_Branch_Chk cursor. Note that the value of variable
    passed to the Crsr_Branch_Chk cursor is set to the value of NAME
    in the current row of cursor Crsr_Branch_Mstr. */
          OPEN Crsr_Branch_Chk (str_BRANCH_NAME);
          FETCH Crsr_Branch_Chk INTO mast_ins_view;
    /* If the record is found then display the Branch details like
    the number of accounts and number of employees in that branch. */
          IF Crsr_Branch_Chk%FOUND THEN
                dbms_output.Put_line('Branch ' || str_BRANCH_NAME ||
                ' exist.');
          ELSE
                dbms_output.Put_line('Branch ' || str_BRANCH_NAME ||
                ' does not exist. Inserting new branch in the
                database');
                INSERT INTO BRANCH_MSTR VALUES (str_BRANCH_NO,
                      str_BRANCH_NAME);
          END IF;
          CLOSE Crsr_Branch_Chk;
    END LOOP;
    CLOSE Crsr_Branch_Mstr;
    COMMIT;
END;
```

OUTPUT: For the first run

```
Branch Mahim exist.
Branch Borivali exist.
Branch Darya Ganj exist.
Branch Thane does not exist. Inserting new branch in the database
Branch Mulund does not exist. Inserting new branch in the database
Branch Chembur does not exist. Inserting new branch in the database
```

```
Branch Khar does not exist. Inserting new branch in the database
PL/SQL procedure successfully completed.
```

OUTPUT: For the second run

```
Branch Mahim exist.
Branch Borivali exist.
Branch Darya Ganj exist.
Branch Thane exist.
Branch Mulund exist.
Branch Chembur exist.
Branch Khar exist.
PL/SQL procedure successfully completed.
```

The above PL/SQL block uses two cursors:

- Crsr_Branch_Mstr, which retrieves all the records of NEW_BRANCHES table.
- Crsr_Branch_Chk, a parameterized cursor which fetches records based on the value passed by the Crsr_Branch_Mstr cursor.

The functionality of the PL/SQL block of code will be as follows:

The cursor Crsr_Branch_Mstr holds all the records of the NEW_BRANCHES table as the active data set. The fetch command holds the values of BRANCH_NO, NAME into the variables str_BRANCH_NO, str_BRANCH_NAME respectively for the first record in the cursor Crsr_Branch_Mstr. The value held in the variable str_BRANCH_NAME indicates the NAME for which the record has to be inserted in the BRANCH_MSTR table.

This str_BRANCH_NAME value is then passed as a parameter to the second cursor, which has to fetch the corresponding record to be inserted from the NEW_BRANCHES table. The WHERE condition of the select statement that defines the cursor Crsr_Branch_Chk gets its value from the variable str_BRANCH_NAME.

Now, if the select statement retrieves a record from the NEW_BRANCHES table and if a corresponding NAME is present in the BRANCH_MSTR table, a message stating 'Branch ______ exist' is displayed. If the select statement retrieves a record from the NEW_BRANCHES table and if a corresponding NAME is not present in the BRANCH_MSTR table, a message stating 'Branch ______ does not exist. Inserting new branch in the database' is displayed.

The above process continues till all the records in the cursor, Crsr_Branch_Mstr are processed. When all the records have been processed the PL/SQL block exists the loop and the all the transactions are completed with the COMMIT statement.

Exception Handling in PL/SQL

Every PL/SQL block of code encountered by the Oracle engine is accepted as a client. Hence the Oracle engine will make an attempt to execute every SQL sentence within the PL/SQL block. However while executing the SQL sentences anything can go wrong and the SQL sentence can fail.

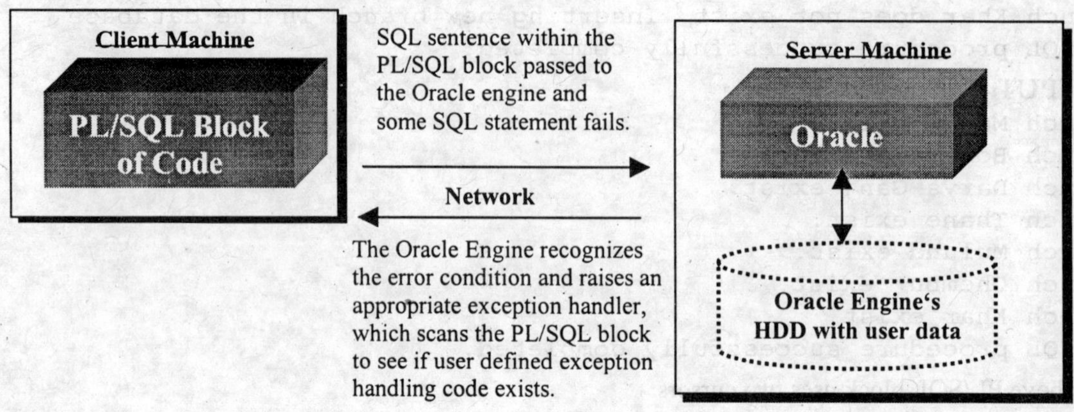

Diagram 17.4: Exception Handling and the Oracle Engine.

When an SQL sentence fails the Oracle engine is the first to recognize this as an Exception condition. The Oracle engine immediately tries to handle the exception condition and resolve it. This is done by raising a built-in Exception Handler.

An Exception Handler is nothing but a code block in memory that will attempt to resolve the current exception condition. The Oracle engine can recognize every exception condition that occurs in memory. To handle very common and repetitive exception conditions the Oracle engine uses Named Exception Handlers. The Oracle engine has about fifteen to twenty named exception handlers. In addition to this the Oracle engine uses more than twenty thousand numbered exception handlers. These exception handlers are identified not by names but by four integers preceded by a hyphen (i.e. -1414). These exception handler names are actually a set of negative signed integers. Each Exception Handler, irrespective of how it is identified, (i.e. by Name or Number) has code attached that will attempt to resolve an exception condition. This is how Oracle's, Default Exception-Handling strategy works.

Oracle's default exception handling code can be overridden. When this is done Oracle's default exception handling code is not executed but the code block that takes care of the exception condition, in the exception section, of the PL/ SQL block is executed. This is an example of a programmer giving explicit exception handling instructions to an Oracle exception handler.

This means that the Oracle engine's Exception Handler must establish whether to execute its own exception handling code or whether it has to execute user-defined exception handling code.

As soon as the Oracle engine invokes an exception handler the exception handler goes back to the PL/ SQL block from which the exception condition was raised. The exception handler scans the PL/ SQL block for the existence of an Exception section within the PL/ SQL block. If an exception section within the PL/ SQL block exists the exception handler scans the first word, after the action word When, within this exception section.

If the first word after the action word When, is the exception handler's name then the exception handler executes the code contained in the Then section of the construct as follows:

```
EXCEPTION
     WHEN <ExceptionName> THEN
          <User Defined Action To Be Carried Out>
```

The first word that follows the action word When must be a String. Hence this technique will work well for the fifteen to twenty named exception handlers. In addition to these the Oracle engine has twenty thousand, numbered exception handlers, which are raised automatically and appropriately when the Oracle engine recognizes exception condition. User defined exception handling code must be permitted even for these (numbered) exception handlers.

Oracles Named Exception Handlers

The Oracle engine has a set of pre-defined Oracle error handlers called Named Exceptions. These error handlers are referenced by their name. The following are some of the pre-defined Oracle named exception handlers.

Pre-determined internal PL/SQL exceptions:

DUP_VAL_ON_INDEX	Raised when an **insert** or **update** attempts to create two rows with duplicate values in column/s constrained by a **unique** index.
LOGIN_DENIED	Raised when an invalid username/password was used to log onto Oracle.
NO_DATA_FOUND	Raised when a **select** statement returns zero rows.
NOT_LOGGED_ON	Raised when PL/SQL issues an Oracle call without being logged onto Oracle.
PROGRAM_ERROR	Raised when PL/SQL has an internal problem.
TIMEOUT_ON_RESOURCE	Raised when Oracle has been waiting to access a resource beyond the user-defined timeout limit.
TOO_MANY_ROWS	Raised when a **select** statement returns more than one row.
VALUE_ERROR	Raised when the data type or data size is invalid.
OTHERS	Stands for all other exceptions not explicitly named.

Example:

Write a PL/ SQL block of code such that depending upon a user supplied account number, the customer to whom the account belongs, the introducer of that account and the nominee of that account are inserted into the ACCT_CUST_INTRO_NOM table. If the user enters an account number that is not in the ACCT_MSTR table, then the PL/SQL block must display appropriate error message back to the user.

CREATE TABLE statement for ACCT_CUST_INTRO_NOM table:

```
CREATE TABLE ACCT_CUST_INTRO_NOM (
    ACCT_NO VARCHAR2(10).
    CUST_NO VARCHAR2(10),
    INTRO_CUST_NO VARCHAR2(10),
    NOMINEE_NO VARCHAR2(10));
```

```
DECLARE
    mACCT_NO VARCHAR2(10);
```

```
      mCUST_NO VARCHAR2(10);
      mINTRO_CUST_NO VARCHAR2(10);
      mNOMINEE_NO VARCHAR2(10);
BEGIN
      mACCT_NO := & mACCT_NO;
/*Retrieving records from the ACCT_MSTR table and assigning them to
memory variables for the ACCT_NO entered by the user */
      SELECT ACCT_NO, INTRO_CUST_NO, CUST_NO, NOMINEE_NO
            INTO mACCT_NO, mCUST_NO, mINTRO_CUST_NO, mNOMINEE_NO
            FROM ACCT_MSTR, ACCT_FD_CUST_DTLS, NOMINEE_MSTR
            WHERE ACCT_MSTR.ACCT_NO = ACCT_FD_CUST_DTLS.ACCT_FD_NO

                  AND ACCT_FD_CUST_DTLS.ACCT_FD_NO =
                  NOMINEE_MSTR.ACCT_FD_NO
                  AND ACCT_NO = mACCT_NO;
/* Inserting values into the ACCT_CUST_INTRO_NOM table*/
      INSERT INTO ACCT_CUST_INTRO_NOM
            VALUES(mACCT_NO, mCUST_NO, mINTRO_CUST_NO, mNOMINEE_NO);
EXCEPTION
/* Using the Oracle engine's named exception handler to handle the
error condition that may occur if the user enters a ACCT_NO that is not
present in the ACCT_MSTR table*/
      WHEN NO_DATA_FOUND THEN
            DBMS_OUTPUT.PUT_LINE('Account No.' || mACCT_NO || ' is
            not present in the ACCT_MSTR table');
END;
```

Output:

When account number exist

```
Enter value for macct_no: 'SB1'
old   9:  mACCT_NO := & mACCT_NO;
new   9:  mACCT_NO := 'SB1';
PL/SQL procedure successfully completed.
```

When account number does not exist

```
Enter value for macct_no: 'SB200'
old   9:  mACCT_NO := & mACCT_NO;
new   9:  mACCT_NO := 'SB200';
Account No.SB200 is not present in the ACCT_MSTR table
PL/SQL procedure successfully completed.
```

USER-Named Exception Handlers

The technique that is used is to bind a numbered exception handler to a name using Pragma Exception_init(). This binding of a numbered exception handler, to a name (i.e. a String), is done in the Declare section of a PL/SQL block.

All objects declared in the Declare section of a PL/SQL block are not created until actually required within the PL/SQL block. However, the binding of a numbered exception handler to a name must be done exactly when declared not when the exception handler is invoked due to an exception condition.

The Pragma action word is a call to a pre-compiler, which immediately binds the numbered exception handler to a name when encountered.

The function Exception_init() takes two parameters the first is the user defined exception name the second is the Oracle engine's exception number. These lines will be included in the Declare section of the PL/SQL block.

Note

 The user defined exception name must be the statement that immediately precedes the Pragma **Exception_init()** statement.

Syntax:

```
DECLARE
      <ExceptionName> EXCEPTION;
      PRAGMA EXCEPTION_INIT (<ExceptionName>, <ErrorCodeNo>);
BEGIN
```

Using this technique it is possible to bind appropriate numbered exception handlers to names and use these names in the Exception section of a PL/SQL block. When this is done the default exception handling code of the exception handler is overridden and the user-defined exception handling code is executed.

Syntax:

```
DECLARE
      <ExceptionName> EXCEPTION;
      PRAGMA EXCEPTION_INIT (<ExceptionName>,<ErrorCodeNo>);
BEGIN
      . . .
EXCEPTION
      WHEN <ExceptionName> THEN
            <Action>
END;
```

User Defined Exception Handlers (For I/O Validations)

The manner of defining and handling an exception in a PL/SQL block of code is shown in the following example.

Example:

Two client machines (Client A and Client B) are accessing the same ACCT_MSTR table using identical PL/SQL code blocks for updating the CURBAL column of the table ACCT_MSTR.

Table name: ACCT_MSTR (Partials Extract)

ACCT_NO	CURBAL	ACCT_NO	CURBAL	ACCT_NO	CURBAL	ACCT_NO	CURBAL
SB1	500	CA2	3000	SB3	500	CA4	12000
SB5	500	SB6	500	CA7	22000	SB8	500
SB9	500	CA10	32000	SB11	500	CA12	5000
SB13	500	CA14	10000	SB15	500		

```
DECLARE
/* Declaration of memory variables and constants to be used in the
Execution section. */
      ACCT_BALANCE  NUMBER (11,2);
      ACCT_NUM VARCHAR2(10);
      TRANS_AMT NUMBER(11,2) ;
      OPER CHAR(1);
/*Declaring a variable of the type exception and associating the variable
to an Oracle error number */
RESOURCE_BUSY EXCEPTION;
PRAGMA  EXCEPTION_INIT  (RESOURCE_BUSY,-00054);
BEGIN
/* Accept an ACCT_NO,OPER and the TRANS_AMT from the user. */
      ACCT_NUM := &ACCT_NUM;
      TRANS_AMT := &TRANS_AMT;
      OPER := &OPER;
/* Retrieving the balance from the accounts table where the ACCT_NO in
the table is equal to the ACCT_NUM entered by the user. Also the select
is with a for update and nowait clause in order to acquire a lock on
the record. */
      SELECT CURBAL INTO ACCT_BALANCE FROM ACCT_MSTR
            WHERE ACCT_NO = ACCT_NUM FOR UPDATE NOWAIT;
/* Checking if the operation specified is debit or credit. If the
operation specified is debit then the balance is reduced by the TRANS_AMT.
If the operation specified is credit then the balance is increased by
the TRANS_AMT of the corresponding ACCT_NO. */
      IF OPER= 'D' THEN
            UPDATE ACCT_MSTR SET CURBAL = CURBAL - TRANS_AMT
                  WHERE ACCT_NO = ACCT_NUM;
      ELSIF OPER= 'C' THEN
            UPDATE ACCT_MSTR SET CURBAL = CURBAL + TRANS_AMT
                  WHERE ACCT_NO = ACCT_NUM;
      END IF;
EXCEPTION
      WHEN RESOURCE_BUSY THEN
      DBMS_OUTPUT.PUT_LINE('The row is in use');
END;
```

Output:

Client A:

```
Enter value for acct_num: 'SB1'
old  13:  ACCT_NUM := &ACCT_NUM;
new  13:  ACCT_NUM := 'SB1';
Enter value for trans_amt: 2000
old  14:  TRANS_AMT := &TRANS_AMT;
new  14:  TRANS_AMT := 2000;
Enter value for oper: 'C'
old  15:  OPER := &OPER;
new  15:  OPER := 'C';
PL/SQL procedure successfully completed.
```

Client B:

```
Enter value for acct_num: 'SB1'
old  13:  ACCT_NUM := &ACCT_NUM;
new  13:  ACCT_NUM := 'SB1';
Enter value for trans_amt: 5000
old  14:  TRANS_AMT := &TRANS_AMT;
new  14:  TRANS_AMT := 5000;
Enter value for oper: 'C'
old  15:  OPER := &OPER;
new  15:  OPER := 'C';
The row is in use
PL/SQL procedure successfully completed.
```

In a scenario where,

1. Client A has fired a select statement for viewing the record SB1 with a FOR UPDATE NOWAIT clause i.e. Client A has acquired a lock on the record SB1 in the ACCT_MSTR table
2. Client A has updated the record SB1 by crediting an amount of Rs.2000. Client A has not yet completed the transaction (i.e. No commit or rollback statement has been fired by Client A)
3. Now, if the second user i.e. Client B also fires the same PL/ SQL block of code and enters the same ACCT_NO SB1, when Client A has locked the record with a SELECT FOR UPDATE clause then:

Observation:

The Oracle engine instead of displaying its own error message, will now display a user?defined message as defined in the exception handling section of the PL/SQL block of code.

```
EXCEPTION
    WHEN RESOURCE_BUSY THEN
    DBMS_OUTPUT.PUT_LINE('The row is in use');
```

In case the above, error condition was not handled by the user in the exception section then the Oracle engine will raise it's own error handler and display the following message to the user:

```
DECLARE
*
ERROR at line 1:
```

```
ORA-00054: resource busy and acquire with NOWAIT specified
ORA-06512: at line 10
```

User Defined Exception Handling (For Business Rule Validations)

In commercial applications data being manipulated needs to be validated against business rules. If the data violates a business rule, the entire record must be rejected. In such cases, the insert SQL DML actually runs successfully. It is the data values that the insert statement is placing in the table, which violates the business rule.

Since the SQL DML did not cause any system error, the Oracle engine cannot object to the erroneous data value being inserted into a table.

To trap business rules being violated the technique of raising user-defined exceptions and then handling them, is used.

All business rule exceptions are completely transparent to the Oracle engine and hence the skill of translating a business rule into appropriate PL/ SQL user-defined exception handling code is vital to a programmer.

User-defined error conditions must be declared in the declarative part of any PL/SQL block. In the executable part, a check for the condition that needs special attention is made. If that condition exists, the call to the user-defined exception is made using a RAISE statement. The exception once raised is then handled in the Exception handling section of the PL/SQL code block.

Syntax:

```
DECLARE
    <ExceptionName> Exception
BEGIN
    <SQL Sentence>;
    IF <Condition> THEN
        RAISE <ExceptionName>;

    END IF;
EXCEPTION
    WHEN <ExceptionName>THEN {User Defined Action To Be
    Taken};
END;
```

Example:

The ACCT_MSTR table records the current balance for an account, which is updated whenever, any deposits or withdrawals takes place. If the withdrawal attempted is more then the current balance held in the account, a user?defined exception is raised displaying an appropriate error message.

Table name: ACCT_MSTR (Partials Extract)

ACCT_NO	CURBAL	ACCT_NO	CURBAL	ACCT_NO	CURBAL	ACCT_NO	CURBAL
SB1	500	CA2	3000	SB3	500	CA4	12000
SB5	500	SB6	500	CA7	22000	SB8	500
SB9	500	CA10	32000	SB11	500	CA12	5000
SB13	500	CA14	10000	SB15	500		

```
DECLARE
/* Declaration of memory variables and constants to be used in the
Execution section. */
     ACCT_BALANCE  NUMBER (11,2);
     ACCT_NUM VARCHAR2(10);
     TRANS_AMT NUMBER(11,2) ;
     OPER CHAR(1);
/* Declaring a variable of the type exception. */
     MORE_THAN_BAL  EXCEPTION;

BEGIN
/* Accept an ACCT_NO,OPER and the TRANS_AMT from the user. */
     ACCT_NUM := &ACCT_NUM;
     TRANS_AMT := &TRANS_AMT;
     OPER := &OPER;
/* Retrieving the balance from the accounts table where the ACCT_NO in
the table is equal to the ACCT_NUM entered by the user. Also the select
is with a for update and nowait clause in order to acquire a lock on
the record. */
     SELECT CURBAL INTO ACCT_BALANCE FROM ACCT_MSTR
          WHERE ACCT_NO = ACCT_NUM;
/* Checking if the operation specified is debit or credit. If the
operation specified is debit then the balance is reduced by the TRANS_AMT.
If the operation specified is credit then the balance is increased by
the TRANS_AMT of the corresponding ACCT_NO. */
     IF OPER= 'D' THEN
          IF TRANS_AMT < ACCT_BALANCE THEN
               UPDATE ACCT_MSTR SET CURBAL = CURBAL - TRANS_AMT
                    WHERE ACCT_NO = ACCT_NUM;
          ELSE
               RAISE MORE_THAN_BAL;
          END IF;
     ELSIF OPER= 'C' THEN
          UPDATE ACCT_MSTR SET CURBAL = CURBAL + TRANS_AMT
               WHERE ACCT_NO = ACCT_NUM;
     END IF;
EXCEPTION
     WHEN MORE_THAN_BAL THEN
          DBMS_OUTPUT.PUT_LINE('Attempted to withdraw more than the
          current balance ' || ACCT_BALANCE || ' from the account
          number '|| ACCT_NUM);
END;
```

Output:

When withdrawal more than current balance:

```
Enter value for acct_num: 'CA2'
```

```
old  13:  ACCT_NUM := &ACCT_NUM;
new  13:  ACCT_NUM := 'CA2';
Enter value for trans_amt: 4000
old  14:  TRANS_AMT := &TRANS_AMT;
new  14:  TRANS_AMT := 4000;
Enter value for oper: 'D'
old  15:  OPER := &OPER;
new  15:  OPER := 'D';
Attempted to withdraw more than the current balance 3000 from the account
number CA2

PL/SQL procedure successfully completed.
```

When withdrawal less than current balance:

```
Enter value for acct_num: 'CA2'
old  13:  ACCT_NUM := &ACCT_NUM;
new  13:  ACCT_NUM := 'CA2';
Enter value for trans_amt: 1000
old  14:  TRANS_AMT := &TRANS_AMT;
new  14:  TRANS_AMT := 1000;
Enter value for oper: 'D'
old  15:  OPER := &OPER;
new  15:  OPER := 'D';

PL/SQL procedure successfully completed.
```

Self Review Questions

Fill in the Blanks

1. The data that is stored in the cursor is called the ______________.
2. When a cursor is loaded with multiple rows via a query the Oracle engine opens and maintains a ______________.
3. If the Oracle Engine for its internal processing has opened a cursor they are known as __________ Cursors.
4. Cursors defined by the users are called ______________.
5. ____________ is always evaluated to false in case of implicit cursors.
6. All LOOP statements must end with an ______________ statement.
7. The __________ statement retrieves the rows from the active set opened in the Server.
8. In case of Explicit cursors the ______________ attribute returns the number of rows fetched from the active set.
9. ____________________ allows passing values dynamically to a cursor while opening a cursor.
10. An ________________________ is nothing but a code block in memory that will attempt to resolve the current exception condition.
11. ____________________ exception is raised when the data type or data size is invalid.

12. The ______________ action word is a call to a pre-compiler, which immediately binds the numbered exception handler to a name when encountered.
13. To trap business rules being violated the technique of raising ____________________ and then handling them, is used.
14. If user defined error condition exists, the call to the user-defined exception is made using a ____________ statement.

True or False

15. The use of cursors provides manipulation of table data in batch processing mode.
16. In Real time processing records are gathered in a table and at regular intervals manipulated.
17. The cursor defined system variables that are associated with a user defined cursor are SQL%IsOpen, SQL%Found, SQL%NotFound, SQL%RowCount.
18. COMMIT can be fired upto a savepoint.
19. Each time a fetch is executed, the cursor pointer remains on the same row in the Active Data Set.
20. The close statement disables the cursor and the active set becomes undefined.
21. Only constant values can be passed as parameters to parameterized cursors.
22. Fetch statement is used to get the data from the table into the cursor.
23. To handle very common and repetitive exception conditions the Oracle engine uses Named Exception Handlers.
24. PROGRAM_ERROR exception is raised when a select statement returns zero rows.
25. The function Exception_init( ) takes two parameters the first is the user defined exception name the second is the Oracle engine's exception number.
26. The user defined exception name may not be the statement that immediately precedes the Pragma Exception_init ( ) statement.
27. The exception once raised is then handled in the Exception handling section of the PL/SQL code block.

Hands on Exercises

1. A Factory maintains records of Stock-On-Hand and Material Requirements in the ITEM_MASTER table and ITEM_REQUISITE table respectively.

Table Name:	**ITEM_MASTER**			
Column Name	**Data Type**	**Size**	**Default**	**Attributes**
ITEM_ID	Number	4		Primary Key. Identity number for the item
DESCRIPTION	Varchar2	20		Item description
BAL_STOCK	Number	3		Balance stock for an item

Data for ITEM_MASTER table:

ITEM_ID	DESCRIPTION	BAL_STOCK
102	Aluminium Sheets	120
105	Steel Sheets	96
151	A14 Iron Rods	50
209	A14 Hexagonal Nut	334
254	A14 Steel Bolts	250
303	Tar Washers	500

Table Name:	**ITEM_REQUISITE**			
Column Name	**Data Type**	**Size**	**Default**	**Attributes**
ITEM_ID	Number	4		Identity number for the item requested
DEPT_CODE requisite	Number	2		Code for the department placing the
QUANTITY	Number	3		Quantity of items requested

Data for ITEM_REQUISITE table:

ITEM_ID	DEPT_CODE	BAL_STOCK
102	10	50
102	20	50
105	10	50
105	20	25
151	10	30
151	20	30
209	10	300
303	20	400

Update the Bal_Stock in the ITEM_MASTER table for each requisite in the ITEM_REQUISITE table. Based on the Item_Id, decrease the Bal_Stock in the ITEM_MASTER table by the Quantity in the ITEM_REQUISITE table. The update operation is completed only when the corresponding record in the ITEM_REQUISITE table is deleted.

Write a PL/SQL block of code based on the conditions:

(a) If at any given point, the value in Bal_Stock becomes negative, the entire update operation for all Item_Id should rollback.

(b) If at any given point, the value in Bal_Stock becomes negative, the update operation for that particular Item_Id should rollback.

2. Write an SQL code block that raises a user defined exception when business rule is violated. The business rule for CLIENT_MASTER table specifies when the value of Bal_due field is less than 0, handle the exception.

18

PL/SQL Database Objects

What Are Procedures / Functions?

A **Procedure** or **Function** is a logically grouped set of SQL and PL/SQL statements that perform a specific task. A **stored procedure** or function is a named PL/SQL code block that has been compiled and stored in one of the Oracle engine's system tables.

To make a **Procedure** or **Function dynamic** either of them can be passed parameters **before** execution. A **Procedure** or **Function** can then change the way it works depending upon the parameters passed prior to its execution.

Procedures and Functions are made up of:

- ❑ A declarative part
- ❑ An executable part
- ❑ An optional exception-handling part

Declarative Part

The declarative part may contain the declarations of cursors, constants, variables, exceptions and subprograms. These objects are local to the procedure or function. The objects become invalid once the procedure or function exits.

Executable Part

The executable part is a PL/SQL block consisting of SQL and PL/SQL statements that assign values, control execution and manipulate data. The action that the procedure or function is expected to perform is coded here. The data that is to be returned back to the calling environment is also returned from here. The variables declared are put to use within this block.

Exception Handling Part

This part contains code that deals with exceptions that may be raised during the execution of code in the **executable** part. An Oracle exception handler can be redirected to the exception handling section of the procedure or function where the procedure or function determines the actual action that must be carried out by Oracle's exception handler.

The flow of code execution from the Exception Handling part **cannot** be transferred to the Executable part.

Where Do Stored Procedures And Functions Reside?

Procedures and **Functions** are stored in the Oracle database. They can be invoked or called by any PL/SQL block that appears within an application. Before a procedure or function is stored, the Oracle engine **parses** and **compiles** the procedure or function.

How Does The Oracle Engine Create A Stored Procedure / Function?

The following steps are performed automatically by the Oracle engine while creating a procedure:

- Compiles the procedure or function
- Stores the procedure or function in the database

The Oracle engine compiles the PL/SQL code block. If an error occurs during the compilation of the procedure or function, **an invalid** procedure or function gets created. The Oracle engine displays a message after creation that the procedure or function was created with **compilation errors**.

The compilation process does not display the errors. These errors can be viewed using the **SELECT** statement:

```
SELECT * FROM USER_ERRORS;
```

When a procedure or function is invoked, the Oracle engine loads the compiled procedure or function in a memory area called the **System Global Area (SGA)**. This allows the code to be executed quickly. Once loaded in the SGA other users also access the same procedure or function if they have been granted permission to do so.

How Does The Oracle Engine Execute Procedures / Functions?

The Oracle engine performs the following steps to execute a procedure or function:

- Verifies user access
- Verifies procedure or function validity
- Executes the procedure or function

The Oracle engine checks if the user who called the procedure or function has the **execute privilege** for the procedure or function. If the user is invalid, then access is denied otherwise the Oracle engine proceeds to check whether the called procedure or function is valid or not. The status of a procedure or function is shown by the use of a **select** statement as follows:

```
SELECT <ObjectName>, <ObjectType>, <Status> FROM <UserObjects>
    WHERE <ObjectType> = <'PROCEDURE'>;
```

Or

```
SELECT <Object_Name>, <Object_Type>, <Status> FROM <User_Objects>
    WHERE <Object_Type> = <'FUNCTION'>;
```

Only if the status is **valid**, will a procedure or function be executed. Once found valid, the Oracle engine then loads a procedure or function into memory (**i.e.** if it is not currently present in memory) and executes it.

Advantages Of Using A Procedure Or Function

Security

Stored procedures and functions can help enforce data security. For **e.g.** by giving permission to a procedure or function that can query a table and granting the procedure or function to users, permissions to manipulate the table itself need not be granted to users.

Performance

It improves database performance in the following ways:

- Amount of information sent over a network is less
- No compilation step is required to execute the code
- Once the procedure or function is present in the shared pool of the SGA retrieval from disk is not required every time different users call the procedure or function **i.e.** reduction in disk I/O

Memory Allocation

The amount of memory used reduces as stored procedures or functions have shared memory capabilities. Only one copy of procedure needs to be loaded for execution by multiple users. Once a copy of a procedure or function is opened in the Oracle engine's memory, other users who have appropriate permission may access it when required.

Productivity

By writing procedures and functions redundant coding can be avoided, increasing productivity.

Integrity

A procedure or function needs to be tested only once to guarantee that it returns an accurate result. Since procedures and functions are stored in the Oracle engine they become a part of the engine's resource. Hence the responsibility of maintaining their integrity rests with the Oracle engine. The Oracle engine has high level of in-built security and hence integrity of procedures or functions can be safely left to the Oracle engine.

Procedures Versus Functions

The differences between Procedures and Functions can be listed as below:

- A function must return a value back to the caller. A function can return only one value to the calling PL/SQL code block
- By defining multiple OUT parameters in a procedure, multiple values can be passed to the caller. The OUT variable being global by nature, its value is accessible by any PL/SQL code block **including** the PL/SQL block via which it was called

Creating Stored Procedure

Syntax:

```
CREATE OR REPLACE PROCEDURE [Schema.] <ProcedureName>
      (<Argument>{IN, OUT, IN OUT}<Data type>,...){IS, AS}
      <Variable> declarations;
      <Constant> declarations;
BEGIN
      <PL/SQL subprogram body>;
EXCEPTION
      <Exception PL/SQL block>;
END;
```

Keywords And Parameters

The keywords and the parameters used for creating database procedures are explained below:

REPLACE	Recreates the procedure if it already exists. This option is used to change the definition of an existing procedure without dropping, recreating and re-granting object privileges previously granted on it. If a procedure is redefined the Oracle engine recompiles it.
Schema	Is the schema to contain the procedure. The Oracle engine takes the default schema to be the current schema, if it is omitted.
Procedure	Is the name of the procedure to be created.
Argument	Is the name of an argument to the procedure. Parentheses can be omitted if no arguments are present.
IN	Indicates that the parameter will accept a value from the user.
OUT	Indicates that the parameter will return a value to the user.
IN OUT	Indicates that the parameter will either accept a value from the user or return a value to the user.
Data type	Is the data type of an argument. It supports any data type supported by PL/SQL.
PL/SQL sub program body	Is the definition of procedure consisting of PL/SQL statements.

Creating A Functions

Syntax:

```
CREATE OR REPLACE FUNCTION [Schema.] <FunctionName>
        (<Argument> IN <Data type>, ...)
        RETURN <Data type> {IS, AS}
        <Variable> declarations;
        <Constant> declarations;
BEGIN
        <PL/SQL subprogram body>;
EXCEPTION
        <Exception PL/SQL block>;
END;
```

Keywords and Parameters

The keywords and the parameters used for creating database functions are explained below:

REPLACE	Recreates the function if it already exists. This option is used to change the definition of an existing function without dropping, recreating and re-granting object privileges previously granted on it. If a function is redefined, Oracle recompiles it.
Schema	Is the schema to contain the function. Oracle takes the default schema to be the current schema, if it is omitted.
Function	Is the name of the function to be created.
Argument	Is the name of an argument to the function. Parentheses can be omitted if no arguments are present.
IN	Indicates that the parameter will accept a value from the user.

RETURN data type	Is the data type of the function's return value. Because every function must return a value, **this clause is required**. It supports any data type supported by PL/SQL.
PL/SQL sub program body	Is the definition of function consisting of PL/SQL statements.

Diagrammatic representation of the working of a Procedure in Server RAM

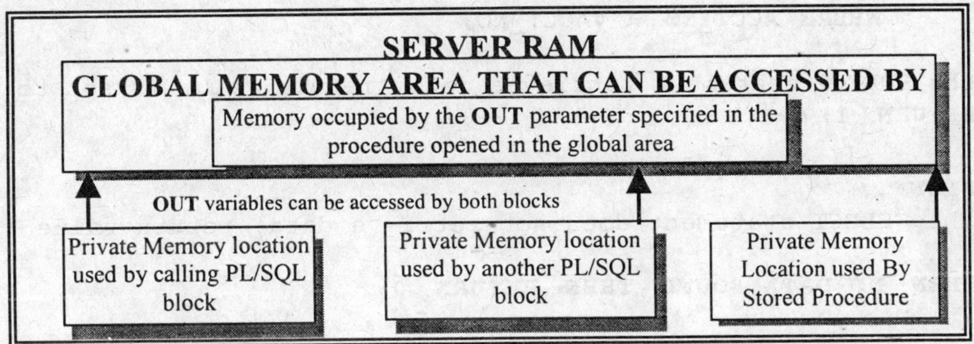

Diagram 18.1: Working of a Procedure within the Oracle Engine

Using A Function

Example:

Consider the tables **TRANS_MSTR** and **ACCT_MSTR**. Both the tables belong to the banking system. The TRANS_MSTR table is used to register the deposits or withdrawals, as performed. As a batch process, the initial opening balance value must be written to the TRANS_MSTR table whenever an account is opened with the bank.

Write a PL/SQL block of code that would insert a record representing the opening balance entry in the TRANS_MSTR table each time an account is opened. The insert in the TRANS_MSTR table depends on **ACCT_NO**. In case the ACCT_NO is not present in the TRANS_MSTR table i.e. there is no entry made for the initial deposit, then a record is inserted in the TRANS_MSTR table representing the initial payment made while opening an account. If there is already an entry made for the initial payment i.e. ACCT_NO is present in the TRANS_MSTR table then the insertion is skipped.

To help simplify this process (of batch insertion) a function called f_ChkAcctNo has been created. The function checks for the existence of ACCT_NO in the table TRANS_MSTR. The function has one argument, which receives a value. The function will search for a matching value in the TRANS_MSTR table when a value is passed to it when being invoked.

The function will return **1** indicating that a match is found or **0** indicating that no match is found. This value returned by the function is used to make a decision to insert a record or skip the insertion in the TRANS_MSTR table.

Creating Function For Use

A stored function is created to perform the ACCT_NO check operation. f_ChkAcctNo() is the name of the function which accepts a variable ACCT_NO and returns a value to the host environment. The value changes from 0 (i.e. if ACCT_NO does not exist) to 1 (i.e. if ACCT_NO exists) depending on the records retrieved.

```
CREATE OR REPLACE FUNCTION F_CHKACCTNO(vACCT_NO IN VARCHAR2)
     RETURN NUMBER IS
/* Variable that hold data from the TRANS_MSTR table */
     dummyAcctNo VARCHAR2(10);

BEGIN
     SELECT DISTINCT ACCT_NO INTO dummyAcctNo FROM TRANS_MSTR
          WHERE ACCT_NO = vACCT_NO;

/* If the SELECT statement retrieves data, return value is set to 1. */
     RETURN 1;

EXCEPTION
/* If the SELECT statement does not retrieve data, return value is set
to 0 */
     WHEN NO_DATA_FOUND THEN RETURN 0;
END;
```

Output:

```
Function created.
```

This function is then called in the PL/SQL block as follows. The return value is then checked and appropriate action is taken.

Calling The Function F_CHKACCTNO In A PL/SQL Code Block

```
DECLARE
/* Cursor SCANTABLE retrieves the required data from the table ACCT_MSTR
*/
     CURSOR SCANTABLE IS SELECT ACCT_NO, TYPE FROM ACCT_MSTR;
/* Variables that hold data from the cursor scantable */
     mACCT_NO ACCT_MSTR.ACCT_NO%type;
     mTYPE ACCT_MSTR.TYPE%type;
/* Variable that stores the value returned by the f_ChkAcctNo function
i.e. 1 or 0 */
     valexists NUMBER(1);
BEGIN
     OPEN SCANTABLE;
     LOOP
          FETCH SCANTABLE INTO MACCT_NO, MTYPE;
          EXIT WHEN SCANTABLE%NOTFOUND;
     /* Call function F_CHKACCTNO to check if ACCT_NO is present in
     TRANS_MSTR table */
          valexists := F_CHKACCTNO(MACCT_NO);
     /* If ACCT_NO does not exist insert a record in the TRANS_MSTR
     table */
          IF valexists = 0 THEN
               IF mTYPE = 'SB' THEN
```

```
                    INSERT INTO TRANS_MSTR (TRANS_NO, ACCT_NO, DT,
                    TYPE, PARTICULAR, DR_CR, AMT, BALANCE)
                        VALUES((SELECT 'T' ||
                        TO_CHAR(MAX(TO_NUMBER(SUBSTR( TRANS_NO,
                        2))) + 1) FROM TRANS_MSTR), mACCT_NO,
                        SYSDATE, 'C', 'Initial Payment', 'D', 500,
                        500);
                ELSE
                    INSERT INTO TRANS_MSTR (TRANS_NO, ACCT_NO, DT,
                    TYPE, PARTICULAR, DR_CR, AMT, BALANCE)
                        VALUES((SELECT 'T' ||
                        TO_CHAR(MAX(TO_NUMBER(SUBSTR( TRANS_NO,
                        2))) + 1) FROM TRANS_MSTR), mACCT_NO,
                        SYSDATE, 'C', 'Initial Payment', 'D', 2000,
                        2000);
                END IF;
            END IF;
        END LOOP;
        CLOSE SCANTABLE;
        COMMIT;
END;
```

Output:

```
PL/SQL procedure successfully completed.
```

The Functionality Of The PL/SQL Block Of Code Will Be As Follows:

A cursor named **SCANTABLE** is created which is responsible to hold the ACCT_NO and TYPE from the ACCT_MSTR table. A call is made to the function and the value held in mACCT_NO is then passed as a parameter. The WHERE condition of the select statement within the function gets its value from the variable mACCT_NO and depending on whether the value exists in the TRANS_MTR table or not, a value of 0 or 1 is returned to the calling PL/SQL block.

If the select statement retrieves a record from the TRANS_MSTR table (**i.e.** the corresponding ACCT_NO is present in the TRANS_MSTR table) the insertion of a new records is skipped.

If the select retrieves no record (**i.e.** the ACCT_NO is not present in the TRANS_MSTR table), a new record is inserted into the TRANS_MSTR table.

The above process continues till all the records in the cursor, **SCANTABLE** are processed. When all the records have been processed the PL/SQL block exits the loop and the all the transactions are completed with the COMMIT statement.

Using A Procedure

Example:

The current example deals with the Fixed Deposit Maturity system. The tables involved with this processing are FD_DTLS, TRANS_MSTR and ACCT_MSTR.

Whenever a fixed deposit is due for payment and if there are instructions given to the bank for crediting the fixed deposit amount on maturity to their account held in the bank, an entry is passed in the TRANS_MSTR table for deposit of the fixed deposit amount as well as the ACCT_MSTR table is updated to reflect the increase of the current balance. Finally the status of that fixed deposits is updated as **M** i.e. Matured in the FD_DTLS table.

In order to simplify the job of insertion and updating, of three tables (TRANS_MSTR, FD_DTLS and ACCT_MSTR) each time a fixed deposit is due for payment, a procedure is created. This procedure is then called in the PL/SQL block while checking for those fixed deposits due for payment.

Creating Procedure For Use

A procedure called **PROC_INSUPD** is created and stored in the database. This procedure when called in a PL/SQL block updates the current balance in the ACCT_MSTR table and the status in the FD_DTLS table. It also inserts an entry to register the credit of the fixed deposit amount in the TRANS_MSTR table.

```
CREATE OR REPLACE PROCEDURE PROC_INSUPD(VFD_NO IN VARCHAR2, VACCT_NO
IN VARCHAR2, vAMT IN NUMBER) IS
/* Variable declarations */
    mCurBal number;

BEGIN
/* Retrieving the current balance */
    SELECT CURBAL INTO mCurBal FROM ACCT_MSTR WHERE ACCT_NO =
    vACCT_NO;
/* Inserting a record in the TRANS_MSTR table */
    INSERT INTO TRANS_MSTR (TRANS_NO, ACCT_NO, DT, TYPE, PARTICULAR,
    DR_CR, AMT, BALANCE)
        VALUES((SELECT 'T' ||
        TO_CHAR(MAX(TO_NUMBER(SUBSTR(TRANS_NO, 2))) + 1) FROM
        TRANS_MSTR), vACCT_NO, SYSDATE, 'C', 'Fixed Deposit Payment',
        'D', vAMT, (mCurBal + vAMT));

/* Updating the CURBAL in the ACCT_MSTR table */
    UPDATE ACCT_MSTR SET CURBAL = CURBAL + vAMT WHERE ACCT_NO =
    vACCT_NO;

/* Updating the STATUS in the FD_DTLS table */
    UPDATE FD_DTLS SET STATUS = 'M' WHERE FD_NO = vFD_NO;
END;
```

Output:

```
Procedure created.
```

Calling The Procedure In A PL/SQL Code Block:

```
DECLARE
/* Cursor CRSR_FDCHK retrieves all the records of table FD_DTLS which
are active and due for payment */
    CURSOR CRSR_FDCHK IS
        SELECT FD_NO, PAYTO_ACCTNO, DUEAMT FROM FD_DTLS
            WHERE TO_CHAR(DUEDT,'DD-MM-YY') =
            TO_CHAR(SYSDATE,'DD-MM-YY')
                AND STATUS = 'A' AND PAYTO_ACCTNO IS NOT NULL;
```

```
/* Declaration of memory variables that will hold values */
     mFD_NO VARCHAR2(10);
     mPAYTO_ACCTNO VARCHAR2(10);
     mAMT NUMBER(8,2);
     mState NUMBER := 0;

BEGIN
/* Opening the cursor */
     OPEN CRSR_FDCHK;
     LOOP
          FETCH CRSR_FDCHK INTO mFD_NO, mPAYTO_ACCTNO, mAMT;
          EXIT WHEN CRSR_FDCHK%NOTFOUND;
          /* Call procedure proc_insupd to perform insert/update
          operations on tables. */
               proc_insupd(mFD_NO, mPAYTO_ACCTNO, mAMT);
          /* Updating the state to 1 i.e. there are fds due for
          payment */
               mState := 1;
     END LOOP;

/* Display a message if no FDs are due for payment based on the mState
variable */
     IF mState = 0 THEN
          DBMS_OUTPUT.PUT_LINE('Currently there are no fixed deposits
          due for payment.');
     END IF;
          CLOSE CRSR_FDCHK;
     COMMIT;
END;
```

Output:

```
Currently there are no fixed deposits due for payment.
PL/SQL procedure successfully completed.
```

The Functionality Of The PL/SQL Block Of Code Will Be As Follows:

The above PL/SQL when fired will open a cursor called **CRSR_FDCHK** that will fetch the fixed deposit number, account number to which the fixed deposit amount will be credited and the fixed deposit due amount from the FD_DTLS table. The cursor will fetch only those records where the fixed deposits are active, due for payment and the account number to which the amount has to be credited is available.

Only when such records are fetched an insert/update operation on tables ACCT_MSTR, TRANS_MSTR AND FD_DTLS is performed via a procedure named **PROC_INSUPD**. This procedure takes three arguments i.e. fixed deposit number, account number that will be credited and the due amount.

On the basis of these three arguments:

- ❑ An insert is fired on the TRANS_MSTR table to register the maturity of the fixed deposit
- ❑ The current balance of the specified account number is increased in the ACCT_MSTR table
- ❑ The status of the fixed deposit is set to **M** i.e. the fixed deposit is now matured

In case no records are fetched by the cursor **CRSR_FDCHK** a message stating "Currently there are no fixed deposits due for payment"

Finally a COMMIT is fired to register the changes.

Deleting a Stored Procedure or Function

A procedure or function can be deleted by using the following syntax

Syntax:

```
DROP PROCEDURE <ProcedureName>;
```

Example:

DROP PROCEDURE PROC_INSUPD;

Output:

```
Procedure dropped.
```

Syntax:

```
DROP FUNCTION <FunctionName>;
```

Example:

DROP FUNCTION F_CHKACCTNO;

Output:

```
Function dropped.
```

Oracle Packages

A package is an Oracle object, which holds other objects within it. Objects commonly held within a package are procedures, functions, variables, constants, cursors and exceptions. The tool used to create a package is SQL* Plus. It is a way of creating generic, encapsulated, re-useable code.

A package once written and debugged is compiled and stored in Oracle's system tables held in an Oracle Database. All users who have execute permissions on the Oracle Database can then use the package.

Packages can contain PL/SQL blocks of code, which have been written to perform some process entirely on their own. These PL/ SQL blocks of code do not require any kind of input from other PL/SQL blocks of code. These are the package's standalone subprograms.

Alternatively, a package can contain a subprogram that requires input from another PL/SQL block to perform its programmed processes successfully. These are also subprograms of the package but these subprograms are not standalone.

Subprograms held within a package can be called from other stored programs, like triggers, precompilers, or any other Interactive Oracle program like SQL* Plus.

Tip

Unlike the stored programs, the package itself cannot be called, passed parameters to, or nested.

Components Of An Oracle Package

A package has usually two components, a **specification** and a **body**. A package's **specification** declares the types (variables of the **Record** type), memory variables, constants, exceptions, cursors, and subprograms that are available for use.

A package's body fully defines cursors, functions, and procedures and thus implements the specification.

Why Use Packages?

Packages offer the following advantages:

1. Packages enable the organization of commercial applications into efficient modules. Each package is easily understood and the interfaces between packages are simple, clear and well defined
2. Packages allow granting of privileges efficiently
3. A package's public variables and cursors persist for the duration of the session. Therefore all cursors and procedures that execute in this environment can share them
4. Packages enable the overloading of procedures and functions when required
5. Packages improve performance by loading multiple objects into memory at once. Therefore, subsequent calls to related subprograms in the package require no I/O
6. Packages promote code reuse through the use of libraries that contain stored procedures and functions, thereby reducing redundant coding

Package Specification

The package specification contains:

- ❑ Name of the package
- ❑ Names of the data types of any arguments
- ❑ This declaration is local to the database and global to the package

This means that procedures, functions, variables, constants, cursors and exceptions and other objects, declared in a package are accessible from anywhere in the package. Therefore, all the information a package needs, to execute a stored subprogram, is contained in the package specifications itself.

Example:

The following is an example of package creation specification. In this example, the specification declares a function and a procedure:

```
CREATE PACKAGE BNK_PCK_SPEC IS
    FUNCTION F_CHKACCTNO(VACCT_NO IN VARCHAR2) RETURN NUMBER;
    PROCEDURE PROC_INSUPD(VFD_NO IN VARCHAR2, VACCT_NO IN VARCHAR2, VAMT IN
    NUMBER);
    END BNK_PCK_SPEC;
```

Output:

```
Package created.
```

Example:

Sometimes a specification only declares variables, constants, and exceptions, and therefore a package body is not necessary. The following example is a package specification for a package that **does not** have a package body:

```
CREATE PACKAGE COSTINGS IS
        TYPE REC IS RECORD(PART_NAME VARCHAR2(30), PART_PRICE NUMBER, PART_COST
        NUMBER);
        PRICE NUMBER;
        QTY NUMBER;
        NO_COST EXCEPTION;
        COST_OR EXCEPTION;
END COSTINGS;
```

Output:

```
Package created.
```

The Package Body

The body of a package contains the definition of public objects that are declared in the specification. The body can also contain other object declarations that are private to the package. The objects declared privately in the package body are not accessible to other objects outside the package. Unlike package specification, the **package body** can contain **subprogram bodies**.

After the package is written, debugged, compiled and stored in the database applications can reference the package's types, call its subprograms, use its cursors, or raise its exceptions.

Creating Packages

The first step to creating a package is to create its specification. The specification declares the objects that are contained in the body of the package. A package is created using Oracle's SQL* Plus interactive tool. A package can include **Functions** and **Procedures**. The variables declared within the package can be accessed by any Function or Procedure within the Package. To create a **specification**, issue the CREATE PACKAGE command:

Example:

```
CREATE OR REPLACE PACKAGE TRANSACTION_MGMT AS
        PROCEDURE PERFORM_TRANS(mACCT_NO VARCHAR2, MD VARCHAR2, AMT
NUMBER);
        PROCEDURE CANCEL_FD(mFD_NO VARCHAR2);
        BAL NUMBER;
        P_ACCT_NO VARCHAR2(10);
        D_AMT NUMBER;
END TRANSACTION_MGMT;
```

Output:

```
Package created.
```

Note

The **OR REPLACE** clause was used to recreate the package specification without loosing any grants that already exist.

After the specification is created, the body of the package needs to be created. The body of the package is a collection of detailed definitions of the objects that were declared in the specification.

These objects, or package subprograms, are accessible outside the package only if their specifications are included in the package specifications.

In addition to the object definitions for the declaration, the package body can also contain private declarations. These private objects are for the internal workings of the package and are local in scope. External PL/ SQL blocks cannot reference or call internal declarations of the package.

If any initialization is done in the package body, it is executed once when the package is initially referenced. The following is an example of the body of the package that was specified in the previous example's specification:

Example:

```
CREATE OR REPLACE PACKAGE BODY TRANSACTION_MGMT AS
    PROCEDURE PERFORM_TRANS(mACCT_NO VARCHAR2, MD VARCHAR2, AMT
    NUMBER) IS
    BEGIN
        SELECT CURBAL INTO BAL FROM ACCT_MSTR WHERE ACCT_NO =
        mACCT_NO;
        IF MD = 'D' THEN
            INSERT INTO TRANS_MSTR(TRANS_NO, ACCT_NO, DT, TYPE,
                PARTICULAR, DR_CR, AMT, BALANCE)
                VALUES((SELECT 'T' ||
                TO_CHAR(MAX(TO_NUMBER(SUBSTR(
                TRANS_NO, 2))) + 1) FROM TRANS_MSTR), mACCT_NO,
                SYSDATE, 'C', 'Deposit', MD, AMT, (BAL + AMT));
            UPDATE ACCT_MSTR SET CURBAL = CURBAL + AMT
                WHERE ACCT_NO = mACCT_NO;
        ELSE
            IF AMT < BAL THEN
                INSERT INTO TRANS_MSTR(TRANS_NO, ACCT_NO, DT,
                TYPE, PARTICULAR, DR_CR, AMT, BALANCE)
                    VALUES((SELECT 'T' ||
                        TO_CHAR(MAX(TO_NUMBER(SUBSTR(
                        TRANS_NO, 2))) + 1) FROM
                        TRANS_MSTR), mACCT_NO, SYSDATE, 'C',
                        'Withdrawal', MD, AMT, (BAL - AMT));
                UPDATE ACCT_MSTR SET CURBAL = CURBAL - AMT
                    WHERE ACCT_NO = mACCT_NO;
            END IF;
        END IF;
    END;

    PROCEDURE CANCEL_FD (mFD_NO VARCHAR2) IS
    BEGIN
```

```
        SELECT PAYTO_ACCTNO, (AMT * (SYSDATE - OPNDT)/365 *
        INTRATE)/100 + AMT
            INTO P_ACCT_NO, D_AMT FROM FD_DTLS WHERE FD_NO =
            mFD_NO;
        SELECT CURBAL INTO BAL FROM ACCT_MSTR
            WHERE ACCT_NO = (SELECT PAYTO_ACCTNO FROM FD_DTLS
                WHERE FD_NO = mFD_NO);
        IF P_ACCT_NO IS NOT NULL THEN
            INSERT INTO TRANS_MSTR(TRANS_NO, ACCT_NO, DT, TYPE,
                PARTICULAR, DR_CR, AMT, BALANCE)
                VALUES((SELECT 'T' ||
                TO_CHAR(MAX(TO_NUMBER(SUBSTR(
                TRANS_NO, 2))) + 1) FROM TRANS_MSTR), P_ACCT_NO,
                        SYSDATE, 'C', 'Fixed deposit
                        payment', 'D', D_AMT, (BAL +
                        D_AMT));
            UPDATE ACCT_MSTR SET CURBAL = CURBAL + D_AMT
                WHERE ACCT_NO = P_ACCT_NO;
            DBMS_OUTPUT.PUT_LINE('Your FD is cancelled. The
            amount is credited to the account number: ' ||
            P_ACCT_NO);
        ELSE
            DBMS_OUTPUT.PUT_LINE('Your FD is cancelled. Collect
            the amount from the cash counter.');
        END IF;
        UPDATE FD_DTLS SET STATUS = 'C' WHERE FD_NO = mFD_NO;
    END;
END TRANSACTION_MGMT;
```

Output:

```
Package body created.
```

The final part of the procedure body in the preceding example is the package initialization. By definition, this runs only once when the procedure's is referenced the first time.

The Functionality Of The PL/SQL Block Of Code Is As Follows:

The above PL/SQL block is a package body named **TRANSACTION_MGMT** based on the package definition created in earlier example. This package consist of following two procedure:

- ❑ PERFORM_TRANS

  Consists of following arguments:

  - mACCT_NO
  - MD
  - AMT

  This procedure will accept the account number, the mode of transaction i.e. deposit or withdrawal and the transaction amount. Based on these arguments it will insert a record in TRANS_MSTR table and update the current balance of that particular account in the ACCT_MSTR table.

Additionally, it also ensures that if the mode of transaction is withdrawal the transaction amount does not exceed the current balance of the account.

- CANCEL_FD

  Consists of following arguments:

  - mFD_NO

  This procedure will accept the fixed deposit number. Based on this argument it will calculate the amount payable on cancellation of the fixed deposit and extract the account number if any to which the fixed deposit amount is to be credited. If the account number is available then:

- Based on this account number a record is inserted in the TRANS_MSTR table registering the credit of fixed deposit amount
- The current balance in the ACCT_MSTR table is updated to reflect the increase in the balance
- A message stating "Your FD is cancelled. The amount is credited to the account number ____"

Otherwise:

- A message stating "Your FD is cancelled. Collect the amount from the cash counter."

Finally the status in the FD_DTLS table is set to **C** i.e. cancelled.

Invoking A Package Via The Oracle Engine

When a package is invoked, the Oracle engine performs three steps to execute it:

1. Verify user access:

   Confirms that the user has **EXECUTE** system privilege granted for the subprogram

2. Verify procedure validity:

   Checks with the data dictionary to determine whether the subprogram is valid or not. If the subprogram is invalid, it is automatically recompiled before being executed.

3. Execute:

   The package subprogram is executed.

To reference a package's subprograms and objects, use **dot** notation.

The Syntax For Dot Notation

- PackageName.Type_Name
- PackageName.Object_Name
- PackageName.Subprogram_Name

In this syntax,

- PackageName is the name of the declared package
- Type_Name is the name of the type that is user defined, such as record
- Object_Name is the name of the constant or variable that is declare by the user
- Sub_Program is the name of the procedure or function contained in the package body

Example:

To reference the variable BAL in the package named **TRANSACTION_MGMT**, the referencing statement would be:

DECLARE

    balance number;

```
BEGIN
    ...
    IF TRANSACTION_MGMT.BAL < balance THEN
        ...
END IF;
```

The first procedure defined in the above package can be executed as follows:

EXECUTE TRANSACTION_MGMT.**PERFORM_TRANS**('SB1', 'D', 5000);

Output:

```
PL/ SQL procedure successfully completed.
```

OR

CALL TRANSACTION_MGMT.**PERFORM_TRANS ('SB1', 'D', 5000);**

Output:

```
Call completed.
```

The second procedure defined in the above package can be executed as follows:

EXECUTE TRANSACTION_MGMT.**CANCEL_FD ('F1');**

Output:

```
Your FD is cancelled. The amount is credited to the account number: CA2
PL/ SQL procedure successfully completed.
```

OR

CALL TRANSACTION_MGMT.**CANCEL_FD ('F1');**

Output:

```
Your FD is cancelled. The amount is credited to the account number: CA2
Call completed.
```

When the Oracle engine executes a package subprogram, an implicit save point will be created. If the subprogram fails with an unhandled exception, before returning to the host environment, the Oracle engine will rollback to the save point, thereby undoing any changes made by the package subprogram.

Alterations To An Existing Package

To recompile a package, use the **ALTER PACKAGE** command with the compile keyword. This explicit recompilation eliminates the need for any implicit run time recompilation and prevents any associated runtime compilation errors and performance overhead. It is common to explicitly compile a package after modifications to the package.

Recompiling a package recompiles all objects defined within the package. Recompiling does not change the definition of the package or any of its objects.

This statement recompiles the package specification.

Syntax:

```
ALTER PACKAGE <PackageName> COMPILE PACKAGE
```

The following examples recompile just the body of a package.

Example:

ALTER PACKAGE TRANSACTION_MGMT **COMPILE BODY;**

Output:

```
Package body altered.
```

Note

 All packages can be recompiled by using an Oracle utility called **dbms_utility**.

Syntax:

```
EXECUTE DBMS_UTILITY.COMPILE_ALL
```

Package Objects - Private V/S Public

Within the body of a package, the definition of subprograms, cursors, and private declarations for types and objects is permitted. For objects that are declared inside the package body, their use is restricted to within that package only. Therefore, PL/SQL code outside the package cannot reference any of the variables that were privately declared within the package.

Any items declared within the package's specification are visible outside the package. This enables PL/SQL code outside the package to reference objects from within the package using dot notation. These objects declared in the package specifications are called **Public**.

Variables, Cursors And Constants

Variables, Cursors, and Constants can change their value over time and have a specific life span. This life duration can vary depending on where the declaration is located. For standalone procedures, variables, cursors, and constants persist only for the duration of the procedure call and are lost when the procedure execution terminates.

If the variable, constant, or cursor was declared in a package specification or body, their values persist for the duration of the user's session. The values are lost when the current user's session terminates or the package is recompiled.

Package State

A package is either valid or invalid. A package is considered valid if none of the source code or objects it references have been dropped, replaced or altered since the package specifications were last compiled.

The package is considered invalid if the source code or any object that it references has been dropped, altered, or replaced since the package specification was last compiled. When a package becomes invalid, the Oracle engine will also make invalid any object that references the package.

Package Dependency

During the recompiling of a package, the Oracle engine invalidates all objects dependent on the package. These objects include standalone package subprograms that call or reference objects declared in the package's section that is being recompiled.

If another user's program calls or references a package's object before it is recompiled, the Oracle engine automatically recompiles it at run time.

During package recompilation, the Oracle engine determines whether objects on which the package depends are valid. If any of these objects are invalid, the Oracle engine will recompile them before recompiling the package body.

If recompilation is successful then the package body becomes valid. If any errors are detected, the appropriate error messages are generated and the package body remains invalid.

Example:

Create a package comprising of a procedure and a function.

The function will:

- ❑ Accept the branch number and calculate the number of employees in that branch and finally return the number of employees

The procedure will:

- ❑ Accept the branch number
- ❑ Using the function created will get the employee count for the branch number accepted
- ❑ Based on the employee count a decision will be taken to delete the employees belonging to that branch followed by deleting the branch

Package Specification

```
CREATE OR REPLACE PACKAGE PCK_DEL IS
    PROCEDURE DEL_EMP_BRANCH(mBRANCH_NO VARCHAR2);
    FUNCTION CNT_EMP_BRANCH(mBRANCH_NO VARCHAR2) RETURN NUMBER;
END PCK_DEL;
```

Output:

```
Package created.
```

Package Body

```
CREATE OR REPLACE PACKAGE BODY PCK_DEL IS
    PROCEDURE DEL_EMP_BRANCH(mBRANCH_NO VARCHAR2) IS noemp NUMBER;
    BEGIN
        noemp := CNT_EMP_BRANCH(mBRANCH_NO);
        IF noemp < 2 AND noemp > 0 THEN
            DELETE EMP_MSTR WHERE BRANCH_NO = mBRANCH_NO;
            DBMS_OUTPUT.PUT_LINE('All the employees belonging
            to the branch ' || mBRANCH_NO || ' deleted
            sucessfully');
            DELETE BRANCH_MSTR WHERE BRANCH_NO = mBRANCH_NO;
            DBMS_OUTPUT.PUT_LINE('Branch ' || mBRANCH_NO || '
            deleted sucessfully');
        END IF;
        IF noemp = 0 THEN
            DBMS_OUTPUT.PUT_LINE('There exist no employees in
            the branch.');
        END IF;
        IF noemp >= 2 THEN
            DBMS_OUTPUT.PUT_LINE('There exist ' || noemp || '
            employees in the branch' || mBRANCH_NO || ' Skipping
            Deletion.');
        END IF;
    END;
    FUNCTION CNT_EMP_BRANCH(mBRANCH_NO VARCHAR2) RETURN NUMBER IS
```

```
        noemp NUMBER;
    BEGIN
        SELECT COUNT(*) INTO noemp FROM EMP_MSTR
            WHERE BRANCH_NO = mBRANCH_NO;
        RETURN noemp;
    EXCEPTION
        WHEN NO_DATA_FOUND THEN
            RETURN 0;
    END;
END PCK_DEL;
```

Output:

```
Package body created.
```

The Functionality Of The PL/SQL Block Of Code with the Package Will Be As Follows:

The above PL/SQL block is a package body named **PCK_DEL** based on the package definition created above it. This package consist of a function and a procedure:

- CNT_EMP_BRANCH - Function

  Consists of the following argument:

  - mBRANCH_NO

    This function will accept the branch number. Based on the argument, it will calculate the number of employees belonging to that branch. The calculated value is stored in a memory variable named **noemp**. This value is then returned by the function on completion of the process. If there are no employees in that branch or there is no such branch available then an exception will be raised on the failure of the query. This exception will be handled by the function by returning **0**.

- DEL_EMP_BRANCH - Procedure

  Consists of the following argument:

  - mFD_NO

    This procedure will accept the branch number. This argument is passed to the function CNT_EMP_BRANCH. This function belongs to the same package. It returns a value (i.e. The number of employees in that branch) that will be stored in a memory variable named **noemp**.

Based on the value returned **i.e.** noemp following processing is done:

- If the employee count is less than 2 then
  - All those employees who belong to that branch are deleted
  - That Branch having less than 2 employees is also deleted
  - A message indicating the deletions is displayed
- If the employee count is 0 then
  - A message indicating the same is displayed
- If the employee count is greater than 2 then
  - A message indicating the number of employees and the branch to which they belong is displayed

Calling The Package

Situation 1: When there are no employees in that branch.

The procedure defined in the above package can be executed as follows:

EXECUTE PCK_DEL.DEL_EMP_BRANCH (**'B5'**);

Output:

```
There exist no employees in the branch.
PL/ SQL procedure successfully completed.
```

OR

CALL PCK_DEL.DEL_EMP_BRANCH (**'B5'**);

Output:

```
There exist no employees in the branch.
Call completed.
```

Situation 2: When there are more than 2 employees in that branch.

The procedure defined in the above package can be executed as follows:

EXECUTE PCK_DEL.DEL_EMP_BRANCH (**'B1'**);

Output:

```
There exist 2 employees in the branch B1 Skipping Deletion.
PL/ SQL procedure successfully completed.
```

OR

CALL PCK_DEL.DEL_EMP_BRANCH (**'B1'**);

Output:

```
There exist 2 employees in the branch B1 Skipping Deletion.
Call completed.
```

Situation 3: When there are less than 2 employees in that branch.

The procedure defined in the above package can be executed as follows:

EXECUTE PCK_DEL.DEL_EMP_BRANCH (**'B6'**);

Output:

```
All the employees belonging to the branch B6 deleted successfully.
PL/ SQL procedure successfully completed.
```

OR

CALL PCK_DEL.DEL_EMP_BRANCH (**'B1'**);

Output:

```
All the employees belonging to the branch B6 deleted successfully.
Call completed.
```

Overloading Procedures And Functions

A package is an Oracle object that can hold a number of other objects like procedures and functions. More than one procedure or function with the **same name** but with **different parameters** can be defined within a package or within a PL/SQL declaration block.

Multiple procedures that are declared with the same name are called **Overloaded Procedures**. Similarly, multiple Functions that are declared with the same name are called **Overloaded Functions**.

The code in the overloaded functions or overloaded procedures can be same or completely different.

Example:

Create a package to check that a numeric value is greater than zero, and a date is less than or equal to sysdate.

```
CREATE OR REPLACE PACKAGE CHECK_FUNC IS
    FUNCTION VALUE_OK(DATE_IN IN DATE) RETURN VARCHAR2;
    FUNCTION VALUE_OK(NUMBER_IN IN NUMBER) RETURN VARCHAR2;
END;
```

Output:

```
Package created.
```

```
CREATE OR REPLACE PACKAGE BODY CHECK_FUNC IS
      FUNCTION VALUE_OK (DATE_IN IN DATE) RETURN VARCHAR2 IS
      BEGIN
            IF DATE_IN <= SYSDATE THEN
                  RETURN 'Output From the First Over loaded Function:
                  TRUE';
            ELSE
                  RETURN 'Output From the First Over loaded Function:
                  FALSE';
            END IF;
      END;
      FUNCTION VALUE_OK (NUMBER_IN IN NUMBER) RETURN VARCHAR2 IS
      BEGIN
            IF NUMBER_IN > 0 THEN
                  RETURN 'Output From the Second Over loaded Function:
                  TRUE';
            ELSE
                  RETURN 'Output From the Second Over loaded Function:
                  FALSE';
            END IF;
      END;
END;
```

Output:

```
Package body created.
```

Overloading can greatly simplify procedures and functions. The Overloading technique consolidates the call interface for many similar programs into a single procedure or function. When executing the procedure or function the Oracle engines **chooses** the **procedure** or **function** whose number of parameters and data type **match the values** passed by the caller.

As seen in the example, a function with the name **VALUE_OK** is created in the package **CHECK_FUNC**. The first function accepts a single parameter of type **date**. The second function also accepts a single parameter of type **number**.

Thus when the **VALUE_OK** function is called and passed a date value, as in

```
    IF CHECK_FUNC.VALUE_OK(TO_DATE('03-JAN-81')) THEN
        ....
    END IF;
```

The Oracle engine compares the data type of the values passed by the caller against the different parameter lists in the package **CHECK_DATA**. The Oracle engine then executes the code for first function that accepts date as in:

```
CREATE FUNCTION VALUE_OK (DATE_IN IN DATE) RETURN VARCHAR2 IS
BEGIN
    IF DATE_IN <= SYSDATE THEN
        RETURN 'Output From the First Over loaded Function: TRUE';
    ELSE
        RETURN 'Output From the First Over loaded Function: FALSE';
    END IF;
END;
```

Similarly, when the **'VALUE_OK'** function is called and a numeric value is passed by the caller, as in:

```
    IF CHECK_DATA.VALUE_OK (23) THEN
        ....
    END IF;
```

the Oracle engine executes the second function that accepts numeric value as in:

```
CREATE FUNCTION VALUE_OK (NUMBER_IN IN NUMBER) RETURN VARCHAR2 IS
BEGIN
    IF NUMBER_IN > 0 THEN
        RETURN 'Output From the Second Over loaded Function: TRUE';
    ELSE
        RETURN ' Output From the Second Over loaded Function: FALSE';
    END IF;
END;
```

Overloading Built-In PL/SQL Functions And Procedures

PL/ SQL itself makes extensive use of overloading. An Example of an overloaded function in PL/ SQL is the TO_CHAR function. Function overloading allows developers to use a single function to convert both numbers and dates to character format.

Example:

```
    DATE_STRING := TO_CHAR(SYSDATE, 'DD/MM/YY');
```

NUMBER_STRING := TO_CHAR(10000, '$099,999');

In this example, the PL/SQL interpreter examines the value passed to the TO_CHAR function. Based on the data type of this value, it executes the appropriate TO_CHAR function.

Benefits Of Overloading

The benefits of overloading are:

1. Overloading can greatly simplify the processing logic of a program by eliminating multiple **IF** constructs or **CASE** constructs that would check the parameters passed and perform appropriate operations.
2. The overloading technique transfers the burden of knowledge from the developer to the software. For example if multiple procedures with different names are written, the programmer will have to remember the names of each of the procedures along with the parameters of each function.
3. If procedures or functions are overloaded, the programmer needs to remember a single procedure or function name and pass values as required.

Where To Overload Functions And Procedures

There are only two places in PL/SQL programs where the procedures and functions can be overloaded:

- Inside the declaration section of a PL/SQL block
- Inside a package

Tip

Standalone programs **cannot** be overloaded nor can two independent modules be created with the same name but different parameter lists.

Example:

If an attempt is made to create or replace the following procedures of **revise estimates**, the second attempt will fail.

```
CREATE PROCEDURE REVISE_ESTIMATES (DATE_IN IN DATE) IS
BEGIN
    ...
END;
```

Output:

```
Procedure created.
```

```
CREATE PROCEDURE REVISE_ESTIMATES (DOLLARS_IN IN NUMBER) IS
BEGIN
    ...
END;
```

Output:

```
ORA-0955: name is already used by an existing object.
```

Because a procedure with the name used is present, PL/SQL rejected the attempt to replace it with the procedure created in the second attempt.

Restrictions On Overloading

There are several restrictions on how the procedures and functions can be overloaded. The following restrictions apply since the PL/SQL engine compares overloaded modules (functions or procedure) before executing the appropriate module.

1. The data subtype of at least one of the parameters of the overloaded function or procedure must differ

   For example an overloaded procedure distinguished by parameters of different types of numeric data types is not allowed. Similarly, an overloaded procedure distinguished by parameters with varchar2 and char data types is not allowed.

Example:

```
CREATE OR REPLACE PACKAGE BODY STRING_FNS IS
      PROCEDURE TRIM_AND_CENTER (STRING_IN IN CHAR, STRING_OUT OUT
      CHAR)
      BEGIN
               . . .
      END;
      PROCEDURE TRIM_AND_CENTER (STRING_IN IN VARCHAR2, STRING_OUT
      OUT VARCHAR2)
      BEGIN
               . . .
      END;
END;
```

Caution

Such procedure overloading is not allowed.

2. The parameter list of overloaded functions must differ by more than name or parameter mode

   The parameter name is replaced by the values sent to the objects when the package is called, so differences in name do not offer a guide to the overloaded objects that must be used.

Example:

A procedure definition will be as:

```
CREATE OR REPLACE PACKAGE BODY CHECK_DATE IS
      FUNCTION VALUE_OK(DATE_IN IN DATE) RETURN BOOLEAN IS
      BEGIN
            RETURN DATE_IN <= SYSDATE;
      END;
      FUNCTION VALUE_OK(DATE_OUT IN DATE)RETURN BOOLEAN IS
      BEGIN
            RETURN DATE_OUT >= SYSDATE;
      END;
END;
```

The call to the function will be:

IS_DATE_OK := CHECK_DATA.VALUE_OK(**TO_DATE**('03-JAN-81'))

The name of the parameter is not available in the module call and thus PL/SQL interpreter **cannot** distinguish objects by name.

Similarly, even if a parameter in the first module is IN and the same parameter is IN OUT in another module, PL/SQL interpreter **cannot** distinguish using the package call.

The overloading attempts will result in the following error messages:

PLS-00307: too many declarations of 'value_check' match this call.

3. Overloaded functions must differ by more than their return data type.

   At the time that the overloaded function is called, the PL/SQL interpreter does not know what type of data that function will return. The interpreter therefore cannot distinguish between different overloaded functions based on the return data type.

Example:

```
CREATE OR REPLACE PACKAGE BODY CHECK_RETURN IS
      FUNCTION VALUE_OK(DATE_IN IN DATE) RETURN BOOLEAN IS
      BEGIN
            RETURN DATE_IN <= SYSDATE ;
      END;
      FUNCTION VALUE_OK(DATE_OUT IN DATE ) RETURN NUMBER IS
      BEGIN
            IF DATE_OUT >= SYSDATE THEN
                  RETURN 1;
            ELSE
                  RETURN 0;
            END IF;
      END;
END;
```

4. All the overloaded modules must be defined within the same PL/SQL scope or block (PL/SQL block or package).

   Two modules cannot be overloaded across two PL/SQL blocks or across two packages.

Example:

```
PROCEDURE DEVELOP_ANALYSIS (QUARTER_END_IN IN DATE, SALES_IN IN NUMBER)
IS
      PROCEDURE REVISE_ESTIMATE (DATE_IN IN DATE) IS
      BEGIN
            PROCEDURE REVISE_ESTIMATE (DOLLAR_IN IN NUMBER) IS
            BEGIN
                  . . .
            END;
            BEGIN
                  REVISE_ESTIMATE(QUARTER_END_IN);
                  REVISE_ESTIMATE(DOLLARS_IN);
```

```
        END;
    END;
```

When the above code is interpreted, the PL/SQL interpreter displays the following error message.

```
Error in Line 12 / Column 3:
PLS-00306: wrong number or type of arguments in call to
'REVISE_ESTIMATE'
```

PL/ SQL displays the error message because the scope and visibility of both the procedures is different. The scope of the date **REVISE_ESTIMATES** is the entire scope of the body **DEVELOP_ANALYSIS**. The scope of the **numeric REVISE_ESTIMATES** is the inner block only and it takes precedence over the date **REVISE_ESTIMATES.**

Function Or Procedure Overloading

Example:

The bank manager decides to activate all those accounts, which were previously marked as inactive for performing no transactions in last 365 days.

Create a package spec and package body named **ACCT_MNTC** that includes two procedures of the same name. The procedure name is **ACT_ACCTS**. The first procedure accepts BRANCH_NO and the second procedure accepts branch name.

Package Specification:

```
CREATE OR REPLACE PACKAGE ACCT_MNTC IS
    PROCEDURE ACT_ACCTS(vBRANCH_NO IN NUMBER);
    PROCEDURE ACT_ACCTS (vNAME IN VARCHAR2);
END;
```

Output:

```
Package created.
```

Package Body:

```
CREATE OR REPLACE PACKAGE BODY ACCT_MNTC IS
    PROCEDURE ACT_ACCTS(vBRANCH_NO IN NUMBER) IS
    BEGIN
        UPDATE ACCT_MSTR SET STATUS = 'A'
            WHERE BRANCH_NO = 'B' || vBRANCH_NO AND STATUS =
            'S';
        IF SQL%ROWCOUNT > 0 THEN
            DBMS_OUTPUT.PUT_LINE(TO_CHAR(SQL%ROWCOUNT) || '
            Account(s) Activated Successfully');
        ELSE
            DBMS_OUTPUT.PUT_LINE('Currently there exist no Inactive
            Accounts in the branch no ' || vBRANCH_NO);
        END IF;
    END;
    PROCEDURE ACT_ACCTS(vNAME IN VARCHAR2) IS
    BEGIN
        UPDATE ACCT_MSTR SET STATUS = 'A' WHERE STATUS = 'S'
```

```
                AND BRANCH_NO IN(SELECT BRANCH_NO FROM BRANCH_MSTR
                    WHERE NAME = vNAME);
            IF SQL%ROWCOUNT > 0 THEN
                DBMS_OUTPUT.PUT_LINE(TO_CHAR(SQL%ROWCOUNT) || '
                Account(s) Activated Successfully');
            ELSE
                DBMS_OUTPUT.PUT_LINE('Currently there exist no Inactive
                Accounts in the  branch ' || vNAME);
            END IF;
        END;
END ACCT_MNTC;
```

Output:

```
Package body created.
```

Execution of the above PL/SQL block will be as follows:

Calling the Procedure by passing the branch number

```
SQL> EXECUTE ACCT_MNTC.ACT_ACCTS(1);
3 Account(s) Activated Successfully
PL/SQL procedure successfully completed.
```

Calling the Procedure by passing the branch name

```
SQL> EXECUTE ACCT_MNTC.ACT_ACCTS('Vile Parle (HO)');
3 Account(s) Activated Successfully
PL/SQL procedure successfully completed.
```

Database Triggers

Database triggers are database objects created via the SQL* Plus tool on the client and stored on the Server in the Oracle engine's system table. These database objects consist of the following distinct sections:

- A named database event
- A PL/SQL block that will execute when the event occurs

The occurrence of the database event is strongly bound to table data being changed.

Introduction

The Oracle engine allows the definition of procedures that are implicitly executed (i.e. executed by the Oracle engine itself), when an insert, update or delete is issued against a table from SQL* Plus or through an application. These procedures are called **database triggers**. The major issues that make these triggers stand-alone are that, they are fired implicitly (**i.e.** internally) by the Oracle engine itself and not explicitly **i.e.** called by the user.

Use Of Database Triggers

Since the Oracle engine supports database triggers it provides a highly customizable database management system. Some of the uses to which the database triggers can be put, to customize management information by the Oracle engine are as follows:

- A trigger can permit DML statements against a table only if they are issued, during regular business hours or on predetermined weekdays
- A trigger can also be used to keep an audit trail of a table (i.e. to store the modified and deleted records of the table) along with the operation performed and the time on which the operation was performed
- It can be used to prevent invalid transactions
- Enforce complex security authorizations

Note

When a trigger is fired, an SQL statement inside the trigger's PL/SQL code block can also fire the same or some other trigger. This is called **cascading** triggers.

Excessive use of triggers for customizing the database can result in complex interdependencies between the triggers, which may be difficult to maintain in a large application.

Database Triggers V/S Procedures

There are very few differences between database triggers and procedures. Triggers do not accept parameters whereas procedures can. A trigger is executed implicitly by the Oracle engine itself upon modification of an associated table or its data. To execute a procedure, it has to be explicitly called by a user.

Database Triggers V/S Declarative Integrity Constraints

Triggers as well as declarative integrity constraints can be used to constrain data input. However both have significant differences as mentioned below:

- A declarative integrity constraint is a statement about a database that is always true. A constraint applies to existing data in the table and any statement that manipulates the table
- Triggers constrain what a transaction can do. A trigger does not apply to data loaded before the trigger was created, so it does not guarantee all data in table conforms to the rules established by an associated trigger
- A trigger enforces a transitional constraint, which cannot be enforced by a declarative integrity constraint

How To Apply Database Triggers

A trigger has three basic parts:

- A triggering event or statement
- A trigger restriction
- A trigger action

Each part of the trigger is explained below

Triggering Event or Statement

It is a SQL statement that causes a trigger to be fired. It can be INSERT, UPDATE or DELETE statement for a specific table. (**i.e.** Table write operations)

Trigger Restriction

A trigger restriction specifies a Boolean (logical) expression that must be **TRUE** for the trigger to fire. It is an option available for triggers that are fired for each row. Its function is to conditionally control the execution of a trigger. A trigger restriction is specified using a **WHEN** clause.

Trigger Action

A trigger action is the PL/SQL code to be executed when a triggering statement is encountered and any trigger restriction evaluates to TRUE. The PL/SQL block can contain SQL and PL/SQL statements, can define PL/SQL language constructs and can call stored procedures. Additionally, for row triggers, the statements the PL/SQL block have access to column values (**:new** and **:old**) of the current row being processed.

Types Of Triggers

While defining a trigger, the number of times the trigger action is to be executed can be specified. This can be once for every row affected by the triggering statement (such as might be fired by an UPDATE statement that updates many rows), or once for the triggering statement, no matter how many rows it affects.

Row Triggers

A row trigger is fired each time a row in the table is affected by the triggering statement. For example, if an UPDATE statement updates multiple rows of a table, a row trigger is fired once for each row affected by the UPDATE statement. If the triggering statement affects no rows, the trigger is not executed at all. Row triggers should be used when some processing is required whenever a triggering statement affects a single row in a table.

Statement Triggers

A **statement trigger** is fired once on behalf of the triggering statement, independent of the number of rows the triggering statement affects (even if no rows are affected). Statement triggers should be used when a triggering statement affects rows in a table but the processing required is completely independent of the number of rows affected.

Before V/S After Triggers

When defining a trigger it is necessary to specify the trigger timing, i.e. specifying when the triggering action is to be executed in relation to the triggering statement. **BEFORE** and **AFTER** apply to both row and the statement triggers.

Before Triggers

BEFORE triggers execute the trigger action before the triggering statement. These types of triggers are commonly used in the following situations:

- ❑ BEFORE triggers are used when the trigger action should determine whether or not the triggering statement should be allowed to complete. By using a BEFORE trigger, user can eliminate unnecessary processing of the triggering statement
- ❑ BEFORE triggers are used to derive specific column values before completing a triggering INSERT or UPDATE statement

After Triggers

AFTER trigger executes the trigger action after the triggering statement is executed. These types of triggers are commonly used in the following situations:

- ❑ AFTER triggers are used when the triggering statement should complete before executing the trigger action

- ❑ If a BEFORE trigger is already present, an AFTER trigger can perform different actions on the same triggering statement

Combinations Triggers

Using the options explained above, four types of triggers could be created

BEFORE statement trigger

Before executing the triggering statement, the trigger action is executed.

BEFORE row trigger

Before modifying each row affected by the triggering statement and **before** applying appropriate integrity constraints, the trigger is executed.

AFTER Statement Trigger

After executing the triggering statement and applying any deferred integrity constraints, the trigger action is executed.

AFTER Row Trigger

After modifying each row affected by the triggering statement and applying appropriate integrity constraints, the trigger action is executed for the current row. Unlike BEFORE row triggers, AFTER row triggers have **rows locked**.

Syntax For Creating A Trigger:

```
CREATE OR REPLACE TRIGGER [Schema.] <TriggerName>
      {BEFORE, AFTER}
      {DELETE, INSERT, UPDATE [OF Column, ...]}
ON [Schema.] <TableName>
      [ REFERENCING { OLD AS old, NEW AS new }]
      [ FOR EACH ROW [ WHEN Condition ] ]
DECLARE
      <Variable declarations>;
      <Constant declarations>;
BEGIN
      <PL/SQL subprogram body>;
EXCEPTION
      <Exception PL/SQL block>;
END;
```

Keywords And Parameters

The keywords and the parameters used for creating database triggers are explained below:

OR REPLACE	Recreates the trigger if it already exists. This option can be used to change the definition of an existing trigger without requiring the user to drop the trigger first.
Schema	Is the schema, which contains the trigger. If the schema is omitted, the Oracle engine creates the trigger in the users own schema.
TriggerName	Is the name of the trigger to be created.
BEFORE	Indicates that the Oracle engine fires the trigger before executing the triggering statement.
AFTER	Indicates that the Oracle engine fires the trigger after executing the triggering statement.
DELETE	Indicates that the Oracle engine fires the trigger whenever a DELETE statement removes a row from the table.
INSERT	Indicates that the Oracle engine fires the trigger whenever an INSERT statement adds a row to table.
UPDATE	Indicates that the Oracle engine fires the trigger whenever an UPDATE statement changes a value in one of the columns specified in the OF clause. If the OF clause is omitted, the Oracle engine fires the trigger whenever an UPDATE statement changes a value in any column of the table.
ON	Specifies the schema and name of the table, which the trigger is to be created. If schema is omitted, the Oracle engine assumes the table is in the users own schema. A trigger cannot be created on a table in the schema SYS.
REFERENCING	Specifies correlation names. Correlation names can be used in the PL/SQL block and WHEN clause of a row trigger to refer specifically to old and new values of the current row. The default correlation names are **OLD** and **NEW**. If the row trigger is associated with a table named OLD or NEW, this clause can be used to specify different correlation names to avoid confusion between table name and the correlation name.
FOR EACH ROW	Designates the trigger to be a row trigger. The Oracle engine fires a row trigger once for each row that is affected by the triggering statement and meets the optional trigger constraint defined in the WHEN clause. If this clause is omitted the trigger is a statement trigger.
WHEN	Specifies the trigger restriction. The trigger restriction contains a SQL condition that must be satisfied for the Oracle engine to fire the trigger. This condition must contain correlation names and cannot contain a query. Trigger restriction can be specified only for the row triggers. The Oracle engine evaluates this condition for each row affected by the triggering statement.
PL/SQL block	Is the PL/SQL block that the Oracle engine executes when the trigger is fired.

Note
 The PL/SQL block cannot contain transaction control SQL statements (COMMIT, ROLLBACK, and SAVEPOINT)

Deleting a Trigger

Syntax:

```
DROP TRIGGER <TriggerName>;
```

where, **TriggerName** is the name of the trigger to be dropped.

Applications Using Database Triggers

Example:

Create a transparent audit system for a table **CUST_MSTR**. The system must keep track of the records that are being deleted or updated. The functionality being when a record is deleted or modified the original record details and the date of operation are stored in the audit table, **then** the delete or update operation is allowed to go through.

The table definition for audit system is given below:

Table Name:	AUDIT_CUST
Description:	This is the table, which keeps track of the records deleted or updated when such operations are carried out. Records in this table will be inserted when the database trigger fires due to an update or delete statement fired on the table **CUST_MSTR**.

Column Definition:

Column Name	Data Type	Size	Attributes
CUST_NO	VarChar2	10	
FNAME	VarChar2	25	
MNAME	VarChar2	25	
LNAME	VarChar2	25	
DOB_INC	Date/Time		
OCCUP	VarChar2	25	
PHOTOGRAPH	VarChar2	25	
SIGNATURE	VarChar2	25	
PANCOPY	VarChar2	1	
FORM60	VarChar2	1	

Details for **AUDIT_CUST** continued:

Column Definition:

Column Name	Data Type	Size	Attributes
Operation	VarChar2	10	
Userid	VarChar2	10	
Odate	Date		

Table Description:

Column Name	Description
CUST_NO	A system generated number auto posted to this table column
FNAME	Customer's first name
MNAME	Customer's middle name
LNAME	Customer's last name
DOB_INC	Customer's date of birth (for individuals) or data of incorporation (for organizations)
OCCUP	Customer's occupation or line of business
PHOTOGRAPH	Location to customer's scanned photograph (for individuals only)
SIGNATURE	Location to customer's scanned signature (for individuals only)
PANCOPY	Holds **Y** if a copy of PAN card has been submitted
FORM60	Holds **Y** if the Form 60 has been submitted
Operation	The operation performed on the CUST_MSTR table
Userid	The date when the operation was performed
Odate	The name of the user performing the operation

Solution

Create table statement for the AUDIT_CUST table:

```
CREATE TABLE "DBA_BANKSYS"."AUDIT_CUST"(
    "CUST_NO" VARCHAR2(10), "FNAME" VARCHAR2(25), "MNAME" VARCHAR2(25),
    "LNAME" VARCHAR2(25), "DOB_INC" DATE NOT NULL, "OCCUP" VARCHAR2(25),
    "PHOTOGRAPH" VARCHAR2(25), "SIGNATURE" VARCHAR2(25), "PANCOPY" VARCHAR2(1),
    "FORM60" VARCHAR2(1), "OPERATION" VARCHAR2(20), "USERID" VARCHAR2(20),
    "ODATE" DATE);
```

Output:

```
Table created.
```

This trigger is fired when an update or delete operation is performed on the table **CUST_MSTR**. The trigger first checks for the operation being performed on the table. Then depending on the operation being performed, a variable is assigned the value **update** or **delete**. Previous values of the modified record of the table **CUST_MSTR** are inserted into the AUDIT_CUST table.

```
CREATE TRIGGER AUDIT_TRAIL
        AFTER UPDATE OR DELETE ON CUST_MSTR
                FOR EACH ROW
DECLARE
/* The value in the OPER variable will be inserted into the operation
field in the AUDIT_CUST table */
        OPER VARCHAR2(8);

BEGIN
/* If the records are updated in the CUST_MSTR table then OPER is set
to 'UPDATE'. */
        IF updating THEN
                OPER := 'UPDATE';
        END IF;
/* If the records are deleted from the CUST_MSTR table then OPER is set
to 'DELETE'. */
        IF deleting THEN
                OPER := 'DELETE';
        END IF;
/* Insert the old values in the AUDIT_CUST table. */
        INSERT INTO AUDIT_CUST VALUES (:OLD.CUST_NO, :OLD.FNAME,
        :OLD.MNAME, :OLD.LNAME, :OLD.DOB_INC, :OLD.OCCUP,
        :OLD.PHOTOGRAPH, :OLD.SIGNATURE, :OLD.PANCOPY, :OLD.FORM60, OPER,
        USER, SYSDATE);
END;
```

Output:

```
Trigger created.
```

The creation of the database trigger AUDIT_TRAIL results in an auditing system for the table **CUST_MSTR**. The owner of the table can keep track of time of modification or deletion of a record in **CUST_MSTR** by querying the table **AUDIT_CUST**.

Observations:

The actual working of the auditing system can be confirmed as follows:

This is the data in the table **CUST_MSTR** before the Database Trigger had been fired.

SELECT CUST_NO, FNAME, MNAME, LNAME, DOB_INC **FROM** CUST_MSTR;

Output:

CUST_NO	FNAME	MNAME	LNAME	DOB_INC
C1	Ivan	Nelson	Bayross	25-JUN-52
C2	Chriselle	Ivan	Bayross	29-OCT-82
C3	Mamta	Arvind	Muzumdar	28-AUG-75
C4	Chhaya	Sudhakar	Bankar	06-OCT-76
C5	Ashwini	Dilip	Joshi	20-NOV-78
C6	Hansel	I.	Colaco	01-JAN-82
C7	Anil	Arun	Dhone	12-OCT-83
C8	Alex	Austin	Fernandes	30-SEP-62
C9	Ashwini	Shankar	Apte	19-APR-79
C10	Namita	S.	Kanade	10-JUN-78
O11				14-NOV-97
O12				23-OCT-92
O13				05-FEB-89
O14				24-MAY-80
O15				02-APR-00
O16				13-JAN-02

16 rows selected.

Following is the data in the table **AUDIT_CUST** before the Database Trigger has been fired.

SELECT CUST_NO, FNAME, MNAME, LNAME, DOB_INC, OPERATION, ODATE, USER
FROM AUDIT_CUST;

Output:

```
No Rows Selected
```

Case 1:

When an update statement modifies a record in the table **CUST_MSTR**.

The following update statement modifies the CUST_MSTR.

UPDATE CUST_MSTR **SET** DOB_INC = '1-FEB-1981' **WHERE** FNAME = 'Hansel';

Once the update is complete the contents of the table **Client_Master** have been modified as shown below. The content of the column Bal_due in the table **Client_Master** where the value was 2000 is updated to 2200.

SELECT CUST_NO, FNAME, MNAME, LNAME, DOB_INC **FROM** CUST_MSTR;

Output:

CUST_NO	FNAME	MNAME	LNAME	DOB_INC
C1	Ivan	Nelson	Bayross	25-JUN-52
C2	Chriselle	Ivan	Bayross	29-OCT-82
C3	Mamta	Arvind	Muzumdar	28-AUG-75
C4	Chhaya	Sudhakar	Bankar	06-OCT-76
C5	Ashwini	Dilip	Joshi	20-NOV-78
C6	Hansel	I.	Colaco	01-FEB-81
C7	Anil	Arun	Dhone	12-OCT-83
C8	Alex	Austin	Fernandes	30-SEP-62
C9	Ashwini	Shankar	Apte	19-APR-79
C10	Namita	S.	Kanade	10-JUN-78
O11				14-NOV-97
O12				23-OCT-92
O13				05-FEB-89
O14				24-MAY-80
O15				02-APR-00
O16				13-JAN-02

16 rows selected.

The changes made to the table CUST_MSTR must be reflected in the table AUDIT_CUST. AUDIT_CUST keeps track of the previous contents of CUST_MSTR whose records were modified as well as the operation and the date when the operation was performed.

SELECT CUST_NO, FNAME, MNAME, LNAME, DOB_INC, OPERATION, ODATE, USER
FROM AUDIT_CUST;

Output:

CUST_NO	FNAME	MNAME	LNAME	DOB_INC	OPERATION	ODATE	USER
C6	Hansel	I.	Colaco	01-JAN-82	UPDATE	13-JUL-04	DBA_BANKSYS

Case 2:

When a record is deleted from the table **CUST_MSTR**.

The following delete statement deletes all those customers from the **CUST_MSTR** table whose names start with 'A'.

DELETE FROM CUST_MSTR WHERE FNAME LIKE 'A%';

The following SELECT statement confirms that four record have been deleted.

SELECT CUST_NO, FNAME, MNAME, LNAME, DOB_INC **FROM** CUST_MSTR;

Output:

CUST_NO	FNAME	MNAME	LNAME	DOB_INC
C1	Ivan	Nelson	Bayross	25-JUN-52
C2	Chriselle	Ivan	Bayross	29-OCT-82
C3	Mamta	Arvind	Muzumdar	28-AUG-75
C4	Chhaya	Sudhakar	Bankar	06-OCT-76
C6	Hansel	I.	Colaco	01-FEB-81
C10	Namita	S.	Kanade	10-JUN-78
O11				14-NOV-97
O12				23-OCT-92
O13				05-FEB-89
O14				24-MAY-80
O15				02-APR-00
O16				13-JAN-02

12 rows selected.

The records deleted from the table CUST_MSTR must be reflected in the table AUDIT_CUST. Records are inserted into this table when an update or delete operation is performed on the table. It can be observed that four more records have been inserted into the table AUDIT_CUST.

SELECT CUST_NO, FNAME, MNAME, LNAME, DOB_INC, OPERATION, ODATE, USER
FROM AUDIT_CUST;

Output:

CUST_NO	FNAME	MNAME	LNAME	DOB_INC	OPERATION	ODATE	USER
C6	Hansel	I.	Colaco	01-JAN-82	UPDATE	13-JUL-04	DBA_BANKSYS
C5	Ashwini	Dilip	Joshi	20-NOV-78	DELETE	13-JUL-04	DBA_BANKSYS
C7	Anil	Arun	Dhone	12-OCT-83	DELETE	13-JUL-04	DBA_BANKSYS
C8	Alex	Austin	Fernandes	30-SEP-62	DELETE	13-JUL-04	DBA_BANKSYS
C9	Ashwini	Shankar	Apte	19-APR-79	DELETE	13-JUL-04	DBA_BANKSYS

Note

If the user performs a ROLLBACK after this, then the records, which were modified and deleted from the table **CUST_MSTR** are restored to their original status. Since all these changes are being done via the SQL* Plus tool at the SQL> prompt, a single ROLLBACK will also cause the records inserted into AUDIT_CUST to be rolled back as well.

If a PL/ SQL code block is performing this type of table operations, the same table behavior will result.

Raise_Application_Error Procedure

The Oracle engine provides a procedure named **RAISE_APPLICATION_ERROR** that allows programmers to issue user-defined error messages.

Syntax:

```
RAISE_APPLICATION_ERROR (<ErrorNumber>, <Message>);
```

where, **ErrorNumber** is a negative integer in the range **-20000 to -20999** while,

Message is a character string up to 2048 bytes in length.

An application can call **RAISE_APPLICATION_ERROR** only while executing a stored subprogram like stored procedures, functions and database triggers. Typically, **RAISE_APPLICATION_ERROR** is used in database **Triggers**.

RAISE_APPLICATION_ERROR ends the subprogram, rolls back any database changes it made and returns a user-defined error number and message to the application.

Example:

Write a database trigger on the TRANS_MSTR that checks the following:

- ❑ The account number for which the transaction is being performed is a valid account number
- ❑ The Transaction Amount is not zero and is positive and
- ❑ In case of a withdrawal the amount does not exceed the current balance for that account number

```
CREATE OR REPLACE TRIGGER TRANS_CHECK
    BEFORE INSERT ON TRANS_MSTR FOR EACH ROW
DECLARE
    v_CNT_ACCT_NO VARCHAR2(10);
    v_CURBAL NUMBER(10);
BEGIN
/* Checking if the account number is a valid account number. */
    SELECT COUNT(ACCT_NO) INTO v_CNT_ACCT_NO
        FROM ACCT_MSTR WHERE ACCT_NO = :new.ACCT_NO;
    IF v_CNT_ACCT_NO = 0 THEN
        RAISE_APPLICATION_ERROR(-20000,'The Account number is
        invalid.');
    END IF;
/* Checking if the transaction amount is a positive number. */
    IF :new.AMT <= 0 THEN
        RAISE_APPLICATION_ERROR(-20001,'The Transaction amount
        cannot be negative or zero.');
    END IF;
/* Checking if the transaction amount exceeds the current balance in
case of withdrawals. */
    SELECT CURBAL INTO v_CURBAL
        FROM ACCT_MSTR WHERE ACCT_NO = :new.ACCT_NO;
    IF v_CURBAL < :new.AMT AND :new.DR_CR = 'W' THEN
        RAISE_APPLICATION_ERROR(-20002,'The amount of withdrawal
        cannot exceed the balance held in the account.');
```

```
    END IF;
END;
```

Output:

Trigger created.

Case 1:

INSERT INTO TRANS_MSTR (TRANS_NO, ACCT_NO, DT, TYPE, PARTICULAR, DR_CR, AMT, BALANCE)

VALUES('T32', 'SB3', '15-DEC-2003', 'B', 'Initial Payment', 'D', -2, 500);

INSERT INTO TRANS_MSTR (TRANS_NO, ACCT_NO, DT, TYPE, PARTICULAR, DR_CR, AMT, BALANCE)

```
*
ERROR at line 1:
ORA-20001: The Transaction amount cannot
be negative or zero.
ORA-06512: at "DBA_BANKSYS.TRANS_CHECK", line 16
ORA-04088: error during execution of trigger 'DBA_BANKSYS.TRANS_CHECK'
```

Case 2:

INSERT INTO TRANS_MSTR (TRANS_NO, ACCT_NO, DT, TYPE, PARTICULAR, DR_CR, AMT, BALANCE)

VALUES('T32', 'SB33', '15-DEC-2003', 'B', 'Initial Payment', 'W', -2, 500);

INSERT INTO TRANS_MSTR (TRANS_NO, ACCT_NO, DT, TYPE, PARTICULAR, DR_CR, AMT, BALANCE)

```
*
ERROR at line 1:
ORA-20000: The Account number is invalid.
ORA-06512: at "DBA_BANKSYS.TRANS_CHECK", line 11
ORA-04088: error during execution of trigger 'DBA_BANKSYS.TRANS_CHECK'
```

Case 3:

INSERT INTO TRANS_MSTR (TRANS_NO, ACCT_NO, DT, TYPE, PARTICULAR, DR_CR, AMT, BALANCE)

VALUES('T32', 'SB3', '15-DEC-2003', 'B', 'Initial Payment', 'W', 99999, 500);

INSERT INTO TRANS_MSTR (TRANS_NO, ACCT_NO, DT, TYPE, PARTICULAR, DR_CR, AMT, BALANCE)

```
*
ERROR at line 1:
ORA-20002: The amount of withdrawal cannot
exceed the balance held in the account.
ORA-06512: at "DBA_BANKSYS.TRANS_CHECK", line 25
ORA-04088: error during execution of trigger 'DBA_BANKSYS.TRANS_CHECK'
```

GeneratinG A Primary Key Using A Database Trigger

Introduction

In a multi-user environment, to allow data entry operators to create and enter a primary key to uniquely identify a record, will always result in a large number of records being rejected due to duplicate values being keyed in due to human error. This will result in a time delay between the record being keyed and the record being accepted for storage.

Automatic Primary Key Generation

If the data entry operator is not allowed to enter the primary key value and the primary key value is generated by the system, it would prevent this type of error from occuring.

Simple but effective approaches that can be used to generate a primary key are:

1. Use a lookup table that stores the last primary key value. The new primary key value must be generated from the value stored in the lookup table
2. Use the MAX function
3. Use a Sequence

As soon as the Oracle engine receives data to be inserted into tables, the Oracle engine must invoke a program that generates the primary key value. The primary key value so generated is merged with the data that has to be inserted into the table. This entire record, now consisting of the primary key as well as the data is then posted into the table.

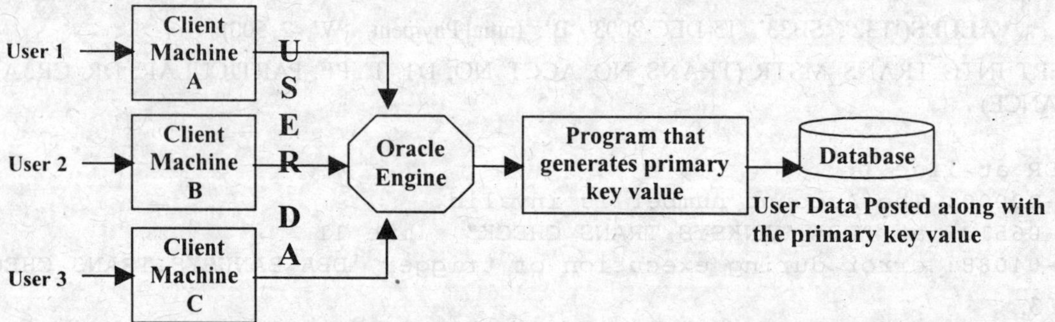

Diagram 18.2: Automatic Primary Key Generation

The program unit that fires automatically before or after any **write** operation is performed on the table is called a **Database Trigger**. Thus a database trigger can be used to generate a primary key value. The primary key value must be generated **before** the data is posted into the table. Thus the database trigger must be written such that it executes **before** the data is posted into the table **i.e.** a BEFORE INSERT database trigger.

Generating Primary Key Using Sequences

The Oracle engine provides an object called a **sequence** that generates numeric values starting with a given value and with an increment as specified by the user. Thus a sequence must first be created using SQL* Plus. Once the sequence is created a database trigger can be written such that it retrieves the next number from the sequence and uses the same as the primary key value.

Example:

Sequence Creation

CREATE SEQUENCE CUST_SEQ **INCREMENT BY** 1 **START WITH** 1;

Output:

```
Sequence created.
```

Example:

Database Trigger Creation

```
CREATE OR REPLACE TRIGGER CUST_NO_GENERATION
     BEFORE INSERT ON CUST_MSTR
          FOR EACH ROW
DECLARE
     PRIMARY_KEY_VALUE VARCHAR2(10);
BEGIN
     SELECT 'C' || TO_CHAR(CUST_SEQ.NEXTVAL)
          INTO PRIMARY_KEY_VALUE FROM DUAL;
     :new.CUST_NO := PRIMARY_KEY_VALUE;
END;
```

Output:

```
Trigger created.
```

The above code gets the next sequence value. The sequence value is concatenated with **C**. So the entire output will look like **C1** if the sequence value is 1.

The data in the last SQL statement can be classified as **New** values and **Old** values. When the user fires an insert statement the values of the columns included in the insert statement can be read or set by using **:NEW.columnname**.

Similarly, if the user updates a record, the value before the updation can be read by using **:OLD.columnname**. The new values set using an update statement will be referenced by **:NEW.columnname**.

In the current example, the value of **CUST_NO** must be set, which will be inserted into the table. Thus the value of **:new.CUST_NO** has to actually be set.

The sequence number value is then assigned to the column CLIENT_NO by using **:new.CUST_NO**.

Since the value inserted into CUST_NO is generated automatically, the user must insert values in all columns **except** the CUST_NO column.

INSERT INTO CUST_MSTR (FNAME, MNAME, LNAME, DOB_INC, OCCUP, PHOTOGRAPH, SIGNATURE, PANCOPY, FORM60)

VALUES('Sharanam', 'Chaitanya', 'Shah', '03-JAN-1981', 'Self Employed', 'D:/ClntPht/Shah.gif', 'D:/ClntSgnt/Shah.gif', 'Y', 'Y');

Generating Primary Key Using The MAX Function

The Oracle engine provides a built-in function that returns the maximum value in a data set. Thus the maximum value retrieved from the table is incremented by 1 to generate a new primary key value.

Example:

```
CREATE OR REPLACE TRIGGER EMP_NO_GENERATION
```

```
    BEFORE INSERT ON EMP_MSTR
        FOR EACH ROW
DECLARE
    MAX_PKEY_VALUE VARCHAR2(10);
    NEW_PKEY_VALUE VARCHAR2(10);
BEGIN
    SELECT NVL(MAX(TO_NUMBER(SUBSTR(EMP_NO,2))), 0) INTO MAX_PKEY_VALUE
FROM EMP_MSTR;
    NEW_PKEY_VALUE := TO_CHAR((TO_NUMBER(MAX_PKEY_VALUE) + 1));
    :NEW.EMP_NO := 'E' || NEW_PKEY_VALUE;
END;
```

Output:

Trigger created.

Since the EMP_NO is generated automatically, the user must insert values in all columns **except** the EMP_NO column.

INSERT INTO EMP_MSTR (BRANCH_NO, FNAME, MNAME, LNAME, DEPT, DESIG, MNGR_NO)

VALUES('B1', 'Ivan', 'Nelson', 'Bayross', 'Administration', 'Managing Director', NULL);

Output:

```
1 row created.
```

Generating Primary Key Using A Lookup Table

A lookup table with one column that holds the next primary key value can be created and a database trigger can be written to retrieve the value from the lookup table. The value so retrieved can be inserted into table and the lookup table can be updated such that it holds the **next** primary key value.

Example:

Creating Lookup Table

CREATE TABLE pkey_lookup (pkey_value **VARCHAR2**(10));

Output:

```
Table created.
```

Create Database Trigger

```
CREATE OR REPLACE TRIGGER BRANCH_NO_GENERATION
    BEFORE INSERT ON BRANCH_MSTR
        FOR EACH ROW
DECLARE
    LOOKUP_PKEY_VALUE VARCHAR2(10);
    NEW_PKEY_VALUE VARCHAR2(10);
BEGIN
    BEGIN
        SELECT PKEY_VALUE INTO LOOKUP_PKEY_VALUE FROM PKEY_LOOKUP;
    EXCEPTION
        WHEN NO_DATA_FOUND THEN LOOKUP_PKEY_VALUE := 'B1';
    END;
    :new.BRANCH_NO := LOOKUP_PKEY_VALUE;
```

```
        NEW_PKEY_VALUE := TO_NUMBER(SUBSTR(LOOKUP_PKEY_VALUE, 2, 1)) +
            1;
        LOOKUP_PKEY_VALUE := 'B' || NEW_PKEY_VALUE;
        IF LOOKUP_PKEY_VALUE = 'B2' THEN
            INSERT INTO PKEY_LOOKUP VALUES (LOOKUP_PKEY_VALUE);
        ELSE
            UPDATE PKEY_LOOKUP SET PKEY_VALUE = LOOKUP_PKEY_VALUE;
        END IF;
END;
```

Output:

Trigger created.

Since the **BRANCH_NO** is generated automatically, the user must insert values in all columns **except** the **BRANCH_NO** column.

INSERT INTO BRANCH_MSTR (NAME) VALUES('Vile Parle (HO)');

Output:

```
1 row created.
```

DBMS_SQL

Processing Of An SQL Sentence In The Oracle Engine

When an SQL sentence is fired from the SQL prompt of a client machine, it travels down the network and reaches the Oracle Server. The SQL statement received by the Oracle engine is treated as a string, which is broken up into words that can be categorized as:

- Oracle verbs like SELECT, INSERT, UPDATE and DELETE
- Oracle objects like user name, table names, column names, and so on

What Is Parsing?

Oracle verbs used in the SQL statement are compared with the verbs in the Oracle **Parse Tree** and checked for syntax. This is done to ensure that the verbs used in the SQL sentence are not only appropriate, but are also placed at correct positions.

Once the SQL verbs and their positions is found correct, the Oracle engine then checks whether the Oracle objects are available in the database and the user who has fired the SQL sentence has valid permissions to use them. In order to perform this check, the Oracle engine references an appropriate Data Dictionary.

Tip

The DBA can locate data dictionary information through System Views, which are held within the Oracle database. These views maintain reference to the Data Dictionary. A user can view the data in the Data Dictionary by executing a select statement on various Oracle system views.

These tables can be described only if the connection is made using **user name** as **SYS** and a **password** as set by the DBA.

The following is an example of a system table held in the Oracle database.

Example:

DESC all_users;

Output:

Name	Null?	Type
USERNAME	NOT NULL	VARCHAR2 (30)
USER_ID	NOT NULL	NUMBER
CREATED	NOT NULL	DATE

If an error is encountered in Oracle verbs or Oracle objects, the Oracle engine raises an exception handler. The exception handler is a block of code that locates the error number and its corresponding error description from the Data Dictionary and sends the appropriate error no and message to the client.

Example:

Wrong Syntax - Error Encountered In Oracle Verbs

SELECT * BRANCH_MSTR;

Output:

```
SELECT * BRANCH_MSTR
         *
ERROR at line 1:
ORA-00923: FROM keyword not found where expected
```

Example:

Column Name Is Invalid - Error Encountered In Oracle Data Directory

SELECT BRANCH_NO, BRANCH_NAME **FROM** BRANCH_MSTR;

Output:

```
SELECT BRANCH_NO, BRANCH_NAME FROM BRANCH_MSTR
                             *
ERROR at line 1:
ORA-00904: "BRANCH_NAME": invalid identifier
```

The process of breaking the SQL sentence into words and then checking them for syntax and object privileges is called **Parsing**.

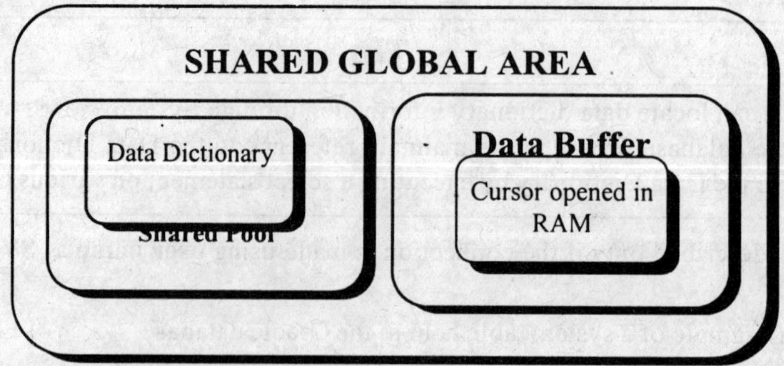

Diagram 18.3: Opening of Cursor in SGA.

Opening A Cursor

If no errors are encountered, the Oracle engine must first reserve space in the Shared Global Area to store data sent by the client if the statement is an INSERT, UPDATE or a DELETE. In case the SQL sentence sent by the client is a SELECT statement then the Oracle engine needs to reserve space for storing data retrieved from the table into memory.

Server RAM

Active Data Set

ACCT_NO	TYPE	CURBAL

Diagram 18.4: Data Binding.

In either of the cases, the area that is allocated is called a **Cursor**. The Oracle engine maintains a pointer to this memory location so that the pointer can be used for further manipulation. The cursor pointer that is maintained by the Oracle engine is called the **Cursor Handle**.

What Is Data Binding?

Based on the SQL statement the cursor is divided into rows and columns, each cursor column is mapped to the Select list specified in the SQL statement for one or more tables. The process of dividing the cursor into appropriate columns as per the SELECT list is called as **Binding**.

Defining A Column

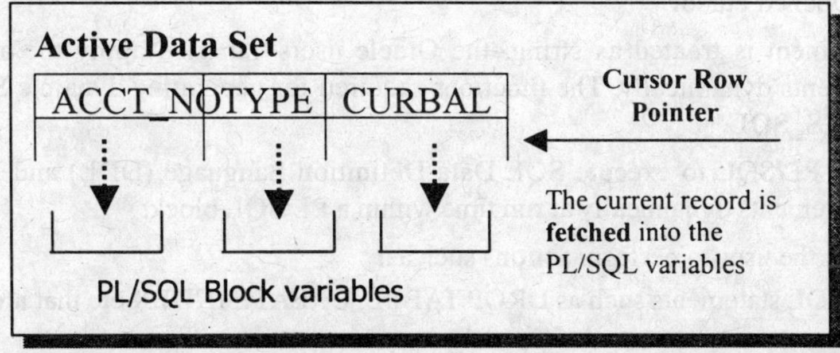

Diagram 18.5: Assigning cursor values to PL/SQL variables.

If a select statement is currently being executed from the SQL prompt, the Oracle engine must retrieve data from table on the hard disk and store it in the opened cursor on the server. The Oracle engine then retrieves one row at a time from the cursor and sends the same to the client machine where each row is printed on the VDU screen.

Thus a set of variables must be defined and mapped to the cursor columns before data is fetched from the cursor. The mapping of variables with the cursor columns is termed as **Defining a column**.

Executing A Query And Fetching Data From The Underlying Tables Into The Cursor

Once the required column and cursor settings are made, data is retrieved from the underlying tables. The process of retrieving data into the cursor is done is called **Query Execution**.

Positioning The Cursor On A Specific Row

Once data is retrieved and held in the cursor, the **row focus** must be set to a specific row starting with row 1. The process of row positioning is called **Row Fetching**.

Getting Values From The Specified Row

Once the row pointer is positioned as desired the cursor column values must be assigned to memory variables.

Processing Of Data

Once cursor column values are assigned to memory variables, they can be used for further data processing.

Closing The Cursor

Once the required processing on data retrieved from the table is completed, the cursor memory area must be freed. This is achieved by closing the cursor.

Thus for any SQL statement Oracle must perform following steps:

- ❑ Open an area in memory and maintain a pointer to that memory location
- ❑ Parse the SQL statement for syntax and Object privileges
- ❑ Bind the select list columns to the cursor columns
- ❑ Define variables to fetch data from the cursor variables
- ❑ Execute the query i.e. fetch data from the tables into the cursor columns
- ❑ Fetch data one row at a time
- ❑ Get cursor column values for a specific row into memory variables
- ❑ Perform required processing
- ❑ Close the Opened cursor

Since the SQL statement is treated as string, the Oracle users can also apply the above technique to generate SQL statements dynamically. The functions required for generating dynamic SQL are stored in a package named **DBMS_SQL**.

This package allows PL/SQL to execute SQL Data Definition Language (DDL) and Data Manipulation Language (DML) statements dynamically at run time within a PL/SQL block.

Dynamic SQL allows the user to perform actions such as:

- ❑ Executing DDL statements such as DROP TABLE, CREATE INDEX etc that are not legal in native PL/SQL
- ❑ Executing a query based on column and table information specified by the user at runtime

Note

To use the **DBMS_SQL** package, the user will require appropriate database privileges.

General Flow Of Dynamic SQL

In order to execute any dynamic SQL with DBMS_SQL package, the following steps must be followed:

1. **Opening a cursor:** When a cursor is opened, the Oracle engine sets aside a valid cursor structure for use with future **DBMS_SQL** calls. The Oracle engine returns an **integer** cursor handle to this cursor. This handle is used for all future calls to the **DMBS_SQL** modules for this dynamic SQL statement. This is done using the **OPEN_CURSOR** function.

Note

 This cursor is completely distinct from normal, native PL/SQL cursors.

The specification for the function is:

```
FUNCTION OPEN_CURSOR RETURN <integer>;
```

Example:

```
CREATE PROCEDURE RAISE (vACCT_NO IN VARCHAR2, vINCBY IN NUMBER) IS
    CURSOR_HANDLE INTEGER;
    ACCT_UPDATED INTEGER;
BEGIN
    CURSOR_HANDLE := DBMS_SQL.OPEN_CURSOR;
        . . . PROCESSING . . .
END;
```

2. **Parse the SQL statement:** The Oracle engine must parse the SQL statement before bind variable values and column structures are specified for the SQL statement. The parse phase verifies that the SQL sentence is properly constructed. It then associates the SQL statement with the cursor handle. This is done using the PARSE procedure

The specification for this procedure is as follows:

CREATE PROCEDURE PARSE(CURSOR_HANDLE **IN INTEGER**, SQL_SENTENCE **IN VARCHAR2**, LANGUAGE_FLAG **IN INTEGER);**

where,

CURSOR_HANDLE	Is the handle or pointer to the cursor originally returned by a call to the OPEN_CURSOR,
SQL SENTENCE	Is the statement to be parsed
LANGUAGE_FLAG	Is a flag that determines how the Oracle 9i server will handle the statement.

There are three valid options for the language flag:

- **DBMS_SQL.V6**: Use the Version 6 behavior when processing the statement.
- **DBMS_SQL.V7**: Use the Version 7 behavior.
- **DBMS_SQL.NATIVE**: Use the normal behavior for the database to which the program is connected.

Example:

```
CREATE PROCEDURE RAISE (vACCT_NO IN VARCHAR2, vINCBY IN NUMBER) IS
CURSOR_HANDLE INTEGER;
ACCT_UPDATED INTEGER;
BEGIN
    CURSOR_HANDLE := DBMS_SQL.OPEN_CURSOR;
```

```
    DBMS_SQL.PARSE (CURSOR_HANDLE, 'UPDATE ACCT_MSTR SET CURBAL =
    CURBAL + :INCBY_AMOUNT WHERE ACCT_NO = :ACCTNO', DBMS_SQL.V7);
        ...PROCESSING...
END;
```

3. **Bind all host variables:** If the SQL statement contains references to host PL/SQL variables, placeholders for those variables must be included in the SQL statement by prefacing their names with a colon. For example, :salary. The actual value for that variable must then be bound into the SQL sentence. This is done using the **BIND_VARIABLE** procedure.

The overload specification supports four data types as follows:

PROCEDURE BIND_VARIABLE (CURSOR_HANDLE **IN INTEGER**, VARIABLE_NAME **IN VARCHAR2**, VALUE **IN INTEGER**);

PROCEDURE BIND_VARIABLE (CURSOR_HANDLE **IN INTEGER**, VARIABLE_NAME **IN VARCHAR2**, VALUE **IN DATE**);

PROCEDURE BIND_VARIABLE (CURSOR_HANDLE **IN INTEGER**, VARIABLE_NAME **IN VARCHAR2**, VALUE **IN VARCHAR2**);

where,

CURSOR_HANDLE	Is the handle or pointer to the cursor originally returned by a call to the OPEN_CURSOR,
VARIABLE_NAME	Is the name of the host variable included in the SQL statement passed to PARSE
VALUE	Is the value to be bound to that variable.

Example:

```
CREATE PROCEDURE RAISE (vACCT_NO IN VARCHAR2, vINCBY IN NUMBER)
IS
    CURSOR_HANDLE INTEGER;
    ACCT_UPDATED INTEGER;
BEGIN
    CURSOR_HANDLE := DBMS_SQL.OPEN_CURSOR;
    DBMS_SQL.PARSE (CURSOR_HANDLE, 'UPDATE ACCT_MSTR SET CURBAL =
    CURBAL + :INCBY_AMOUNT WHERE ACCT_NO = :ACCTNO', DBMS_SQL.V7);
    DBMS_SQL.BIND_VARIABLE (CURSOR_HANDLE, ':INCBY_AMOUNT', vINCBY);
    DBMS_SQL.BIND_VARIABLE (CURSOR_HANDLE, ':ACCTNO', vACCT_NO);
        . . . PROCESSING. . . .
END;
```

4. **Define columns in the SELECT statement:** Each column in the SELECT statement must be defined. This step sets up a correspondence between the expressions in the list of the SQL statement and local PL/SQL variables receiving the values when a row is fetched. This step is roughly equivalent to the **INTO** clause of an implicit SELECT statement in PL/SQL. This is done using the COLUMN_VALUE procedure. The overloaded specification for the procedure is:

CREATE PROCEDURE COLUMN_VALUE(CURSOR_HANDLE **IN INTEGER**, POSITION **IN INTEGER**, VALUE **OUT DATE** [, COLUMN_ERROR **OUT NUMBER**] [, ACTUAL_LENGTH **OUT INTEGER**]);

```
CREATE PROCEDURE COLUMN_VALUE(CURSOR_HANDLE IN INTEGER, POSITION
                 IN INTEGER, VALUE OUT NUMBER [, COLUMN_ERROR
                 OUT NUMBER] [, ACTUAL_LENGTH OUT INTEGER] );
CREATE PROCEDURE COLUMN_VALUE(CURSOR_HANDLE IN INTEGER, POSITION
                 IN INTEGER, VALUE OUT VARCHAR2 [, COLUMN_ERROR
                 OUT NUMBER] [, ACTUAL_LENGTH OUT INTEGER] );
CREATE PROCEDURE COLUMN_VALUE(CURSOR_HANDLE IN INTEGER, POSITION
                 IN INTEGER, VALUE OUT RAW [, COLUMN_ERROR
                 OUT NUMBER] [, ACTUAL_LENGTH OUT INTEGER] );
CREATE PROCEDURE COLUMN_VALUE(CURSOR_HANDLE IN INTEGER, POSITION
                 IN INTEGER, VALUE OUT ROWID [, COLUMN_ERROR
                 OUT NUMBER] [, ACTUAL_LENGTH OUT INTEGER] );
```

where,

CURSOR_HANDLE	Is the handle or pointer to the cursor originally returned by a call to the OPEN_CURSOR,
POSITION	Is the relative position of the column in the SELECT list
VALUE	Is a local variable that will receive the outgoing value.

There are two **optional** parameters:

COLUMN_ERROR	Returns an error code for the specified value (the value might be too large for the variable, for instance)
ACTUAL_LENGTH	Returns the actual length of the returned value before any truncation takes place. This could be due to difference in the size between the retrieved value in the cursor and the variable.

A COLUMN_VALUE procedure is called after a row has been fetched to transfer the value from the SELECT list of the cursor into a local variable.

Note

 The column must be defined using the DEFINE_COLUMN procedure. The defined column is then passed to the COLUMN_VALUE procedure along with the cursor handle and the cursor column position.

The DEFINE_COLUMN Procedure

When a **DBMS_SQL.PARSE** procedure is used to process a SELECT statement to pass values from the database columns to the local variables, the columns or expressions in the SELECT list must be associated with the local variables. The **DEFINE_COLUMN** procedure is used for the purpose.

The **DEFINE_COLUMN** procedure is called after the call to **PARSE** is made. After the execution of the SELECT sentence the **COLUMN_VALUE** procedure is used to grab a column value from the SELECT list and pass it to appropriate local variables.

The overloaded specification for the procedure is:

CREATE PROCEDURE DEFINE_COLUMN (CURSOR_HANDLE **IN INTEGER**, POSITION **IN INTEGER**, COLUMN **IN DATE);**

CREATE PROCEDURE DEFINE_COLUMN (CURSOR_HANDLE **IN INTEGER**, POSITION **IN INTEGER**, COLUMN **IN NUMBER);**

CREATE PROCEDURE DEFINE_COLUMN (CURSOR_HANDLE **IN INTEGER**, POSITION **IN VARCHAR2**, COLUMN **IN INTEGER**, COLUMN_SIZE **IN INTEGER);**

where,

CURSOR_HANDLE	Is the handle or pointer to the cursor originally returned by a call to OPEN_CURSOR.
POSITION	Is the relative position of the column in the SELECT list
COLUMN	Is a local variable or expression whose data type determines the data type of the column being defined.

Note

When the column is defined as a varchar2 column, the maximum expected size of the column value must be specified.

column_size IN integer

5. **Execute the SQL statement:** The SQL statement associated with the specified cursor is to be executed. The **EXECUTE** command returns the number of rows processed by the SQL sentence if the statement is an UPDATE, INSERT, or DELETE. In any other case the return value must be ignored. This is done by using the **EXECUTE** function.

   The specification of the function is as follows:

   ```
   FUNCTION EXECUTE (<CursorHandle IN INTEGER>) RETURN INTEGER;
   ```

6. **Fetch rows for Dynamic SQL query:** This is similar to the **FETCH** statement for regular PL/SQL cursors. It fetches the next row from the cursor.

   The specification for the function is:

   ```
   FUNCTION FETCH_ROWS (<CursorHandle> IN <INTEGER>) RETURN <NUMBER>;
   ```

   The function returns **0** when there are no more rows to fetch. The **FETCH_ROWS** function can therefore be used like the **%FOUND** (or **%NOTFOUND**) attribute is used in normal cursors.

Example:

In case of a normal or static:

```
FETCH ACCT_CUR INTO ACCT_REC;
IF ACCT_CUR %NOTFOUND THEN
        ...PROCESSING...
END IF;
```

In case of DBMS_SQL used to fetch rows:

```
IF DBMS_SQL.FETCH_ROWS (CURSOR_HANDLE) > 0 THEN
        . . . PROCESSING . . .
END IF;
```

7. **Retrieve values from the execution of the Dynamic SQL:** If the SQL statement is a QUERY, then the values from the **SELECT** expression list can be retrieved using **COLUMN_VALUE** procedure. If the call is made to the procedure using a PL/SQL block then the **VARIABLE_VALUE** procedure is used to retrieve the values returned by the procedure.

   The overloading specification for this procedure is as follows:

```
CREATE PROCEDURE VARIABLE_VALUE (CURSOR_HANDLE IN INTEGER, VARIABLE_NAME
                                    IN VARCHAR2, VALUE OUT NUMBER);
PROCEDURE VARIABLE_VALUE (CURSOR_HANDLE IN INTEGER, VARIABLE_NAME
                                    IN VARCHAR2, VALUE OUT DATE);
PROCEDURE VARIABLE_VALUE (CURSOR_HANDLE IN INTEGER, VARIABLE_NAME
                                    IN VARCHAR2, VALUE OUT VARCHAR2);
```

where,

CURSOR_HANDLE	Is the handle or pointer to the cursor originally returned by a call to OPEN_CURSOR.
VARIABLE_NAME	Is the name of the host variable included in the PL/SQL statement passed to **PARSE**.
VALUE	Is a local variable that receives value from the cursor.

8. **Close the cursor:** Using the **CLOSE_CURSOR** procedure, the specified cursor is closed. All memory associated with the cursor is released. Also the **cursor_handle** is set to **NULL**. The **cursor_handle** is the handle or pointer to the cursor which was originally returned by a call to **OPEN_CURSOR**.

   The specification for the procedure is as follows:

```
CREATE PROCEDURE CLOSE_CURSOR (cursor_handle IN OUT INTEGER);
```

Example:

```
BEGIN
        . . . PROCESSING . . .
    DBMS_SQL.CLOSE_CURSOR (CURSOR_HANDLE);
END;
```

Applications Using Dynamic SQL

The following are the examples of certain areas where Dynamic SQL can be used:

1. Primary Key Validation
2. Data Definition Language programs

Primary Key Validation

Example:

While developing any commercial application, using Oracle, there is an input/output validation that checks that the value entered in the Primary key column of the table is unique. Each time a record is inserted in the table, unique and NOT NULL value checks have to be performed. This means scanning through the **Primary Key** column and verify if the newly inserted value already exists or not. If a corresponding value is found, the entire record needs to be rejected and appropriate message displayed to the user.

This check needs to be carried out irrespective of the table on which data entry is taking place. To avoid redundant code a database function can be created and stored. This function being a generic function will accept the table name, column name/s when it is called and will return a numeric value of **0** or **1** depending upon whether a corresponding value exists in the table or not. It will return **1** if a match is found and **0** if no matching row is found.

The function can be called in any PL/SQL block where a primary key check is to be carried out and depending upon the return value of the function further processing can be done. An insert is allowed to go through if the function returns a 0, else the Insert is prevented and an appropriate error message is displayed.

Solution:

```
CREATE OR REPLACE FUNCTION PKEY_CHK (TABLE_NAME IN VARCHAR2, COL_NAME
                                     IN VARCHAR2, COL_VALUE IN
                                     VARCHAR2) RETURN NUMBER AS
/* Declaring a handle to the Dynamic SQL cursor. */
    CURSOR_HANDLE INTEGER;
/* Variable that holds the return value from the EXECUTE. */
    EXECUTE_FEEDBACK INTEGER;

BEGIN
/* Open new cursor and return cursor ID. */
    CURSOR_HANDLE := DBMS_SQL.OPEN_CURSOR;

/* Parse the query with the columns in the SELECT list. */
    DBMS_SQL.PARSE (CURSOR_HANDLE, 'SELECT ' || COL_NAME || ' FROM
    ' || TABLE_NAME || ' WHERE ' || COL_NAME || ' = ''' || COL_VALUE
    || '''', DBMS_SQL.V7);

/* Execute the SQL statement. */
    EXECUTE_FEEDBACK := DBMS_SQL.EXECUTE(CURSOR_HANDLE);

/* Returning values 0 or 1 depending upon whether the select returned a
row or not and closing the cursor. */
    IF DBMS_SQL.FETCH_ROWS (CURSOR_HANDLE) = 0 THEN
        DBMS_SQL.CLOSE_CURSOR (CURSOR_HANDLE);
        RETURN 0;
    ELSE
        DBMS_SQL.CLOSE_CURSOR (CURSOR_HANDLE);
```

```
        RETURN 1;
    END IF;
END;
```

Output:

```
Function created.
```

Calling the above function in a PL/SQL block

```
DECLARE
/* Declaring a variable that will hold the return value of the function.
*/
    ROWS_FOUND NUMBER;
BEGIN
/* Calling the function PKEY_CHK that takes the table name and column
name/s as the IN parameter and returns a number. */
    ROWS_FOUND := PKEY_CHK ('&TABLENAME', '&COLUMNNAME',
    '&COLUMNVALUE');
/* Displaying message to the user */
    IF ROWS_FOUND = 0 THEN
        DBMS_OUTPUT.PUT_LINE ('The column value is unique');
    ELSE
        DBMS_OUTPUT.PUT_LINE ('The column value is not unique');
    END IF;
END;
```

Output:

```
Enter value for tablename: ACCT_MSTR
Enter value for columnname: ACCT_NO
Enter value for columnvalue: SB1
```

Output: (Continued)

```
old    6:  ROWS_FOUND  :=  PKEY_CHK  ('&TABLENAME',  '&COLUMNNAME',
'&COLUMNVALUE');
new   6:  ROWS_FOUND := PKEY_CHK ('ACCT_MSTR', 'ACCT_NO', 'SB1');
The column value is not unique
PL/SQL procedure successfully completed.
```

Data Definition Language Programs

A regular PL/SQL code block cannot include references to database objects such as tables and stored procedures. If CREATE TABLE syntax was being executed with a regular PL/SQL code block, the PL/SQL compiler would check the code and try to validate that all the tables are present before executing the PL/SQL code block. Since the table does not exist the compiler will throw an error.

Example:

```
BEGIN
    CREATE TABLE ACCT_MSTR (ACCT_NO VARCHAR2 (10), . . .); —ILLEGAL
        . . .
END;
```

Example:

Similarly in the next example, the compiler cannot bind the table reference in the DROP TABLE statement because the table name is unknown until the procedure is executed.

```
CREATE PROCEDURE DROP_TABLE (TABLE_NAME IN VARCHAR2) AS
BEGIN
      DROP TABLE TABLE_NAME; —ILLEGAL
            ...
END;
```

This is where Dynamic SQL comes to the rescue.

Example:

Write a procedure that drops the objects specified by the user. This procedure also takes wildcards for object names. For example, if the user wants to drop all object with name like 'FD%'. The following procedure uses both static and dynamic SQL.

Solution:

```
CREATE OR REPLACE PROCEDURE DROP_OBJECT_PROC (TYPE_IN IN VARCHAR2,
NAME_IN IN VARCHAR2) IS
/* The static cursor retrieving the object. */
      CURSOR OBJ_CUR IS
            SELECT OBJECT_NAME, OBJECT_TYPE FROM USER_OBJECTS
                  WHERE OBJECT_NAME LIKE UPPER(NAME_IN)
                        AND OBJECT_TYPE LIKE UPPER(TYPE_IN) ORDER BY
                        OBJECT_NAME;
/* Declaring a handle to the Dynamic SQL cursor. */
      CURSOR_HANDLE INTEGER;
BEGIN
/* For each matching object. */
      FOR OBJ_REC IN OBJ_CUR
      LOOP
      /* OPEN NEW CURSOR AND RETURN CURSOR ID. */
            CURSOR_HANDLE := DBMS_SQL.OPEN_CURSOR;
      /* CONSTRUCT THE SQL STATEMENT AND PARSE IT IN VERSION 7 MODE. */
            DBMS_SQL.PARSE (CURSOR_HANDLE, 'DROP ' ||
            OBJ_REC.OBJECT_TYPE || ' ' || OBJ_REC.OBJECT_NAME,
            DBMS_SQL.V7);
      /* CLOSE THE CURSOR. */
            DBMS_SQL.CLOSE_CURSOR (CURSOR_HANDLE);
      END LOOP;
END;
```

Output:

```
Procedure created.
```

Calling The Above Procedure In A PL/SQL Block

```
BEGIN
```

```
/* Call to the procedure DROP_OBJECT_PROC. The two parameters the procedure
takes is the type of object and the name of the object.*/
     DROP_OBJECT_PROC ('SEQUENCE', 'CUST_SEQ');
     DBMS_OUTPUT.PUT_LINE ('Object Dropped Successfully');
END;
```

Output:

```
Object Dropped Successfully
PL/SQL procedure successfully completed.
```

Self Review Questions

Fill in the Blanks

1. A ____________ or __________ is a logically grouped set of SQL and PL/SQL statements that perform a specific task.
2. Procedures and Functions are stored in the ______________ __________.
3. When the procedure or function is invoked, the Oracle engine loads the compiled procedure or function in the memory area called the ______________.
4. Only ________ copy of procedure needs to be loaded for execution by multiple users.
5. A ______________ is an Oracle object, which holds other objects within it.
6. A package has usually two components, a ____________ and a ________.
7. The body of a package contains the definition of ________ objects that are declared in the specification.
8. A package can include ________________ and ______________.
9. The ______________ clause is used to recreate the package specification without loosing any grants that already exist.
10. All packages can be recompiled by using an Oracle utility called ______________.
11. Multiple procedures that are declared with the same name are called ______________.
12. A ________ trigger is fired each time a row in the table is affected by the triggering statement.
13. ____________ ____________ should be used when a triggering statement affects rows in a table but the processing required is completely independent of the number of rows affected.
14. __________ trigger executes the trigger action after the triggering statement is executed.
15. The Oracle engine provides a procedure named ______________ that allows programmers to issue user-defined error messages.
16. The Oracle engine provides an object called a ___________ that generates numeric values starting with a given value and with an increment as specified by the user.
17. Oracle verbs used in the SQL statement are compared with the verbs in the Oracle __________ __________ and checked for syntax.
18. The process of breaking the SQL sentence into words and then checking them for syntax and object privileges is called __________.
19. The process of dividing the cursor into appropriate columns as per the SELECT list is called as ______________.

20. A ______________ procedure is called after a row has been fetched to transfer the value from the SELECT list of the cursor into a local variable.

True or False

21. An Oracle exception handler can be redirected to the executable section of the procedure or function.
22. One cannot transfer the flow of execution from the Exception Handling part to the Executable part.
23. The Oracle engine checks if the user who called the procedure or function has the write privilege for the procedure or function.
24. A function or a procedure can return only one value to the calling PL/SQL code block.
25. All users who have execute permissions on the Oracle Database can use the package.
26. A package cannot contain a subprogram that requires input from another PL/SQL block to perform its programmed processes successfully.
27. Packages enable the overloading of procedures and functions when required.
28. The objects declared privately in the package body are not accessible to other objects outside the package.
29. Recompiling a package does not recompile all objects defined within the package.
30. Triggers are fired implicitly.
31. A trigger is executed implicitly by the Oracle engine itself upon modification of an associated table or its data.
32. A trigger restriction specifies a Boolean (logical) expression that must be False for the trigger to fire.
33. BEFORE and AFTER apply to only the statement triggers.
34. The PL/SQL block in the trigger cannot contain transaction control SQL statements i.e. COMMIT, ROLLBACK, and SAVEPOINT.
35. An application can call 'raise_application_error' only while executing a stored subprogram like stored procedures, functions and database triggers.

Hands On Exercises

1. Create a function that accepts a Client_No and checks if the Client_No exists in the table CLIENT_MASTER. If the Client_No exists, display a message Valid Client and if the Client_No does not exist then display an appropriate error message.
2. Drop the function created in exercise1.
3. Create a package named **myPackage** that will hold the function created in the exercise1. Write the package specification and package body for the package **myPackage**.
4. Write an Update trigger on CLIENT_MASTER table. The system should keep track of the records that are being updated. The old values of the updated record should be added in the AUDIT_TRAIL table.

Table Name:	**AUDIT_TRAIL**			
Column Name	**Data Type**	**Size**	**Default**	**Attributes**
Client_no	Varchar2	6		
Name	Varchar2	20		
Bal_due	Number	10,2		
Operation	Varchar2	8		
Userid	Varchar2	20		
Odate	Date			

5. **Delete the trigger created in exercise 4.**

19

Import And Export Of Data

An Overview

Oracle provides two utilities, which are complementary to each other. They are the EXPORT and IMPORT Utilities. The export utility is used to perform backups and the Import utility is to perform a restore of the backup taken by the Export utility.

The export utility is also known as the Logical Backup utility. The reason is that the DBA can take a backup of Logical objects within a database such as Tables, Views, and so on. The export of these logical database objects can be taken with or without data being resident in them.

The DBA can use the export utility to perform various tasks such as:

- Saving a database object's definition in Oracle Binary file format.
- To move data from one Oracle database version to another version.
- Create a copy of the entire data of a database **or** of selective data within the database to an export file, which is in Oracle Binary file format.

Using The EXPORT Utility

Export utility can be invoked at the operating system prompt by typing the following command.

For Windows NT:

```
C:\ORANT\BIN>  EXP80
```

For Unix:

```
$ exp
```

Different Modes of Export

Following are three modes in which a DBA can export database objects.

- Full Database Mode
- User Mode
- Table Mode

Full Database Mode

When an export utility is performed using **full database** mode, the entire database's objects (except the objects owned by the user SYS) are exported to the export **dump** file. This dump file will contain the exported object's business data, and the Object Definitions (DDL statements) of the objects exported.

The use of this mode is restricted to users with DBA privileges **or** to users bound to the EXP_FULL_DATABASE role.

User Mode

When selecting USER mode for an export, all the objects owned by a particular user can be exported. In fact as the name suggests, this is a mode in which the export dump file is created which contains objects **bound** to specific users of the database.

Table Mode

When selecting table mode for an export, a DBA can export database table objects on a table-by-table basis. In this mode, the DBA can also export a **specific portion** of a table.

Different Levels of Export

There are three levels of **logical** exports that can be performed on a database.

- ❑ Complete
- ❑ Cumulative
- ❑ Incremental

Complete Exports

This is the desired level of exports for a sound backup strategy. A complete export is **same as** a full database export.

Cumulative Exports

Cumulative export is where the export is performed on tables that have changed since the last Cumulative or Complete Export.

Incremental Exports

Incremental Export is where the export is performed on tables that have changed since the last Incremental, Cumulative or Complete Export.

Note
 Oracle recommends taking a **full export** of a database at regular intervals.

Using The Import Utility

The import utility is used for recovering the business data of select database objects. The Import utility can read only the data stored from an Oracle Export dump file.

Different Modes of Import

The Import utility has the same modes that are available with the export utility. They are:

- ❑ Full database mode
- ❑ User mode
- ❑ Table mode

Full Database Mode

In full database mode, a DBA can import data from the Export file, which was taken with the option of Full database export. Only a DBA or the user with IMP_FULL_DATABASE privileges can import data using full database mode.

User Mode

In user mode, all database objects belonging to a particular user can be imported.

Table Mode

In Table mode, the DBA can import data on a table-by-table basis.

Answer To Self Review Questions

14. SQL Performance Tuning

	Fill in the Blanks		True or False
1.	Indexing	37.	False
2.	two	38.	False
3.	ROWID	39.	True
4.	Data Blocks	40.	False
5.	Duplicate	41.	True
6.	Simple	42.	True
7.	Composite	43.	False
8.	Composite Unique	44.	True
9.	REBUILD NOREVERSE	45.	False
10.	Bitmap	46.	True
11.	global	47.	False
12.	Local	48.	False
13.	USER_IND_COLUMNS	49.	True
14.	subquery	50.	True
15.	Parent SQL	51.	False
16.	View	52.	False
17.	Updateable	53.	True
18.	cluster	54.	False
19.	cluster key	55.	True
20.	Columns	56.	False
21.	INCREMENT BY	57.	True
22.	NOMINVALUE	58.	True
23.	MAXVALUE	59.	False
24.	NOCACHE	60.	True
25.	response time	61.	False
26.	complex	62.	False
27.	simple	63.	True
28.	STORAGE	64.	False

29.	CLUSTER	65.	True
30.	ROLLBACK SEGMENT	66.	False
31.	MASTER	67.	True
32.	FORCE	68.	True
33.	WITH ROWID	69.	False
34.	subqueries	70.	True
35.	ALTER SNAPSHOT	71.	False
36.	COMPLETE	72.	True

15. Oracle Object Oriented Features

	Fill in the Blanks		True or False
1.	Objects	22.	False
2.	standards	23.	False
3.	de facto	24.	True
4.	object	25.	False
5.	Abstract	26.	False
6.	standard	27.	True
7.	nested	28.	True
8.	VARRAYS	29.	False
9.	LOB	30.	True
10.	CLOB	31.	False
11.	BFILE	32.	True
12.	varying	33.	False
13.	References	34.	False
14.	Object	35.	True
15.	methods	36.	True
16.	data	37.	False
17.	attributes	38.	True
18.	constructor	39.	False
19.	SCOPE	40.	True
20.	ROWID	41.	True
21.	OID	42.	False

16. Introduction to PL/SQL

	Fill in the Blanks		True or False
1.	call	23.	True
2.	block-structured	24.	False
3.	declaration	25.	False
4.	Exception	26.	True
5.	End	27.	False
6.	Lexical Units	28.	True
7.	literal	29.	False

8.	period	30.	True
9.	Numeric	31.	False
10.	%TYPE	32.	False
11.	binary	33.	True
12.	2GB	34.	False
13.	Rowids	35.	True
14.	ROWID_BLOCK_NUMBER	36.	True
15.	ROWID_TO_ABSOLUTE_FNO	37.	False
16.	BLOB (Binary LOB)	38.	True
17.	locator	39.	False
18.	Locator	40.	False
19.	PUT_LINE	41.	False
20.	ROWID_TO_RESTRICTED		
21.	loop		
22.	GOTO		

17. *Cursors and Exceptions*

Fill in the Blanks		True or False	
1.	Active Data Set	15.	False
2.	row pointer	16.	True
3.	Implicit	17.	False
4.	Explicit cursors	18.	False
5.	SQL%ISOPEN	19.	True
6.	End Loop	20.	False
7.	fetch	21.	True
8.	%ROWCOUNT	22.	False
9.	Parameterized Cursor	23.	True
10.	Exception Handler	24.	False
11.	VALUE_ERROR	25.	True
13.	Pragma	26.	False
14.	user-defined exceptions	27.	True

18. *PL/SQL Database Objects*

Fill in the Blanks		True or False	
1.	procedure, function	21.	False
2.	Oracle database	22.	True
3.	System Global Area	23.	False
4.	one	24.	False
5.	package	25.	True
6.	specification, body	26.	False
7.	public	27.	True
8.	Functions, Procedures	28.	True

9.	OR REPLACE	29.	False
10.	dbms_utility	30.	True
11.	Overloaded Procedures	31.	True
12.	row	32.	False
13.	Statement triggers	33.	False
14.	AFTER	34.	True
15.	raise_application_error	35.	True
16.	sequence		
17.	Parse Tree		
18.	Parsing		
19.	Binding		
20.	COLUMN_VALUE		

Solution To Hands On Exercises

14. SQL Performance Tuning

1. **Writing appropriate SQL statements for the following:**

(a) Creating a simple index idx_Prod on product cost price from the Product_Master table.

```
CREATE INDEX idx_prod ON Product_Master (CostPrice);
```

(b) Creating a sequence inv_seq.

```
CREATE SEQUENCE inv_seq
    INCREMENT BY 3 START WITH 1
    MINVALUE 1 MAXVALUE 9999 CYCLE Cache 4;
```

(c) Create view on OrderNo, OrderDate, OrderStatus of the Sales_Order table and ProductNo,ProductRate and QtyOrdered of Sales_Order_Details.

```
CREATE VIEW vw_Sal_Ord AS
    SELECT s.OrderNo, s.OrderDate, sod.ProductNo, sod.ProductRate, sod.QtyOrdered,
    s.Orderstatus
    FROM Sales_Order s, Sales_Order_Details sod WHERE s.OrderNo = sod.OrderNo;
```

15. Oracle Object Oriented Features

1. **Creating the Address_Ty type:**

(a) **Type Name**: Address_Ty

```
CREATE TYPE Address_Ty AS OBJECT (
    Address1 varchar2(30), Address2 varchar2(30), City varchar2(20),
    PinCode number, State varchar2(20));
```

2. **Creating the Salesman_Master table:**

(a) **Table Name**: Salesman_Master

```
CREATE TABLE Salesman_Master(
    Salesman_no varchar2(6), Salesman_name varchar2(20), Address Address_Ty,
```

SalAmt number(8,2), SaleTrgt number(6,2), SaleAchvd number(6,2),
Remarks varchar2(60));

3. **Inserting data into the Salesman_Master table:**

(a) Data for **Salesman_Master** table

INSERT INTO Salesman_Master
VALUES ('S00001', 'Aman', **Address_Ty**('A/14', 'Worli', 'Mumbai', 400002, 'Maharashtra'), 3000, 100, 50, 'Good');

INSERT INTO Salesman_Master
VALUES ('S00002', 'Omkar', **Address_Ty**('65', 'Nariman', 'Mumbai', 400001, 'Maharashtra'), 3000, 200, 100, 'Good');

INSERT INTO Salesman_Master
VALUES ('S00003', 'Raj', **Address_Ty**('P-7', 'Bandra', 'Mumbai', 400032, 'Maharashtra'), 3000, 200, 100, 'Good');

INSERT INTO Salesman_Master
VALUES ('S00004', 'Ashish', **Address_Ty**('A/5', 'Juhu', 'Bombay', 400044, 'Maharashtra'), 3500, 200, 150, 'Good');

4. **SQL statement for retrieving records from a table:**

(a) Retrieving the list of city and state from Salesman_Master

SELECT sales.address.city, sales.address.state FROM salesman_master sales;

(b) Changing the **CITY** value for salesman who live in Bombay to Chennai

UPDATE Salesman_Master Sales SET Sales.Address.city='Chennai'
WHERE Sales.Address.city='Bombay';

(c) Deleting the record for the salesman who live in **Chennai**

DELETE FROM Salesman_Master Sales WHERE Sales.Address.city='Chennai';

5. **SQL statement for creating object types:**

(a) Creating type Dependent_Ty

CREATE OR REPLACE TYPE Dependent_ty AS OBJECT(Relation varchar2(15),Age number);

(b) Create nested table Dependent_List consisting of Dependent_Ty

CREATE OR REPLACE TYPE Dependent_List AS TABLE OF Dependent_Ty;

(c) Create type Salesman_info_ty with the following columns

CREATE OR REPLACE TYPE Salesman_info_ty AS OBJECT(
id number(5), name varchar2(20), dependents dependent_list);

(d) Create the TABLE Salesman_info of the TYPE Salesman_info_ty

CREATE TABLE Salesman_info OF Salesman_info_ty
NESTED TABLE dependents STORE AS Dependents_ty;

17. *Cursors and Exceptions*

1. Writing a PL/SQL block of code based on conditions:

(a) The entire update operation for all **Item_Id** is rollback, if the value in Bal_Stock becomes negative.

```
DECLARE
/* Cursor Crsr_Item_Rqst retrieves all records from the Item_Requisite
table. */
     CURSOR Crsr_Item_Rqst IS
          SELECT Item_Id, Dept_Code, Quantity FROM Item_Requisite;
/* Cursor Crsr_Item_Mstr accepts the value of Item_Id from the
Item_Master table based on the value passed as a parameter. */
     CURSOR  Crsr_Item_Mstr (num_Item_Id number) IS
          SELECT Item_Id FROM Item_Master WHERE Item_Id =
          num_Item_Id;
 /* Variables that hold data from the cursor Crsr_Item_Rqst. */
     num_ItemId number(4);
     num_DeptCode number;
     num_Qty number(3);
/* Variable that hold data from the cursor Crsr_Item_Mstr. */
     num_Mast_Uptd number(4);
/* Variable to check negative values in Bal_Stock after updation. */
     num_BalStock number;

BEGIN
     num_BalStock := 0;
/* Open the Crsr_Item_Rqst cursor. */
     OPEN Crsr_Item_Rqst;
/* Defining a savepoint */
     SAVEPOINT svpnt_No_Change;

     LOOP
     /* Fetch the records from the Crsr_Item_Rqst cursor. */
          FETCH Crsr_Item_Rqst INTO num_ItemId, num_DeptCode, num_Qty;
          EXIT WHEN Crsr_Item_Rqst%NOTFOUND;
     /* Open the Crsr_Item_Mstr cursor. Note that the value of variable
     passed to the Crsr_Item_Mstr cursor is set to the value of
     Item_Id in the current row of cursor Crsr_Item_Rqst. */
          OPEN Crsr_Item_Mstr (num_ItemId);
          FETCH Crsr_Item_Mstr INTO num_Mast_Uptd;
     /* If the record is found then update quantity else insert a
     record in the Item_Master table. */
          IF Crsr_Item_Mstr%FOUND THEN
          /* If the record is found, then update the Bal_Stock in
          Item_Master table.   */
               UPDATE Item_Master SET BalStock = BalStock - num_Qty
```

```
                    WHERE Item_Id = num_ItemId;
        /* Deleting the record from the Item_Requisite table. */
                DELETE FROM Item_Requisite
                    WHERE Item_Id = num_ItemId AND Dept_Code =
                    num_DeptCode;
        ELSE
                DBMS_OUTPUT.PUT_LINE('Item ' || num_ItemId || ' is
                not available for department ' || num_DeptCode ||
                '!!');
        END IF;
        CLOSE Crsr_Item_Mstr;
    END LOOP;
    CLOSE Crsr_Item_Rqst;
/* Storing the total negative values in BalStock from the 'Item_Master'
table into a variable. */
    SELECT SUM(BalStock) INTO num_BalStock FROM Item_Master WHERE
BalStock < 0;
/* Checking it the value of num_BalStock is equal to zero. */
    IF num_BalStock = 0 THEN
    /* Make the changes permanent. */
        COMMIT;
    ELSE
    /* Undo the changes made to the 'Emp' table. */
        ROLLBACK TO SAVEPOINT svpnt_No_Change;
    END IF;
END;
```

(b) The update operation for a particular **Item_Id** is rollback, if the value in Bal_Stock becomes negative.

```
DECLARE
/* Cursor Crsr_Item_Rqst retrieves all records from the Item_Requisite
table. */
    CURSOR Crsr_Item_Rqst IS
        SELECT Item_Id, Dept_Code, Quantity FROM Item_Requisite;
/* Cursor Crsr_Item_Mstr accepts the value of Item_Id from the
Item_Master table based on the value passed as a parameter. */
    CURSOR Crsr_Item_Mstr (num_Item_Id number) IS
        SELECT Item_Id FROM Item_Master WHERE Item_Id =
        num_Item_Id;
/* Variables that hold data from the cursor Crsr_Item_Rqst. */
    num_ItemId number(4);
    num_DeptCode number;
    num_Qty number(3);
/* Variable that hold data from the cursor Crsr_Item_Mstr. */
    num_Mast_Uptd number(4);
/* Variable to check negative values in Bal_Stock after updation. */
    num_BalStock number;
```

```
BEGIN
     num_BalStock := 0;
/* Open the Crsr_Item_Rqst cursor. */
     OPEN Crsr_Item_Rqst;
     LOOP
     /* Fetch the records from the Crsr_Item_Rqst cursor. */
          FETCH Crsr_Item_Rqst INTO num_ItemId, num_DeptCode, num_Qty;
          EXIT WHEN Crsr_Item_Rqst%NOTFOUND;
     /* Open the Crsr_Item_Mstr cursor. Note that the value of variable
     passed to the Crsr_Item_Mstr cursor is set to the value of
     Item_Id in the current row of cursor Crsr_Item_Rqst. */
          OPEN Crsr_Item_Mstr (num_ItemId);
          FETCH Crsr_Item_Mstr INTO num_Mast_Uptd;
     /* If the record is found then update quantity else insert a
     record in the Item_Master table. */
          IF Crsr_Item_Mstr%FOUND THEN
          /* Defining a savepoint */
               SAVEPOINT svpnt_No_Change;
          /* If the record is found, then update the Bal_Stock in
          Item_Master table. */
               UPDATE Item_Master SET BalStock = BalStock - num_Qty
                    WHERE Item_Id = num_ItemId;
          /* Deleting the record from the Item_Requisite table. */
               DELETE FROM Item_Requisite
                    WHERE Item_Id = num_ItemId AND Dept_Code =
                    num_DeptCode;
          /* Storing the total negative values in Bal_Stock from the
          'Item_Master' table into a variable. */
               SELECT BalStock INTO num_BalStock FROM Item_Master
                    WHERE Item_ID = num_ItemId;
          /*Checking it the value of num_BalStock is equal to zero.*/
               IF num_BalStock < 0 THEN
               /* Undo the changes made to the 'Emp' table. */
                    ROLLBACK TO SAVEPOINT svpnt_No_Change;
               ELSE
               /* Make the changes permanent. */
                    COMMIT;
               END IF;
          ELSE
               DBMS_OUTPUT.PUT_LINE('Item ' || num_ItemId || ' is
               not available for department ' || num_DeptCode ||
               '!!');
          END IF;
          CLOSE Crsr_Item_Mstr;
     END LOOP;
     CLOSE Crsr_Item_Rqst;
```

```
END;
```

2. **Writing SQL code block that raises a user defined exception when business rule is violated. The business rule for CLIENT_MASTER table specifies when the value of Bal_due field is less than 0, handle the exception.**

```
DECLARE
     less_than_target  EXCEPTION;
     mclient_no  Client_Master.Clientno%type;
     mbal_due  Client_Master.Baldue%type;
BEGIN
     SELECT Clientno, Baldue INTO mclient_no, mbal_due FROM
     Client_Master
          WHERE Clientno  = &mclient_no;
     IF mbal_due > 5000 THEN
          RAISE less_than_target;
     END IF;
EXCEPTION
     WHEN less_than_target  THEN
          DBMS_OUTPUT.PUT_LINE ('Balance cannot be less than Rs.0');
END;
```

18. PL/SQL DATABASE OBJECTS

1. **Creating a function that accepts a Client_No and checks if the Client_No exists in the table CLIENT_MASTER. If the Client_No exists, display a message Valid Client and if the Client_No does not exist then display an appropriate error message.**

```
CREATE FUNCTION f_Client_no_chk(vClientno IN varchar2) RETURN number
IS
     dummyClient varchar2(6);
BEGIN
     SELECT client_no INTO dummyclient FROM CLIENT_MASTER
          WHERE client_no = vClientno;
     DBMS_OUTPUT.PUT_LINE('Valid Client');
EXCEPTION
     WHEN NO_DATA_FOUND THEN
          DBMS_OUTPUT.PUT_LINE('Invalid Client');
END;
```

2. **Drop the function created in exercise1.**

   DROP FUNCTION f_Client_no_chk;

3. **Creating a package named myPackage that will hold the function created in the exercise1. Include the package specification and package body for the package myPackage.**

```
CREATE OR REPLACE PACKAGE myPackage AS
     FUNCTION f_Client_no_chk(vClientno IN varchar2) RETURN number;
END myPackage;
/* Package body */
```

```
CREATE OR REPLACE PACKAGE BODY myPackage IS
     FUNCTION f_Client_no_chk(vClientno IN varchar2) RETURN number
     IS
          dummyClient varchar2(6);
     BEGIN
          SELECT client_no INTO dummyclient FROM Client_Master
               WHERE client_no = vClientno;
               DBMS_OUTPUT.PUT_LINE('Valid Client');
     EXCEPTION
          WHEN NO_DATA_FOUND THEN
               DBMS_OUTPUT.PUT_LINE('Invalid Client');
     END;
END myPackage;
```

4. **Writing an UPDATE trigger on CLIENT_MASTER table, which keep track of the records that are being updated. The old values of the updated record are added in the AUDIT_TRAIL table.**

```
CREATE TRIGGER audit_client AFTER UPDATE ON Client_Master
     FOR EACH ROW
DECLARE
     oper varchar2(8);
     client_no varchar2(6);
     name varchar2(20);
     bal_due number(10, 2);
BEGIN
     IF updating THEN
          oper := 'update';
     END IF;
     client_no := :old.client_no;
     name  := :old.name;
     bal_due := :old.bal_due;
     INSERT INTO audit_trail VALUES(client_no, name, bal_due, oper,
     user, sysdate);
END;
```

5. **Deleting the trigger created in exercise 4.**

   DROP TRIGGER audit_client;

Section - VI

Appendix

A. Test Records For Retail Banking

Table Name: BRANCH_MSTR

BRANCH_NO	NAME	BRANCH_NO	NAME
B1	Vile Parle (HO)	B2	Andheri
B3	Churchgate	B4	Mahim
B5	Borivali	B6	Darya Ganj

Table Name: EMP_MSTR

EMP _NO	BRANCH _NO	FNAME	MNAME	LNAME	DEPT	DESIG	MNGR _NO
E1	B1	Ivan	Nelson	Bayross	Administration	Managing Director	
E2	B2	Amit		Desai	Loans & Financing	Finance Manager	
E3	B3	Maya	Mahima	Joshi	Client Servicing	Sales Manager	
E4	B1	Peter	Iyer	Joseph	Loans & Financing	Clerk	E2
E5	B4	Mandhar	Dilip	Dalvi	Marketing	Marketing Manager	
E6	B6	Sonal	Abdul	Khan	Administration	Admin. Executive	E1
E7	B4	Anil	Ashutosh	Kambli	Marketing	Sales Asst.	E5
E8	B3	Seema	P.	Apte	Client Servicing	Clerk	E3
E9	B2	Vikram	Vilas	Randive	Marketing	Sales Asst.	E7
E10	B6	Anjali	Sameer	Pathak	Administration	HR Manager	E1

Table Name: CUST_MSTR

CUST_NO	FNAME	MNAME	LNAME	DOB_INC
C1	Ivan	Nelson	Bayross	25-JUN-1952
C2	Chriselle	Ivan	Bayross	29-OCT-1982
C3	Mamta	Arvind	Muzumdar	28-AUG-1975
C4	Chhaya	Sudhakar	Bankar	06-OCT-1976
C5	Ashwini	Dilip	Joshi	20-NOV-1978
C6	Hansel	I.	Colaco	01-JAN-1982

C7	Anil	Arun	Dhone	12-OCT-1983
C8	Alex	Austin	Fernandes	30-SEP-1962
C9	Ashwini	Shankar	Apte	19-APR-1979
C10	Namita	S.	Kanade	10-JUN-1978
C11				14-NOV-1997
C12				23-OCT-1992
C13				05-FEB-1989
C14				24-MAY-1980
C15				02-APR-2000
C16				13-JAN-2002

Table Name: CUST_MSTR (Continued)

CUST_NO	OCCUP	PHOTOGRAPH	SIGNATURE	PANCOPY	FORM60
C1	Self Employed	D:/ClntPht/C1.gif	D:/ClntSgnt/C1.gif	Y	Y
C2	Service	D:/ClntPht/C2.gif	D:/ClntSgnt/C2.gif	N	Y
C3	Service	D:/ClntPht/C3.gif	D:/ClntSgnt/C3.gif	Y	Y
C4	Service	D:/ClntPht/C4.gif	D:/ClntSgnt/C4.gif	Y	Y
C5	Business	D:/ClntPht/C5.gif	D:/ClntSgnt/C5.gif	Y	Y
C6	Service	D:/ClntPht/C6.gif	D:/ClntSgnt/C6.gif	N	Y
C7	Self Employed	D:/ClntPht/C7.gif	D:/ClntSgnt/C7.gif	N	Y
C8	Executive	D:/ClntPht/C8.gif	D:/ClntSgnt/C8.gif	Y	Y
C9	Service	D:/ClntPht/C9.gif	D:/ClntSgnt/C9.gif	Y	Y
C10	Self Employed	D:/ClntPht/C10.gif	D:/ClntSgnt/C10.gif	Y	Y
C11	Retail Business			Y	N
C12	Information Technology			Y	N
C13	Community Welfare			Y	N
C14	Retail Business			N	Y
C15	Retail Business			Y	N
C16	Marketing			Y	N

Table Name: SPRT_DOC

ACCT_CODE	TYPE	DOCS
0S	Individuals / Savings Bank Account	Driving Licence / Ration Card / Passport
0S	Individuals / Savings Bank Account	Birth Certificate / School Leaving Certificate
1C	Propriety / Sole Trading Concerns	Letter From The Propriety
2C	Partnership Concerns	Letter From The Partners

2C	Partnership Concerns	Partnership Deed / Registration Certificate
3C	Hindu Undivided Family Businesses	Letter From The Karta
3C	Hindu Undivided Family Businesses	List Of Members
4C	Limited Companies	Copy Of Board Of Directors'' Resolution For Opening The Account
4C	Limited Companies	Memorandum and Articles Of Association
4C	Limited Companies	Certificate Of Incorporation
4C	Limited Companies	Certificate Of Commencement Of Business / Registration Certificate
5C	Trust Accounts	Trust Deed
5C	Trust Accounts	Resolution Of Trustees
5C	Trust Accounts	List Of Trusties
6C	Clubs / Societies	Resolution
6C	Clubs / Societies	Constitution And Bye-laws
6C	Clubs / Societies	Certificate Of Registration
7C	Legislative Bodies	Letter From The Authority

Table Name: ACCT_MSTR

ACCT_NO	SF_NO	LF_NO	BRANCH_NO	TYPE	OPR_MODE	CUR_ACCT_TYPE
SB1	SF-0001	NOV03-05	B1	SB	SI	0S
CA2	SF-0002	NOV03-10	B2	CA	JO	1C
SB3	SF-0003	NOV03-22	B3	SB	SI	0S
CA4	SF-0004	DEC03-05	B5	CA	AS	2C
SB5	SF-0005	DEC03-15	B6	SB	JO	0S
SB6	SF-0006	DEC03-27	B4	SB	ES	0S
CA7	SF-0007	JAN04-14	B1	CA	AS	6C
SB8	SF-0008	JAN04-29	B2	SB	SI	0S
SB9	SF-0009	FEB04-05	B4	SB	JO	0S
CA10	SF-0010	FEB04-19	B6	CA	AS	1C
SB1	SF-0011	MAR04-10	B1	SB	SI	0S
CA2	SF-0012	MAR04-10	B2	CA	JO	1C
SB3	SF-0013	MAR04-22	B3	SB	SI	0S
CA4	SF-0014	APR04-05	B5	CA	AS	2C
SB5	SF-0015	APR04-15	B6	SB	JO	0S

ACCT_NO _NO	INTRO_CUST _NO	INTRO_ACCT _SIGN	INTRO _NO	VERI_EMP _SIGN	VERI	MANAGER_SIGN
SB1	C1	SB1	Y	E1	Y	Y
CA2	C1	SB1	Y	E1	Y	Y
SB3	C4	SB3	Y	E4	Y	Y
CA4	C4	SB3	Y	E4	Y	Y
SB5	C1	SB1	Y	E1	Y	Y
SB6	C5	SB6	Y	E4	Y	Y
CA7	C8	CA7	Y	E4	Y	Y
SB8	C9	SB8	Y	E1	Y	Y
SB9	C10	SB9	Y	E4	Y	Y
CA10	C10	SB9	Y	E4	Y	Y
SB11	C1	SB1	Y	E1	Y	Y
CA12	C1	SB1	Y	E1	Y	Y
SB13	C4	SB3	Y	E4	Y	Y
CA14	C4	SB3	Y	E4	Y	Y
SB15	C1	SB1	Y	E1	Y	Y

ACCT _NO	TITLE	CORP_CUST _NO	APLNDT	OPNDT	CURBAL	STATUS
SB1			05-NOV-2003	05-NOV-2003	500	A
CA2	Uttam Stores	O11	07-NOV-2003	10-NOV-2003	3000	A
SB3			20-NOV-2003	22-NOV-2003	500	A
CA4	Sun''s Pvt. Ltd.	O12	02-DEC-2003	05-DEC-2003	12000	A
SB5			14-DEC-2003	15-DEC-2003	500	A
SB6			27-DEC-2003	27-DEC-2003	500	A
CA7	Puru Hsg. Soc	O13	14-JAN-2004	14-JAN-2004	22000	A
SB8			27-JAN-2004	29-JAN-2004	500	A
SB9			05-FEB-2004	05-FEB-2004	500	A
CA10	Ghar Karobar	O14	19-FEB-2004	19-FEB-2004	32000	A

Table Name: ACCT_MSTR (Continued)

ACCT _NO	TITLE	CORP_CUST _NO	APLNDT	OPNDT	CURBAL	STATUS
SB11			05-MAR-2004	10-MAR-2004	500	A
CA12	Suresh Stores	O15	07-MAR-2004	10-MAR-2004	5000	A
SB13			20-MAR-2004	22-MAR-2004	500	A
CA14	Moon''s Pvt. Ltd.	O16	02-APR-2004	05-APR-2004	10000	A
SB15			14-APR-2004	15-APR-2004	500	A

Table Name: FD_MSTR

FD_SER_NO	SF_NO	BRANCH_NO	ACCT_NO	TITLE	CORP_CUST_NO	MANAGER SIGN
1	SF-1001	B2	CA2	Uttam Stores	C11	Y
2	SF-1002	B5	CA4	Sun's Pvt. Ltd.	C12	Y
3	SF-1003	B1	CA7	Puru Hsg. Soc	C13	Y
4	SF-1004	B6	CA10	Ghar Karobar	C14	Y
5	SF-1005	B4				Y

FD_SER_NO	INTRO_CUST_NO	INTRO_ACCT_NO	INTRO_SIGN	VERI_EMP_NO	VERI_SIGN
1			N	E1	Y
2			Y	E1	Y
3			Y	E4	Y
4			Y	E4	Y
5	C7	SB6	Y	E4	Y

Table Name : FDSLAB_MSTR

FDSLAB_NO	MINPERIOD	MAXPERIOD	INTRATE
1	1	30	5
2	31	92	5.5
3	93	183	6
4	184	365	6.5
5	366	731	7.5
6	732	1097	8.5
7	1098	1829	10

Table Name: FD_DTLS

FD_SER_NO	FD_NO	TYPE	PAYTO_ACCTNO	PERIOD	OPNDT	DUEDT
1	F1	S	CA2	365	02-APR-2003	01-APR-2004
1	F2	S	CA2	365	02-JAN-2004	01-JAN-2005
2	F3	S	CA4	366	25-MAR-2004	25-MAR-2005
2	F4	S	CA4	366	15-APR-2004	15-APR-2005
3	F5	S	CA7	183	24-APR-2004	24-OCT-2006
4	F6	S	CA10	732	19-MAY-2004	20-MAY-2006
5	F7	S	SB6	366	27-MAY-2004	27-MAY-2005

Table Name: FD_DTLS (Continued)

FD_SER_NO	AMT	DUEAMT	INTRATE	STATUS	AUTO_RENEWAL
1	15000	16050.00	6.5	A	Y
1	5000	5350.00	6.5	A	N
2	10000	10802.19	7.5	A	Y
2	10000	10802.19	7.5	A	Y
3	2000	2060.16	6	A	Y
4	5000	5902.47	8.5	A	Y
5	15000	16203.30	7.5	A	N

Table Name: ACCT_FD_CUST_DTLS

ACCT_FD_NO	CUST_NO	ACCT_FD_NO	CUST_NO
SB1	C1	CA2	C2
CA2	C3	SB3	C4
CA4	C4	CA4	C5
CA4	C5	SB5	C1
SB5	C4	SB6	C5
SB6	C7	CA7	C6
CA7	C8	SB8	C9
SB9	C3	SB9	C10
CA10	C10	CA10	C9
SB11	C1	CA12	C2
CA12	C3	SB13	C4
CA14	C4	CA14	C5
CA14	C5	SB15	C1
SB15	C4	FS1	C2
FS1	C3	FS2	C4
FS2	C4	FS2	C5
FS3	C6	FS3	C8
FS4	C9	FS4	C10
FS5	C5		

Table Name : NOMINEE_MSTR

NOMINEE_NO	ACCT_FD_NO	NAME	DOB	RELATIONSHIP
N1	CA2	Joseph Martin Dias	17-SEP-1984	Colleague
N2	CA2	Nilesh Sawant	25-AUG-1987	Colleague
N3	SB1	Chriselle Ivan Bayross	25-JUN-1952	Daughter
N4	SB3	Mamta Arvind Muzumdar	28-AUG-1975	Friend
N5	SB6	Preeti Suresh Shah	12-FEB-1978	Friend
N6	SB8	Rohit Rajan Sahakarkar	30-MAY-1985	Relative
N7	CA10	Namita S. Kanade	10-JUN-1978	Niece
N8	FS1	Rohit Rajan Sahakarkar	30-MAY-1985	Relative
N9	FS2	Joseph Martin Dias	17-SEP-1984	Colleague
N10	FS2	Nilesh Sawant	25-AUG-1987	Colleague
N11	FS3	Chriselle Ivan Bayross	25-JUN-1952	Colleague
N12	FS3	Mamta Arvind Muzumdar	28-AUG-1975	Friend
N13	FS4	Namita S. Kanade	10-JUN-1978	Relative
N14	FS5	Pramila P. Pius	10-OCT-1985	Niece

Table Name: ADDR_DTLS

ADDR_NO	CODE_NO	ADDR_TYPE	CITY	STATE	PINCODE
1	B1	H	Mumbai	Maharashtra	400057
2	B2	B	Mumbai	Maharashtra	400058
3	B3	B	Mumbai	Maharashtra	400004
4	B4	B	Mumbai	Maharashtra	400045
5	B5	B	Mumbai	Maharashtra	400078
6	B6	B	New Delhi	Delhi	110004
7	E1	N	Mumbai	Maharashtra	400056
8	E2	C	Mumbai	Maharashtra	400078
9	E3	N	Mumbai	Maharashtra	400059
10	E4	C	Mumbai	Maharashtra	400058
11	E5	C	Mumbai	Maharashtra	400058
12	E6	N	Mumbai	Maharashtra	400076
13	E7	N	Mumbai	Maharashtra	400016
14	E8	C	Mumbai	Maharashtra	400016
15	E9	N	Mumbai	Maharashtra	400028
16	E10	C	New Delhi	Delhi	110016
17	C1	C	Mumbai	Maharashtra	400056
18	C2	C	Mumbai	Maharashtra	400056
19	C3	C	Mumbai	Maharashtra	400060
20	C4	C	Mumbai	Maharashtra	400016

21	C5	C	Mumbai	Maharashtra	400016
22	C6	C	Mumbai	Maharashtra	400028
23	C7	C	Mumbai	Maharashtra	400016
24	C8	C	Mumbai	Maharashtra	400016
25	C9	C	Mumbai	Maharashtra	400016
26	C10	C	Mumbai	Maharashtra	400016
27	N1	C	Mumbai	Maharashtra	400058
28	N2	C	Mumbai	Maharashtra	400016
29	N3	C	Mumbai	Maharashtra	400056
30	N4	C	Mumbai	Maharashtra	400060
31	N5	C	Mumbai	Maharashtra	400067
32	N6	N	Mumbai	Maharashtra	400102
33	N7	C	Mumbai	Maharashtra	400016
34	O11	H	Mumbai	Maharashtra	400058
35	O12	H	Mumbai	Maharashtra	400057
36	O13	H	Mumbai	Maharashtra	400016
37	O14	H	Mumbai	Maharashtra	400016
38	N8	N	Mumbai	Maharashtra	400102
39	N9	C	Mumbai	Maharashtra	400058
40	N10	C	Mumbai	Maharashtra	400016
41	N11	C	Mumbai	Maharashtra	400056
42	N12	C	Mumbai	Maharashtra	400060
43	N13	C	Mumbai	Maharashtra	400016
44	N14	C	Mumbai	Maharashtra	400102
45	C4	N	Mumbai	Maharashtra	400059
46	O15	H	Mumbai	Maharashtra	400057
47	O16	H	Mumbai	Maharashtra	400058

Table Name: ADDR_DTLS (Continued)

ADDR_NO	ADDR1	ADDR2
1	A/5, Jay Chambers,	Service Road, Vile Parle (East),
2	BSES Chambers, 10th floor,	Near Rly. Station, Andheri (West),
3	Prabhat Complex, No. 5 / 6,	Opp. Air India Bldg., Churchgate
4	23/A, Swarna Bldg., Smt. Rai Marg,	Eastern Express Highway, Kurla (East)
5	Vikas Centre, Shop 37, Near National Park,	Western Express Highway, Borivali (East),
6	24/A, Mahima Plaza, First Floor,	Darya Ganj,
7	F-12, Diamond Palace, West Avenue,	North Avenue, Santacruz (West),
8	Desai House, Plot No. 25, P.G. Marg	Near Malad Rly. Stat., Malad (West),
9	Room No. 56, 3rd Floor, Swamibhavan,	J. P. Road Junction, Andheri (East),

10	301, Thomas Palace, Opp. Indu Child Care	Yadnik Nagar, Andheri (West),
11	456/A, Bldg. No. 4, Vahatuk Nagar,	Amboli, Andheri (West),
12	201, Meena Towers, Nr. Sun Gas Agency,	S. V. Rd., Goregoan (West),
13	Patel Chawl, Rm. No. 15, B. P. Lal Marg,	Mahim (West),
14	A - 10, Neelam, L. J. Road	Mahim (East),
15	1/12 Bal Govindas Society, M. B. Raut Rd.	Dadar (East),
16	Pathak Nagar, Cadal Road	Mahim (West),
17	F-12, Diamond Palace, West Avenue,	North Avenue, Santacruz (West),
18	F-12, Silver Stream,	Santacruz (East),
19	Magesh Prasad	Saraswati Baug, Jogeshwari(E),
20	4, Sampada Kataria Road, Mahim,	
21	104, Vikram Apts. Bhagat Lane	Shivaji Park, Mahim,
22	12, Radha Kunj, N.C Kelkar Road	Dadar,
23	A/14, Shanti Society, Mogal Lane,	Mahim,
24	5, Vagdevi, Senapati Bapat Rd.	Dadar,
25	A-10 Nutan Vaishali	Shivaji Park, Mahim,
26	B-10, Makarand Society	Cadal Road, Mahim,
27	307/E, Meena Mansion,	R. S. Road, Andheri (West),
28	Smt. Veenu Chawl, Sawant Colony Rd.,	Opp. Veer Road, Matunga (West),
29	F-12, Silver Stream,	Santacruz (East),
30	Magesh Prasad	Saraswati Baug, Jogeshwari(E),
31	Rita Apartment, Room No. 46, 2nd Floor,	J. P. Road, Andheri (East),
32	106/A, Sunrise Apmt., Opp. Vahatuk Nagar,	Kevni-Pada, Jogeshwari (West),
33	Pathak Nagar, Cadal Road,	Mahim (West),
34	Shop No. 4, Simon Streams,	V. P. Road, Andheri (West),
35	230-E, Patel Chambers,	Service Road, Vile Parle (East),
36	G-2, Puru Hsg. Society,	Senapati Bapat Rd., Dadar,
37	B-10, Makarand Society,	Cadal Road, Mahim,
38	106/A, Sunrise Apmt., Opp. Vahatuk Nagar,	106/A, Sunrise Apmt., Opp. Vahatuk Nagar,
39	307/E, Meena Mansion,	R. S. Road, Andheri (West),
40	Smt. Veenu Chawl, Sawant Colony Rd.,	Opp. Veer Road, Matunga (West),
41	F-12, Silver Stream,	Santacruz (East),
42	Magesh Prasad,	Saraswati Baug, Jogeshwari(E)
43	Pathak Nagar, Cadal Road,	Mahim (West)
44	405,Vahatuk Nagar, Kevni-Pada,	Jogeshwari (West),
45	203/A, Prachi Apmt.,	Andheri (East),
46	Shop No. 4, Sai Compound,	Service Road, Vile Parle (East),
47	G-4, Sagar Chambers,	G. P. Road, Andheri (West),

Table Name: CNTC_DTLS

ADDR_NO	CODE_NO	CNTC_TYPE	CNTC_DATA
1	B1	O	26124571
1	B1	F	26124533
1	B1	E	admin_vileparle@bom2.vsnl.in
2	B2	O	26790014
2	B2	E	admin_andheri@bom2.vsnl.in
3	B3	O	23457855
3	B3	E	admin_churchgate@bom2.vsnl.in
4	B4	O	25545455
4	B4	E	admin_sion@bom2.vsnl.in
5	B5	O	28175454
5	B5	E	admin_borivali@bom2.vsnl.in
6	B6	O	24304545
6	B6	E	admin_matunga@bom2.vsnl.in
8	E2	R	28883779
9	E3	R	28377634
10	E4	R	26323560
11	E5	R	26793231
12	E6	R	28085654
13	E7	R	24442342
14	E8	R	24365672
15	E9	R	24327349
16	E10	R	24302579
17	C1	R	26405853
17	C1	O	26134553
17	C1	O	26134571
17	C1	M	9820178955
18	C2	R	260455754
18	C2	O	26134571
19	C3	R	28324567
18	C3	O	26197654
19	C4	R	24449852
19	C4	O	28741370
20	C5	R	24302934
20	C5	O	22819964
21	C6	R	24217592
22	C7	R	24372247
23	C8	O	26480903
24	C9	R	24313408
25	C9	M	9821176651

26	C10	R	24362680
26	C10	O	28973355
26	C10	M	9820484648
27	N1	R	26762154
28	N2	R	24307887
29	N3	R	260455754
30	N4	R	28645489
31	N5	R	30903564
32	N6	R	26793771
33	N7	R	24304455
34	C11	O	26790055
34	C11	F	26784409
35	C12	O	26120455
35	C12	O	26120456
35	C12	F	26121450
35	C12	E	admin@sunpvtltd.com
35	C12	W	www.sunpvtltd.com
36	C13	O	24301090
36	C13	O	24301196
37	C14	O	24321122
38	N8	R	26793771
39	N9	R	26762154
40	N10	R	24307887
41	N11	R	26045754
42	N12	R	28645489
43	N13	R	24304455
44	N14	R	26790180
44	N14	R	26771275
45	C6	R	28274784
46	O15	O	26170055
46	O15	F	26174409
47	O16	O	26790455
47	O16	F	26781450
47	O16	E	admin@moonmltg.com
47	O16	W	www.moonmltg.com

Table Name: TRANS_MSTR

TRANS_NO	ACCT_NO	DT	TYPE	PARTICULAR	DR_CR	AMT	BALANCE
T1	SB1	05-NOV-2003	C	Initial Payment	D	500	500
T2	CA2	10-Nov-2003	C	Initial Payment	D	2000	2000
T3	SB3	22-NOV-2003	C	Initial Payment	D	500	500
T4	CA4	05-DEC-2003	B	Initial Payment	D	2000	2000
T5	SB5	15-DEC-2003	B	Initial Payment	D	500	500
T6	SB6	27-DEC-2003	C	Initial Payment	D	500	500
T7	CA7	14-JAN-2004	B	Initial Payment	D	2000	2000
T8	SB8	29-JAN-2004	C	Initial Payment	D	500	500
T9	SB9	05-FEB-2004	C	Initial Payment	D	500	500
T10	SB9	15-FEB-2004	B	CLR-204907	D	3000	3500
T11	SB9	17-FEB-2004	C	Self	W	2500	1000
T12	CA10	19-FEB-2004	B	Initial Payment	D	2000	2000
T13	SB9	05-APR-2004	B	CLR-204908	D	3000	4000
T14	SB9	27-APR-2004	C	Self	W	2500	1500

Table Name: TRANS_DTLS

TRANS_NO	INST_NO	INST_DT	PAYTO	INST_CLR_DT
T4	98324	02-DEC-2003	Self	05-DEC-2003
T5	232324	14-DEC-2003	Self	15-DEC-2003
T7	434560	14-JAN-2004	Self	14-JAN-2004
T10	204907	14-FEB-2004	Self	15-FEB-2004
T12	100907	19-FEB-2004	Self	19-FEB-2004
T13	204908	01-APR-2004	Self	05-APR-2004

TRANS_NO	BANK_NAME	BRANCH_NAME	PAIDFROM
T4	HDFC	Vile Parle (East)	2982
T5	India Bank	Andheri (West)	30434
T7	ICICI Bank	Bandra (West)	4882
T10	Memon Co-operative Bank	Jogeshwari (West)	1767
T12	Memon Co-operative Bank	Jogeshwari (West)	2001
T13	Memon Co-operative Bank	Jogeshwari (West)	1767

Index

%

%FOUND 349
%ISOPEN 349
%ROWCOUNT 349
%TYPE 336

A

ABS 194
Active Data Set 348, 352
ADD_MONTHS 204
Advantages of PL/SQL 333
Aggregate Functions 192
Alias 182
ALTER PACKAGE 390
ALTER SEQUENCE 300
ALTER SNAPSHOT 304
ALTER TABLE
- ADD PRIMARY KEY() 175
- ADD() 147
- DROP COLUMN 147
- MODIFY() 146

Altering A Sequence 300
AND Operator 183, 184
Archive log files 90
Archiver (ARCH) 34
Arguments 192
Arithmetic Operators 181
ASCII 198
AVG 192

B

Before Triggers 404
Benefits of Overloading 397
BETWEEN Operator 186
BIND_VARIABLE 422
Binding 419
Bitmap Indexes 285

C

CACHE 299
CEIL 197
Check 11
Checkpoint 31
CLOSE 354
CLOSE_CURSOR 425
Cluster Key 297
COLUMN_VALUE 423
Combinations 404
Complete Export 433
Components of an Oracle Package 385
COMPOSE 198
Composite Index 283
COMPUTATIONS 181
Conditional Control 341
Constants 337
Constraints 155
- ON DELETE CASCADE 159
- Business Rules 167
- CHECK 167
- Restrictions 172
- Column Level 167
- Composite 156
- DEFAULT 175
- Dropping Integrity 175
- FOREIGN KEY/References 160
- Foreign/Detail Table 159
- Integrity 174
- Naming 163
- NOT NULL 170
- PRIMARY KEY 158
- Primary/Master Table 159
- Table Level 168
- UNIQUE 166

Control Files 26

Conversion Functions 192
COUNT 193
COUNT(*) 193
CREATE INDEX 283
CREATE PACKAGE 385
CREATE SEQUENCE 298
Create Table 134
  AS SELECT 143
CREATIVE UNIQUE INDEX 283
CREATE VIEW 292
Cumulative Export 433
Cursor 349
Cursor for loops 358

D

Data Blocks 279
Data Dictionary Cache 33
Data Files 279
Data Integrity 10
Data Models 8
  File-Based Systems or Primitive Models 10
  Hierarchical Model 9
  Network Data Model 9
  Relational Data Model 9
  Semantic Data Models 8
  Traditional Data Models 8
Database Buffer Cache 29
Database Files 88
Database integrity 10
DATABASE TRIGGERS 401
  FOR EACH ROW 408
  Trigger Action 402
  Trigger Restriction 402
  Triggering Event or Statement 402
Database Writer (DBWR) 34
DATATYPE 130
  CHAR (size) 130
  DATE 131
  LONG 131
  RAQ 131
Date Functions 192
DBA 40
DBA Studio 55
  Creating A DBA 64
  Creating A User 70
  Creating Tablespace 46
  Database Connect Information 56
DBMS_SQL 417
DECOMPOSE 199
DEFINE_COLUMN 423
DELETE 144
  WHERE 145
DELETE CASCADE 177
DELETING A STORED PROCEDURE 384
DELETING A TRIGGER 406
DESCRIBE 151
Dirty Buffers 30
Dispatcher 37
Displaying User Message
  dbms_output 341
  Put_line 341
DISTINCT 192
DROP TRIGGER 406
DROP FUNCTION 384
DROP INDEX 286
DROP PROCEDURE 384
DROP SEQUENCE 301
DROP SNAPSHOT 305
DROP TABLE 149
DROP VIEW 296
DUAL 191
Duplicate/Unique Index 282

E

Entity Relationship Model 8
Equi Joins 238
ERROR HANDLING IN PL/SQL 364
Exception Handler 364
EXECUTE 424
EXP 194
Explicit 352
Explicit Cursors 352
Explicit Cursor Attributes 354
Export Utility 432
EXTRACT 195

F

FETCH 354
FETCH_ROWS 424
FLOOR 196
FOR LOOP 346

G

GOTO STATEMENT 344
GRANT 77
ADMIN OPTION 67
GRANTING AND REVOKING PERMISSIONS 76
GREATEST 195
GROUP BY 217
Group Functions 192
GROUPING DATA 217

H

HAVING Clause 217

I

Implicit Cursor 349
Implicity Utility 433
Incremental Export 433
Indexes 278
Init.ora 26
INITCAP 197
INSERT INTO 136
SELECT ... FROM 143
INSTR 199
Intersect Clause 259
Iterative Control 340

K

Key-Compressed Index 286

L

LAST_DAY 204
LEAST 195
LENGTH 200
Like 188
Literals 336
Lock 37
Log Files 89
Log Groups 89
Log Writer (LGWR) 36
Logical Backup Utility 432
Logical Comparisons 339
Logical Operators 183
LOWER 197
LPAD 201
LTRIM 200

M

MANIPULATING DATES 206
MAX 193
MIN 193
Minus Clause 261
MOD 196
MONTHS_BETWEEN 204

N

Nested Query 226
NEXT_DAY 204
Nextval 299
NOT IN 190
NOT NULL 337
NOT Operator 185
NOTFOUND 349
NULL 168
Numeric Functions 192

O

OBJECT PRIVILEGES 76
Off-line Redo Log Files 90
On-line Redo Log Files 89
OPEN_CURSOR 419
OR Operator 184
Oracle Background Processes 26
Oracle Database 27
ORACLE FUNCTIONS 192
Oracle Instance 26
Oracle Memory Components 26
Oracle Physical File Structure 25
Oracle's Named Exception Handlers 365

P

Parallel Server 37
Parameter File 26
Parameterized Cursors 360
PARSE 421
PATTERN MATCHING 188
Physical Database Structure 88
PL/SQL Character Set 335
PL/SQL Comments 341
POWER 194
Pragma Exception_init() 366
Privileges 76
Process Monitor (PMON) 34

Program Global Area (PGA) 34

R

RAISE Statement 370
RAISE_APPLICATION_ERROR 412
Range Searching 186
RDBMS System 24
Read-Only View 292
REBUILD NOREVERSE 285
Records 279
Recoverer (RECO) 36
Redo Log Buffer 32
Redo Log Files 26
Renaming Columns 182
Renaming the Columns of a View 292
Reverse Key Index 284
REVOKE 78
Revoking of Privileges 77
Role 66
Rolliing Forward 90
ROUND 194
Row Fetching 420
Row Pointer 348
Row Triggers 403
ROWID 279
ROWNUM 290
RPAD 203
RTRIM 201

S

Scalar Functions 192
SELECT 137
- DISTINCT 141
- FROM 138
- FROM ... ORDER BY 143
- FROM ... WHERE 140
- FROM TAB 150

Self Joins 250
SEQUENCES 297
Server 37
SET SERVEROUTPUT [ON/OFF] 339
Shared Global Area 419
Shared Pool 33
Shared SQL Area 33
Simple Index 282
Simple Key 176
Simple Unique Index 283
Snapshot 301
Sorting 142
SPTH 210
SQRT 194
String Functions 187
SUBQUERIES 226
SUBSTR 198
SUM 193
Sysdate 192
System Global Area (SGA) 25
System Monitor (SMON) 34
System Privileges 67

T

Tablespace 39
- AUTOEXTENT 42
- CHUNK 42
- DATAFILE 41
- DEFAULT STORAGE 42
- EXTENT MANAGEMENT 42
- LOGGING 42
- MINIMUM EXTENT 41
- NOCACHE 42
- NOLOGGING 42
- OFFLINE 42
- ONLINE 42
- PERMANENT 42
- STORAGE 42
- System 39
- TABLESPACE_NAME 41
- TEMPORARY 42

TH 209
The Declare Section 334
The Exception Section 334
The Generic PL/SQL Block 334
The Package Body 391
The PL/SQL Syntax 335
TO_CHAR 203
TO_DATE 204
TO_NUMBER 202
TRANSLATE 200
TRUNC 196

U

Union Clause 254
UPDATE 146

SET 146
SET ... WHERE 146
Updateable View 292
UPPER 198
User 210
CREATE USER 91
DEFAULT TABLESPACE 91
IDENTIFIED BY 91
PROFILE 91
TEMPORARY TABLESPACE 91
User Defined Exception Handlers (For I/O Validations) 367
User Defined Exception Handling (For Business Rule Validations) 370
USER_CONSTRAINTS 173

V

VARIABLE_VALUE 425
Variables 337
VIEWS 291
Views Defined from Multiple Tables (Which have been created with a Referencing clause) 294
Views Defined from Multiple Tables (Which have no Referencing Clause) 294
VSIZE 202

W

Where Clause 140
WHILE LOOP 341
Wildcard 188
With Grant Option 76